MW01014929

The Gospel of Hip Hop

First Instrument

Presented by

KRS ONE

For the Temple of Hip Hop

powerHouse Books
Brooklyn, NY

I AM HIP HOP

ORDER OF OVERSTANDINGS

PAGE

A NEW COVENANT 006

THE LOVE 024

THE PROMISED LAND 034

THE FIRST OVERSTANDING
REAL HIP HOP 058

THE SECOND OVERSTANDING
THE REFINITIONS 102

THE THIRD OVERSTANDING
THE DIVINE PERFORMANCE 143

THE FOURTH OVERSTANDING
THE H-LAW 201
HEALTH 206
LOVE 227
AWARENESS 235
WEALTH 253

THE FIFTH OVERSTANDING
THE INNER CITY 282

THE SIXTH OVERSTANDING
THE SEASONS 314

THE SEVENTH OVERSTANDING
THE SEVENTH SENSE 336

THE EIGHTH OVERSTANDING
ENDARKENMENT
TRACK ONE 355
TRACK TWO 365
TRACK THREE 371
TRACK FOUR 375

THE NINTH OVERSTANDING
THE FREE STYLES   384
THE TENTH OVERSTANDING
THE SPIRIT OF GRAFFITI ART   438
THE ELEVENTH OVERSTANDING
THE TEACHA   465
THE TWELFTH OVERSTANDING
THE MOVEMENT   494
THE THIRTEENTH OVERSTANDING
THE HIP HOP ACTIVIST   530
THE FOURTEENTH OVERSTANDING
THE HIP HOP DECLARATION OF PEACE   549
THE FIFTEENTH OVERSTANDING
DOWN BY LAW   558
THE SIXTEENTH OVERSTANDING
OUR GOD – THE GREAT EVENT
            TRACK ONE   598
            TRACK TWO   618
            TRACK THREE   627
THE SEVENTEENTH OVERSTANDING
THE TEMPLE OF HIP HOP   643
THE EIGHTEENTH OVERSTANDING
THE ORIGINS OF HIP HOP
            TRACK ONE   708
            TRACK TWO   724
            TRACK THREE   740
            TRACK FOUR   768
            TRACK FIVE   799
SHOUT OUTS   819

"HEAVEN IS NOT A PLACE YOU GO TO,
IT IS A PLACE YOU GROW TO."

—*Edgar Cayce*

A NEW COVENANT

¹ IN THE END, the last days of others became the first days for us! ALL PRAISE, GLORY AND WORSHIP BE TO GOD—the Love that rescued us from oppression and ignorance!

² And to all future generations of Hip Hop, know this; it is this Love that has delivered this gospel to OUR PEOPLE for OUR correction and survival. This gospel comes to us as the physical manifestation of GOD's grace and love for Hip Hop.

³ I am but one of many who was saved by such *Love*. In my time (your past) I am called *teacha*; I was present at the *first time*. I am the *first born*. I am from the *Age of Leo*, and I have come to call our Hip Hop nation into existence.

⁴ To all future generations of Hip Hop, I am the b-boy who destroys all negative circumstances everyday spiritually.

⁵ I am the emcee who reaches above poverty skillfully; the divine word-warrior known in my time as the *Blast Master*.

⁶ I am the graffiti writer who thinks and grows spiritually; I *draw* peace, love, unity and joy.

⁷ I am the DJ who delivers justice while cuttin', mixin' and scratchin' with life.

⁸ I am the beat boxer whose body expresses art through sound; I play GOD's instrument.

⁹ I am the fashion that uncovers the fear and shame hidden in oppressive nations.

[10] I am the language that loves and never gets understanding amongst grown-up educators; I am the utterance of my culture.

[11] I am known as Knowledge Reigning Supreme; I build and destroy, heal and inspire with the right combination of words.

[12] I am the entrepreneur who presents expert negotiating that repeatedly escapes poverty's routine experiences, never exploiting unlimited resources. In my time I am self-created and self-sustained.

[13] I AM HIP HOP! I am not just doing hip-hop, I am Hip Hop! I am the *Watchman* in the tower of Hip Hop's *Inner City* urging my people to turn from sickness, hatred, ignorance and poverty, and be restored to health, love, awareness and wealth. I am "the Teacha"—a witness to the activity of GOD within and around Hip Hop.

[14] I was present at the beginning of this World Age, August 11, 3114 B.C., and I was again present at the births and transformations of Hip Hop since its artistic organization at 1520 Sedgwick Avenue in the Bronx, August 11, 1973. I am a true witness to the divinity and cultural history of Hip Hop. Hip Hop is my family; I am like the people I teach, I am like the people I am among, and I am not ashamed or afraid of my family—I AM HIP HOP!

[15] In my time (your past), I am called the "conscience of Hip Hop." I am the step-father and legal guardian of Hip Hop. This, I confirm to those truth-seeking Hip Hop scholars in my future. Emceein is my craft and I have mastered my craft. I am Hip Hop and in my time I have mastered myself.

[16] To all my hustlers, thugs and gangstas trying to survive in these mean streets, this is YOUR gospel! To all my Gods, Goddesses, revolutionaries, street scholars and conscious Hiphoppas, this is YOUR heritage and birthright!

This is the "good news" for YOU! ALL PRAISE, GLORY AND WORSHIP BE TO GOD—the Love that loved us first as Hip Hop.

[17] GOD IS REAL! And Hip Hop is evidence of GOD's real existence and Love. Hip Hop is GOD's response to our suffering and this gospel celebrates that response and the personal character that caused such divine responses to occur. ALL PRAISE, GLORY AND WORSHIP BE TO GOD—the Love that topples whole kingdoms and sets up new civilizations from the debris of the unrepentant!

[18] We are humbled before GOD—the author of Hip Hop. Other cultures and nations were created in other ways for other reasons and have certain divine responsibilities that they must adhere to. Other cultures have a certain *grace* over their communities and we are not authorized or encouraged to demean or disrespect in any way the faith and/or religious practices of others.

[19] But as for us, as for our group commonly known in the World as "Hip Hop," this gospel acknowledges and celebrates the Love that has saved OUR people from self-destruction. It is time to repent and grow up! Rapping about crime and murder may sound good amongst those who have never committed such acts, but for those of us who are REAL IN THE FIELD, we send this message to our young people—YOU DON'T REALLY WANT IT!

[20] For with this first instrument we remember GOD and how we were rescued by unseen forces more powerful than any government on Earth. For when all seemed hopeless and oppression seemed permanent, a caring, protective, nurturing creative force independent of all the World's political, business, educational and religious institutions, swept through our hearts and homes and we were rescued from sickness, hatred, ignorance and poverty with a behavior that we eventually began to call "Hip Hop."

And we must NEVER forget this.

21   With this first instrument written at the time of Hip Hop's cultural beginnings, we remind all future generations of Hip Hop to NEVER FORGET THE LOVE that has saved us from self-destruction. Hip Hop has no other creator, no other savior and no other architect.

22   Love alone takes credit for the creation and further development of Hip Hop because before we even knew we were Hip Hop, GOD—the Love that saved us from corruption, had already ordained us as such and set us free in the World with power.

23   What a great gift! What a great Love! What a GREAT GOD! But how soon did we forget after we had eaten and were satisfied, how hungry we were just a moment ago. How quick did we forget our own strategies to our own success. We ate the fruit but never replanted the seed. We drove the car far but never looked at the gas tank meter.

24   Know this. GOD's Love (Hip Hop) is like a car that many people found with a full tank of gas topped off and ready to go; a gift freely given to all who would hop in. Now that we have driven this car for over 30 years through all kinds of terrain the time has come to repair and replenish our beloved vehicle so that it may last another 30 years. However, now that everyone has gotten where they intended to go using the vehicle, there seems to be little motivation toward the upkeep of the vehicle itself, the cause of everyone's good fortune.

25   GOD's Love (Hip Hop) is like a banquet laid out before hungry people. Many people today are eating well but they are not the chefs of their own meals. They eat but they don't really know where their food comes from or even how it was prepared. They themselves were never truly hungry or homeless or even had to prepare their own food for themselves, they just sat down and started eating at an

already laid-out table. Therefore, the life-lessons learned from being hungry and homeless which accompany the skills of the *chef* are absent from the copied presentations of the imitator, and any success found during this state of ignorance is indeed short-lived.

26   This is how many today treat GOD and Hip Hop. They seek the hand and not the face. They seek the luxury but not the culture, the food but not the appetite, the house but not the home, the medicine but not the health, the bed but not the rest. They would rather use GOD/Hip Hop than live GOD/Hip Hop.

27   But such are acts of desperation, and such behaviors are expected of a People who have been traumatized as we have been. Hip Hop saved us and made us not only rich, but important and well respected worldwide. How then can we forget GOD—the Love that protected us and raised us up? How can we forget about Hip Hop—the craft that feeds us and gives us identity?

28   However, in my time (your past) many have already forgotten the Love of GOD. Desperate and impoverished and suddenly propelled to the top of the World's social circles, they marvel at the effects of their own artistic skills caring little for the cause of such skills; they just want to eat.

29   And because they know not what causes their good fortune they have become frantic and greedy, content with being imitators of the original presenters of the saving force—Hip Hop. Such an approach works fine for those who are not really serious about living Hip Hop for real. Such an approach to Hip Hop works fine if you are only participating in Hip Hop to get out of poverty or make a name for yourself. This approach works if you got something else to do and/or somewhere else to go.

30   But for those of us who live Hip Hop and seek enlightenment through Hip Hop and are seeking to raise a

family while being an emcee or DJ, etc; those of us who are without purpose as well as those of us who are burdened with purpose, we have NO TIME TO WASTE! At this very moment while you read this gospel you are being called out of the World again for your own protection and development. Will you answer the *call* this time?

³¹   Repent, GOD is closer to you than your nose. Now is the time to take your Hip Hop spiritual life more seriously. Now is the time to align your Hip Hop identity with God's nature and not be distracted by the doubts and suspicions of others. Now is the time to declare "I AM HIP HOP" and begin living from that realization in GOD. HIP HOP IS YOUR BIRTHRIGHT! It may not be anyone else's birthright, but it is indeed yours. And if you decide to throw away your birthright because of the doubts of others it is only you that suffers, because they are maintaining their birthrights and cultures with faith while you destroy your heritage with doubt.

³²   Now is the time to actually become Hip Hop, to actually be the nation that we know we are. Such a life, however, is not for everyone. Many amongst us are just trying to use Hip Hop's artistic elements to escape poverty, and when they have attained the money, power and Worldly respect of escaping poverty through Hip Hop, we don't see or hear from them any more; they and their careers vanish.

³³   This is why TODAY IS THE GREATEST MOMENT FOR HIP HOP AND HIPHOPPAS. Now that the desperate part of our family has been fed, clothed and sheltered they are gone. Hip Hop itself was never their focus. They just wanted to use hip-hop to relieve their own suffering and once such suffering was dealt with they (the desperate) went on to do acting, open businesses, and basically live as the rest of the World does. But this was NEVER the intention for Hip Hop or Hiphoppas.

[34] As we have observed now within our 36-year history (1973–2009), Hip Hop was a saving force. If Hip Hop didn't do anything else, what it actually did in real history is rescue the children of a scattered and impoverished people from certain death. Yes, Hip Hop has inspired the development of Breakin, Emceein, Graffiti Art, Deejayin, Beat Boxin, Street Fashion, Street Language, Street Knowledge and Street Entrepreneurialism; but all of these elements basically did one thing—THEY SAVED US!

[35] So, now that we and the desperate part of our family have been satisfied, they (the desperate) are no longer *in our way*. We now have the liberty to explore the true meaning and purpose of Hip Hop (the Love that freed us from oppression) because the music industry has finally collapsed in my time. ALL PRAISE, GLORY AND WORSHIP BE TO GOD—the Love that freed us from exploitation and slavery.

[36] We are indeed happy that the impoverished part of our family has eaten and has been clothed and sheltered; we pray for their continued security. But their *ways* are not our *ways*, and their results are not our results. They are indeed our family, but within our family structure we are the *firstborns*. We are the elder sisters and brothers—GOD EXPECTS MORE FROM US. We are Hip Hop's original cultural architects, its caretakers, its teachers.

[37] We are Hip Hop's janitors cleansing and restoring Hip Hop for the next generation of Hiphoppas. Know this. With every generation Hip Hop gets dirty because of how it is used in the World by that generation. Hip Hop is then cleansed and restored for each generation by its janitors who work within the *Temple of Hip Hop*.

[38] Therefore, if you love Hip Hop and appreciate all that Hip Hop has done for you so far, regardless of your artistic expression, take up your broom and mop and begin

the clean up of YOUR CULTURE! If you are not the desperate part of our family prove it now by taking your Hip Hop life seriously; join in on the clean up! Your reward shall be greater than anything the World can ever offer!

[39] This gospel is a strong disinfectant, which is poured onto our rags (clothing fashions), our brooms (dances), our air fresheners (microphones), our mops (markers and spray cans), our scrub brushes (turntables), and our buckets (culture). While cleaning, we make our own music with our own bodies. It doesn't matter what you may rap about; now is your chance to become a serious participant in the preservation of the Hip Hop arts and sciences.

[40] In Hip Hop and within Hip Hop's real history we have NEVER been the desperate and impoverished part of our family; we were and still are the faithful, the humble, the loyal, and most of all the grateful. And this is what begins the *seeing* of the vision that GOD has for Hip Hop.

[41] It is first our appreciation for GOD and for what GOD has done for us with Hip Hop that leads the grateful to start asking some real questions regarding not Hip Hop, but the Love that sent Hip Hop to us. For we can never posture like we are somehow better or more holy than others when GOD's actual grace is upon us now! We are humbled by GOD's obvious mercy.

[42] It is first our respect for GOD and our acknowledgement that something was given to us that we did not work for nor even deserve that leads us to explore the spiritual meaning and purpose of Hip Hop. It is our acknowledgement of the *force* that has saved us that reveals to us the plan and purpose such a *force* has for us.

[43] Something happened to us over a 30-year period that resulted in our complete transformation and restoration. Hip Hop baffles the World today. Those who knew that we were trapped because of the traps they set for us were

amazed and baffled not only when we didn't die, but when we rose up and took everything our oppressors of the 20th century had—including their children.

44   We (Hip Hop) belong to no political, religious, financial or educational institution or group in the World. Yet, each of these institutions have used Hip Hop in their own desperateness to attract new followers to their causes.

45   For a culture with no central home base, no financial backing, no religious affiliation, no political organization, not even a race or an ethnicity that it can call its own; this culture Hip Hop created out of the historical activities of America's inner cities has risen up and has completely established itself in the minds of youth everywhere and has completely side-stepped the entire World system and ways of achieving success and stability in the World. Such a culture is indeed beyond this World and its power structure. Such a culture reveals the activity of GOD—the Love that rescued us.

46   This is the beginning of the Hip Hop spiritual life. Not a lot of bells and whistles, not a lot of claims to divinity, just simply living a life that shows appreciation for the *force* that rescued us. It's about living a life of gratitude which is expressed by asking the Great Rescuer, *for what purpose did you save me, and how may I serve your interests, which are clearly in harmony with my own?* Such a question is asked not in words, but in deeds.

47   The way in which you live is what actually shows GOD your level of appreciation for all that has been gracefully given to you. Appreciation for GOD's Grace is shown in how you treat others. Such an appreciation causes righteousness, the opposite causes judgment. This gospel is not about the critique of other religions. This gospel is not about Moses, Abraham, King Solomon, King David or Jesus. This is not about Krishna, the Buddha, or the

prophet Muhammad. This is not about Earth worship, or even Satanism, or Paganism. This is not even about atheism or some other philosophy. *To each their own*; we seriously respect them all and even see ourselves within all of these faiths and philosophies—ALL OF THEM!

⁴⁸ However, I must say here that the only consistent minister/prophet Hip Hop has ever heard advocating its divine existence and authority is the Honorable Minister Louis Farrakhan who has repeatedly warned us and asked us, *Who are you? You are the bearers of either light or darkness. If you continue to make your people think that the way we act is right, you are an emissary of darkness; you are not a bearer of light. It's one thing to talk about the condition out of which we live and say 'we keeping it real.' But hell, is that the way you wanna continue to live, and keep the reality of what the slave master and his children have placed our people in? Is that the reality that you want? Or do you want something better for yourself and better for your people? Well, how will you get something better if you don't raise their consciousness to aspire for something better? That's our job. The artist is the most important person! YOU ARE THE TEACHAS! The people listen to you, they don't listen to their preachers! Preacher's day is done!*

⁴⁹ What we are dealing with here is a NEW COVENANT, a new vision, the birth of a NEW PEOPLE. What we are dealing with here is the rediscovery of our ancient birthright, our original culture which is our true religion. We have no time or authority to critique and judge the covenants GOD has made with others. We are concerned with how GOD is dealing with us today.

⁵⁰ If we can acknowledge the fact that Hip Hop came to us as a saving force, we are then encouraged to ask, *For what purpose were we saved?* <u>Why</u> did Hip Hop happen? Not <u>how</u> did Hip Hop happen, but <u>why</u> did Hip Hop happen.

Yeah, Hip Hop has made a lot of people wealthy, including myself, but the real question for a grateful and highly appreciative Hiphoppa is "WHY?" Why is Hip Hop Hip Hop? What is its real purpose?

51   These questions reach far beyond getting a little money. These questions lead to salvation and peace. For if we have evidence of an unseen *force* operating amongst us (and we do), such evidence should lead us to ask more questions regarding such a *force* that seems to love us very much. What kind of *force* is it? Is it GOD or is it our own egos? How can we know?

52   Well first, if we can acknowledge that GOD—the great unified field of infinite possibilities—is one Great Event, and we, Hip Hop, are not separate from the oneness of such an Event, then Hip Hop too is an idea of GOD. And because we exist in the mind of GOD, we too belong to GOD and are heirs to a certain unique divinity unmatched by any other in our time. We can even see historically how other cultures have described the God-force that saved them from certain death as a voice, an inner-*urging*, a *Word* that instructed them and guided them to victory.

53   Such an *urging* is accompanied by seeming coincidences, miracles and natural events that line up with the intent of that *urging*. It is not words that GOD speaks, it is life, and the Voice of Life is Love—this is GOD's Word, and this is what saved us! *Public Enemy heard a Word. KRS ONE heard a Word. Big Daddy Kane heard a Word. Professor Griff heard a Word. So when they heard the Word, the Word inspired new thought. Yeah, pain, but then they started rappin'. There was no beat to it then, it was just spittin' out lyrics, but the lyrics were powerful! And the lyrics were not popular in those circles that produced us. So they were producing themselves! They were distributing themselves, and becoming rich! And so those who always watch us for trends [would ask], what's the*

new trend among them? Ooooh, it's called 'Rap,' bring some of it, let me hear it. When they took that in the room, they said we can't..., (gasp) uh, why, the 'negras' are listening to this? Why if they keep listening to this our police won't have work to do! They [Hip Hop] *gonna start building something.* (Minister Louis Farrakhan, 2007)

54   When I was wandering around Brooklyn and Manhattan without a house or a home it was this *Word* that guided me. It was this *Word* that showed me where to sleep, how to eat, and when to study. This is how I became The Teacha; I heard the Voice of GOD and followed it.

55   It was this *voice* that led me to leave home at 16 years of age and drop out of high school to pursue Hip Hop. It was this *voice* that taught me things that I had never read or heard before only to substantiate such knowing later in life.

56   It was this *voice* that recited to me the poetry that I recite to others. It was this *voice* that instructed me in battle. It was this *voice* that inspired the Stop The Violence Movement (1989), and Human Education Against Lies (1991), and the Temple of Hip Hop (1996), and this gospel for Hip Hop (2009).

57   It was this *voice* that first called me "teacha" and instructed me on how to inspire both elementary and college students without ever having attended college myself. It was this *voice* that told me what to say at Yale University, at Harvard University and at Oxford University in London. In fact, it was the instruction of GOD's voice, GOD's urging, that guided me though all of the colleges and universities I've taught at even though I didn't even hold a junior high school diploma.

58   It was this *voice* that taught me how to teach. It was this *voice* that first called me "KRS ONE," and I've repeated it ever since. Obedience to this *voice* is indeed the source

of my intellectual strength and artistic longevity. ALL PRAISE, GLORY AND WORSHIP BE TO GOD—the Love that has lifted us up. This is exactly why this gospel is before you now; it is because that same *still small voice* that has guided KRS thus far is guiding you now. This is real! And if you are indeed Hip Hop *you must learn* that there is a divine blessing and grace upon your life that you cannot afford to continue ignoring, and this is what the Gospel of Hip Hop is all about.

59   This training is all about getting you to recognize your spiritual reality and begin living your life outside of the fear and worry caused by excessive material want. This gospel acknowledges Hip Hop as an idea of Divine Mind and reunites the Hiphoppa with the existence of such a Mind. This is how I became KRS ONE. Others may have entered the Rap music industry in other ways, or may have been hooked up by *this one* or *that one*. But as for KRS ONE, it was (and still is) the mystical life and its real effects that got me started as an emcee/rapper, and this awareness is what I teach to all serious apprentices.

60   For I am not who I am today just because I can rap. Study KRS's history closely. If my life is not a living example of what I teach, then you have no reason to believe anything that I am saying here. But if my life is evidence of my claims then why deny your own blessing and the gospel that speaks directly to YOU for YOUR salvation. I am who I am so that you may clearly see who you are.

61   But the question we are dealing with here is *how do we know if it was GOD that has rescued us?* The quick answer is because I just told you so, and if you join with me in faith you too can become heir to this New Covenant. But a longer answer explores what others have experienced in history regarding the saving Grace of the one GOD.

62   One thing we know for sure is that when GOD raises

up a *people* it has historically been the most downtrodden, impoverished, powerless group of people that GOD chooses to restore and raise up. And part of the reason for this historically has been that GOD chooses the most powerless people to raise up, the most ignorant to educate, the most unorganized to order so that they and the World may know once again that GOD IS GOD! And nothing in the World is above the power of GOD.

63   It doesn't matter what the World is doing or what the World has, when GOD decides to move, no force on or in the earth can stop such a movement. Historically, over the past 36 years, Hip Hop has been such a movement in the United States. *And now this people, who were once destroyed, have found favor with GOD, as he has always favored the enslaved, the oppressed, the downtrodden. And he has favored us, not just with a prophet, but with his presence. And out of us chose one to lead, teach, and guide us to the path of his divine favor. And with that presence, he's offering to us the scepter of rulership. That, that which was not becomes that which is. And that, that which was the bottom rail, he will bring it to the top. And that which was last, he would make it first. This is the Lord's doing and it is marvelous in our eyes.* (Minister Louis Farrakhan, 2007)

64   The strength and power that Hip Hop has did not come from us, we received it, yet it was already within us when we received it—this is GOD. In addition, it is clear that Hip Hop operates within a certain moral immunity. There is clearly a grace over us and we must ask, for what reason are we being excused like this? For what reason do we have this grace? And for how long?

65   Know this. Grace is a kind of mercy. It implies that you are undeserving of the mercy you are receiving. That for the activity of your selfish, inconsiderate needs you should have been dead, injured or imprisoned. But GOD's Grace

comes and rescues you from the judgment that you truly deserve. Some people realize the Grace of GOD over their lives and they humble themselves in thanksgiving and praise for the Love they didn't deserve. Others walk blindly.

66   Now when you realize that in GOD's eye all of us are basically animals grunting and groaning before GOD, and that our attempts at righteousness can never match GOD's, you realize that you are under GOD's Grace, that you are being protected from your own ignorance and excused of your own immaturity RIGHT NOW! Others are being killed, injured and/or incarcerated for what you are doing every day.

67   But when you get truthful with yourself and you look at the amount of illegal, unhealthy and stupid things you are doing and saying yet you are never really caught by the system, you are never really sick, and danger always seems to escape you, you realize that it is GOD's Grace that is protecting you. Not your intellect, not your knowledge, not your reputation, not your respect, not your money, not even your faith has protected you from the effects of your own immaturity; IT WAS GOD!

68   When you realize this for real, you also realize that something bigger than you, something stronger than you, something smarter, faster and calmer than you is trying to communicate with you. When you can actually recognize the grace on your life you seek not more of the grace, but more of the grace-giver. If you actually care, you will want to know why such a gift is being given to you?

69   The first obvious reason is love. GOD cares about us. The second obvious reason is understanding. GOD understands us more than we understand ourselves. We belong to GOD. And finally, there's a plan, a purpose, a work that needs to be done. The blessing in all of this is that for some reason GOD believes we can get the work done.

Or in this case, GOD seems to believe that Hip Hop can get the work done.

70   Now when you look at this closely, you see that GOD's Grace is also GOD's faith in the belief that we (Hip Hop) are worthy of grace; that we will get the work done. For when GOD gives a people grace it is because of the work they've been called to do, it is because of a purpose that will be fulfilled. We are being excused of our wickedness and immaturity right now because we are obviously victorious in our future. GOD can see that, and we are encouraged to see that also.

71   But such grace is not a free pass for continued ignorance. Don't get it twisted; if you are not fulfilling the vision GOD has place upon your life, suddenly and without warning your grace can disappear. Grace is only provided for you to catch up to the vision GOD has for you. If you are not perfecting yourself and moving toward the vision GOD has shown you, grace will not save you from your own stagnation and ungratefulness.

72   GOD's vision for Hip Hop is also GOD's promise to Hip Hop. But GOD's people are called long before they even know that they have been called, this is where grace comes in. Grace gives you a chance to catch up to GOD's already in-progress plan and vision.

73   Know this. GOD calls us things before we actually become them. GOD's vision for us is not a far-off dream, it is an actual promise as to what GOD has in store for us. However, if you don't rise to the promise you don't get it. It is not that the promise will not happen, it is more that you just won't be part of it.

74   The Hip Hop spiritual life acknowledges GOD's already in-progress grace and inspires the Hiphoppa to walk worthy of that already received grace. The Hip Hop spiritual life acknowledges the standards, practices and principles of

the grace-giver. We respect the promise and the promiser. For it is our respect for the promiser that motivates us to rise to the level of the promise.

⁷⁵ Just imagine, if someone promised you something, you would have to respect the promiser in order to receive the promise. You have to believe that the one promising is actually capable of delivering such a promise. If you don't believe or respect the promiser, even if the promiser can deliver the promise, you will never achieve it simply because you don't respect nor believe the promiser.

⁷⁶ A promise is like a two-way street; both the giver and the receiver have to cooperate for a promise to be fulfilled, especially a promise that is like a received gift. If you don't join in on the faith of the promiser, it is you who walks away from your own gift. In this case, the promiser is GOD and Hip Hop is the receiver of the promise/gift.

⁷⁷ All those who join in on this faith, join in on a new covenant complete with health, love, awareness and wealth; a covenant that provides peace and prosperity to all who claim Hip Hop as their culture and lifestyle. This is real.

⁷⁸ GOD has already made us a holy nation, the challenge for us now is to rise to the character of GOD's Vision of us before this season of grace runs out. And the key word here is "vision." Vision gives us direction, purpose and restraint. When you have a vision to achieve and you are seriously committed to it, the World's temptations don't affect you.

⁷⁹ When you have a vision to achieve and you are achieving it, you are in harmony with not only GOD's Vision, you are in harmony with GOD's Law. In such a condition grace is unnecessary; it is the living Law of GOD that protects and guides you now. Grace is always needed in some form or another, but at this level of awareness you are no longer unaware, or immature, or ignorant so grace is not

really necessary for you.

80   Grace is for those who unknowingly break spiritual laws because of immaturity or ignorance. However, when the Hiphoppa atones for past ignorance and attunes herself to the vision GOD has promised her nation, that Hiphoppa becomes GOD's Vision and thus GOD's Law; fulfilling the promise and thus saving herself and her whole World from destruction. This is the *good news* for Hip Hop. This is the gospel.

81   The Gospel of Hip Hop comes to Hip Hop at this time because our grace period is running out again. This word keeps GOD's judgment at bay and gives us time to catch up to GOD's Vision for Hip Hop. This is not about possessions, this is about *position*. This is about getting into position to receive the Promise of GOD.

82   Therefore, the time has come to make a final decision regarding how deeply involved you shall explore your Hip Hop reality. Is Hip Hop still just a side thing to you, or is it really your birthright and heritage? There it is.

THE LOVE

[1]   Before and beyond the collective history of our recording contracts, platinum sales awards and tour dates, we have been the direct recipients of a saving force, a spiritual form of intelligence which can only be described as *Love.*

[2]   But how soon did we forget who fed us when we were hungry, who taught us when we were ignorant, who clothed us when we were naked, who sheltered us when we were houseless? We were quick to pray for what we wanted in our time of need, but after we were out of the danger or satisfied in some way we forgot that we've just prayed to "something" that actually responded.

[3]   The question is, how serious are you about GOD? Many people believe in GOD but only a tiny few actually appreciate GOD and show it with a life dedicated to union with GOD. How soon did we forget how helpless and vulnerable we were before the threats of our enemies were miraculously dealt with? How can we forget? Such forgetfulness is almost always reminded by a return to hunger and powerlessness.

[4]   Miracles happen every day, all day. But most people don't expect them so they don't see them, or experience them. Strange, kooky-type events go on all the time and people simply disregard them as coincidences or they ignore them altogether, then they criticize their own spiritual experiences as not real, childish and/or naïve.

[5]   Most people cannot deal with the possible fact that

what they are seeing is not all of what they are getting. That there is a deeper, faster, stronger reality that can actually override the mechanics of their known physical universe and its laws. That things might not actually be the way we think they are.

6   For most people such a revelation is indeed scary and not even to be discussed. But for a select few, such a revelation is inspiring and encourages such people to learn more, seek more and live more!

7   This is what the Gospel of Hip Hop is all about. It is about the restoration and further development of one's love for Hip Hop because it is through Love that we learn of the deeper lessons regarding the nature of GOD.

8   The Gospel of Hip Hop points the way to a spiritually lived Hip Hop life—however, Love is the code that tells the universe that you can be trusted with information that must be lived in order to be learned. Know this. The universe thinks and responds to your thinking, and this is the essence of what Hip Hop is for us; it is our relationship with divinity. Hip Hop is what we are doing with our portion of GOD.

9   When we are performing the role of a pimp, a hustler, drug dealer, stick-up kid, whore, murderer, etc., this is what we are doing with our portion of GOD—the Love that has rescued us from self-destruction. When we are performing the role of teacha, minister, parent, volunteer, emcee, etc., this is also what we are doing with our portion of GOD—the Love that inspires us to self-create.

10   For if Hip Hop was created explicitly for self-destruction then self-destruction would be fine and we would thrive upon such a condition. But Hip Hop was not created to self-destruct, it was created to self-create—*"Hip Hop, ya don't stop!"* And this is how we know that its inspiration was of GOD; Hip Hop came from within us, yet

we still had to learn it. In our early days, we felt the fullness of it but still had to develop artistic techniques to express it in Nature. Hip Hop came to us, from within us.

11   Hip Hop is the name of the Love that rescued us from oppression. It (Hip Hop) is the term given to the inner force that inspires us to self-create. This gospel is a tribute to the Love that has saved us and brought us together under the title of HIP HOP. And this is the message. LOVE IS THE MESSAGE! This is what we originally did our artistic elements for, we did it for the Love. That unspoken collective intelligence that is shared psychically by all who belong to the group.

12   Those who belong to the group feel the Love. Those who care for the group feel the Love. Those who seek love feel the Love, and it is this god that we serve. Without form, without name, without origin, the Love is that saving force in the World many civilizations have written about and have called "GOD" for thousands of years.

13   We have observed now that Love is a divine activity, an intelligence unto itself that saves, rewards, inspires and teaches all who are part of its group. LOVE IS GOD! But Love seems to also be selective; it thinks and judges.

14   Many follow the tradition that "God is Love" and yes, such is the Truth. But when you really begin to live out this statement you find that it is more the fact that "Love is GOD." "GOD" is a term that makes Love understandable to us. The term "GOD" is not anything unto itself, but what the term "GOD" describes is actually Love and the activities of Love.

15   Yes, for many people "God is Love," but for us, Love has been our GOD. Love is what we have served, and it is Love that has saved us. "GOD" is not above Love. Love is GOD. Love is not from GOD, Love is the only god we have ever known.

[16]   The term "GOD" is not above the term Love because without Love the term "GOD" has no meaning and ceases to exist. For it is Love that defines GOD and empowers GOD to act. Love is the true god and to love is GOD.

[17]   For it is not GOD that governs and orders the universe, it is Love. And it is not GOD that destroys the universe, it is the illusory absence of Love. Therefore, let us return to our ancient understanding of GOD as an event of Great Love that operates as the universe itself. Let us return to our ancestral wisdom formed from the real experiences we have had with GOD—the Love that has enlightened us.

[18]   Before the kidnap, rape, theft, deception and murder of our ancestors and grandparents which forced upon us our modern-day view and perception of GOD, we worshipped the power of Love. We saw it, we felt it and we expressed it toward one another—even to those who would eventually enslave our parents.

[19]   Over many years some of us would track its patterns and repeated behaviors in an effort to communicate and be more in harmony with such a *being*. Of all the virtues available to humanity, Love is truly the god of them all.

[20]   This gospel for Hip Hop acknowledges the Love that set us aside in the World and has made us Hip Hop. This gospel acknowledges the grace bestowed upon Hip Hop and Hiphoppas, and urges the Hip Hop community to rise to the promise GOD has made to us.

[21]   And what is the promise GOD has made to us? The promise is that if we turn from our own ignorance and immaturity, and seek the face of GOD, we shall experience that ancient blessing that topples the most powerful nations and establishes the nation that has repented and has obeyed. The promise is that if we ever dare to rise to our divinity, GOD promises to meet us there. Our divinity begins with the proper understanding of love and what it means to

forgive and care for one another.

22   With this understanding we learn that we can never really love GOD; we can only be Love (God) toward each other. We have observed now that the way to experience GOD is to experience true Love, and this is achieved not by receiving love, but by being Love itself.

23   Such an approach to spiritual living begins one's understanding of Hip Hop's spiritual life. And again, this has nothing to do with the spiritual concepts and experiences of other cultures far older than ours. For we have realized now that your culture is your religion, and it is impossible for us (Hiphoppas) to have a relationship with GOD through a culture that is not inherently ours. OUR culture is OUR direct connection to GOD. Our cultural life is the actual path that we must take to arrive at the presence and power of GOD.

24   Much respect to all who seek the face of GOD. However, this gospel reflects the actual notes taken over a 14-year period with over 40 years of living Hip Hop spiritually. Others may have discovered other truths, but this gospel documents the spiritual truths we as a Hip Hop community have discovered at the birth of our civilization. These are the principles WE must never forget.

25   This is what it means for us to be and remain free, to take responsibility for ourselves, to be able to chart our own path toward the divine and make our own humble observations regarding spiritual, cultural and political matters. Are we not free-thinking adults? Does GOD not speak to us as well? Well, let us begin acting as such, beginning with the documentation of what we have seen, heard and felt regarding the activity of GOD for ourselves.

26   Let us as scholars and Hip Hop citizens acknowledge the presence of the Love that has saved us. With this gospel let us proclaim our reconnection and trust for the Love

that has guided us thus far. We respect the experiences older civilizations have had with GOD, but now it is time we experience GOD for ourselves. We no longer need an interpreter, OUR CULTURE IS OUR RELIGION AND OUR RELIGION IS OUR CULTURE!

27   Such a life is not for everyone though. Hip Hop is alive, it is a thinking faculty of the universe itself and it chooses who it shall reveal its secrets to. Those of us who have committed ourselves to observing the divine activities of Love in human affairs have observed that the force that brought Hip Hop into existence planned, protected and nurtured us long before we knew we were being developed into Hip Hop. Hip Hop started for us before we were aware of it.

28   Our observations show that Divine Love was the first act that got Hip Hop started. Something cared about us. Something cared about our group. Long before we knew what we would become, a loving-caring force was at work guiding our steps and molding our collective character to become Hip Hop today, and we acknowledge the existence of this guiding force. It is to this force that we owe our existence. ALL PRAISE, GLORY AND WORSHIP BE TO GOD—the Love that has made us Hip Hop!

29   For us, it is Love that produces the intentions of our minds and we live and perceive our reality in GOD— the Love that fights for us. And because nothing exists outside of Love, including Hip Hop, we accept our divinity as Hiphoppas (as GOD's intention).

30   For we now know for sure that we belong to GOD knowing that Hip Hop itself has its source in Eternal Being along with everything else in the known and unknown universe. Know this. Hip Hop exists for divine reasons and we have come into material existence as part of the divine order of the universe. We (Hip Hop) are not a mistake; we

are a manifestation of Divine Love.

[31]   We are NOT here to just sing and dance! WE ARE PART OF THE DIVINE ORDER OF THINGS! Hip Hop is a product of human genius clearly inspired by Divine Mind. Therefore, our first work as a young nation is to take the source of our *being* more seriously, and this is what the Temple of Hip Hop is all about. Here, we approach the *being* of Hiphop seriously.

[32]   Announced in 1996, *The Temple of Hip Hop was formed to work in 3 phases. (1) As an organization that protects, preserves and promotes Hip Hop Kulture. (2) To open a cultural learning center and facility for Hip Hop Kulture, featuring a museum exhibiting artifacts of Hip Hop Kulture. (3) To build a school recognizing and teaching Hip Hop as the consciousness of our common culture, and (4) to create an authentic collaborative history for the culture.* (Men of Hip Hop calendar series, 1998)

[33]   In short, the Temple of Hip Hop is a Hip Hop preservation society and ministry established to ensure the longevity and further development of traditional Hip Hop in the World. Our society is made up of exceptional Hiphoppas who are united in the cause for Hip Hop's cultural, political and spiritual expansion.

[34]   However again, the Temple of Hip Hop as well as the Gospel of Hip Hop are not intended for all people, even those who are participating in Hip Hop's culture and elements. Both the Temple of Hip Hop and its gospel attract those Hiphoppas who intuitively feel what is already presented in this *first instrument* and only need to be reminded of such Truth in a culturally relevant way. For many, this gospel will be more of a confirmation than an education.

[35]   Nothing that is taught here is actually new. However, the way in which it is taught is indeed new. Truth

is Truth no matter where it comes from. It is only in the way that such Truth is presented that gives the impression that what is being taught is somehow new or original.

³⁶ Much of what is taught here is ancient and timeless, and you will be able to find many of our principles in a variety of spiritual circles. But the reason for this gospel is that no one in my time seems to be speaking directly to the Hip Hop community regarding its spiritual, cultural and political development, and part of the reason for this I suspect is that no one can do this work for us—this work we must do for and by ourselves.

³⁷ This is that part of our journey where we must "go it alone," blazing our own path toward union with the divine. Know this. Revolution only works for those who participate in it. Tradition reveals its secrets and its powers only to those who are committed to the tradition.

³⁸ GOD speaks to those who speak to GOD. GOD listens to those who listen to GOD. The Hip Hop life that we live can only really be experienced by true Hiphoppas committed to living Hip Hop spiritually. Others can read this gospel, watch instructional Hip Hop DVDs, even watch us, imitating the effects of OUR real Hip Hop lives, but ultimately if you have not committed your entire being to the spiritual exploration of Hip Hop it will be a long time before you begin to experience the awareness of a spiritually lived Hip Hop life. And this goes for anything, really.

³⁹ Even further, those who choose not to develop themselves or the *craft* which feeds them and their children become subject to the agendas of those who have. And on a more personal note, if the people around you are not participants in the revolution you have embarked upon they will not be able to comprehend your ways or take part in the fruits of your success; they have not traveled your path, therefore they will not have (know) your

experience or perception.

40   You can help them, you can give to them, you can assist them, you can teach them, you can love them, you can feed them and you can advise them, but you cannot share your space and time with those who have not traveled your path or have not gained your experience.

41   You cannot trust those who haven't traveled your path with the commitments your path requires. Your path is for you! Your blessings are for you! Your talents are uniquely yours. Yes, you are special. Everything else can be shared except the actual living of your own life experiences, these are authentically yours. You should keep a journal; such is your personal gospel.

42   The Love in your heart will want to unite with those who suffer and are in need. But please remember that everyone is <u>where</u> they are because of <u>who</u> they are. To truly save a person from their own illusions and hardships it is not you that must unite with them, it is they who must unite with you! You uniting with the ignorant and the immature will only lead to your own suffering.

43   Your natural humility and care for others will direct you to suffer with those who surround you because without you they would be lost! You know it and they know it but they front like "you ain't special" and you agree, *I ain't special, I'm not above anyone, what I do anyone can do if they put their minds to it.*

44   All of this is simply not true. Because of the life-path that you have chosen and mastered you ARE actually *special*. Yes, you ARE respectfully above everyone else who has not mastered even their own life-path and purpose. And no, everyone cannot do what you do or even what you have done. Realize your uniqueness right now and let no one degrade you or lead you to doubt yourself with the experiences of their lives.

45   Yes, you are special! YOU ARE HIP HOP! Your only challenge is your own belief in the existence of your own Hip Hop reality. Repent now, your victory is closer to you than your hands!

46   Prophet Farrakhan has already said to us, *YOU ARE NOT CONSCIOUS OF HOW POWERFUL GOD HAS MADE YOU; IN THE WRONG DIRECTION! BUT IF YOU TURN IN THE RIGHT DIRECTION YOU WILL SPARK REVOLUTION ALL OVER THE WORLD! But it's not a revolution of bloodshed.*

47   The prophet continued, *I can't be like Jonah anymore and neither can you; hiding from your mission, running away from what your real assignment is! So the fish is swallowing you up. But when that boy learned to pray, he was spit up on dry land and he said 'I surrender GOD; I've been fightin' you, but I know it's time.' I hope that you will say I surrender GOD I know it's time, that I can do better than what I'm doing. Money is not more important than the rise of a suffering people into the fulfillment of the promise of GOD. Nothing is more important than your people becoming truly free.* There it is.

THE PROMISED LAND

¹ Peace and much love to all generations of Hip Hop—past, present and future. Hip Hop is our *Word*, and this *Word* is the Truth of our *being*. From this *Word* all of our words come. For it is our words that are the Truth of our thoughts and intentions. Words are the fragrance of our being.

² Know this. Words are Truth's physical image, and we are made into the image of the words that we think and intend. WE ARE NOT JUST DOING HIP HOP; WE ARE HIP HOP! We are that word, and the abilities we give that word are the abilities we give to ourselves and to our children forever. Our word is our name, our name is our nature, and our nature is our specialized ability in physical reality.

³ Hip Hop is clearly a divine response to our particular suffering in the World, and it has been the study of this "response" that has revealed to us the nature of GOD—*the Love* we serve.

⁴ Hip Hop has clearly given us all purpose. Hip Hop has even made many of us rich, famous and influential. However, no one person can ever take full credit for the creation and artistic development of Hip Hop itself—it just happened! Yes, Kool DJ Herc, Afrika Bambaataa, Grandmaster Flash, Crazy Legs and others are indeed the architects of Hip Hop, and can even be called "fathers." But there were simply too many unseen, supernatural forces that assisted in Hip Hop's birth and development

for any one person to claim exclusive credit for the creation of Hip Hop.

5   Even Kool DJ Herc, Afrika Bambaataa, Grandmaster Flash, Crazy Legs, Phase II and others were all unaware that what they were doing in the 1970s would eventually become Hip Hop in the 1980s. In fact, these great icons of the Hip Hop arts and sciences were more created by Hip Hop, than Hip Hop was created by them. We actually discovered Hip Hop as we participated in it.

6   In the early days of our development, Hip Hop first appeared as a saving force; a form of recreation, a neighborhood pastime. It wasn't about making money initially; it was more about expressing what you would do when you acquired money. Hip Hop was what we did because we had limited resources and little money for anything else.

7   Know this. It was the lack of money and other resources that caused Hip Hop to exist. Hip Hop existed outside of the mainstream and its validations. Hip Hop was what WE did independent of the World's value systems. Hip Hop was (and still is) our only salvation. Hip Hop is what saved us—nothing else!

8   For it is known by all the sages and learned spiritual teachers of all the ages that GOD responds to suffering. That when all human strength is exhausted and all Worldly avenues of success have been closed, it is at that precise moment that GOD appears and we are saved again!

9   THE EXISTENCE OF HIP HOP IS EVIDENCE FOR THE EXISTENCE OF GOD AND GOD'S LOVE AND CONCERN FOR HIPHOPPAS. Hip Hop itself is a miracle! A divine solution! No human hand can ever take full credit for the true birth and development of Hip Hop. HIP HOP IS GOD'S DIVINE ACTIVITY EXISTING AMONGST US TODAY. For it was GOD that made us

Hiphoppas, and this is the good news!

10   It was GOD that inspired Kool DJ Herc. It was GOD that inspired Afrika Bambaataa. It was GOD that inspired Crazy Legs. It was GOD that inspired Phase II, Taki 183, and Cornbread. It was GOD that inspired Grandmaster Flash, GrandWizzard Theodore as well as the Furious Five. It was GOD that inspired Run-DMC and Jam Master Jay.

11   It was GOD that inspired LL Cool J, Doug E. Fresh, Salt-N-Pepa, MC Lyte, Public Enemy, Poor Righteous Teachers, Niggaz With Attitude, MC Hammer, and so on, and so on, and so on. And this is the good news; through Hip Hop GOD HAS OPENED TO US A NEW WAY TOWARD UNION WITH THE DIVINE!

12   The *good news* is that GOD IS REAL! And this is our faith (experience). For us, the existence of Hip Hop proves the existence of GOD's presence within us, around us and for us. Yes, for us! GOD is with us! The spirit realm is all around us! GOD is actually present with us right now! GOD is at this very moment reading this gospel with us, to us, for us right now! Feel the presence! GOD actually likes you as Hip Hop; this is why you exist.

13   The existence of Hip Hop proves for all Hiphoppas that there is a divine intelligence looking out for us (or rather looking out from us). Something divine is concerned about Hip Hop, and this is the focus of our study. As Hip Hop scholars, we are seeking and tracking the patterns and nature of The Force that made us Hip Hop—and this is right for us.

14   As a community, we love GOD. Even though we may fall short of what GOD truly intends for us, still we yearn for the presence of GOD. We know that Rap music is only the early leaves of a very young Hip Hop fruit that we, in immaturity and ignorance, continue to eat before it has

fully grown into the fruit-bearing tree that it was intended to become. We are so much more than the leaves that bud up first to catch the sunlight. We have so much more growing to do.

15   Hip Hop today is like the seed of a great fruit tree given to a poor and desperate people in an effort to save them from the effects of the terrorism their parents faced. But because of their own desperateness, fears and doubts caused by such terrorism, today they eat the seeds as opposed to planting the seeds to grow the tree.

16   Hip Hop is like a seed that, if planted in your heart and watered by your faith, will spring up in you like a mighty fruit tree that feeds you and everyone around you *all year 'round*. But in our own desperateness to eat something, anything, we eat the seeds of our own salvation, ultimately remaining hungry and unsatisfied, never truly attaining the harvest that the seed was meant to produce for us.

17   Another way of looking at this is to say that we are stuck eating eggs because we never nurtured the eggs long enough for them to become chickens. It is like we are eating raw food because we haven't yet learned to cook. In other words, when we plant the seed (Hip Hop) we never wait long enough for the seed to grow into the tree (peace and prosperity) that it was intended to become.

18   This is the actual state of Hip Hop today. We have been given the seeds to a great new civilization but the seeds themselves are so valuable in the World that we just sell the seeds and eat the seeds without ever thinking about planting the seeds or from whom such seeds come.

19   Many have become rich participating in Hip Hop's artistic elements, but they are only rich in their accumulation and consumption of seeds. They would be even richer if they would plant the seeds in their own minds and in the minds of those who need the seeds the most. But such is

the state of a desperate and traumatized people; we may be outside of the prison walls but we are still lining up to eat.

20   This is why we as a people are not yet out of the dark in my time. Yes, we have been liberated, but we are not yet free. Yes, the chains are off of our feet, but we haven't yet begun to walk OUR path. Yes, the chains are off our hands, but we haven't begun to reach or grasp for those things necessary to OUR healing and growth. Yes, today the chains are even off of our minds, but we still have not begun to actually THINK FOR OURSELVES!

21   Yes, think for ourselves! We have the "Hip" (the awareness) of Hip Hop, but as a group we have yet to attain the actual "Hop" (the movement) of Hip Hop. We think like Hiphoppas, but we do not yet move like Hiphoppas. We are aware of ourselves as a specific social group, but we are simply not moving collectively as the group we perceive ourselves as. This is why the Temple of Hip Hop exists.

22   Such a movement requires mass motivation caused by mass inspiration. This type of inspiration is deliberately caused by those who are the caretakers of the culture they seek to expand; they are the physical embodiment of what they teach. Others can perform the artistic elements of Hip Hop; this is good and highly respected. But if those same performers have no clear idea as to why they perform, then longevity, even as a performer, is out of their reach.

23   Hip Hop is so young in my time that we haven't yet produced authentically committed, serious cultural caretakers, and again, this is why our temple for Hip Hop exists. Our temple is not a physical location, it is a society of Hip Hop culture-keepers who not only perform Hip Hop artistically, but also spiritually.

24   Our goal as a learning institution is to produce some real Hip Hop scholars capable of not only studying and teaching Hip Hop, but also producing it. As Hip Hop's

scholars, we are also Hip Hop's gardeners; we beautify and maintain the Hip Hop landscape, assisting GOD in the growing of our Hip Hop environment.

25   For us, such an environment is the *land* promised to us by GOD if we would walk with GOD never forgetting that it is not Hip Hop that sustains us, it is GOD. Hip Hop is simply the name of our interaction with GOD. Hip Hop is the solution GOD sent to relieve our suffering. Hip Hop is the seed (solution) of a new vine (people).

26   Those that walk this life path are shown the secrets and the mysteries to the fabric of life itself. The *good news* is that we have identified the Love we belong to, and as Hip Hop scholars we are encouraged to seek and document the nature and pattern of this Love which continues to guide us, protect us and teach us.

27   As Hip Hop scholars, our study of the Love begins at August 28, 1963 when our King—the true king, Dr. Martin Luther King Jr.—stood before the World in Washington, D.C. and stated…

28   *I am happy to join with you today in what will go down in history as the greatest demonstration for freedom in the history of <u>our nation</u>.*

29   *Five score years ago, a great American, in whose symbolic shadow we stand today, signed the Emancipation Proclamation. This momentous decree came as a great beacon light of hope to millions of Negro slaves who had been seared in the flames of withering injustice. It came as a joyous daybreak to end the long night of their captivity.*

30   *But one hundred years later, the Negro still is not free; one hundred years later, the life of the Negro is still sadly crippled by the manacles of segregation and the chains of discrimination; <u>one hundred years later, the Negro lives on a lonely island of poverty in the midst of a vast ocean of material prosperity</u>; one hundred years later, the Negro is still languished*

in the corners of American society and finds himself in exile in his own land.

31   *So we've come here today to dramatize a shameful condition. In a sense we've come to our nation's capital to cash a check. When the architects of our republic wrote the magnificent words of the Constitution and the Declaration of Independence, they were signing a promissory note to which every American was to fall heir. This note was the promise that all men, yes, Black men as well as White men, would be guaranteed the unalienable rights of life, liberty and the pursuit of happiness.*

32   *It is obvious today that America has defaulted on this promissory note in so far as her citizens of color are concerned. Instead of honoring this sacred obligation, America has given the Negro people a bad check; a check which has come back marked 'insufficient funds.'*

33   *We refuse to believe that there are insufficient funds in the great vaults of opportunity of this nation. And so we've come to cash this check, a check that will give us upon demand the riches of freedom and the security of justice.*

34   *We have also come to this hallowed spot to remind America of the fierce urgency of now! This is no time to engage in the luxury of cooling off or to take the tranquilizing drug of gradualism.*

35   *Now is the time to make real the promises of democracy; now is the time to rise from the dark and desolate valley of segregation to the sunlit path of racial justice; now is the time to lift our nation from the quicksands of racial injustice to the solid rock of brotherhood; now is the time to make justice a reality for all GOD's children.*

36   *It would be fatal for the nation to overlook the urgency of the moment. This sweltering summer of the Negro's legitimate discontent will not pass until there is an invigorating autumn of freedom and equality.*

[37] *Nineteen sixty-three is not an end, but a beginning.* And those who hope that the Negro needed to blow off steam and will now be content, will have a rude awakening if the nation returns to business as usual.

[38] There will be neither rest nor tranquility in America until the Negro is granted his citizenship rights. The whirlwinds of revolt will continue to shake the foundations of our nation until the bright day of justice emerges.

[39] But there is something that I must say to my people who stand on the warm threshold which leads into the palace of justice. *In the process of gaining our rightful place we must not be guilty of wrongful deeds.*

[40] Let us not seek to satisfy our thirst for freedom by drinking from the cup of bitterness and hatred. *We must forever conduct our struggle on the high plane of dignity and discipline.*

[41] We must not allow our creative protest to degenerate into physical violence. *Again and again we must rise to the majestic heights of meeting physical force with soul force.*

[42] The marvelous new militancy which has engulfed the Negro community must not lead us to a distrust of all White people, for many of our White brothers, as evidenced by their presence here today, have come to realize that their destiny is tied up with our destiny and they have come to realize that their freedom is inextricably bound to our freedom.

[43] *This offense we share mounted to storm the battlements of injustice must be carried forth by a biracial army. We cannot walk alone.*

[44] And as we walk, we must make the pledge that we shall always march ahead. We cannot turn back. There are those who are asking the devotees of civil rights, "When will you be satisfied?"

[45] *We can never be satisfied as long as the Negro is the victim of the unspeakable horrors of police brutality.*

[46]   *We can never be satisfied as long as our bodies, heavy with fatigue of travel, cannot gain lodging in the motels of the highway and the hotels of the cities.*

[47]   *We cannot be satisfied as long as the Negro's basic mobility is from a smaller ghetto to a larger one.*

[48]   *We can never be satisfied as long as our children are stripped of their selfhood and robbed of their dignity by signs stating 'for whites only.'*

[49]   *We cannot be satisfied as long as a Negro in Mississippi cannot vote and a Negro in New York believes he has nothing for which to vote.*

[50]   *No, we are not satisfied until justice rolls down like waters and righteous like a mighty stream.*

[51]   *I am not unmindful that some of you come here out of excessive trails and tribulation. Some of you have come fresh from narrow jail cells. Some of you have come from areas where your quest for freedom left you battered by the storms of persecution and staggered by the winds of police brutality.*

[52]   *You have been the veterans of creative suffering. Continue to work with the faith that unearned suffering is redemptive.*

[53]   At this point our King was overcome by GOD's spirit and turned away from his prepared speech and began free-styling from his heart. As author Drew D. Hansen points out in his book *The Dream: Martin Luther King, Jr., and the Speech that Inspired a Nation,* Dr. King was supposed to end his speech with: *And so today, let us go back to our communities as members of the international association for the advancement of creative dissatisfaction. Let us go back and work with all the strength we can muster to get strong civil rights legislation in this session of congress. Let us go down from this place to ascend other peaks of purpose. Let us descend from this mountaintop to climb other hills of hope.* But he did not say this part of his written speech publicly.

⁵⁴ As Mr. Hansen points out, prophetess/gospel singer Mahalia Jackson urged him on, saying, *Tell us about the dream, Martin!* And the King began speaking from his heart, unscripted and unrehearsed.

⁵⁵ *Go back to Mississippi; go back to Alabama; go back to South Carolina; go back to Georgia; go back to Louisiana; go back to the slums and ghettos of northern cities, knowing that somehow this situation can, and will be changed. Let us not wallow in the valley of despair.*

⁵⁶ The prophetess called out to him again saying, *Tell them about the dream, Martin!* And the King continued.

⁵⁷ *So I say to you, my friends, that even though we must face the difficulties of today and tomorrow, I still have a dream. It is a dream deeply rooted in the American dream that one day this nation shall rise up and live out the true meaning of its creed—we hold these truths to be self-evident, that all men are created equal.*

⁵⁸ *I have a dream that one day on the red hills of Georgia, sons of former slaves and sons of former slaveowners will be able to sit down together at the table of brotherhood.*

⁵⁹ *I have a dream that one day, even the state of Mississippi, a state sweltering with the heat of injustice, sweltering with the heat of oppression, will be transformed into an oasis of freedom and justice.*

⁶⁰ *I have a dream that my four little children will one day live in a nation where they will not be judged by the color of their skin but by the content of their character. I have a dream today!*

⁶¹ *I have a dream that one day, down in Alabama, with it vicious racists, with its governor having his lips dripping with the words of interposition and nullification, that one day, right there in Alabama, little Black boys and Black girls will be able to join hands with little White boys and White girls as sisters and brothers. I have a dream today!*

[62] *I have a dream that every valley shall be exalted, every hill and mountain shall be made low, the rough places shall be made plain, and the crooked places shall be made straight and the glory of the Lord shall be revealed and all flesh shall see it together.*

[63] *This is <u>our hope</u>. <u>This is the faith</u> that I go back to the South with. With <u>this faith</u> we will be able to hew out of the mountain of despair a stone of hope. With <u>this faith</u> we will be able to transform the jangling discords of our nation into a beautiful symphony of brotherhood.*

[64] The King then returned to his written speech, *With <u>this faith</u> we will be able to work together, to pray together, to struggle together, to go to jail together, to stand up for freedom together, knowing that we will be free one day.*

[65] But the cheering crowd and the overwhelming spirit of GOD led our King away from his prepared text again and back to his freestyle. The King continued.

[66] *This will be the day when all of GOD's children will be able to sing with new meaning—'My country 'tis of thee; sweet land of liberty; of thee I sing; land where my fathers died, land of the pilgrim's pride; from every mountain side, let freedom ring'—and if America is to be a great nation, this must become true.*

[67] *So let freedom ring from the prodigious hilltops of New Hampshire.*

[68] *Let freedom ring from the mighty mountains of New York.*

[69] *Let freedom ring from the heightening Alleghenies of Pennsylvania.*

[70] *Let freedom ring from the snow capped Rockies of Colorado.*

[71] *Let freedom ring from the curvaceous slopes of California.*

[72] *But not only that. Let freedom ring from Stone*

Mountain of Georgia.

[73]   *Let freedom ring from Lookout Mountain of Tennessee.*

[74]   *Let freedom ring from every hill and molehill of Mississippi, from every mountainside, let freedom ring.*

[75]   *And when we allow freedom to ring, when we let it ring from every village and hamlet, from every state and city, we will be able to speed up that day when all of GOD's children— Black men and White men, Jews and Gentiles, Catholics and Protestants—will be able to join hands and sing in the words of the old Negro spiritual, 'FREE AT LAST! FREE AT LAST! THANK GOD ALMIGHTY! WE ARE FREE AT LAST!'*

[76]   And with this decree, our nation was born! Our King, Dr. Martin Luther King Jr., in the midst of war, injustice and poverty, saw the coming of a new raceless, classless, unified nation built upon the timeless principles of freedom, justice and equality. He saw the beginnings of what we now call "Hip Hop."

[77]   Our King spoke us into existence. He spoke to and for the generation of his immediate children; those born between the years 1960 and 1970. This generation is the group that would eventually produce Hip Hop.

[78]   When our King said, *I have a dream that my four little children will one day live in a nation where they will not be judged by the color of their skin but by the content of their character,* most people assumed that the only nation our King could have been talking about was the United States of America. That one day IT would live up to ITS creed of "all men" being "created equal" with the "unalienable rights of life, liberty and the pursuit of happiness."

[79]   Indeed our King was talking about America as a nation, but it is clear that he was NOT talking about the America that he was protesting against at the time. He saw

a radically different America than even the one that exists today! However, the King's vision of true racial unity and equal citizenship under the law never fully materialized for the people of the United States.

[80]   Most Americans at the time felt that the King's *"I Have A Dream"* decree was simply a powerfully moving speech. However, the King's *"Dream"* in the realm of prophesy, prediction and instruction was not just (as the average American mind remembers it) protest words for his time. On the contrary, our King was not even speaking for his time; he was speaking for OUR TIME! He said, *Nineteen sixty-three is not an end, but a beginning.*

[81]   Most of what the King said in that famous decree was said in future tense: *One day right there in Alabama, little Black boys and Black girls will be able to join hands with little White boys and White girls as sisters and brothers.*

[82]   Most people, because of their own prejudices, refer to the phrase "...as brothers and sisters" figuratively and symbolically. They doubt that "little Black boys and girls" and "little White boys and girls" can actually be real brothers and sisters. And they doubt this because for Black children and White children to become real blood brothers and sisters this would mean the creation of a new race, a new sect of people, a new culture, a new nation.

[83]   As prophesy, the King's *I Have A Dream* decree calls a new people and nation into existence. And because he was speaking to the future of those youths (us) born between 1960 and 1970 (Generation X) who became the pioneers of modern Hip Hop and instinctively created the alternative multicultural, multiracial, omni-faithed community that the King predicted, we have realized today that WE are the true citizens of the nation Dr. Martin Luther King Jr. dreamt about. HIP HOP IS THE PROMISED LAND!

[84]   Nowhere else in the World is the King's *Dream*

so accurately expressed as within Hip Hop. Nowhere else in the World is there an international culture that is truly home to all races, classes, ethnicities and religious beliefs without prejudice other than Hip Hop. Sure, individuals may practice such a vision, but as for the social structures and foundations of whole communities, none can match the inclusive nature of Hip Hop today—even the African American community itself has not risen to the character and vision of Dr. Martin Luther King Jr.

[85]   Nowhere else in the World is a person truly judged by the "content of their character" as opposed to the "color of their skin" than within Hip Hop. Hip Hop even fulfills the King's economic strategies for lower income and poor people. HIP HOP IS THE PROMISED LAND.

[86]   Our King said, *One day on red hills of Georgia, sons of former slaves and sons of former slave owners will be able to sit down together at the table of brotherhood.* Nowhere has this happened in the World culturally on a mainstream level except within the international community of Hip Hop. In fact, nowhere in the World could this type of unity happen because our King was specific to the historical relationship between Africans and Europeans in America.

[87]   As pimped-out, thugged-out, materialistic and drugged-out as we may appear to be today, Hip Hop is still NOT a racist culture. Our existence as a Hip Hop community literally fulfills the prophecy of our King spiritually and historically. Hip Hop is the "freedom" spoken of by the King.

[88]   Within our Hip Hop community a person gains money, power and respect through a display of high skill in one or more of Hip Hop's unique artistic elements. Here, you are truly judged by the "content of your character" (your attributes, your principles, your abilities, your reputation, who you associate with) not by your race or ethnic origin

or financial status. Real Hip Hop is beyond all of that. HIP HOP IS THE PROMISED LAND!

[89] When we look closely at the King's *Dream* we see too many so-called coincidences and symbols that directly relate to Hip Hop and its real development in the World. Like Barack Obama becoming the 44th President of the United States approximately 40 years from the assassination of our King, where he predicted that "We as a people will get to the Promised Land!" This we cannot ignore, especially when organizations like the National Association for the Advancement of Colored People (NAACP) started approximately 100 years ago (1909–2009) after a race riot in Illinois.

[90] We refuse to passively accept the *Dream* of our King as just a dream. We can see ourselves within the King's *Dream* in real life. We can clearly see the King prophetically outlining the mystical path of Hip Hop (*freedom*) in his *Dream* years before we began to actually travel such a path.

[91] When we were very young the King stated; *So let freedom ring from the prodigious hilltops of New Hampshire.*

[92] *Let freedom ring from the mighty mountains of New York.*

[93] *Let freedom ring from the heightening Alleghenies of Pennsylvania.*

[94] *Let freedom ring from the snow-capped Rockies of Colorado.*

[95] *Let freedom ring from the curvaceous slopes of California.*

[96] *But not only that. Let freedom ring from Stone Mountain of Georgia.*

[97] *Let freedom ring from Lookout Mountain of Tennessee.*

[98] *Let freedom ring from every hill and molehill of Mississippi, from every mountainside, let freedom ring.*

[99]   Here we can see how the King has laid out the symbolic path that Hip Hop was to follow years later. First we have New Hampshire, which is located in the State of Vermont which is above New York State geographically.

[100]   If you look at any map of the United States, you will see Vermont in the upper northeastern region of the country. With this we can see the flow of Hip Hop's creative spirit starting from the northeastern region of the United States, moving downward toward New York. We can even track the spirit of Hip Hop as far north as Africville in Nova Scotia, Canada. Symbolically as well as literally, the spirit of Hip Hop comes from above, from on high, from mountainous regions.

[101]   We know today that modern Hip Hop got its artistic start on the east coast of the United States, and the east has always symbolized spiritual awakening, wisdom and light— even birth. But the north signifies the top, on-high, above; the realm where both curses and blessings come.

[102]   Hip Hop beginning in the northeastern region of the United States has huge spiritual, cultural and historical significance especially when it comes to Caribbean people, the history of the Maroons and the establishment of Africville in Nova Scotia, Canada. Our King saw Hip Hop symbolically coming from above (New Hampshire) in the 1960s. His very next line takes the creative spirit of Hip Hop into New York in the 1970s. The King stated; *Let freedom ring from the mighty mountains of New York.*

[103]   New York is where Hip Hop began culturally in the 1970s. This is where Hip Hop got its artistic start. We can see the creative spirit of Hip Hop symbolically entering New York because we know in real life that this is what actually happened.

[104]   In fact, right after Hip Hop establishes itself in New York our King states; *Let freedom ring from the heightening*

Alleghenies of Pennsylvania. And we know that the spirit of Hip Hop left New York and went into the City of Philadelphia in the State of Pennsylvania during the 1980s. Philadelphia was the very next place the spirit of Hip Hop went after its time in New York.

[105]   After Pennsylvania the spirit of Hip Hop went over to the west coast of the United States in the 1990s. Our King stated; *Let freedom ring from the snow-capped Rockies of Colorado.* And again, we can see the spirit of Hip Hop coming down from mountain regions into well-populated urban areas.

[106]   The *mountains* of Colorado, just like the *hilltops of New Hampshire* and the *mountains* of New York, are symbolic of high spiritual consciousness, peace, strength, knowledge, protection and salvation. Again, mountains have always symbolized the realm of GOD. It is from the *mountain top* that GOD delivers staggering victories and astounding Truths.

[107]   But our King accurately continues the prophetic journey of Hip Hop when he states in his very next line; *Let freedom ring from the curvaceous slopes of California.* And we know that after Hip Hop established itself on the East Coast of the United States it traveled directly over to the West Coast of the United States and settled in Los Angeles, California. In fact, this migration brought with it much resentment from artists on both coasts, who would battle each other for artistic and street supremacy during the 1990s.

[108]   Symbolically the *west* has always represented spiritual death and dying; it is where the *sun* (spiritual light) rests and darkness begins to take over. It is not the people of the *west* that symbolize death and dying, it is the symbolism of the sun setting in the *west* and darkness following that gives the *west* this ancient symbolism.

[109]   But as we know, in real life this is what actually happened. In Hip Hop's earlier days on the East Coast, Hip Hop produced both *gangstas* as well as revolutionaries, but the mainstream emphasis was placed upon its revolutionaries and overcoming the injustices of the United States. Hip Hop was conscious of itself in the 1980s on the East Coast of the United States.

[110]   However, when Hip Hop entered the *west* in the 1990s, its priorities and public image began to change. Hip Hop went from being socially conscious to being about everything the World offered materially. Even artists from the East Coast joined in on the seeming success of West Coast hip-hop.

[111]   And remember, Hip Hop on the West Coast of the United States produced some of the greatest Hip Hop revolutionaries of that time, but the mainstream emphasis of that time was placed upon Hip Hop's West Coast *gangstas* not Hip Hop's East or West Coast revolutionaries.

[112]   But our King saw even further when he stated in his very next line, *but not only that. Let freedom ring from Stone Mountain of Georgia.* And we know that when Hip Hop left California in the 2000s it went to the south of the United States. In fact, as our King predicted, Hip Hop went into Georgia; into Atlanta, Georgia, where the King was born. And we can see here the reference to the *mountain* again.

[113]   Our King stated; *Let freedom ring from Lookout Mountain of Tennessee,* which again is just above Atlanta, geographically symbolizing the need for Hip Hop's people during this time to raise their consciousness from criminal-minded to spiritual-minded.

[114]   And then our King states; *Let freedom ring from every hill and molehill of Mississippi.* And we know that right now in our time the spirit of Hip Hop is flourishing in the southern regions of the United States.

[115]   The *south* symbolizes foundation and fire. Change coming from the south means change coming from below to the top, from the streets to the institutions, from the People to its government. In fact, we can see the migration and completion of Hip Hop with its appearance and influence upon the *south*.

[116]   Hip Hop in the *south* means that Hip Hop is returning to the *east*—to its spiritual consciousness. We can see now how Hip Hop went all over the United States in a circle liberating and strengthening its people only to return to its place of origin in GOD.

[117]   It is here that the prophecy of our King seems to end, and strangely enough Hip Hop has nowhere else to go in the United States today. Our King ended his prophecy in the south and then stated, *From every mountainside, let freedom ring!* Some may call these facts "coincidences" but for us these facts are indeed Hip Hop's spiritual confirmation.

[118]   *From every mountainside* symbolizes the whole World and all of the spiritual places in it; this statement symbolizes Hip Hop's international influence which we are clearly experiencing today.

[119]   Here, the King refers to *freedom* as a sound (a ring, a ringing, a tone). The King says *let freedom ring,* meaning let the vibratory tone of freedom ring, let the vibration of freedom reverberate in the lives of the oppressed.

[120]   Here, the *freedom* that our King was referring to was clearly Hip Hop—the only *sound* that has freed us thus far. Hip Hop is OUR freedom. Hip Hop breaks the chains of OUR bondage to the American mainstream workforce and its crippling institutions. Hip Hop is OUR Promised Land. Hip Hop may not mean anything to anyone else, but for us Hip Hop is the fulfillment of the prophetic promise of our King.

[121]   When our King says *freedom* we hear *Hip Hop*, and

when our King says *Negro* we hear *Hiphoppa* regardless of race, class, religion or ethnicity. This is OUR faith, *That every valley shall be exalted, every hill and mountain shall be made low, the rough places shall be made plain, and the crooked places shall be made straight and the glory of the Lord shall be revealed and all flesh shall see it together.*

122   Peace, love, unity and safely having fun has always been OUR faith! From before the American Revolution this has been OUR faith—the unity and further freedom of humankind.

123   So when our King writes, *Let us go back to our communities as members of the international association for the advancement of creative dissatisfaction,* we can see that Hip Hop has been the loudest voice in our time for the advancement of such *creative dissatisfaction.*

124   In fact, this is what Hip Hop is; Hip Hop IS the advancement (the voice) of OUR dissatisfaction. No other social voice or movement since the days of our King has expressed so distinctly and so creatively our dissatisfaction with American injustice.

125   Although it was not said publicly in the original "I Have A Dream" decree, we now know that the King wanted us to engage in politics not for the sake of our own careers but to achieve *strong civil rights legislation.* The need for such work continues even today. Yesterday we needed *civil rights,* today we need *civilization rights*—the right to create, define and govern ourselves.

126   The King stated; *Let us go back and work with all the strength we can muster to get strong civil rights legislation in this session of congress.* This is a call to be pro-active in politics toward nation building.

127   But then the King states; *Let us go down from this place to ascend other peaks of purpose.* This indicates that the Civil Rights Movement was not to stop with what the

King achieved in his lifetime. Our King intended for us to climb *other peaks of purpose*. He stated; *Let us descend from this mountaintop to climb other hills of hope*. WE MUST CONTINUE THE WORK OF THE KING!

[128]   The question is really simple; what are we doing today to continue the work of the only true king we have ever known? And this is the challenge right here. It is not that we are without leadership, it is more the fact that we don't respect the leadership we have, and as a result, we delay our own salvation and freedom as a people.

[129]   Everyone claims to respect Dr. Martin Luther King Jr. but really that's because he's dead. Many respect the King's death, but not his life. Sub-consciously they respect the assassin's death-work over the King's life-work. It's time to ask yourself, am I a citizen of the nation Dr. Martin Luther King Jr. spoke of in his "I Have A Dream" decree? Everyone is NOT a citizen of the King's Dream.

[130]   When our King walked the Earth he had very little support from the very people he was trying to help. In fact, many ridiculed and even betrayed the King's strategies toward freedom, justice and equality. Everyone did not agree with our King when he walked the Earth, everyone did not love our King, protect our King and serve our King when he walked the Earth.

[131]   Everyone did not enter the King's dream nation and as a result many delayed their own salvation and freedom; this is why we are where we are today socially, politically, economically and spiritually. It seems that we keep ignoring the Truth and disregarding the warnings of our own prophets.

[132]   We are doing the same things today that our parents did yesterday; we are killing prophets and ignoring the Truth! For everyone who claims to love freedom and justice and non-violent conflict resolution the question is really

very simple; *What are you doing today right now to bring such conditions into material reality?* THIS IS THE WORK OF THE KING!

133   The question is, *how often do you remain silent in the face of injustice? How often do you ignore the cries of the poor, the abused, the sick and the homeless?* Are you one of those people who hide behind the statement "I'm just doing my job" even though your job contributes to the suffering of others?

134   Our King spoke to all of this, and the citizens of the nation that he saw are those people courageous enough to continue his work toward freedom, justice and equality for all today. Our King saw a raceless, classless, spiritual community that would hasten the day of peace and human unity.

135   Are you a citizen of the King's community? I am. And this is what the Gospel of Hip Hop is all about. It has been only 40 years since the King's assassination and already many have forgotten him. In my time many within the Hip Hop community say of themselves, *"I ain't no role model."* And in many ways I truly understand where they are coming from, however it is also clear that they simply are not interested in influencing others positively!

136   However, I am a role model; I model the role of the King. Actually, everyone is a role model really. Everyone is modeling a role that is influencing someone else in some way. Everyone plays a role in the public; the question is, *what role do YOU play?* Do you play the role of a murderer? or a theif? or a ruthless drug-dealer? Or do you play the role of a prophet? Or a minister? Or a loving parent? What role do YOU willingly and voluntarily play?

137   Most people equate the term "role model" with presenting a good public image, someone others can look up to, and this is why many choose to say, *I ain't no role*

model. But every physical thing in nature is modeling a role that can affect the development of others. Everyone is a role model; the question again is what role are you modeling?

138   I am modeling the intentions of the King. I model the role he played as a leader and as a freedom fighter. Some are clothes models, others are hair models, car models, dance and acting models, but I model (show off, display, present) the role and intentions of Dr. Martin Luther King Jr. and all fighters for freedom. My role is to model these intentions.

139   My role is to CONTINUE THE WORK OF THE KING WHICH IS HAPPENING RIGHT NOW! The King's work may be going on in other fields of human life, but when it comes to Hip Hop the King's work continues here. Hip Hop shall forever honor its kings by courageously continuing their struggles for freedom and human unity.

140   This is why the Gospel of Hip Hop exists. Not to lay down some sort of law upon Hip Hop, or exalt ourselves above others practicing Hip Hop. No. Our aim here is to offer our unique community a matching spirituality and lifestyle capable of producing real peace and real prosperity. Our gospel is not for everyone, it is for those Hiphoppas who are serious about either the spiritual life or Hip Hop's preservation. This gospel is for the seriously committed Hip Hop scholar who has not forgotten the words of the King.

141   Our King promised us that, *When we allow freedom* (Hip Hop) *to ring, when we let it ring from every village and hamlet, from every state and city, we will be able to* <u>*speed up that day*</u> *when all of GOD's children—Black men and White men, Jews and Gentiles, Catholics and Protestants—will be able to join hands and sing in the words of the old Negro spiritual, 'FREE AT LAST! FREE AT LAST! THANK GOD ALMIGHTY! WE ARE FREE AT LAST!'*

THE FIRST OVERSTANDING
REAL HIP HOP

[1]   PEACE AND MUCH LOVE. Know this. Like Hip Hop itself, the Gospel of Hiphop is to be lived; not just read. It is to be done; not just watched. It is to be expressed; not just studied and taught to others.

[2]   For when you ARE Hip Hop you FEEL Hip Hop. And it is through the feelings and the emotions (the heart) that Hip Hop's inner secrets are revealed.

[3]   Studying Hip Hop, debating Hip Hop and writing about Hip Hop are like observing a fashionable suit in the window of a clothing store; while doing Hip Hop, being Hip Hop and living Hip Hop are like putting the suit on and walking around town. There is simply no comparison, and this is what we call "real Hip Hop."

[4]   A *real* Hiphoppa believes (be and lives) Hip Hop. For it is wise for a *real* chef to believe in the reality of cooking, and a real doctor to believe in and live from the reality of medicine, and a *real* Christian to believe and live in Christ (as examples). Therefore, is it not equally wise for *real* Hiphoppas to believe and live in Hip Hop? On the other hand, why participate in something that you really do not fully "be" or "live" in?

[5]   "Real" relates to fixed or immovable things like land. When Hip Hop is real to you, when it is fixed and immovable from your being; YOU ARE PRACTICING REAL HIP HOP. When something is "real" it is considered to be genuine and/or authentic; it is what it proposes to be, it is not imaginary, it is actually existing and occurring to

our physical senses. The term "real Hip Hop" relates to the fixed conditions and genuine nature of Hip Hop as it appears to our physical senses today.

6   Breakin, Emceein, Graffiti Art, Deejayin, Beat Boxin, Street Fashion, Street Language, Street Knowledge and Street Entrepreneurialism are all fixed conditions of Hip Hop. These elements are permanent and immoveable from the existence of Hip Hop. These elements are "real Hip Hop", and those who promote and preserve these elements promote and preserve "real Hip Hop." When these elements are not present in one's self-expression one is not doing or being "real Hip Hop."

7   The true Hip Hop scholar/apprentice is studying to <u>become</u> Hip Hop; not to just <u>observe</u> Hip Hop. How can anyone claim any authentic scholarship on something that they themselves are not and equally cannot actually do? Where, then, is your authority to teach? Our perspective on Hip Hop and its culture is not an objective one. We love Hip Hop, we live Hiphop and we are not ashamed or afraid to say; *we are Hiphop!* We are "REAL HIP HOP!"

8   However, it should be clearly understood that even though we place great emphasis upon the mastery of one or more of Hip Hop's real elements, I must confess here as well that it is really one's love for and loyalty to Hip Hop that rests at the fundamental foundations of Hip Hop's scholarship and citizenry. For there are those who have mastered Hip Hop's real elements but have yet to truly love and care for Hip Hop itself and its future development.

9   For there are those who rap, break, deejay, piece, tag and beat box very well but still find it difficult to consider the real lives of those who are influenced by them artistically and culturally. Many have mastered Hip Hop's artistic elements but only a few have mastered themselves. Many who have mastered Hip Hop's artistic elements

still find it difficult to contribute even towards Hip Hop's artistic preservation.

[10] However, other Hiphoppas have not mastered any of Hip Hop's artistic elements, but the passion and loyalty that they have brought to Hip Hop, their very contributions to the understanding of Hip Hop in many ways are more substantial than even the contributions of those who have mastered Hip Hop's artistic elements. For it is one's love for Hip Hop that truly makes one a Hip Hop scholar and citizen. And your love is proven within your commitment, your works and your sacrifices.

[11] It is through your works (your words and actions) that your true love is revealed. It is through your sacrifices that your true nature is revealed. The nature (name) of your true Self is revealed within the creation and expression of your true Self which requires a real commitment toward the building of your true Self, not the role that you may model but your authentic Self.

[12] This is what most of humanity has had taken away—our true nature which gives all people the ability to govern themselves. This is what we are missing—KNOWLEDGE OF OURSELVES! Without such knowledge we have no way of controlling and/or directing ourselves.

[13] By not speaking our ancient native languages, by not eating our native foods, or dressing in our native clothing, or playing our native games, or hearing ancient stories that pertain to us and our circumstances, combined with no clear and definitive community leadership, or group plan or revolutionary scholarship, it is indeed very difficult to hold on to our ancient humanity—the awareness of our true *names*.

[14] However, WE ARE GOD'S! And the absence of such self-knowledge is actually the trigger that sets the universe in motion toward self-knowledge. Mystery

(not ignorance) is indeed the greatest motivator toward knowledge. As it turns out, not totally knowing our ancestral past has created the possibility of starting a new and even brighter future. We can create and re-create ourselves right now!

15   Not knowing is what causes one to know. And so, the same force that built our civilizations 10,000 years ago (seeking, searching, discovering, not knowing) is the same force that has given life to Hip Hop today. This is one reason why the whole World understands our cultural language. We are the return of the original human spark that caused all great civilizations to exist.

16   This instrument establishes the existence and preservation of our Hip Hop community. Our Truth is self-evident; we must first <u>believe</u> that we exist and then we must perceive the powers of our own existence.

17   This instrument (The Gospel of Hip Hop) begins the creation of Hip Hop's (Hiphop's) faith in itself and its powers. Our first Truth must be an awareness of our own reality as *Hiphoppas*. We must first believe that we exist if we are to develop ourselves into a strong Hip Hop community capable of raising our collective quality of life.

18   Only we can do this for ourselves, no one else is responsible for us and our spiritual/cultural development. We must align our collective thoughts and actions as Hiphoppas with what we know to be *real* for us in the material World. We must see the physical results of that which we claim to spiritually believe; otherwise we are living in denial and fantasy as others do.

19   Hip Hop is made up of real people and real events. We must explore the <u>facts</u> of OUR experiences as Hiphoppas in search of achieving the <u>Truth</u> about ourselves as Hiphoppas. We must finally mature to the faith of confirming our own spiritual reality as Hiphoppas.

[20]   This is what KRS really means to Hip Hop. I am the actual historical evidence that Hip Hop was conscious of itself in its early days, and I am not the only one of my time.

[21]   We practice *real* Hip Hop. We practice the immovable and fixed conditions of the Hip Hop spirit. Whether Hip Hop is accepted or not by those of the corporate mainstream is irrelevant. Real Hiphoppas come to Hip Hop with no other interests but to authentically manifest it. This is *real* Hip Hop.

[22]   I AM HIP HOP! And upon this evidence our culture is born! Hip Hop's culture now exists <u>factually</u> as a real divinely guided community because you and KRS exist as its first citizens. Our unity declares the reality of Hip Hop. And because we willing choose to fix ourselves to the spirit of Hip Hop and not move from it, it is a fact when we say, "THE REAL HIP HOP IS OVER HERE!" We make Hip Hop real by authentically being it. This is *real* Hip Hop and this gospel is presented by some *real* Hiphoppas.

[23]   I AM HIP HOP! And upon this faith (our belief in ourselves as Hiphoppas) we can achieve Truth. Through Hip Hop we have a paradigm by which to create ourselves and document our own body of Hip Hop knowledge and history. Our faith in ourselves as a community of conscious Hiphoppas is what we call Hip Hop's *culture* or *Hiphop Kulture.*

[24]   Unfortunately, people today have grown accustomed to equating Rap music and the images portrayed in mainstream Rap music videos with the whole of Hip Hop's culture and history, and this is why we say that such material is NOT "real" Hip Hop. It is NOT authentic to the original Hip Hop spirit or tradition, and does not represent what is actually occurring to our physical senses in the present. Most of the mainstream Rap videos of my time are

imaginary tales of crime, sex and street adventure. They are good, they are entertaining, but they are not "real."

25   Real Hip Hop is real life, and it is from the experiences of our real lives that our songs and dances, our graphic arts and our language come from. This is why we teach that Hip Hop and Rap music are not the same things; that Rap is something we <u>do</u>, while Hip Hop is something we <u>live</u>, and the living of Hip Hop is "real" Hip Hop. Let us get more orientated by taking a look at the following terms closely.

26   **Hiphop** is the name of our creative force in the World. It is our lifestyle and collective consciousness.

27   **Hip Hop** is the name of our culture and artistic elements.

28   **hip-hop** is Rap music product and its mainstream activities.

29   With this original cultural learning system we reveal the more real nature of Hip Hop beyond the average mainstream understanding of *hip-hop*. Here, we introduce a Hip Hop spiritual code of conduct capable of producing enhanced states of health, love, awareness and wealth for those engaged in the mastery of Hip Hop's *real* elements. This is the gospel, and this is what really works for Hiphoppas.

30   Here, *Hip Hop's* real elements can be pursued and developed in any way that one feels. However, *"Hiphop"* is a specific term that deals with the spiritual nature of *Hip Hop*. Study this paragraph and the above terms carefully before going forward.

31   Remember, the Gospel of *Hip Hop* is the instructional book and the Gospel of *Hiphop* is a spiritually lived Hiphop life. This instrument is called the *Gospel of Hip Hop* because Hip Hop is commonly spelled as such amongst the Hip Hop populace today. However, we teach

Hiphop, Hip Hop and *hip-hop* so that our discoveries regarding the spiritual nature of Hip Hop do not contradict or hinder the free study of others seeking to uncover the nature of Hip Hop for themselves. We hold no monopoly on the interpretation of the nature of Hip Hop, spiritual or otherwise. Our understandings and approaches to Hip Hop are unique to <u>our</u> *Hiphop* preservation society.

32   These are <u>our</u> discoveries and notes and no one is obligated to believe or acknowledge that which we believe and acknowledge as the Truth for us. This Gospel is what we know successfully works for those practicing Hip Hop, and this is what we teach. We are called *Hiphoppas* and not *Hip Hoppers* or *hip-hoppers* because we actually practice *Hiphop*, which for us is the spiritual living of *Hip Hop*.

33   Our community is called <u>*Hiphop*</u> *Kulture* and not *hip-hop culture*. Although we do sometimes spell the name of our community as *Hip Hop Kulture*, it is *Hiphop's* culture that we are actually referring to. For a clearer, deeper understanding of what is being taught throughout this instrument you will have to train your eye to recognize the spellings and meanings of *Hiphop, Hip Hop* and *hip-hop*.

34   Our approach to Hip Hop is indeed unique in our time. We teach that Rap (rhythmic speech) is but ONE expression that comes out of the total Hip Hop experience. For us, Hip Hop is the combination of Breakin, Emceein, Graffiti Art, Deejayin, Beat Boxin, Street Fashion, Street Language, Street Knowledge and Street Entrepreneurialism. For us, Hip Hop is the amplification of human expression and awareness. At its core, Hip Hop is not just an art form; it is the pursuit of one's authentic being through the Arts.

35   For those who consider themselves true Hip Hop scholars, Hip Hop is defined as, *The artistic response to oppression. A way of expression in dance, music, word/song. A culture that thrives on creativity and nostalgia. As a musical*

art form it is the stories of inner-city life, often with a message, spoken over beats of music. The culture includes Rap and any other venture spawned from the Hip Hop style and culture. (Alonzo Westbrook, *Hip Hoptionary: The Dictionary Of Hip Hop Terminology*)

[36] For those who live Hiphop, Hip Hop is not *over there* somewhere external of one's self—we ARE Hip Hop! Hip Hop itself is not a person, a place or a physical thing. You cannot actually go to Hip Hop, or wear Hip Hop, or eat Hip Hop. Hip Hop exists as a shared *idea.* You cannot drink a can of Hip Hop and suddenly know how to rap. You cannot put Hip Hop on as clothing, or read a book in order to understand Hip Hop. Hip Hop begins as an awareness, as an alternative behavior. Again, Hip Hop is a shared idea. Rapping, break dancing, graffiti art, beat-boxing and deejayin are all expressions OF this collective urban idea commonly called *Hip Hop.*

[37] Hip Hop is a new global urban understanding that communicates an alternative reality through art. Hip Hop is a new faculty in the collective consciousness of urban America. Hip Hop is understood psychically by those who participate in it. More than just a music genre, Hip Hop is an international agreement as to how ALL peoples may come together in peace on neutral ground. Hip Hop is indeed a psychic "True World Order."

[38] We've discovered that Hiphop, Hip Hop, hip-hop and the Hiphoppa are all aspects of the same creative force; that one cannot fully function without the others because Hiphop, Hip Hop, hip-hop and the Hiphoppa are all really one event. This is why the Temple of Hip Hop teaches that TO PRESERVE HIP HOP WE MUST PRESERVE THE HIPHOPPA!

[39] Preserving the specific artifacts and memorabilia of Rap music has its place and its importance, and

someone should be doing that work; such work is indeed a strength to the preservation of our culture. However, as a 'temple' we are more concerned with the essence, substance, force, being, cause and identity of Hip Hop as a creative force—"Hiphop."

40   Hiphop is not a physical thing or things; it is a metaphysical principle, a shared urban idea, an alternative human behavior, a way to view the World, a collective consciousness. We must finally leave the finite room of *hip-hop* as Rap music entertainment, and enter the infinite realm of *Hiphop* as consciousness. We are far more than just the World's entertainment.

41   For us, Hip Hop is a mass 'event' that was captured on record, cassette, CD, video, DVD, clothing, etc. for the purpose of selling its *elements* to relieve poverty. It is *Hiphop* that inspires *Hip Hop's* elements to exist, but it is only *Hip Hop's* performed elements that appear in the physical World. *Hiphop* itself never enters the physical World. We imitate the inspiration of *Hiphop* through its elements (Hip Hop) but again, *Hiphop* (the collective consciousness) never enters the physical World; it remains a shared idea of OUR collective consciousness. Study this paragraph again carefully.

42   For serious apprentices of the Temple of Hip Hop, Hiphop is a perceptual ability that transforms subjects and objects in an effort to express the character of one's inner being. Hiphop is the ability to make physical objects and social subjects perform according to your perception of them.

43   When we say "I AM HIPHOP," the *Hiphop* idea then enters the physical World as *Hip Hop* which is then captured on CD, etc., and sold as *hip-hop*. By becoming *Hiphop*, by allowing the Hiphop idea to dominate our 'being', *Hip Hop* enters the physical World through our

66

physical bodies and artistic expressions. This "expression" (and for some, their physical bodies) is then captured in some way and sold as *hip-hop*.

[44]   Before Hip Hop can even be recorded and/or documented, it must first be brought into the physical World through people who have voluntarily surrendered to its *force* and *essence*. Everything else is a recording, an imitation or a documentation of the real effects of the original Hip Hop creative force (*Hiphop*).

[45]   The preserving of such a perceptual *ability* has little to do with the preserving of its products; it has to do with understanding the *ability* itself; the essence that causes such products to exist. To preserve Hip Hop we must preserve Hip Hop's perceptual abilities. We must preserve the actual living thinking Hiphoppa with a knowledge of Hip Hop beyond entertainment.

[46]   From our perspective, the preserving of Hip Hop has more to do with the preservation of its people than with the preserving of its products. It has to do with the preserving of certain customs, traditions, abilities and techniques unique to the Hip Hop experience. Such a style of cultural preservation is about preserving the essential causes that bring Hip Hop into physical existence. This is the essence of <u>our</u> Hip Hop preservation movement.

[47]   Traditionally, Hip Hop has been approached as an art form that consists of four core elements; b-boyin (break dancing), MC-ing (rap), aerosol art (graffiti writing) and DJ-ing (the cutting, mixing and scratching of recorded materials). These are called the "core four." However, Hip Hop's "core four" elements also encompass specific and unique urban clothing styles, language styles, business and trade techniques as well as a collective body of knowledge derived from its internal experiences with itself and the World.

[48]   The experiences produced by Hip Hop's "core four" have created uniquely rich Hip Hop stories, Hip Hop legends and myths, original Hip Hop arts, popular Hip Hop music and thought-provoking Hip Hop poetry that critiques and interprets the World in which the Hip Hop community exists. At first glance, Hip Hop can be seen as simply an urban music genre inspired by the African American and Latino youths of the Bronx during the early 1970s. However, upon closer observation Hiphop becomes a way of life; a specific way of being and seeing the World; a unique view of the World and World events.

[49]   We are uniquely Hiphop because the repetition of such a unique *being* and *seeing* has created our specific *Hiphop* way of life. And the *Hiphop* way of life is what we call Hip Hop's *culture* or *Hiphop Kulture*. As culture, Hip Hop is the specific behaviors, traits, expressions, patterns and institutions of OUR unique collective consciousness. It (Hip Hop) is OUR intellectual and artistic activity as well as the works produced by it.

[50]   In the past, some argued that Hip Hop was not a culture. They made the mistake of comparing their knowledge of traditional cultures to Hip Hop's culture. But as the great Hip Hop professor Zizwe Mtafuta-Ukweli (Professor Z) has pointed out, *Culture is the character of a living entity. That entity could be an organism or an entire generation functioning as an organism. Every culture has its linchpin aspects, or that which makes its membership pledge allegiance to it. Culture also provides a fence around the collective epic memory of the group which accepts this memory as its philosophy and history.*

[51]   Professor Z continues, *Our culture* [Hip Hop] *is strengthened through a heightened self-awareness and a heightened awareness of the surrounding environment. For every young culture, the relationship between it and its*

environment is dynamic and determinant. The culture seeks to absorb all it can from the environment yet must prevent itself from being totally absorbed by the environment. Total absorption by the environment means certain death for any culture. Part of any cultural identity is distinctiveness. This is why Hip Hop is so successful; as a young culture Hip Hop absorbs the music of Blues, Gospel, Rock, Soul and Jazz but is absorbed by none of them.

52   Over the years Hip Hop's absorption of older musical and artistic traditions helped to create a certain lifestyle and worldview unique to the total Hip Hop experience. This is what we now call Hip Hop's *culture*. Rap is something we <u>do</u>; Hip Hop is something we <u>live</u>. And the living of Hip Hop's culture has more to do with your sense of security, peace, self-development and well-being than it has to do with performing one or two of Hip Hop's artistic elements. <u>Living</u> Hiphop is far more involved than <u>performing</u> Hip Hop.

53   For if you do not <u>live</u> a productive Hiphop lifestyle you increase your difficulty in maintaining a lasting success in any of Hip Hop's traditional elements or artistic expressions. This is why Hip Hop is not regarded as simply a music genre here. For us, such an approach to Hip Hop is indeed dangerous to the practicing Hiphoppa.

54   The music and dances of Hip Hop come from a collective urban view of the World that inspires such music and dance to exist. It is Hip Hop's worldview that inspires (or rather causes) its music, art and dance to exist. This is why so many of the hip-hop history books of my time are so culturally limited. They focus primarily upon the money-making effects of hip-hop and not upon what causes such effects to occur.

55   Music and art are very important elements that assist in the make up of hip-hop as a whole. However, it

is Hiphop itself (our collective consciousness) that brings into manifestation Rap music, Breakin and Aerosol Art as well as the other urban expressions that derive from our unique life experiences. Our unique life experiences and the performances that occur as a result of such unique life experiences are called "real Hip Hop."

[56]   For us, *real* Hip Hop is a transformative power that has its beginnings at the genesis of human awareness. Its *elements* are seen throughout human history and all over the World. And this is no accident. We did not arrive at our place in the World by luck. GOD IS TRULY WITH US! And we must never forget to honor GOD in our writings and performances. Hip Hop is the return of the ancient ways, the healing ways, the natural ways—the way of God.

[57]   Whether on the cave walls of northern Africa 20,000 years ago, or as Egyptian hieroglyphics with its letters and characters describing ancient life some 10,000 years ago, or as the Mayan and Inca pyramid and temple hieroglyphs (Graffiti Art), or as the Griots and Djeli who performed for the royal courts of Ghana, Song hai (present-day Mali) some 2,000 years ago (emcees/deejays), or as the Capoeira martial artists of 16th-century Angola (breakers), or as the social organization of aboriginal Americans since the dawn of creation Hip Hop has always existed as a unique awareness that enhances one's ability to self-create. Hip Hop is a *sight*, an ancient behavior, today an alternative way to view the World.

[58]   *Hip Hop* is the correct pronunciation of *Hiphop*. As an acronym/affirmation, *H.I.P.H.O.P.* can be interpreted as Her Infinite Power Helping Oppressed People. Or, Having Inner Peace Helping Others Prosper. Or, Holy Integrated People Having Omni-present Power. Hip Hop means all of this.

[59]   Those who show little respect for Hip Hop still

spell Hip Hop as *hip-hop*. True Hiphoppas are advised to spell Hiphop as well as *Hip Hop* with a capital *H* as it is the name of our collective consciousness; it is the 'force' that animates our way of life, our culture, our tribe, our nation. When Hiphop and/or Hip Hop are spelled as *hip-hop* it refers to Rap music product and its related activities. We'll go deeper into this later.

60   *Hiphop* or *Hip Hop* when misspelled as *hip-hop* means (*hip*) trendy, (*hop*) jump or dance. However, we are not just a *trendy dance*. We love and respect the art of dance, but dancing is not the only thing *Hip Hop* is about.

61   Those who approach Hip Hop like it is exclusively a *trendy dance* (or entertainment) are usually those who repeatedly speak and spell the term incorrectly and care little for Hiphop as a community of real people.

62   To spell *Hip Hop* incorrectly as *hip-hop* is to deny our right to exist as a people. The use of the term *hip-hop* to describe real people reduces those people to products. However, *Hip* (spelled here with a capital *H*) from the ancient African *hipi* means *to know* or *to be aware*. It is a form of intelligence; a knowing.

63   On the other hand, *Hop* (spelled here with a capital *H*) from the Aboriginal American *hopi* (*Hopi*) means *good* and/or *peaceable*. Together *hipi* and *hopi* (the original union of cultures in the Americas) can symbolize not only the unity of African and Native American civilizations, but can also symbolize *peaceful awareness, good awareness* or *the awareness of peace* or *of goodness*.

64   However, according to the English language, to be *hip* means *to have knowledge of*. Again, it is a form of intelligence. *Hop* is a form of movement. And together *hip* and *hop* when spelled correctly as *Hip Hop* means *moving or jumping intelligence*, even *knowledgeable movement*. Hip Hop—*moving intelligence, active intelligence, intelligence*

71

moving, conscious movement or *intelligent movement!*

[65]   The etymology of the term *Hip Hop* as it relates to the English language begins with the Old English term *hype,* meaning the joint formed by the upper thighbone and pelvis. Additionally the term *hype-banes* appears around 1149 meaning *hip bones.* This is the joint used the most in our breakin moves and most urban dance moves.

[66]   In addition to the term *hip* being interpreted as part of the skeletal structure of the human body (we *hop* out of the *hips*), *hip* is also the seed pod of a rose bush (*hipe,* 1414) and is also interpreted as *to be informed* or *to be up to date* (1903).

[67]   Later (1952) the term *Hippie* was designated to a specific group of people (*Hipsters*) that were considered *hip,* meaning *keenly aware of what is new and in style.* In many ways, Hip Hop is a continuation of the *Hippie* movement of the 1960s. Being also politically aware, the *Hippie* preferred to *turn-on* to legal and illegal drugs, *tune-in* to peace and sexual promiscuity, and *drop-out* from conventional society, wearing unconventional clothing, sporting long and sometimes uncombed hair, preaching peace and universal love for all humankind.

[68]   *Hippies* were at the center of the Civil Rights, Gay and Lesbian Rights, Women's Rights, Free Love and Anti-War movements of the 1960s, and Hip Hop is a direct effect of this earlier freedom movement. However, we've now seen the errors of the *Hippie* movement and it is our responsibility today to go beyond such tragic events. Drug overdoses, murders and lawlessness simply DO NOT WORK toward our goals for freedom.

[69]   Spontaneity is good, but continuous spontaneity doesn't offer stability. We have seen now that when there is no permanence there is no reliability. The *Hippie* movement seems to have been killed by media hype and

drug abuse; many other *Hippies* just *burned out* or became part of the same government and corporate structure they were fighting against. Hip Hop can learn a lot from this early protest movement.

⁷⁰ *Hop,* on the other hand, appears in the English language as *hoppen* sometime before 1200, meaning to *spring,* or *to move by springing* (usually upon one foot). This term *hoppen* seems to come from the Old English *hoppian* (about 1000) meaning *to spring* or *to dance.* This term corresponds with the Old Icelandic *hoppa,* the modern Dutch *hoppen,* and the German *hopfen,* all meaning to *hop* or to *spring.*

⁷¹ Like the term *hip,* the term *hop* is also associated with plant life. *Hop* is interpreted as *a vine having flower clusters* (1439). The *hop* plant was (and still is) used to flavor malt drinks like beer, something the Hip Hop community is very familiar with.

⁷² These are the English etymologies of the term *hip hop,* and we can see here within these definitions how even *hip* and *hop* come together to mean hip—*informed,* and hop—*springing or dancing.* Together the term *hip hop* (even when spelled in lower case *h*) can mean *an informed springing,* or *an up to date modern dance,* or *an informed movement upward.* A *hip* (updated) *hop* (movement) is an intelligent movement—a movement aware of itself.

⁷³ To be *hip* means to be *up to date, relevant, in the know.* Therefore to *hip* something or to make something *hip* is to modernize it. To *hip* a *hop* is to *modernize* an *upward movement.*

⁷⁴ However, it is interesting to point out the correlation of these two terms as they apply to plant life. Both *hip* and *hop* refer to plant life. One (*hip*) refers to *the seed pod of a rose bush.* And the other (*hop*) refers to *a vine having flower clusters.* The relation between *seed* and then *vine* within the symbolic interpretations of *hip* and then *hop* cannot be ignored.

[75]   In terms of spiritual symbolism, we focus upon how *hip* comes before *hop* like *seed* comes before *vine*. Spiritually, it appears that *hip hop* is the *seed* of a new *vine* (the new people/the new way). However, when you add the etymology of *culture* to these interpretations even more symbolism is revealed.

[76]   The term *culture* (1439) from the Latin *cultura* (*cul-too-ra*), meaning *tending, care* and *cultivation,* seems to come from *cult-,* the past participle stem of the Latin *colere,* meaning to *till, cultivate, tend to* and *inhabit.*

[77]   *Cult* (1616) originally meant *worship* or *homage*; not *to worship* or *to pay homage. Cult* comes from the Latin *cultus* (*cul-toos*), meaning *cultivation, care, attention, worship.* We can see here that the term *worship* was originally associated with the *cultivating, caring for,* and *attending to,* of something or someone. Attuned Hiphoppas are advised to *worship* GOD in this way; to *care* for GOD.

[78]   For as we belong to GOD, GOD equally belongs to us. GOD is to be worshipped (meaning *cultivated* and *cared for*), not just acknowledged in thanks. For when we hear that *they fell down and worshipped him/her* we must understand that in ancient times to *worship* a person or GOD meant that they took *care* of that person or GOD. Know this. GOD IS TO BE CARED FOR AND CULTIVATED! Not just thanked. Let us continue with the word *culture.*

[79]   The suffix *ure* in culture forms abstract nouns of action or the means or result of action. To *ure* is to -*ing*, -*ed*, or -*s*; like the act of fail-*ing* = fail-*ure* or failure, the condition of being pleas-*ed* = pleas-*ure* or pleasure, something or someone that legislate-*s* = legislat-*ure* or legislature.

[80]   Therefore, by adding the *ure* to *cult* we get *cult-ure* or culture, originally meaning the act of cult-*ing* or *cultivating, caring, attending to, worshipping.* Looking at the etymology of *hip* and *hop* and *culture* together we can

interpret such a phrase as meaning; the *cultivation, care, attention* and *worship* of the *seed* (plan/vision) of the new *vine* (people/way).

81   Another interpretation of *hip hop culture* could read; the *cultivation, care, attention* and *worship* of the *intelligent movement.* The term *hip hop culture* seems to imply the *cultivation of,* and *care for,* the *upward springing of intelligence.*

82   There seems to be a symbolic connection to farming when it comes to the etymology of the words *hip, hop* and *culture* as defined within the English language. Symbolically, we seem to be growing an ancient intelligence with an ancient meaning and purpose.

83   This is important to meditate upon because ancient humans watched animal behavior to understand and develop human behavior, and they observed flowers and plants (their colors, shapes and functions) to discover what was possible in Nature and within themselves. Nature taught early humans through the symbolisms produced by Nature's activity.

84   The activity of fire taught us about the nature of our emotions. The activity of water taught us about character. The activity of air and wind taught us about the nature of spirit and the invisible. The activity of the life-giving Earth, the very ground itself, farming taught us how to survive and revealed to us the nature and cycles of the universe and the effects of its celestial bodies (stars, the sun, the moon, etc) upon life on Earth. Truly, Nature itself is our teacher and provider.

85   However, plants are the first of our direct teachers; the ingestion of certain medicinal plants showed us all kinds of sciences and revealed to us the mysteries of the Earth and of the universe itself. Indeed, the first knowledge was delivered through play and the ingestion of certain plant-

types which then revealed the symbolism of Nature itself. Symbolism and metaphor are indeed important elements in the building of human understanding and awareness. As poet Robert Frost suggested, *If you are not properly educated in metaphor you are not safe to be loose in the World.*

[86] We (Hiphoppas) are the genetic return of an ancient people. For it is known by all true seekers of Truth that Nature produces knowledge through symbolism, comparison and metaphor. It appears that we (Hiphoppas) are responsible for the gathering of symbolic information on this planet and then teaching it to others through art for guidance and the relief of human suffering. By oppressing Hiphoppas you stagnate the gathering and distribution of symbolic knowledge and thus stagnate the progress of human understanding.

[87] Finally within the etymology of *hip hop* we come to the Hiphoppa or *hip hoppa*. Looking at the Old Icelandic term *hoppa* (meaning *to spring upward*) it becomes obvious that the way in which the Temple of Hiphop describes and spells *Hiphoppa* is influenced by the two terms *hip* and *hoppa*.

[88] The term *hip*, meaning *keenly aware of what is new and in style,* and *hoppa,* meaning *to spring upward* or *to hop,* reveals the *hip-hoppa* (Hiphoppa) as the actual intelligence that is springing forward. The *hip-hoppa* can also be said to be a modernized life-dancer *keenly aware of what is new and in style; a conscious mover,* or *one who moves with awareness.*

[89] And know this. What we have done in our early days as Hiphoppas, how we have defined ourselves and how we have expressed ourselves in the material World, was done spontaneously (spiritually). We were calling ourselves *Hiphoppas* and *hip hoppers* long before the refinitions, definitions and interpretations of this gospel. It is truly amazing to discover our real natures and characters

as Hiphoppas (even the term *hip hoppa*) already existing within the very structure of the English language itself as us. Meditate upon this fact.

90   If we were a community of doctors, or lawyers, or architects, or even politicians, then the idea that *hip hop* can be defined as a *trendy dance* or as an *intelligent movement* would not apply to us; it would not mean much. But the very fact that these terms *hip* and *hop* and *culture* and even *hip-hoppa* which we spontaneously gave to ourselves in childhood play within a so-called *slang* dialect intuitively corresponding to the etymology of these words and terms only proves once again the depth into which the Hip Hop mind can go if left to its own development.

91   In the 1970s we did not define ourselves in this way. We did not have this knowledge. However, the fact that we can accurately identify ourselves and our specific artistic expressions (like dance for example) within ancient English, Latin, African, German, Dutch and French languages, and that the etymology of these words and terms matches accurately with our modern self-expression (even though we've never formally studied these words and terms to know them) says something about our divine role as *Hiphoppas*.

92   We are truly the return of an ancient people, with ancient skills rooted in the earliest experiences of human consciousness. All that we need to know is OURSELVES! We simply need to be left alone to contemplate the depths of our own consciousness. We truly have something important and forgotten to teach and remind the World. All we have to do is BELIEVE IN OURSELVES!

93   As Hiphoppas we operate in a spiritual reality when we handle and manipulate Hip Hop. The fact that we created ourselves points to our divinity. The fact that we spontaneously and randomly choose names and characters for ourselves that can be matched with a

history and knowledge that we have not studied proves that we (as a community) are not just singing, rapping and dancing. There seems to be more to Hip Hop than our ability to sing and dance—we are connected to something divine and timeless.

[94]   The fact that we created Hip Hop first and then the explanation as to how our creation came about later proves that we are working with spiritual energy, awareness and law. The opposite is the way of the World; that is to plan and explain your plan of action before you act or create.

[95]   Spiritual Law works differently; the creation is created first, and the explanation as to how it was created comes later. And usually when natural and spiritual events are later explained they align with the mathematics and harmony of Nature and the universe itself. However, this is usually discovered years later by future generations equipped with better instruments and a broader knowledge.

[96]   This is why the Great Pyramids of Egypt are so mathematically in alignment with the Earth and the universe. Those ancient builders were simply not an oppressed people. They were truly their natural selves with no restrictions. They simply did not know what they couldn't do, and so they did it all! Through play, art and experimentation, great things are accomplished unconsciously and with little or no effort at all. We will explore this theme more later. For now, let's get back to Hip Hop and the English language.

[97]   It is also a common linguistic rule of the English language that the titles or names of all cultures, nations, civilizations, ethnicities, etc. be spelled beginning with a capital (uppercase) letter. Hip Hop is our culture, therefore it must be always spelled with the same grammatical respect one would give any other culture in the English language.

[98]   In addition, the term *Hip Hop* can be interpreted as a proper noun, as a specific thing. Unless the term *Hip Hop*

is being displayed in an art presentation or if translated into another language or culture where the grammatical rules of the English language do not apply, it (Hip Hop) should be spelled beginning with a capital *H* – *Hiphop* or *Hip Hop*.

99   Those using the English language to describe Hip Hop while misspelling *Hiphop* and/or *Hip Hop* as *hip-hop* are not only grammatically incorrect, they also undermine the importance of what Hip Hop really is to Hiphoppas. They participate in Hip Hop's enslavement by reducing our culture and way of life to a music genre and product to be bought and sold.

100   Again, Hiphop is the name of our collective consciousness. Hip Hop is not a product to be bought and sold (see Hip Hop Declaration of Peace; Principle Seven). It is the inalienable right of all Hiphoppas. Hiphop (Hip Hop) is OUR name!

101   *Hip Hop*, spelled here with two uppercase H's is also called the phonetic spelling of Hiphop. It is also the traditional and general spelling of Hip Hop.

102   This spelling is politically correct. Again, it means *moving* or *active intelligence*. When used to describe us as a people *Hip Hop* can mean *the awareness of peace*. True Hip Hop scholars are advised to use this spelling (*Hip Hop*) when educating the public on how to correctly pronounce *Hiphop*. Writers who have spelled Hip Hop in lower case (*hip-hop, hip hop*) before the publishing of the Gospel of Hip Hop are excused from criticism and/or retaliation. However, now that the Gospel of Hip Hop is published, writers are advised to approach Hip Hop as the nation that it is with the importance that it deserves.

103   *Hip Hop* spelled in this way is also used in titles, introductions, invitations and artwork or when *Hiphop* is being explained in a general or historic sense. Failure to comply with this *style* undermines Hip Hop's effort to

develop, unify and strengthen itself. Those who continue to spell Hip Hop in lower case (hip hop) when describing Hip Hop place themselves outside of our community and cannot be called true scholars of the Hip Hop arts and sciences. Let's take a look at these terms again.

• **Hiphop** = our unique Spirit, our unique collective consciousness, the creative force behind Hip Hop's elements. Hiphop is the name of our lifestyle and collective consciousness.

• **Hip Hop** = the creation and development of Breakin, Emceein, Graffiti Art, Deejayin, Beat Boxin, Street Fashion, Street Language, Street Knowledge, and Street Entrepreneurialism. It is what we call ourselves, and our activity in the World. Hip Hop is the name of our culture.

• **hip-hop** = Rap music product and those things and events associated with Rap music entertainment—hip-hop is a music genre.

[104]   *Hiphop Kulture* is the name of our unique community of consciousness. Hiphop is the name of our collective consciousness and Hiphop's culture is the manifested character, patterns, beliefs and arts of our collective consciousness as Hiphoppas. We are a very real community of specialized people.

[105]   Those that live the principles of our culture are called *Hiphoppas* and not *Hip Hoppers* because to live *Hip Hop* is to think *Hiphop*. A Hiphoppa is the manifestation of Hiphop. Technically, a Hiphoppa is *Hiphop* and performs or presents *Hip Hop,* which is then sold as *hip-hop.*

[106]   Or, you can say *Hiphop* (spirit) creates the *Hiphoppa* (mind), which creates *Hip Hop* (body), which creates *hip-*

hop (product). **Hiphop** is born of GOD; the Great Spirit, the Great Event. It is the light of our World.

[107] **Hip Hop** is born of cultural syncretism, meaning the blending of different cultures to create a new culture. It is the combination and unity of several independent cultures creating a new heterogeneous culture. And finally, **hip-hop** is born of corporate business interests—it exists when the effects of *Hiphop* and *Hip Hop* become tradeable material products.

[108] As a title, true Hiphoppas spell the full name of our culture with a *K* signifying our cultural uniqueness and right to define ourselves—*Hiphop Kulture*. Hiphop Kulture can also be spelled as *Hip Hop Kulture* in certain specific writings, artwork and/or advertisements.

[109] Even beyond the right to define ourselves, *Hiphop Kulture* is the creation of our Hip Hop atmosphere, our Hip Hop environment, our Hip Hop climate, our Hip Hop reality. The principles of our *Hiphop Kulture* are the paradigm that we create ourselves with and interpret the World through.

[110] As a City-State, *Hiphop Kulture* is the place where Hiphoppas can achieve their true life purposes in peace with no hostile *beefs* between Hiphoppas and with no interference from anyone unless such a purpose interferes with other Hiphoppas seeking the fulfillment of their life purposes. Our Hip Hop city is where there is no economic high class that manipulates and/or forces an economic low class to work for it, where no person is above another person, where the public education of our children helps them to know and fulfill the potentials of their natural talents, where the life purpose of all men and women is nurtured and fully respected.

[111] Hiphop Kulture (the City-State) is a place where the *elements* of Hiphop can be further developed and

mastered by Hiphoppas in peace leading to our lasting prosperity. As opposed to a president, a king or a warrior, Hiphop Kulture as a nation is guided by its *teachas* who lead by productive examples.

[112]   Hiphop Kulture is an international tribe of peace and prosperity whose unique World view expresses certain arts and opinions that unite people around some simple yet common principles shared all over the Earth regardless of racial, cultural, financial or religious background.

[113]   Our culture is all about peace, love, unity and safely having fun. Here, Hip Hop is the common ground that all people can meet upon. Hip Hop itself is the World's common spirit—the True World Order.

[114]   In our culture it is the accumulation of knowledge that reigns supreme, not the accumulation of money, property, weapons, tools, food or clothing; these are the effects of knowledge. And as useful as these things are, they are still not valued above wisdom, knowledge and overstanding. Our civilization is based upon advanced human interaction, not advanced human accumulation or even annihilation.

[115]   Again, our community is all about peace, love, unity and safely having fun. This vision is what is common to most of the peoples of the Earth, and this is why Hip Hop appeals to most of the Earth's people; we speak a universal language.

[116]   We seek the deeper meanings of Hip Hop beyond entertainment and we are inspired by our discoveries; symbolically as well as literally. For example, Hip Hop can be seen as $H_2 I_1 P_2 H_2 O_1 P_2$ or Hydrogen, Iodine, Phosphorus, Hydrogen, Oxygen, Phosphorus. Such chemical elements create a variety of useful substances, some of which are indeed life-sustaining.

[117]   Symbolically, H-I-P-H-O-P is chemically made

up of two hydrogen atoms and one oxygen atom which produces water—a necessary element for the creation and sustainment of life in its physical form.

[118]   Iodine not only kills unwanted bacteria, but hydrogen, iodine and phosphorus (H-I-P) are essential minerals used to restore vitality to the physical body. Hydrogen, oxygen and phosphorus (H-O-P) are three of the nine macronutrients essential for plant growth (again the reference to plant life).

[119]   Hydrogen, oxygen and phosphorus (H-O-P), properly combined, produce phosphoric acid, which is commonly used to make soil-enriching fertilizer. In essence, H-I-P-H-O-P (in its chemical interpretation) is a life-giving, life-sustaining, life-enhancing compound—one that we already have within us. And this interpretation (symbolically) is what our culture represents to the World.

[120]   Even further, looking at "H" as an individual symbol, and not just as a letter, sheds more light upon the deeper symbolic meanings of Hip Hop and its existence in the World. In many metaphysical circles "H" symbolizes twin pillars, justice, mercy, "the Gate to Heaven" and the ladder. "H" as a symbol is made from the union of two "I"s. "H" itself is a symbol for unity and togetherness—two "I"s coming together. "H" is truly a symbol for the preservation of our community.

[121]   Hip Hop can also represent the breath or the act of breathing. Hip = inhale, Hop = exhale. With every breath, attuned Hiphoppas confirm their Hip Hop existences. We are not just breathing, we are inhaling and exhaling our collective Hip Hop consciousness. With every breath we are confirming the existence of our Hip Hop Kulture and community.

[122]   Therefore, Hip Hop Kulture (the name of our community), when misspelled where *Kulture* does not begin

with a *K* but instead is spelled as *culture* with a c (*hip-hop culture*), refers to the condition of Hip Hop's development as music. It does not relate to the mature community of responsible and unified *Hiphoppas,* the *Hiphop* City-State or the *Hip Hop nation.*

[123]   To become a citizen of *Hiphop Kulture* one must be willing to adopt and defend the *Hip Hop Declaration of Peace* and begin the study and mastery of one or more of Hip Hop's nine *elements.*

[124]   To be a Hip Hop citizen one must simply be loyal to the preservation of Hip Hop's principles, elements and lifestyle above all else. One must be willing to direct the productive effects of Hip Hop's principles, elements and lifestyle back toward the advancement of Hiphop Kulture above all else. However, the most important factor in Hip Hop's citizenry is Hip Hop's own internal unity and collective maturity.

[125]   As WE all have learned now, our increased freedom, peace, prosperity and defense are all linked to OUR own level of unity. Those of us who continue to ignore the importance of unity above all else are the very people holding us back. HIP HOP MUST REMAIN UNITED— otherwise, with our own hands we defeat ourselves and we should stop complaining about the actions of those who are unified against our interests.

[126]   We (the international Hip Hop community) are not criminals! We do not support crime and lawlessness even from our own countries and governments! For if we are to truly enjoy higher states of freedom, peace and prosperity, we must conduct ourselves in manners that surpass the current state of World affairs.

[127]   Where there is injustice, we MUST remain just! Where there is corruption, we MUST remain honest! And where there is disunity, WE MUST REMAIN UNIFIED!

The Truth is: our freedom, peace and prosperity are based solely upon how we decide to govern ourselves.

[128]   We can talk, talk, talk, complain, complain, complain, protest and rally all day about the injustices of oppressive government agencies, the police and insensitive corporate business practices, but if WE are unwilling or incapable of governing ourselves then the natural result of such an inability is oppression and cops getting away with murder. The point is unity! As our parents chanted during the rise of the Civil Rights movement; THE PEOPLE UNITED CAN NEVER BE DEFEATED!

[129]   We believe that every human being has a duty and a right to govern themselves, and the way in which one governs one's self begins the structure as to how whole communities govern themselves. Before we can even think about the governing of our Hip Hop nation, we must first consider the governing of our own homes, our own businesses, our own lives.

[130]   The decision to ignore this duty or seek to prevent Hiphoppas (and others) from exercising this duty is oppression. Whether self-imposed or induced in some way by outside forces, those who deny us (and others) the right to govern ourselves and live as we believe is best for our development are our oppressors and history shows that the universe itself will remove such oppression from ITS path toward increased order and independence.

[131]   Know this. Restriction of thought, action, expression and/or speech is oppression even if one does it to oneself. On the other hand, freedom of thought, action, expression and speech is self-governance even if one is ignorant of the effects of one's own thoughts, actions, expressions and speech. Either way, it is your own self-expressed thoughts, actions and words that shape and directly affect the circumstances of your physical life.

[132]   Sometimes to leave the ignorant to themselves is to equally oppress them as if you kept them in chains and in prison. Allowing the ignorant to remain ignorant actually destroys the ignorant and the community the ignorant rely upon.

[133]   Our work, therefore, is to lift Hip Hop out of ignorance and onward toward increased knowledge. Our work is to inspire the Hip Hop community to be a *community* through a unified understanding of its own existence beyond entertainment. Our work is about building and maintaining a sustainable Hip Hop culture and protecting our people from themselves first, and then from the non-productive forces that tempt us to our own demise. In short, we are cultivating an authentic Hip Hop citizenry.

[134]   Here, loyalty implies a strict adherence to the principles of our culture; this is the center of unity for any group or community. For when one consciously and deliberately breaks the principles of one's community, one is engaged in the act of destroying one's community and even one's self.

[135]   We can now see that a community's defeat and collapse is almost always brought on by the disunity, disrespect, and disobedience of its own people. It is always a *snitch* or a betrayer of the cause that hands victory over to the enemy. It is always one's disloyalty to the principles of the group and to its leadership that destroys the group from within and hands victory over to that group's enemies. This fact simply cannot be avoided.

[136]   Infighting is another cause for the destruction of any group. OUR COMMUNITY CANNOT AND MUST NOT BETRAY ITSELF IN THIS WAY! Betrayal is not always the act of giving up the secrets and/or plans of the group. Giving away or selling the group's resources for one's own gain is another cause for group destruction from

outside forces. However, infighting (or fighting amongst oneselves) is the number-one cause of any group's defeat.

137   UNITY IS THE KEY! Not only must we never sell our elements and expressions to interests that go against our own existence, we must equally not wage war with ourselves. We must find the strength and the courage within ourselves to resolve our conflicts peacefully and without violence. This is what it means to be loyal to Hip Hop.

138   Loyalty to Hip Hop also means the protection of our own artistic and cultural *elements*; this is the beginning of independence and self-governance for Hiphoppas. We are financed by our cultural *elements*, these are our intellectual properties. If we are to become and remain politically and socially strong we cannot continue to give our intellectual property (our *elements*) away to those who care little for our continued development and well-being as a people.

139   Know this. A Hip Hop *element* is one of Hip Hop's cultural expressions. It is a material good. It is our intellectual property. It is our capital. It is an act, art or idea that further expresses Hip Hop's culture and consciousness. It is a skill that reflects the character of the Hiphop consciousness and enhances the Health, Love, Awareness and Wealth of the truly committed Hiphoppa.

140   An *element* is usually created when the Hiphop *sight* (awareness/perception) is applied to a subject or object (material or immaterial).

141   Presently Hiphop's elements are: *Breakin, Emceein, Graffiti Art, Deejayin, Beat Boxin, Street Fashion, Street Language, Street Knowledge,* and *Street Entrepreneurialism.* These *elements* are symbolized throughout this instrument as B.E.G.D.B.F.L.K.E.

142   Hiphop's or Hip Hop's *elements* are the sources of Hiphop Kulture's political power. They are also the sources of a Hiphoppa's livelihood. They are how the

Hiphoppa provides for and protects her *Self* and her family. True Hiphoppas are specialized in at least one or more of Hiphop's *nine elements*.

[143] By itself one Hip Hop *element* is not the totality of Hip Hop's culture. It is a representation or an introduction to the culture itself. To fully comprehend Hip Hop's *elements* artistically one must gain an *overstanding* of Hip Hop culturally, even legally.

[144] In the United States, human beings are thought to have certain inalienable rights; rights that are natural to the existence of a human's *being*. In his book, *Cases and Materials on the Law of Real Property*, law professor Ray Andrews Brown writes, *Man, by virtue of his very existence, is endowed with certain natural desires and claims. Among the most common and apparent of these are the freedom of his body from injury or restraint; the exercise of his faculties in order that he may obtain the material things essential to his life and comfort; and the possession and enjoyment of these physical things of the world which he has brought under his control.*

[145] Professor Brown mentions the above as part of an explanation as to "Man's" natural right to property and how the state or community in which "Man" may live can override such a right for the good of all. Mr. Brown writes, *Organized society also has its own de facto interests, the most important of which is the preservation of peace and order,* which can come in direct conflict with "Man's" natural rights to exist and be happy.

[146] However, in return for giving up one's natural rights and freedoms, *The state recognizes, protects, controls and adjusts individual and social claims and interests.* The state, although determined to preserve peace and order, still recognizes (or should recognize) the rights of the individual.

[147] As professor Brown points out, *When an individual claim or interest receives recognition and protection from the*

state, it achieves the status of what is technically known as a 'legal right.' Thus a landowner under normal circumstances has the right, which will be vindicated by the state, to exclude others from entrance to his premises. The correlative to this right is the 'duty' which others have to observe this right.

[148]   I bring this up because when it comes to Hip Hop it seems that the United States is not yet recognizing or protecting our right to our own property. It seems that the United States does not recognize our real existence as Hip Hop and thus cannot protect our interests under law. And what does this mean legally?

[149]   First it means that if we are unprotected by law and the state's obligation to protect our interests as Hiphoppas practicing Hiphop is nonexistenant, then corporate bodies of all sorts can invade our culture and freely take from our culture whatever they choose because not only have we not put up a legal fence around our own intellectual property (B.E.G.D.B.F.L.K.E.), but we also have not invoked our inherent rights to our own property.

[150]   It is not that corporate entities exploited our artistic elements for the good of their own interests; it is more that because we were ignorant of our rights to property, others with knowledge took advantage of our ignorance. Through unfair contracts and even blatant theft they made OUR property THEIR property and the states in which we lived did not protect us, or our interests as a group. However, we were and still are expected to pay the taxes and abide by the laws of a nation that didn't and still doesn't protect us, or our property.

[151]   But what is property? Property in its common sense is thought of as something owned, a possession of some sort. Hip Hop's elements are indeed our property in a common sense, they are the tangible physical results to our intangible cultural reality. However, in a strict legal sense,

property as explained by Mr. Brown *denotes not the physical things themselves but the rights that the individual concerned has in them.*

[152]   *In a strict legal sense, land is not 'property,' but the subject of property. The term 'property,' although in common parlance frequently applied to a tract of land or a chattel, in its legal signification means only the rights of the owner in relation to it.*

[153]   This is important for true Hip Hop scholars to know because when seeking to preserve our culture (Hip Hop) we must also know the legal route of such preservation as it relates to real property. You cannot fully preserve something that you do not actually own. But as we can see ownership in a legal sense has less to do with what is actually possessed as it has more to do with one's right to property; one's ability to use what is said to be owned. *Use is the real side of property.*

[154]   Professor Brown continues, *If property in land consists in certain essential rights, and a physical interference with the land substantially subverts one or more of those rights, such interference takes the owner's property.*

[155]   *The right of indefinite user (or of using indefinitely) is an essential quality or attribute of absolute property, without which absolute property can have no legal existence. Use is the real side of property. If the right of indefinite user is an essential element of absolute property or complete ownership, whatever physical interference annuls this right takes property.*

[156]   It is not so much that our physical property has been taken from us, it is more the fact that our ability or inability to use, control, direct, alter, etc. our own Hip Hop elements for our own good has been interfered with, even stifled by greedy corporate interests and our own ignorance, and such an act is the taking or giving away of our property.

[157]   Our *indefinite* use of Hip Hop's artistic and

intellectual elements still remains our property today. It is us as a specialized group in the World that must invoke and lawfully demand our rights to property as it pertains to Hip Hop and its cultural elements and products.

158   *Property itself is an intangible thing. It is the right that a person has to make use of and enjoy a tangible thing, and not the tangible thing itself. If we stop to think, we will discover also that 'property' is not one single protected interest or claim to a thing but the totality of a number of different though related interests: the interests of possessing, of using, of altering, of conveying, etc., the thing in question.*

159   Hip Hop is an intangible thing that produces tangible things, and our inability to possess, use, alter, etc., our own Hip Hop tangibles is the beginning of our lost of property. We simply have got to stop giving away in ignorance our resources and rights to real *property*. This we must seriously begin to *overstand*.

160   Moving along now, we come to this frequently used term in our culture: *overstanding*. Here, *overstanding* is a state of awareness developed primarily from having a firsthand experience with learned subjects and objects. It is different from *understanding*, which is a comprehension of learned subjects and objects gained primarily from having been taught.

161   Someone who *understands* has a comprehension of taught information (acquired knowledge). Such is the objective approach to Hiphop and Hip Hop.

162   Someone who *overstands* actually experiences the information that has been taught and comprehended (acquired wisdom). Such is the subjective approach to Hiphop and Hip Hop.

163   Know this. Along with being loved, and being needed, most people just want to be understood. For the more you understand life, the easier your life shall be. Above

all learning we must truly seek understanding, and if we are blessed—*overstanding*.

[164] For life is to be *under* and *over* -stood, not just lived. But to truly lend your mind to the understanding of something other than yourself requires a certain appreciation for what is about to be studied. Therefore, let us seek to understand before we seek to form opinions and views on things we know little about. Let us also be unified in our overstanding of ourselves as *Hiphoppas*.

[165] What does this mean? It means that we must continuously seek the Truth and the true nature of our authentic being as Hiphoppas. This is what shall ensure our success. Relying upon Rap music's incomplete history is NOT how we are going to truly understand the divinity of our Hip Hop nature.

[166] Hip Hop's true history is NOT the history of Rap music entertainment. Rap music's entertainment history can be included in Hip Hop's history, but to interpret Hip Hop's cultural history through mainstream Rap music entertainment is a mistake.

[167] Most people today approach Hip Hop as a music genre because that's how Rap music is promoted. Icons such as Kool DJ Herc are referred to as "rap pioneers" even though they (he) are Hip Hop's "cultural architects," even spiritual leaders. In my observations, this perception of people like Kool DJ Herc (the recognized Father of Hip Hop) stagnates our collective development today as a Hip Hop community. We simply do not value one another and it is this devaluing of each other that keeps us in a valueless state.

[168] Approaching Kool Herc (the Father) historically as simply a DJ is like approaching Jesus (the Christ) historically as simply a carpenter. Not only does such a perception limit the potential of the community influenced

by such a perception, but such a view of Hip Hop is simply inaccurate historically. Kool DJ Herc is far more than a DJ, and Hip Hop is far more than a music genre!

169   Arriving in the United States from Jamaica sometime around 1967, Kool DJ Herc (an abbreviation for Hercules) was known for having the biggest and the loudest sound system in the Bronx, which attracted many street kids, young poets, graffiti writers, DJs and especially b-boys.

170   Kool DJ Herc would attract huge crowds to the playgrounds and parks of the West Bronx playing the instrumental *breaks* of songs by recording artists such as James Brown as well as the Amazing Bongo Band. In fact, James Brown's popular recordings would become Kool DJ Herc's main records to play.

171   And while many DJs in the Bronx, like El Marko, Mandingo, DJ Maboya, Elvis 007 and others, were also playing James Brown recordings, Kool DJ Herc was considered a street DJ because he would play his music on a huge sound system outside in the playgrounds and parks of the Bronx regularly for free! These events were called *Jams*.

172   One place where we were able to hear Kool DJ Herc *jam* was at the 1520 Sedgwick Avenue community center in the Bronx. This community center, which was part of the housing tenement where Kool Herc lived, was connected to a playground park where Herc was known to "deejay" on his huge sound system. This is one of the main places where Hip Hop as an art form is said to have started sometime around 1972-1973.

173   The apartment building directly on the other side of the playground park was 1600 Sedgwick Avenue and this is where I lived from about 1972-1974. During these times (1970s) the whole political and social structure of

the United States was changing. During this time major recording artists, actors, athletes and academicians were all openly protesting and speaking out against war and social injustice. Revolution was in the air!

[174]   Being influenced by the living conditions and national events of the day (unemployment, drug addiction, the Vietnam War, police misconduct, poverty, racism, civil rights, etc), the population at both 1520 as well as 1600 Sedgwick Avenue were very much politically and socially active. This community was NOT just singing and dancing; we were also praying and protesting.

[175]   In his time, Kool Herc was not just a DJ; he was also a popular activist in his community; a believer in GOD. He was *conscious* and talented and was known as a community leader. Kool Herc's street credibility was solid; he was *down by law.*

[176]   The actual idea of a *jam* was to set up a time and a space where the true intentions of our hearts and minds could be manifested through our various forms of *street* recreation, and Kool Herc was the guy that brought everyone together through his *deejayin.*

[177]   *Jams* were not only outdoor party spaces and places (Cedar Park, 123 Park, the 161 street Yankee Stadium Park, Stevenson High School park, all in the Bronx), *jams* were also a creative escape. It was a time to step outside of the confinement of mainstream life and create ourselves, to dress up in the clothes ("gear") that amplified what we thought of ourselves, to talk, walk and live according to our perception of ourselves without compromise.

[178]   A *jam* was a time to either show-off your own unique talents or watch the unique talents of others. A *jam* wasn't just about a crowd of people listening to a DJ (or, years later, to an MC), a *jam* was a community event—a social gathering. It was a time and space were the young

neighborhood school kids as well as the young outcasts, the outlaws and young revolutionaries would all come together to exchange ideas, street products, plans, gossip and of course talents.

179   To understand the true birth of Hip Hop, one must understand what the 1970s was really like. One must also remember that those who attended Kool Herc's *jams* were not exclusively b-boys, DJs and/or graffiti writers; many were the activists, intellectuals and revolutionaries of their time.

180   B-boyin, Aerosol art, Deejayin and Emceein were not the only things going on in the public parks of the 1970s and Kool DJ Herc was not the only DJ of his time in those areas. However, Kool DJ Herc and his sister Cindy (Pep) were also activists in their community and their free service to their community is what caused Hip Hop to exist.

181   As I mentioned earlier, I too was present at the birth of Hip Hop in 1973 and I remember being more concerned with the mystical life and with the development of myself spiritually than with being a *fresh* MC; yet I too was attracted to the *jams* and all that the *jams* represented. I too was Hip Hop! So, what is Hip Hop's true history? Gang culture? I don't remember Hip Hop's birth like this.

182   The point here is that when Kool Herc began playing music in the community center of 1520 Sedgwick Avenue and its neighboring parks, attracting and gathering together b-boys, graffiti writers, kung fu martial artists, poets, MCs and other DJs, he also attracted gang members as well as young philosophers from a wide variety of spiritual views and traditions, and I am only one survivor from this era.

183   In Truth, many young men and women of the early 1970s were very spiritual and philosophically-minded. Early Hip Hop was surrounded by a variety of World philosophies; many of which we adopted for ourselves.

As an example, the 1973 film *Enter The Dragon* starring Bruce Lee was a huge success in the 1970s and inspired millions of urban kids all across the United States to begin practicing kung fu.

[184]   The spirit and fighting skills of Bruce Lee (and Jim Kelly) were a major influence upon the values and principles Hiphoppas still hold sacred today. It wasn't so much that Bruce Lee was explicitly teaching ancient Chinese philosophies in his films, it was more his attitude toward life and living that captured our hearts.

[185]   Bruce Lee was not just a Chinese martial artist or an actor, he was sensitive to the times in which he lived and his films always tried to convey some sort of message aimed at self-control, self-mastery and social justice. WE LOVED BRUCE LEE! He symbolized what early Hip Hop aspired to be.

[186]   Although censored at the time, *Enter The Dragon* (Bruce Lee's version) opened up with a conversation between Bruce Lee and his spiritual teacher. His teacher begins the film saying, *I see your talents have gone beyond the mere physical level. Your skills are now at the point of spiritual insight. I have several questions.*

[187]   *What is the highest technique you hope to achieve?* Bruce answers, *To have no technique.* The teacher continues, *Very good. What are your thoughts when facing an opponent?* Bruce replies, *There is no opponent.* The teacher asks, *And why is that?* Bruce answers, *Because the word I does not exist.* The teacher then says *So, continue.*

[188]   Bruce Lee explains; *A good fight should be like a small play, but played seriously. A good martial artist does not become tense, but ready; not thinking, yet not dreaming. Ready for whatever may come. When the opponent expands, I contract. When he contracts, I expand. And when there is an opportunity, I do not hit, IT hits all by ITself.*

189   The teacher replies, *Now you must remember; the enemy has only images and illusions behind which he hides his true motives. Destroy the image and you will break the enemy. The IT that you refer to is a powerful weapon easily misused by the martial artist who deserves his loss.*

190   Further into the conversation the teacher asks Bruce, *Tell me now the Shaolin commandment number 13.* Bruce replies, *A martial artist has to take responsibility for himself and accept the consequences of his own doing.*

191   This attitude is basic to Hip Hop. However, one month before *Enter The Dragon* was released, Bruce Lee mysteriously died and this whole dialog was cut from the film. I often wonder what the World would be like if so many great minds like Bruce Lee were not sabotaged and/or murdered. Minds like Dr. Martin Luther King Jr., Malcolm X, John Lennon, Gandhi, and again Bruce Lee to name a few.

192   I am from that group of young people that were inspired by these minds. We went to the *jams* and philosophied in a *cipher* (a circle) with others of like mind about the state of the Black man and woman in America. My group did not grab the mic, or break, or DJ at first; we were more concerned with hidden Truths and attaining freedom from injustice *by any means necessary.* Kool Herc's *jams* attracted us also.

193   Some of us grew up Baptist, or Catholic, or Jehovah's Witness. Others of us grew up Muslim; even others of us grew up Rastafarian, and Jewish, and as Hebrew Israelites, and as Five Percenters. I grew up in all of these spiritual traditions. I can remember feeling all kinds of spiritual traditions at the places where Kool DJ Herc played and later where Afrika Bambaataa and Jazzy Jay played.

194   Even later where Red Alert, Chuck Chillout, DJ Breakout and Brucie B. played, Christians were there,

Rastafarians, Five Percenters, Freemasons were there, Muslims were there, Hindus and Buddhists were there, even Witches, Satanists and Atheists were in attendance. It was a *jam!* It was open and anyone who wanted to be there was there.

195   At these early *jams* I remember everyone being in harmony with one another through the music, the clothing and our unique styles of communication (hand shakes, head nods, street games and street news, etc.).

196   Even when we argued philosophically we were always able to work things out in the end without violent confrontations because in the end we knew that we were all united in the idea of freedom from oppression. And yes, our debates did get heated! But this is why we created Hip Hop to begin with.

197   Hip Hop was created as a neutral zone, an alternative form of recreation, an escape from street-violence, corruption and boredom. This is a major part of Hip Hop's history that seems to always be left out of Hip Hop's historical presentations.

198   The very subjects and activities that rappers rap about today are exactly what Hip Hop was created to avoid and even overcome. The point here is that knowledge and *overstanding* were also at the birth of Hip Hop right along with b-boying, MC-ing, graffiti writing and DJ-ing. However, the desperate quest to exploit Hip Hop's artistic elements for profit (in Hip Hop's later years) buried the principles and life skills that accompanied Hip Hop's early artistic elements.

199   Early Hiphoppas united around Kool DJ Herc's sound system because it was the biggest and the loudest of the time. However, even with talent the actual character of Kool DJ Herc himself was one of leadership and social activism. He and his sister Cindy actually cared about the

young kids in their neighborhood and this is what caused Hip Hop to exist. In fact, this was the general attitude of even the gangs at the time.

200   Kool Herc wasn't just playing music in the park; he was trying to keep young kids like me out of trouble by playing his music in the park for free. Kool Herc would play the songs of James Brown which represented the Black Power movement and most people's feelings at the time of struggling against oppression.

201   James Brown with Alfred James Ellis would publish the song "Say It Loud—I'm Black and I'm Proud" which was a huge success in 1968. As youths, we sang along with James Brown as he shouted, *SAY IT LOUD!* And we would all say, *I'M BLACK AND I'M PROUD!*

202   James Brown would tell us, *I worked on jobs with my feet and my hands, and all the work I did was for the other man! And now we demands our chance to do things for ourselves, we tired of beating our heads against the wall and working for someone else!* This advice would follow me all of my life—this is Hip Hop!

203   For youngsters like me growing up in New York, the *good life* was all about independence from the rigid order of the World's work-force, and non-attachment to the ways, the people and the things of the mainstream. Like many of my time I just wanted to be at peace and happy. I just wanted to *chill.*

204   The group of youngsters I grew up with were not really interested in making careers out of their MC-ing and DJ-ing abilities. These were our pastime recreations; we simply wanted freedom from the oppression that we witnessed our parents and grandparents experiencing. This inspired many of us (the original MCs, b-boys/b-girls and DJs) to enroll in college and become professionals later in life.

[205] For others of us (the artists), Hip Hop became our new identity. It became our interpretation of the World. At very young ages we confirmed to our skeptical parents that we were going to make a life for ourselves practicing the artistic elements of Hip Hop. And even though many of us would have to leave home at early ages in order to pursue our goals as MCs, dancers and DJs, our group (influenced by the events of the Civil Rights movement) still saw Hip Hop as the continued struggle for true freedom, justice and equality.

[206] For our group, as we got older we began to turn our Hip Hop view of the World (our *sight*) toward the subjects of philosophy, history, religion and politics. Beyond music and dance, Hip Hop was the life that we began to live. So the question became, *how would we live the Hip Hop life?* Beyond rapping, how should the rapper's life be lived?

[207] This is how I, and many others, have always approached Hip Hop. For us, Hip Hop is NOT just art and entertainment. For us, Hip Hop is a metaphysical principle that ensures one's health, love, awareness and wealth through the arts, and the Gospel of Hip Hop is the documentation and instruction of such a view.

[208] For us, Hip Hop is GOD's response to OUR suffering, it is the answered prayer of our grandparents and ancestors, it is the PROMISED LAND, it is the *idea* that unites us. Such an *idea* teaches us to cooperate with one another, to help one another and support one another.

[209] For we have now learned that life is all about cooperation. That the power which causes several portions of a plant or even a human (for example) to come together to help one another is called "life," or produces "life." We have now learned that life intensifies with the increase of helpfulness and cooperation. The intensity of life is also the intensity of helpfulness, unity and cooperation. The ceasing

of these powers causes deterioration, therefore the ceasing of help is called "corruption."

[210]   We (Hip Hop) have a unique opportunity to join the World's peace process and establish the sovereignty our parents envisioned without violence and/or war. But first we must cooperate with one another, and this is why the Gospel of Hip Hop physically exists and why the Temple of Hip Hop culturally exists. Let us get to work on the realization of this vision. Let us cooperate with one another. For us, THIS IS REAL HIP HOP! There it is.

THE SECOND OVERSTANDING
THE REFINITIONS

¹   Peace and much Love. Know this. The term *refinition* means "redefined definitions." This overstanding deals with the redefining of Hip Hop, Hip Hop's artistic elements and the Hiphoppa in an effort to strengthen the methodology of Hip Hop's actual preservation and lifestyle.

²   *The Refinitions* are not only the Temple of Hip Hop's collection of Hip Hop cultural terms and codes designed to organize and raise the self-worth of the Temple Member that teaches Hip Hop for a living, *The Refinitions* encourages Temple Members to redefine themselves as Hip Hop above all else.

³   Here, Hip Hop is not just a music genre or some other kind of art form. Here, Hip Hop is the name and divine nature of our present lifestyle. Hip Hop is the name of our ritual; it is the utterance of our being.

⁴   *Rap fans* are told about the *fathers* and *mothers*, *Godfathers* and *Godmothers*, *Pioneers*, *Teachas* and history of Hip Hop for the sake of building Hip Hop's political common Spirit and cultural continuity in the World. Such knowledge promotes respect for those Hip Hop pioneers that have contributed to Hip Hop's physical manifestation and cultural continuity in the World.

⁵   However, knowing the history of *Hip Hop* and/or the names of *Hip Hop's* pioneers will not defend against the everyday happenings and temptations of the material World. For Hip Hop itself to be strong and vibrant,

its practitioners must become strong and vibrant when practicing the Hip Hop lifestyle. The purchasing of Rap CDs is NOT the Hip Hop lifestyle.

6   The Hip Hop lifestyle prescribed in these writings establishes the foundations of Health, Love, Awareness and Wealth in preparation for a life lived in peace, love, unity and joy while practicing Hip Hop.

7   Critics of our movement can say whatever they like, however amongst average Hiphoppas who have bills to pay, families to raise, mouths to feed and goals to achieve, Hip Hop cannot be just about music and dance, beefs and scandals. What kind of lifestyle is that!

8   After you've reached 20 years of age Hip Hop must be able to sustain your well-being or you will be forced to associate with another movement or way of life that can. And there begins the death of Hip Hop for real! The inability to enhance the quality of the Hip Hop life can lead to the death of Hip Hop itself.

9   For if Hiphoppas cannot sustain their own well-being with Hip Hop, or if the Hip Hop lifestyle leads to prison, then sooner or later some of our best minds and the most talented of our group will be forced to take up other lifestyles and careers just to feed and protect themselves. And even beyond the protecting, feeding, clothing and sheltering of one's self, if Hip Hop cannot offer the Hiphoppa peace then what is it offering?

10   This teacha has achieved peace through his contentment with Hip Hop, and this is what he teaches. I really don't need anything else to be happy. Hip Hop is total living for me, I would live no other way. Therefore, by being true to the "love" in my life, GOD is revealed, my purpose is fulfilled and peace is produced. People can betray you; family and friends can be unreliable, selfish and unreasonable. But GOD, revealed through an attuned

Hiphop lifestyle, is a firm foundation upon which to stand. Let GOD be your strength, not people.

11   Forty years of living Hip Hop has also revealed to us an order, a plan, a pattern, some sort of divine direction that guides and develops Hip Hop. This *knowing* produces peace and knowing this produces peace. Knowing for a fact without a doubt that Hip Hop is divinely guided creates peace in the life of the attuned Hiphoppa. Practicing Hip Hop in this way and being content with Hip Hop in this way produces an inner security that satisfies your outer perception, causing a state of peace.

12   Know this. PEACE PRESERVES HIP HOP. And peace is not attained after one is successful; peace is practiced at the beginning of one's journey toward success. This is why those who have not mastered their own inner-workings first will find themselves enslaved to their own outer-workings later. And one of the first tasks of one's inner-work is to live a life that one can be proud of, a life that can be commended before GOD. Such a lifestyle causes peace, and this is why such a lifestyle should begin when you are young; like 15.

13   Knowledge also causes peace in the sense that being able to accurately and impressively explain what you do as well as who you are produces a sense of inner-security about yourself. Being impressed with yourself, that you are your Self, causes peace. Being satisfied with your Self causes peace.

14   Mastery of *the Refinitions* presents a professional personality that draws needed opportunity through the curiosity and admiration of those who hear you speak. However, *the Refinitions* have been known to backfire upon those who simply speak the terms and don't live the life. It is like claiming to be a gangster so that you may impress your ignorant friends. But when your own gangster speech begins to draw gangster situations to you, you are unprepared

because you really don't live a criminal life; you were only speaking about criminal behavior because you thought you needed to do so to be considered cool.

15   The same can be applied to good and productive situations like when you claim to have something that you don't really have only to achieve it and have not the hands, the mind, or the space to receive it. Know this. Lifestyles are created by the rituals of one's tribe which corresponds with the nature of one's being. Hip Hop is the name of our tribe, and the mastery of one's own tribal rituals sets up a confident character about one's self even before one enters the World as an adult or as a professional of some sort.

16   When one has matured and has completed the ritual "stages" of one's own tribe and holds the respect of one's own group one then earns a certain importance and respect in the World not for what one has done in the World, but for what one has done for one's self amongst one's own people. Such a character invites peace.

17   The World respects a man whose tribe respects him. The World protects a woman whose tribe protects her. The World feeds and educates the children whose tribe feeds and educates them.

18   The World is also confident in the leader who is confident in himself, and such confidence comes by way of one's own mastery of one's own culture and self-expression. Hip Hop is the name of our tribe, and the way we present ourselves to the World is the way the World shall present itself to our children and their children's children forever.

19   For when we finally accept our tribe and commit to it, we see ourselves more clearly because we know what we belong to. The problem with so many of our young people today is that they don't feel as though they belong to anything and so peace in their adult years is almost impossible because they are not comforted by a satisfying tradition.

20   Mastery of *the Refinitions* begins one's journey toward contentment and peace as a Hiphoppa because the mastery of *the Refinitions'* language and approach to Hip Hop makes the practicing Hiphoppa sure about the Hip Hop he/she lives and practices. Such surety causes a sense of peace and self-satisfaction well into one's elder years.

21   *The Refinitions* make the best parts of Hip Hop a repeatable science—a science that when mastered offers special intellectual and creative abilities unique to the Hip Hop experience. For as long as we stay within the mastery of our own self-expression we shall always possess a special strength in the material World against all challenges, foreign or domestic. The problem is when you doubt the authority and value of your own self-expression, then everyone else must doubt you as well.

22   Sure, we can all talk about preserving Hip Hop and teaching its true history, but if there is no clearly outlined strategy to actually preserve Hiphoppas themselves, how then shall Hip Hop actually be preserved? What are we actually preserving of Hip Hop?

23   Hip Hop's many activist organizations are right to preserve Hip Hop's artistic memorabilia and real history— respect to that. However, the Temple of Hip Hop is more concerned with the preservation of Hiphoppas themselves than with the study and/or glorification of Hip Hop's artifacts and/or possible history.

24   In fact, Hip Hop does not actually need to be preserved, because nothing real can ever be destroyed. And Hip Hop is real! However, if the Hiphoppa is ignorant of Hip Hop's productive lifestyle then it is the Hiphoppa's participation in Hip Hop that can lead the Hiphoppa to suffering, affecting the very fabric of Hip Hop itself. No, Hip Hop cannot actually be destroyed, but it can be distorted and made to serve interests it was not initially intended for.

This is one of the real challenges facing Hip Hop today, its belief in its own existence.

25   Many people (mostly Rap fans) are convinced that Hip Hop is just music. They approach Hip Hop as a music genre with no principles or social awareness and then wonder why "hip-hop's" music doesn't offer its consumers anything more than gangstas, bitches, pimps, hoes and niggas. Indeed they got it twisted!

26   This is why many rappers don't make it past two albums or even 10 minutes live on stage, because talent never got anyone anywhere! It is the way in which you live your life that ensures your success and longevity. Talent does help. Being highly skilled does help. But ultimately, if people don't like you then you are going NOWHERE! If people don't trust you, you are going NOWHERE! If you have no faith, no courage or credibility you are going NOWHERE!

27   Hip Hop's music alone never got anyone killed or made anyone live any longer. It was always one's own lifestyle or even one's own life decisions that produced such results either way. So, how ya livin? What principles do you conduct your life by? Do they cause peace, contentment and joy in your life?

28   Hip Hop reaches far beyond music and lyrics, as we've been learning; Hip Hop is a conscious way to be. But some have suggested that Hip Hop is simply an art form; a genre of music to be compared to other music genres and performing arts. They insist that Hip Hop is no more than music entertainment, as if "Breakin" and "Graffiti writing" do not exist as Hip Hop as well. As if Hip Hop actually exists outside of GOD!

29   But is there really a debate here? The real issue is faith. What do YOU believe? If you believe that hip-hop is just music then you shall live with the manifestations of

your own beliefs. And if I believe that Hiphop is a conscious behavior that produces health, love, awareness, and wealth for the believer then I too shall live with the manifestations of my own beliefs.

30   But, even if we limit Hip Hop's activity to the realm of just music, many still fail to meditate upon the actual depths of music itself. Even hip-hop journalists, music executives and so-called *hip-hop scholars* refuse to ask themselves surface questions like: Where does music come from? What is it that inspires the human mind to create music? What is the purpose of music itself? More importantly, what is the purpose of OUR music? What should OUR music inspire OUR listeners to feel? And, what is art?

31   How many of our critics are really asking these questions? If Hip Hop is just good music, then what is its purpose as "good music?" Not that we should give our music a fake purpose that it did not originally have, but instead shouldn't we be seeking the Truth and deeper existence of the music that WE are inspired to create?

32   Shouldn't we be investigating the deeper aspects of our OWN creativity? An inquiry into just Rap music's existence would reveal to us the true nature of our OWN being. Such an inquiry would explore Hip Hop far beyond DJ-ing, MC-ing and CD sales.

33   If we are truly Hip Hop's artists (and not just fans) is it not OUR responsibility to seek the deeper meaning to OUR Hip Hop art? Who else is supposed to do this inquiry for us? Who else CAN do this inquiry for us? Even if it is just to get better as artists and master the performances of our own artistic expressions, shouldn't WE be investigating the deeper meaning to OUR creative activity? And this is if we limit Hip Hop to just "Rap music."

34   These are just the basic questions of those that

truly love Hip Hop. Others (even with lengthy recording contracts and various sales awards) expose themselves as *"desperate fans of the music"* by never taking the time to investigate the deeper mechanics of their own craft and livelihood. They themselves act as if they are visitors to Hip Hop's culture and elements simply by their non-caring attitude toward Hip Hop's preservation.

35   For if they were even true musicians and not "hustlers" hustling or peddling Rap music to a gullible public their greatest joy would be to probe the sacred path of music creation into the very depths of poetry and even sound vibration itself.

36   The young emcee seeking a deeper understanding of hip-hop even as music would ask; *"if hip-hop is just good music, then what is music?"* The origin of music is not the radio, nor is the origin of art the artist, nor do CD sales equate to artistic excellence.

37   Know this. Music is the art of arranging sounds into harmonious melodies and rhythms. Sound is a vibration that passes through any elastic material and/or medium; either solid, liquid, gas, or other.

38   Music and sound are not the same things. Sound must vibrate at the frequency of 16 to 20,000 hertz (or cycles per second) to be detected by the human ear. The vibration frequency of sound hitting the ear at 20 hertz must be almost 70 dB higher (2000 hertz or 10 million times more energy) to produce human hearing. The ear actually magnifies sound vibrations so that we can hear them.

39   In our time, the frequency range for human beings to hear speech is between 600 to 4,800 hertz. The energy output of the male voice peaks at about 350 hertz and the energy output of the female voice peaks at about 700 hertz, which is then magnified by the eardrum to produce hearing. However, even if there was no eardrum to detect sound in

the human ear, sound would still exist because sound is energy; you just would not hear it.

40   Again, music is not sound. Music is the arrangement of various sounds. Sound is vibration; it is the ingredients of music. Sound is vibration and vibration is energy. Energy is produced by atomic forces.

41   We exist in a universe of energy. In fact, we and our material environments are the forms which this energy takes. The most commonly understood manifestations of this energy are heat, light and sound. Music is the arrangement of energy in its form as sound. Each sound communicates an idea to us based upon how we have been educated (trained) to interpret such sounds.

42   *This now leads us to another aspect of music, to the process of hearing. This process is not an isolated phenomenon which only entails the ears, it involves the whole body. Everybody knows the feeling that runs down your back when someone scratches on a hard surface; you have to shudder. Music can also affect you like this through and through. Indeed, happy are those who hear the chords of joy and ecstasy. Happy are those familiar with the tones of our planet, happy are those who let these tones resound within, attuning them to the basic motion and rhythm of the earth.* (Hans Cousto, *The Cosmic Octave*)

43   The point here is that even if Hip Hop is just "good music," we must still seek the deeper meaning and uses of music and sound to arrive at a deeper understanding of *hip-hop* even as music. Such an inquiry is bound to lead the inquiring Hiphoppa beyond *hip-hop* as entertainment and into *Hiphop* as consciousness and energy.

44   This is what makes the Temple of Hip Hop unique in its approach to Hip Hop in our time, and those that master *the Refinitions* as well as their approach to GOD won't <u>use</u> Hip Hop or God, they will inherit the ability to <u>produce</u> Hip Hop and/or God for others to use. Our needs are met

in the production of Hip Hop and/or God itself.

[45]   *The Refinitions* approaches Hip Hop as a repeatable science and lays out a practical framework for the explaining of Hip Hop's elements to younger Hiphoppas and even to those foreign to Hip Hop.

[46]   However, mastery of *the Refinitions* and its magical uses can only come alive in real-life situations. Ultimately, mastery of *the Refinitions* is an experience, not a speech. It is a perceptual reflex that reveals the inner-workings of Hip Hop's creative spirit.

[47]   Teaching *the Refinitions* creates employment opportunities for the truly committed members of our Hip Hop preservation society. In addition, *the Refinitions* gives the apprentice an organized view of Hip Hop's activities in the physical World beyond entertainment.

[48]   And even though the Temple of Hip Hop does teach the nine elements of *the Refinitions* in nine days, it is suggested that each of the nine elements which interprets Hip Hop for us be taught within a one month period. Each *element* should be studied for 30 days before moving on to the teaching and/or study of the remaining elements. In all, it is suggested that these *elements* be taught over a nine month period; one *element* per month.

[49]   As a templist, do not allow yourself to be caught unstudied. Such neglect will only affect your ability to overcome the World and its traps. These *Overstandings* are for YOUR empowerment. Take yourself seriously!

[50]   *The Refinitions* are true Hip Hop codes and terms based upon Hip Hop's historical facts, not upon emotion and folklore. It is designed to give the templist an empowering lifestyle, an empowering authoritative conversation and an organized view of Hip Hop's elements.

[51]   Seriously committed templists are advised to seek and study all knowledge, organizations and interpretations

of Hip Hop available. However, knowing and speaking the language of *the Refinitions* is a good first start for any Hiphoppa; it opens new doors of opportunity, defense, self-worth and longevity.

52   Other Hip Hop organizations may practice a different set of elements and terms. However, *the Refinitions* remain the primary teaching tool of the Temple of Hip Hop. With this body of knowledge we raise our self-worth as *Hiphop Kultural Specialists*. Like Hip Hop itself, *the Refinitions* is a social art that offers its practitioners an escape from poverty and purposelessness.

53   It is this approach to Hip Hop that assisted in OUR freedom and has delivered OUR *victory over the streets* in our time. And it has been our experience that this approach to Hip Hop (*the Refinitions*) truly preserves Hip Hop because it truly empowers the Hiphoppa.

54   By learning how to speak and teach the language of *the Refinitions;* and by performing Hip Hop's elements in this way, the true Hiphoppa raises her own self-worth and artistic longevity. In addition, the language of *the Refinitions* raises the value of those that teach *Hiphop, Hip Hop* and *hip-hop* for a living.

55   This begins your intellectual training of Hiphop, Hip Hop and hip-hop, and here your training is directly connected to your doing. Reading about Hip Hop is NOT how one experiences *Hiphop*. It is in the doing, being and living of *Hiphop* that one gains the spiritual essence of Hip Hop.

56   Remember, an athlete was never made by mere instruction, and no soldier was ever trained simply by studying her manual. Both are made by the continuous practice of their drills and exercises. It is not the hearers of Truth, but the doers of Truth that are justified before their God.

[57]   So let us perfect ourselves in this way. Let us work in our own sphere and with what GOD has provided to us. Let us perfect ourselves before seeking the ways of those outside of ourselves and our experiences. *The more we are sustained by internal strength, the less we demand of life around us. Each must keep his own happiness in his own name. No man is so rich or powerful that he can hire another to sleep for him or to eat for him. Each must perform the essential requirements of survival, and this is true of the inner-life as well. To depend for strength upon that which is not ourselves is folly.* (Manly P. Hall, *The Mystical Christ*)

[58]   A perfected *Self*, meaning a life purpose fulfilled, inherits the intellectual ability to know anything. Focus now upon the perfection of your *Self-expression*. Be not envious of the blessings and skills that GOD has given to others, ignoring the blessings and skills that GOD has given to you. Take a moment now to review and reflect upon our list of Hip Hop elements, terms and codes.

[R-10]   **BREAKIN:** (*The study and application of street dance forms.*) Originally called the *Go-Off, Burnin'* and/or *Boy Yong Yong,* Breakin is commonly called *Break Dancing* or *b-boying* today and it now includes the once independent dance forms *Up-Rockin, Poppin and Lockin, Jailhouse* or *Slap-Boxing, Double Dutch, Electric Boogie* and *Capoeira* martial arts. It is also commonly referred to as *freestyle street dancing.* The practitioners of traditional *Breakin* are called *b-boys, b-girls* and *Breakers.*

[I]   *Breakin* moves are also used in aerobics and other exercises that refine the body and relieve stress. Dance and other rhythmic body movements appear at the genesis of human awareness and remain the center of good health.

[II]   *Breakin* gets our hearts pumping at about 120

beats per minute, and if we can *break* or dance at least three times a week for only 20 minutes we will have enhanced our physical health and prolonged our very lives by years. Like letters, dance is also a form of communication. In fact, Poppin, Lockin, and Electric Boogie are all body symbols; even body letters.

III   Dance is often used as a form of self-expression; it is like a language (body language). It is also a form of healing and rejuvenation. *Break-dancing: acrobatic style of street dancing.*

IV   *While breakdancing (a term disowned by all b-boys) began with crews like the Nigga Twins, the Zulu Kings, the Salsoul Crew, the City Boys, Freeze Force, Starchild La Rock, the Disco Kids, and the KC Crew, the most influential was undoubtedly the Rock Steady Crew. Formed in 1977 by Jojo Torres, Jimmy Lee, Mongo Rock, Spy and Jimmy Dee, the Rock Steady Crew gathered together the best of the second wave of Latino b-boys who had come to dominate the field since it migrated out of the Bronx in the early 70s.*

V   *The RSC main innovation was to make b-boying more athletic, more gymnastic. Many of these moves were pioneered by the two b-boys who are generally considered the greatest: Richie 'Crazy Legs' Colon and Ken 'Swift' Gabbert. Moves like the windmill, the whip, the 1990, the chair and the spider are credited to Crazy Legs and Ken Swift, who helped the RSC become the dominant crew in legendary battles against the Dynamic Breakers, the Floor Masters and the New York City Breakers.*

VI   *Meanwhile, in Los Angeles, a kid called Don Campbell invented* Locking *(freezing in between moves). The dance became so popular that he formed his own troupe in 1973, the Campbellock Dancers, which included such minor celebs as Fred 'Rerun' Berry, Toni Basil and 'Shabba-Doo' Quinones. The style was expanded by The Electric Boogaloos ('Boogaloo*

Sam' Solomon, Timothy 'Poppin' Pete' Solomon, Skeeter Rabbit, Twist-O-Flex Don, Creepin' Cid and Tickin' Will), who invented moves like poppin', boogaloo, tickin', twist-flex and the old man while dancing to Zapp records. (Peter Shapiro, *The Rough Guide to Hip-Hop*)

VII   In a letter written to the Temple of Hip Hop, b-boy historian Mickey Ice explains how the dance style of Poppin was created in Fresno, California sometime around 1977 by a man named Boogaloo Sam dancing to Roger Troutman and Zapp records. He explains in this letter *The group was called the Electric Boogaloos, a group of young Black kids from Edison High School on the West Side of Fresno...My uncle was hyped by the whole movement, this was around 1977 until 1984, Poppin got exposure to the world, then came Oakland etc.*

VIII   Mickey Ice continues, *Just like the Bronx, this style of dancing was only going on here* (Fresno, CA), *nowhere else in California, not even Los Angeles, except Lockin which was Don Campbell. He was Lockin at Compton Community College, then came Rerun. Big ups to the Rock Steady Crew for taking it across the oceans! But there was some nasty brothas before the Rock Steady Crew like the Nicholas Brothers, Sammy Davis Jr., and Sandman. I got some footage of Black folks on the cotton plantation with the illest footwork and Up-Rocking before Hip Hop.*

IX   Popularized by: James Brown, Don Campbell and the Campbellock Dancers, the Nigga Twins, Poppin' Pete, Dennis Vasquez—the Rubber Band Man, Rock Steady Crew, Pee Wee Dance, the New York City Breakers, the Los Angeles Breakers, Boogaloo Shrimp, "Shabba-Doo" Quinones, Demons of the Mind, the Breeze Team, Michael Jackson, and others.

R-11   **EMCEEIN:** *(The study and application of rhythmic* *talk, poetry and divine speech.)* Commonly referred to as *rappin* or *Rap*, its practitioners are known as *emcees* or *rappers.*

I   The *emcee* is a Hip Hop poet who directs and moves the crowd by rhythmically rhyming in spoken word. The *emcee* is a cultural spokesperson. Technically, the *emcee* is a creation of one's community whereas the *rapper* is a creation of corporate interests.

II   The word *emcee* comes from the abbreviated form of *Master of Ceremonies* (M.C.). In its traditional sense, M.C. referred to the hosting of an event—the <u>master</u> of a <u>ceremony</u> or an event.

III   In its ancient sense, to *emcee* meant to pray or to communicate with GOD. It was used by the Greeks to communicate with their oracles and to pray to their gods.

IV   The earliest known forms of *Emceein* were done by the ancient priests, sages and philosophers of Africa and Asia. Later in history, the ancient art of *Emceein* would be practiced by African Griots and Djelees as they went from village to village teaching (or rather performing) history and important life lessons.

V   *Emceein* (or rhythmic speech/divine speech) also appears at the genesis of human awareness. It is the language of the heart.

VI   Early Hiphoppas transformed the traditional character of the *Master of Ceremonies* to include crowd participation routines and poetry. Today, the *emcee* seeks to be a master of the spoken word, not just the best rapper or poet.

VII   *Emceein* (when properly understood) manipulates air through sound vibration in an effort to alter or expand consciousness.

VIII   *Emcees* also deliver lectures and other forms of public instruction. Most *emcees* rate themselves on their ability to *rock a party*, speak clearly and/or tell a good story.

IX   *Emcees* (different from MCs) seek the mastery of the spoken word. For in the mastering of *emceein* we also express our inherit understanding of rhythm, linguistics, physics, mathematics, memory, logical reasoning and high communication skills. Emceein expresses a total integration of right and left brain coordination.

X   Know this. A talented *emcee* almost always becomes a respected rapper. But a talented rapper usually never becomes a respected *emcee*.

XI   The *emcee* expresses through rhyme what is already on your mind, whereas the *rapper* tells you all about his or her self. True Hiphoppas are encouraged to study both styles for maximum success.

XII   Popularized by: Cab Calloway, Coke La Rock, Pebblie Poo, Sha Rock, Chief Rocker Busy Bee, Keith Cowboy, Melle Mel, Grandmaster Caz, Rakim, Queen Lisa Lee, Slick Rick, Big Daddy Kane, MC Lyte, Roxanne Shanté, Muhammad Ali, and others.

R-12   **GRAFFITI ART:** *(The study and application of street calligraphy, art and handwriting.)* Commonly called *Aerosol Art, Writing, Piecing, Burning, Graff* and *Urban Murals*. Other forms of this art include *Bombin'* and *Taggin'*. Its practitioners are known as *Writers, Bombers, Graffiti writers, Aerosol artists, Graffitists* and *Graffiti artists*.

I   Also at the genesis of human awareness, writing on walls, trees, stones, clothing, etc. plays an important part in the development of human intelligence and self-expression. Most urban children instinctively begin learning to write by writing on walls.

II   Ancient humans of prehistoric times would put certain berry juice in their mouths and blow or spit their images onto cave walls sometimes in total darkness just as the modern graffiti writers of the 1970s and 1980s would do with their aerosol spray cans on the sides of subway trains.

III   Today, *Graffiti* artists seek to be masters of handwriting and art. *Graffiti* writing is mostly about letters. It's about actualizing one's artistic style and expression through letters. *Graffiti* artists rate themselves on their letter styles, characters and ability to write and/or draw a good story. Many *writers* have become graphic artists, fashion designers, photographers and motion picture directors.

IV   Know this. *Graffiti* as art is not vandalism! *Graffiti Art* is the revolutionary control of public space. *Graffiti Art* does to letters what emceein does to language. Traditionally, the word *Graffiti* originated from the Italian term *Graffito*, meaning *a scratch*—thus its connection with *deejayin* (Graffiti writing—*visual deejayin*).

V   *Graffiti* was a term given to Hip Hop's graphic art animation when it appeared legally and illegally on public and private properties as an act of social protest (especially on subway trains).

VI   Similar to the way Emceein was labeled *Rap* and Breakin was labeled *break dancing*; so it became with *writin', bombin', piecin', burnin'* and *taggin'*, which have all come to be labeled *graffiti*.

VII   *Graffiti—writing or drawing that is scribbled, scratched, or sprayed onto a surface.*

VIII   Popularized by: Cornbread, Taki 183, Phase 2, Cay 161, Barbara 62 and Eve 62, Lady Pink, Stay High 149, Kase 2, Lee, Chico, Cope 2, TATS CRU, Presweet, Iz the Wiz, Seen, Quik, O.E., Revolt, Dondi, Papo 184, Zephyr, Futura 2000, and others.

R-13   **DEEJAYIN:** (*The study and application of Rap music production, cuttin', mixin' and scratchin' as well as on-air radio broadcasting.*) Commonly refers to the work of a disc jockey. However, *Hip Hop's* disc jockey doesn't just play vinyl records, tapes and compact discs. *Hip Hop's* DJ interacts artistically with the performance of a recorded song by *cuttin, mixin,* and *scratchin* the song in all of its recorded formats.

I　　Originally presented by two turntables, first designed by Edward P. Casey of the Bronx in 1955, and connected to a mixer with a "cross-fader" first designed by Grandmaster Flash in 1976, Hip Hop's DJ used the turntable and mixer as instruments that manipulated the playing of vinyl records.

II　　Deejayin, different from "DJ-ing," includes speaking, even rapping while presenting recorded music. Caribbean people still use the term *deejayin* to describe the vocal performances of rhythmic speech over music.

III　　Deejayin is also about knowing the moods that certain music can put an audience in. Deejayin detects and orchestrates the *mood* of music presentations. Deejayin explores the relationship between music melodies, song production, and their effects upon the moods of people.

IV　　Even beyond music and other forms of entertainment, *Deejayin* as a conscious awareness not only inspires our style of musical instrumentation, it also expresses the desire and ability to create, modify and/or transform music technology.

V　　Its practitioners are known as *turntablists, deejays, mixologists, grandmasters, mixmasters, jammasters,* and *funkmasters. Disc Jockey—presenter of recorded music.*

VI　　Popularized by: El Marko, Kool DJ Herc, Afrika Bambaataa, Jazzy Jay, Grand Master Flash, GrandWizzard Theodore, Kool DJ Red Alert, DJ Cash Money, Marley Marl, Brucie B., Chuck Chillout, Kid Capri, Afrika Islam, Jam Master Jay, and others.

R-14　　**BEAT BOXIN:** (*The study and application of body*

music and body language.) Commonly refers to the act of creating rhythmic sounds and language with various parts of the body; particularly the throat, mouth and hands. Its practitioners are known as *Human Beat Boxes* or *Human Orchestras.*

[I]   *Beat Boxin* is about seeing and using the body as an instrument. Earlier versions of this expression included *Hand bone* or *Hambone.* However, modern Beat Boxin originates from the act of imitating early electronic drum machines.

[II]   The early electronic drum machines were some of the original *beat boxes;* and to skillfully imitate them was called *Beat Boxin.* However, ancient *Beat Boxin* was the ability to imitate the sounds of Nature with one's own body parts.

[III]   Not only is *Beat Boxin* a form of communication; it is Hip Hop's actual language. *Beat Boxin* is also found at the genesis of human awareness. In fact, imitating the sounds of Nature (or one's natural environment) to communicate ideas and feelings is at the very beginning of human awareness, knowledge and survival.

[IV]   Popularized by: Doug E. Fresh, Biz Markie, the Fat Boyz, (the original) DMX, Greg Nice, Bobby McFerrin, Emanon, Click Tha Supah Latin, K Love, Rahzel, and others.

[R-15]   **STREET FASHION:** *(The study and application of urban trends and styles.)* Commonly refers to the clothing trends of urban centers. However, *Street Fashion* deals with all trends and styles of Hip Hop's culture—what's in and what's out, regardless of the expression. Its practitioners are known as *Hiphoppas.*

[I]   Self-expression through *Street Fashion* is an important way to present Hip Hop's unique identity to the

World. *Street Fashion* represents the prominence of all Hip Hop cultural codes, forms and customs.

II   Not only is fashion a very ancient form of communication, but our expressed consciousness was (and still is) also represented in the way in which we adorned, colored and dressed ourselves.

III   Popularized by: the Black Spades, the Black Panthers, the Crips, the Bloods, Jew Man, Ron 125th, Dapper Dan, Shirt Kings, Lugz, FUBU, Karl Kani, Sean John, Wu Wear, Fat Joe 560, Phat Farm and others.

R-16   **STREET LANGUAGE:** *(The study and application of street communication.)* Commonly referred to as *Black English, Urban Slang* and *Ebonics.* It is Hip Hop's urban language and linguistic codes—the verbal communication of the *streets.*

I   Advanced *Street Language* includes the correct pronunciation of one's native and national language as it pertains to urban life. In addition, advanced *Street Language* deals with one's communication skills even beyond what one says.

II   *Street Language* is not always spoken words. Hip Hop's *Street Language* includes Beat Boxin and certain *street* codes that may not be communicated in words at all.

III   Still, *Street Language* (as it pertains to the spoken word) is Hip Hop's effort to free itself from the confinement of standard language and standardized views of reality.

IV   English (for example) does not have enough words or definitions to describe how we (Hiphoppas) feel about the World. This is what makes our *Street* (slang) *Language* so important to our state of freedom.

V   Our speech publishes to others the thoughts and perceptions of OUR minds. *Street Language* helps Hiphoppas interpret THEIR World THEIR way. Its practitioners are known as *Hiphoppas.*

VI   Popularized by: Richard Pryor, Martin Lawrence, the Last Poets, Chris Rock, the Watts Prophets, James Brown, Gil Scott-Heron, E-40, DJ Hollywood, Lovebug Starski, Nas, Fab 5 Freddy, Frankie Crocker and others.

R-17   **STREET KNOWLEDGE:** *(The study and application of ancestral wisdom.)* Commonly refers to the basic common sense and accumulated wisdom of urban families. It consists of techniques, phrases, codes and terms used to survive within the inner cities.

I   It involves the ability to reason soundly with or without the ideas or validation of the traditional academic mainstream. *Street Knowledge* is the accumulation of Hip Hop's cultural self-awareness.

II   Its practitioners are known as *Hiphoppas* as well as *Sisters, Brothers, Goddesses, Gods, Mothers, Fathers, Teachas, Queens, Kings, Princesses, Princes, Lords* and *Divine.*

III   Contrary to the myth that knowledge is only accumulated in quiet, ordered, academic environments, much of Hip Hop's communal knowledge can be found with its comedians, poets and authors. Hiphoppas learn and transfer knowledge through laughter and having fun. *Streetwise—knowing how to survive modern urban life.*

IV   Popularized by: Malcolm X, Dr. Cornel West, Martin Lawrence, Afrika Bambaataa, Clarence 13X, Minister Louis Farrakhan, Kwame Ture, Chuck D, Nas, Dick Gregory, Chris Rock, Tupac Shakur, the Wayans Brothers, Wise Intelligent and others.

R-18   **STREET ENTREPRENEURIALISM:** *(The study and application of fair trade and Hip Hop business management.)* Commonly referred to as *street trade, having game, the natural salesman,* or *the smooth diplomat.* It is the readiness to engage in the creation of a business venture that brings about grassroots business practices. Many of Hip Hop's apprenticeships begin here.

[I] Different from *entrepreneur-ism* which may include the techniques and practices of the entrepreneur, *entrepreneurial-ism* focuses upon the motivating <u>Spirit</u> to be self-employed, inventive, creative and self-educated.

[II] It is this Spirit; the Spirit of self-creation, the urge to create and sell one's own talents, discoveries and inventions that is encouraged by these teachings. Its practitioners are known as *hustlers* and *self-starters*. *Entrepreneur—a self-motivated creative person who undertakes a commercial venture.*

[III] Popularized by: Madame C.J. Walker, Russell Simmons, Luther Campbell, Sean "Puffy" Combs, Jack the Rapper, Robert Townsend, Eazy-E, Too Short and others.

R-19 **The Dark Age:** (Age of Revolution) 1961–1971. This was a time when every institution in the United States was being questioned and challenged on its authenticity and value. It was during these turbulent times that the first generation of Hiphoppas were born. Our first gatherings were held in our homes as *house parties*. Later, we moved outside into the public parks. Originality in one's artistic skill was Hip Hop's first cultural status symbol.

R-20 **The Light Age:** (Age of Light) 1971–1981. During this time Hip Hop began to emerge as a distinct and unique urban movement. This was a time when Hiphoppas displayed the *sight*. As our *house parties* became over-crowded, we (Hiphoppas) began using electric power from the city streetlights to generate as much energy needed to run huge sound systems in New York City's public parks. *Hip Hop was set out in the dark, they use ta do it out in the park...*(MC Shan). *Power from a streetlight made the place dark...*(KRS ONE).

^I Intercepting city power was literally and symbolically one of the ways in which the Hiphop *sight* was first expressed. The light of the street or the awareness of the street; the street-Light (*sight*) had some Hiphoppas creating community recreation by unleashing the fire hydrants on hot summer days.

^{II} Some wrote their names and other messages on city subway trains and buses, while others danced for money in the downtown areas of their cities. Still others would express new fashion and language trends.

^{III} At the close of this age Hip Hop began to slowly influence the American mainstream in a variety of ways. However, the *hip-hop* community began to want what the mainstream offered as opposed to being satisfied with what it had already accomplished.

^{IV} This was an age when Hip Hop realized it was unique and self-evident. There were no limits in our sight. By the middle of this age, most of our gatherings were held in public parks, nightclubs and community centers.

^V Those with loud sound systems and/or boom boxes (large portable radios) were considered important. Self-recorded cassette tapes of *Deejayin* and *Emceein* became Hip Hop's industrial and cultural status symbols. It was through the symbolic power of the *street-light* that we empowered ourselves.

R-21 **The Golden Age:** (Age of Awareness) 1981–1991. This was a time when Hip Hop became self-aware and began to establish itself in the World. This was when most of Hip Hop culture's foundation work was inspired.

^I Many of Hip Hop's cultural icons emerged during this time. The Hip Hop community was still inexperienced and many Hiphoppas were angry at the mainstream for ignoring them. Kurtis Blow would be the first MC to sign

to a major recording corporation (Mercury Records).

^{II} During this time, a gold album (500,000 recordings sold) and gold jewelry became the Hip Hop community's industrial and cultural status symbols. Those with a gold album sales award and/or an assortment of gold jewelry were considered *large* or important.

^{III} During this age, some Hiphoppas remained *cultural* while others chose to be *corporate*. It was a time of great debate and image-building. It was during this time that many Hiphoppas began to lose the *sight*.

R-22 **The Platinum Age:** (Age of Power/ The Ice Age) 1991–2001. This was an age when the Hip Hop community began to benefit from the techniques set down by those of the *Golden Age*. This age was influenced by a so-called *war on drugs* which many said was really a *war on families*.

^I Most of the artistic expressions of this era were makeovers, do-overs, remixes, rewrites and samples; very little originated from any of Hip Hop's nine elements during this time. Emphasis was placed upon media ratings, sales chart positions, fame and money which came about through the basic copying and remaking of the already popular songs, dances and street trends of the 1970s and 1980s.

^{II} During this time, Rap music became the dominant expression of the inner cities, influencing millions of people from a variety of ethnicities, classes and professional occupations.

^{III} It was during the *Platinum Age* or *Ice Age* that *hip-hop* accumulated enough wealth to independently provide for its families. A platinum album (1,000,000 CDs sold) and platinum jewelry became the hip-hop community's status symbols. True Hip Hop went undaground.

^{IV} And even though Hiphoppas cried out for *peace and*

unity during this age, it was the pursuit of money, power and respect that was called...*the key to life!*

R-23 **The Information Age:** (Age of Culture) 2001–2011. In this age Hiphop Kulture and all of its elements became common knowledge in the inner cities and within the institutions of the World.

I   Many Hiphoppas matured during this age, becoming aware of their spiritual natures and higher purpose as Hiphop. Many Hiphoppas raised families in productive Hiphop lifestyles.

II   This age was influenced by a so-called *war on terror.* This age also experienced the moral collapse of corporate and religious institutions in America due to widespread greed, lust and corruption. In addition, this age saw some of the worst weather in history! Whole cities and coastlines began to disappear during this age.

III   During this time, Rap music lost some of its mainstream CD-selling appeal. Many argued that it was the availability of free music over the Internet and bootlegged mixtapes that caused Rap music to lose its ability to sell like it did in its previous ages.

IV   However, another perspective suggests that Rap music lost some of its mainstream appeal and commercial dominance because of the irresponsible, unbalanced and vulgar images hip-hop portrayed daily through mainstream media outlets that were controlled by two or three recording companies, as well as continuously over-priced CDs which lacked any real artistic talent.

V   Rap music's original production styles of hard aggressive drums and samples were replaced by a more rhythm-and-blues style of production. With more popularity and money, Rap music became more musical and less confrontational.

VI   With its acceptance into the mainstream, Rap music lost its rebellious street-edge and thus its ability to compete in the corporate world. Diamonds became the hip-hop community's industrial and cultural status symbols while true Hip Hop became more *undaground* and socially conscious.

VII   But the many cultural campaigns, songs, articles and conferences that were launched by Hip Hop's conscious organizations against the unbalanced presentations of hip-hop to the World were largely overlooked by the mainstream. These campaigns forced many Hiphoppas to revisit their Hip Hop roots, causing new ways of thinking about one's self and one's environment to manifest within the hip-hop community.

VIII   In this age, which was also during the completion of this first instrument, attuned Hiphoppas became well-respected political and spiritual forces for social change. Many of the mistakes made in our previous ages were corrected in this age when we became the executives, teachers, writers, politicians, athletes, actors and technicians of mainstream media outlets.

IX   During this time, the Temple of Hip Hop established itself as a legitimate Hip Hop preservation society and Hip Hop ministry.

X   Never again was there *no way out* of sickness, hate, ignorance and poverty for our people. Never again did we have to accept the exploitation of the mainstream just to be heard. Those Hiphoppas that stayed committed to Hip Hop's original principles would be repeatedly honored in this age.

XI   However, the Hip Hop community would still have to outsmart many of the counter-intelligence programs launched against it. However, our victories over such challenges proved our divinity.

It was during this age that *The Hip Hop Declaration of Peace* became common knowledge and Hip Hop was declared an official international culture for peace and prosperity. It is during this age that people begin to approach Hip Hop more seriously. And a new age of peace began.

---

59 From the very beginning of modern Hip Hop, around 1973, Hip Hop has struggled for self-determination. Within the development of our identity, character, and intellectual uniqueness, the creation of our own dialect was inevitable.

60 For many years Hip Hop has communicated with itself by developing a language that relies upon the transformation of already existing languages. The need for an outcast wing of society to create its own system of discourse has always been felt; slave days are a primary example.

61 Since words were only one of the weapons for early Africans in America, a sophisticated system of code had to be developed that inverted meaning, cloaked irony and allowed for a free and open exchange of ideas when such free speech was not permissible or, like today, unacceptable.

62 For years Hip Hop's dialect has been scorned as incorrect, ignorant ghetto talk, and for us to believe this from the same orthodoxy that ignores our intelligence and condescends to our lifestyle is suicidal for us.

63 To further understand the language of Hip Hop's culture one must avoid condemnation of the unfamiliar. The belief that "Hiphoppas" have no intellectual agency in their self-expression and that the World must be interpreted for us is unfounded.

64 Similarly, the incredibly prejudiced notion that Hiphoppas are incapable of critical and abstract thinking—

that we excel only at primal expressions like song, dance, and sport (like these too are of lesser importance)—still exists in society, albeit in a much subtler form. Unfortunately, it seems to be natural for society to look down upon offshoots of its language.

65   People who speak "high" German look down on those who speak "low." Cajun pronunciations of words like "Pontchartrain," "Carondelet," and "Banquet" continue to make French people cringe.

66   These dialects are clearly breaking the rules, but the idea that a language isn't self-governing, that it needs rules to keep it in check, is absurd. Language comes first, then comes grammar. To say that a language is "wrong" is ethnocentric!

67   Language is constantly evolving and dictionaries of all sorts constantly change to reflect this evolution. New words are admitted into a variety of dictionaries every year, although it is interesting to note that common Hip Hop phraseology is continually denied entry into many "well-known" dictionaries.

68   Language is the gateway to culture, and the first step in killing a culture is killing its language. The British paid Irish teachers not to teach Irish Gaelic; Koreans were forced to learn Japanese; Africans, Native Americans— English, etc.

69   Language serves the *internal* communication of a group; in a social sense it serves the internal communication of the dominant group. It allows a group to share pleasures, pains, dreams, and creative intelligence. It records the history of the group. It is the utterance of the culture. The problem today is not really Rap lyrics; it is actually cultural illiteracy on the part of those who criticize Hip Hop's artistic expressions and language that is the problem.

70   As rapper Ludacris pointed out in *The Source*

magazine when asked about Oprah Winfrey's opinions of him and his lyrical content, *They need to understand that every time people in Hip Hop say 'bitch' we're not degrading women. They need to understand that in this language Hip Hop built, some words don't always mean something negative. What I'm saying is that in Hip Hop, there is a language. I feel like people should understand where we are coming from. We live it, and the people that criticize it so much have never lived it and are just hearing us talk.* (*The Source,* August 2006, 202)

71   Now either you respect Ludacris as an intelligent representative of Hip Hop's culture, explaining his language and content clearly for all to learn, or your OWN prejudice only sees Ludacris as a foul-mouthed rapper with nothing worthwhile to say or add to society.

72   The problem seems to be that those who criticize Hip Hop's artistic expressions are simply ignorant of Hip Hop. They don't know how to interpret what they are seeing and hearing of Hip Hop in mass media. Some do, but most don't. And the "most" that don't know of Hip Hop's true meaning, purpose, intent, and history are those who criticize us and our language today. But there is also an academic silence or passiveness on our (Hip Hop's) part when it comes to educating Americans as to what is going on with us and our cultural existence. This is why the movement to teach Hip Hop in its OWN private schools is so important.

73   In a 1980 Reader's Digest book entitled *Word Power: The Entertaining Way To Enrich Your Language Skills,* one of its contributors, Roderick MacLeish, writes: *Today, young white Americans are adopting, wholesale, the language of black America. In the process they are telling us that they identify and sympathize with the struggle of black America to find its deserved place in our society. Meanwhile, some*

wonderfully articulate phrases are swirling into our language...
We had no precise word for lively, direct communication until
'rapping' appeared.

[74]   Some of what the public doesn't understand
about language can be explained in elementary linguistics
or sociology. But I don't hear too many scholars speaking
publicly on this subject—the subject of language and its
role in society. To criticize Hip Hop on the basis of its
word usage is again unscholarly on the criticizer's part.
In the same Reader's Digest book, State Department
linguist James Bostain explains, *If you can be understood,*
if you project the social image that you want to, you are
speaking correctly.

[75]   Most scholars are aware that words affect
little without definition. All words yield a definition or
definitions, which in turn yield a graphic description
between the user and the receiver. The challenge seems
to be the want of our criticizers to understand what we
are saying, to decipher our coded language. And so, it is
not the words in their minds that need to be changed, it is
the pictures that certain words create in their minds that
need to be updated. They are attempting to understand
the meaning of our coded words with their traditional
linguistic images. This is the challenge.

[76]   Words affect very little without definitions and
definitions affect very little unless one can graphically
picture it in his mind. Do you "see" what I'm saying? So
when Hiphoppas say "bitch" or "nigga" whatever image
comes to your mind is your business! But if my friend
comes to me and says "what's up my nigga" and the
graphic description of his greeting affects my psychology
in positive and productive ways, how then is our (Hip
Hop) language offensive or even degrading? THIS IS
OUR LANGUAGE!

[77]   However, it is within our sincere respect and love for our elders that we should consider our language and the terms we use to describe the World. At the *end of the day,* our most important responsibility (culturally) is to stay in communication with our parents and elders. Therefore, if the use of certain words creates certain graphic images and symbols in *their* minds we must consider altering our language when communicating with them. They deserve our utmost respect and admiration; if we don't respect our elders no one else will either.

[78]   However, today's arguments against Rap lyrics by others outside of our community imply that we are not allowed to define "our world" or "the World" for ourselves our way. Such arguments imply that we (Hip Hop) are not allowed to give our own definitions and interpretations of the material World in which we live.

[79]   As I listen to the criticisms against Rap lyrics I can't help but feel that the whole debate over Rap lyrics stems from an emotional base and not from a logical base. Logically, to imply that we are disrespecting ourselves and our heritage as if we are not "ourselves" and "our heritage" stinks with the stench of prejudice and arrogance on the criticizer's part.

[80]   Hip Hop is treated as if it just came out of nowhere! From the very beginnings of Hip Hop in the late 1970s we were always treated like aliens or "outsiders" who had to fend for themselves while being criticized along the way. The sad thing, though, is that "outsiders" are not studied or taken seriously at all—even if they are your children.

[81]   Without studying our culture and language you cannot critique our culture and language. I'm sure the whole material World is offensive and threatening to those who remain ignorant of it. But that doesn't mean that one must remain ignorant. Those who don't know, criticize

because they don't know. Those who know don't need to criticize—they know.

[82]   So for those who don't know, or for those who act like they don't know, allow me to say explicitly; HIP HOP ITSELF IS NOT A VIOLENT MUSIC GENRE THAT DEGRADES WOMEN AND PROMOTES ILLEGAL ACTIVITY! These events are the products and effects of corporate marketing in an entertainment arena.

[83]   However, it is still interesting to note how other music genres get to enjoy a certain immunity from the "fantasy" of their poetry no matter how graphic, while rappers are held accountable for the "fantasy" of their poetry. Everyone agrees and understands that other music genres are simply telling a story using metaphors and symbols when telling their graphic tales, even when those tales are true, but Hip Hop doesn't seem to enjoy such an understanding.

[84]   If a Rhythm and Blues (R&B) singer sings a song that implies adultery, betrayal and deceit between husband and wife (as an example), the R&B singer is not questioned about the content of her lyrics. It is basically understood that the R&B singer is "performing" and the lyrics to the song as well as the performance of the song may not be real—it's an act, it's entertainment.

[85]   An R&B singer can sing about cheating on his wife (as an example) and then be seen at the supermarket with his wife and children and no one will associate that R&B singer's lyrical content with the actual character of the man that sings that song.

[86]   But anything a rapper says, she is expected to actually live. And this "rule" is even understood amongst Hiphoppas; this is what separates hip-hop from every other major music genre on Earth. It's a bit unfair, but such unfairness has its advantages.

[87]   One of which is the ability to become anything you desire through the mastery of one or more of Hip Hop's nine elements. Imagine, through the mastery of an artistic performance you can attract the resources and support to become that which you rap about.

[88]   Different from every other music genre on Earth, Hip Hop's magical elements actually actualize the character and intentions of the performance. This is why we are also burdened with the biased opinion that our lyrics have real effects on people and environments while other styles of entertainment simply do not—and there is some Truth to this.

[89]   However, to label Hip Hop "violent" or "misogynistic" is again one-sided and unscholarly because the very criticism against Hip Hop should operate in two ways. On one hand if Hip Hop's violent, graphic, "gangsta" performances transform the performer into a violent, graphic Hip Hop gangsta in the eyes of the public, then Hip Hop's enlightened, revolutionary, "conscious" performances should transform those same performers into enlightened, revolutionary, "conscious" Hip Hop leaders in the eyes of that same public, but this is not the case.

[90]   We are acknowledged publicly for our negative influences but our positive influences go unnoticed, unacknowledged and unappreciated by our critics. That's why the core of the Hip Hop populace doesn't care what these "outsiders" have to say about a cultural movement they don't know and care little about. For the first time in a long time, a social movement (Hip Hop) has emerged that side-steps the conventional methods and means of achieving social success, prestige and mainstream access, and such a movement does it in its own unapologetic way. This is the real problem. This is the real threat.

[91]   In the past one had to attend college, or military

service, or borrow money to start up a business, or work up the corporate ladder until retirement if one was going to make it out of one's lot in life. It was through America's major social institutions that opportunity was found and when those institutions began to deteriorate, the needs of the *People* fell upon Hip Hop's artistic upsurge in the 1980s and 1990s.

92   Hip Hop may have remained just a great music genre if the people participating in Hip Hop's artistic elements didn't need it to also fulfill their cultural, spiritual and financial needs. So, is Hip Hop violent for real? Of course not. Is Hip Hop itself misogynistic toward women? I can't be.

93   The last time I checked, the term "misogyny" meant "the hatred of women by men." HIP HOP IS NOT MISOGYNISTIC TOWARD WOMEN. Hip Hop does not hate women; I can't! Hip Hop is made up of women. It was women who taught us (men) how to be the men that we are. In fact, male Hiphoppas may actually blindly love and wildly lust after Hip Hop's women a bit too much. Hate? No. Lust? Yes. Respect? Always.

94   Hiphoppas know that as men, the disrespecting of women is unnatural to our being. Hip Hop is an urban behavior that has saved millions of urban people from the collapse of America's social institutions and the corruption prevalent throughout America's corporate communities. We (Hiphoppas) are trying to survive and escape the collapse of America's institutions just like everyone else.

95   As Dr. Cornel West has pointed out, *The basic aims of hip-hop music are threefold—to provide playful entertainment and serious art for the rituals of young people, to forge new ways of escaping social misery, and to explore novel responses for meaning and feeling in a market-driven world.*

96   When I hear people complain about Rap music's

lyrical content I tend to ask them, so what rappers do you like? Most people can't go into it that far because if you could compare and critique rappers with a knowledge of their history and style, nothing one rapper says would offend you; you would know how to critique the Hip Hop event happening before you.

97   The problem is that mainstream America is ignorant of Hip Hop because when it first emerged, mainstream America only sought to exploit hip-hop not understand it. To "understand" Hip Hop you would have had to respect the people you were engaging, not use them as products— and the same rings true today.

98   The last time I checked, the term "violence" meant deadly physical force. *Violence: behavior involving physical force intended to hurt, damage, or kill someone or something.* Legally, "violence" is *the unlawful exercise of physical force or intimidation by the exhibition of such force.* In most social circles "violence" has to do with "physical force." So are Rap lyrics violent? Can they be? Can a lyric that is said in an entertainment setting and/or over an entertainment medium actually be violent? Lyrics are not physical. Or are they?

99   I always thought that art and poetry were exactly the arenas where ideas and images controversial to mainstream society were expressed. Art and poetry in my mind are exactly the arenas to explore the otherwise inexpressible regions of human thought and activity. The term "nigger," for example, should have its existence in art, education and poetry and not in politics, religion or trade. If violence and obscenity are not explored in art and/or education, where should they be explored?

100   Violence and obscene behavior are simply American entertainment, and in many ways they should remain American "entertainment." Violence and/or

obscenity shouldn't be anywhere in the public arena. We should lessen violence and obscenity in public life and enjoy more freedom to explore violence and obscenity in artistic life. In my observation, art is where extreme ideas should be expressed.

101   Turning to Bob Colacello's book, *Ronnie and Nancy: Their Path to the White House—1911–1980,* Mr. Colacello points out while writing about Harry Warner being *called before the U.S. Senate Subcommittee on Moving Picture Propaganda* in 1941 that Ronald Reagan's films showed *one fight per every 1,000 feet of film.*

102   I bring this up not to pass the buck by saying "See; look at da Prezadant, he vylent too." Not at all; I won't even bring up "the Governator" Governor Arnold Schwarzenegger and the violent content in most of his early motion picture work, many times shooting police officers and destroying government property—not at all.

103   I bring this point up to shed light on the true nature of the argument. It is not violent lyrical content that threatens America, nor is it over-sensualized images of sex acts and foreplay throughout mass media. None of this actually threatens America's social order and economic structure. In fact, in many ways such images and acts actually strengthen America's social order and economic structure.

104   The problem is not Rap lyrics, the problem is that your child likes them and is influenced by them and "you" have no control over such foreign influences. "You" believe that your child's participation in Hip Hop lowers her self-worth. Because of your own fears "you" want your child to conform to the same success "you" have conformed to; you want your child to "play the game" like you did. But like First Lady Nancy Reagan, it is authentically American to look up to the foul-mouthed, down-to-earth, real people who are most times having the best times of their lives.

105   We all want to be like "the rebel," the "outsider," the "outcast," "the one not to mess with." Is this attitude not authentically American? The State of Texas makes it clear in its State motto: DON'T MESS WITH TEXAS!

106   The issue is that violence was cool when Al Pacino did it. Violence was cool when the "Governator" did it, when John Wayne did it, when the bible depicts it, even when cartoons portray it. But if a rapper even speaks about violence within a poetic entertainment setting we are called the "cause" for the corruption of America's youth and moral fortitude.

107   In fact, we are accused of "influencing" America's youth negatively with our words and imagery, yet none of our critics will ask about the events and people that directly influenced us. But this too is a weak argument. A stronger argument points to our collective power as "Hiphoppas" based upon the criticisms laid before us.

108   The character and self-expressions of any public figure are indeed "roles" that will be "modeled" by that public figure's audience, even if that public figure is the President of the United States. This is human nature; we grow and develop through adaptation and imitation. Every responsible "emcee" or DJ recognizes this fact and his influence upon his audience.

109   We (rappers/DJs) tell the crowd what to say and how to say it. They wear what we wear, they drink what we drink, and they watch what we watch on television and elsewhere. Our audiences repeat what we tell them to, so how are we (or any other public figure) not to be held accountable for our own self-expression?

110   However, if we are to be held accountable then let us also seize the power that comes with accountability. If the World's youth are listening to and following Hip Hop's culture and arts then why are we not taken more seriously as

the World's leaders even beyond artistry and entertainment? Sort of like the path of President Ronald Reagan.

[111]   If we (Hip Hop) have that much influence over the children of the United States then Hip Hop needs to be advising the President and governing America's inner cities. If most of the students in the United States are influenced by Hip Hop's arts and culture why then is Hip Hop not taught in every public school in the United States? If we have the power that the critics claim we have, then respect us for who we are and for what we have accomplished—Hip Hop is a new American institution and Americans would do well to embrace us!

[112]   Americans need to know that the real Hip Hop community has never been free to present itself to the World on its own terms. We've always had an interpreter, and our early interpreters only sought to exploit our resources at a time when we were simply too young to defend ourselves or even know what was going on.

[113]   The Truth is that America's supposed addiction to porn and violence gives radio and television stations the excuse to put my music aside so that they may play "what the people request." And of course, what the People "request" is what the radio and television stations have been paid to program all week.

[114]   But this is just obvious! Everyone knows this already! Everyone knows why the radio sounds like it does—THEY'RE BEING PAID TO SOUND LIKE THEY DO! The government knows it, they know it, we know it, but still we engage in these bullshit arguments over Rap lyrics when KRS ONE and others struggle to get their music played on a regular basis on any radio station.

[115]   In my time, White "girls" seem to "go wild" lifting up their T-shirts and blouses to expose their breasts for the cameras of sexually explicit *infomercials* and music videos.

Does Hip Hop cause young girls to act this way or are Rap music and rappers brought into the production of the infomercials because Rap music is considered "cool" and/or "attractive" to youth?

[116]   Why blame Hip Hop for what people are already doing of their own free will? The issue is that America's foundation, its moral authority and Christian social structure are losing ground; it may even be transforming and growing. Just as Christianity evolved out of Judaism and Paganism, Hip Hop as evolved out of Christianity and Islam. We are the new lights of the World.

[117]   In any event, rappers represent the new popular heroes. We have the global trust of the People. We (Hip Hop) are the gunslingin', rootin'-tootin' cowboys of this day and age. And if we (Hip Hop) *are* trusted and respected by the public through the inspiration of our arts, we owe it to those who empower us with their love, trust and respect to assume the responsibilities of leaders in the solving of the World's social ills.

[118]   We are not the problem; Hip Hop and its view of the World are actually the solution. We can see right through the assumptions of our critics who claim that it is Hip Hop that incites and glorifies violence. Yes, we are extreme in our art; our art reflects the violent and unjust conditions in which we live.

[119]   And yes, we enjoy gun battles either as entertainment or as self-defense. And yes, our lyrics and graphic art can glorify the power and use of guns, but where are graphic images and forbidden language to be expressed if not within the confounds of art and/or science? Our view is that it is not the gun that is dangerous or irresponsible; it is the person holding the gun that can become dangerous or irresponsible.

[120]   But for some reason our critics do not hear nor

respond to any of this. They know what the real is! They know the statistics just as we do! But still Hip Hop is blamed for what is already occurring in the World and in our individual communities.

121   The Truth is so obvious and so accessible to anyone who wants to know that some of us even wear such statistics as designer fashion statements. As the clothing company Scifen has pointed out on the back of one of their popular *hoodies* worn by many Hiphoppas in my time: *Every minute someone is killed by a firearm.*

122   The graphics on the upper back of the pull-over *hoodie* continue: *Each year an estimated 500,000 people will die worldwide from small arms: about 300,000 people in wars, coups d'etat, and other armed conflicts, and another 200,000 people in homicides, suicides, unintentional shootings and shootings by police.*

123   *In that same minute in which someone dies from armed violence, 15 new arms are manufactured for sale. There are nearly 640 million small arms in the World today, that's one for every ten people. The total value of the combined arms sales by the top 100 arms-producing companies in the World is about $236 billion per year.*

124   *This total is roughly equal to the combined national output of the 61 lowest-income countries in the World. Of the 100 arms manufactures, 38 are based in the United States. Do the math. The only groups who win armed struggles are the arms manufacturers.*

125   This and other, similar clothing statements are what many Hiphoppas wear in my time, and this is what is common knowledge in our communities even as our critics blame us for the violence we were born into. We must evolve pass this level of immaturity.

126   It is now obvious that we must mature past our own self-destruction and assist the World toward peace and

good will toward all. As a specialized social group we must become self-directed. In fact our immaturity, the incapacity to use our own intelligence without the guidance of others, will be the only thing capable of holding us back.

[127]   Our very survival depends upon our continued maturity. Sisters, Brothers, Mothers and Fathers, let us begin today writing a new history in the World. Let us tell a new story about ourselves to the World! Our activity today is the origin of Hip Hop's history and heritage tomorrow. Be conscious of this always.

[128]   These are *the Refinitions* for the Temple of Hip Hop's committed membership. However, it must be emphasized that Hip Hop is a continuously growing culture so your comprehension of this *Overstanding* is bound to grow as well. Such terms and codes are designed to organize and raise the self-worth of those who love Hip Hop and may teach Hip Hop for a living. There it is.

THE THIRD OVERSTANDING
THE DIVINE PERFORMANCE

1   Peace and much love. Let us continue. After you have made the decision to be Hiphop, and after you have declared to three of your closest associates *I am Hip Hop,* it is time to enter your *temple.*

2   For it is not enough to read about what spiritual righteousness is. The true Hiphoppa must act out (or perform) spiritual righteousness in order to experience the peace and power of the spiritual realm, and this requires strength. For without spiritual strength (endurance) no spiritual virtues or principles can be achieved.

3   At the top of this discipline it should be clearly pointed out that the Divine Performance reveals only the first steps in Hiphop's spiritual living. This study gets the true Hiphoppa ready for the deeper mysteries of GOD which must be lived in order to be understood.

4   Such an *Overstanding* is designed to build up the spiritual character and awareness of the Hiphoppa in preparation for the deeper spiritual knowledge to come. The Divine Performance centers the Hiphoppa's life around a simple set of timeless spiritual life skills that open the gates of the spiritual realm and preserves the actual life of the Hiphoppa thus preserving Hip Hop for real.

5   For it is never one's talent that ensures one's longevity. Even with great talent and/or inheritance it is one's personal character that truly ensures one's professional success and longevity. We have seen too many talented people (artistic and otherwise) fail to acquire and/or maintain successful

careers, even with great skills, because of the shortcomings of their own personal characters.

6 The hurts, the betrayals, the loneliness, the failures; all of this can hinder the development of both the ignorant and the enlightened. But if you put GOD first in your life and lend your heart to the reality of GOD only, all else shall fall into place. The ignorance, immaturity and insecurity of others shall be revealed to them in time, while you shall be protected by your divine performance.

7 In addition, we've also seen too many Hip Hop activists fail to actualize their plans and goals because of their own outdated perceptions and stubborn attitudes toward life. Know this. Life is about growth, and if you are not growing you are not living. Yes, there will be times of hurt and loneliness. Yes, you will wonder why people do what they do. But in the end, if you remain strengthened and transformed by your performance of divinity, peace and justice shall become your permanent condition.

8 Therefore, in accordance with our strategies to actually preserve Hip Hop, those who take the vow *I am Hip Hop* and have decided to live and grow in Spirit are given these instructions for atonement:

A) From where you stand, sit or lie, cleanse your mind with the following affirmation given to me by my mother (Jacqueline) years ago. Say the following affirmation three times every night before you sleep and once in the morning when you awaken for 21 days. Feel this! Expect this!

I am not afraid! Today I give myself permission to be all that I can be. New fields of divine activity now open for me. Unexpected doors fly open! Unexpected channels are now free! My mind is focused and directed toward my victory! I now create what I need with divine energy. Good things come to me easily in peace and at the right time. There it is!

B)   At this very moment you must decide to change your diet toward the consumption of healthier foods and thoughts. If you are above the age of 18 you should gradually withdraw from the consumption of all processed and junk foods, meats and meat products. Even before you finish these *Overstandings* you should gradually begin to accustom your mind and body toward a healthier diet.

I   You should begin to gradually lessen your intake of dairy, flour, salt, sugar and all other addictions like hate, worry and fear. Resist overeating and lessen your intake of drugs that can cause irregular eating or overeating. Respect yourself by committing to your Self.

II   Remember, the future you is depending upon you now to make the right decisions for its survival. This is the attitude one must adopt in order to protect, preserve and develop one's Self productively.

III   Therefore, realize the Truth of GOD's actual presence and cleanse your body inside and out; for it is now GOD's temple. Prepare now for the arrival of your God.

C)   At this very moment and before you prepare to sleep, confess to GOD the things you've thought, said and done that you felt were not right.

I   Forgive your enemies first by acknowledging that they were young and ignorant and then ask GOD to forgive you for your immaturity and ignorance. Ask GOD to guide you toward increased knowledge.

II   Trust no man or woman with your confession. Confess your mistakes only to GOD. Ask GOD to forgive you of your anger and discourteous responses even while driving, working and walking. Humble yourself and truly contemplate the pain you've caused others.

III   Ask GOD to forgive you and bless those whom you have performed ignorantly and destructively toward. You can also directly seek the forgiveness of those you have hurt by performing the superhuman act of apologizing.

IV   Cleanse the guilt from your own heart. Apologize, repent and let it go. Seek to resolve the conflicts and misunderstandings in your own life (see *Perform Forgiveness*).

D)   Right now, at this very moment, think about a space close to where you sleep where you can set up an area to pray and study. It can be a space on the floor, a table, a shelf or a window. It can be as small as a shoebox in a corner or as large as the entire bedroom. In any event, at your beginning the space you set aside to pray and study should be near to where you sleep if possible.

I   After you've designated a space, choose a surface (a table, a shelf, a box, a crate, etc.) to place in your sacred space. Such a surface is commonly called an *altar*. It is the physical place you go to *alter* your awareness from natural to divine. It is the place where you talk in the presence of GOD. It is in this place that you affirm your past, present and future victories.

II   Here, you can cover your designated surface with a new and clean cloth. Then place upon your covered surface a candle or candles, your favorite oils, sprays, waters, incense, pictures of those you truly love and/or admire and this *Gospel of Hip Hop* opened to either *The Free Styles* or your favorite *Overstanding*. After you have done this, thank GOD for your sacred space and then repeat your affirmation three times and go to sleep in faith; in peace.

III   Cleanse your environment with the establishment of your sacred space and let not your space be violated!

Believe in YOUR spiritual reality and it shall become real in YOUR life.

---

9   Let us continue. At an average Rap music concert there is usually an opening act or acts followed by a headliner.
10   Attuned Hiphoppas and experienced *Rap fans* alike have learned that great opening acts that have been successful have always shouted praise to the headliner and have always sought to align their performance to that of the headliner's.
11   The opening act performs with an overstanding that the headliner is sure to follow with an even more elaborate performance. It is the headliner who closes the show. Similarly, attuned Hiphoppas know that GOD is the true headliner in every arena of life.
12   Even if the Hiphoppa is a headliner in the World, the attuned Hiphoppa remains an opening act to GOD. As an opening act, the attuned Hiphoppa performs life in Spirit knowing that GOD will close the show.
13   Whatever the attuned Hiphoppa does, it is done with the overstanding that GOD will complete whatever has started. When this Truth is realized, one's actions will reflect such a realization.
14   How often do we forget that the Hip Hop-lived life is a performance, and that imitating the performance of GOD sets one apart from the World and its troubles? Attuned Hiphoppas live life as a great performance. When we are at work we are performing. When we are with family we are performing.
15   Every day and at every moment of the day we are performing. Even while asleep there are a variety of performances taking place within one's mind, body and environment. It is our performances in life that manifest (or

form) the circumstances of our lives.

16   Each performance is literally a *pre-formed dance* or a *pre-form-ance:* an action that creates and forms life circumstances. Therefore, attuned Hiphoppas align their *pre-formances* to GOD's performance, remaining protected, prosperous and at peace, in harmony with the Will of God in their lives continuously.

17   For when God's personality is a habit in your life, *victory over the streets* is inevitable and constant. And when GOD is enough for you, peace shall always be with you. This performance ensures one's longevity as an emcee, deejay, graffiti writer, etc.

18   *Rap fans* are trapped in the lure of lyrical freestyling, while attuned Hiphoppas enjoy a life that is free. *Rap fans* focus only upon sales and the performances of the marketplace while attuned Hiphoppas focus upon the performance of their God and receive all things freely.

19   To perform correctly is to live and act totally aware of your life and actions. The *arena* is your environment.

20   The *stage* represents your level of mentality and the *audience* is the World.

21   The *show* is an act of one or more divine performances.

22   Therefore, give a good *show.* As we perform throughout life we should be drawing the applause of GOD! Hiphoppas are advised to perform the following:

---

1)   Perform God. Act consciously with the intelligence/ force that guides your life. Make the decision to finally acknowledge and <u>expect</u> GOD's actual presence. Turn your conscious attention away from the reality of the material World as valuable and turn your conscious attention toward the value of GOD above all else in and as your life.

¹ Put GOD first in your life! Throughout the day make an effort to raise your heart and mind to the acts of God. Act like your God would act. Speak like your God would speak. Love like your God would love. God is not a name, it is a nature. Acknowledge the *nature* that has governed and guided your life.

² Be God's Will on Earth; be "the Love." Align your Spirit through visualization to the totality of your God. Act out of your highest comprehended good. Act and speak on behalf of your God—*the Love*. Develop the ability to care unconditionally for your *Self* and others. Be the actual personality of your God in the lives of others; answer the prayers of those in need. Do God's work in the World.

³ Act out the personality of your God and live in the character of your wiser Self. Express the Love of your God and *see* your God's finished work in everything and everyone. The most important training you can do for your *Self* in life is to practice living in the presence and personality of your God—the Love that is a true friend to all in its presence. Such a practice leads to peace and strength.

⁴ Practice thinking through the mind of your God. Perceive in God. Openly perform the personality of your God everywhere and anywhere you are. And do not be ashamed or become discouraged by your own uniqueness; God is your nature. Perform your God in GOD. Direct your Self, teach your Self, govern your Self, heal your Self, guide your Self and most of all LOVE your Self.

⁵ GOD, the totality and unified consciousness of all existence, THE ALL, is one event! Ultimately, there is no other god (power) but GOD! Without name, without form, everywhere and nowhere GOD is GOD! As an attuned Hiphoppa God is the nature that sustains you.

⁶ Happy and secure is the one who acknowledges no other power as their god except GOD. Value only GOD!

See only GOD! Trust only GOD! Live and act in the image of your God. It is indeed a fact that you can never be hurt by the immaturity of others when you act selflessly on behalf of GOD. Hurt comes when you place your immediate interests over the presence of GOD. Remember, the key is to keep GOD first in your life.

[7]   However, it is of extreme importance that you not force your interpretation of GOD upon others. GOD is real, but GOD is not real for everyone. As difficult as this may sound try to understand that knowledge of GOD is a privilege. Do not force your privilege upon others or expect others to see what you see.

[8]   For us, God is a bloodline—everyone does not possess the nature of God. They may respect and revere the godly life but they themselves are not yet prepared to commit to such a life themselves. Only those who are born for God shall commit to such a life.

[9]   Just as some are born with the ability to cook, and others are born with the ability to build houses, and even others are born healers; some of us are born God. Just as some of us are born with certain psychic abilities, others of us are born with the nature of God—our existence balances human affairs.

[10]   This is not to place anyone above anyone, nor is this an effort to claim some sort of authority, but in all Truth, some people were born to love GOD. Are you one of those people? We are not above anyone; in fact we serve and teach the World on GOD's behalf. Our aim is to relieve human suffering.

[11]   This is why we argue with no one over the existence of GOD. If you do not know GOD it is because GOD is not part of your nature. It doesn't mean that you are a bad or immoral person; it simply means that you were not born for that understanding and/or purpose. And likewise, if you

do not know GOD or simply doubt the existence of GOD do not make the mistake of applying such doubt toward others who do claim to know GOD.

12 Let us all accept each other as we all are, and let us hold each other accountable to the natures that we claim to possess. Those who truly know GOD express God; in fact, we have no choice in such expression. God is our nature. God is in our blood. And there is no condemnation of atheist communities who are free to act according to their own Godless nature.

13 For it doesn't matter what you believe or don't believe, the real point is how do your views and values make you a better person, more tolerant and understanding of people? How do your views, values and beliefs benefit those around you? How are you making things better?

14 However, if God is your nature and you truly feel the presence of GOD and you are naturally drawn toward the things of the spirit it is of extreme importance that you outwardly perform the nature of your God whenever and wherever you are invited to do so.

15 Performing God is also about bringing spiritual reality into physical reality when needed. It makes no sense to claim a relationship with GOD and then have no real power on Earth and no real power in the World.

16 At some point we must mature from being consumers of God to becoming producers of God. Temple Members produce the effects of God as needed toward the relief of human suffering; we perform the nature of God openly for the benefit of all.

17 Nothing is more empowering than a real relationship with GOD. As John Bunyan has pointed out, *"He who runs from GOD in the morning will scarcely find him the rest of the day."* Perform God.

2)   Perform Listening. More than being a good speaker, be a good listener. Develop the ability (through practice) to truly listen and comprehend the subjects, topics, concerns and causes of others without judgment or prejudice.

[1]   Practice giving your full attention to a person. Practice the art of temporarily setting aside your own desires and concerns so that you may experience the speaker's world from within yourself.

[2]   For until you are willing to enlarge your Self as to include others unconditionally it shall be difficult for you to truly <u>listen</u> to another. The act of truly listening to someone requires some love or care for that person.

[3]   It is difficult to truly understand another person without first making room for that person within yourself. True listening requires the total acceptance of the one speaking. True Listening is about true sharing. It is a union of interests.

[4]   GOD listens and speaks through many kinds of people as well as circumstances and situations. Perform your listening. Don't just hear; train yourself to listen. Like your eyesight, you can direct your hearing. You actually can hear what you want to hear. You can hear the ignorance and immaturity of others, or you can hear GOD. The decision (freedom) is always yours. You can hear ignorance but you do not have to listen to it.

[5]   Direct your ear to hear and then listen to God's instructions instead of the World's insecurities. Know God's voice. It is difficult to live by faith (or in spirit) if you cannot truly hear (and even speak) the voice of your God.

[6]   Know this. The brain selects certain sounds to hear, and you select out of those sounds what you want to hear. Throughout the day direct your brain to hear the messages of GOD. They may come when you least expect it from

unusual and non-traditional places. Practice your spiritual sensitivity and train/use your intuitive abilities daily. You can begin with prayer, then affirmation, then visualization, then actualization.

7   Through each stage of growth it is the discipline to listen and comprehend the voice of GOD that provides the greatest guidance through the obstacles of the *streets*. Listen for your purpose and listen through your purpose.

8   Those who know their divine purpose can practice listening to that small, inner, background voice inside of them. It usually tells them what to do as well as what not to do. But most people ignore their *still small voice* only to regret making a decision contrary to the Will of that *still small voice*. In sorrow and regret they say, *I knew I should have...or something told me to....* It is this cycle that must be reversed.

9   You must eventually develop the ability to hear clearly and obey that inner voice that warns, guides and teaches. You must learn how to act upon the messages of God. Take some time to <u>listen</u> to silence. God speaks silently and quietly.

10   When a split-second decision must be made in the material World, or when you get that feeling to choose *left* or *right, yes* or *no, him* or *her, them* or *me*, a helpful technique to hearing and obeying your inner-voice has traditionally been to act upon your first impression.

11   For those who live spiritual lives, usually it is the *wiser-Self* that advises us first, then the *younger-Self* doubts the advice of the *wiser-Self* in the decision making process.

12   Even if your first impression (or feeling) proves to be an immediate failure always remember that what appears to be a failure in the present isn't always a failure in the future. Trust <u>in</u> GOD!

13   Just because you cannot immediately see the success

of your decision does not mean that your decision has led you to failure. Trust in GOD!

14   Those who truly live in Spirit and take their gospel seriously are guided and protected even when they cannot see it or do not even know it. Trust GOD! All throughout life you will be guided toward the fulfillment of your divine purpose.

15   Even when you appear to be lost, you are moving toward your divine purpose. Even when you believe that you are late, you shall escape danger and arrive right on time! Even when you lose you shall win. Trust GOD.

16   Even when adversity arises, fear not; indeed you are moving toward your divine purpose. When things are taken from you or damaged or it appears that you cannot get the things that you want, do not be discouraged; it is for your own protection and development.

17   The key to understanding life and flowing with life is in the knowing of your life purpose and in the knowing that it is your life purpose that God is actually fulfilling and that you are ultimately achieving your vision of your *Self*. Listen to your purpose. Feel and follow the direction of your purpose.

18   Those who do not yet know their life purpose should ask their God to reveal it to them. Search your heart and listen. GOD has already given you purpose. Look around your environment and into what you do best. Listen out for those activities that truly make you the happiest. You are already being called to your purpose right now! Do not be discouraged. Release all doubt, LISTEN and be guided! Perfrom Listening.

3)   Perform Study. Study the progression of your own life experiences. Write them down! Study your life and practice repeating the actions of your own success. Study

GOD's Ways, study GOD's Voice, study GOD's Laws and most of all study GOD's Love and selfless care. Familiarize yourself through study with the way of the *Great Spirit*.

1   Every week investigate on a mental level a new idea that you are unfamiliar with or only partially familiar with. Design your style of conversation through study.

2   Seek out new spiritual, philosophical and political books, seminars, cassettes, compact discs, videos and other information that specifically builds your spiritual and political knowledge. An infinite, all-knowing, all-seeing, omni-present GOD does not speak one language or through one religion or political party. GOD is infinitely limitless and speaks through a variety of sources.

3   Therefore, Hiphoppas are encouraged to explore and respect all spiritual materials, thoughts, people and places. Such a study expands the spiritual experience of the Hiphoppa and builds character.

4   Perfect yourself. For the more you perfect your *Self* the more perfect you shall become. You cannot expect spiritual results in the physical World if you are spiritually unstudied. For if you are truly serious about enhancing your spiritual reality and you truly value the presence of GOD in your life, then you must take your spiritual study time seriously. Don't just study this gospel; study all gospels! Know this. The true Hiphoppa lives this gospel, and studies all others.

5   Watch television shows that inform as well as entertain. Do not waste your time criticizing the use of television, computers, motion pictures, print media, the Internet and radio. Simply choose very carefully the programs you expose yourself (and your family) to.

6   Whatever the program, seek to create a lesson out of it. Extract the hidden meaning behind all that you are exposed to. Create meaning even when there appears to be

none. Know this. To the pure in heart, all things are pure. But to the troubled, all things are troubling. See only GOD and experience only peace.

7   Look for the lesson even if one does not appear to exist. Expand your comprehension. Do not just study knowledge; create knowledge out of the experiences of your own life. Add to the things that you already know. Do not just study to know, bring your knowing to your study. STUDY WHAT YOU NEED TO KNOW.

8   All true Hiphoppas should know something of World history, commerce and trade, philosophy, politics, art, music, medicine, religion, geology, science, mathematics, psychology, public speaking, cooking, cleaning, parenting and this *Gospel of Hip Hop*.

9   The true Hiphoppa is familiar with (and knows how to use) a variety of holy books, standard dictionaries, the solar and lunar calendars, his country's constitution and the interstate highway and road maps of his country. This knowledge is very helpful and empowering to the free, traveling, entrepreneurial Hiphoppa.

10   Visit and use your public library if you are privileged to be near one. Be prepared to copy information and take notes at all times. Perform your study. Seek, memorize and create new knowledge.

11   Study is about the building and knowing of one's self, it is not about the building of state institutions and the knowing of others and their achievements. Study is about getting educated; it is about the building of one's self. As Ernest Thompson Seton once said, *"Manhood, not scholarship, is the first aim of education."* Perform your study.

4)   Perform Discipline. Every day we are faced with opportunities to perform discipline (self-control). The attuned Hiphoppa uses moments of temptation to practice restraint, moments of fear to practice faith, and moments of anger and anxiety to practice patience and inner calmness. These are divine performances.

1   In all actions use moderation. Temptation, fear, anger, etc., can be used as tests that strengthen your mind and body. Seek balance. Do not over indulge; for this act leads to suffering. Control yourself! Self-control is your only friend, while temptation is your only enemy. Never forget this!

2   A Hiphoppa's spiritual strength is not measured by what can be resisted in the flesh; it is measured by that which is resisted in the mind. In order to change or modify your behavior you must first change or modify the picture you hold of yourself in your mind. What is your perception of your Self? What do you mean to you? How valuable are you to you? How serious do you take yourself?

3   On the inside, what do you look like to you? Do you say often,...*ain't nobody perfect!* If this is how you see yourself (imperfect), then you shall never be even close to perfect. Your affirmation is final. The World shall have its way with you. Temptations of all sorts attack unperfected people constantly. Such people actually weaken themselves by affirming and believing that they are imperfect. It's like saying to the World; *come and get me!* Such an affirmation leads nowhere!

4   However, if you even reach for perfection in your own imperfect life (which is perfectly imperfect), such an act will indeed protect you from the World and its temptations. For in the material World it is not perfection that is needed to protect you from temptation; it is the actual desire <u>for</u> perfection that is an indestructible shield and sword against the World and its agents of temptation. Never give up! Keep trying. Seek Truth!

[5] The Truth is that temptation is always temporary. All temptations are spiritual tests. Therefore, when you are tempted it is very important to be still and not say or do anything; indeed the temptation shall pass. Try to remember that temptation is always temporary, but if you give in to it all the time its unpleasant after-effects can last a long time, even a lifetime.

[6] In addition, resisting temptation strengthens one's faith. It is like lifting spiritual weights or exercising. Resisting temptation strengthens one's spiritual vitality. However, the question here is, why should I resist temptation? Answer: because satisfying the call of temptation (as opposed to the call of purpose) leads to guilt which can weaken your faith.

[7] Therefore, we must take advantage of temptation. We cannot allow temptation to take advantage of us! When you know in your heart that you live righteously and your mind is focused only upon the fulfillment of your divine purpose, you expect the favor of GOD. And it is this expectancy that is at the center of one's faith and courage.

[8] But when you know in your heart that you are guilty of actions that you perceived as spiritually weak, evil or immoral you do not expect the favor of GOD; you hide from the presence of GOD. And it is this expectancy (expecting not to receive the favor of GOD) that is at the center of your doubts and fears.

[9] It is your own guilt that diminishes your faith and thus your ability to achieve your divine purpose. Ultimately we judge and then weaken ourselves through guilt caused by our submission to temptation and other weaknesses.

[10] Self-control and virtuous living strengthens your faith in GOD's favor upon you, which in turn enhances your ability to achieve your purpose and even perform miracles in your life and in the lives of others. Self-control makes

you certain of your trustworthiness before GOD. And it is this trustworthiness that empowers your faith to achieve your divine purpose and perform miracles.

11   Spiritual strength is also measured by one's patience and endurance. For when you know in your heart that you live a righteous life and that GOD's favor is upon you; those things that you do not have, those people that you do not see and those places that you do not go are all for your own good.

12   For one of the keys to lasting discipline is when one becomes serious about actually acknowledging the real presence of GOD. For when you know that GOD is with you, watching you, listening to you, etc., you need not try to be disciplined; you are automatically disciplined by the presence of GOD in your midst.

13   Undisciplined people can be said to simply not believe in the presence of GOD or their own spiritual abilities. They ignore their God and their own access to their own God-force. Truth is always with them but they ignore it. Love is always with them. Peace, wealth, knowledge, healing, etc. are always available to us but we simply ignore them because we really don't believe that we deserve these gifts. We know to ourselves that we are imperfect because of the temptations that we have fallen to, and with such knowledge we judge and limit ourselves.

14   Discipline over the desires of the body and mind come when you truly acknowledge the existence and presence of GOD right next to you! Know this. A true awareness of GOD causes discipline to automatically happen to you.

15   One does not have to be actually disciplined to keep one's hand off of a hot stove. It is not that you need to restrain yourself from touching the hot stove. It is more the fact that you do not want to burn your hand. In this example, discipline is not only a matter of awareness; it

is also a matter of taking care of your Self. It is a matter of self-respect. Again, seek the Truth of GOD's actual presence, and discipline is sure to follow.

[16]   For the attuned Hiphoppa, discipline has more to do with realizing Truth and having respect for one's *Self* than the practice of restraint. The whole *Divine Performance* is a disciplinary training exercise designed to produce a Hiphop character/behavior that prepares one for leadership and victory over the obstacles of the *streets*.

[17]   Therefore, we must remember to use moments of anxiety to perform patience and calm. Use moments of depression to perform joy. Commit to yourself. Bring order to yourself by recognizing and truly respecting only the existence and value of GOD in your life. Make the conscious decision to value your God. Stop burning your hands upon the hot stoves of the World's temptations! This is spiritual strength. This is a divine performance.

[18]   Start your discipline practice small by resisting your favorite cake (as an example). Try not to overeat. Speak less. Turn off or unplug the television. Cease listening to the radio. Go on to resist argument and gossip. Begin repeating an affirmation or prayer regularly. You might want to attend places of prayer.

[19]   Practice fasting from junk foods, recreational drugs, intoxicating drinks, lustful desires, unproductive conversations and even the careless spending of money. In these examples the achievement of discipline is a matter of spiritual self-respect which leads to physical self-control. Now may be the time to truly care for your *Self* and most of all value your *Self!* These lead to discipline.

[20]   The teacha practices withdrawing his senses from the happenings of the material World. With this performance the teacha escapes the inconsistent and sometimes dangerous events of the World. But the teacha

is mindful not to become too distant from those whom he is teaching. Balance is the key.

21   If you have proven your discipline and self-governance, you can indulge in Worldly temptations at times. The practice of discipline is not to abstain from the happenings of the physical World, it is to be strong enough to stop and start such activities at will. The teacha is simply free from addiction.

22   In fact, when it is pleasurable to abstain from pleasure one can be called *teacha*. When one looks forward to moments of self-restraint one can be called *teacha*. The teacha is unattached and mentally independent.

23   The teacha is not lured nor tempted toward pleasure; the teacha freely and willingly chooses pleasure. The World and its temptations do not move the teacha. As Henri-Frédéric Amiel has pointed out, *The man who has no refuge in himself, who lives, so to speak, in his front rooms, in the outer whirlwind of things and opinions, is not properly a personality at all. He floats with the current, who does not guide himself according to higher principles, who has no ideal, no convictions—such a man is a mere article of the World's furniture—a thing moved, instead of a living and moving being—an echo, not a voice. The man who has no inner life is the slave of his surroundings, as a barometer is the obedient servant of the air at rest, and the weathercock the humble servant of the air in motion.* Perform Discipline.

5)   Perform Forgiveness.   Guilt is self-imposed. Begin by forgiving yourself for all of your indiscretions. Yes, you do have the power to repent and forgive yourself. Yes, you do have the power to let it go. Hold no grudge, harbor no anger and release resentment and guilt.

1   Remember, an act that you may have perceived as evil may have turned out to be a blessing in disguise. At the

beginning of your spiritual studies do not judge yourself and/or others, only make observations and learn.

2   Turn away from evil thinking and never return. Show Love, not revenge. Be ready to forgive others by restoring some level of resolve into the relationship. Forgive others just as you would want to be forgiven. Be patient with others just as you would want GOD to be patient with you. This is a divine performance.

3   Give the transgressor a chance to repair the situation. If this is not possible, take steps to insure that the evil and/ or selfish act will not happen to you again. But still, perform forgiveness, not resentment or revenge. Show Love, not hate. Teach, do not judge. Show your spiritual strength through understanding and patience, not through emotion and/or criticism.

4   Always know that you are working on behalf of GOD, not yourself. This will help you with the resentment you may feel because of the selfish acts of others. For every selfish act committed against you your God shall indeed restore you. Work for GOD; not for yourself or others.

5   Do not ask GOD to use you as a *tool of peace* or as a *vessel of love* if you are not prepared to be stuck into the dirt and the stench of the World itself. Know this. GOD shall use <u>you</u> to clean up the vomit of the World and to catch its feces. GOD shall use <u>you</u> to be stuck into the soil of the World in an effort to plant new seeds. Is this not the work of our God?

6   Try to remember that symbolically you are the tool of GOD. That it is the universe (not you) that is doing the work. You (the teacha) are the tool that helps the work get done. Just as we use tools to go into places that we ourselves cannot go into, so it is with GOD. GOD is Spirit! And those that commit to their God are like that of valuable tools in the material World.

[7] Indeed, GOD is an artist, a master builder, a great architect, and we (the teachas) are the tools. When a great architect finds a good tool that is indispensable to the building of the World, that tool is preserved and repaired, cleansed and restored repeatedly for the sake of the work that is necessary to achieve. Eventually, the good tool is set aside and remembered for its faithful service.

[8] You are the tool (teacha) in your environment. And tools are used to go into those difficult and hard-to-reach places of the World. You cannot run and hide when difficult people and/or situations arise. This is like a plunger that refuses to go into a stopped-up toilet! Or even a hammer that refuses to hit the nail into the wall!

[9] Teachas that refuse to teach difficult people in difficult places at difficult times are like broken tools. And if tools break where they cannot be restored, they are indeed thrown away! You are the representation of your God. Indeed you may be the only hope in your environment.

[10] With every sincere act of forgiveness you gain another degree in your spiritual development. And it is these degrees that prove your usefulness, strength and trustworthiness before GOD. Forgiveness proves your endurance. Take advantage of every evil and/or selfish moment brought before you. Tell the selfish one, *you are forgiven*.

[11] Look into the face of those who tried to harm you and say, *you are forgiven*. Even while the evil and/or selfishness is occurring, subdue your emotions, take advantage of the moment, and tell the evil and/or selfish one; *you are forgiven*. And really mean it! GOD is examining your heart to determine YOUR level of spiritual maturity and trustworthiness.

[12] Remember your own times of ignorance and/or fear and correct your own past errors by performing

patience with those who are blind, immature, fearful, confused, or have wronged you today.

13   Learn to forgive yourself and others. Forgiveness leads to freedom and health, while resentment leads to bondage and sickness. Take care of your *Self*. Heal your *Self*. Release guilt! Through virtuous living, turn your own ignorant past into a testimony or a ministry for the correction of others today. For no one can minister or teach upon a subject they themselves have no experience with.

14   Instead of feeling guilty for your own past actions, use them as evidence of your wisdom and as evidence of your victory over the World's obstacles. Use your corrected failures as the textbook that you shall teach others from. Allow your corrected errors to qualify your wisdom to teach. This very gospel is a product of such advice.

15   Let the immature thinking of others bounce off of you like rain. Do not drink the immaturity of others by responding to their ignorance with more ignorance. In hostile situations, protect yourself first through immediate forgiveness! Never empower the weaknesses of others with resentment and/or your immediate impulse to act as they did. Be the Light in all situations!

16   Once you have performed the act of forgiveness you can believe that GOD is sure to follow up with justice. This is a divine performance. Work for GOD, not for self. For it is selflessness that gives strength to forgiveness. No one can hurt or betray a self that doesn't exist. If you are hurting it is most likely because you have accepted someone else's immaturity onto your *self*. You have allowed the immaturity of others to change your God-like nature.

17   Therefore, do not waste time on revengeful, resentful and angry performances. For with your divine performance GOD is sure to close the show! Only seek to help. Even in argument, only seek to correct the ignorance of others.

Never argue angrily or resentfully; only teach.

[18]   Mature Hiphoppas never argue just to prove their point. Such an argument is pointless. Instead, try to learn and truly understand the opposing view. Show respect for the thinking of others and with a forgiving heart remind them of their own ignorance for their own sake. Perform Forgiveness.

6)   Perform Patience.   Practice expressing calm endurance, silent strength and inner resolve—these lead to patience. Be tolerant of others and their views and always be willing to wait. Whatever is yours is yours by Divine Right. Within the spiritual life there is very little need to rush or to be anxious. Simply ask and then wait in an expectant manner.

[1]   Usually what you do not receive is for your own good. Here, patience is the ability to be still and allow opportunity to fall into your lap. Do not run after opportunity; only position yourself to receive opportunities. Usually it is the righteous that remain still through the changes of the World (in a strategic position) so that when the World unexpectantly changes again opportunity falls into their laps.

[2]   Remember that opportunity is not to be chased down, it is to be searched for. Opportunity is not to be hunted, it is granted. It is not taken, it is received. Hiphoppas are encouraged to find strength in the things they already have. Be patient, even with ignorant selfish people. Be patient with them as well as with yourself and prepare for the fall of the ignorant; it is inevitable!

[3]   Sometimes the fall of the ignorant will temporarily hinder the rise of the Hiphoppa. In this case, the attuned Hiphoppa has already prepared for the inevitable fall of the ignorant through independence and a variety of divine performances and rises while others are trapped under their

own rubble!

4   In all things perform patience. Even with difficult people be patient. No matter how ignorant or inconsiderate people may appear to be, always remember that ultimately everyone is growing, learning and developing according to their own level of consciousness, and if they are not then they will not be around you much longer. Be patient.

5   Some people will simply not see it your way—be patient, you and they are always growing. Eventually, everyone sees the Truth; however, everyone grows at their own pace. What is obvious to you today may not be so obvious to others. But if you stand in Truth and in righteous humility they shall eventually see what you see. Be patient. Everyone arrives at the Truth eventually.

6   Finally, we must continue the practice of being patient with ourselves. Let us remain committed to our principles, performances and disciplines but let us not be too anxious to receive spiritual insight and power—all shall come in time.

7   For we have seen for over 40 years that it does not matter how much meditation one does or how virtuous one may live, spiritual insight and power happen on their own, in their own time. You simply must continue your practice until you are granted the results that you desire. Be patient and learn the art of waiting.

8   The spiritual life is not the material life; it moves within its own time. When you are being delayed for some trivial reason do not get upset or worried; simply go with the flow. Go with the flow because your very steps are counted and guided by spiritual forces; be patient. Be willing to wait.

9   Practice performing patience while waiting in line. Practice patience with difficult people. Practice patience with your own spiritual development, with your career, with

your children, with your parents. In all areas of life learn how to apply the virtuous performance of patience. Many disasters have been avoided and many have come to see the light by the correct use of patience. As the philosopher Carlyle once said, *"Every noble work is at first impossible."* Perform Patience.

7)   Perform Charity. Be of a giving nature. Be of service to the progression of life itself. Perform charity often and do not concern yourself with whether your giving shall be returned to you. Give for the sake of giving. Give of your talent as freely as GOD has given it to you.

[1]   Freely giving away samples of one's talent actually opens unexpected doors for the giver and for the receiver. Give of yourself, give opportunity, give knowledge, give time, give money and other resources. Charity actually relives human suffering. Be willing to forgive the debt of those who owe you.

[2]   Through your own actions, be the example to society as to what charity looks like. Do not attach yourself to anything. All that you have should be able to be given away in a second's notice. The one who gives never loses. The one who owns nothing cannot experience theft, loss, foreclosure, seizure or confiscation.

[3]   Charity also proves the wealth of an individual even if that individual has little or no money. Only a wealthy mentality (even with little money) can freely give. And likewise, only a poor mentality (even with an abundance of money) has nothing to give.

[4]   If it is wealth (which includes money) that you seek, it is very important that you <u>act</u> wealthy first through charity. Seek to perform charity in public and in private. Charity raises your self-worth. Public charity sets a good example within your community and private charity sets a

good example before your God.

5   Find ways to perform charity, but also be careful not to make those who you are charitable toward dependent upon you. Give with the intention of relieving one's suffering. Sometimes a free gift can prolong one's suffering and/or prevent one from learning a much-needed lesson.

6   So remember, as you seek to help and assist people, always remember that everyone is where they are for a reason. We have found that some people are exactly where they need to be in life regardless of how impoverished and/ or dangerous their circumstances may seem to be. GOD is engaging us all.

7   At all times we must walk and talk with a giving heart, but if a person is not also willing to help himself, there is little that anyone can do for such an individual. Therefore, be wise in your giving. Give with the intention to truly help and empower. Sometimes the giving of nothing is the greatest gift of all. Perform your charity.

8)   Perform Love. Show your Love. Be compassionate and caring. Give others the devotion that you expect from GOD. For our God is Divine Love and this *Love* is not blind. It is *lust* that is blind. Love is unconditional. It makes itself available to the loved. Love is patient. Love suffers long. Love is kind. Love proves and empowers one's ability to teach and guide others.

1   Allow GOD to manifest through you toward others. It is from GOD that your Love comes and it is from here that we correctly express our Love.

2   Love all and hate none; but when all hate, Love none. To truly Love is to unite with the being of others, and at the beginning of your spiritual understanding it is important to guard your heart. For Love is healthy and hate is diseased. Love all who deserve your Love, and hate no

one. For in Love you are truly protected and empowered.

3   The attuned Hiphoppa knows that GOD is the headliner in every arena of life, and that it is GOD's performance that is sure to follow the Hiphoppa's opening act of true Love. Be the Love to those that truly deserve it. See the holiness in those people even when they cannot see it in themselves.

4   Their divinity is the Truth of their being. Therefore, let us practice speaking only to the divine nature of people; such is their true essence, but do not live in denial of those who do not truly Love you. Even when you are cursed out and/or disrespected, remain calm and centered, knowing that such responses are not the Truth of anyone's being; such responses are indeed temporary.

5   This is why the immature always regret what they say and do and often wind up apologizing for it. Wait for the apology because those who return to their right mind and seek your pardon of their immaturity deserve your Love and understanding.

6   If you remain calm in the midst of such temporary fits of rage, ignorance, immaturity or sadness, eventually you will see those angered, ignorant, immature, depressed people return to their true state of peace, awareness and normalcy. And if they truly respect you, even Love you, they will apologize not for their own well-being but for yours.

7   Anger and sadness are not normal for any human being, therefore such states are always temporary. Joy is normal. Peace is normal. LOVE is normal. The opposite of this is abnormal.

8   At all times perform with Love. Search your heart for the people you Love most and LOVE THEM. Look at the people you love and say with your inner voice, *I Love you*. Make this a habit.

[9] Despite the emphasis others may place upon doing things strictly for payment, in whatever you do, perform it with Love. If you hate or dislike what you do, stop doing it!

[10] If you dislike or hate what you do even if you are paid for it, ultimately the result of your compensation will not be fulfilling. In fact, it will only depress you. Therefore, do what you Love to do. And do not be afraid to do whatever it is that you Love to do. Find time for it.

[11] Although forgotten, Hip Hop was created out of Love. Early Hiphoppas performed their elements out of Love. With or without payment, early Hiphoppas loved Hip Hop. With all tasks and people *show Love*.

9)   Perform Faith. Demonstrate your faith. Do not live exclusively by your natural reasoning or believe exclusively what your senses tell you. Live by faith.

[1] Faith is not just a belief in unseen things; it is an unconditional confirmation of the finished work. It is a knowing or expectancy that comes from living a spiritual and virtuous life. Faith is not an invisible thing, it is a very visible thing; it has physical effects. In fact, faith is the invisible substance of visible things. Faith is simply what you perceive as real. Is God real to you? Are God's abilities real to you?

[2] Whatever you believe your God can actually do shall be done! Because of unrighteous and non-spiritual living, if you do not truly perceive your Spirit abilities and the strength of your God, then it is your own doubt that weakens the supernatural abilities of your own Spirit over the material World. Live a virtuous life and every month do something or say something that requires faith. Practice faith. Expect results!

[3] As an example, as simple and as easy as it is

to faithfully order food from a restaurant you should likewise faithfully order Health, Love, Awareness and/or Wealth from the universe. In this example, the universe is the restaurant.

4   When you know that you have money to eat, you effortlessly and confidently enter the restaurant, sit down and order whatever you have a taste for. Such is the same with spiritual living. When you know that you have an abundance of spiritual money (faith; the effect of righteous/virtuous living, helpfulness, patience, etc.), you boldly order from the universe those things that you need.

5   Just as easily as you might order a beer from a bar, with the confidence that comes from righteous living, order for yourself peace and prosperity with the same expectancy. Point to the unseen and translate the unheard. Practice exercising your faith by ordering things in faith.

6   Temple Members are united in the faith that Hiphop is GOD's response to our suffering. Our faith as Hiphoppas is established through our trust in the divinity of our unique historical experiences.

7   At the heights of our faith (knowing) we believe that our God has called a new nation into being and WE are they who are called of GOD. We are a new people; a truly free people. We are not subjected to the blessings, curses or prophecies of other nations and faiths. GOD is dealing with us right now! Today, we are a Holy Integrated People Having Omnipresent Power.

8   The truly attuned Hiphoppa performs and walks in this faith (knowing). Those who walk in this faith and both regularly and randomly perform acts of this faith, are truly inspired and rarely depressed. They are joyous and strong while others remain anxious and weak. They are at peace even when others are afraid—these are the effects of faith.

9   For GOD is an exact god. Those that live by faith

need not an abundance of anything. They always have exactly what they need exactly when they need it; in fact this is the abundance. Never too soon, never too late, never too much and never too little, the faithful always have exactly enough!

[10] Faith and the knowing that comes from righteous living eliminate fear and doubt. And likewise, fear and doubt caused by ignorance and unrighteous living eliminate faith. Decide right now which of the two you shall serve—fear or faith, doubting or knowing, surviving or living!

[11] Practice faith by performing random acts of faith. In troubling situations, be still and know that your God is GOD! Store up your spiritual money (faith) in righteous/virtuous living and then order whatever you need from the universe.

[12] Immerse yourself in something that your God must follow up on and complete. Believe in your God! Expect the presence, power and activity of your God! Believe God, not the World.

[13] Regularly perform faith. Accumulate and then spend your spiritual faith-money wisely. Bruce Barton reminds us that *"The ablest men in all walks of life are men of faith. Most of them have much more faith than they themselves realize."* Perform Faith.

10) Perform Overstanding. In all things seek the deeper meaning. Truly seek to know the pain, joy, needs and wants of those who you may come into contact with. Cultivate your mind to truly overstand the situations and circumstances of others.

[1] Even just for a moment, join them in their life experience. Know this. To understand is to comprehend whatever you have been taught. However, to overstand is to experience whatever you have been taught. Such is the

essence of wisdom and spiritual leadership.

2   At all times perform overstanding. Seek to know through experience your own views as well as the views of others. Never settle for simply being educated. For with spiritual overstanding comes discernment and with discernment comes agreement, resolution, conclusion and solutions.

3   While knowledge makes you aware of things, overstanding makes you aware of the character and nature of things. For it is not enough to know whatever you know. You must also experience the things that you know in order to truly know them and correctly apply them. More than just knowing something, it is far better to experience whatever you know. This is the essence of wisdom and true leadership.

4   Overstanding proves the validity of one's acquired knowledge. Know this. Just because you have been educated, does not mean that your education is truly productive to your real life. Theories must be tested and facts change all the time. The true Hiphoppa does not just read the Gospel of Hip Hop; she performs the *Overstandings* of this gospel and proves to herself the value of this gospel in real life.

5   The teacha must know for sure that the Gospel of Hip Hop truly works in real life before she can seek to teach it to others! The teacha must be certain of the trueness and authenticity of the Gospel of Hip Hop. Such certainty is found in the heart. The trueness of this *gospel* is determined by its compatibility with your heart. Does this path feel right to you? You cannot teach this *gospel* if you are uncertain of its *overstandings*; if you are still in doubt.

6   Know this. The teacha argues on behalf of the Gospel of Hip Hop not for the sake of winning, but for the sake of offering others the possibility of experiencing Health, Love, Awareness and Wealth. He argues only

from experience and for the sake of reaching harmonious agreements between parties of conflicting opinions.

7   You must always seek to overstand the things that you know; and always seek to experience the *Overstandings* of this gospel. Live by the productive experiences of your life. Learn to repeat the actions of your own success. Learn from the mistakes as well as from the achievements made by your actions as well as the actions of others. Discipline is a result of wisdom and overstanding.

8   Applied wisdom is overstanding. A Hiphoppa's wisdom is manifested in that Hiphoppa's life. It proves that he truly overstands. More than just talking about what they have experienced, you can see the results of a Hiphoppa's wisdom by the effects in and of that Hiphoppa's life.

9   Joy is an effect of overstanding. Peace is an effect of overstanding. Mercy, compassion, justice and patience are also effects of overstanding. However, you can be wise and not experience any of these virtues. Be guided. Wisdom and knowledge are two different things.

10   Wisdom can be achieved through life experiences, while knowledge can be acquired through educational/ intellectual studies. But to overstand is to have experienced them both. To overstand is to act upon what you know and have experienced.

11   Knowledge proves that you know some things. Wisdom proves that you have experienced some things. But overstanding proves that you are active in both your knowledge and wisdom of things. For it is the guidance of our God that adds valuable experiences to our knowledge. Such experiences create wisdom. But even the wise are not always motivated to act. They have experience, yet they are not always experiencing!

12   Know this. Wisdom is not righteousness. In fact, to be wise one must go through some very unrighteous situations;

one must experience things that can only be experienced in failure, fear and ignorance. And after one has learned from such fearful and ignorant experiences, one then becomes wise. For when knowledge is backed by experience and the Hiphoppa can skillfully apply them both while performing life, that Hiphoppa is said to be *overstood*.

[13] For it has been said that *the experience gathered from books is of the nature of learning; the experience gained from actual life is of the nature of wisdom; and a small store of the latter is worth vastly more than any stock of the former.* (Samuel Smiles, *Self-Help* [New York: American Book Company, 1904]). Perform Overstanding.

11) Perform Truth. Don't just seek to know the Truth; seek to perform the Truth, be as genuine and as real as you can. While everyone else performs behind their variety of masks and phony personalities, you must be the Truth in such illusionary and fake circles.

[1] This is what it means to *keep it real!* It means to be true to yourself—be your true self. Don't hide behind falsities and illusions. Such a performance leads to nowhere. Knowing Truth is to know what is real. Performing Truth is to manifest or actualize what is real. But what is real as it pertains to Truth?

[2] What we know to be real and what is real are two different things. Truth is the ultimate reality of reality itself. It is the real reality of reality; it is the whole, it is what it is. To perform Truth means that what we believe to be real corresponds with what is actually real.

[3] Most people experience all kinds of things in their lives, and their experiences are indeed real to them. But in Truth, their experiences are not real at all! Experiences in material reality are more the opinions of the observer than that of actual Truth.

4   Yes, your experiences are T.R.U.E. They are The Reality U Experience. However, they may not be the T.R.U.T.H.; The Reality U Truly Have. The material World is true. But the spiritual realm which projects the material World into existence is the Truth. It may be true that you are in prison. But the Truth is that prison was first inside of you. Deal with the Truth and you shall be free.

5   Know this. There is reality, and then there is your perception of that reality. Reality is the Truth, but your perception of that reality is a fact. It is true for you. In the material World, what is called *Truth* is actually an agreement as to what is real. These are called *facts*. And so many people rely upon the facts of life as opposed to the reality of life.

6   Perform Truth. For Truth is the whole, while lies are its fragments. Falsity is the fragmentation of the Truth. Falsity takes a fragment of the Truth and treats it as if it is the Truth itself. Do not be led by falsities, illusions and lies. Seek Truth! Speak Truth! Perform Truth! Be a whole person as often as you can. Be mindful of how many times you fragment and hide your true *Self* for the sake of others. Practice being whole and transparent.

7   Truth is also freedom from the bondage of ignorance. Truth is the revelation of what already exists but just could not be comprehended or seen before. Truth is the cause of awareness or ahhh-wareness. Truth is happening right now as you read this gospel. For Truth is the ultimate gospel, but no gospel is the ultimate Truth.

8   Truth cannot be actually written down. In reality, Truth cannot even be described in words. All words, numbers, shapes and letters are symbols which assist us in understanding the realm in which Truth exists. Words, numbers, shapes, and letters, even dancing, rapping and singing are all translations of what is really the Truth.

9   Therefore, we must seek Truth beyond the material

World and its symbols. And we must seek Truth beyond our physical senses. These tools (symbols and senses) fragment the Truth so that we may create an ordered World out of the Truth that is a chaotic oneness. Seek Truth! Be truthful, and perform your Truth.

12)   Perform Skill.   Because the Hiphoppa is independent and self-sufficient in the World, perfection of a chosen skill (that is in demand) gives the Hiphoppa a lifestyle that supports the seeking of her purpose in peace. As with the performance of discipline; seek the perfection of your chosen skill. Practice perfecting your skills.

[1]   Most people want many things for themselves. Some have dreams and goals they wish to achieve for themselves, but they just continue to admire the achievements of others because they simply have not mastered the skills needed to manifest their own dreams and goals. All goals require skill mastery to be achieved.

[2]   The most important questions a Hiphoppa can ask when daydreaming, visualizing, praying and/or wishing for things and desirable situations are: *What am I actually capable of doing? What can I really accomplish? What have I mastered?* And *what are my skills?*

[3]   Those without a perfected skill that is in demand will find it difficult to lead an *inner-city* spiritual life. Having a skill that is in demand is what separates the one who is chasing resources and opportunity from the one who is chased by resources and opportunity.

[4]   Attuned Hiphoppas are experienced in Hiphop's nine elements and we are experts at two or more of Hip Hop's artistic elements. We seek to sharpen our skills in every phase of life that requires skill.

[5]   In parenting, in teaching, in nurturing, in apologizing, in loving, in playing, in fighting, in speaking, in

cooking, in working, in cleaning, in eating and with all the elements of Hiphop and with all of the performances of the *Divine Performance*, perform with skill. Seek to be an expert at all that you do. Do nothing haphazardly.

6   When performing your skill you must be conscious of how skillful you are. Attuned Hiphoppas who perform the *Divine Performance* learn that each performance requires spiritual skill.

7   In many cases, such skill is found and perfected in battles, confrontations and threatening situations. Never seek confrontation, but never be afraid to fight or display your skill!

8   It is when we are challenged by people, places, things and events that we are made strong and skillful in life. For at the end of all human knowledge and strength GOD shall appear! Once fully practiced in overcoming the challenges of life, the attuned Hiphoppa is spiritually strong and prepared to teach and lead others.

9   Perfect your cultural, spiritual, artistic and intellectual skills by performing your skills often. As Henry W. Longfellow once stated, *I will be a man among men; and no longer a dreamer among shadows. Henceforth be mine a life of action and reality! I will work in my own sphere, nor wish it other than it is. This alone is health and happiness.* Perform Skill.

13)   Perform Intelligence.   Our intelligence is creatively inquisitive. Therefore, practice asking questions especially about the things that you are already familiar with. For it is the question that drives us toward our God, not necessarily the acquired answer. Asking the right questions leads to spiritual awareness and peace.

1   At the start of one's quest for spiritual awareness one must ask the correct questions that will expand one's

ability to acquire and apply correct spiritual knowledge. We must question GOD to know more about our God.

2   For it is indeed true that your God will answer all of your questions with astonishing accuracy. The Hiphoppa uses *faith* to see what is not yet physically there and uses *action* to bring those things into existence. Intelligence (the ability to know and perceive) questions the two. Be careful. Question GOD, but never doubt God.

3   Just as our faith sees and confirms what is not yet physically possible, our intelligence must ask questions concerning the possibilities of what is perceived to be possible. But do not allow the performance of your intelligence to override your faith.

4   For we are guided by the questions we ask, not necessarily by the answers we get. But once our intelligence has given its performance it must be put back in its place; in the dimension of question, perception, logic and rationale. This is what it means to perform your intelligence. Do not allow your intelligence to just rule over your life. Apply its sharp inquiry and sense of perception when necessary to shape the reality that you truly desire.

5   We (Hiphoppas) should pay more attention to how we view the World because the solutions for many of society's ills lie inside of us. Hiphoppas must question the so-called facts of the physical World but after gaining an awareness of one's spiritual nature, question not (only) believe) the Truth of one's *Spirit*. As Colton reminds us, *Doubt is the vestibule which all must pass before they can enter the temple of wisdom*. Perform Intelligence.

14)   Perform Communication. Be aware of what you are communicating to the World. Do not just talk for the sake of talking. Be mindful of every word, thought and action that you may communicate to others. Instead of speaking out of idleness, perform silence. Most events, good and/or evil, begin with thoughts and then words and then actions.

1   The attuned Hiphoppa creates a productive life arena through the thoughts and words he chooses to express. Every thought and spoken idea creates an awareness around the Hiphoppa. This awareness attracts the people, places and things that help to openly manifest the intentions of that Hiphoppa's heart.

2   By speaking for the sake of joy and peace the attuned Hiphoppa creates an awareness that attracts joy and peace in one's life. Attuned Hiphoppas speak of good things so that good things may manifest in their lives and in the lives of others. Do not label your work *Ready to Die* unless you are ready to die. Do not claim to be *Criminal Minded* unless you are prepared for the results of criminal activity.

3   Do not think and/or speak those things that you wish to avoid in your life, and be careful of what you continuously listen to. Be aware of those who speak with bad intentions and perversion as the main subject of their conversation. Seek to correct them humbly if they are simply unaware; or simply avoid their company if they reject Truth.

4   When others are frustrated, use diplomacy and speak from the perspective of wisdom. You can say: *Just let it go... You're bigger than that... Don't let this situation steal your joy... Forget them... GOD has bigger plans for you... Are they really worth it?*

5   Do not judge. Simply make observations and show others, with wisdom and overstanding, the causes and the effects of what they communicate. People should know that your character and personality is one of maturity and trustworthiness. Lead by example. Advise others with your very personality and the results of your life experiences.

6   Do not linger around those whose conversation

carries impurity and scandal. Seek the companionship of those who you study and pray with. Know this. Communication is not just speech. Hiphoppas communicate through writing, drawing, fashion, personal character, dancing, rapping, eating, etc.

7   For when the attuned Hiphoppa finally acknowledges the Truth that GOD is present; that Hiphoppa's character changes. And when that Hiphoppa's character is one of righteousness others are disciplined and inspired not only by that Hiphoppa's words, but also by that Hiphoppa's character and very presence. For there are certain things that people just cannot do in the presence of holiness. For the very character of the attuned Hiphoppa disciplines, teaches and inspires those who surround her.

8   Attuned Hiphoppas care more about the totality of what is being transmitted or passed on to others than about the way in which one actually speaks. While others communicate hatred, we communicate love. While others communicate anger, we communicate joy, not by speaking it but by being it.

9   Even in fierce argument we must practice and strengthen our spiritual reflexes. We must train ourselves to never enter into the insanity of anger, bitterness and/or hatred while arguing. We must perform our communication, not just communicate. For example, we should NEVER ARGUE IN FRONT OF CHILDREN or where they can hear the thoughts of our angry, resentful, fearful minds.

10   Discipline yourself! Guide your inward and outward communication. Learn to speak well, read well and write well; these lead to good communication skills. Learn to deliver your point of view quickly and accurately—get to the point. And remember, sometimes the best communication is silence. Never be afraid to say nothing at all.

11   For it is in the performances of one's life that one's

intentions are communicated and then manifested. Perform your communication and be aware at all times of what you are communicating as well as what is being communicated to you.

[12] Quarles reminds us that *If any speak ill of thee, flee home to thy own conscience, and examine thy heart; if thou be guilty, it is just correction; if not guilty, it is a fair instruction; make use of both, so shalt thou distill honey out of gall, and out of an open enemy create a secret friend.* Perform Communication.

15) Perform Responsibility. Regularly check your *response-ability*. This means to regularly check the character of what you respond to. Prepare for what you must respond to and be mindful as to how well you respond. Ask yourself daily, *What is my ultimate responsibility? Have I met my responsibilities?*

[1] True Hiphoppas always seek to help, which proves their selflessness. True Hiphoppas always seek to uplift, enhance, and strengthen those who rely upon them. Even if it is personally uncomfortable; the true Hiphoppa does what is required of him. Such an *ability* is not for everyone, nor can such an *ability* even be performed by everyone. Responsibility is a spiritual skill.

[2] It is maturity, self-respect, and self-sacrifice that helps to develop the *response-ability* of the true Hiphoppa. Without maturity, self-respect and the ability to sacrifice for others, it is difficult to be a responsible person. This is why many young *Rap fans* start off irresponsible. They simply lack the ability to respond to issues beyond *my clothes, my rent, my car, my thirst,* and so on. They cannot see past their own individual wants and needs. Self-sacrifice is the essence of responsibility.

[3] The Temple of Hiphop encourages Hiphoppas to

do what they are supposed to do when they are supposed to do it. Most people are led by their *wants* and not by their needs. Most people do what they *want* to do as opposed to what they *must* do, and this is just irresponsible.

4   Hiphoppas are encouraged to do what they *must* do first, then do whatever they *want* to do later. Always doing what is pleasurable and/or easy to do sets one up for a weak foundation in life. For there is nothing special about *easy*, it is the conquering of the difficult that makes one special and even appreciated.

5   The one who goes out of her way to remove a difficulty is respected by everyone. The one who can be depended upon is respected by everyone. The one who makes sacrifices for the good of the whole is respected by everyone, and this is what it means to be responsible. It means that you and others are clear as to where your commitment lies.

6   The attuned Hiphoppa is not afraid of commitment. In fact, the attuned Hiphoppa builds a character that demands respect by selflessly performing her commitments and responsibilities. At times, we must even sacrifice for those who depend upon us.

7   We will not always like what we must do, but if the greater good depends upon our commitment, then those dependant upon our sacrifices must not be let down. Attuned Hiphoppas are dependable people.

8   The attuned Hiphoppa upholds an image of maturity and can always be depended upon. Remember, with whatever you must do; if you want to do it then it is not a sacrifice. It is when you do those things that you personally do not want to do that you are indeed sacrificing. However, to be responsible is to be dependable.

9   Hiphoppas are encouraged to be dependable people, responsible people, committed people. For us, the "balanced

life" is *when you want to do what you have to do*. When your responsibilities are a joy to complete, your life is balanced. When you are committed and responsible to something or someone you truly love, when your sacrifices bring you peace and joy, your life is balanced.

¹⁰ Charles Kingsley reminds us to *thank GOD every morning when you get up that you have something to do which must be done, whether you like it or not. Being forced to work, and forced to do your best, will breed in you temperance, self-control, diligence, strength of will, content, and a hundred other virtues which the idle never know.* Perform Responsibility.

16) Perform Action. The most important thing to know of one's *Self* is one's purpose. The fulfillment of one's life purpose is the cause of true joy and happiness. Do not become idle or live without purpose. Although you may be still seeking your purpose, perform action. Never just sit around being unaware of the effects of your actions or your non-action.

¹ The attuned Hiphoppa shows others through example what righteousness, love, justice, charity and overstanding looks like. The attuned Hiphoppa is aware of how her actions teach society. Such a Hiphoppa knows that every social act is a lesson performed in and for one's family, friends and larger society.

² For every cause or act there is an effect or response. Be aware of what you *cause* to exist through your thinking and your actions. We are the offspring of our own actions. We actually create ourselves through action which is motivated by purpose. So, what's your purpose? If you lack direction or purpose in life, focus your mind upon the actions of your teacha.

³ Pay attention to the way that your teacha performs an action and imitate those performances. Know that your

teacha is impartial to success or failure. See how your teacha is not attached to the effects of the act. Feel how your teacha not only gives but sacrifices.

4   The attuned Hiphoppa overstands that even while acting we do nothing at all. The attuned Hiphoppa knows that all is the _Great Oneness Deity_ and it is only _G.O.D._ that actually acts.

5   When we are eating, breathing, talking, walking, working, driving, etc., we really do nothing at all. Only GOD through Nature is moving which gives us the temporary appearance of movement. The attuned Hiphoppa does not act nor cause action when it is overstood that all action is the divine performance of GOD. We are actually the effects of GOD in action.

6   Like when the wind blows dried leaves across a road. The leaves have no sense of the wind blowing them along, yet the leaves move. Physical bodies have movement in a similar way. Forces (winds) blow against us and push us toward this circumstance or that circumstance. We must learn to navigate the forces (winds) of life toward the fulfillment of our life's purpose.

7   However, such navigation has more to do with allowing _the force_ to carry you without you getting in your own way. Spiritual navigation has to do with allowing GOD to guide your life; it's about GOD's leadership in your life. Some people regard GOD's leadership in their lives as a choice. They say; _I now give my life to GOD_, as if they had the authority to do such a thing!

8   The leadership of GOD in your life is not a choice. It is the Truth! It's a realization, an awakening, a new awareness, a sense of giving up and letting go on your part. The leadership of GOD is happening now! It is you who must realize this by releasing your fears, doubts and disbeliefs about your own God-force. We must get in

harmony with what GOD is already doing in our lives!

⁹ Know this. When our will is not the Will of our God we naturally begin to experience pain and suffering. The Will of our God is for Hiphoppas to be joyous, at peace and prosperous. Our God's Will is occurring long before we come to realize it. And those things which happen against our will are usually for our own good. For GOD sustains life itself. You do not choose GOD; GOD chooses you.

¹⁰ Because life is sustained by GOD, every act of the Hiphoppa should be performed as a tribute and sacrifice to GOD. No work (or person) is too difficult to deal with when all is done as a tribute and service to your God. With this, the attuned Hiphoppa escapes the cycles of cause and effect because the attuned Hiphoppa causes nothing and is detached from everything. Only GOD is moving, acting and speaking.

¹¹ Perform difficult activities knowing this. E.L. Magoon once said, *Existence was given us for action, rather than indolent and aimless contemplation; our worth is determined by the good deeds we do, rather than by the fine emotions we feel. They greatly mistake who suppose that GOD cares for no other pursuit than devotion.* Perform Action.

17) Perform Prayer. Both regularly and randomly raise your heart to GOD in prayer. Make time to pray. Take time to pray. Pray in the shower. Pray while driving, while walking, working, etc. Thank GOD often and find peace in the security of GOD's presence. Do not concentrate on the proper words to say. Focus more upon expressing the joys, questions, cries and groans of your own heart.

¹ Prayer is relaxing; it lowers one's heart rate and blood pressure. For us (templists), prayer is not ritualistic or repetitive speech. Do not posture before GOD; allow your heart to cry out to GOD, with GOD. For it is the

sincere cry of the heart in joy or in sadness that attracts the response of the Great Spirit, not words.

2   Know (through righteous living) that you are loved and cared for and that your God will always make a way for you. Know in your heart that your God already sees what you need. So when you pray, thank GOD for satisfying your needs in advance. Thank your God for the finished work.

3   For everything already exists and is readily available to you now! It is only your doubts that block or deny the existence of everything happening to you at once so that (out of your own fear of chaos) you can bring order to your World. When praying, simply allow things to happen by ceasing your doubt and/or fear of them happening.

4   Stop doubting and/or denying the existence of those things that you want. Everything you need already exists in your reality. Stop doubting and/or denying that those things you desire are separate and distant from your immediate reality. Simply allow them to exist in your World. Let there be *this*…and let there be *that*. Expect what you want in prayer.

5   However, it is important to remember that GOD is an exact god. Everything that you need you really already have. Most of the time we simply are not looking clearly enough into our own environments. Sometimes we also become convinced of the importance of things that we really do not need. Be careful!

6   With your whole heart repeat the following prayer regularly:

> *Great and Holy Spirit I AM—the light of my World! The Love that guides me. Enter now into this temple fulfilling the purpose for which it was built. I AM— clean and unafraid. Great Spirit, keep my foot upon the path of holiness that I may give without watching*

the cost, and endure without stress. I am in your care and protection. For when my eyes cannot see a way, Your Love reveals the obvious and I am saved again. There it is!

7   Say this with your whole heart. Feel it, see it, believe it and know it! Use your heart and expect GOD's response. Move in this faith. But remember, your prayers are more likely to be answered when your prayer requests are also in harmony with your being, your intentions, your true thoughts and actions.

8   Know this. Hiphoppas do not always get what they want in prayer; most of the time they receive exactly who they are in life. For it is who you are that shall determine what you shall receive in prayer. You receive what you believe, and you achieve what you perceive! You get what you expect and respect! You can only attract that which you really are.

9   Therefore, care not for what the World believes is valuable and care not for how things may appear to be to your intellect. Recognize only the oneness and simply allow things to come to you. Everything you want is already with you now. Your reality is really a World of possibilities. You decide what comes in and out of your reality based upon your level of expectancy.

10   When praying, you not only expect GOD, but you also respect GOD. Prayer proves one's respect for GOD, and you get more of what you respect. Therefore, after you have opened your door of *respectancy,* open your door of expectancy!

11   Be still, and allow things to happen. This will take courage because it is your own fears and disbelief that keeps all of the chaos of actual reality away from your conscious awareness. This is what prayer is all about; it's about access, not excess. Prayer is a special language humans use to

communicate to the guiding force in their lives.

12   Know this: the prayer of the attuned Hiphoppa has to do with spiritually accessing the productive resources and circumstances that are already available to one's self.

13   The attuned Hiphoppa prays (communicates) with GOD. And notice how I am writing this; *the attuned Hiphoppa prays with GOD*, not to GOD. When you pray to GOD there is distance between you and GOD. In a way, your prayer must still reach GOD. But when you pray with GOD there is no distance, no space and no intervals of time. Your prayer request can happen instantly!

14   When you pray, thank GOD and know that the blessing has already been granted and that it must only be revealed to you (through you). Thank GOD for what you already have and ask to always be enlightened of GOD's plan. You always want your prayer request to be in harmony with GOD; sometimes GOD will give you your request only to show you how useless and silly your "needed" request actually was. Before you ask about what you want, ask first to know what GOD wants.

15   GOD is concerned with human development, so when you pray for yourself sincerely pray for others; even those people that you do not personally know or do not even personally like. The heart that can sincerely do that is always heard by GOD. Remember, GOD is praying with you.

16   The Great Spirit answers ALL prayers! No prayer goes unanswered. For if you are truly not in possession of that which you are praying for, GOD will truly provide it. But if you already possess that which you pray for GOD will not answer your request twice. Therefore, if your prayer goes unanswered either you are being protected from your own ignorance or you already have that which you are praying for and you simply have not comprehended it yet.

17   We must remember to pray that you may see the

solutions that we already have and always thank GOD for the protection that we cannot see. For when you pray you do not always get what you pray for; most of the time you actually get exactly what you need!

18   Those things that you don't have, you don't need! Those places that you can't go are also dangerous for you! Trust the love of the Great Spirit!

19   Remember, all prayers are answered. The question is, are you in the environment or awareness of your answered prayer? Many people receive their answered prayer many times and simply don't see it because they are expecting it to come from a familiar place or source.

20   Therefore, as attuned Hiphoppas we must be open and receptive to the unexpected activities of GOD. We must be willing to identify and retrieve our blessings and answered prayers from, through and in unconventional, unexpected, and beyond-normal circumstances, sources and places.

21   Remember, you are speaking with GOD when you earnestly pray, and your God has an infinite amount of ways to deliver to you the desires of your heart. The challenge for many is that they reduce God to their own understanding, which blinds them from seeing GOD for real. You cannot ask an infinite source to communicate back to you in only one way, on one day, through one person, or one thing.

22   GOD is spirit, and to communicate to spirit you yourself must become spirit. As a spirit being operating effortlessly in the spirit realm, you can then see GOD and GOD's activity ultimately leading to your fulfillment.

23   So, when you pray or communicate with GOD seek understanding into the Mind of GOD, the Will of GOD, and the plan of GOD. Your God already has your best interest in mind, everything is already working in your favor; the challenge for you is to really believe this. Do you truly

perceive and expect GOD's love and care? When you pray, perform your prayers in faith. Act upon them. Perform Prayer

18)   Perform Hip Hop. Be conscious of Hip Hop as GOD's response to our suffering. For Hip Hop is the strategy that has freed us from sickness, hatred, ignorance and poverty.

[1]   Be conscious of Hip Hop as a divine blessing with divine purpose. That Hip Hop is beyond entertainment and Worldly validations.

[2]   Be conscious of *Hiphop* as a lifestyle and as an awareness. That *Hiphop* is a unique and empowering identity that has developed into an international community/culture of specialized people.

[3]   Be conscious of Hip Hop as its nine elements, B.E.G.D.B.F.L.K.E., and teach them by example.

[4]   At all times perform Hip Hop's elements with perfect skill. Whatever the specific element might be, the attuned Hiphoppa has mastered it and has perfected it.

[5]   The attuned Hiphoppa is Hiphop and is conscious of how Hip Hop is expressed in society. Performing Hiphop is all about having the courage to be your true self—to express your true identity. Self-creation is the ultimate Hiphop performance. We are not just doing Hiphop; we are H.I.P.H.O.P.—a Holy Integrated People Having Omnipresent Power!

[6]   Those who criticize Hip Hop today as being obscene, misogynistic and criminal are just as immature and limited in their thinking as we appear to be in ours. If we were approached with any kind of respect, or even compassion, or even logic, our critics would see us not as a bunch of irresponsible, money-hungry thugs but as a forgotten group of people trying to survive in an already corrupt World, making the best out of the conditions we

found ourselves in at birth.

7   This is in no way an excuse for our own immaturity. However, our immaturity today will be the warnings to future Hiphoppas as to what not to do and where not to go.

8   As long as Hip Hop is regarded as a music genre it shall always be criticized in the way that it is being criticized today. However, when Hip Hop is viewed as the international culture that it is, we come to the realization that Hip Hop is going through the same growing pains that most of the World's cultures have gone through at their origins.

9   Any logical, compassionate eye would see that Hip Hop is need of help. Instead of criticizing Hip Hop, show us your "better way" of life. Reveal to us the folly of our ways and point us in the right direction. And while you're at it, try listening to our concerns and grievances and try to remedy them.

10   We are fully aware as to what we look and sound like in mass-media today and we are even frustrated with ourselves. But we also overstand the struggles of our people and why we look and sound the way that we do. In fact, the Hip Hop community is known for warning other communities about the fallacies of living a criminal life; our advice comes from experience.

11   We know that cultures are like people and just as people teach people, cultures teach other cultures. Hip Hop is no different in this regard.

12   It is only natural that as a young community we will make mistakes. However, we will not be young forever and we will not be immature for long—yes, we will grow up! However, in the meantime, our immaturity should motivate others toward their own maturity.

13   Our immature behavior today is teaching all the World's cultures (including future Hiphoppas) what not to do and what not to become. When you see us acting stupid

you should check yourself to see if you are not acting just as stupid in another area of life.

14   The Truth is, every culture teaches other cultures, and today Hip Hop is teaching the World about the inevitable path of suffering caused by putting Worldly prestige and power above GOD.

15   We shall outgrow this lesson and produce other lessons with our collective life experiences, but while we are young we are in the process of relearning the World for ourselves and this process is not easy. We are in the process of knowing the World and GOD for ourselves—such is a painful process.

16   Therefore, let us perform *Hip Hop on a higher level*. Let us as Hiphoppas strive to be better than we were yesterday. Everyday let's seek ways to be responsible toward one another and collectively mature with our handling of Hip Hop. We may start out criminal minded but indeed we shall all end up spiritual minded.

17   As James Freeman Clarke teaches, *Progress in the sense of acquisition, is something; but progress in the sense of being is a great deal more. To grow higher, deeper, wider, as the years go on; to conquer difficulties, and acquire more and more power; to feel all one's faculties unfolding, and Truth descending into the soul—this makes life worth living.*

---

23   These are all divine performances. Make these performances your daily habits. Learn them while you are young and teach them to your children. This collective character is the personality of the attuned Hiphoppa.

24   The character and personality prescribed in *The Divine Performance* offers the true Hip Hop activist an empowering code of conduct capable of achieving lasting peace and uninterrupted prosperity.

²⁵ More importantly, the character presented in *The Divine Performance* opens up the realm of the *Inner City,* the Kingdom of Heaven, the realm of supernatural events and miracles.

²⁶ Although each *performance* can be used as an individual teaching or meditation; it is all eighteen performances that make up the total character of the spiritually attuned Hiphoppa. Templists who are studied in the Divine Performance can teach this *Overstanding* to others. Such a character draws the favor of GOD.

²⁷ Once we realize how awareness, blessings and Worldly resources come through us and not to us, we are encouraged to give, to help, to love, and to listen. As we look to GOD for guidance and strength; others look to us. We are the blessing, the answered prayer, the needed assistance in the lives of those that surround us. And this life is not an easy one to achieve or even to maintain at the beginning.

²⁸ At the beginning of such a *path*, your friends will desert you, your family will disrespect you, your place of employment will terminate you, and your school will fail you—you may even wind up houseless. As your new awareness begins to become your new reality, others who do not possess your new awareness will cease to understand you—but hold on!

²⁹ Your closest associates (family included) will show their true natures. Those who didn't like you in the past will like you now and those who like you now will not like you in the future. However, you MUST stay focused upon the creation of the new you. This is a time where you must place your interests above everyone else's interests, wants, needs, desires and fears.

³⁰ This is an act of *selfistness*—not selfishness, but *selfistness*. To be *selfist* simply means to tend to the critical needs of one's self above the temporal needs of others. It is

when one takes one's self seriously and stands up for one's self. And remember, this is not selfishness, where you think, care and are concerned only with your own self interests, regardless of who you hurt in the process. Not at all.

31   *Selfistness* still includes a care for others as you care for yourself. However, the difference between being *selfish* and being *selfist* has to do with whether you are using people for your own goals and achievements or whether you are using yourself for your own goals and achievements.

32   The *selfist* <u>uses</u> himself to achieve his goals, whereas the *selfish* <u>uses</u> others to achieve his goals. The *selfist* gets to a point where he simply must gather up all that is generated by his name and work so that he may properly organize his life; the selfist simply needs time to himself. Whereas the *selfish* gets to a point where he must deprive others of his resources in an attempt to have more. The *selfist* still empathizes and cares for others but has simply reached a point where he must now care for himself. The selfish cares only for himself.

33   For it is usually the selfishness of others that causes the *selfist* to withdraw into seclusion. You will learn that those who care little for your spiritual growth have not the capacity to truly care for you. Therefore, cling only to GOD. Give your heart to GOD only; express your deepest thoughts and emotions to GOD only. Others will only continue to hold you to their own needs and wants.

34   In fact, many spiritual teachers have failed to reach their full potential because they've spent too much time debating, arguing and trying to convince others of GOD's Love without taking some time to experience such Love for themselves. It is known by the wise that NO PERSONAL TIME or thought should be given to those who do not respect the Truth. They'll get it one day.

35   Many spiritual teachers have painfully learned that

when they have given up their spiritual lives for the comfort of others who care not for the things of the spirit, they (the teachers) end up with nothing. They do not gain the spirit, nor the friendship or resources they've forfeited their spiritual path for.

36   In the end, the spiritual teacher that has given up the pursuit of perfection for family and friends finds that such family and friends never really cared for the teacher to begin with; they were only looking to secure their own needs and insecurities at the time.

37   In the end when you are left unfulfilled and ultimately unhappy in your older years, you will find your own family and friends apologizing to you, saying that *you should have stayed on your path* and not have listened to them because they were only *thinking of themselves at the time*. In the present moment while the argument, debate and questioning is going on, everyone seems right.

38   Everyone is a master spiritual teacher expounding upon THEIR wisdoms and truths when they are arguing for THEIR interests. However, in the end it is you who suffers for not having the courage to follow your own heart and vision. Be strong.

39   The questions for you are: *How serious are you about GOD? How serious are you about the development of YOUR spiritual character?* Many millions of people are familiar with the World's spiritual teachings, but fail to actually practice them when the path of life turns turbulent. Many people desire to live in paradise, in peace, love, unity and joy, but in actuality they really don't believe such states are possible for them. For them, these states of awareness are only words, and this is what makes life difficult for them.

40   They say "I believe in GOD" until they experience the death of a loved one. They thank GOD for their good fortune, but then forget about GOD when they cannot

seem to achieve what they want for themselves. They read spiritual texts of all sorts, only to pick out the parts that they are comfortable living with. All of this makes life hard for them, and if you continue to align yourself with such people you will NOT experience all that the true and living GOD has in store for YOU.

[41]   If you believe in GOD, then BELIEVE IN GOD! If you believe in a spirit realm then don't cry at funerals. If you believe in universal order and "what goes around comes around" then don't be disappointed when things don't go your way, or when others suffer because of their own thinking and actions. Make the decision to finally take your spiritual life seriously. BELIEVE IN YOUR SELF!

[42]   As you grow spiritually, stressful decisions and/or life events will all be part of your growth and maturity. Stay focused! Even if you fall at times and revert back to your old self and feelings, simply get back up and re-align yourself to the desire in your own heart for self-improvement. For there is no final judgment for the one who is truly seeking perfection. Such a seeking is the true character of a spiritually alive Hiphoppa.

[43]   However, the worst thing that you can do is ignore the Truth when it is in your face. Many people suffer today because when real Truth was in their presence they debated it, they disrespected it, they ignored it. You cannot afford to make such mistakes. Do not criticize or judge anyone too harshly, and do not run from challenging situations. Give a divine performance in all areas of life.

[44]   For it is truly wonderful to be alone in the desert, mountains and/or forests at peace practicing one's disciplines. But the true test of your discipline is to be in the stressful, depressed and/or lustful influences of the *inner city* and still maintain your discipline, principles and peace. Such is truly a divine performance.

45   However, at the beginning stages of one's spiritual development it is almost impossible to be around those who care little for spiritual reality. In fact, it is at the very beginning and at the very end of your spiritual training that you will find it most difficult to associate with others.

46   For when your character is one of righteousness others, suffering from guilt, will feel uncomfortable around you. When you are succeeding because of your principles others without success will become jealous and bitter toward you. For it is the most difficult thing to endure, having your own family and friends bitter and jealous because of your success.

47   If you choose to remain within the company of such people, you will find yourself in a very strange situation where you are constantly compromising yourself for others; always putting your happiness aside for others, always turning your *light* down so that others can feel comfortable and secure.

48   In such an unfair situation you will often have to turn *your* light down for the sake of others. You will have to alter your true personality so that others may feel comfortable around you. All of this is destructive to the development of your true SELF! Yes, it is the selfless life that eases the pain of other people's immaturity, but the attuned Hiphoppa does not live in denial. You have the right to preserve yourself and your inner joy. Don't let people take advantage of your God-nature. God is to be understood, not used.

49   Please remember, those who do not walk your path cannot experience your reality. You can share your reality with them but in the end they will betray you; they have no choice. It is not that they actually want to betray you; it is more the fact that they are simply acting from their level of awareness, from their insecurities, from their character which in many ways is contrary to yours.

50   Therefore, it is important that you develop a habit of non-attachment. This life requires that you remain independent and self-sufficient. Not in a non-trusting or in an *"I'm better than everyone else"* attitude, but very strategically and with care for all who surround you, remain independent and self-sufficient in all dealings. Maintain your own space; this is the creation of your Temple of Hiphop.

51   Your heart is full of love, yet you are surrounded by jealousy and bitterness. You actually care about people, yet very few actually care about you. At some point you must get to your place of peace. At some point you are going to have to build your sacred space; your temple. Every man and woman of God must have a place outside of the World, family and friends in which they can go to receive rest, rejuvenation and instruction.

52   At some point you are going to have to STAND UP for your SELF! Now may be the time to truly and unapologetically LOVE YOUR SELF! If no one around you is willing to truly love you, care for you and make you happy as you are doing for them, then it is of extreme importance that you take responsibility for your Self and love, care for, and make your Self happy—such is truly your only real purpose in life.

53   You cannot allow your loving heart to lead you down a sucker's path. You cannot allow your humility to keep you in a subservient position in your own life, in your own house and with your own family and friends.

54   You cannot keep running around putting out everyone else's fires, neglecting your own burning house! You cannot continue to compromise yourself and expect to be fulfilled in your life. You cannot continue to love those who do not or cannot love you back. These events will destroy you. GET OUT NOW!

[55] Be the higher, wiser, stronger YOU at all costs and may your performances always draw the applause of GOD. There it is!

THE FOURTH OVERSTANDING
THE H-LAW

[1]   The H-LAW is an acronym for Health, Love, Awareness and Wealth. This code of conduct, the H-LAW, governs and protects the quality of the Hiphop lifestyle. This is what Hip Hop actually produces for the Hiphoppa.

[2]   Hiphoppas who are true to Hiphop as a strategy toward self-improvement and empowerment comply with this advice and seek not to transgress it. The H-LAW is actually the divine condition (or nature) of the true Hiphoppa.

[3]   The natural condition (or nature) of other cultures produces for them the laws that govern the development of those cultures. All cultures are not the same, and therefore are not governed by the same laws of development as their neighbors may be. Every thought and act of the attuned Hiphoppa can be checked against the H-LAW. For this law/condition is one of the first foundations needed to understand an attuned Hip Hop lifestyle.

[4]   The H-LAW is sometimes called *Hiphop's laws* because, in addition to being a time-tested set of virtues to observe, it is the actual life guide used by Temple Members to achieve and maintain personal peace and lasting prosperity. The H-LAW can also be contemplated as <u>H</u>iphop's <u>L</u>essons <u>A</u>nd <u>W</u>isdom.

[5]   However, the H-LAW is not to be observed as four individual codes of conduct. Instead, the H-LAW is to be observed as one collective behavior toward peace and sustained prosperity. Health, Love, Awareness and Wealth

are all principles that work together toward one's total well-being and joy. This is what Hiphop is all about; Hiphop is all about producing health, love, awareness, and wealth for Hiphoppas. But remember, the gifts of the spirit are reserved for those who live in spirit. Many people desire the gifts of supernatural health, everlasting love, expanded awareness and abundant wealth, but fail to live the life that causes such conditions.

6   When the H-LAW is one's regular habit the traps and obstacles of urban life lessen dramatically. Commit to this lifestyle and try not to contradict it! Stay committed to the perfection of your Self, but engage the H-LAW cautiously and gradually. This is real! We can send our minds and bodies into shock when we suddenly change the habits that we have engaged in for so long.

7   Therefore, gradually adopt the lifestyle that is prescribed here. Do not try to swallow everything at once. However, when you have adopted it, do not send your mind and body into shock by contradicting your principles. Perfect your Health! Perfect your Love! Perfect your Awareness! Perfect your Wealth! But do it gradually. Do not say; *Ain't nobody perfect.* Say instead; *I am not perfect yet!* Or; *I am being perfected.*

8   Get in the habit of visiting and then living the reality of your Higher Self. Reach for a habitual lifestyle that includes no intoxicants, no excessive eating, control of sexual desires, a vegetarian and health-conscious diet, cleanliness, the practice of your chosen skill, the study of important facts and updated knowledge, prayer, visualization, exercise and rest.

9   These repeated activities lead to personal peace and power while the opposite leads to personal stress and worry. Rise up! Arise to your Higher Self! YOU ARE A GOD FORCE.

10   The Truth is that being attracted to the spirit realm only means that you belong there. Other people belong other places, but you are attracted to the things of the spirit because that is who you are. Your very being is divine and is moving toward its ultimate fulfillment. The question is, will you be ready when you become your Higher Self?

11   The Hiphop spiritual life is not so much about adding to one's self or seeking a new knowledge of some sort. Spiritually living Hip Hop seems to be about preparing for the inevitable coming of your Higher Self into physical manifestation. Instead of adding to one's self, Hip Hop's spiritual path is all about subtracting useless ideas and outdated education from the memory of one's soul.

12   Most people make the mistake of thinking that the spiritual life is to be attained after a rigorous practice of self-restraint and prayer. This is not altogether true. Yes, self-restraint and prayer are critical to one's spiritual development, but we've learned now that once you have committed even one time to the actualization of your Higher Self it is inevitable that such a *Self* will materialize at some point in your life.

13   The issue is not whether you will attain a higher, deeper level of spiritual awareness, the issue is will you be prepared when your higher, deeper level of spiritual awareness arrives? Will you be still doing the same immature things you've been doing when your Higher Self arrives? Such contradictions are indeed dangerous and even embarrassing.

14   The language you spoke as a child you can no longer speak as an adult, and the language you spoke as an adult you can no longer speak as a teacha. Right now you are pregnant with your Higher Self. However, the question is, will you be prepared when such a Self is born?

15   Much of the H-LAW's practice has to do with first

strengthening one's will to even achieve such a condition. We are talking here about health, love, awareness and wealth, and to achieve any one of these conditions the *will* of the Hiphoppa will have to be strong. For without willpower nothing that the mind wants to do will ever get done.

16   Know this. It is the *will* of the Hiphoppa that directs that Hiphoppa's electro-magnetic energy. It is the *will* of the Hiphoppa that causes that Hiphoppa's Hip Hop life to begin. Hip Hop is *willed* into existence. Hip Hop is deliberately produced, it is *willed* into existence by God. And this is what every attuned Hiphoppa must know; God *wills* things into existence.

17   God's Work is God's *Will*. Here, we observe that spiritual strength is found in one's mastery of one's *will*. It is the *will* that resists temptation. It is the *will* that seeks GOD. It is the *will* that pushes you and urges you onward toward your completion. It is the *will* that achieves goals and manifests visions. All of these are possible with a strong *will*, and strength of *will* is produced by uniting your will with the *Will* of God.

18   *Will* is spiritual energy, and it requires spiritual management. *Will*-power begins as an attitude. "I will" is forward movement, but "I won't" is also forward movement. The first, "I will," affirms the strength to proceed into a new experience. The second, "I won't," affirms the strength to remain in the same condition. Neither is good or bad, but one ("I will") moves you forward to achieve, while the other ("I won't") moves you forward as you are.

19   "I won't" is just as powerful a statement as "I will" because "I won't" is really "I will not," and whether you affirm "I will" or "I will not" you are still *willing*. You either *will* move or you *will* not move, but both require *will*-power to achieve. To do nothing requires *will*-power, and to do something requires *will*-power.

20   Know this. A spiritual man without a strong *will* is like a beautiful car without a steering wheel. *Will*-power is your inner-energy emanating from your inner-G; your inner-guidance, your inner God, *the Love*.

21   Everyone is moving forward. However, the question is, are you moving in the right direction? Some people are moving forward but away from their purpose. Others are moving forward toward disaster and hard times. However, the direction of your Hip Hop life is determined by the power and intensity of your *will*.

22   The ability to fast, to resist temptation, to study, to exercise, even to practice B.E.G.D.B.F.L.K.E. all has to do with *will*-power and your level of *will*-power. The H-LAW strengthens the *will* of the Hiphoppa because it takes a higher level of *will*-power to create the habitual life prescribed here.

23   Know this. Hip Hop's spiritual lifestyle must be *willed* into existence because technically we are the first of our holy nation. And those Hiphoppas that are to come after us, future Hiphoppas, will have to follow the same technique in their (your) time because even then they (you) shall be the first in their (your) environment to seriously commit to such a practice.

24   Commit to the H-LAW and then teach it to others. Many people do not even have a point of reference as to where they should begin the correction and further development of themselves. Help them! Help them with these instructions; you may actually save someone from a life of hardship, frustration and pain. Blessed are those who achieve and sustain their Higher Selves through the practice of the H-LAW.

HEALTH:

[1]   Health is a state of being at peace in one's mind and body. It is the state of being well or whole. For Hiphoppas, health is the state of total physical, mental, social and spiritual well-being.

[2]   A healthy Hiphoppa has a positive attitude about life itself and is at peace with the state of his physical body as well as his mind. A healthy Hiphoppa, even when sick, is undefeated! In fact, being healthy does not mean freedom from sickness; it means continuous healing.

[3]   For we are all healing everyday. Right now as you read or hear this instrument you are healing. Your body and mind are all regenerating themselves and dissolving potential sicknesses right now at this very moment! The question is; what are YOU doing to assist in such a process?

[4]   The body is in need of life-giving, nutritious foods, physical exercise and rest. The mind is in need of stimulating ideas, purpose and knowledge; especially knowledge about itself. The Spirit is in need of peace, love, unity and joy. Together they are all in need of a stable and nurturing environment. For Hiphoppas, this is a healthy lifestyle.

[5]   Health is one of the only true forms of material wealth a Hiphoppa has. Therefore, throughout our lifetime we must seek to spend our health (wealth) wisely. Health is also about overcoming sickness. Not that you will never be sick, but how fast do you overcome and/or recover from sickness? Even prevent sickness? All of this points to good health.

[6]   However, we must not wait until we are sick to try to be healthy. Instead, when we are healthy we should try to be even healthier. Isn't it funny how when we are sick and we wish to recover, we eat all the right things and get plenty of rest? Then when we fully recover because of the healthy

foods, drugs and rest we have taken, we go right back to the very foods, drugs and nonstop activities that got us sick in the first place. We must reverse this.

7   Be wise about your health. Prevention is the key! Don't use the hospital to patch yourself up after you've become sick. Use the hospital and the expertise it provides to prevent sickness and physical harm to yourself. Before you become a diabetic you should eat as if you are recovering from diabetes now. Before you are diagnosed with cancer you should eat, think and live as if you are trying to overcome cancer now!

8   If you know that certain foods, drugs and even rest periods are responsible for the recovery of your health when you are sick, then why not make these certain foods, drugs and rest periods a regular habit in your daily life before you get sick? Why not eat healthy now and rest as often as you can so that you may dramatically decrease your chances of being sick at all? This is what it means to be conscious, or *aware*.

9   Isn't it funny, even ironic, how you can never find time to rest and care for yourself until you get sick? As long as you can move around you will. You will work, work, work, work, work and even work some more with no time toward the upkeep of yourself until you get seriously ill. You can never find time to rest or read, or commune with GOD, or listen to soothing, relaxing, healing music until you are confined to a bed, sick and in pain. We must reverse this.

10   Why must your God slap you down in sickness for you to focus upon your own well-being today? Is this not immature on your part? Shouldn't you be voluntarily seeking and planning your own well-being through moments of rest, right thinking, right eating and exercise? Or is this the true purpose for sickness, to get you to focus upon those

things that truly matter?

11   Isn't it equally ironic how your friends, family and even employers will deny you time to yourself unless you are sick and in pain? It seems that only when you are sick can your so-called friends and family, as well as your bosses, treat you the way that they are supposed to in order to maintain your good health. When you were up and about, healthy and working, it was actually them and their situations that made you sick!

12   When you are sick and in pain, it seems to be at that time that you focus upon all that you should have done to remain healthy. All of your goals and dreams seem very important when you are sick. Nothing going on in the World seems to be of much importance when you are sick and focused upon your recovery. Grow up, Hiphoppa! Prevention is the key to good health.

13   Achieve your goals now while you are in good health. Seek your God now while you are in good health! Eat right, think right, and live right while you are in good health. Do not squander the riches of your good health on lust, drugs, overeating, partying, anger, worry and/or depression. Respect your Self! Do not neglect your Self! Every day that you are healthy is a day to rejoice! Every healthy moment that you experience is an opportunity to achieve your life purpose. Cherish and make wise use of your healthy days.

14   Without good health all Worldly goals will be difficult to achieve. Joy is an effect of good health. Peace is an effect of good health. Every act or thought should be checked against one's status of good health. For in the World there is nothing more important to preserve than one's good health. If you are healthy there is no need to ever really be depressed. Health is happiness. Be happy today. Do not wait until you are sick to then realize this Truth.

15   Good physical health can be sustained with

discipline (self-control), while sickness almost always begins with temptation (spiritual weakness). Not that you will never be sick in life, but discipline (self-control) minimizes your chances of attracting certain illnesses that could have otherwise been avoided.

16   To ensure good health the attuned Hiphoppa must first adopt a habit of responsible thinking and eating. In this *Overstanding* the Temple of Hiphop offers a standard strategy toward responsible thinking and eating and good overall health. However, the attuned Hiphoppa must discover, study and know the make-up of his own mind and physical body in order to reach a maximum level of personal health. Study yourself.

17   The attuned Hiphoppa must know what foods, thoughts and environments he is allergic to and which enhance his well-being.

18   The attuned Hiphoppa must know or begin to pay more attention to the foods, thoughts and environments that settle the body, mind and Spirit. What is healthy to some can easily cause sickness in others. One man's poison is another man's cure. *Know thy Self.*

19   Even if you are sick today do not allow such sickness to overcome your ability to cure yourself. All sickness is curable. Listen to your own inner-voice and be guided. Do not be led by the negative or positive reports of doctors and nurses. They have been baffled over and over again by the human body's own miraculous healing abilities. Go wherever you must go and do whatever you must do to achieve maximum health. Listen and be guided. *Know thy Self!*

20   In addition to knowing the deeper essence of your *Self,* it is just as important to consciously take care of your *Self.* Neglect is the number one cause of fatal illnesses. Do not neglect your Self! Respect your Self! Check your status

of health regularly. Not just by getting a physical check-up, but by seriously examining what works for the sustainment of your well-being and what simply does not.

[21]   Others may be able to indulge in fast foods, smoking, drinking, etc., but because of the life path that you have chosen such simple pleasures may indeed be toxic to you. Others may vomit at the very smell of bitter herbs and raw vegetables. However, because of the life path that you have chosen such foods may be exactly what you need to survive. Do not force your way upon anyone, and equally allow no one to force their way upon you. *Know thy Self!*

[22]   On the subject of good physical health there is no *one strategy fits all* recipe. And those who refuse to modify and/or change their destructive thinking habits will have little success with maintaining good physical health even if they change their diet. Sickness is almost always caused by self-neglect and/or destructive thinking habits. However, there are some general principles to achieving good physical health that can get anyone started toward realizing the H-LAW. They are as follows:

[23]   **First Principle.** First the attuned Hiphoppa must come to the realization that the term *food* is a misleading title. Most people believe the term *food* means anything that you can eat. This is not true. Food is any substance that provides nutrition or maintains life. Ideas are also food. In fact, it is usually the consumption of the food *idea* that leads us to the physical eating of a specific food item. One should first avoid eating bad *food* ideas.

[24]   The body is nourished by life-sustaining foods while the mind is nourished by life-sustaining ideas. The Spirit is nourished by love while society is nourished by order. If any one of these *foods* (proteins, water, carbohydrates, vitamins, minerals, productive ideas, love, purpose, peace, order, etc.) is missing from one's regular diet, sickness (spiritual

disharmony/weakness) is bound to manifest.

25   *Food* is a misleading term because everything one eats does not maintain the vitality of one's life. The attuned Hiphoppa must find life-giving food and eat it. Everything edible is not food. Every new idea is not nourishing. Every environment does not enhance your well-being. *Know thy Self!*

26   Actually, the term *food* should be thought of as either energy/vibrations or as chemicals. For the stomach knows not what is warm, cold, hot, or freezing and the mind eats both love and hate.

27   The small and large intestines know not sour or sweet, salty or bitter. All foods are read by the internal organs as chemicals. It is mostly the tongue that determines what is sweet, sour, salty, bitter, hot, cold, warm, or freezing. But these are sensations that mostly happen in the mouth, whereas such sweet, salty, and bitter, tastes can produce some very harmful effects upon other areas of the body once leaving the mouth.

28   Likewise, all ideas are eaten by the mind as vibrations. Both harmonious and dis-harmonious ideas are eaten and digested by the mind, which in turn manifests the essence and intention of such ideas in the life of the (eater) thinker. The act of reflection is the mind's digestive process. The more you think about something the realer it becomes. Such an idea is digested in the mind as good, evil, happy, or sad based upon the experiences of one's life and what set of values one has chosen to live by.

29   The attuned Hiphoppa must begin to eat not just for the tongue but for the total well-being of the body and mind. For sickness is almost always an indication that one is out of harmony with one's true being. However, on the subject of food when one's mind is fresh and clean one will seek and eat foods that are fresh and clean.

[30] Most people judge how they are going to eat and think based upon the reactions of the tongue and/or the emotions. These acts are immature. Taste has little to do with health and likewise, basing one's expanded awareness on if it feels good or not prevents the true Hiphoppa from gaining wisdom.

[31] For it is when we are challenged and threatened that we learn of our strengths and weaknesses, and we become wise. However, most people simply don't want to go through pain, suffering and/or hard times to become wise; yet most people desire to be wise.

[32] Likewise, few people voluntarily invite the bitter and sour tastes of life. But everyone desires to be prosperous and strong. Sure, there are some stimulating benefits to good tasting foods, as well as emotionally stimulating ideas, but taste and soothing emotional ideas alone cannot compare to the benefits of simply eating and thinking to productively live and develop.

[33] Most people despise rain, for when it is raining and/or snowing everyone appears to be inconvenienced. However, it is during these seasons that the Earth is preparing to bring forth its harvest. No rain, no harvest!

[34] Hiphoppas must begin to get accustomed to the delight of bitter, raw, sour and/or room-temperature foods just as we would delight in sweet, cooked, salty, hot and/or cold foods. Hiphoppas must get use to the rainy and stormy seasons of life and use those difficult times as moments to spiritually learn, grow and seek opportunity. Such habits create wisdom.

[35] In our time there is no way around this discipline. Just as rainy days are bound to happen in one's life so that the harvest can come later, all foods (bitter or sweet) are chemicals and all food combinations (causes) are like mixing chemicals in the laboratory of your

physical body (manifesting an effect).

36   When we feel sick because of what we have eaten, it is because we have violated the delicate balance of our physical bodies by disregarding the very real reality of what nurtures the body, mind and/or even the Spirit. In reality, when we disregard Truth we suffer. However, all suffering is temporary. In fact, the attuned Hiphoppa has realized that suffering is actually a purifier. It is a director. It is a common creator of wisdom. Suffer once or twice, but learn your lesson!

37   It is with wisdom (and usually in hindsight) that people see how their hardest and most difficult times in life were actually the times that they grew up and realized more Truth. It is for these reasons that wise people are scarce and hard to come by. It is because no one chooses to suffer so that they may become wise.

38   Likewise, few people are willing to eat the bitter and sour foods of the Earth even if such foods are healthier for them than the sweeter and tastier foods they are accustomed to. Yet when they become ill, they seem to find the discipline to eat the necessary foods required for healing. But again, why must we wait until we are suffering to simply eat right, rest and exercise? It is obvious that if we always eat as if we are recovering from illness, we shall never be sick.

39   Know this. To spiritually grow we must get accustomed to (and even invite at times) the suffering, failures and disappointments of life, for they are not actually setbacks, they are the way in which many human beings learn. Such suffering is usually caused by not taking your *Self* seriously.

40   If you have declared your spiritual identity, then you must seriously live it out or you shall physically deteriorate. Things that others can do freely and effortlessly in the physical World, you will not be able to do. However, the

things that you can do freely and effortlessly in the physical World as well as in the spiritual realm, others will not be able to do. *Know thy Self!* Love thy Self! And most of all, respect thy Self. Don't apologize for your blessing, don't hide your Self; reveal your Self!

41   One of the most difficult things for any seeker of Truth to achieve is to simply take his or her spiritual *Self* seriously. Sometimes it is just too much to believe that you are actually the one chosen by GOD to fulfill the purpose of the universe. What an honor, and what a burden! However, if you continue to doubt, fear and/or fail to put aside old habits and pleasures in exchange for the manifestation of your true life purpose, then you shall truly suffer and deteriorate, achieving nothing in the end. Grow up!

42   GOD has but one purpose for you, and if you fail to fulfill it, the universe itself has no use for you! This is where sickness and suffering begins. Through suffering the mind of the universe teaches and directs those that have a special purpose. *Know thy Self!*

43   Seeing suffering, failure and disappointment as purifiers, life-guides and wisdom builders, the Hiphoppa learns quickly what to do and what not to do in order to establish a lasting peace in one's life. Suddenly wise advice, or the privilege of learning without suffering, becomes very useful and important. Perform Listening.

44   For just as the body reads material food items as chemical compounds and digests these foods according to physics, not according to whether it tastes one way or another, the Hiphoppa has realized that all life circumstances are created for the further perfecting of one's *Self*. All circumstances (good or bad, tasty or bitter) are to be used toward one's own advancement and the advancement of others.

45   Remember, Love and forgiveness replenish while

hate and resentment deplete. If you wish to sustain the health of your body you must sustain the health of your mind. Remember, whatever the mind creates, the mind must maintain. Believe in your *Self!* Take your divine *Self* seriously! Do not neglect your *Self!*

46   **Second Principle.** Foods are moods. All foods are drugs. Food can stimulate certain physical and mental activities as well as hinder the same. Ideas are the same. Ideas motivated by hate, worry, and fear have real chemical reactions upon the physical body. Love, faith and knowledge have their physical effects as well.

47   The attuned Hiphoppa must begin to break away from the addictions of poisonous edible items, some of which are: caffeine, worry, alcohol, anger, sugar, hate, guilt and salt. These drugs/moods are almost as addictive as heroin, revenge, cocaine, anxiety, stress and morphine. In some instances, sugar, salt, guilt, hate, caffeine, selfishness and alcohol are even harder to resist and/or release one's self from simply because of the World's acceptance of these drugs/moods.

48   Hiphoppas must begin to train themselves to accept and eat foods/ideas that are free from these drugs/ moods. In our time there is no way around this discipline. Slowly but surely the Hiphoppa must lessen his intake of all drugs/moods until it is clearly a choice to ingest them and not an addiction.

49   **Third Principle.** The Temple of Hip Hop advises all members to lessen their intake and eventually abstain from the eating of animals and animal products. This includes milk, cheese, butter, lard, eggs and other animal products.

50   There is simply too much evidence that points to the destructive results of continuously eating animals and their products. If at all possible, try to add more wheat,

barley, tomatoes, beans, peas, strawberries and garlic to your diet. Try to eat more *organic* green vegetables that are free from pesticides and other harmful chemicals, and drink an abundance of distilled water if available.

51   Although we recognize that all of nature is eating itself and even though we do not criticize, condemn, nor judge those that are carnivorous, it is our conscious respect for life and the suffering of all life-forms that concerns us most.

52   The philosophy of our temple on this matter is that no living creature should be subjected to serve another against its free will. With the discovery of alternative food sources, one day Hiphoppas will not have to participate in the destruction of other life-forms just to eat. One day we shall be able to feed ourselves without the use of plant and/ or animal body parts.

53   We regard all life as part of the *Great Event*. We (Hiphoppas) are not superior to any living creature. All life is participating in the same *Great Event* and therefore belongs to the same common family. We all have a right and a purpose to be here. We anticipate the day when we are able to communicate with other life-forms and not just eat them or have them eat us to live! The answers to many of our human challenges are found in those life-forms that we continuously kill and eat.

54   Although in our time it may be difficult or seemingly impossible for even attuned Hiphoppas to discontinue the consumption of other life-forms it is clearly a goal that all attuned Hiphoppas are required to consider and possibly achieve. Every time we sit down to eat, let us also thank the Spirit of the life-forms that we are eating as well as those that have paid for and prepared the meal. Simone G. Parker provides us with a meal prayer. Let us affirm...

Thank you GOD, for you have once again showered us with an abundance of food. Let our mouths enjoy the taste as our bodies receive the blessings, and the angels of digestion and nutrition guide us through this meal toward a healthy and happy outcome. There it is!

55   **Fourth Principle.** With the third principle in mind, every seven days Hiphoppas should increase their water intake. One should drink water and water-based soups and eat or drink fruits and vegetables often.

56   Medicinal teas, tonics, love, herbs, faith and certain roots are also acceptable. But if these items are already part of one's regular diet a physical fast will not be necessary.

57   Every seventh day is called a *day of abnegation*—a time when attuned Hiphoppas not only abstain from certain foods, but also abstain from certain pleasures, desires, environments, the careless spending of money and non-productive ideas and/or people. Seek silence. Quiet yourself. Not just your mouth and/or voice, but your desires and emotions, your wants and needs.

58   We must voluntarily abstain from pleasure and desire before the universe itself forces us into this position through sickness and/or accident. We must not overindulge in the pleasures of life or eventually they will lead to suffering. And in such suffering we may acquire a dislike and disinterest in such pleasures. Then how shall we be happy?

59   Be happy! And take time to make your body happy as well. Do not deny your flesh that which makes it happy. However, with all pleasures and desires use moderation so that such pleasures and desires remain pleasures and desires. Reward yourself with pleasure only after you have a firm grip upon the disciplines of your life. Pleasurable desires such as sex for example are actually healthy; an active sex

life actually prolongs your life. Use your pleasures; do not let them use you!

60   Prove to yourself that you have total control over the pleasures and passions of the flesh by not always indulging in them. Only then can you truly enjoy them. Practice *pleasure-fasting* regularly. In the beginning days of your spiritual training, every seven times that you deny yourself pleasure, you may give in to your pleasurable desires once. Perform Discipline.

61   Remember, the flesh can be controlled and subdued but it will not be denied until you are totally in Spirit and away from the happenings of the material World. To be happy, seek this balance.

62   **Fifth Principle.** The Temple of Hip Hop advises its members to walk often, visualizing one's *Self* healthy and at peace. Go outside and walk! Some might walk in the evening while others may walk in the morning. Do whatever works for you. But walk and/or run as often as you can. The idea is to get your heart pumping at about 120 beats per minute for 20 minutes, three times a week. While walking, breathe through your nostrils, visualizing a healthy body, mind and Spirit.

63   Although it is almost forgotten today, walking is a necessary part of the philosophical life. To stimulate one's reasoning abilities as well as other faculties of the brain, one must walk. Higher consciousness and critical thinking are greatly stimulated by regular periods of walking. Try to remember that it is not just air that we breathe. We are also inhaling and exhaling consciousness. Mastery of one's own breathing is another key to good health. Therefore, do not become addicted to sitting and/or allowing your mind to continuously wonder. Be active! Walk and run as often as you can. Breathe! And study the benefits of certain breathing techniques.

[64]   **Sixth Principle.** The Temple of Hip Hop advises its members to stop eating solid foods at least two hours before sleeping. Attuned Hiphoppas should wake up to the daily diet of prayer as food then water or tea, then fruit, then soup and then solid food. Such a process can also be reversed as one prepares for sleep.

[65]   Hiphoppas are advised to eat little meals throughout the day, as opposed to several big meals at certain times of the day, and with alcohol to use moderation. One shot of whiskey, or four glasses of beer, or a half bottle of wine three times a week is moderate.

[66]   **Seventh Principle.** Attuned Hiphoppas are prohibited from consuming food/drugs to which there is no purpose. The Temple of Hiphop recognizes the medicinal uses of all food/drugs but advises its members against using, abusing or misusing any food/drug just because it might be considered *cool* or even popular to do so. With all foods and drugs be responsible, follow the given directions and use them in moderation.

[67]   If a Hiphoppa consumes a food/drug for the purpose of relaxation, that Hiphoppa should also find out what is stressing, aggravating or agitating her well-being. The Hiphoppa should seek the total elimination of the stress, etc., and avoid the habitual consumption of the food/drug. Seek freedom.

[68]   Although it is easier said than done, Hiphoppas must practice controlling their emotions. Do not allow yourself to become upset to the point of openly expressing an angry or depressed response. Practice making awareness your habit, peace your habit, love your habit; not drugs or foods.

[69]   If a Hiphoppa consumes a food/drug for the purpose of relieving depression, the Hiphoppa should seek to find out why she is depressed. Hiphoppas are encouraged

to take control of themselves! This does not always mean self-restraint. Here, control of one's self means that the Hiphoppa has made a choice not to become over-worried, over-saddened, or even over-angered. Ultimately, YOU are in control of YOU!

70   Acknowledging only GOD as real and valuable, the attuned Hiphoppa lives life fearlessly! For every challenge (or life circumstance) is a test to make the Hiphoppa a stronger, wiser and better person.

71   The Hiphoppa should finally realize that she is in control of all emotions, moods, desires and feelings experienced in the mind, body and Spirit. While foods and drugs may offer temporary relief, the Hiphoppa should seek the real cause of such discomfort and heal it. Remember, what is <u>true</u> may not necessarily be the <u>Truth</u>. Seek freedom.

72   Hiphoppas should never assume that food/drugs are the cure for sickness or discomfort. The cure is usually found in the balancing or fine-tuning of one's life.

73   The questions one must ask are: *Where am I out of balance? Why am I not satisfied? What am I afraid of? What am I worried about?* Sometimes the body can be relieved or temporarily restored, even strengthened with the correct use of a certain food/drug. However, food/drugs should not be a substitute for simply eliminating the bad habit, situation or inadequacy that has caused the imbalance in one's life.

74   When under the influence of a medicinal food/drug the Hiphoppa should use that time of relief to seek, learn from and ultimately eliminate the real problems in her life if there are any. This was (and still is) the original reason for ingesting a food/drug—it was to expand awareness, heal and/or find answers; even see one's future. It is a known fact that the origins of knowledge and many useful inventions began with the use of mind-altering drugs.

75   Although some food/drugs like marijuana seem to stimulate the Hiphoppa's artistic, intuitive and/or academic abilities, the effects are temporary. Hiphoppas are advised to ingest and offer all foods/drugs with a specific purpose in mind. However, if the Hiphoppa cannot achieve academic, intuitive, spiritual or creative greatness without the assistance of a specific food/drug, that Hiphoppa must investigate the reasons for such mental or intuitive shortcomings and use such food/drugs in moderation, ceasing her dependency upon the use of such a food/drug.

76   In no way whatsoever does the Temple of Hip Hop advise its members or the general public to engage or not engage in the legal or illegal drug trade. Our aim here is to advise our people about their health and expand the discussion on food and drug use within our communities. Drugs like marijuana are used to sustain or enhance human performance and induce a feeling of well-being and relaxation. From shamanistic knowledge to the oracles at Delphi certain natural hallucinogenic food/drugs have been part of the development of human awareness since the dawn of human awareness.

77   In fact, to speak against ALL drug use as somehow wrong or shameful is irresponsible and it impedes upon a person's Freedom of Mind. No, we don't want young children experimenting with unsafe foods and mind-altering drugs. However, adult Hiphoppas do retain the right to self-medicate. Drug use is not the problem, it is drug abuse that is the problem and that's why young people shouldn't have free access to such substances. To abuse or misuse any food/drug is indeed irresponsible and even dangerous. Drugs are to be used, not abused.

78   The deeper questions here are, what is the criteria as to what state of mind a person should be in? Is it even right to judge what kind of mind-state is good or bad

for someone other than yourself? Caffeine, Viagra, anti-depressants, alcohol, aspirin, cold and cough medicines and even medicinal teas are all drugs, or rather conventionally accepted stimulants. In the name of freedom, can anyone judge the enhancement of another person's quality of life?

[79]   Marijuana (as an example), different from aspirin, is a quality of life drug. Aspirin is more of a quantity of life drug; it may help you to live longer. However, upon closer observation the line between quantity and quality of life may be interpreted one way or the other based upon the experiences of the user. Sometimes the use of certain drugs enhances both the quality and quantity of one's life.

[80]   Still, Hiphoppas should know why they have chosen to ingest a drug. What's the point? The Temple of Hip Hop advises its members against the continuous use of ALL food/drugs especially illegal food/drugs as it may cause legal harm to the Hiphoppa. Be careful! Agencies of all sorts are trying to trap Hiphoppas with our uses of legal and illegal foods and drugs.

[81]   Take extra care especially when traveling. Think ahead. Follow all the traffic laws, even the ones that seem unfair and outdated, and wait until you are in a safe and stable place before you decide to ingest your food/drug of choice. Again, stay alert and be careful! If you are going to use drugs don't abuse drugs. Be responsible!

[82]   The Temple of Hip Hop advises its members to be extra careful when buying any food/drug in an unjust society. The safest course of action is to minimize or eliminate one's dependency upon certain legal and illegal foods and drugs altogether. In addition, practice fear, doubt, anger and food/drug fasting regularly. Prove to your *Self* regularly that you can stop. Don't make excuses! Conquer your addictions!

[83]   Know this. The best time to quit an addiction is when you get sick. The next time you are physically sick,

use that time to fully abstain from those addictions that may have helped to make you sick. Use the breakdown and recovery process of sickness to free yourself from addiction. Don't make excuses! Conquer your drug addictions! Such acts prove your spiritual strength and trust before GOD.

[84]   **Eighth Principle.** Hip Hop Kulture's undisciplined and immature experiences with alcohol, tobacco and firearms have been devastating. For these reasons, Hiphoppas are advised to limit their alcohol intake and never operate heavy machinery like motor vehicles, factory machinery, exercise machinery, guns, etc., while under the influence of an intoxicating food or drug. And again, the Temple of Hip Hop advises against the habitual consumption of any food/drug product. This includes smoking. Prove to yourself that you can stop. Stop now! Be a friend to yourself; not an enemy. Establish your freedom and independence today!

[85]   Weapons are to be kept safely and secretly in the house. Hiphoppas are not advised to carry their weapons outside of their homes unless they are teaching, participating in a weapons show or practicing, or there is an immediate danger threatening the safety of a Hiphoppa's home, family or general well-being.

[86]   All Hiphoppas have the right to defend themselves and master the use of their weapons through practice. Using one's weapons for anything other than practice and/or self-defense can eventually jeopardize one's peace of mind, freedom and good health.

[87]   **Ninth Principle.** The Temple of Hip Hop advises its members to plan for periods of rest. Attuned Hiphoppas enjoy rest and we rest often.

[88]   Different from sleep which is a state of temporary unconsciousness and a decrease of bodily movement and responsiveness to the external World; rest is the easing of mental and/or physical exertion and/or activity. We

sleep to achieve rest.

89   Know this. Freedom is found in one's ability to rest at will. Slaves cannot rest at will. Workaholics cannot rest at will. Those who place results above peace of mind cannot rest at will.

90   Rest comes as a result of completion and/or victory. Rest is the actual manifestation of peace. Rest is freedom or relief from movement. It is the opposite of working. The decision to rest is evidence of one's self-respect. Deciding to rest proves that you care about your mind and body and their abilities to perform. Rest is owed to the one who has worked.

91   True Hiphoppas are never ashamed of rest, for rest is mental and emotional tranquility. The Temple of Hip Hop advises its members to plan for eight hours of sleep per day and at least one hour of rest; even more if necessary at times.

92   Contrary to the belief that such regular amounts of sleep waste the years of one's life, attuned Hiphoppas overstand that during sleep the total body (mind and Spirit as well) repairs and rejuvenates itself.

93   During sleep the body replenishes its life-force and vital fluids. It prepares to operate at its peak when you return to it (wake up).

94   During sleep the mind is made aware through dreams, while the Spirit replenishes its life-force. Attuned Hiphoppas cherish sleep and rest, for sleep and rest are not wastes of time. They are requirements for maximum health, love, awareness and wealth.

95   Seek to sleep and rest often. By studying and then practicing the science of breathing the Hiphoppa can achieve a rejuvenating rest without sleeping. Just thirty minutes of slow and long, deep abdominal breathing through the nostrils brings one's mind and body rest. Prove

your freedom and independence by resting at will.

96 **Tenth Principle.** Personal hygiene also maintains good health. Hiphoppas are advised to wash their hands regularly and be mindful of their cleanliness and appearance.

97 Although exposures to certain strands of bacteria have been found to actually strengthen one's immune system, attuned Hiphoppas are advised to regularly disinfect and dust the rooms of their homes with antibacterial sprays and soaps, for these acts minimize the continuous accumulation of bacteria that can hinder one's maximum health.

98 Likewise, safe sex and abstinence has been a longstanding tradition amongst attuned Hiphoppas. In our time, sexually transmitted diseases and their causes cannot be immediately seen by the physical eyes.

99 Invisible sexually transmitted diseases can only be seen by the mind's eye. The physical eyes are deceived by beauty just as the physical ears are deceived by *soft* and *sexy* sound vibrations.

100 Discipline is your only friend while temptation is your only enemy. With all matters dealing with sex and personal hygiene, perform discipline and self-respect. Seek to be physically and spiritually clean and not dirty.

101 Show yourself the highest respect by committing to your own well-being. Self-control and self-respect are the best preventers of physical illness. Respect your *Self!* Do not neglect your *Self!*

102 **Eleventh Principle.** Finally, attuned Hiphoppas are advised to pay more attention to their sense of smell. The sense of smell is directly connected to one's memory. And a lot of times our actions, emotions and behaviors are influenced by certain smells even without us being conscious of those smells.

103 Each smell that we encounter triggers or creates

specific memories in the mind that directly influence our behaviors, emotions, etc. This is why it is important to burn only one fragrance of incense at a time. This is because the sense of smell is our primal way of learning and hearing Nature.

104   The sense of smell and the fragrances that it detects communicate valuable information to the mind. We don't just hear, see and talk to communicate with Nature and each other, we also smell. Fear has a smell to it. Anger has a smell to it. Sex has a smell to it. Happiness and joy, even sadness all have smells (fragrances) to them.

105   Vegetarians smell different from carnivores. Smokers emit a certain odor, as do alcoholics. Many animals can smell a storm coming, even earthquakes. Most mothers in Nature identify their children through smell and odor. People speak unconsciously about *the smell of money, the smell of trouble,* or *something smells fishy.* These metaphoric phrases actually have some reality in the realm of smell, fragrance and memory.

106   The sense of smell is a very powerful trigger for the recall of certain memories. And this is why it is always best to document your good times and moments of peace, or victory, or courage, or love to a fragrance that captures that moment. This way, you may train your emotions to respond to your set of specific fragrances. Such a practice is commonly called *aromatherapy,* and there is more to this science than what is written here.

107   The point here is for you to be conscious of what you and your environment smell like. Not just physically, but more importantly, on that sub-atomic spiritual level.

108   Try to emit a pleasant fragrance through a peacefully lived life. Peace has a smell to it as well. Let us try to smell like peace, love, unity and happiness. Let us seek to emit the fragrance of Health, Love, Awareness and Wealth to all of

Nature's beings. Such leads to good health.

109 However, having outlined now these eleven basic principles to good health, let us remember that sickness is often a time to reflect upon what is most important in life. Often good-hearted people that are in good health still get sick so that they may focus upon becoming even healthier in Spirit, mind and body. Others of the spiritual path are protected by sickness; it prevents them from engaging in other activities that might have become worse for them than the actual illness they experience.

110 Too often we will overwork or stress ourselves out, eventually causing ourselves an even greater harm than the sickness that we actually experience. Sometimes through sickness we are forced to stop our own activities and/or avoid the activities of others for our own greater good. Most minor sicknesses that are easily curable are often warnings against some life activity we are engaged in that shall eventually cause us an even greater suffering.

111 True Hiphoppas are advised to pay attention to the minor illnesses of their lives to avoid the more major illnesses that can occur through neglect. Again, respect your *Self!* Do not neglect your *Self!*

LOVE:

1 Know this. Love is the essence of one's *being*. It is a very real motivating, healing, nurturing force. It is you.

2 One's feeling of Love is the actual existence of one's non-physical being. To Love is to care, to protect, to heal and to nurture. To Love is to surrender or transfer one's being toward someone or something. Love is the essence of one's *being*—one's caring *being*.

[3] The act of loving is an act of self-enlargement; it is an act of spiritual growth. To Love is to extend one's being; to enlarge the essence of one's self to include the survival and comfort of one's self and others.

[4] When Hiphoppas express Love we are transferring the essence of our being toward the person, place, thing, or event we are *in Love* with. To be *in Love* means that you have made a conscious decision to share or transfer the essence of your being to whomever or whatever you are *in Love* with.

[5] To Love yourself is to transfer the vital animating essence of your *Self* to yourself. It is a form of Self-strength. To Love others is to consciously transfer the essence of your being to them. However, to *Love* something or someone other than your *Self* more than you *Love* your *Self* will eventually lead to your weakness.

[6] For when you Love someone it is very important that they Love you back. If you are not receiving the Love you are giving, such an unbalanced relationship will eventually lead to your suffering. In fact, most people suffer in their relationships because they usually Love people who do not truly Love them back.

[7] However, when one loves others on behalf of GOD or even loves others unconditionally because of one's own life principles, one's suffering is diminished dramatically. The attuned Hiphoppa expresses Love because such a principle is the essence of life itself, not because an individual deserves it. Love is to be lived, not given.

[8] There is no *Love at first sight*. There is only lust at first sight. Love comes with a knowing that is acquired over time. Love is committed. Love is not sex!

[9] The term *making Love* is misleading. Sex, no matter how gratifying, is not Love. To Love someone is to seriously know and care for the essence of that person. It is

an acquired familiarity with the essence of a person. Love is a oneness in being. Like Hip Hop and Rap, Love and sex are two different things.

10   Sex may be part of loving relationships, but love is not necessarily part of sexual relationships. Sex can be part of love, but Love is not part of sex. Love comes with trust. Lust does not, and sex is mostly an act of pleasure or reproduction which in and of itself is good and right.

11   However, the need for Love is a thirst of the Spirit. The need for sex is a thirst of the flesh. The decision between Love and lust is made in the mind. When people are *in Love* it means that they have decided to create a bond in being.

12   When people are *in lust* it means that they have decided to pleasure one another through a variety of physical bonds and stimulants. Again, lust is a thirst of the flesh, while Love is a thirst of the Spirit; neither is above or below the other.

13   Nevertheless, the Temple of Hip Hop teaches that lust is natural. For without lust there would be very little physical attraction. Lust can also be calming, relaxing and even rejuvenating. However, lust is a craving that must be overcome or else it will strip you of your freedom, your good health and your peace of mind. Use lust; do not allow it to use you.

14   Know this. Love holds together what lust attracts. Lust cannot hold any couple together; eventually, the decision to Love must come into play or the lust-driven couple will not remain committed to what has stimulated their physical senses in the beginning. In this example, lust is temporary attraction, while Love is a bond formed by an emotional commitment.

15   *Falling in Love* is also a misleading term. You do not actually *fall* into Love. In actuality you *stand in Love!*

For Love strengthens and rejuvenates. Love is a spiritual progression, unlike lust, which is a physical sensation. Most of the time, it is our flesh that is attracted to other flesh. In most cases if it were not for lust people would not have stayed together long enough to experience Love.

[16]   The Temple of Hiphop advises its members to practice overcoming lustful thirsts but not to discard lust as evil. It is not. Lust is natural, while Love is supernatural. However, even Love must be practiced in discipline. Loving those who hate you is self-destructive. Loving those who do not appreciate your Love is emotionally painful.

[17]   This is not to say, *love only those who love you*. More accurately, live Love and those who surround you will benefit from your Loving nature; others, because of the hardness of their own hearts, will find you incompatible with their hateful, resentful, revengeful nature and they will be compelled to get away from you.

[18]   However, like Love, lust can be dangerous without discipline. But on the other hand, lust is healthy for those who are truly in Love. Sometimes committed men and women forget to lust after one another although they may still deeply Love one another.

[19]   Know this. The flesh will not be denied. It can be trained and controlled, but it will not be denied. If trust is established in the relationship between consenting adults then lust should not be forgotten. The flesh is not evil, it is just younger and freer than the spirit on earth. Remember, the flesh belongs to the earth; it is the spirit that is the foreigner.

[20]   The Temple of Hip Hop encourages Hiphoppas to not only Love one another, but Love all of creation—be Love itself. For Love is everlasting and lust is temporary; use them both in balance toward your own good. However, we have seen now how Love replenishes the body, mind and

Spirit while hate deteriorates the body, mind and Spirit. And lust challenges the mind, body and Spirit. Seek freedom. True freedom is to be free from guilt and addiction to one's own lustful desires.

21 Remember to use lust toward your own happiness as well as the happiness of others; but do not allow lust to use you. Practice fasting from lust often, and refrain from multiple sex partners; attuned Hiphoppas are self-sufficient even with lust. However, if you do not have your lustful thirsts under control, such lustful activities shall indeed lead to your own suffering. With all of the Temple of Hip Hop's teachings...*Love is the message!*

22 But know this. Guard your heart, and while being Love give your love to those who deserve your Love; others who do not deserve your Love will receive it anyway from being in the presence of your Loving nature.

23 So, how does one experience Love? What is an act of Love? The answer begins with attention. For when we truly Love someone we give that person our full attention. We attend to that person's growth, happiness, protection and general well-being whenever we can. When you Love someone you are compelled to care for that person.

24 Love actually rides the act of attention. And you can always tell what a person truly loves by what that person is focused upon and willing to put time into. Hiphoppas must never forget this. Whatever you Love, you put time into. Whatever you Love, you care for. Whatever you Love, you protect. Whatever you love, you will nurture and develop.

25 Hiphoppas must Love themselves, Love GOD and Love their true families; this is healthy and right. We cannot put our full attention upon those who do not really Love us; this is an act of self-destruction. To Love all unconditionally sounds good when preached, but it does not actually work out to one's benefit in real life.

26   Therefore, Hiphoppas are advised to be Love. Be of a loving, nurturing, caring nature so that those who do not love you may still receive a portion of your automatic Love. This is a supernatural act.

27   On the other hand, you are natural, you are affected by your natural flesh. Do not deny this; such denial leads to suffering. Therefore, Hiphoppas are equally advised to give their unconditional Love to those who equally Love them unconditionally.

28   For us Hiphoppas, we have learned that Love is truly precious, and to give attention (Love) to those who wish to enslave us or use us has proven to be nonproductive! We have now seen for ourselves that when you Love everyone unconditionally you wind up hating everyone unconditionally, meaning that you become distrustful of people and even resentful of people because of their own unworthy conduct toward your sincere act of Love.

29   However, had you been selective with your Love and attention, you would have grown stronger in Love, because such worthy people would have returned to you the Love that you gave to them many times over. Giving your Love freely to anyone and everyone makes you a poor judge of character, which eventually leads to your own sorrow because you have now surrounded yourself with those who did not really deserve to be in your presence.

30   Such people did not receive your Love gratefully, they took your Love selfishly. Eventually you wound up confused, wondering what went wrong when all you were trying to do was "Love your neighbor" as you loved yourself. But now you've learned that everyone cannot Love you as you Love yourself because everyone is NOT you, nor has everyone experienced your life and level of Love.

31   Now you've turned old and those who truly deserved your Love did not actually get it because you were spending

so much time loving those who could care less about you. You did not Love those who really deserved your Love, you neglected them and yourself for those who squandered your Love and time. This leads to resentment and a dislike for humanity.

³² Therefore, Hiphoppas are advised to help and try to understand those who do not Love us, but nothing in this gospel says that we must Love those who hate us. Instead of hating those who hate us or have no Love for us, let us simply ignore them; give them neither Love nor Hate. Let us give them no attention and no more of our time at all. Simply leave them alone.

³³ Reserve your Love for your true family. True Love is a precious and rare jewel; like faith, Love is spiritual currency. Therefore, be selective in who you spend your Love with. You don't ever have to hate anyone, but you equally do not have to Love them either.

³⁴ For when Hiphoppas seek a permanent loving union together they vow to care, nurture, support and protect one another. For what the World calls *marriage* we call *adoption*. For when Hiphoppas seek a loving union, all parties agree to adopt each other just as foster parents adopt children.

³⁵ Each member of the union vows to care for the other, nurture the other, protect the other, advise the other, and listen to the other. For us, marriage is the adoption of our lover. It is a nurturing unit to which one finds empowerment and peace to achieve one's purpose and tackle the challenges that may come in pursuit of that purpose.

³⁶ All members of the union are independent and bring to the unit whatever skill or resource is necessary for the survival of the unit. Love is the bond, the glue, the essence of what keeps the unit together. Love is not the only thing that keeps a union together, but without Love it is difficult for any lasting union to exist.

[37] Therefore, Hiphoppas are advised to evaluate their union every five years, and live with one another at least three years before officially adopting the other. It is neither the belief nor the practice of the Temple of Hip Hop that two people should be wedded to each other for their entire lives. Evaluating one's union and true commitment to one another every five years is healthy and right.

[38] Every Certificate of Union issued by the Temple of Hip Hop expires five years from the date of its issue. In this way, Hiphoppas can evaluate their commitments to each other without legal harm. In addition, if both members of the union decide to renew their commitments to each other in five years then truly they belong together.

[39] However, if one or both members of the relationship decide not to renew their commitment at the end of five years, their Certificate of Union shall expire and the union shall be automatically dissolved.

[40] The Temple of Hip Hop advises Hiphoppas under 25 years of age to wait the first two years of their relationship before producing or adopting children. And even if two Hiphoppas produce and/or adopt children it must be clearly understood that such children are the sole responsibility of both Hiphoppas individually for life.

[41] NEVER DO WE ABANDON OUR CHILDREN! Hiphoppas are advised to Love their children. You experience Love itself when you Love and care for your children. Reserve a special Love for them. Give them your time and your attention. Hug them, play with them and be sure to teach them, advise them, protect them and most of all listen to them.

[42] One of the best ways to teach our children that they are valuable is to value them. Often we must compliment them, point out their special qualities to them, fulfill their prayers, support their legitimate dreams and aspirations, let

them know that we are interested in them above the World and our individual careers.

43   For all of this is healthy and right. To Love is to always be doing the right thing. You can never be called wrong living the habitual character of LOVE.

AWARENESS:

1   If an electrician walked into a room with a person untrained and unskilled in electronics, it is safe to say that the electrician and the unskilled individual would view the room in two different ways.

2   The electrician would walk into the room and see things that the untrained, unskilled individual would not. It's the same room but the electrician sees the room in one way and the untrained individual sees the room in another way. Neither person is wrong in their interpretation of the room; it is just that the electrician has a certain knowledge that gives her the ability to see the room in a different way, even in a more expanded way.

3   The electrician, just by glancing at the room, would habitually take special notice to the room's electrical outlets, lighting fixtures, wiring, etc. The electrician could ascertain certain things about the room that the untrained person simply could not.

4   It is not that the electrician is a better person or even more intelligent than the untrained individual, it is simply a matter of awareness. Because of a certain knowledge, the electrician has access to a different *sight*—a broader view.

5   Even deeper, we can see how the one room changes several times according to the observer's knowledge (or awareness) of that room. The electrician sees one kind

of room and the untrained individual sees another kind of room; but in reality there is only one room. The room could change again if a professional painter accompanied the untrained individual and the electrician into the same room.

6   The painter's knowledge of paint and wall textures would reveal an entirely different room to the painter than the electrician and the untrained individual might be capable of *seeing*. Because of their levels of awareness, the painter, the electrician and the untrained individual would all see the same room in three different ways, and each view of the room would be correct and true for the viewer.

7   The room would change a fourth time if the painter, the electrician and the untrained individual were then accompanied by a professional plumber. The point is that your perception of your environment is created by the amount of awareness (or knowledge) that you have. Your reality is based upon your knowledge.

8   Awareness comes to us by way of knowledge or inspiration. The more things we know and feel, the more things we can see. Any *thing* that the brain doesn't have a word for it cannot see. It sort of overlooks the object or subject. Therefore, the more words we know, the more things we can see and experience.

9   Every *thing* that our eyes sense must be pictorially identified in our minds in order for us to actually see it, or more accurately, notice it. In fact, you don't see what you have never seen. You don't notice what you don't have a previous reference for. Things are going on all around you right now but because these *things* are not in your immediate vocabulary you remain unaware of such *things* and their happenings until they are pointed out to you; you don't actually *see* them, nor do they actually affect you consciously. Know this. We see, act and feel according to our vocabulary.

In physical nature we respond to our vocabulary. Whatever is not in our vocabulary we don't notice or respond to.

10   The untrained individual entering a room with an electrician is analogous to the apprentice walking in the World with a teacha. Just as the electrician is trained to identify and restore electrical wiring and power, a teacha is trained to identify leaks, breaks and clogs in one's creative flow and life circumstances.

11   The teacha is trained to see GOD's movements and look past the projected illusions of the material World. It is not that the teacha is somehow above everyone else, it is that the teacha has committed himself to *seeing* the spiritual World more than choosing to *see* the material World. The teacha notices spiritual reality.

12   The teacha practices *seeing* his dreams in the physical World. Such a practice is commonly called *Creative Visualization* or *Spiritual Actualization*. The question is, what do you see? Or rather, what are you trained to see? What are you aware of? Are you really *conscious*?

13   Awareness is an ability of consciousness. Consciousness and being conscious are not the same things. Consciousness is generally thought of as awareness and/or sensitivity. However, consciousness is more of a field, a substance, a realm, a force that we are all immersed in. Consciousness gives us the ability to be conscious.

14   Consciousness makes us conscious, and to be conscious one must be aware of one's own thoughts, identity, surrounding environment and sensations. One must be awake to one's reality. However, the Hip Hop community has used the term *conscious* to also mean having a *conscience*—a moral sense of right and wrong.

15   Those of our community who have displayed high moral character and ethical behavior, an aura of spirituality and peace in addition to social activism and protest, have

always been called *conscious*. Artists who may Rap about social conditions or point out possible solutions to the challenges facing our community have also been called *conscious rappers,* distinct from being called *gangsta rappers* as a comparison.

16   But when being *conscious* is applied to being *aware* we must ask ourselves, what we are conscious of? What are we actually aware of? What are we awake to? For if the brain processes 400 billion bits of information per second yet we are only aware of 2000 bits of that same information, which is mostly assigned to physical reality and bodily functions, then what is our true reality?

17   For if it is our own senses that tell us what is real according to their nature, then what is reality? Our sense of touch, taste, smell, sight, and hearing gives us their interpretation of the physical World. But what exists outside of our sense perception? For if reality is only electrical signals or choices being made and interpreted by our brains through the senses, then the reality of your life is truly what you perceive it to be.

18   With more and more awareness you should be able to do and see more and more into the true nature of your reality. You are doing what is happening to you. The observer affects the observed. We only see what we want to see.

19   Therefore, if at the sub-atomic quantum level of reality the observer and the thing observed are really two aspects of the same event, it is accurate to teach that *life is what you make of it,* and that you truly *get what you expect;* that it truly is *all in your mind*—GOD willing. At the quantum level, two supposedly separate things like an observer and an atom seem to affect each other in such a way that if the observer looks at an atom it is a particle in a fixed position in space, yet if the same observer is not

looking at the atom it remains a wave in superposition in space—meaning that it is everywhere at once until we look at it again.

20   Our true being seems to exist in a unified field of infinite possibilities that we call GOD. Everything seems to be going on at the sub-atomic level at the same time in the same space until we choose one outcome by denying all others. It is perception that creates reality.

21   It seems that physical matter is both particles and waves at the same time. Meaning that there are physical as well as a non-physical existences to everything our senses can detect. Even we are physical/non-physical beings. Actually the body is the mind in particle form and the mind is the body in wave form.

22   The Truth of the *matter* is that physical reality and the observer of physical reality are two aspects of the same unified field/event. The observer affects what the observer sees. We basically see what we want and need to see.

23   This goes for our other four senses as well. We are telling physical matter through our sense perception what we want it to smell, feel, taste, sound and look like based upon what we have decided over many years shall be real for us. In essence, everyone affects the reality they see, hear, touch, smell, and taste.

24   The physical World is a potential until we choose it to be what we desire. Space is the substance/environment that helps us to see separate things; it blocks reality so that we can get specific things done. At this level of understanding, we are the universe itself focused upon who we are (it is) and where we are right now. Meditate upon this paragraph before going further.

25   As spirit/human beings, the universe is seeing what it is capable of as us! To know that you are not in the universe, but that you are the universe itself, is self-awareness. To

know that you are an idea, a possibility, a hope, a try-out in GOD's mind; this is self-awareness. To know that GOD is depending upon you to fulfill the purpose designed for you is self-awareness.

26   To create yourself is self-awareness. For when you create yourself, you know yourself. And when you know your *Self*, you know God. Not that you are GOD, but that you are GOD's. You belong to the very fabric of the spiritual realm itself.

27   Your intention is your answer to GOD's purpose for your existence. Your intention is what affects the very fabric of your space-time reality. It is not about your words so much as it is about the intention behind your words, the emotion you put into your statements, the feelings and graphic mental pictures that occur simultaneously in the mind while speaking, the moaning and groaning of one's being, these are what the universe listens and responds to.

28   Therefore, by believing in ourselves as attuned Hiphoppas with special abilities to complete our tasks in this reality, we command the fabric of life itself toward the aim of our desires. Again, everyone affects the reality they see and experience, so what do you see and experience?

29   Do you see and experience Hip Hop as an international culture of peace and prosperity? Do you even think something like this is possible? Is such a vision truly the intention of your heart, or are you really, truly, deep down inside, just looking to make a little more money and maybe a better quality of life for yourself and your family?

30   This is fine. But you are going to have to keep it real with your SELF! Maybe you just want to rap, or break, or tag, or deejay; maybe you just like to be in the presence of Hip Hop's artistic elements. All of this is fine, and no one can judge a person who is upfront with others and honest with himself.

31   But those who are compelled to do Hip Hop's preservation work must *keep it real* with themselves or life can get more difficult than it probably already is. And *keeping it real* with one's self has to do with one's awareness of one's self, one's abilities and one's destination or goal— what is your intent? YOUR REAL INTENT?

32   If you truly intend to preserve Hip Hop then Hiphop shall truly preserve you. The issue is your intentions, this is what GOD is listening to; this is what the universe is responding to. To be true to one's self is to live for and from one's true intention without compromise or excuse—this takes courage.

33   However, with this understanding, if our true intention as a group is to preserve and expand Hip Hop, then the very fabric of the universe itself will respond to our heartfelt intentions if it is safe for us. In fact, the universe gives the *intention* special abilities to actualize itself and it protects and guides such *intentions* toward actualization. Those whose intentions match the group's collective intention inherit the powers and abilities to complete the actualization of the collective intent. But remember, GOD is not mindless; GOD is thinking with you. Meditate upon this paragraph; read it again slowly.

34   For us, Hip Hop is not a product of the physical World to be bought and sold, but instead *Hiphop* is a principle in the very real cosmic order of the conscious universe. We know that Hip Hop is an event of the universe, and not a Rap music CD. This is what it means to be a *conscious Hiphoppa* or an *attuned Hiphoppa*. It means that you are aware of Hiphop's total nature as an event of the conscious universe itself.

35   As a *conscious Hiphoppa* you have the ability to go beyond yourself. In a more cultural sense, a *conscious Hiphoppa* or a Hiphoppa that is said to be *aware* is one who

feels a connection to the visions, dreams and desires of her ancestors, children and parents. The aware (or *attuned*) Hiphoppa is conscious of the fact that she/he was born into an already underway movement toward peace and justice in the World; that we owe our activist ancestors the respect of continuing their dreams within our own.

[36]   Those in the Hip Hop community who are aware of their place within their ancestors' visions and their children's historical heritage are said to be *conscious*. We are aware of our roles in the continuation of our own ancestors' struggle for freedom and justice as well as the dependency of our children upon our success. We (the conscious) do not live exclusively in our present, or past, or future; we live in all dimensions of time at once.

[37]   When we speak in the present, we are also speaking into our so-called past and into our so-called *future*. When we lift our arm and move our hand, we are lifting and moving information that has a variety of existences on a variety of different atomic and sub-atomic levels. I am aware that when I speak today in my present, my past as well as my future are listening and feeling what I am saying. My existence today is the hope and faith of yesterday as well as the heritage and foundation of tomorrow.

[38]   We (conscious Hiphoppas) are *aware* that we are the dream characters of Dr. Martin Luther King Jr.'s dream. We are the thoughts of our parents, the outcome of their intentions. Yes, we can transform ourselves into whatever we desire, but it is the conscious Hiphoppa who shows respect and acknowledges the vision of those whose intentions created him.

[39]   Such an awareness has very little to do with the content of one's artistic expression. Just because you may write and then perform a song that expresses the social ills of society doesn't mean that you are a *conscious* person.

[40]   The idea of judging a person's level of civilized conduct, spiritual awareness or aptitude for revolutionary action based upon their artistic expressions is a fairly new concept and I would say a poor judge of a person's real revolutionary, spiritual or civilized character.

[41]   A *conscious* artist is NOT necessarily a *conscious* person. And likewise, a *thug* or *gangsta* artist is NOT always on his way to prison. In fact, many true revolutionaries have actually developed from criminal-minded to spiritual-minded, inspiring others through productive life examples to do the same. In fact, in our culture wisdom is NOT achieved by living a righteous life.

[42]   Wisdom and true understanding are achieved through a series of failures, mistakes, insecurities and doubts, which one overcomes, turning such life experiences into degrees and credentials for the warning and teaching of others. A *conscious* artist is simply aware of his non-physical nature and seeks to develop it just as one would develop his physical nature. To be aware is to also be awake; it is to be alert or not asleep; it is to be conscious and not unconscious.

[43]   However, many people are stagnated in life not by being ignorant, unaware or unconscious, but by being *inconscious,* which is the inability to act upon one's own productive thoughts and plans. To be *inconscious* is to not be fully awake to the will of one's true *Self*—different from *unconscious,* which is a mental/physical condition more related to sleep or immobility. To be *inconscious* means to exist, yet be unaware of one's own existence and weak in the execution of one's own will—to be, yet not actually BE.

[44]   *Inconsciousness* can be said to be a state of self-awareness that is foreign to one's natural and true state of being. To be *inconscious* means that you are awake and alert through an awareness that is artificial to your real *Self*. To

be asleep to one's true *Self* or to rest from one's true *Self* can also be called *inconsciousness*.

45   *Inconsciousness* can be called the seat of unhappiness because it denies one the ability to actualize one's innate potentials. It handicaps the development of one's character and personality. An example of an *inconscious* human being is one who knows not his own purpose yet is stimulated to the purpose of others. To surrender to this condition of mind can be called *inconsciousness*.

46   Another example of *inconsciousness* is to feel your true purpose, character, identity and personality, yet fail to actualize them because of your own fears, insecurities, doubts or other kinds of emotional and/or mental inabilities. The emotional and/or mental state of knowing yet not doing can be called *inconscious*. Drug addiction is another form of *inconsciousness*. It is that act of consciously doing things that you consciously don't really want to do—it is like observing yourself sleepwalking through life, bumping into things along the way.

47   To be *conscious* is to know your potential nature and to fulfill it. To be *conscious* is to activate one's natural powers and talents. And in the activation of one's innate abilities one becomes aware. For to know one's *Self*, one must create one's *Self*.

48   For we have seen that some people, in spite of the traps and obstacles of the *streets*, are still able to achieve their purposes in life. Others are hindered and stagnated by the traps and obstacles of street-life. Why is this? The difference lies in what they see.

49   Everything is an opportunity, and everything is a failure. It's all in how you *see* it. Whether you allow life's circumstances to control you or whether you control life's circumstances. The issue is, is your mind controlling you, or are you controlling your mind? Are you *conscious*

or *inconscious?*

50   Ask yourself now even on an intellectual level, *Am I the slave of my own mind or am I the master of my own mind? Do I passively allow the circumstances of my own life to control me or do I control the circumstances of my own life? Am I afraid of my own life or am I living my own life?*

51   Attuned Hiphoppas practice experiencing the essence of *Spirit* beyond the fears and limitations of the body, and experience an empowerment and strength that ensures victory over the traps and obstacles of the *streets*. However, practicing the essence of spirit requires a certain single-mindedness which is the essence of spiritual awareness. But that same single-mindedness left unchecked has prevented many from growing and developing in the physical World and accepting new and valuable ideas and discoveries. Seek balance.

52   Still, it is a single-minded spiritual awareness that prevents fear and it is fear that prevents single-minded spiritual awareness. Duality in thought is what prevents spiritual awareness. In Truth, the only things that can prevent you from achieving spiritual reality are fear, doubt and disbelief.

53   Above all, it is fear that hinders the most. Fear is of the flesh. It is an instinctive craving for the protection and safety of the physical body. It is manifested by the body's will to live. However, fear is not Truth.

54   The Truth is that there is one permanent reality— The Great Oneness! The unified field! GOD! And all of life's creations and circumstances (good and/or evil) are really different manifestations of the one reality, the one power, the fully aware cosmic ocean of potentiality, the one Great Spirit! GOD!

55   When the attuned Hiphoppa realizes that all is GOD, including the Hiphoppa, this very awareness frees

the Hiphoppa from living exclusively through the fears of the flesh. When you realize that you are made from GOD's imagination, that you are a divine idea of GOD, you will live as infinitely as the Divine Mind that thought of you.

56   Know this. Peace is a decision of the Spirit. The Spirit (You) decides whether it believes in (places its focus upon) the peace of God or the fear of flesh. The flesh does not cause peace. Only the Spirit (You) makes this decision, and having to make decisions on spiritual matters as opposed to being single-minded on spiritual matters is what causes the fear, doubt and disbelief that stagnates the growth of one's spirit.

57   Problems are only problems when you focus upon certain events as problems. It all lies in your interpretation of life's events and situations. Nothing is all bad and nothing is all good. All is subject to your interpretation based upon your values.

58   What you call a *problem* might be the very opportunity you have been looking for. And what you interpret as an *opportunity* may indeed be a problem! But how can anything be a problem when every situation can be used as an opportunity? Only a limited and defeated mind interprets life's challenges exclusively as problems.

59   Therefore, use the circumstances of life to your advantage. Do not attach yourself to your limited understanding of the material World. If you have made the decision to live as a *Spirit Being* in the material World, then all of life's circumstances are to your advantage; even your so-called *problems* or disappointments. Let go! Stop trying to fix it all yourself. It's all good! It's all GOD!

60   The mind is a tool of the Spirit—*You*. You are infinite and eternal. Therefore, *You* need not fear or worry. But the flesh is finite and destructible and instinctively manifests fear and worry through the mind as survival

mechanisms for its own preservation. This is when the animal instincts of your body are controlling and leading you and your mind, as opposed to the opposite.

61   The material World is a challenge for an unaware Spirit. The Spirit does not live here, yet in ignorance it tries to adopt an existence it is not of. The unaware Spirit believes that it is separate from all forms and circumstances when it is not.

62   The Spirit that is not at peace has made a decision not to be at peace through ignorance and/or denial of itself. Fear arises out of our own denial of being one with everything. Through your own limited interpretations of life circumstances *You* have decided to create the fears and/or disappointments of your life. This happens when the unaware Spirit is *in Love* with the happenings of the physical realm as opposed to being aware of the happenings of the spiritual realm. Know this. Everything is working to your advantage right now!

63   When the unaware Spirit is *in Love* with the flesh, it transfers the essence of its being into the flesh, eventually forgetting its alternative (true) existence as a spark of the divine. It actually believes it is the physical body and thus values material reality over spiritual reality. This can be said to be a form of *inconsciousness.*

64   Such a belief arises out of continuously focusing one's conscious attention upon the past and/or the future as well as upon separate and individual things, as opposed to realizing that ALL is one and ALL is now!

65   Constantly focusing upon the past causes guilt, depression, and judgment. Likewise, constantly focusing upon the future causes over indulgence, worry and anxiety. Both cause stress. Live now! Love now! Be here; NOW! Your past is with you now! And your future is with you now! And all is one reality NOW!

66   When Hiphoppas cease submitting to the cravings, disappointments and fears of the flesh, Hiphoppas will become courageous in the face of all physical threats and unpleasant circumstances. When the attuned Hiphoppa realizes that GOD is the true force behind all people, places, things and circumstances, then that Hiphoppa approaches life as its master, not as its slave. Live now! Love now! Be now! You are creating the *future* you now, and you are actualizing the *past* you now. Your challenge is fear.

67   Practice facing the fears of the body. Some fears will be legitimate instincts to prevent harm to one's body or circumstances. Most fears are illusions and assumptions based upon either a lack of knowledge (awareness) or a chronic attachment to the happenings of the physical World and its temporary circumstances. In any event, it is fear that stagnates spiritual and cultural growth.

68   For we are not the physical body, we are the Light within it! We are literally beings of consciousness or Light. Fear prevents this awareness and likewise, this awareness prevents fear. The more we are aware of ourselves as non-material beings with the ability of *mind* to affect the physical World, the less fearful and disappointed we shall be. Realize this now and live free!

69   Stop doubting and going back and forth with your spiritual development. Eliminate the contradicting dualities in your character and simply choose to be the powerful spirit that you already are. Be spiritually single-minded. For in Spirit, what is impossible with the body is possible in the *Oneness of Mind*. For if you are to truly overcome the traps and obstacles of the physical World you must finally decide to live as a *Spirit Being,* acknowledging the very real existence of the great *Oneness* all around and within you. You are truly an event within a greater event.

70   Practice living as a *Spirit being* or as a dream character

in the material World. For when we are aware of (and practice) our *Spirit/dream* existence in the material World the results are wonderful! Take your spiritual *Self* more seriously by putting its character and activity before everything else and it shall become more and more real for you daily.

71   The object of the Hiphop spiritual life is to learn how to make one's spiritual reality the dominant activity of one's physical life—to bring spiritual reality into physical manifestation. Ask yourself, *if you are reading this instrument silently to yourself, where is the voice that is repeating the words that you are reading? Where is this voice that speaks without the use of a larynx, tongue, or mouth?*

72   Try to remember that it is not your two physical eyes that actually <u>see</u> the past or the future, yet you do <u>see</u> your past and you do <u>see</u> your future. You can close your physical eyes and still <u>see</u> your past and future. It is just a different type of sight. Ask yourself; *with what sight do I see my dreams? Where is that place? Who am I in that place? Where exactly is the inner-voice that I hear reading the words of this gospel? Is this voice in my (your) head or is it actually somewhere else?*

73   Ask yourself now, *in what dimension outside of space-time are my other non-physical senses?* The answering of these questions leads to *Spirit* awareness.

74   For this inner-voice, sight, hearing, etc., is You! You are not your mouth, your ears, your eyes, your hands, your feet, etc., you are the conscious being that uses these tools to affect and interpret the physical World. You are Light! You are the knowing of the universe concentrated into your immediate time and space. You are an address in the universe. You ARE the essence as well as the utterance of your name.

75   This is what it means to be a *conscious Hiphoppa* or an *attuned Hiphoppa*. It means that you have created

yourself! You are not a product of someone else's purpose. Through your striving to experience reality directly, you have expanded your awareness and thus your abilities in the physical World.

76   Release fear and doubt caused by your own duality of thought and be the real YOU now! Be single-minded about your spiritual nature. While others spend their time acquiring temporary material goods and pleasures, you seek to rise to the Truth, to the true nature of your being. Not just communicating and functioning in the symbolic reality of words, but experiencing the true reality of what those word-symbols represent.

77   We now know that to exist and operate in and from the Truth is the ultimate strength an attuned Hiphop activist can possess on Earth. It's all about what you are aware of. You can only do what you know. Therefore, KNOW THY SELF! Before you can manage large sums of information you must first manage your *Self*.

78   Know this. *Self*-management is spiritual, *Self*-organization is intellectual, *Self*-esteem is emotional, and *Self*-governance is political. Before you can truly learn something you must first learn your *Self* and then manage and cultivate who you have discovered. For when you are your authentic self without excuse or limitation you see with your real eye, you listen with your real ear, and you speak with your real mouth. You are awake; you are aware! Now you can learn.

79   Like the painter and the electrician walking into a room with a person untrained in electronics and painting, the spirit realm is all around us physically, people just do not see it. And they don't see it because they have not been trained to see it.

80   The spirit realm (or the kingdom of heaven) is not invisible; the issue is that you are blind. You are simply

untrained in this specific subject. It is your ignorance that makes the spirit realm invisible to you, and likewise it is your awareness that makes the spirit realm visible to you. What do YOU see?

[81]   In fact, the more ignorant we are the less we see; and the more aware we are the more we see. However, we must also remember that it is this balance between knowledge and ignorance or knowing and not knowing that forms the totality of what we perceive of ourselves and our environment. Here, the term *ignorance* is more accurately the *mysterious*. And to teach the *mysteries* is to reveal the Truth. True ignorance (motivated by fear and doubt) rejects the Truth.

[82]   However, ignorance (as the great mystery) is also a form of knowing; it is unknowing, or the unknown, which is actually a form of knowing. You know that you don't know, and the knowing that you don't know is an awareness unto itself.

[83]   Mystery is a force like knowledge; it too can transform a human being for the better. The assumption that ignorance is somehow wrong and to be avoided in and of itself is not a wholistic thought. Ignorance and mystery are to be used toward one's total awareness. As is said often, ignorance is bliss. Sometimes the best knowing is to not know at all.

[84]   Many people have achieved great things in life simply because they didn't know that they couldn't achieve them; they didn't know of the risks so they proceeded with what appeared to be courage, but in fact was ignorance. This is how Hip Hop got started.

[85]   We have observed and experienced the fact that it is mystery that prompts one to know; it is <u>not</u> knowing that prompts one <u>to</u> know. But we can also say that it is knowing that produces more knowing because it is the knowing that

you are ignorant that motivates you to become more aware.

86   Mysteries and secret knowledge help you to humbly remember all that you do not know, and how important it is to know; even if what you know is that you don't know.

87   Actually, knowing relaxes the mind, while it is mystery that motivates the mind. It is when we DO NOT know something that we seek to know of it. But should we seek to know of everything that we may become partially aware of from time to time?

88   Most people run from ignorance and toward knowledge, not realizing that some things are not to be known. The knowing of things alters one's physical condition, one's physical appearance, and the circumstances of one's physical life. All knowledge (or knowing) is not good knowledge or even useful knowledge.

89   In fact, too much information at one time can cause an overload in the mind and produce a nervous breakdown in a person. Ignorance can do the same. Not enough information at one time can also cause the nervous breakdown of a person. Of course, the issue here is balance.

90   In addition, unpleasant information can also do the same; as with doubtful information, and fearful information, as well as information that turns out not to be true, or reveals itself as false after you've set your life up around the reality that such false information provided to you.

91   We can see here that awareness is a balancing act between knowing and unknowing; awareness is unknowing and knowing at the same time. We create ourselves and our life circumstances based upon what we want to know and what we refuse to know. We are that which we accept and that which we do not accept at the same time.

92   It is your knowing and your unknowing together that creates your total awareness. Therefore, in your quest to know and to become educated, do not look down upon

ignorance. Instead, learn to live consistently within the awareness of the total YOU! Live wholistically.

93   Live without duality in thinking; be only one character. Be your Higher Self. Fix your mind upon only one character and it shall become real for you. But remember, whatever the mind creates, the mind must maintain. Doubts, fears and anxieties hinder the mind from maintaining the productive perceptions you have created for it. The same applies to the body, the spirit, and the tongue.

94   Do not allow yourself to become so overwhelmed by the World that you cause emotional confusion and uncertainty in your own my mind, body, and spirit. Such will deteriorate those things and ideas created by your mind, body and/or spirit. Remember, whatever the mind creates, the mind must maintain. Create your Self and be consistent and content with your creation. This is what it means to be aware and alive.

WEALTH:

1   Know this. True wealth is associated with prosperity and well-being, even good health. Wealth is not just money or an abundance of valuable material possessions. Wealth also deals with anything one possesses in abundance that has value in terms of exchange or use. Knowledge is wealth. Skill is wealth. Love is wealth. Any valued exchangeable thing that one has in abundance is wealth.

2   However, pertaining to money, wealth is created by one's skill mastery and knowing things that others simply do not know. Those who have mastered a useful skill that is also in public demand are often wealthy. Those who possess secret knowledge or advanced knowledge are also often

wealthy. Money is not wealth, but money can assist in your wealthiness (your well-being).

3   Many people believe that money is the cause of evil in the World and as a result they remain in poverty. As J. P. Wingate has pointed out, *Money is NOT the cause of evil in the World; it is poverty that is the cause of many of the World's evils.* Because of poverty many people do, say and believe things that they would never have done, said or believed had it not been for their state of impoverishment. It is in their attempt to escape poverty that many people (even the rich) do some very devious things.

4   Money in and of itself is a neutral social force that brings out and advances the true nature of a person; whatever that nature may be. This is why it is better to arm yourself with the habits of the Divine Performance before and while you seek riches for yourself—and be clear as to why you desire such riches.

5   Most people want to be rich and not necessarily wealthy. Most people want more money as opposed to well-being. Most people are simply afraid of being poor so they believe that being rich will prevent such a condition. Hiphoppas are advised to seek wealth over riches, but never be ashamed of acquiring money.

6   Being rich is not just about living a luxurious life; it is more about access to better living and being appreciated and accepted by talented and influential people who would otherwise ignore us. Being rich is about having the ability to help those in need—beginning with one's self. It is about relieving the suffering of the poor and assisting in the common good of the society in which one's lives.

7   Being rich is also about being respected and admired. It is also a form of protection and security, even happiness. Yes, money does buy happiness! However, money does not buy joy. Happiness is temporary, whereas joy is everlasting.

Ultimately it is joy we want, and such joy is connected to one's state of well-being.

8   Money is good. However, money without knowledge can be dangerous. Money without friends, freedom and a virtuous life will still lead to loneliness, stagnation and depression. For even if we possess huge houses, cars and cash, without love, trust and respect it is as if we had none of these material things at all!

9   What's the sense in having expensive linen sheets but too much stress and anxiety to sleep at night? Or a luxurious car but no freedom to drive it? What's the sense in even owning a bank if you must run the bank's affairs from a hospital bed because of poor health?

10   The Temple of Hip Hop encourages its members to be financially independent but not at the expense of one's health, love, awareness and true wealth. Temple Members learn to acquire their own sources of money and save it as well as invest it; we may even give it away.

11   Temple Members depend only upon themselves for their financial well-being. We are self-motivated, self-directed, self-disciplined and self-sufficient. We are not solely dependent upon anyone for our well-being.

12   And the key word here is DEPENDENT! Yes, you will need the assistance of others to acquire money—however, depending upon another for your financial stability, or giving others total control or authority over your finances and/or life decisions, almost always leads to disaster.

13   As attuned Hiphoppas, very seldom do we borrow but often we give. We are not looking to only *get paid;* we are also looking to pay others. Know this. The key to wealth is found in one's ability to usefully serve and empower others. Wealth is an attitude. In fact, wealth is the attitude that attracts riches (money). DO FOR YOUR SELF!

14   True Hiphoppas are entrepreneurs. For when one

works for one's *Self* one is truly free. But with such freedom comes responsibility. One must be honest with one's *Self*. If one has not the skill or discipline or even desire for self-employment, which includes self-control, moderation, a healthy savings and the preservation of one's source of income, one must find no shame in getting a job.

15   Some jobs are great sources of income and stability and should not be looked down upon or done haphazardly. Hiphoppas are encouraged to take pride in their jobs (whatever that job may be) knowing that the strength of one's employment, family, community and nation depends upon *a job well done*.

16   But we must also remember that jobs do not lead to freedom or wealth. It is work that leads to freedom and wealth. *Jobs* provide temporary social stability and security. *Work* is more connected to one's purpose in life. You must know your purpose, decide upon what you really want and then get up and go get what you really have the skills, education and discipline to achieve. But remember, it is ignorance that causes poverty and knowledge that causes wealth.

17   Although a great sense of personal achievement and self-esteem can be achieved through the completion of a rewarding job or task, for a Hiphoppa to be trained solely for the workforce violates the H-LAW. The Temple of Hiphop promotes the realization of one's GOD-given talents and real purpose in life—these lead to wealth.

18   For these reasons, not only does the Temple of Hip Hop promote the acquiring of jobs for those in need of a steady income, but entrepreneurships and the start-up of small businesses are encouraged even more. Hiphoppas should eventually seek to go into business for either themselves or with their families before they are robbed of the time and energy that comes with youth.

[19]   The principles of wealth (as it pertains to money) are grounded in the laws of Intention. If you really don't have a wealthy attitude or a natural expectancy for money you will not achieve the riches that you desire. Money will come, but you will never be able to hold on to it. Becoming rich is simply a matter of attitude. The first step toward millions of dollars is having a million-dollar attitude! You have to actually expect money to get money.

[20]   However, on the other hand, in our life journeys we also pick up things that we don't really need. Not just worthless items, but also people and certain activities, such as being ripped off, cheated, exploited, and the like. These experiences not only can make you angry, bitter, fearful and resentful toward others and future business possibilities, but you can also pass such negative, non-productive life experiences on to others simply out of habit and/or reflexes.

[21]   This is why it is very important to choose your close friends and business partners wisely, because not only can you receive certain unproductive experiences from your closest associates, you can also express these same unproductive experiences toward others. Be mindful not to continuously repeat the disappointing and hurtful experiences others have displayed toward you.

[22]   Through the performance of forgiveness discontinue the disappointing and hurtful experiences others have displayed toward you. Be spiritually responsible. Do not pass on the bad habits that you may have learned growing up. Treat all business dealings as a game that, whether you win or lose, you can always return to the next day—don't take it personal.

[23]   Most people become bitter and angry in business because of their own fear of failure. No one wants to lose. They despise their losses and failures because they

believe that such disappointments are final. Or those disappointments reflect badly upon their character. This could not be further from the Truth.

24   The Truth is that everyone fails. Failure is a part of life; it is a part of growing up. In fact, failure is the great teacher of the wise and the most important tool of the inventor. The quicker you learn that, the quicker you shall take advantage of your failures and cease to allow your failures to take advantage of you.

25   Going through failure and being a failure are two entirely different things. No one can be called a *failure* if they continue to try. It is only when you give up and cease to grow that you have truly failed. Imagine the amount of failure we had to endure just to write this gospel and establish our temple. No, it was not easy! But had we given up, you would not be reading such a gospel today, nor would the Temple of Hip Hop be standing as a beacon of Light for all true Hiphoppas.

26   Know this. The road to riches is paved with one failure after another, one disappointment after another, one rip-off after another. Do not be discouraged! The key to wealth is found in one's ability to manage failure and see the opportunity in disaster. Read this paragraph again and again until you fully comprehend its meaning.

27   Even in the midst of non-supportive people, mistrust, criticism, envy, greed and even your own personal failures, you MUST press on! Never give in to the immaturity that surrounds you, simply plan around it—and remember, don't take it personal. Always take the *high road*; such is the essence of business success.

28   You cannot give disorganization and expect to be organized. You cannot have a nasty attitude and expect to attract pleasant customers/consumers, business partners, investors, etc. You cannot have a poverty consciousness

and expect to attract wealth. These are called *the Laws of Attraction*. You attract to yourself exactly who you are inside.

29   Although Hiphoppas are advised to save their money, you cannot hoard your money and resources and expect to attract more money and resources. You cannot cheat people and expect not to be cheated. The Temple of Hip Hop encourages its members to always remain fair in all business transactions and competitions.

30   Likewise, if you are cheated resort to the principles of charity instead of revenge so that you do not harm yourself or pass on such actions to others. Revenge, deceit and hostility in the long run only destroy and/or hinder your ability to succeed.

31   If you wish to be successful, help someone else become successful, even your competitors. This is a divine performance. The best way to attract opportunity is through charity. Everyone needs help, even your competitors. Therefore, give of your *Self*. Advertise your superior skill openly and freely. By empowering others, you empower yourself!

32   The principles of wealth also rest in the mastery of a specific skill that is in demand. Basically, it makes no sense to devote your time to the comprehension of a skill that in years to come will not be in demand. The principles of wealth (in terms of money) rest in your ability to learn from the needs of the past, know the needs of the present and predict the needs of the future.

33   Know this. If money is your ultimate goal, you shall never achieve it. With any goal it is important to reach beyond what you want so that you are sure to pick up the specific things you want along the way.

34   By setting a higher goal than the one that you truly desire, you will achieve all mediocre goals along the way.

Money is always a mediocre goal when compared to peace of mind. Money can always be collected along the way. Never love the accumulation of money or money itself. However, if money is not important to you, you will never keep it. If you want money you must get serious about acquiring and keeping money.

35   If money is what you want, advertise the mastery of your skill. Give portions of your skill away for free. Others will be sure to pay for it once they have seen the benefit of it.

36   The Temple of Hiphop suggests seeking the personality of your God first so that all other material possessions can be picked up along the way in peace. If you are serious about acquiring money, seek God. For with God (or rather, in the character of God) you shall always have enough money.

37   However, the Temple of Hip Hop further advises its members to seek ways to live with little or no money at all. Different from living in poverty; live a simple life. Learn to live according to your means. Extravagance and excessiveness lead to stress and worry.

38   True wealth is not based upon how much one has; true wealth is based upon how much one can do without. It is not just about what one possesses, it is more about what one can let go of. For when one is content with one's self, no material loss can ever overwhelm such a person—self is the ultimate value.

39   An attuned Hiphoppa invested in herself can never really experience loss—she is self-sufficient. She is sufficient unto herself; self is enough for her. If she loses her eye, or ear, or arm, or leg, she makes use of whatever is left knowing that these things (arms, legs, ears, eyes, etc.), as valuable as they are, are still not as valuable as one's self.

40   Self-sufficiency, or rather the state of being sufficient

with only one's self is one of the truest conditions of real wealth. This is also why Hip Hop's artistic elements are so important to the life of the Hiphoppa. Beyond being money-makers, Hip Hop's artistic elements focus the Hiphoppa upon the value of one's self. These elements preserve the privilege of producing and eating from one's own hands, from one's own self-expression.

41   As is mentioned throughout this instrument, Hip Hop's artistic elements are human skills which bring value to one's own self-expression. The emcee is sufficient in his Emceein, the DJ is sufficient in her Deejayin, beat-boxers are sufficient in their Beat Boxin. The wealth and value of each Hip Hop element produces riches as well as well-being for the practicing Hiphoppa.

42   The attuned Hiphoppa is first content with herself, with her own skill and self-expression, and such contentment produces a wealthy mentality which then produces money and other valued resources. Self is the true wealth and from this true source comes riches.

43   However, being rich with an abundance of money should only be a preferred condition, not a necessity to one's condition. Yes, we want money! But even without money we are still content with ourselves.

44   Know this. Those who are unhappy with a little will be equally unhappy with a lot. And those who are happy with a little will be equally happy with a lot. Nothing satisfies the one who is not first satisfied with a little. Even deeper, nothing satisfies the one who is not first satisfied with himself.

45   Do not allow abundance and large sums of money to trap you. Be grateful for what you already have. Most of the time, it is your lack of money that is actually protecting you from the World as well as from your own ignorance.

46   While practicing Hip Hop's elements, be content

with GOD. This is important because without Hiphop's spiritual *sight* Hip Hop's elements cannot really be productively experienced or accurately taught.

47   In this state of spiritual blindness, instead of Hip Hop's elements liberating and freeing the Hiphoppa from incarceration or an oppressive workforce, Hip Hop's elements practiced through excessive want, greed, anxiousness and guilt are reduced to mere alternative work programs themselves, eventually robbing the Hiphoppa of his freedom and peace.

48   Without the *sight* that sees beyond time and forms, even sincere Hiphoppas will sell (and have sold) the mastery of their element for only a fraction of what it is really worth. And what is the true worth of one's skill mastery? Answer: peace of mind through a real and solid *victory over the streets!*

49   Not just more money, but more freedom! Not just more popularity, but more respect! Not just a sense of security, but a sense of contentment and peace! These are the effects of mastering one's spiritual skill through Hiphop's spiritual *sight*.

50   At some point you must take off the makeup, the designer clothes and the jewelry and face your God! At some point everyone has to grow up. And growing up has to do with realizing your immature ways and outgrowing them.

51   Know this. Poverty is a personal choice, and so are wealth and riches. Greed does not make one richer. It is the attitude of already being wealthy that attracts and maintains steady streams of wealth and riches. However, without Hiphop's spiritual *sight*, those who exploit Hip Hop's elements usually reduce <u>themselves</u> to marketable products.

52   Again, Hip Hop is not a product, nor is it exclusively

a performing art. Hiphop is not even a material thing. Hiphop creates products and inspires artists, ministers, politicians, comedians and professors of all styles, but Hip Hop (in and of itself) is not a material thing. It is a shared idea, a feeling, an awareness.

53   Others may still be stuck with the idea of Hip Hop being just good music. This may work if you are a *Rap fan*. But if you consider yourself to be a true Hiphoppa and you seek a lasting success living Hip Hop and performing its elements professionally, you are going to have to approach Hip Hop with more wisdom, organization and skill than all the employees, C.E.O.'s, ministers, professors and artists of the entire entertainment, academic, religious, fashion and media industries. Otherwise, you will be eaten alive by these industries and professionals. Be clear with this.

54   For these reasons the Temple of Hip Hop starts the training of its members with the comprehension of Hiphop as a collective consciousness; a unique urban attitude, an empowering identity, an international culture, a life-improvement strategy, a creative self-evident awareness, and an international cultural movement—not just music or even entertainment!

55   Such an awareness brings Light to those whose grievances are ignored and identity rejected. Such an approach to Hip Hop is the seat of political power and the birth of true freedom for us. With this new *sight*, we can begin transforming ourselves, our environment and eventually our personal circumstances.

56   For these reasons the Temple of Hip Hop encourages Hiphoppas to think beyond the normal social definitions and conditions of things. Rethink your World! Hiphop's spiritual *sight* transforms subjects and objects for the enhancement and protection of the Hiphoppa. Yes, the current financial situation in the United States is terrible for

many families and it seems like our government and many global corporations today just don't care—or do they? More importantly, can they?

57   Nations grow and societies do move forward. As we have seen many times with the rise of America's homeless population, if you cannot *keep up* you will be left behind, trampled, even eaten. Whether this is right, or just, or fair is irrelevant. The object here is survival—survival of the richest. Therefore, let us not personally complain about high prices, let us outthink, or rather rethink the whole situation we may be experiencing.

58   Remember, it is not what happens to you that is real; it is actually your interpretation of what is happening to you that is real. You decide to be happy or miserable based upon your own interpretations of life's events. Everything is perception, and perception is based upon knowledge. If your nation's prices have become too high for you it only means that that part of your nation has become smarter than you. They are using certain techniques, skills and knowledge to render you dependent upon not only their products, but also their prices for such products. But there is always another way around high prices.

59   Your task then is not to complain, but to outsmart the situation by applying some kind of skill, technique or knowledge capable of making high prices low prices for you. You simply need to either make more money, which usually requires the acquiring of more knowledge and more skill, or you need coupons, savings tags, and sale days. Either way, you can always rethink your condition. If you find yourself unable to *make ends meet* it may mean that it is time for you to invent something or engage in some new experience that clearly requires you to adopt new skills and new knowledge, or even new relationships.

60   Know this. Poverty is about applied ignorance, while

riches are about applied knowledge. If you really don't know where the money is then you cannot have it. Prices are going up because most people in the World CAN afford them! If prices are too high for you it only means that the World is passing you by. Everyone is not as poor as you are. You may be poor simply because you don't know where money is, you are not part of that money-making community. You don't speak their language, nor do you hang out in their circles. And why? Maybe because you don't believe you can.

61   Inspired by the Spirit of God, Hip Hop was about the renaming and redeveloping of a *corny*, bland and segregated society. Our ultimate transformation was of the entire American mainstream popular culture itself, and this is what saved us. We simply perceived our World differently and suddenly everything changed around us! Early Hiphoppas realized intuitively that everything was also something else. This spiritual *sight* (awareness) gave us the ability to begin transforming our surrounding subjects and objects in an effort to create new ways to survive and develop in a society that ignored and rejected our very existence.

62   The original Hiphop *sight* began with the conscious awareness that everything was also something else and that everything could be renamed and reinterpreted and thus reused or modified in its use. With this kind of awareness we were instantly transformed from insignificant and rejected to important, free and accepted. No one handed us such validations, we simply declared ourselves "fresh" and within immense poverty and injustice we were made fresh again.

63   Our new perception of reality (*sight*) would transform the very clothes on our backs, our shoes, our language, everything! For example, what was once a rag used to wipe sweat or clean dishes, or what was once an

insignificant construction worker's boot were transformed into important fashion statements worth millions of dollars and worn upon the heads and feet of many mainstream clothing models, sports personalities, artists and politicians alike, just because we (Hip Hop) gave these products a value they did not originally have.

64   Such a transformation occurred when we were inspired to give our dirty rags, worn shoes, old jackets and even outdated furniture value. By *seeing* our dirty rags, torn clothing and broken furniture as valuable we escaped poverty by reinterpreting the value of what we already had. In addition, Hip Hop brought with it new techniques, skills and knowledge. And with these new skills and techniques we outsmarted the poverty of our parents and carved out a whole new life path for ourselves.

65   Likewise, by seeing the expensive clothes, music, foods and tastes of the mainstream as *corny* (no longer cool or even necessary) we devalued the riches of the World and forced the mainstream popular culture to accept our values!

66   We simply stopped trying to participate in the 1970's and 1980's mainstream, and everyone came to us! This is what Hip Hop's political power is; it dictates what is valuable in urban areas. It defines the urban reality of the Hiphoppa for the empowerment of the Hiphoppa.

67   In fact, it was the strength of our collective Spirit rebelling against what was being force-taught to us that first introduced our Hip Hop awareness or *sight*. We simply stopped participating in our own oppression by not valuing the music, art, fashion, foods, politics, education, etc. of the 1970s mainstream.

68   This is why the continuous promotion of mainstream values like expensive cars, clothes, jewelry, houses, etc., without the balance of cultural values like faith, courage

and wisdom weakens Hip Hop's political position in the World. It makes our people devalue their own possessions and self-worth in an effort to acquire something outside of their own socio-political reach.

[69] So while we chase the temporary values of the mainstream, the mainstream exploits the everlasting values of our souls, and this causes our poverty.

[70] The true Hiphoppa values Hiphop! True Hiphoppas reject the reliability and authority of mainstream commercial resources and values as valuable. For they are truly worthless when compared to the everlasting and priceless essence of Hip Hop itself.

[71] Although the American mainstream of the 1970s and 1980s would tell us that our material possessions were worthless and that Hip Hop itself would not last but *three more years,* we rejected such opinions and appreciated the little bit that we did have.

[72] 30 years later, we discovered that the ability to change and/or improve one's situation was based upon one's ability to transform the things and ideas already available to one's self. We did not accept our condition, we changed it!

[73] It was here that we learned how Hip Hop's political power (even economic power) begins when you can appreciate and value what you already have as opposed to envying the resources and achievements of those who do not respect you.

[74] Self-empowerment begins when you can bring value to those people, places, things and events already around you or in your possession. We simply took responsibility for ourselves. We did not accept the conditions of our parents; we decided to become active participants in our own survival. We simply gave ourselves value. We began to define ourselves.

[75] Know this. Poverty begins when you envy those

things outside of your immediate reach. Wealth begins when you learn to value and make use of those things that you already have.

76   This is why early Hiphoppas would avoid *crossing over from the undaground* to the mainstream. *Crossing over* into the mainstream meant that you no longer had the ability to define yourself.

77   Through your voluntary participation in an environment that did not truly respect you, you ultimately devalued yourself. By remaining independent with the power to define ourselves and our environment we maintained our ability to compete.

78   This is the only real reason Hiphoppas were accepted into the mainstream arena. It was (and still is) because in competition what we had (Hip Hop) was a force that no one in any mainstream market could compete against. So, as the old saying goes, *if you can't beat em, join em!* And join us they did.

79   No mainstream business that depended upon urban areas to survive was able to compete with the force which Hip Hop exploded onto the national scene with. Therefore, many Hiphoppas were immediately paid large sums of cash (which was only a fraction of their true worth) before they realized the magnitude of what GOD had really blessed them with.

80   Only now have we realized that the ability to compete is the essence of power in business and politics. Indeed, integration and conformity weakened our ability to remove our oppression using our unique business and political-competition tactics. In fact, even though we were poor, we were not impoverished. With little or no money we still lived well. We may have not been rich but we were indeed wealthy. We lived wisely, not poorly.

81   Ironically, it was our lack of money and access that

protected us from the excessive and often toxic lifestyles of the rich. The idea of eating bacon, eggs, sausage, butter, cereal, milk, toast and orange juice all at once as a balanced breakfast was ignored by most low-income Hiphoppas of the 1970s and 1980s, who ate oatmeal, cream of wheat and cold cereals instead.

[82]   Certain professional exercise techniques that were later proved to be damaging to the physical body were also ignored by early Hiphoppas. Our aerobics was Breaking, Popping, Locking, walking, handball, stickball and basketball, which the mainstream would later incorporate into ITS plans for a healthy body.

[83]   Attuned Hiphoppas who could afford the steak and eggs advice dined on fish, fruits, juices and vegetables long before it was a popular health trend to do so. Because of our low incomes, we were already walking, jogging and riding bicycles long before such activities became popular health trends.

[84]   Later in life we learned that not having access to mainstream living actually saved us from certain diseases and sicknesses that were caused by the excessive lifestyle of the American mainstream of the 1970s and early 80s. We learned early that in the short term, the lifestyles of the rich and famous might have looked appealing and desirable to many, but in the long term, such lifestyles proved to heighten one's chances of disease, stress and injury.

[85]   Know this. Sometimes it is those things that you do not have as well as those places that you do not go that are actually saving and enhancing your life. As contradictory as it may sound, it was actually our low incomes that protected us. And this is not about living poorly, this is about living simply. Living according to your means, in proportion to your work.

[86]   This has always been the balance for those

communities born in urban environments: *Be in the mainstream, but not of the mainstream.* Be content with the mastery of your chosen skill and live within the means that your skill provides. This leads to peace.

87   However, those who have mastered a skill that is in demand never have to look for money or chase opportunity; they are chased by money and opportunity. The objective is not to get more money; it is to get more skill! It is to be more influential, more inspiring, and more useful; this will get you more money in the long-run.

88   Believe it or not, staying out of trouble and presenting a pleasant and *easy-to-get-along-with* attitude will also help you to attract real money-making situations and strengthen your position in business competition. Most times competition is not about defeating your opponent directly; it's about being able to endure long enough to overcome life's challenges.

89   From a spiritual perspective, most times the one to succeed in fierce business competitions is simply the one who has endured the longest. And usually endurance has to do with remaining focused, fair and just while others remain anxious, greedy, unfair and unjust. Most of the time those greedy and unjust people who compete against the righteous eventually trip themselves up with their own greedy and unjust personalities and practices.

90   Know this. A selfish, non-caring, *I'm-just-doing-my-job* attitude always increases one's impoverished situation. For if your skill, technique, knowledge, or service is one that shapes, protects and/or further develops the society in which you live, you cannot work just for money or go along with exploitative business trends that place money over the sanctity of human life. This will lead to your own depression in your older years. The life of the Hiphoppa must mean more than the accumulation of money and property.

[91] Ultimately, to exist without the need to compete is Godlike, and living in a non-competitive environment is peace. Living a simple life within your means protects you from participating in certain stressful activities that are caused by having to compete to maintain more than you actually need. With all business transactions, employees, employers and products, be fair, be tolerant, be clear and be just. Live simply.

[92] Practice equality amongst employers, employees and tasks. Show no favoritism and lead by example. Most of all, seek the perfection of your chosen occupation. Always seek to improve your industry. Be the best at what YOU must do. Such perfection leads to lasting wealth, the opposite leads to sustained poverty.

[93] Everything is perception. Wealth is also created by perception; the Gospel of Hip Hop is evidence of this. Perception is everything and it is knowledge that creates one's perception. It is not that you are actually poor, it is that you may perceive yourself as being poor.

[94] No one is actually poor, most people simply don't know how to get money or where the money actually is. Money is everywhere, but if you don't know how to grab it, or who to talk to, or even how to talk money, you will simply not have any of it. Being rich is about having a certain knowledge and/or skill that is in demand.

[95] However, for the spiritually minded this very overstanding goes a bit deeper. Everything is perception, and perception has to do first with knowledge. However, that word *knowledge* takes on a slightly deeper meaning when applied spiritually.

[96] To *know* something or someone spiritually is to have an intimate relationship or understanding of that something or someone. So when asked, *do you know GOD?,* the answer is not achieved only intellectually. There is also

a healthiness, a wealthiness, a liveliness to one's being when one truly knows GOD. Even during times of sickness or some other challenging situation, those who truly know GOD are comforted and strengthened by such knowing. There are physical effects to your union with GOD.

97   People say things like, *You haven't aged at all,* or, *Why do I feel like I know you?* Knowledge of GOD affects you physically. You can see the Light of GOD on a true truth-seeker's face. However, this is not the case for most people. Most people use GOD in the same way that the World uses them. They want GOD to pay their bills and heal their sicknesses. This is the value that they themselves place upon their own God.

98   For their god is not the God of the universe itself. Their god is truly the god of their little houses, represented by wall ornaments, body trinkets, spiritual guides and books. Such a god is not GOD at all! Such a god is more of a self-induced invisible baby-daddy/mama.

99   Most people, due to their own attachment to their own material World, do not want their God to rescue them completely from sickness, hate, ignorance and poverty, which would mean giving up the pleasurable addictions of their material World and changing some unproductive habits. They prefer to have their god help them from a distance to live with sickness, hate, ignorance and poverty. They want their god to live with their demons. And this they call...*being blessed!*

100   Hiphoppas must mature beyond this level of spiritual understanding. We must realize that there is only GOD manifesting in different forms! And that we have the spiritual ability to create and control all situations, circumstances, people, places and things in the physical World through an awareness of everyone and everything's true source in the one GOD. We must believe, perceive and

achieve in God! Control of one's life is achieved by giving up the ultimate control of one's life. Be guided.

[101]   Everything is possible within the nature of God! But too many spiritual people don't really believe this. Is this you? Do you really *know* GOD? Do you really *know* your true God-force, your true spirit name/nature? Do you answer the *calling* of your higher-Self, or do you continue to answer the *cravings* of your physical body?

[102]   If you have matured to the awareness of having what you need when you need it, then this particular lesson may not be for you. However, too many so-called *spiritual people* walking a so-called *spiritual path* tend to live some very poor lives. This too Hiphoppas must mature from.

[103]   If you live a spiritual life then you should be practicing your spiritual skills in real life. If we are not content with ourselves yet, or at this particular moment, we should be visualizing ourselves better than who and/or where we presently are. Whether it is a health issue, love issue, awareness issue or wealth issue; see your situation through the eye of God. Use your spiritual skill!

[104]   Don't just believe in GOD; perceive through the reality (emotional intelligence) of God. The question here is, why are you still broke, yet you claim to walk in the Spirit? Maybe you are still reading about GOD's nature as opposed to adopting God's nature? Maybe you are still thinking and not being?

[105]   In any event, we must try to remember that the spirit realm is chaos to the human intellect. Rational thought limits the supernatural ability of Spirit and this is why so many truth-seekers still don't have what they need to survive in the material World. They are still seeking as opposed to *being*.

[106]   When it comes to spiritual reality, they <u>know</u> it but they don't <u>feel</u> it yet. So, they are definitely able to recite

Socrates, Moses and Jesus, even interpret ancient spiritual texts, but still they are behind in their mortgages, losing their investments, can't afford healthcare, and are hungry, sick and tired.

107   Remember, the top of the World is still the bottom of heaven. Those who walk a spiritual path through life may not be richer than anyone else, but we are indeed wealthier than everyone else—we live life abundantly. As true beings of Spirit we are wealthy for the purpose of relieving human suffering, beginning with our own.

108   If you are true to your spiritual principles and lifestyle then there should be some evidence of your fidelity. If your training is of a supernatural nature, then we should be able to experience your supernatural skill.

109   Those who live in the spirit realm live above the material World; we live deeper lives. Therefore, from the spirit realm we should be able to manipulate the material World because it is the spirit that quickens the flesh, not the other way around.

110   I am the Teacha! I am KRS ONE! This is my opinion of myself. But in order for anyone to actually agree with me and/or respect the validity of my opinion so that I may be treated the way in which I perceive myself, there must be some evidence to the claim that I am making.

111   And this is the point. There is a ton of evidence everywhere to substantiate every claim that I've made of myself, because really I only claim to be what the people already say of me; I only repeat their critiques, praises and expectations of me. However, I still practice hard because it is still I who that must produce the initial evidence of my own claims.

112   But the point here is to apply these examples to your own spiritual life. Do you claim to be a mystic, a minister, a prophet, a teacha? If you do, then where is the evidence of

your claims? If you claim to walk with GOD then why are you frustrated, addicted, afraid, depressed, unfulfilled, etc., against your own will?

113   On another note, if you claim to walk with GOD why are the people around you still lost and bitter? NO! If you claim to possess the Light, then let us see you use it! Let us see you transform your block. Let us see the miracles in your life. Save your children! Secure your spouse.

114   And get what I am saying here. This is no place for posturing and puffing one's self up, this is not the case at all! However, it is of extreme importance that we understand the urgency in being who we say that we are, and I am using myself as an example as to what such urgency actually looks like.

115   As an example, I am not the richest rapper in our community. I am Hip Hop's first official teacha; I live a simple life—a principled life. I am not pushing my lifestyle upon anyone. You do you and I'll do me. But if the doing of me includes my claim of "teacha," then where is the evidence of my claim? What you call yourself is your business. But what I call myself is indeed my business; it's my actual bread and butter!

116   So, yes I may push (drive) that new Benz, or spend $700 on dinner for two, or purchase a rare book for $1200. Sure, I am a popular rapper today, but in the end what am I teaching, and is it effective? Am I following my purpose? I humbly reply "yes."

117   This is why you are listening/reading this instrument right now, because I am being right now exactly who I claim to be, *the Teacha*, and this nature is what makes my life magical.

118   This gospel took years to write and thousands of dollars to produce, years that I didn't have and money that I couldn't see when I first began to gather the notes for

this gospel, yet here it is! The Gospel of Hip Hop stands as evidence not only of GOD's love and concern for Hip Hop, but such a gospel is evidence to all of my own claims and beliefs about myself as a spiritually guided Hip Hop Teacha.

[119]   The point is that as a spirit-being you should have very few challenges creating yourself in the material World. Yes, there will be challenges, but if you remain within the boundaries of your principles and life purpose you shall not really be affected by such challenges. As long as you are following your purpose, you shall have everything you need to manifest your purpose. And this is real!

[120]   If you are truly of a divine nature then the state of your country's economy shouldn't affect you. Gas prices shouldn't stop you from traveling. Home foreclosures shouldn't prevent you from buying the home of your dreams. School tuition shouldn't stop you from pursuing the best education available for yourself and your child. Bad credit in the World shouldn't prevent you from making God's investments on Earth.

[121]   The real issue is knowledge, knowledge of GOD over the World's knowing. The body of knowledge that you presently possess right now may be useless to you if it is not sufficiently matching your needs and making your life comfortable. Even your present knowledge of GOD may need to be modified or changed completely in order for you to achieve the state of consciousness required for a peace-filled and prosperous life.

[122]   Remember, it is not GOD that makes you rich, it is knowledge and skill that makes you rich. GOD makes you aware, and your Godly awareness attracts wealth and opportunity as needed. However, if you don't *have* something it's really because you don't *know* something. Having or not having is a matter of knowing or not

knowing. For those on a Hip Hop spiritual path, poverty happens when your spiritual knowledge does not keep up with your material needs.

123   For spiritual people to achieve those material things that we may need to survive we must truly <u>feel</u> that we deserve whatever we desire and then expect it to come in some unplanned, unexpected way (GOD Willing). To achieve true wealth we must practice <u>using</u> the expectancy of our minds. It's not just about reading books and watching metaphysical DVDs; it is more about actually putting to the test that which we read and believe is true.

124   I don't know how everyone else did it, how everyone else became successful, but for me, for KRS ONE, my success began with the proper use of my own mind. This was the first lesson GOD brought to my understanding. I visualized my entire career. Everything that I am doing today, including the writing of this gospel, I first visualized years ago when I was houseless in New York and I've continued to use these spiritual techniques throughout my 22-year Rap career.

125   This is the essence of what I teach today—self-creation, self-construction. As far as wealth goes, we must affirm in our minds those things that we want for ourselves and then forget about them so that the thought leaves our human intellect and enters the realm of Spirit (divine intelligence) where all things are possible. Do you really believe that such a technique is possible?

126   Do you really believe that you can affirm whatever you desire and then forget about it, knowing that it is on its way? For we do not dwell upon the things that we already have; we simply know (feel) that we already have them. And likewise, we do not dwell upon those things that we <u>expect</u> to come; we simply wait for them to appear. But really, what do you expect? What do you accept as real?

127   This is the beginning of health and wealth for those who claim a Hiphop lifestyle. First, we affirm in our mind's eye the object that we desire, then we purchase or acquire a small accessory to the object we desire, like an air-freshener if it is a car, or a lamp if it is a house. Then we FEEL how we would feel when we have the object in our possession, such feelings draw your desires to you. As mentioned earlier, expectancy creates wealth.

128   We repeatedly practice this *feeling* technique once before sleep and once as we awaken for about a week, then we forget about our desire, knowing that it is on its way. This is a standard technique for the spiritual-minded; it is commonly called "creative visualization." However, such a technique goes even deeper and further once practiced in real life.

129   Know this. Thought is like a cloud, or a mist, or rather a form of temperature. The mist of the mind is what actually influences things to happen and even causes things to appear. Whenever we think of something it is just a thought until we put some kind of feeling to it, that magical heat that makes things move. Whether that feeling is one of fear, or sadness, or excitement, once that feeling/heat is part of a thought, that thought takes on a life of its own.

130   Thought by itself is nothing without one's true feelings and intentions (the heat) within it. The mind is like a faucet, thought is like running water and your intentions and feelings are what warms the water up or cools the water down. Study this example closely.

131   When you are showering you will notice that even though you may adjust your faucet to add more warmth to the water, in most cases the water temperature does not change instantly. Only if you are in a modern state-of-the-art designer bathroom does the temperature change exactly when you turn the faucet.

132   In this example we can see how the mind works. You may think of something today, but it will take some time for your thought to manifest. You may turn on the faucet of your mind to heat up or even cool down your situation but you must realize that the mind affects your life in the way that temperature affects water; the effects are gradual for the beginner, and some people do burn themselves with the heat of their own intentions.

133   Most of our minds are old and worn, and so we find it almost impossible to intend and feel our desires into physical manifestation. We need relief now, and our minds simply do not work like this. Because of the worn-out conditions of our own minds due to worry, fear, depression, doubt, resentment, etc., it simply takes too long for such a technique to have any real effect upon our real lives. But this can be corrected.

134   Creative Visualization is reserved for those who have given their lives over to the reality of mystical experiences. There is a certain character that goes along with each level of spiritual awareness. You cannot expect any results from your spiritual practice if deep down inside you still doubt that such mystical experiences are even possible.

135   When you direct your mind to heat up or cool down your situation, patience is a must. Patience is crucial for beginners because beginners are very distant from the effects of their own mind. It is this distance that creates the illusion of time passing and the need for patience because you are waiting for the manifestation of your own intentions.

136   Such distance is indeed safe for beginners because you really don't want the manifestations of your own immature thinking to materialize instantly. Until you have matured to the level where your thoughts are habitually healthy to your own well-being, your God-nature shall remain a safe distance away from your material reality—for

your own good.

137   This is why things take time to manifest, it is because your own doubt and fears have placed you in a safe distance from your own power for your own good. Time gives beginners the ability to change their thinking before such thoughts become reality.

138   It is when you have matured spiritually that you eliminate the distance between you and the effects of your own mind. This is when you decree something and it happens instantly or the next hour, or the next day, or the next month! Know this. The closer you get to your own mind, the closer you get to God.

139   Attuned Hiphoppas are advised to practice eliminating the distance between themselves and their thoughts in an effort to secure and enhance the state of their well-being. This takes time and practice. The technique goes as follows.

140   First, get in the habit of decreeing with feeling the desires of your heart and see how long it takes for such desires to manifest. When I first started my creative visualization exercises it took years for my visualizations to materially manifest, but they did! And each time my dreams came true, my faith in such an ability was strengthened.

141   I began to believe in the power of my own mind, but with the realization of such a powerful ability came the character and nature that goes along with such an ability. I had to discipline myself to speak in a certain way, to cancel out certain feelings and visions I may have had toward certain adversaries, critics and situations—and it was not easy. But after a while, I began to experience the manifestations of my thoughts materializing faster and faster in my material reality.

142   Today I intentionally put distance in front of my mind and my feelings so that I can take advantage of time.

Some things are not meant to occur instantly when you want them to occur. Today, I've learned that it is easier to simply put one's spiritual nature on auto-pilot and allow one's self to simply flow with GOD's intention, which is found in one's purpose, as opposed to always trying to make things happen.

143   Sure you can create any life you desire for yourself with your mind. But you must always remember that GOD is thinking too. And GOD is actually looking out for your best interests—your well-being.

144   Practice eliminating the distance between you and your own mind. Measure how long it takes for your mental reality to become your physical reality, and seek to shorten the time it takes to manifest such a reality. Being within seven days of one's thinking is actually a safe distance for a powerful mind.

145   Therefore, we must affirm our needs several times in an earnest prayer, affirmation or visualization and then prepare for their arrival with a matching character. Practice often. Everything is already with you NOW, including your Higher-Self! Simply let it be; point to your perceived reality and say to yourself... *There it is!*

THE FIFTH OVERSTANDING
THE INNER CITY

1   Peace and much Love. Know this. It is not a coincidence that such a testimony is before you now.

2   At this very moment you are being *called* out of the World again for your own protection and further development. Will you answer the *call* this time? Will you believe in your *Self* this time? You are who you think you are.

3   Why say that Hip Hop is your lifestyle yet continue to doubt your own *Self* and the Gospel of Hip Hop, which exists to protect and empower you? Why fight against your *Self* and the reality of your own life experiences? Why deny your own empowerment? Believe in your *Self* and in the gospel that speaks highly of YOU!

4   Don't let those who surround you overwhelm you with their doubts and fears. You are the light! You are the light of <u>your</u> World! And you are NOT alone. Others are content with being ordinary and average, they do not strive to attain the character of God! In Truth, they are afraid of it.

5   But you have dared to explore the unknown. You are indeed different. And this is what may have angered and/or depressed you in your early stages of spiritual maturity. It is the fact that you feel average and ordinary but in Truth you are not. Many of us have suffered as you do, and many of us have overcome our frustrations living with the weak in Spirit, the doubtful of mind and the guilty at heart.

6   We know what it feels like to give, and give, and give,

and still get no result, or in most cases no appreciation or even respect. We know exactly what it feels like to give your life-force to those who do not replenish your life-force, to love those who refuse to show you the same love in return, to willing assist those who exploit you.

7   We know what it is like to assist in the freedom of those who refuse to free themselves, to give charitably to those who receive with expectant hands, to argue with others about THEIR well-being, to be the one that everyone relies upon to get them out of trouble and difficulty!

8   Yes, I know your struggle and I also feel your pain. Your compassion for those around you is your only weakness. Your care for people is the cause of most of your headaches! At times you feel that if you were more selfish, or that if you were by yourself, you would be at peace. You wouldn't have to help those who were going to turn around and diss you!

9   Like you, I also yearned for the presence of GOD above all else only to be surrounded by stressful, fearful, doubtful people who never seemed to ever be at peace. They want what you got without having done the work or endure the sacrifices that you did to achieve what you got.   And on top of this, such people trapped by their own chronic state of denial, continuously blaming and criticizing you for their shortcomings in life, are leading to your depression and anxiety. I've been through this as well in my younger years.

10   My character and reputation would be called into question quick if I decided to have a carnal moment, yet everyone around me, even my criticizers, continued in the very ways that they falsely accused me of. But wait! GOD is real. And you are who you think you are. DON'T GIVE IT UP! Stay your course!

11   There IS light at the end of this tunnel, and it begins

with your entrance into your *Inner City*. Often spoken of as the *Middle Way, the Kingdom of Heaven, the Kingdom of GOD, walking the path*, etc., *the Inner City* is that condition of being habitually moved to spontaneous right choices—it is the *good life*.

12   Without thinking, without planning, without assistance you arrive right when you are supposed to, you get exactly what you need at the exact moment you need it, you are protected and guided by a larger intelligence than that of any person, group or institution. Whenever a decision must be made toward your forward movement, peace and/or survival, somehow you always make the right choices or rather, the right choice is always made for you.

13   This is *the Kingdom of GOD, the realm of Heaven, the Middle Way, the Shining Path*. This condition is what we call the *Inner City*, and it is produced by enduring the ignorance and temptations of the World and its people.

14   It is when you have walked in righteousness and nobility for so long that you develop certain spiritual reflexes to material challenges. You no longer respond to the World like everyone else does, or like everyone else would like you to. They live in denial and their actual lives confirm their false view of the World.

15   However, you are not in denial, you are in Truth. Your reflexes are spiritual, not physical. For many years you have walked in love and with a caring heart. You've immediately sought to help those in danger, you've felt for people that you didn't even personally know, you went out of your way to bring comfort and relief to those in need, you are reliable and you've been reliable.

16   Therefore, be encouraged in the Truth of your being, which is clearly defined by your intentions, actions and by what you lend your time and resources to. You are attracted to this *gospel* not only because it has something

important and personal to tell you about your Hip Hop life, you are also generally attracted to the things of the Spirit. You spend your time and money seeking Truth, and GOD sees that.

[17] This *gospel* is now in your presence because obviously it is time that you turned up the volume on your own spiritual life, on your own dreams, on what is important to you. However, you've been waiting for everyone else to understand what you understand, and see what you see for too long, and they're not seeing it yet. But you must not give up on your *Self* or give up on the reality of your OWN spiritual experiences. Obviously you see (sense) something more than your *Self*, something greater than your *Self*; you feel that your nature is divine.

[18] Others have laughed at you, ridiculed you, and have even conspired against you, but you've also seen their plans fail completely or never reach the full magnitude of what such plans intended. In Truth, it is your very nature that protects you and guides you.

[19] Know this. Cats are attracted to cat reality; dogs are attracted to dog reality. Birds do bird things and fish do fish things. Each acts according to the nature each naturally possesses. A culinary student is attracted to cooking, an attorney—law, a doctor—medicine, a teacher—knowledge. But only a few are really attracted to GOD and the *ways* of the Spirit.

[20] GOD must be in your nature for you to even be interested in GOD. Sure, everyone would like their prayers answered, but YOU seem to be attracted to GOD. You seem to yearn for the face of GOD, not just the hand. You seem to want to know the mysteries of spiritual living; others are simply not interested in such subjects because it is NOT in their nature to know.

[21] You are a person who truly seeks peace, love, unity

and good times in your personal life, but it seems that everyone around you is becoming increasingly depressed and confused. You must save yourself from this or you will be limited, even destroyed, by this. This is why those who are called to a life in Spirit and are constantly assisting others through life's challenges frequently and regularly take time to themselves. We go away for *40 days and 40 nights* so that we may rejuvenate our spiritual and emotional vitality.

22   This is important because you are always asked to help. You are always lending yourself to others—baby sitting, doing someone's hair, giving money, giving advice, speaking on behalf of others, teaching, giving bail money, feeding, etc. You MUST tend to YOUR needs or you will not be of any use to anyone! You are the dependable one in your group and it seems that people take advantage of your good nature. However, YOU ARE NOT ALONE in this! You are truly one of the great minds of your time. Do not doubt yourself!

23   Recently (like in the last three months) you've been feeling an urgency to complete your projects and realize your goals. You have been feeling like you are at the crossroads of your life, like now more than ever you have to decide WHO you are going to become over the next three to five years.

24   Your future is always on your mind. Your only challenge is what you believe you are capable of. But like many who finally realize what their true purpose is, you too have doubted yourself for too long. How good are you, will you be accepted, will you get ripped off, will you fail? Deep down inside you may fear your own success more than your own failure.

25   Like most who are instructed by GOD to do a seemingly impossible task, GOD seems to be urging you to act upon your true purpose despite your fears and doubts. It seems to be TIME FOR COURAGE!

26   This seems to be the year for GOD to become more real in your life because only gods are attracted to GOD. Only divine people are attracted to the things of the divine. Regardless of your artistic or academic self-expression, you are a divine being. It's time to stop being what everyone else thinks you should be, and be who you <u>know</u> you are.

27   Remember, the universe is exact. There are no mistakes. You are hearing this *word* now because it is time for you to hear this *word* now. You are the light of your world. You are being *called* to help others because you have the power to help others. Others don't have the abilities that you have just as you don't have the abilities they have. Your ability is God—and it's time that you start being it!

28   People ask you to help them because THEY BELIEVE that you can. They *feel* that you can. People don't ask those who they *feel* are helpless to help them. People don't ask the powerless to empower them. People are asking for your help because they know that you can help them. So why not join in on THEIR FAITH IN YOU and express more FAITH IN YOURSELF?

29   Everyone can see your aura, your character and your reputation clearer than you can. It is you who doubts you; everyone else believes in what they feel about you until you say or act otherwise. So what are you affirming to yourself and others? *Nobody's perfect, I ain't nobody special, I can't..., I don't..., I hate...,* etc.?

30   Ya know, the only difference between a "demo" recording and a "master" recording is your interpretation of what has been recorded. What do you feel about your own being and self-expression? What do you believe you are capable of?

31   This is the year that you make the *inner* you the *outer* you. For your own survival, you must believe more in your *inner* reality than in your *outer* circumstances. You

are clearly the light of YOUR World, the savior of YOUR home, the teacher of your neighborhood.

32   Even when you don't see how you can help, your very involvement or attention toward others create solutions that didn't even exist before. And this is the challenge; you are a healer by nature. However, it is not your intellect that heals; it is your loving presence, your time, your attention, your care that heals.

33   Your wanting to comfort another, to selflessly give attention to what someone else is going through, to help others along their way and realize their goals—these acts shall raise you up and actualize your own purpose successfully because blessings come THROUGH you, not TO you.

34   The more you are giving, the more you shall be receiving. The more you love and care, the more you will be loved and cared for. The more peace you provide to others, the more peace GOD shall provide to you. But remember, cats are cats by nature and dogs are dogs by nature. Those who seek certain professions and fields of life do so out of their very nature. And so it is with you.

35   Your thirst for Truth is evidence of your nature— USE IT! Your ability to care for others unconditionally is evidence of your true nature—USE IT! Your yearning for the presence of GOD is evidence as to what your true nature really is—USE IT!

36   Your only challenge is doubt; therefore your only strength is faith. BELIEVE IN YOURSELF! Be and live in your inner-Self. You have help in places that you have not even touched upon yet. Search yourself; YOU ARE NOT ALONE! You have a divine power that only YOU can express <u>for</u> others. For if you do not express your divinity, the people of your world suffer.

37   Remember, if you go to a person that you believe

is a doctor and that person refuses to heal you; you suffer. If you go to a person that you believe is an attorney and that person refuses to defend or argue for your rights you suffer. The point is that people are suffering today because many divine people simply don't believe that they are divine and capable of divine work; the activity of the World overwhelms them.

38   For divine people like you there's nothing special about yourself or your life circumstances. For you, little miracles happen often, but they are normal to you so you don't celebrate your divinity. Plus, many divine people keep their divinity to themselves or turn their spiritual *light* down so that others are not uncomfortable around them. It's time for all of this to change.

39   It's time for GOD's people to stand up! Evil and suffering occurs in the World when divine people ignore their divinity—their responsibilities. Others cannot do what we can do, that's why it is not being done. We must get to work quickly. YOU ARE THE SAVIOR OF YOUR WORLD!

40   You have a tremendous responsibility to promote health, love, awareness and wealth to your people with your Hip Hop existence and activity in the World. Acts of kindness and assistance, acts of mercy and forgiveness, disattachment from the material World, mentoring, charity, trustworthiness, commitment, responsibility, etc., are all acts of holiness, and each act strengthens and proves your own divinity.

41   These repeated *acts* of holiness eventually become the habits of your life, and after a while you have no choice in any situation but to habitually act from this place of holiness and care for life and freedom—and this is where YOUR frustration with others began!

42   You have become habitually addicted to the Ways of

the Spirit, yet others have not. Where others habitually react physically and carnally to physical and carnal situations, you have been habitually compelled to react spiritually to physical and carnal situations, and such habitual actions have not been easy for you in the material World around materially-minded people. But hold on! You are entering your *inner city*.

43   Even though certain outcomes have not always worked out in your favor, and even though you've been embarrassed, and cheated, and lied about; and even though it has been lonely and unfair for you, even though you've done what was right while others enjoyed their wickedness, behold! You have defied the World and its many temptations with your habitual right actions motivated by the Will of your Spirit, and it is now time to receive your reward—the Crown of Life.

44   Such a habit of righteousness eventually creates a reality that we call the *Inner City*, where the physical World and its material conditions seem to act in accordance with your will. Your physical, spiritual and mental surroundings seem to walk and talk with you. Everything seems to work in your favor. The good, the bad, the faithful and the fearful; the victories, the setbacks and the so-called *defeats* all seem to work in your collective favor.

45   People that you need to meet show up unexpectedly, while those who you care not to meet seem to somehow always just miss you. The numbers that randomly show up around you are always exact, like 101, 202, 303, 404, etc., or 11, 22, 33, 44, etc., or 10, 20, 30, 40, and 100, 200, 300, 400, etc., and 111, 222, 333, 444, etc.

46   Even when you are late it is because you shall arrive right on time. You begin to notice how opportunity keeps coming your way even while others are convinced that the World has gone mad!

47   Without any effort on your part you are protected, promoted, guided and secure. Health, love, awareness and wealth surround you. People see the *light* in you and on you, and strangers feel that they know you like a family member. Others claim that you resemble someone that they admire.

48   No matter what you look like physically, or have materially, you are beautiful. You are truly attractive. Even beyond your physical appearance, people are attracted to you and your beauty. You never seem to really age.

49   When you are entering your *Inner City* your spiritual receptivity becomes very sensitive. You enter a condition of making unconscious spontaneous right choices. Without really thinking about your choices, the right choice seems to always be made for you.

50   You arrive at places just before or after the accident. You feel the essence of people beyond what they are saying. You have become *the right guided one*—the Teacha!

51   Your continuous habit of righteous living and generous giving over many years has opened the gates of the heavenly realm which many wise teachers have written about and have said was all around and spread out across the Earth but that people just did not see it, or more accurately, didn't care to see it. Most are not even really looking for it.

52   But because of who you are, and the way in which you have freely chosen to conduct your life, you have died to your material reality, only to be resurrected to your spiritual reality. The things that you took pleasure in before as a human being, you must now set aside for your completion and enjoyment as a Spirit being.

53   Take courage in this Overstanding and allow it to strengthen you. It is the Truth. Those who walk in righteousness and in love, speak with care, fight against oppression and corruption, cannot be bought or tempted, hear no gossip or schemes of evil, and seek not to cause

conflict and war, are blessed beyond blessings! They are guided, fed, clothed, taught, promoted, advertised and protected by truly divine forces!

54   This is why the World doesn't work for you. This is why the World doesn't validate you, and why you cannot seem to succeed in conventional styles of living; you are simply not of the World! Your home is the *Inner City*, and your frustrations come from YOU wanting the pleasures, securities and validations of the World as a human being, yet you are clearly a Spirit being operating in a habitual spiritual reality but in the material World.

55   The issue is that you must finally decide to *make up* your mind. You must actually create (make) your mind. For it is you (the Spirit) that creates (makes up) your Mind, and the Mind then goes on to create the physical Body and life circumstances. The question is, are you going to live and be moved by your *Inner-City* reality or are you going to live and be moved by your outer-city environment? Which has more value to you? Which one brings you peace?

56   At some point in your training you must finally accept the spiritual life and its powers and cease trying to live two lives in two opposing realities, one spiritual/mystical, and the other material/worldly. You should repeat to yourself: *I am a resident of GOD's spiritual Inner City. I prefer to walk with GOD in the realm of the Spirit. I have freely chosen God over the World, and I am content with my choice.*

57   Say all of this to yourself over and over again: *I am content with my free choice. I am content with GOD's presence. Spiritual awareness is more important to me than the temporary sensations of the World.* At some point in your training you will be surrounded by fearful, desperate, doubtful people, most of which will be your closest associates, even members of your own family. But do not be depressed by this, they are there to help build your strength. Humble yourself

and Perform Listening; this will be one of your greatest challenges.

58   For when you are surrounded by the fears and doubts of others, it means that it is time for you to exercise the faith and principles that govern YOUR life. Often it is your compassion that opens your heart to suffering people; however, you cannot become them because you are NOT them. Perform Listening knowing that the fearful and the doubtful cannot do what you do nor can they see what you see. They have not done the work to arrive at your level of spiritual skill; perform patience.

59   In Truth, your random acts of righteousness and love have led you toward the realm of Heaven which we call the *Inner City*. Just don't doubt who you are. Don't give up on your SELF! Don't abort the birth of the divine you! Remember, those who are born to comprehend the mysteries of GOD have no choice in their comprehension—GOD is in their blood! Even when they do not want to see, they see. Even when they do not want to hear, they hear. Even when they do not want to know, they know.

60   And you must be clear with this. You may be surrounded right now by people who are confident and sure of THEIR fears and doubts but you CANNOT make their fears and doubts your fears and doubts. Don't make other people's problems your problems. Always seek to help wherever and whenever you can, but as sure and confident as they are in their fears and doubts, you must be just as sure and confident in your faith and principles.

61   Others seem to live their lives doing any unrighteous thing they desire while those who are born for spiritual comprehension and leadership lack the skills for unrighteous living. Those who are born for righteousness will continuously fail at unrighteousness, while those who are born for unrighteousness will continuously fail

at righteousness.

[62]   For the righteous have no choice but to be righteous while the unrighteous limit their decisions to unrighteousness. You cannot try to be righteous; you either are or you are not. Likewise, those who are Hiphop really have no choice in their Hiphop identity; it is simply who they are! Therefore, let us accept ourselves and in doing so, accept the powers that come with the acceptance of ourselves.

[63]   You cannot try to be Hiphop; you either are or you are not. The same principle is applied to spiritual living; you either are of the Spirit or you are not! And again, the free choice is always yours. God is a privilege, not a right, and again, this gospel for Hip Hop is not a new spiritual idea, it is a confirmation of the spiritual ideas Hiphoppas already hold.

[64]   For the unrighteous are called <u>into</u> the World while the righteous are called <u>out</u> of the World. You will know if you are called out of the World simply by your failure to succeed in the World. Those who are successful in the World have been called to do so by the World. And likewise, those who are Hiphop are called for that purpose.

[65]   Be yourself! Envy not the riches and/or longevity of those cultures foreign to your own. Respect the beliefs of all believers but put no faith in those beliefs and traditions that do not respect the experiences of your life. Be and enjoy yourself! Learn from the history that your God has made for you. Live your Hip Hop tradition and it shall become real for you!

[66]   Respecting and even learning the traditions and basic teachings of all cultures expresses one's maturity and wisdom. But denying and/or neglecting the Truth of <u>your</u> own being to associate with foreign cultures and beliefs expresses one's immaturity. Be yourself! And if you are Hip

Hop, don't front! Be Hip Hop!

67   For the righteous hurt themselves envying and chasing the success of the World while the unrighteous hurt themselves envying the victories of the righteous. At some point the Hiphoppa must evaluate her *Self* and be reborn to the path which she is prepared to commit to. All paths lead to the one GOD.

68   The heart does not lie. You know exactly who you are and what you truly desire. Be not ashamed of your past or your future; neither of them are exclusively yours. Your life experiences were (and still are) necessary for you to have arrived at this very moment. And here you are—blessed beyond any blessing!

69   Through practice you shall acquire that sensitive *sight* that sees the exactness of GOD. Beyond rational explanation, you must learn to trust in divine intelligence and the timely alignments that come with such a trust. GOD speaks to you in this way, so pay close attention and be guided.

70   Know this. Anyone can read the Gospel of Hip Hop but only those that are born of the *Inner City* shall have the ability to put it to use. You may be one of these people. Are you? Are you a *C.I.T.Y.* planner? One who plants Consciousness In The Youth. Are you a builder of civilization?

71   For GOD has risen up a new people from the dust of the *Inner City* who are not afraid to hear GOD's voice and do their God's work. GOD has opened the eye of a new people to continue the renewing of the human spirit. Are you one of these new people? Are you Hiphop? When the elements of Hip Hop are before you do you feel excited or do you feel aggravated? Does Hip Hop bring you joy or anxiety? The truthful answering of these questions will reveal if you are Hiphop or not.

[72]   On another note, even though the results of an infinite intelligence are shown and proven throughout the existence and history of Hip Hop itself, still many religious people doubt Hip Hop's divine nature. They doubt us, doubt our teachas and doubt GOD. Others mock us, mock our teachas and mock their own GOD. Indeed, they mock us just as they did all of the young prophets and nations of World history. Such disbelief is the way of the World.

[73]   But we hold no grudge and we harbor no anger. GOD has already revealed to the spiritual-minded the coming of Hip Hop as a spiritual force for the uplifting and empowerment of the forgotten and rejected youth of the World. As Bishop Clarence E. McClendon preached in 1999 during his X-blessing series, *I submit to you that it's not some of their eyes that have been blinded, it's some of ours! I submit to you that the reason a lot of people are not coming to the kingdom of GOD right now is not because their eyes are blind, but because our eyes are blind. 'Cause we think they gotta look a certain way and walk a certain way and talk a certain way to come in. And GOD said, 'If you open your eyes I'm a show you brothers of yours, sons of mine, that you haven't even identified yet.'*

[74]   Bishop McClendon continues, *You got to be spiritual for this. Church folk can't do this. Religious people will not be able to walk this line, because they're going to be looking for cookie cutouts of themselves. They're going to be looking for folk who look like them and talk like them and walk like them and 'oh bless GOD,' 'hallelujah,' 'praise the lord,' 'thank you Jesus,' 'we were sharing the other day,' and these folks ain't gonna talk like that. They gonna be like 'what up, what up, what up!' And GOD says, 'THEY ARE MINE! THEY'RE MINE! THEY'RE MINE! THEY'RE MINE!'*

[75]   For it is true that to the righteous all things are righteous, and to the wicked all things are wicked. To the

beautiful all things are beautiful, and to the ugly all things are ugly. And likewise, to the godly all things are godly, and to the ungodly all things are ungodly. For the voice of GOD lives within all creation, and those who live with GOD can hear it.

76   GOD's true gospel speaks to all living things; it is not just words in a book, it is *the Love*. But if you cannot truly hear the voice of GOD, then you cannot truly hear the instruction of GOD. And if you cannot hear the instruction of GOD, it is the World that shall instruct you.

77   And what is the instruction of the World? It is an instruction that convinces one to doubt everything—even the way of one's own God. It is an instruction that convinces one to express individual desires over the common good of all. It is an instruction that leads to the sinking *S.H.I.P.* (<u>S</u>ickness, <u>H</u>atred, <u>I</u>gnorance and <u>P</u>overty).

78   Such an instruction convinces men that they are boys and boys that they are men. Such an instruction convinces women that they are girls and girls that they are women. Such an instruction has adult men and women justifying their own enslavement and the enslavement of others with statements like, *Well I'm just doing my job!* For such is the *Way* of the World!

79   Such an instruction creates slaves for the World's workforce. For it is disunity, disbelief and disrespect amongst people that keeps the World's workforce unified. The way of the World is to doubt everyone and trust no one, while the way of the Spirit is to believe and trust the one GOD. For these reasons we are obedient to GOD and we recognize the divinity in all whom we may encounter.

80   For it is only the enslaved who cannot see what the one GOD is doing with Hip Hop. For the mind of the enslaved cannot rejoice in the freedom of others, and for these reasons they judge us. For many successful slaves say,

"I hear GOD's voice." But if GOD does not speak their written language, it is as if GOD never spoke at all! Let us seek to ease their suffering with our divine performances.

81   For them, GOD must speak English and abide by the laws of the World in order to convey divine instructions. But we hold no grudge and harbor no anger. For our God has truly spoken through our hearts and we did hear. For these reasons we are obedient to GOD. The World can say whatever it likes; we are NOT obedient to its ways.

82   Rather than believe, in disbelief the World and its representatives cut themselves off from even their own God. Such people are truly lost! And it is for this reason that the Great Spirit has raised us up from nothing! That the whole World shall see from whence we came, and be inspired again to reunite with their God and their religion. For everyone shall give their God credit for the success of Hip Hop! And *this is how it should be done.*

83   Our existence as a temple for Hip Hop points people back to the timeless ways of GOD and their own religious traditions. This is why all true and attuned Hiphoppas are encouraged to study the principles of all religious faiths so that we may steer the people of those faiths back to the essence of their own principles and traditions. Our aim is to inspire truth-seekers from all backgrounds to continue seeking Truth. Simone G. Parker has taught us to be R.E.L.I.G.I.O.U.S.: to Realize Every Life In GOD's Image Offers Useful Solutions.

84   Discrimination and elitism have no place within the Temple of Hip Hop. Our gospel exists at a time when we (Hiphop Kulture) are at the lowest level of political power and organized social influence ourselves. So when we become politically powerful and socially organized, we shall know for sure that it is truly GOD who has lifted us up. For GOD has instructed us to enter our *Inner City* and

transform its *streets*. Therefore, open your eye, Hiphoppa! For the mind of every Hiphoppa is a city of ideas.

85   Enter your *Inner City* today and transform your *streets!* Rename your avenues and repair your roads. Focus not upon the criticisms or the praises of the World; focus only upon the achievement of your life's purpose. Behold! We have already defied the institutions of the World! Imagine what we can achieve by believing in the divinity of ourselves. Enter your *Inner City!*

86   The population of one's *city* is the ideas one has allowed citizenship to in one's mind. For every Hiphoppa is the mayor of her city. And it is the wise mayor who productively directs the population of one's city toward peace and prosperity. Crime does not exist in the city that nurtures the dreams and goals of its population.

87   Do not be afraid to walk the *streets* of your own *Inner City!* Enter your *Inner City* and transform the *streets* of your own mind! Such teaching is the essence of the Gospel of Hip Hop. For we know who we are! We need not the validation of anyone or anything to substantiate who and what we are. For it is GOD alone that builds nations, and for these reasons we are obedient to GOD—the Love that continues to bless us.

88   *What is the X-Blessing? The X-Blessing is the drawing near of unidentified sons and daughters. It's when GOD begins to draw near those that have not yet been identified, and then begins to open the eyes of His people so that they can recognize them. And this is why I am preaching to you, because you got to know what GOD is up to. The religious will miss it, the regular church going folk are not going to be a part of this, but the spiritual will be.* (Bishop Clarence E. McClendon, *The X-Blessing*, Part Three, 1999)

89   This is us. This is Hip Hop. GOD has chosen us for a great work! Let us not reject the invitation of GOD. Let

us finally get prepared to answer the door!

90   GOD now seeks refuge in the temples of our Inner Cities. Open your door of awareness and let GOD in! Hiphop Kulture appreciates GOD. We shall feed our God, clothe our God, love our God and restore our God to strength in our Inner Cities! For our God shall find strength in the *Templists of Hiphop*.

91   The last days of other nations shall be the first days for the Hip Hop nation. We must believe in ourselves! We must enter our own Inner Cities and make them worthy of GOD's presence. Behold Hiphoppas! The presence of the one GOD is now! Prepare your Inner Cities for the presence of your God! Such is the teaching of our temple. And for these reasons we are obedient to GOD—the Love that Guides Our Direction.

92   Prepare yourself now! The presence of GOD is sudden! For it is always some unseen disaster or even blessing that instantly changes the World and its power structure. So let us be prepared. Let us always be prepared for the activity of GOD in the World.

93   We know that when the World rejoices, the Spirit of justice mourns. And when the Spirit of justice rejoices, it is the World that mourns. The failed plans of an unjust and disobedient World are a victory for justice!

94   Choose today who and what you shall represent. Through your own thoughts, speech and actions choose today who you shall be and become. If you are Hiphop, do not deny your own protection and power by doubting your true identity and disrespecting the gospel that is before you now. Don't be a hypocrite! Be what GOD has given you your strength and skill for.

95   For we would rather appear contradictory to the World, yet be consistent with God, than to be contradictory to God so that we may appear consistent with the World!

[96] The opinions of an ignorant and temporary World are valueless when compared to the wisdom and heavenly conditions of the loving and eternal GOD. Choose today whose approval you shall prepare for. Such a choice shall eventually relieve your frustrations and doubts.

[97] But it does not stop there. For as more Hiphoppas begin building up their *Inner Cities*, such a process shall bring our Hip Hop (outer) city into physical manifestation. Such an inward process shall firmly establish our outer reality. This begins our social movement and the true meaning of our Hiphop civilization. Our concept of civilization begins with a serious focus upon one's human skills independent of technological knowing and/or assistance.

[98] *Black's Law Dictionary* describes "civilization" *as A law, an act of justice, or judgement which renders a criminal process civil. Black's Law* continues, *A term which covers several states of society; it is relative, and has no fixed sense, but implies an improved and progressive condition of the people, living under an organized government. It consists not merely in material achievements, in accomplishments in culture, science, and knowledge, but also in doing of equal and exact justice.*

[99] Advancing the concept of the *Inner City* outside of the spiritual realm and into the social realm, we find that just because a nation has made a variety of advancements in the field of technology, does not mean that such a nation has become civilized. A nation's inner cities must be peaceful, prosperous and secure for that nation to have domestic tranquility.

[100] Technology does not measure the extent of one's humanity. Neither does technological skill, nor does intelligence; nor do power and influence measure and/or define *civilized* human behavior. Tech skills, etc., are the tools for human survival, they are not survival itself. Indeed these tech tools are very important to the survival and

further development of the human being, but still, tools do not define one's humanity.

101   How you love defines your humanity. Your ability to solve problems, and the way in which you do so, defines your humanity. The ability to think and act beyond your own personal wants and achievements defines your humanity. Your character defines your humanity.

102   What kind of human are you? What can YOU do without technological assistance? What can YOU command your body and/or mind to do independent of your tools? Self-control, as an example, is a human skill that technology cannot really produce. Care is a human skill. Speech is a human skill. Writing is a human skill. Thinking is a human skill. Hip Hop is a human skill. Even the creation of technology itself is a human skill.

103   Technology is commonly thought of as the science of mechanical and industrial arts, whereas civilization is commonly thought of as an advanced stage in developing societies. Which do you value more?

104   Civilization includes intellectual, cultural and material development. It includes progress in the arts and sciences as well as writing, record-keeping and the development of social institutions, all of which are present and gradually maturing within Hip Hop today.

105   Technology is the scientific method and/or material used to achieve a commercial or industrial objective. This is how hip-hop is used today; it is used as a tool of commerce, not as a means toward better human relations. In light of this, Hiphop Kulture shall always make use of its technologies and technological innovations not just for industrial and/or commercial interests but also for the actual sustainment of its civilized society.

106   Technology is the application of a refined science, whereas civilization is an application of a refined mind.

Technological advancement is not civilization. To be truly civilized, human beings must interact with each other in advanced manners. To be truly civilized we must first be human. We must reinforce our quest for human rights with an unshakable commitment toward our human duties.

[107]   Know this. Humanity is GOD's technology; the more you master GOD's technology, the less you will need to depend upon the World's technology. GOD's technology heightens productive human interactions, creating the effect of civilization. It does not matter how technologically advanced a nation is; government corruption, racism, murder, theft, deceit, selfishness, greed, cruelty, etc., are not advanced human interactions. To be truly civilized one must first be humane. One must be refined in learning, morality and social manners—the causes of civilization.

[108]   Integrity, peace, love, unity, happiness, charity, respect for life, respect for one's environment, artistic, intellectual, spiritual and political refinement, etc., are indeed advanced human interactions. And it is these advanced interactions amongst human beings that the Temple of Hip Hop seeks to promote and preserve.

[109]   Such a promotion and preservation of civilized human behavior begins with us. As Hiphoppas, we must be civilized if we expect others to be. And those who live the Hiphop lifestyle are indeed civilization builders.

[110]   This not only means having concern for the public good and the peace of a society's citizens, this also means respecting and perfecting our human abilities over the advancement of our technological achievements. This is what Hip Hop's nine elements are all about. Each element commits the Hiphoppa to the perfection of her human abilities.

[111]   In fact, Hip Hop may be one of the last truly human expressions free from technological dependency. Yes, we

use, have used, and will continue to use technology to advance our lives and art. But when technology fails, the true Hiphoppa can still express *Hip Hop* because Hip Hop does not need technology to exist; it is a human skill, it is GOD's technology.

[112]   A deeper understanding of Hip Hop can give us a deeper understanding of technology and its productive uses. In the fast-moving, rapidly growing World of technological innovation it is this awareness (human awareness and skills) that is most important to preserve if we are to preserve true Hip Hop as well as our own peace of mind in a technological World.

[113]   The questions are: What can YOU do without technological assistance? What valuable thing can your hands or body produce without technological assistance? Again, Hip Hop is a human skill. Breakin, Emceein, Graffiti writing and Beat Boxin are human skills. Deejayin as cuttin', mixin' and scratchin' is also a human skill. However, it is the cuttin', mixin' and scratchin' aspects of Deejayin that make it a human skill.

[114]   It is not just the creation of technology that is the human skill; it is what you do with such technology that is the value of one's human skill. Human intelligence in manipulating existing objects produces technologies of all sorts. But after such technology is produced we cannot forget the mind or the creative process that produced it. Yes, turntables are a form of music technology, but it is cuttin', mixin' and scratchin' that are indeed the human skills brought to turntable technology.

[115]   This is what many DJs lack today. They rely upon music technology to define their DJ-ing as opposed to relying upon their *Deejayin* to define the use of their music technologies. In addition to knowing little about the other elements of Hip Hop, many of today's DJs focus more

upon the manipulation of technological innovation to exist (beat-making) rather than on the perfection of their cuttin', mixin' and scratchin' abilities.

116 Still, Breakin, Emceein and Beat Boxin require no technologies at all to exist. You can produce and perform the act of Breakin, Emceein and Beat Boxin anywhere and at any time! Without any money, or clothing, or even a microphone, or any recording devices, without even light you can still produce Breakin, Emceein and Beat Boxin at will. These sacred elements to our culture require no technology to exist; they are human skills. And this is where one's Hiphop lifestyle (habit) begins.

117 Hiphop reminds us of what it means to be truly human. Hiphop conditions us to communicate with one another in person and not just over the Internet or through a cellular phone. True Hip Hop was born out of the Great Spirit and remains a mental and physical human activity.

118 As we perfect our human skills we also strengthen ourselves against the technological dominance of those who wish to exploit us and our resources. The Truth that we Hiphoppas must never forget is that NO POWER ON EARTH CAN DEFEAT THOSE WHO HAVE PERFECTED THEMSELVES!

119 True Hip Hop will always seek to empower and free human beings as human beings. Not that we are against technological innovations or those who survive by way of technological assistance, but to be clear here, we must never get into the habit of believing that Hip Hop (like most products) is produced by television, radio, CD manufacturing, office buildings, distribution centers, music stores, recording studios and high-speed computers.

120 Yes, these tools are very important to the presentation and sustainment of Hip Hop's activity and history in the World but again, Hip Hop in and of itself is a human skill

produced by the human Spirit, and it must remain this way. Such is *real* Hip Hop.

[121]   This we must never forget. And even though most of us are already totally dependent upon an outside technological system of some sort to live, pay bills and eat, it is always liberating to know that Hip Hop as a human skill offers some balance, even relief from mainstream technological employment dependency. Such knowledge keeps us and our children's children free and entrepreneurial, well-grounded upon what is real.

[122]   Never should we be totally reliant upon technological innovation to eat and pay bills. As Hiphoppas we should be able to cause our wealth (well-being), and teach and protect ourselves with the activities of our innate abilities.

[123]   As thinking human beings, technology should never exclusively define our humanity. Let us walk more. Let us write more. Let us talk face-to-face more. Let us learn or re-learn how to depend upon our divine natures more. Let us re-learn how to fight without guns, and communicate without phones, and travel without cars or airplanes, and even live without money!

[124]   Growing up in the World's ever more rapid acceleration toward total technological dependency strips many human beings of some of the greatest yet most basic human skills we have, like environmental survival skills, natural instincts, our psychic abilities and even such mental/ emotional human skills as intimacy, courage, understanding and patience. These are human skills. And as the growth of technology attempts to tighten its grip upon the production of our very being it is wise to promote and never forget those skills that make us truly human.

[125]   So, while still in the process of building Hiphop Kulture and while using the best of what technology has to offer to expand our culture, we (Hiphoppas) must seriously

consider for ourselves the meaning of our group, the use of technology and the true concept of *civilization* in World history.

[126]   If we are serious about our children's well-being in just the next 10 years, Hip Hop's World image is going to have to continuously improve. Our activities yesterday and today are setting up the heritage that our children shall claim and promote for the World's respect and trust tomorrow.

[127]   Just ask yourself, if Hip Hop was to stop tomorrow, what would be the *human* history and heritage of the Hip Hop community in World history? What would OUR children rely upon as their credible and authentic human heritage? What will the dictionaries and encyclopedias say of us as a distinct human group?

[128]   As Hiphoppas let us never forget our humanity. Let us eat and live off of the talents of our own existence. Let us never become dependent upon things outside of ourselves to actualize that which is already within us. Let us become a nation of exceptional human beings—independent and self-sufficient.

[129]   As Hiphoppas, we must become the civilization that we expect others to be. We can talk and dream all day about living a better quality of life, but if we are unwilling or incapable of governing ourselves then (for the safety of the World) we deserve to be governed by others.

[130]   For if GOD is GOD then GOD is also Hip Hop! And regardless of anyone else's union with GOD, we Hiphoppas must have a union with GOD for ourselves if we are to be truly free, living in peace and prosperity as an independent World culture.

[131]   Different from *spiritual enlightenment* or even praise and worship, our most pressing challenge is to simply live by the principles we have established for ourselves. Endurance, not conquest, shall be our greatest strength.

Other communities shall fall because they contradict their very foundations, while we shall rise by simply being consistent with ours.

[132] For there is no need to fight those who have contradicted their own foundations (their principles); they shall fall by their own hands! However, we Hiphoppas are a principled nation which produces principled people.

[133] The question is, who and what are you actually creating your *Self* to be? Yeah, you might have a goal to achieve or you may be a professional right now but really, who are YOU becoming? Where is all of your effort actually going?

[134] And there is no wrong answer or better answer to these questions. Every truly serious seeker of Truth knows that faith makes all things possible. And those ideas that we think on continuously and desire in our hearts secretly eventually come to pass. The deeper question here is, upon what story shall you place your faith? Even deeper, what exactly is YOUR birthright? What heritage do YOU claim? What is the style of YOUR life?

[135] The importance in answering such questions for yourself rests within the fact that we are only living the stories that we have come to accept as Truth. Change the story; you change your life.

[136] Our work as templists re-establishes a spiritual heritage, a cultural birthright and a daily code of conduct, a lifestyle for all who seek peace, love, unity and safely having fun through the culture of Hip Hop. Although it may have been called many different names throughout human history, that which we call *Hip Hop* today is a very ancient experience.

[137] This first instrument speaks to the spiritual observations of our tribe. Our tribe is called *Hiphop* and/ or *Hip Hop,* and our experiences belong to us! We need not

borrow anyone else's experiences to substantiate or interpret our own. We need not borrow the gods of other cultures to have a relationship with our own.

138   Why borrow or adopt the birthright and/or heritage of a foreign culture when you can clearly point to the richness of your own? Or do you borrow the customs of foreign cultures because you know not the divinity of your own? Wake up! Wake up to the reality of the LOVING GOD who loves you as you are; as a Hiphoppa!

139   And this is the *good news* for OUR PEOPLE today searching for identity and meaning to their lives! WAKE UP! Believe in your *Self!* Believe in the divinity of your own everyday experiences and you shall live in the reality of who you believe your *Self* to be. For we are all made up of the stories that we choose to believe. So what do you believe of yourself and of Hip Hop's story?

140   If you are not prepared to live this culture (Hip Hop) to its fullest, then please close this instrument and hand it to someone who is. However, the real question is, *where do YOU place YOUR faith?* And is it really working out for you?

141   Ask yourself seriously, *are you at peace? Are you in love? Are you whole? Are you empowered by your faith? Is God really real in your life?* And only you can truthfully answer these questions. Why live in denial when you can live in real Health, Love, Awareness and Wealth as an attuned Hiphoppa for real? Why deny that which you already are?

142   Here, we approach Hip Hop as the subject that we put our faith into because we know this subject to be true. In our time (and possibly in yours) we have learned that the history that we are taught as the facts and as the Truth about ourselves cannot be trusted. In my time, ALL AMERICAN HISTORY IS INACCURATE AND INCOMPLETE, especially when it comes to us and our

experiences in the United States. Therefore, to regain and know of the Truth about ourselves, we must BE ourselves and not our education.

[143]   Even if this means starting our history over again from today, or rather continuing our history from what we <u>know</u> to be true, we must at some point begin the re-creation of ourselves and our civilization through the accurate documentation of our past, present and future activities in the World. WE must tell our OWN story to our OWN children.

[144]   WE must seriously begin to believe in ourselves and the historical documentation that we are inspired to create for ourselves. We must stop saying that we have lost our history, culture and heritage and begin proclaiming the rebirth of our divinity and the establishment of a new history, culture and heritage.

[145]   Let us not see our ignorance or *loss* of accurate historical data, resources, land, etc., as a handicap but rather as an opportunity to be truly born again! In fact, whoever we were as a People led to our enslavement and present state of oppression. However, we can recreate ourselves today. This is what Hiphop is all about.

[146]   And yes, we <u>can</u> believe in what is true for us, and Hip Hop is what is true for US! It may NOT be true for anyone else. Others may find peace and prosperity in the strict observances of other faiths and the histories of their religions, and they are right to do so. But here, WE ARE HIP HOP! And we are right to BELIEVE IN OURSELVES!

[147]   Here, Hiphop is the unique activity of our collective consciousness. Hip Hop is our collective faith in action. Hiphop is what WE are being and Hip Hop is what WE are doing!

[148]   When WE appear Hip Hop appears; and when WE are gone Hiphop is gone. Indeed, *life IS what you make of it,*

and Hip Hop is what God has made of our lives. Let us live and learn the gospel that reflects the experiences of OUR unique history as Hiphoppas.

149   Let us learn from the accumulated wisdom of OUR ancestors. Is GOD not with us also? Did GOD not create us also? In fact, the real question here is, where is an omnipresent GOD not? Even deeper, what exists outside of GOD?

150   For if GOD is ALL then GOD IS HIP HOP! And we need not borrow anyone else's interpretation of GOD to have union with GOD. Are we not GOD's children also? Let us then begin to act like the sons and daughters of the Most-High GOD and draw the blessings that can only come by way of a pure heart, a clear mind and an upright character. Is this not the whole point to even the most ancient of spiritual practices?

151   You can be a very talented Graffiti writer, Emcee, Deejay, etc, but if your personal living habits and views on life are not in alignment with the Truth of YOUR being; you cannot expect to achieve any real fulfillment doing whatever you do in life, even if you do it well.

152   One thing that we have learned for sure is that it is the Hiphop lifestyle itself (not one's talent) that empowers one to live a peaceful and prosperous life approaching Hip Hop's artistic elements with success. So let us begin the study of ourselves seriously.

153   Let us stop aligning OUR faith with those who don't respect us. WE ARE HIPHOP! And ALL peaceful people are welcomed within our *city*.

154   For we have seen now that those who are destined and chosen for spiritual awareness only need to prepare for their inevitable transformations. For us (the spiritually minded), spiritual growth is not just about adding to yourself, it is more about preparing for the inevitable

appearance of your own intentions.

155   Once you have made up your own mind to live a spiritual/mystical life, it is inevitable that such a reality will eventually reveal itself to you. The idea then is to simply prepare for the inevitable coming of your Higher-Self. Such an awareness is not to be attained, it is to be prepared for. You are already your Higher-Self.

156   The question is, are you prepared for the inevitable actualization of your own Higher-Self? It is like giving birth to a child. Under normal circumstances, once mom realizes that she is pregnant it is inevitable that a child will be born. However, the question here is, how healthy shall this child be?

157   Yes, it is inevitable that a child is on its way. But such a child can still be born prematurely or even late. Such a child may be born with certain health issues because of the conduct of the mother and/or father. Such a child can still be abused, neglected, aborted, or even born dead. The same examples can apply to the birth of your Higher-Self.

158   From the time you make up in your mind that it is the spiritual life that you want to live, you are at that very moment pregnant with the intention to achieve your Higher-Self. At this moment it is of extreme importance that you begin to eat right, think right and live right or you can hinder the development of your own Higher-Self and, more importantly, its delivery.

159   Therefore, ENTER YOUR INNER CITY and nurture the development of your Higher-Self. WE ARE HIPHOP! And we need nothing else to survive and grow. We are content with the burden GOD has given to US!

160   Bishop Clarence E. McClendon explains in an advertisement for his sermon entitled *The X-Blessing* that *while the World has labeled this generation as 'Generation X,' and has written them off as rebellious, uncommitted and lazy,*

GOD says that He has chosen to mightily use this generation for His supernatural purpose and plans.

[161]   Bishop McClendon proclaimed in 1999 that "believers" need to *adjust their thinking and to understand that there is an unusual blessing and endowment upon this generation.*

[162]   Bishop McClendon reveals through scripture how *GOD has once again today chosen the ones that nobody expected to deliver a generation and impact the World. God is raising up a generation that He has called and anointed with a special grace to spark revival throughout our nation.*

[163]   So, let us rise now! Let us mature into those *Holy Integrated People Having Omnipresent Power.* Let us NOT squander OUR gifts or smother the development of OUR Higher-Selves this time. Let us actually begin to reveal and un-Rap them. We have great work to do, let's get to it. There it is.

THE SIXTH OVERSTANDING
THE SEASONS

[1] Peace and much love to all future Hiphoppas! Rejoice! For we are truly blessed people! Do not be discouraged or depressed by the criticisms of the World. For ignorance is always bold and certain. However, ignorance is also temporary. For it is better to be *fresh* in the sight of your God and *wack* to the World, than to be *fresh* in the sight of the World and *wack* to your God!

[2] For the same World that hails you up in praise is the same World that can tear you down in judgment! The same World that condemns you is the same World that hails you up! Such is the way of the World. Be prepared!

[3] Therefore, focus not upon the praises or the criticisms of the World. Focus only upon your performance before GOD! Stand only in Truth! For the correction of GOD is like that of a loving mother while the criticisms of the World are like those of rebellious children. For the World will hate you one day and then love you the next.

[4] Likewise, the rewards, awards and validations of GOD are like the handmade clothing of a protective mother that is given to her child to guard against the harsh elements of those rainy and cold seasons.

[5] However, the rewards, awards and validations of the World are like the mass-produced clothing of an impersonal corporation that is sold to you for a price. Such clothing offers only temporary protection against the harsh elements of those rainy and cold seasons because the clothing manufacturer needs you to keep coming back to purchase

clothing. Eventually such clothing even goes out of style.

6   For the mass-produced clothing of the World impresses only the immature, while the handmade clothing of God impresses only the wise. Choose today the garment you shall wear! For we have learned that sunny and warm days are followed by cloudy days which are followed by rainy and stormy days which return to sunny and warm days.

7   Those who are unaware of the spiritual seasons of life believe that when the storms of life beat upon their circumstances they are doomed to that situation for the rest of their lives. It seems as if the storm will never end! And in desperation they make decisions under pressure, which force them to make the wrong decisions in life. In the long run, such desperate decisions only prolong their suffering.

8   Attuned Hiphoppas who have acquired the knowledge of life's seasons and cycles occasionally go through the same storms everyone else goes through. However, with an awareness that the storm is always temporary, attuned Hiphoppas remain calm and mentally still, allowing the storm to pass over them. Others without knowledge of life's seasons try to run from the storm, only to wind up running with it! Even more people miss valuable opportunities and lessons that can be found in the midst of the storm by running away from the storm. The same applies to the sunny days.

9   Not realizing that everything has its season, the unaware *Rap fan* believes that he is running ahead of the storm when he is actually keeping up with the storm! For when the storms of life beat against your clothing it is usually best to remain still and allow the storm to pass you by. The same applies to the sunny days.

10   With difficult people and circumstances, be still. Be on good terms with all people, even if you must be silent in the face of those that disrespect you. Develop the habit of

not saying things that you may regret later when the storm of hostility and/or depression has passed. Be silent, be still. Even with all forms of temptation, be silent, be still. Allow the storms of those tempting desires to pass over you. Do nothing! When tempted, do nothing.

11   But know this. Only those who wear the handmade clothing of God—Purpose, Mercy, Peace, Charity, Love, Overstanding, Truth, Discipline, Inspiration, Wisdom, Gratefulness, Self-Sacrifice, etc.—can stand still in the midst of life's storms (changes/temptations). These are the designer labels of our everlasting God. For only divine clothing can withstand the various storms of life.

12   For when it is sunny and warm, meaning that everything is going your way, such a season is not to be used to relax and indulge in the pleasures of the World. Such a season is always used to prepare for those rainy days. And such preparation is not done in fear. Such a preparation is done with an overstanding that all Worldly relationships, validations, rewards and opportunities are indeed temporary.

13   Attuned Hiphoppas preserve their Health, Love, Awareness and Wealth during those sunny and warm seasons in preparation for the inevitable storms (changes) to come. After a while the storms do not even affect the attuned Hiphoppa's H-LAW. With wisdom the attuned Hiphoppa sees that it is during those rainy days that the people of the World are fed.

14   For it is through challenges, changes and disappointments that the people of the World gain wisdom. For it is the storms of life that humble and teach the people of the World. However, Spirit beings remain still and protected in the most terrifying and difficult of life's storms. For they are not taught (or fed) during the stormy seasons or during the sunny seasons. They are taught (or fed) by an

acknowledgement of the Truth which comes to everyone first but is rejected by those who value the World more than they do their own God.

15   Actually, Spirit beings find opportunity in the very midst of the storm. While others attempt to run from the storm, or fight the storm, or criticize the storm, Spirit beings find their opportunities within the storm!

16   For true power is not gained through conquests and takeovers, it actually falls into the laps of those prepared to catch it! Those who take by force prove that they were unprepared to freely receive what they have stolen. Whatever they took they did not truly earn and it is not theirs to keep. It shall return to its rightful owner!

17   For true power is given when GOD upsets the normal order of human civilization, causing shifts in public demand, which causes a redistribution or reallocation of Worldly wealth and influence. Everyone eventually gets an opportunity to govern their World. The question is, what are you prepared for? How shall you govern? Even the sunny days are temporary.

18   With a knowledge of life's seasons we know that it is always some unexpected turn of events that changes everything and opens doors that did not even exist before. Therefore, stay true to your purpose in life. Perform patience. No matter how humble or grand, be true to your life's purpose and envy not the achievements of others.

19   For the material World is truly temporary. Therefore, do not become aggravated, angry, worried or disappointed with those who appear to be in Worldly power today, for in a minute they shall be in power no more and the effects of their temporary power and prestige shall also fade away. We have seen this too many times.

20   Not that we wish harm or failure upon anyone; such is not the character of an attuned Hiphoppa. However, it is

a fact that the World and Worldly circumstances are indeed temporary. For those who chase after the pleasures, powers and items of the World chase after things that are temporary in their very existence. Be still, be committed to your life purpose and perform patience. It is inevitable that your day will come again. Stay focused!

21   For in the reality of the material World, everything is deteriorating. Every material thing, every physical structure, requires maintenance for its continued existence in the material World! Nothing physical is permanent. And likewise, every person that holds Worldly power today will not hold such power tomorrow. And those who have not Worldly power today shall indeed have an abundance of such tomorrow. For this is the way of the World! Be prepared when it is your turn to govern! Treat all people with respect when you are in power and they shall remember you and your children.

22   Hiphoppas who hold Worldly power, prestige and/or popularity should never forget that such powers are indeed temporary. That when it is sunny and warm one should be prepared for rainy and cold! And vice versa. For those who praise you today shall curse you tomorrow. And those who curse you today shall praise you tomorrow.

23   Therefore, focus not upon the praises, the criticisms or the curses of the World, for they are truly powerless! Instead, focus only upon the Truth of your God animating your purpose. Indeed you are a projection of the universe itself! You are what the universe is doing right now! Your existence and purpose are part of the balance of the entire universe. Know this. It is of extreme importance to the unfolding of the universe that you be your true *Self!*

24   As mentioned throughout this gospel, the most important practice attuned Hiphoppas can do for themselves is to actually BE themselves. And after that is achieved, one

must literally become one's own best friend.

25   You must realize rather quickly that the 20-year-old you has depended upon the 10-year-old you for its very survival. And the 30-year-old you is depending upon the 20-year-old you for its very survival. And the 40-year-old you is depending upon the 30-year-old you for its survival.

26   As an example, just think for a moment about the decisions that you made, as well as the decisions that were made for you, at just 10 years of age. Whether you were conscious or unconscious of the decisions made at 10 years of age, they have nonetheless had a profound effect upon your life at 20 years of age. And yes, the decisions that you possibly made at 20 years of age will have and/or have had a profound effect upon the well-being of your life at 30 years of age.

27   In fact, if you are 30 years of age now, for example, it was the 10, 15, 20, and even 25-year-old you that was actually more important to your survival at 30 years of age than your 30-year-old self is now. For if the 10, 15, 20, and 25-year-old you did not make the right decisions, it is likely that the 30-year-old you is suffering for it today.

28   For it is not only the you of today that is responsible for your well-being and status in life today, it is more that your past self is responsible for your total well-being right now and that at this very moment you are the manifested thoughts of your past self. Do you like what you have created so far? The future you is truly depending upon you today to make the right decisions for its well-being and social status tomorrow. This is what it means to be a friend to your own *Self!*

29   Do not wait until you are 40, 50, or even 60 years of age to ponder how stupid and careless you may have lived your life at 20, 25, 30 and 35 years of age. Grab hold of your life now! Perform responsibility now! Achieve your purpose

now! Be your own best friend NOW! Do not become stagnated by your own *inconsciousness*.

30   However, it gets even deeper than this. Yes, you may understand how your past self has affected you today. But consider the idea that your future *Self* can also affect you today. Being your own best friend includes the concept of being your own guardian angel.

31   Consider the seventh sense where there is neither time nor space, where everything is actually one thing, where the concept of time simply does not exist. Everything is *here* and *now*. You at 10 years of age and you at 70 years of age exist right now at whatever age you believe yourself to be today.

32   Consider your mind a time-traveling device that can take you far into your so-called *past* as well as far into your so-called *future*. All of you at different ages exist together as one *being* right now. This means that if you are truly aware that time does not govern your mind, the 70-year-old you can literally act as the spiritual guardian of the 20 or 30-year-old you now.

33   You can begin at 20 years of age (for example) visualizing yourself watching over, protecting and guiding your 15-year-old self. This would mean that when you were physically 15 years of age, the mind of the 20-year-old you actually did *look out* for the body of the 15-year-old you. This would explain a lot of the miraculous things that happened to you during your teenage years. It would be because the future versions of you (which is you right now) learned of this technique and applied it.

34   Try to understand this. Read the previous paragraph again slowly to really understand what is being taught here. If you begin to regularly visualize yourself guiding and protecting the younger versions of yourself today, then by continuing this practice for the duration of your physical

life, your 70 year old self (as an example) is guiding and protecting you now! Just as you are appearing to your 15-year-old self as its guardian angel today, so it is that your 70-year-old self is appearing to you now if you continue this practice into your future.

35   This means that the decisions that you make in the future are also affecting your life now, just as the decisions that you have made in the past are also affecting your life now. All things are one thing. In your seventh sense, at the deepest levels of your being, there are no separate spaces and there are no past, present or future intervals of time. Everything is actually *here* and *now*.

36   The memories of your future self are the imaginations of your present self. And the memories of your present self are the imaginations of your past self. Whatever you desire or are doing in the future is also affecting you now in your present. You can see who you are in the future by your desires today. This is why it is of extreme importance that you lead a virtuous life. Every thought and desire that you act upon in some way affects your total well-being in the so-called *past, present* and *future*.

37   So be careful with this technique. With your own mind go into your own past with love (not judgment) and protect and guide the younger versions of yourself. Do not seek to change anything; just give your younger *Self* strength to arrive at your present self. Free yourself from the bondage of time! Learn through your seventh sense to manipulate the illusion of time in your life. Use your time wisely. Do not allow it to use you ignorantly!

38   When you pray; pray not just for your future self, but pray also for your past self. And when you meditate, meditate upon the victory of your youth. Give yourself the habit of watching over the younger versions of yourself with the wisdom and overstanding that you have acquired

today. There is no time! You can be 5 years of age or 50 years of age right now.

39   If you continue this practice of praying and/or meditating back onto yourself for the duration of your physical life, then indeed the future you is correcting, guiding and protecting you right now with what you have yet to learn. Remember; the 16-year-old you cannot actually see the experiences of the 60-year-old you. But the 60-year-old you can see the experiences of the 16-year-old you. Let your future *Self* advise you.

40   The 16-year-old you (now aware of this gospel) must listen out for the warnings and inspiration of the 60-year-old you. And likewise, the 16-year-old you must be a friend (even a servant) to the 20, 30, 40, 50 and 60-year-old you. This is also the essence of a disciplined Hiphop life; *Self*-creation, *Self*-control and *Self*-direction.

41   The attuned Hiphoppa who is *Self*-created, *Self*-directed and in control of one's cravings is rarely depressed, insecure or confused. The attuned Hiphoppa commands the environment she enters; not by force but by the spiritual character she openly displays. For this reason, the attuned Hiphoppa is safe wherever she goes. She is rarely insecure or confused within her environment because in fact she is no longer living within her environment; her environment is now within her.

42   In other words, most people feel vulnerable within their own environments as well as foreign environments because they lack the ability to influence the happenings of either. Things are going on in their environments which they believe they have no control over. This causes all kinds of insecurities, worries and doubts.

43   However, if you are to have any victory over the chaotic happenings of your own environment as well as the environment that you may enter then you must be able to

exert some kind of influence over the happenings of such environments. This kind of influence over one's physical environment begins with the ability to project your own mind (through Spirit) beyond the confinement of your own insecurities, doubts and fears and onward toward Truth.

[44]   For when the Hiphoppa lives in doubt and in ignorance of his higher *Self*, the Law (or Way) of the universe confines that Hiphoppa to his lower self. The one who has not even tried to perfect himself shall never go beyond the confinement of himself. Fear, doubt, selfishness and spiritual ignorance turns one's own mind against one's own *Self*, and confines such a person to the prison of his own perceptions.

[45]   The true Hiphoppa must make an effort to complete *himself* if he desires to exert any real influence beyond *himself*. An incomplete person is unable to direct himself. It is like having a broken leg or a broken wing. Only a *Self*-directed person can get to where he needs to be. Everyone else is drifting or being directed by the intentions and influences of others.

[46]   Very simply, when you gain control of your *Self* you shall be able to command your *Self* to do whatever you wish. The real issue as to why you cannot heal yourself, feel good about yourself or achieve those things that you really want for yourself is because you have very little control of your *Self*. Your mind does whatever IT wants to do! Your body does whatever IT wants to do! Your emotions are out of YOUR control! And YOUR own environment acts as if you are not even there! The master of your *house* is asleep. WAKE UP, HIPHOPPA!

[47]   When you gain control of your *Self* you shall tell yourself what to do, and where to go, and what to be and it shall have no choice of its own but to do, or go, or be that which you have commanded it. But first, you must get

control of your SELF!

⁴⁸ Just think. If you wanted to pick up a glass of water but your arms were doing whatever they wanted to do on their own, and the glass of water was doing whatever it wanted to do on its own, and the table and everything else were all moving on their own, it would be impossible to pick up the glass and drink. In fact, there would be no glass to drink from.

⁴⁹ This is how most people live their lives! They have no control of themselves or their environment. They are tempted by this and disciplined by that. They are helplessly blown across life like a leaf in the street! This type of life can make anyone insecure, fearful, doubtful and stressed out! It is only when you have complete control of your arms and hands that you can then effortlessly move them toward that which you desire.

⁵⁰ Even deeper, when you realize that what you call your *Self* is actually the table, the glass and the water as well as your arms and hands, then the table, the glass, the water, your arms, your legs, your mind, your physical environment and your life circumstances shall all stop doing their own things. They shall hear your commands and obey them because at this level of awareness they have no movement outside of your *Self*—outside of your perception. Your very presence brings everything into harmonious order with each other; *each other* meaning the totality of your *Self!*

⁵¹ It is only your limited perception that allows your environment to do what IT wants. In fact, because of your own doubt and disbelief you allow your environment to do whatever IT wants—no one is directing it. This is why it is of extreme importance that you first gain control of your own *Self* if you are to attain any kind of real peace or lasting prosperity. Such a control begins as a consistent learned habit of the mind. First YOU must get your mind

right! First YOU must make the decision to direct your OWN mind, which is done through a defeat of your bodily cravings. Then when you have *made up your mind,* when you have created your mind-state outside of your cravings, stick to it! STAND YOUR GROUND! Do not be moved!

52   Know this. An uncontrollable, imperfect mind is a prison for the true Hiphoppa. For if you cannot direct your own mind and body beyond your own temptations, fears and doubts then it is obvious that you are led not by what YOU desire for your *Self* but by what your mind and body crave for themselves. You are their slave. This is why you cannot seem to get anything done for yourself. In spirit you must finally *make up your mind,* create and build your own mind-state.

53   It is YOU (Spirit) that must order your mind and body to think and move toward YOUR success; otherwise they will think and move toward the fulfillment of their own successes which is your spiritual failure. Right along with the knowing of one's *Self* and even the creation of one's *Self* is the true directing of one's *Self.* Once your tempting desires and cravings no longer have a hold on you, you can properly direct your *Self.*

54   For it is the will to direct your *Self* even in the most confusing and uncomfortable situations that proves your spiritual maturity. In fact, the ability to actually direct one's thoughts and actions above the cravings of the flesh is a skill that every true Hiphoppa growing along a spiritual path must attain.

55   This is why many people feel stagnated in their lives, even with success. Most of the time it is because they either lost the ability to direct themselves or they never had the ability to direct themselves. They've become slaves to their situations. Whenever they think of something that they would like to do for themselves it is always their OWN

uncontrollable fears, doubts, cravings, temptations and other immaturities that prevent them from achieving that which they say that they want for themselves.

⁵⁶   In this case someone will say, *I want X but I'm too afraid to do what it takes to achieve X*. Or they will say, *I want X* but deep down in their very being they really don't believe that they deserve X, or can actually achieve X. Here, it is fear and/or doubt that is not only stagnating one's life, but this same fear and/or doubt is actually guiding one's life. Such a person is not led by his will to achieve X (purpose). Such a person is led, guided and directed by fear and/or doubt.

⁵⁷   The cure is to direct your *Self* beyond your fears and/or doubts with awareness. Being *Self*-directed is the beginning of peace and prosperity. And this skill begins with taking your *Self* seriously. This means to finally make the decision to be that which you say you are. Whatever that is, be it NOW! *Bloom where you are planted!* Love your *Self*.

⁵⁸   Don't wait for the best opportunity or some favorable situation to arrive before you actually begin the process of self-transformation; *grow from what you already know!* Practice the control of your emotions (sadness, anger, even happiness) when you are confronted by selfish, depressed and/or angered people. Begin today to seize control of the environment in which you live and the mind in which you have. Do not allow the environment, people's attitudes, or the cravings of your mind to move you exclusively; at this very moment make the decision to begin moving them!

⁵⁹   Most people will say that they are looking for peace and prosperity but in actuality they are looking for the cravings and temptations of their own mind and body. If you are serious about peace you must look for it with your eyes, ears and other physical senses. Most people have no

control of their own eyes! This is crazy! Most men cannot stop themselves from looking at the breasts and asses of women passing them by in the street. And get what I' m saying here: THEY CANNOT CONTROL THEIR OWN EYES!

60   They may say that they are "looking for GOD," but this statement is actually said figuratively. In reality their eyes are in control of them. They say that they are looking for GOD (as an example), but their own eyes disagree with them. The eyes themselves look wherever they choose to look regardless of what the man says he wants for himself. This is crazy! This is self-oppression.

61   On the other hand, women in need of attention, knowing that men are looking at their breasts and asses, put on the tightest and most revealing costumes in order to tempt men into associating with them. And many women will say that they are "seeking to attract the favor of GOD," but in reality they are seeking to attract sexual favors. This too is crazy! They claim to be listening for the voice of GOD, but in reality their ears are listening to the problems and scandals of the World around them.

62   As Hiphoppas we must gain direction of our own physical senses. We must direct our eyes, ears, etc., toward that which we claim to be searching for. Know this. In any given environment there are millions of things going on, but if you chose to allow your physical senses to focus only upon what stimulates the physical body, you will in no way see GOD or enter the realm of Spirit.

63   Likewise, we must ask ourselves, *Am I the tempter/ temptress in other people's lives, tempting them with my good looks, breaking up marriages and families, preventing people from reaching their own spiritual potentials with my own desire for sex and vanity? Am I a walking distraction?* You will in no way enter the realm of Spirit if you present yourself to the

World as a tempter of others.

⁶⁴   Wear only the God-made garments of Wisdom, Love, Faith, Discipline, Truth, Charity, Mercy, etc., holding as a mighty weapon this Gospel of Hip Hop, and you will attract the same to you. With this character, not only shall you be protected against the temporary storms of life, but indeed you shall maintain your VICTORY OVER THE STREETS!

⁶⁵   We have seen now that Life does move in seasons, and if we can be still and observant we will begin to see the seasons (patterns) of Life as well as of our own lives and be able to predict changes and heed warnings.

⁶⁶   One of the most important spiritual practices one can learn is how to detect the repeated patterns (the seasons) of Life and of one's own life. Yes, the seeming chaos that we call "Life" is predictable and it speaks through natural occurrences, symbolic natural signs and repeated occurrences.

⁶⁷   The Temple of Hip Hop tracks and records the naturally repeated patterns of our Hip Hop life and harmonizes such patterns with the patterns of Life itself. The synchronizing of these patterns (repeated occurrences) makes up the natural reality of our Hip Hop lifestyle. Our patterns are unique to us; we are not linked with the life patterns and prophecies of other cultures. We respect and love them all but we are indeed free to discover and live our own prophecies and life patterns—this is freedom for our people.

⁶⁸   There are things that we as a group (Hip Hop) repeatedly do, and these repeated activities make up the character and language that we speak and understand. Likewise, there are things that Life itself repeatedly does, and these activities make up the character and language that Life speaks and understands.

[69] To know the naturally repeated patterns of Hip Hop not only causes peace and security for the knower, but knowing Hip Hop's repeated patterns puts the knower in direct relation with the essence of Hip Hop's existence and movement in the World. Without such knowledge it is almost impossible to correctly guide the Hip Hop community or one's self within it.

[70] Likewise, knowing the repeated patterns of Life itself puts the knower in direct relation with the existence and movement of GOD—the Love that moves our movement. And without knowledge of GOD we are blind to GOD's activity in our lives. Often what we call *errors* and *mistakes* are actually GOD's guidance. To get us to arrive at where we are supposed to be, we are often led through a variety of *other* seemingly unrelated activities and events.

[71] Instead of moving harmoniously with GOD, in ignorance we get in our own way trying to correct ourselves, preventing GOD from guiding us toward our ultimate peace and joy. In such ignorance we must settle for guessing what GOD is doing in our lives as opposed to knowing what GOD is doing in our lives, assisting GOD in the perfection of our lives.

[72] Everything happens in season, in its proper time, and failure to move within Life's seasons is what causes stress and loss. Knowing that *yours* is coming in due season produces the virtue of patience and gives one strength to endure while waiting for one's *season* to kick in.

[73] Those with knowledge of Life's seasons refrain from doing things outside of one's *seasons*. We plant our dreams in the cold and rainy seasons of life only to harvest the grains of success in the cool and sunny seasons. Others of us with different styles of seed plant our dreams in the sunny and cool seasons, reaping our harvest in the cold and rainy seasons.

74   You simply have to know who you are and why you are. Your Hip Hop spiritual path may begin with your own knowledge of your own seasons and life cycles. Hip Hop has its own seasons but such knowledge is secret at this time because of the exploitive way hip-hop is being approached in my time. As scholars, just because we know doesn't mean we must reveal.

75   However, Hip Hop's seasons, as well as Life's seasons, can be discovered on one's own through the study of one's own life patterns. You can also apply fractal mathematics and the living (wearing) of Life's most celebrated virtues (garments)—Peace, Love, Unity, Joy, Patience, Charity, Forgiveness, etc.—to achieve such knowledge. In order to learn from Life you must submit yourself to the service of Life; do what Life does and Life will do what you do.

76   Life serves the interests of all without judgment. Life does justice, not judgment.

77   Life sustains all in its environment. Life is a provider, a sustainer. Life endures.

78   Life heals and self-creates. Everything about Life is healing, nurturing and creative.

79   Life teaches and makes its participants aware of themselves and their environment. Life is good.

80   This is the character that we must align ourselves with if Life is to reveal its secrets. One thing that we know for sure about Life itself is that it repeats. Life is all about repetition, and repetition is also about consistency.

81   Therefore, one way of submitting to Life is to be as consistent as one can be with one's true nature. Once you have decided to commit to a lifestyle that reflects your true nature, be consistent with that lifestyle. Life itself will teach you not only about the seasons of your own life but about the seasons of Life itself.

82   As scholars of the Hip Hop arts and sciences we are

encouraged to observe the character of Life itself and repeat its ways. As scholars, let us join in on the work that Life itself does. Take some time and observe Life, how it seems to function, its likes and dislikes, its causes and its effects, as well as its repeated patterns. Know this. The study of Life is the study of GOD's Will.

83   However, as Hiphoppas we have learned that consistency itself is actually a season. We've learned that there are times to be consistent and then there are times to be inconsistent. We've learned that Life itself is alive, and it does contradict itself in many ways because it offers us choices. The same exact events never repeat themselves; it is the exact same conditions that cause the occurrence of certain events that repeat themselves.

84   It is then up to us. How we choose to handle such conditions determines whether the events of the past shall happen again as they did in history. The repeated patterns of certain conditions are indeed consistent, but not repeated events in history. Consistency and inconsistency are creations of logical and rational thought trying to make sense of a seemingly chaotic natural World. Such terms, when applied to human affairs, are what we call "social virtues"—virtues that spring up based upon the survival needs and comfort of a dominant social group. But in the end, we do have choices.

85   Today, being consistent is completely overrated, especially when compared to simply living one's life. In my time, African Americans still have to be consistent with the collective character of the White mainstream, religious groups and political parties in order to even exist in the United States successfully. This form of consistency is indeed destructive to African American well-being and growth. How can any group discover what is right for them while being consistent with the purpose, prophecies and

life-path of another group? Can such a condition even be called "freedom?"

86   When it comes to Hip Hop, being consistent with anyone or anything outside of our Hip Hop experience is self-destruction and this is why continuous consistency with someone or something foreign to our Hip Hop experience is simply not right for us. We must study and discover our own life patterns and seasons in order to be truly free and productive.

87   Being consistent generally means being constant, predictable and dependable, whereas being inconsistent or contradictory simply means to be of an opposite view, to break with tradition or be in conflict with an accepted normality. In a real effort to preserve and further develop Hip Hop it is now time that we break our spiritual, physical and psychological ties with many of the World's prophecies and psychological patterns. In our quest for real freedom, now is the time for us to respectfully contradict many of the traditions that were forced upon our parents in an effort to truly discover what GOD has in store for us. This is true freedom for our people.

88   Most people however, confuse *contradiction* with *hypocrisy*, and most often accuse a contradictory person of being a hypocrite. A hypocrite is someone who makes false claims to virtue. Hypocrisy has to do with virtue, or rather the lack thereof, whereas contradiction has to do with change of view; the two are not the same. This is why spiritual-minded people should not attempt to be too organized in worldly affairs. Those of spiritual mind operate within a different timing, and so at times we may contradict the timings of the World by being behind the *times* and/or ahead of the *times*.

89   Yes, we are encouraged to be consistent, but with ourselves, our own principles and with our own spiritual

nature. In this case, we are ordained to be consistent with Hip Hop because we are Hiphoppas. And such a consistency with Hip Hop creates a slight inconsistency with that which is not Hip Hop. As spiritual beings we must get comfortable with arriving late sometimes or arriving early at other times. Our consistency is grounded in our true nature; it is not grounded in the ways of the World.

90 That which is not consistent with Hip Hop cannot be consistent with us. We have the right to grow as a social group, and growth is contradiction. Nothing that is consistent grows or changes. It is when you contradict your present reality that you really get a new one. A seed that is consistently a seed never becomes a flower, a plant, a tree, or a vine.

91 If you like your present lifestyle, if it fulfills you, then by all means be consistent with that which is consistent with you. But if your present lifestyle is unfulfilling and stagnating then you must contradict your present life for a new one. Examine yourself for real.

92 Being consistent with something or someone going nowhere is self-destruction. However, self-creation is the result of properly contradicting one's self and one's lifestyle for a better one. To think and to change one's mind, to hold two opposing thoughts within one's mind, to grow intellectually is to contradict some aspect of your present reality and character in exchange for a new one.

93 Without a wholistic view of reality everything seems to contradict everything else. Nature is very contradictory to human awareness because we cannot yet see how all the *pieces* fit together. Things change in physical Nature. Adulthood contradicts childhood. Life contradicts death. Hot contradicts cold. Man contradicts Woman. Humanity contradicts Nature.

94 But when you realize that most of what we sense as

physical reality is really the effects of consistent invisible forces, you begin to see the unity of things and how all things work together for those who's eye is open to the activity of GOD. GOD's activity has been known to contradict humanity's activities because humanity is not consistent with GOD. The question then becomes, who are you going to be consistent with, them or GOD?

[95]   Only in spirit is there any real consistency, any real constant, and even the spirit realm has seasons to it. The physical World with its condition of dualities—up and down, right and left, back and forth, in and out—makes you have to *choose sides* and be consistent so that others can label and identify you for their own understanding of their own reality. Ultimately, consistency in my time is used as a character meter, some kind of morality check which informs others whether you are O.K. to deal with or not.

[96]   This is not altogether a bad thing though. People like consistency because it is predictable and so the consistent person appears trustworthy. Therefore, as Hiphoppas, let us be consistent with GOD—the Love that made us Hip Hop.

[97]   Let us as Hiphoppas be consistent with a Hip Hop character that glorifies GOD and produces health, love, awareness and wealth for all who participate in the Hip Hop experience.

[98]   Let us be consistent with the principles of our temple which teach us to be consistent with GOD—the Love that Guides Our Direction.

[99]   Let us be consistent with our own history which reveals the activity of GOD—the Love that brought us this far.

[100]   Let us be consistent with our own dreams, our own visions and our own future, which teaches us the promise that GOD has declared to OUR people. THE LAST DAYS

OF OTHERS ARE THE FIRST DAYS FOR US! We are Hip Hop, and we shall survive the prophecies of foreign nations and cultures. We now know that it is our consistent focus upon the law, overstanding, voice and exactness of GOD that shall raise us up and establish our holy nation in due season.

[101]   In a way, we can see what GOD is doing today. This gospel for Hip Hop is not even really for the time in which it is written. This gospel is for the true Hip Hop nation that is to come after this age is complete. Those who can comprehend this instrument today and walk in its principles are indeed blessed. But really, the citizens of our Hip Hop nation are not even born yet; they are waiting for this instrument to arrive in the hands of their parents. And as you can see it just did, in due season. There it is.

THE SEVENTH OVERSTANDING
THE SEVENTH SENSE

[1]   Know this. We are seeds. We are spiritual seeds planted in this dark World. It is not the body that we are, it is the flower within it, the fruit within it, the spirit within the seed/body that we are. The body is our protective shield, our husk that houses the spirit/seed inside, planted within this World to sprout at our time of shedding.

[2]   In reality, there is only creation. In reality, there is only one thing Going On Daily—GOD! The true concept of creation has no room for destruction. *All is creation!* This *Overstanding* explores the illusion of death, and gives some examples that might point the way to the reality of LIFE.

[3]   Know this. There is only creation and further creation; death as destruction is an illusion. The term *destruction* only implies the act of deconstructing or breaking something down. However, even to destroy is to create. Even destruction must be created; even death is a new birth—a new creation, a new reality, a new thing that your essence is experiencing.

[4]   Consider the fact that destruction, for the most part, is simply another form of creation. Again, destruction must be created. Therefore, whatever is real cannot be destroyed—it can only be changed. Therefore, creation cannot be destroyed; it is the only real thing happening. Energy cannot be destroyed; it only changes.

[5]   Once You *are* or it *is;* YOU and/or IT can never not be. You and/or IT can only be changed, transformed or further created. Your physical form can change but YOU

will never not exist. YOU are the essence of you. And if you are to overcome the illusion of death, it is you who must decide to be and live as the real YOU right now. Nothing real can ever be destroyed. The real YOU is not physical. YOU are the actual breath of GOD.

6   The real YOU is the animating essence (the breath) of the Great Spirit. YOU are not your body. YOU are the breath (or consciousness) that must continuously enter the body for the body to have life and ideas. If YOU (the breath) are separated from the physical body for just a minute or more, the first thing that the body loses is consciousness.

7   Therefore, let us consider humanity as not the billions of people on this planet, but instead let us consider that humanity is found in the air/substance that such human animals are breathing. As an aid to our disciplinary practices over the cravings of the body, let us enter our physical bodies as opposed to being them.

8   Let us consider ourselves as consciousness, the breath of GOD, Spirit. And when such a Spirit/consciousness is inhaled into the animal, that animal is made to act like the consciousness that has entered it. Such an animal is *being* human or acting human. However, the *true* human (the breath of GOD) is what is causing your physical body or animal/natural self to act human. This is what we call a *human being*. Human beings are natural Earth creatures (animals) *being* or acting human.

9   However, the *true* human is not a physical creature at all. The *true* human is actually a non-physical being invading the body of an animal. And this is where the struggle between the natural self and the spiritual *Self* begins.

10   Know this. Your physical body is formed by the Earth's animal intelligence in preparation for the incoming breath of GOD—YOU. However, it is YOU who must tame the cravings and desires of your natural/animal *self* so

that you may ride, work and stir your animal *self* toward the fulfillment of YOUR true life's purpose.

11   For if YOU have not tamed and trained the animal that YOU have entered, such an animal will lead you everywhere but where YOU need to be. This is the beginning of Hiphop's spiritual training; subdue the animal that YOU have entered first, so that YOU may travel through life in peace. Still, some people spend their entire lives taming and training their animal selves, never becoming fully human.

12   Hiphoppas don't have time for this! True Hiphoppas are advised to subdue their animal instincts and get to their spiritual work quickly. Be all of yourself! For when you are all of yourself there is no more need to subdue or train any aspect of yourself. When you are your whole *Self* other aspects of your animal-self will automatically fall in line with the Truth of your being. Be one with your *SELF*!

13   You are REAL! And you are eternal! Death, as in the end, is an illusion. Sickness, as in deterioration, is an illusion. Poverty, as in lacking, is an illusion. All that the universe is, YOU are. All that the universe has, YOU have. All that the universe does, YOU are doing. Go with the flow!

14   Know this. Spiritual Awareness is not about you doing anything! It is about YOU being in harmony with what is already going on. Life and death are already with you now. When you close your eyes you don't see only blackness, you see your ideas. So when you no longer have physical eyes (in death) you are left with your own thoughts to see.

15   For what is truly man-made when human beings are products of the conscious universe itself? For what idea is originally human when it is the Great Spirit alone who thinks, creates, inspires and acts?

16   Consider the idea that we are doing exactly what

Nature wants us to do. That it is our own sense of *I, Me* and *My* on an unconscious level that has us believing that we are doing something separate from Nature itself!

[17] For it is only the unaware mind that thinks it is separate from the universe, separate from Nature, separate from Eternal Mind! And in thinking so, it limits its own authority and capabilities for Health, Love, Awareness and Wealth in the physical World. Separate selfhood is an illusion, and this is why so many people are lonely and/or insecure.

[18] For the only way to truly prove that you are separate from Nature is to use your limited intellectual perception of reality to create something contrary to what Nature is all about. And so, in the name of an undeveloped *I, Me* and *My*, unaware human beings have used their limited perception of reality to contradict and challenge Nature by creating the illusion of sickness, hate, ignorance and poverty for themselves!

[19] It is like saying, for the sake of maintaining the illusion of being separate from Nature, look Mother (Nature), I will perceive and accept suffering for myself because it is the only thing that you are actually incapable of! And so we suffer in our own attempt to perceive ourselves as separate from the universe, Nature and Eternal Mind!

[20] Many people have traded the Truth of an infinite creation for the illusion of a final destruction. Such a mindset is the equivalent of children who wish to have their own identity and make it on their own, so they rebel against their parents and cut themselves off from what is rightfully theirs only to struggle throughout life ignorant to the fact that they are heirs to all that their parents have, being only smaller versions and/or continuations of their parents in reality.

[21] WAKE UP HIPHOPPA! You are a sleeping God.

Not a sleeping god, but in fact God asleep; an unaware God. You are like a spirit-seed planted in this Worldly reality, awaiting your time to sprout! The Hiphoppa is God asleep, while God is the attuned Hiphoppa awake! The Hiphoppa is an unaware God, while God is a fully aware attuned Hiphoppa. Let's go deeper.

22   Human beings are said to have five senses: seeing, hearing, smelling, touching and tasting, with a sixth sense that is called *human intuition* or the ability to perceive without the use of the other five senses or rational thought. However, human beings possess even more senses than these. In fact, "balance" is a sense that is very seldom mentioned among the human senses.

23   Actually, "balance" can be called a "sixth sense" while human intuition can be called a "seventh sense." But for the sake of mass understanding we shall not include "balance" as a "sixth sense," although Hiphoppas do acknowledge that they possess more than five or six senses.

24   For there is a seventh sense (technically an "eighth sense") that is even beyond balance and intuitive perception. Know this. To perceive is to become aware through the senses; even through the "sixth sense" or intuitive perception. It is to apply one's senses to material objects in order to understand and operate them. However, the seventh sense is the awareness of oneness and wholeness; it is to sense the oneness and interconnectedness of life itself, it is a knowing, a being.

25   Technically, there is nothing to perceive (or sense) because nothing is separate from one's *Self*. In fact, there is no *Self* separate from the conscious universe. There is no *you* and *them*, *yours* and *theirs*, *this* and *that*, so there is nothing to "sense" or perceive or try to understand. Here, you can only be! There is nothing you do not know, nothing you do not have, and nowhere that you are not.

26   In the seventh sense all existence is one! And your particular identity or sense of *Self* is simply the conscious gathering of the universe into your particular time and space.

27   Here, we realize that whenever we think (or perceive) that we are *this* or *that* we limit our access to the entire conscious universe to our individual identities. And it is this type of an awareness that gives us our sense of order, independence, security, *I*, *Me*, *My*, etc.

28   However, the seventh sense is to feel the Truth of the one great unified conscious event as one's *Self*. It is to return to one's non-physical essence while still physically aware. It is to *wake up* to the reality of the conscious, chaotic universe while voluntarily dreaming the ordered material World!

29   Most people do it at their time of death (awakening). But some, though meditation and/or some dramatic life event, actually wake up to the oneness of the conscious universe while still dreaming the perceived reality of physical life! What a revelation!

30   Consider the idea that this life, as we know it, is simply the dream of our true existence as beings of Light (consciousness). For it is Light (consciousness) that we are, and it is more Light (consciousness) that we shall become. At the time of our physical deaths, we simply wake up! For this physical life is only a temporary rest for our real existence as beings of conscious Light.

31   Consider this. Conscious awareness uses an enormous amount of energy—even in the physical world. This is why those who think often also sleep often. Just by being conscious we wear our bodies out!

32   Likewise, as beings of Light, (consciousness) we use an enormous amount of energy in the universe just to remain conscious. Therefore, as non-physical beings of the conscious universe we rest from our true existence as Light only to dream the life we are living now. The

physical World is the dream or idea of the spiritual realm and spiritual beings.

33   The longer we live (dream) in this physical World the more rest we are getting as beings of Light in the conscious universe. And when we have fully rested (lived) in this physical World we simply wake up (die)!

34   However, while resting, some beings of Light experience nightmares (traumatic life experiences) such as physical injury, worry, sickness, hate, ignorance, poverty, etc., which cause them to be awakened from their sleep (die) before they are fully rested as Spirit beings.

35   Such people, at their physical deaths, awaken to their true selves as beings of conscious Light, only to find themselves still tired or unfulfilled. Such people (beings), for a lack of energy (fulfillment) fall back to sleep, returning to the dream of physical life, repeating the process again until they are fully rested.

36   However, those people (beings) that do get a full life's rest awaken at the time of their physical deaths fully rested. Such people (beings) acquire the energy needed to stay awake as beings of Light. They do not have to rest again for a long, long time. They do not need to sleep again, having dreams of physical life, with its traumatic and stressful experiences. As fully rested beings of conscious Light they live in the peace of Eternal Mind.

37   If you notice, when you are sleeping, your dream world is just as real as the physical World you are resting from. In your dream world you have friends, relatives, memories, material goods, concerns and responsibilities that are all very real and very important to you while you are asleep. However, when you awaken from your sleeping you care nothing for the people, places, things and events of your dream world—especially if your dream (life) was a nightmare!

[38]   While you are dreaming, nothing except the happenings of your dream world is important to you until you wake up. In fact, when you are asleep in the physical World you literally look dead. It is only the automatic physical functions of the body that continue to operate when you are asleep. However, conscious awareness (You) is gone! And without *You* (conscious awareness) the body is semi-lifeless, even fully lifeless!

[39]   For death (just like your dreams) is so real, so relaxing, so important, such an escape to you that when you die you care nothing for the happenings and relationships of the physical World that *You* have left behind unless you choose to.

[40]   For the consciousness that you suddenly remember at your so-called *time of death* is the Truth of your being! And in that Truth is a peace that is simply unattainable in the illusion of physical life.

[41]   In death you escape the illusions of physical life. You are in Truth! You may even wish that all your relatives and friends were dead so that they may experience the peace and joy that you have attained by escaping the nightmares of physical life. However, the reality is that in death you *wake up* and care little for the World you have left behind.

[42]   Just as when you awaken from sleep, caring little for the people, places, things and events that you have left behind in your dream world unless you choose to, so it is at the time of your physical death. The only thing you take with you, the only thing of any true value from one dream world to the next is the love, respect and ultimate lesson you have acquired while dreaming.

[43]   Consider this. Your physical existence is simply the dream of your non-physical existence at rest. And likewise, your non-physical existence is simply the dream of your physical existence at rest. But oh what a joy when you

actually *wake up* in your physical dream. Such an experience is indeed the essence of spiritual empowerment!

⁴⁴ What an empowerment! What a great revelation it is when one becomes conscious to one's true *Self* as a being of conscious Light while still dreaming one's physical reality! To realize that everyone in your conscious awareness, including your environment, is part of your self-induced dream state, is the beginning of spiritual awareness. In fact, your physical body is the vehicle that is carrying you through your dream—a dream created by your mind.

⁴⁵ For when one is spiritually conscious while physically dreaming, all things become possible. For what in the physical World is impossible to the one whose physical body is asleep, yet whose conscious awareness is awake to the Spirit in the physical World?

⁴⁶ For when you reverse your conscious perception to perceive this physical World as the dream world, anything becomes possible! Fear is eliminated because death becomes simply an awakening, a transformation, a realization, an exit, as birth becomes simply an entrance. All is creation!

⁴⁷ Everything is one! The universe is one! And all that proceeds from the universe is one! There is no other material reality. Therefore, there is no death for the being of conscious Light that leaves the physical body every night at sleep! There is only transformation and rejuvenation.

⁴⁸ Destruction (as in the end of a thing's existence) is actually the illusion of an undeveloped and unaware mind that has not carried the essence of things to their final and ultimate conclusion. For the only thing that is truly impossible in the physical universe is destruction.

⁴⁹ For we hold and limit the universe to our particular time and space out of fear and/or doubt. Like a security blanket, we create and hide ourselves within our physical bodies. And out of fear and ignorance we use our conscious

perception to deny the terrifying presence of the infinite and chaotic conscious universe! We are hiding in our dreams.

50   The seventh sense produces a kind of *sight* that sees the material World as an effect of conscious Light-energy—a dream. Everything physical is changing its form before your very eyes. The things of the material World are indeed temporary and illusionary.

51   Only Spirit itself (conscious Light-energy) is real and everlasting. Everything else is an effect of Spirit. And the intelligence of all people, places and things have their origin in Spirit, which has its origin in the Light-energy of Eternal Mind.

52   Here, the attuned Hiphoppa becomes the teacha! Having realized that there is no separation in Light-energy, and that everything and everyone is simply another manifestation of intelligent Light-energy, the teacha looks beyond the temporary effects, cravings and temptations of the material World, manipulating and affecting the intelligence of the material World at its source, which is Light-energy.

53   There are no separations in Light-energy or the intelligence that produces it. All is one, including space and time or space-time. Light-energy simply manifests in a variety of forms and effects; forms and effects that we create and manipulate with our perceptions.

54   But you can manipulate Light-energy with your mind simply by expecting it to obey your commands. Yes, it is really that simple! And this is why the Temple of Hiphop teaches spiritual <u>training</u> before and beyond traditional <u>praise</u> and <u>worship</u>.

55   The training of one's Spirit is all about the releasing of one's fears and doubts, and getting past the cravings of the physical body for real! The spiritual training offered by the Temple of Hiphop is a re-education as to what is real

and possible spiritually. Here, learning to live beyond one's physical senses is all about freeing one's self from living exclusively within the interpretations of one's physical senses of physical reality.

56 Beyond faith, once you know and operate within the reality of the Spirit realm, you shall habitually expect the laws of such a realm to obey your commands.

57 Just as when you are born to this World; weak, helpless, dependent and unaware of your life as a human being, so it is with your birth in the Spirit World.

58 When you are an infant in the physical World you live within the wants and needs of an infant in the physical World. An infant expects to drink milk. An infant expects its mother to be there. An infant expects to play. An infant expects to sleep. An infant expects to learn.

59 As you become a teenager your wants and needs change based upon your level of maturity. Teenagers expect certain things that infants do not expect. And likewise, adults expect certain things based upon their level of maturity that neither teenagers nor infants expect.

60 It is not that such things as cars, houses, a job, a career, relationships, etc., are out of a teenager's reach; these things exist around all teenagers. But most teenagers are uninterested in mortgages, car notes, and career choices; others are not qualified to possess such items and ideas.

61 Yeah, they may say, *That's a hot car!* Or, *I want a house like that!* But the Truth is that, they don't really <u>expect</u> to have a car or a house like that. The adult (on the other hand), who knows and operates within an adult World, expects to acquire in this World whatever she has worked to achieve. And the key phrase here is…*whatever she has worked to achieve.*

62 However, beyond adult maturity exists Spirit maturity. And here, Spirit beings require things and

circumstances that adult human beings do not require. Know this. If you are beginning to require the things of the Spirit more than the things of the World, YOU are indeed becoming an aware Spirit being. The challenge now is, do you actually believe that?

63   Do you truly believe that you are Spirit? Do you actually operate within a Spirit reality? Do you expect spiritual results? What have you actually worked to achieve spiritually? This is what spiritual training is all about.

64   How can anyone expect to communicate with anyone or anything if they do not speak the language of who or whatever they wish to communicate to?

65   How can you speak to GOD without knowing GOD's language? GOD does not speak English, French, or Spanish. GOD speaks Health, Love, Awareness, and Wealth and hears intentions, not words. Through your thinking, feeling and daily activities do you speak GOD's language? Are you even in communication with GOD for real?

66   GOD, the Light of Eternal Mind, speaks through all of existence. Are you listening? GOD, the Great Spirit, does not speak through temples, churches, synagogues, mosques or lodges exclusively. GOD is more likely to speak through the circumstances of your life.

67   Know this. Everything is GOD! If it exists it is GOD and it is aware. All that your senses perceive is intelligent and aware at some level. The challenge for many is that through undisciplined and unrighteous living (immaturity) they come to believe through guilt that they cannot expect to command the intelligent forces of the universe and Nature. We expect Nature to govern us, so it does.

68   Just as certain adults will not share certain information with certain children, so it is with the many manifestations of GOD toward immature human animals.

Through undisciplined and immature living the intelligence of the spiritual realm and Nature itself stops communicating with the immature. Such immaturity cannot be trusted.

69   Everything is intelligent and aware of you. You simply may not be aware of the intelligence that flows through everything. Our physical body is intelligent; it is an effect of Light-energy, yet we seldom speak to it.

70   Your material possessions, your ideas, sickness, health, poverty, wealth, as well as the circumstances of your life are all intelligent beings caused by the effects of conscious Light-energy; an energy that you can communicate with because your own mind is made active by the same intelligence.

71   For when you fully realize (expect) that reality itself is one intelligence moving and manifesting (thinking) in a variety of ways, and that you are one of the ways in which it is thinking, moving and being, you shall speak to the oneness of all reality with a certain confident expectancy and it shall respond to you.

72   For when you truly realize that there really are no separate spaces, you shall appear everywhere! And when you truly realize that there really is no such thing as time for you, you shall reinterpret your own past for yourself and create the future that you desire for yourself NOW. And when you truly realize that everything is conscious at some level you shall seek to learn the secret language that communicates to all Light.

73   This is what it means to live beyond your immediate time and space. Such concepts as separate things, times and spaces are indeed illusions. Try to adopt this understanding.

74   Say to yourself: *I am Hip Hop! Such a realization frees me from the restraints of separate things, times and spaces because Hiphop itself is beyond separate things, times and*

spaces. *This is why Hip Hop affects everything and can be applied to anything! It is an idea of Divine Mind.*

75   *Through affirmation, visualization and practice I have adjusted my consciousness to the identity of Hiphop itself. I have given up the ethnicity that I was forced-taught to be, and I have united with a timeless, formless and spaceless intelligence called* (for political identity) *"Hiphop."*

76   For the ancient statement, *As a man thinketh, so is he,* is indeed true. Again, try to adopt this understanding. Say to yourself: *I am the activity and survival of Hip Hop itself! The collective consciousness* (intelligence) *that is called "Hiphop" will not allow me to be defeated. As long as my challenges rely upon intelligence for their existence and survival I shall never be challenged.*

77   *As Hiphop itself I move and think much faster than those who are just performing "hip-hop's" artistic elements. Any battle or challenge within Hip Hop is simply me battling or challenging some aspect of my Self.*

78   *I move and do things much faster in the material World because speed is a concept that comes with distance, time and separate places, and for us there are no separate places. We are already there!* Adopt this understanding of Hip Hop.

79   WAKE UP HIPHOPPA! Your role as a Hiphoppa is a divine decision. Your challenge is to finally believe in your *Self.* You are more than just a rapper, dancer, or graphic artist. You are an idea of Divine Mind choosing to perform such activities, and all of existence knows this except you.

80   At some point you must put aside the immaturity of fear and doubt, and move at the speed of your own thoughts. At some point your thinking, acting and being must come into harmony with one another. At some point YOU must be the total YOU. This is an act of spiritual maturity.

81   The Hiphoppa who thinks one way, feels another way, and acts yet another way is spiritually immature. At

some point you must decide to be what you say that you are and do what you say that you do.

⁸²   Maturity or adulthood is when one has made the decision to live as one perceives one's *Self*. If you perceive yourself to be a Hiphoppa but you are living a life contrary to Hiphop, then it is your own immaturity (doubt) that stagnates your life.

⁸³   If you perceive within yourself that you are a minister, teacha, prophet, a man or woman of GOD, then you must bring your perception of yourself and your daily activities into harmony with one another.

⁸⁴   You cannot feel like a prophet yet talk like a pimp. You cannot feel like an emcee yet spend your day working a nine-to-five job. At some point there will be conflict between the true nature of your being and the activities of your physical body in the World. This process is not easy.

⁸⁵   This is why spiritual training is so important. Such training helps you to center and balance the activities of your mind and body toward the Spirit. For if YOU instruct your body to do something and the body is unwilling or has something more pressing to do, such a body instantly becomes your prison, even your master. And this is the state that many people live within daily.

⁸⁶   They say; *I know that I am a very talented Emcee* (as an example) *and I would truly like to only do this with my life. In my heart I want to live this!* But then the circumstances of the physical World operating upon the physical body have such a person following the desires, cravings, fears and doubts of the physical body, as opposed to fearlessly following the Truth of his being, which is not physical at all.

⁸⁷   Know this. If you are to achieve anything in this World you must be willing to suffer for it. And not that suffering is a requirement of achievement, or that you will

even have to suffer at all. But in Truth, if you are not <u>willing</u> to suffer to actualize your true *Self*, then you are simply not worthy of your true *Self*. This path that leads toward eternal joy is paved by denying temporary happiness.

88   It is the power of one's creative Spirit that brings non-physical ideas into physical manifestation. During this process the intelligence of the physical body doubts and fears the activities of the Spirit. And this conflict is what causes suffering. Decide now who you are going to be and stick with that!

89   For when YOU (Spirit) are in conflict with the desires, cravings, fears, and doubts of the physical body, such conflict confuses the mind and then nothing can get done. You must decide right now if you truly are who you say you are.

90   If you are an emcee for real, then you should be doing nothing else but actualizing your *Self* as you truly are. Everyone and everything is indeed second to the actualization of your true *Self*. But what does this mean for real?

91   It means this: Are you willing to give up all Worldly desires for the actualization of your true *Self*, or are you going to give in to the demands of the physical World and its hold on YOUR physical body? It is just that simple. Sure, you may have to get a job to support your family or live somewhere that you do not really want to live. However, these decisions are always temporary and should only be a last resort.

92   When you make this decision in your life for real the whole <u>Y</u>oung and <u>O</u>ld <u>U</u>niverse (Y.O.U) comes to your aid. Yes, in the beginning there will be an adjustment period where the physical body will rebel and life itself will seem too hard to bear. But HANG ON! After a short while your true *Self* shall begin to emerge.

93   Once you become YOU, which is everything in existence, then everything in existence must obey YOU because it actually is YOU! Your *sight* changes. And behold, you can see! You are your daily events. You are your day.

94   You now *see* that when the sun rises and creates a new day that everyone has a different experience in that same day according to their own perceptions? For if the concept of a *day* truly existed outside of your *Self* (as most people believe) everyone would have the experience that the *day* wanted them to have. Everyone would have the same experience in a *day*. And in many ways people do share the same daily experiences.

95   However, the Truth is that you do not live within the day; the very reality of the *day* lives within you. So any interpretation you have of your *day* is undoubtedly true for you as well as those who take part in your *day*.

96   Wake up Hiphoppa! You are your *day!* Speak to the intelligence of your *day*. Tell it what you want and how you would like it to present itself to you. And expect an answer.

97   With an awareness of your seventh sense, you become the very *day* itself! Everything that goes on in your *day* first goes on in you. Therefore, when you bring peace to your *Self* through the habits of your divine performances you are actually speaking the secret language of peace to the intelligence of your *day*.

98   Know this. The seventh sense is a sense of being one's whole *Self*. It starts with you being who you say that you are. You can be anything! So why not be exactly who you see yourself as?

99   The problem for most people is that they cannot be their true selves because of the consequences related with being one's true *Self*. Everyone would be their true selves if such consequences as loss of employment, expulsion from school, divorce, death, argument, etc., were not looming in

the background of one's decision to be one's *SELF*.

100   Fear and/or doubt are always the root causes as to why people don't actualize themselves. Attachment is another hindrance. Ignorance is another. However, all of these hindrances are indeed illusions created by our own minds.

101   In Truth, you really don't know what will actually happen if all you did was be YOU. Something great can actually happen to you! Your friends and family may even accept you more. Why do you believe that it is difficult to be you? What are the real obstacles?

102   Ask yourself; *"Why do I immediately envision disaster whenever I think of being the _real_ me or expressing my _real_ feelings? Why am I not inspired to overcome when faced with an obstacle? Why do I believe that in a challenging situation I will lose or be hurt? Why do I believe this?"*

103   What you think can turn out to be the worst experience may actually turn out to be exactly what you need to survive. And most of the time this is exactly what happens.

104   Face your fears! If you are truly pursuing your purpose nothing can stop or hinder you from achieving such a purpose. Do not base your expectations as to what may happen to you upon what may have happened to others, even those doing the same things as yourself. Where others have failed YOU will succeed! Your blessing is unique! GOD is truly with YOU!

105   Remember, your purpose is not only yours; it belongs to GOD also. Your purpose is GOD's Will and GOD's activity. Nothing on or in the Earth can stop or hinder the divine Will of GOD! And once you feel this, you are in your seventh sense. You expect your spirit reality. You have taken total responsibility for your *Self* knowing that GOD is responsible for you, that GOD is

ultimately Guiding Our Direction.

[106]   For it is the responsibility of every attuned Hiphop activist on the path of self-actualization to develop his/her seventh sense. For your society is yours to create and shape; everything makes a difference. The question is, what kind of productive *difference* are you making in your community?

[107]   For when you realize that every moment of your life affects every other moment of your life, you shall become more aware of the choices that you make (create) in life. James Allen points out in his book *As A Man Thinketh: Man is made or unmade by himself; in the armory of thought he forges the weapons by which he destroys himself; he also fashions the tools with which he builds for himself heavenly mansions of joy and strength and peace. By the right choice and true application of thought, man ascends to the Divine Perfection; by the abuse and wrong application of thought, he descends below the level of the beast.*

[108]   For it is always our decision who we become in the World. GOD has already made us perfect in spirit; now it is up to us to consciously unite with GOD's vision of us. For it is obvious that GOD intends for us to be HIP HOP in our time, so with this awareness KRS has become Hiphop conscious of itself! Such is the seat of OUR power and strength in the material World as Hiphoppas, and as you can see, IT WORKS! There it is.

THE EIGHTH OVERSTANDING
ENDARKENMENT

TRACK ONE

[1]   Consider this. Spiritual life is reflected more in natural circumstances and symbolic ideas. To be more specific, the natural/physical World is an effect or rather a temporary flickering, a spark caused by the activity of Light-energy (electromagnetic radiation). All is Light-energy! It is only our perception and interpretation of Light-energy that actually presents the material World to us.

[2]   All is Light. All is Eternal Mind. At the essence of all material things are vibrations of electromagnetic waves commonly called *Light*. What we call the material World is simply our interpretation of these electromagnetic waves. Everything that we see or sense is really our interpretation of *Light*. And you can perceive and then use *Light* as anything that you wish.

[3]   The material World is our interpretation of various forms of *Light*. The vibration of *Light* is constant; however, it is our interpretation of *Light* that creates our material World.

[4]   Anything that you desire you can have, because nothing is actually separate from your *Self*. Simply act and feel like you already have whatever you desire, and it must materialize. You and whatever you desire are really the same things in essence.

[5]   Having an attitude of expectancy regulates the speed at which we detect Light-energy, and focus (or

conscious attention) directs expectancy. However, it is one's values, which are created by the principles one has come to accept in life, that organize and direct one's focus. Read this again until you fully understand its meaning.

6   Together, one's life principles, which create one's values, which direct one's conscious attention or focus, which then directs the force of one's expectancy, manipulate our interpretation of Light-energy and certain people, places, things and circumstances manifest in our lives. You truly get whatever you expect.

7   Your awareness of yourself (or focus upon your *Self*) as a certain kind of person controls the speed at which certain kinds of human necessities (values) vibrate into your environment. Remember, principles + values + focus = expectancy. What do you expect?

8   Know this. The awareness of human beings vibrates at a much slower rate than the awareness of Spirit beings. Human beings tend to focus upon (or rather expect) slower material vibrations than Spirit beings. Likewise, the values and necessities of Spirit beings lead those beings to expect bigger results from Light-energy than human beings are capable of perceiving.

9   Vibrations such as health, love, wealth, faith, forgiveness, etc., vibrate at much faster speeds of awareness than sickness, hate, ignorance, poverty, doubt, hate, revenge, etc. The question here is, which group of vibrations do you truly value the most? What do you expect? Of course, at first glance one is quick to value health over sickness or forgiveness over revenge. However, upon a closer observation we can see that most people value the power of sickness more than they value the power of health. They actually expect sickness more than they expect health. They actually believe more in the possibilities and powers of sickness than in the possibilities and powers of perfect

and continuous health.

10	Sure, on the surface we agree that forgiveness is better than revenge and that love is better than hate, until we (ourselves) are wronged in some kind of way. Then our real principles and values come to *Light*. And it is our focus (or expectancy) upon these real principles and values that speeds up or slows down our awareness. You are the Truth! And you cannot truly lie to your *Self*.

11	Human awareness vibrates at the speed of all it sees. It is our own focus (conscious attention) that interprets Light-energy itself. The more we focus upon things, the more we become aware about things, eventually expecting the actualization of what we are aware of.

12	Therefore, when one truly expects one's own spiritual reality and begins to truly value (focus upon) the principles of Spirit as opposed to the temporary effects of the World, one will eventually manifest the reality of Spirit in the temporary reality of the physical World. Such activity appears supernatural and miraculous in the physical World. However, such supernatural and miraculous activity is simply about adjusting your expectancy of things by adjusting the value you place upon things. Everyone affects the physical reality they see and perceive.

13	When you truly value (see/perceive) your God, the presence of GOD shall be with you always. When you begin to truly value Spirit, spiritual things shall begin happening to you. Most people <u>want</u> GOD in their lives but they do not really <u>expect</u> GOD in their lives. Either they do not really <u>value</u> GOD or they do not really <u>value</u> themselves.

14	When you expect GOD in your life, God then appears! However, if you expect to fight your devil when you wake up every morning, such a devil will be right there ready to do battle with you every morning! Attuned Hiphoppas must be mindful as to what they place their focus (conscious attention) upon. Again, the question here is, *What do you truly expect? Even respect? What do you truly value?*

15　　　For it is through the repetition of certain words, affirmations and prayers that one focuses one's awareness upon the values of one's heart. It is also what one places one's money and time upon that determines what one values most.

16　　　This is why it is so important that you freely give abundantly and from your heart to whomever (or whatever) is your spiritual guidance. Not just because tithing, donating, volunteering, etc., helps your *man* or *woman of GOD* financially and releases him/her from chasing the values of the World just to eat and pay bills. But tithing, etc., and the amount that you tithe, etc., prove to your *Self* how much you value the people, places and things of the Spirit.

17　　　Such giving strengthens your own sense of expectancy. Such high value placed upon the things of Spirit speeds up (or intensifies) the awareness of the human being that is focused upon Spirit. Such acts eventually transform those human beings into Spirit beings because such acts can only come from human beings who expect to be and live in Spirit.

18　　　For, Spirit awareness vibrates at a much faster speed than human awareness. Therefore, the Spirit being out-runs, out-feels and out-thinks the human being on all levels of physical reality. Spirit beings see and operate in a much faster non-physical World/vibration than human beings. So, human awareness cannot even see the movements of Spirit awareness because of its (human awareness) own slower (material) vibratory speed (awareness). This is what makes the Spirit realm invisible to us; we simply vibrate too slow.

19　　　Human beings are commonly thought of as

intelligent animals—the bridge between the spiritual and the material World. The more you realize (value) your *Self* as a Spirit being, the faster you will vibrate. In fact, the more aware you are of your God, the faster you shall vibrate.

20   Know this. The closer you arrive to your source (the oneness), the faster you shall vibrate, intensifying your Light-energy until your flesh is completely consumed in it.

21   Such speeds in awareness give one a considerable advantage over the illusionary traps and obstacles of the physical World. Through different speeds/levels of awareness, the attuned Hiphoppa travels through different speeds/levels of Light-energy, affecting and manipulating the people, places, things and circumstances of the physical World.

22   The same concept can be applied to time and space. Time and space are really two aspects of the same thing. Commonly, such a reality is called *space-time*. *Space-time* is the reality in which we exist. It is believed to be absolute. However, our *space-time* reality responds to our perception of it.

23   *Space-time* reality is in the eye of the beholder. Everyone has their own inner-clock that measures time and everyone has their own inner-ruler that measures space. Yet the total *space-time* dimension remains the same for everyone.

24   It is like two people with one knife each about to slice up the same loaf of bread. No matter how they decide to carve up the bread there is still only one loaf. Daily we manipulate time, space and Light in the same way.

25   Sort of like flour, or even water. For example: flour is the source of a variety of breads, crackers, cakes, cookies, etc. All of these items are indeed different but the binding essence of them all is the same. In this example, flour is Light-energy.

26   Just like water, as another example. You can freeze water, steam water or allow it to remain in liquid form. But whether as ice, steam or liquid, water is water. In fact, it would be very accurate to see your physical body as a glass made of ice (Light), with your Spirit (more Light), being poured into the glass as semi-hot water. Your thoughts (more Light) are the steam. And the very Light (or heat) of you (Spirit) melts away at the physical body (the glass made of ice or more Light).

27   Everything is Light-energy. Whether it is solid, gas, liquid or other, all is vibrating Light-energy. Whether as people, places, circumstances or things, all is still Light. When you realize (value) your *Self* as Light and when you realize (value) everything you see as Light, you will see the oneness of everything as different forms of Light. With such an awareness of oneness (the seventh sense), the attuned Hiphoppa exists in harmony with the cycles and patterns of the universe itself.

28   The attuned Hiphoppa has freed his mind and can now see (sense) GOD. Know this. The strength of a free mind is in not knowing what it cannot do. An uninstitutionalized mind is free to really think and create! It doesn't know what it can't do.

29   For when your mind is truly free and in harmony with the intention of the universe, your thinking, your speaking and your actions all unconsciously match the mathematics and patterns of the universe itself. It's like the universe plays with you, advises you and walks with you throughout the day like another presence (person) that you can actually rely upon. And this is what really gets the work done EFFORTLESSLY!

30   For as a teacha, you will also be an activist and a helper of the lost. On behalf of GOD, we literally sacrifice our peace at times for the sake of the World's maturity.

However, it is GOD—the unified field of infinite possibilities —that is actually doing the work. When you are aware of this, it shall be easier to deal with those who surround you with their worries, doubts and fears.

31   Imagine, the Great Spirit has sent you (or rather sacrificed you) for the sake of your World. You are the Light of your World! You are GOD's representative to all the people in your World. And they would be wise to listen to your advice.

32   For as far as your influence shall reach, so shall you be the Light to all in your influence. This is the meaning of self-sacrifice. And such sacrifice can only be performed by the Lights of Eternal Mind. Know this. Hip Hop's spiritual practice has to do with becoming more spirit than flesh, more God-like than man-like; it has to do with becoming more energy than matter, more principle than politics, more Hip Hop than Rap.

33   Knowing, feeling, and living in the great boundless cosmic event is the Truth! Actually knowing (without any doubt or fear) that GOD is with you, and that there is nothing after GOD, that there is only GOD projecting everything, that everything and everyone (good or evil) is connected and projected by the one great cosmic event—GOD—the attuned Hiphoppa becomes the teacha, fully aware.

34   As the teacha, the attuned Hiphoppa sees the World beyond time and separation. For in the oneness of GOD everything moves in harmony with your being. Everything is ONE! Everything is HERE! This awareness has been called "Knowledge of Wholeness" where reality becomes a matter of what you allow to materially exist out of the great chaotic boundless event that surrounds you, where you are a participant in the unfolding of life itself. Take some time to truly understand this.

35   Once the attuned Hiphoppa realizes that there

really is no *then* and *now*, *this* and *that*, *him* and *her*, *them* and *us*, that in reality everything is happening in the oneness of the Great Now Event, the attuned Hiphoppa matures and begins to further create the actual flow of reality itself. No event is wrong or bad if you live in a reality where all events and circumstances work out in your favor in the end. Life itself moves with the attuned Hiphoppa.

36   In his book *The Mystical Christ*, Manly P. Hall puts it this way: *It is difficult to explain such a term as 'knowledge of wholeness.' The Greek mystics defined it as 'participation in causes,' by which they meant soul-awareness of the divine plan. As the intent and purpose of God is inwardly known, the consciousness is filled with a wonderful understanding that cannot be defined.*

37   By adjusting your conscious awareness to the substance (Light) that is all around you, you simply allow Health, Love, Awareness, Wealth, people, food, the new car, house, clothing, etc., to effortlessly appear to your senses and the senses of others as needed. Life was not meant to be random; such is caused by ignorance. You can plan your future. If you really and truly live the Hiphop spiritual life, then you can simply feel that you already have whatever you desire and it shall eventually appear to you. It's really that simple! Try to <u>feel</u> how you would feel when you actually have the thing or things that you want. Thank GOD (divine intelligence) in advance for supplying you with all of your needs. Expect and respect what you desire.

38   Know this. Spiritual power comes not with just believing in your God. To truly walk in power we must also perceive in our God! To believe is to trust, but to perceive is to become aware. You can believe in your God, but until you perceive through your God-nature your true spiritual power shall remain undeveloped. To achieve what GOD has for us we must see the World through God's eye. We

must perceive in (or through) God! After we <u>believe</u> that there is a substance/event/spirit commonly referred to as "GOD," we must take the next step to <u>perceive</u> ourselves working through that substance/event/spirit.

39   As the teacha, the attuned Hiphoppa recognizes the value of GOD projecting Light as the physical World. Whether the seasons of life appear to be temporarily favorable or disappointing, the teacha recognizes only the source of all things (Light-energy) as credible, not its effects. Cars, clothing, food, jewelry, etc., are all temporary effects. They are not original things. They flicker and spark for a moment and then they are gone. Only the one GOD is permanent.

40   Many people <u>believe</u> that GOD exists but they do not <u>perceive</u> themselves within such an existence. They do not operate within the reality of their own God-force. They operate within their own perceived reality, separate from their God-force. They <u>believe</u> in GOD but they do not <u>perceive</u> through God. Hiphoppas must mature beyond this level of spiritual understanding.

41   However, one of the main reasons why many Hiphoppas do not graduate past their beliefs of GOD, is because to really see GOD and begin living from your God-nature you have to be shown your God-nature through a series of trials, tests and tribulations and not many people are willing to go through such experiences in order to see the strength of their own God-force.

42   Remember, Pharaoh's army has to be chasing you down into the sea in order for you to see that you can split the sea and walk right through it. It is within battle and adversity that you truly see and experience your God-nature. For there are real divine forces that protect the elect of GOD, but you won't ever discover them until you are put in some dangerous or compromising position. As long

as you are protected and living in perfect peace you will not know what you are really capable of.

43   Face your fears. Debate your doubts and dis your disbeliefs. If you cannot do this, you cannot grow spiritually. This is how many truth-seekers become cowards. It is because they know the Truth but they don't yet actually live the Truth. To live the Truth of one's *being* one must display a sense of courage, one must be tested for the validity and strength of such *being*. I am the greatest live emcee of all time! And so, I am often tested on this claim.

44   Jealous producers, envious rappers and disinterested sound engineers often attempt to sabotage my performances and undermine my sound quality. Yes, some of our most celebrated Rap icons do try and have tried to sabotage KRS ONE's live performances. Yes, the promoters do try to cut corners and penny-pinch when it comes to sound equipment, and yes they do lie about the amount of equipment and hospitality they are providing. Yes, the sound does cut off! Yes, the microphones do go out! Yes, fights break out in the audience!

45   Yes, all kinds of things can and do go wrong, but the teacha is unaffected. In fact, it is here that the teacha begins to see and experience his own strength and divine abilities. I've been conspired against and disappointed so many times by my own Hip Hop peers that now I've come to see it for what it really is—many are simply afraid of my skill, however many more simply don't understand it! It's like they enjoy putting obstacles in my way just to see me overcome them, or they try to prove me wrong about something so that they may appear knowledgeable; others are just plain afraid of me!

46   And they are afraid because I have a history of battling other rappers, and yes, I am vicious for my time. It doesn't matter who's on the show with me, KRS ONE is

usually the last one to go on; I am usually *the headliner*, and I say this with humility. However, having such a reputation as a live emcee, being the greatest emcee of my time, does have its drawbacks and this is what I am trying to say here.

47   When you are the best in your field others will try their best to undermine your skill and even sabotage your performances, but if you are truly who you say that you are, all of their trying will only aid you in the pursuit of your own excellence and the achievement of your own purpose. The teacha battles with the intent to correct the opposing force. The teacha battles with knowledge and awareness.

48   We never invite confrontation—however, adversity actually strengthens us. As truth-seekers we must never be afraid to confront adversity and sabotage head-on, knowing that we truly are who we claim to be. When you are truly who you claim to be, your *being* effortlessly operates above the effects of any low-level attack; you are the correction. You are actually there to put an end to the ignorance attempting to sabotage and/or criticize you.

TRACK TWO

49   For the one GOD can be perceived as our Father and the Earth as our Mother, but these are figurative and symbolic terms. The realm of Spirit is beyond rational/ intellectual thought. The challenge is that GOD is a oneness—a boundless conscious event. Yet, rational/ intellectual thought must individualize, label, question and define each temporary effect in an effort to make sense of the physical World. The intellect wants order out of chaos. But the true reality of the one GOD is chaos to the intellect.

50   Therefore, stories, parables, angels, devils and other

symbolism are used to explain spiritual concepts simply because the realm of Spirit cannot be fully comprehended through intellect alone. Such a technique of symbolism and parable is also used throughout the Gospel of Hip Hop to explain some very real concepts in spiritual living. Let us continue.

51   Consider this. Heaven is not just where you are going; heaven is where you came from. Nirvana is not just a state of awareness to attain; it is the very state of awareness you have forgotten. The Gospel of Hip Hop should not be the only authentic Hip Hop lifestyle; it is simply the way that GOD has instructed us to come at this time.

52   The World of nature, with its system of prey and predators, is a projection of spiritual reality. Just as the deer is hunted by the lion, human beings are hunted by devils. Not half-man, half-animal caricatures, but in fact, jealousies, greeds, hatreds, fears, temptations, etc. In the realm of Spirit these predators are real!

53   They eat and eventually deplete one's life-force. We will become aware of our true reality and be better equipped to protect ourselves when we overstand that we are part of a spiritual food chain system just as the deer is part of a natural food chain system.

54   All day and night we are giving and receiving the conscious breath of life. But spiritual beasts (devils) seek to deplete our life-force (consciousness) for their own nourishment. Randomly, these packs of predators seek our life-force to sustain themselves. Jealousies, greeds, hatreds, lusts, fears, etc. are like real beasts that have no life unto themselves so they seek the life-force emanating from us to survive.

55   In the *Spirit realm* thought is as real as a cloud or a mist or a fog. In the physical realm thought is temporary material things and circumstances. Either way,

thought is real! And the thought-energy of others (if left unrestrained), whether good or evil, will roam around looking to fulfill its purpose in the lives of random people. Like stray animals looking for food, the random thinking of others will wander around until it is either fulfilled or transformed (further created).

56   Both good and evil undirected thoughts wander aimlessly, like the way certain airborne bacteria wander throughout the air until a series of life circumstances brings them into the nostril, eye and/or ear of some random individual. And it is not that such airborne bacteria (wandering thought) in and of itself is harmful to us. It is more the fact that our immune systems (principles and values) may not be as strong as we may need them to be. Such weaknesses in our own natural defense system (mind) give airborne bacteria (wandering thought) the advantage over us and we become sick (imbalanced).

57   Such wandering and undirected thought roams around until we run into it, and then it seems like some unexpected circumstance always seems to come our way. People usually call such circumstances *good luck* or *bad luck*. However, it is the thinking of unaware Spirit beings (human beings) that create such wandering thought-energy and random life experiences.

58   Some thought-energy is created with the intention to help (so-called *good luck*) while other thought-energy is created with the intention to harm (so-called *bad luck*). The intellect cannot see itself; only the Spirit can accurately look at the mind of reason and intellectual awareness. And only in Spirit can the teacha see and manipulate thought-energy of all kinds.

59   Knowing that the ultimate force behind all thought-energy is Light, the teacha accepts all random life experiences (both good and evil) as manifestations of

properly directed Light or misdirected Light. Dealing with physical reality from its source (which is thought-energy), and dealing with thought-energy from its source (which is Light-energy), the teacha manipulates the physical World itself (causing miracles) with the empowering awareness of the oneness, for there are no separate things or events.

60   It is because of our own ignorance (or denial) that we become prey for wandering spiritual predators. Traditionally, evil and unpleasant people, places, things and circumstances were (and still are) called the works of *devils* or *beasts*, even *vampires* sucking the life-force out of you. However, in reality such predators are simply the manifested ignorance of people we may or may not consciously know. And there are many of them!

61   Ignorance seeks Light (awareness) because it has little of its own. Ignorance is attracted to awareness but awareness is not attracted to ignorance. Ignorance seeks awareness; however, awareness does not seek ignorance. Therefore, the teacha does not fight ignorance to destroy it. The teacha feeds ignorance Light (awareness) and defeats ignorance by further creating (transforming) and/or redirecting it.

62   Know this. The teacha uses creation, awareness, knowledge and/or transformation as weapons against random ignorance. When the teacha is hit with an unpleasant and random situation, the teacha transforms the situation or redirects the thought-energy of the situation toward her highest good with an awareness of that situation's ultimate source in the Light of Eternal Mind: the one GOD.

63   Hiphoppas must overstand that as long as they remain in the born state of animal/human being they are subject to the natural laws of nature. When the attuned Hiphoppa comes to the realization that she is a Spirit being and that the only Truth is oneness, then the deer defeats the

lion, the mouse defeats the cat, the cat defeats the dog, and You defeat the World! In other words, the prey becomes the predator. The employee hires or fires the employer. The child teaches the parent. The patient heals the doctor!

64   In the meantime, human beings are being hunted and preyed upon not by one devil but by several. One vice (devil) is no match for any human being. It is the accumulated pack of devils that continuously attack and devour one's life-force.

65   Packs of devils, such as hatreds, angers, insecurities, worries, greeds, etc., lure us to our defeat through a variety of temptations. Randomly, these packs of spiritual predators seek our shells (bodies) and eat them by eating the conscious life-force that sustains the physical body.

66   This is what it really means when someone asks, *What's eating at you?* Or when someone says, *Hate just ate him up!* But know this. We are protected by our natural weapon—the mind!

67   The mind of an attuned Hiphoppa is the weapon used to fight off *devils* as the attuned Hiphoppa develops (rests) spiritually in the physical World. The mind is our natural camouflage...our porcupine back...our venom...our turtle, snail and crab shells. It is our speed, our strength, our wings, etc.

68   Devils attract and lure us to physical harm through smell, touch, taste, sight and sound—even intuition. But a disciplined and sharp mind protects us. Every human being has this weapon or natural defense. But only Spirit beings ever really learn to use it. And even fewer Spirit beings learn to actually master it!

69   The natural technique (or strategy) of a devil is to use temptation and deception. Our technique (or strategy) is discipline and Truth. Therefore, when we are confronted by devils (lies and cravings), the mind must not be clouded

by ignorance, drug abuse, self-doubt, fear, guilt, etc., or we lose the fight, and our shells (bodies) are cracked and our life-force is devoured.

70   This is how *Inner-City* pain and suffering is manifested. Both are the manifestations of being constantly hunted by spiritual predators. Sometimes our life-force is bitten and scratched and we manage to escape with injuries such as depression or anxiety. Other times, our life-force is completely devoured and our physical bodies collapse and/ or we are driven to insanity.

71   However, when we remember (or realize) that we are Spirit we can effectively use the mind as a weapon against such devils. Such a realization (or enlightenment) is the Truth. And it is in the knowing of this Truth (that you are Spirit and not the physical body) that we automatically become disciplined, avoiding the unnecessary suffering caused by the temptations of devils upon the physical body.

72   Spiritual awareness is enlightenment. And it is enlightenment that causes discipline. Separate your conscious awareness from your physical body, even your mind, and you shall be better able to fight off the devils. Practice <u>observing</u> the cravings of your physical body and always seek Truth. Do not give in to temptation and lies.

73   For, anyone who deceives and/or tempts people does the work of devils. Not that they themselves are devils, but that they are possessed by devils, devils control their motives. Attuned Hiphoppas must always examine themselves to be sure that they are not wearing or saying something that is deceptive and/or tempting to others.

74   The public image, appearance and words of the attuned Hiphoppa should always promote Health, Love, Awareness and Wealth. With what we say, do and wear we must always seek to help those who are victims of deception

and/or temptation. Most people do not even know that they have a devil. With a sincere care for the well-being of others we must always advise (even through our clothing and jewelry) the seeking of TRUTH!

TRACK THREE

[75]   Enlightenment is a revelation, an awakening, a new way to interpret your reality. It is figuratively called *Light* because it assists your ability to understand or *see*. To be enlightened is to become aware. Enlightenment is a state of awareness; it is the awareness of leaving one's self-caused immaturities. However, for those Hiphoppas who live in the physical World there is no prolonged mentally sustained sensation of enlightenment. For the most part, enlightenment comes and goes. Great ideas and revelations appear like flashes of Light in the mind.

[76]   The results of your new awareness (or enlightenment) can remain with you for a long while, even a lifetime and beyond, but the actual moment of enlightenment is temporary. Like a flash, it exists for only a moment. What you are left with is the revelation achieved by such a flash of enlightenment. Once enlightened, you can never return to ignorance again. This is what gives the impression that the actual experience of enlightenment remains with you throughout your life.

[77]   On the contrary, it is through the experience of being enlightened or becoming aware that one's attitude and outlook on life changes, giving the impression that one has remained in the actual moment of enlightenment. For the attuned Hiphoppa, enlightenment is not the final stage of spiritual development while in the World. Enlightenment

happens throughout one's life.

78   For the attuned Hiphoppa, enlightenment has to do with realizing one's true *Self* as Spirit, detached from the senses and sense objects of the World. However, this is only part of what is needed for those who are living in modern inner cities and are still faced by spiritual predators.

79   The one who is enlightened is usually the one who is the recipient or achiever of spiritual Light or awareness. The enlightened one is the one who receives Light and radiates Light. But in the reality of a chaotic *Inner City,* enlightenment (or awareness) is not enough to combat the perceived devils of others.

80   Devils are attracted to Light and beings of Light. When God is with you, you are a target for devils. Likewise, when you assist others you become a target for devils. Be prepared! Ignorance seeks to eat awareness. But like a moth that is attracted to a flame, devils are attracted to beings of Light only to be incinerated when they finally make contact with such enlightened beings.

81   This is one of the reasons why many *enlightened* souls leave the city to find comfort and peace in the mountains, forest, suburbs and other more secluded and private environments. They care not to sacrifice themselves for the good of those around them. And such is their decision to make. Such is their privilege. They have earned their escape. They are indeed free!

82   For when one is enlightened it is difficult to live around those who are not. In fact, not only is it depressing and spiritually depleting to constantly witness other human beings being helplessly devoured by devils, but even when you have become *unplugged* and *unattached,* wandering devils (through people and circumstances) will not cease attacking you!

83   But some Spirit beings are indeed sent into the

World to do battle and free people from their own demons. Some Spirit beings are prepared to sacrifice themselves for the sake of the World's maturity. In the Hiphop Kulture these Spirit beings are called *teachas*. At times we deny ourselves the comforts of the mountains and lakes to enter the *Inner City* for the purpose of freeing people from their own demons. And we are divinely equipped for such a task.

84   Devils run from us! Demons hide from us! Our very presence makes the carnally-minded uncomfortable, the criminally-minded repent, and the spiritually-minded rejoice! For while others enjoy their enlightenment far from the chaos of the *Inner City,* teachas enjoy endarkenment right in the center of the *Inner City*. Chaos does not baffle us.

85   For the teacha, the state of endarkenment also helps in one's spiritual survival while working in the *Inner City*. Endarkenment is not a state of ignorance and it does not imply a lack of spiritual Light. On the contrary, endarkenment is the ability to move in the World without the aid of intellectual awareness or a plan, a sign, etc.

86   Endarkenment is the ability to see in the dark chaos without the aid of rational/logical thought. It is a level of spiritual awareness where the teacha appears to operate harmoniously and effortlessly in chaos. It is a stage in one's spiritual development when intellectual awareness—a plan, a script, a book, a map, etc.—is no longer needed for one to move victoriously in the physical World. One is aware of one's God and sees the World beyond time and separation. Everything is NOW! And all is GOD!

87   For when we are spiritually young we are in need of Light (order/awareness). The one GOD provides Light (order/awareness) so that we may develop and see our way. But if the one GOD provides Light (order/awareness) or decrees that there should be Light (order/awareness), then where is this GOD?

88   The one GOD does not exist in the Light (order/ awareness) that is provided. GOD's Light is for us. GOD exists as Light, not in Light. The one GOD is Light! And we are sparks of that Light! However, the World cannot see its own Light or GOD as the ultimate unified Light-energy.

89   To the World, the one GOD exists in the Dark. For it, GOD exists in those highly chaotic and dangerously forbidden, hidden, secret places that incite fear in the hearts of those who forever seek comfort in the temporary security of predictable events.

90   The practice of endarkenment begins with the understanding that it is the constant search for Worldly/ intellectual security which is usually the idea of never doing without, always having an abundance of whatever is needed, always knowing ahead what is going on that keeps us from being totally developed as spiritually mature beings.

91   For as long as we depend upon our intellectual pre-planning abilities exclusively, we shall never develop the ability to see and act spontaneously in the dark with GOD where most times there is no foreseeable plan! At this state of awareness things are effortlessly and spontaneously created as needed.

92   Here, the teacha overstands that abundance and wealth are great resources to have but having the ability of true faith is worth even more! It is here that the attuned Hiphoppa realizes what faith actually is.

93   Here, Faith is about having what you need exactly when you need it. Quite different from asking GOD (in fear) for an abundance of *this* or *that*, the attuned and boundless teacha gets exactly what he needs exactly when it is needed. In the one GOD the teacha truly trusts.

94   Miraculously and with little effort the teacha receives the perfect weapon just before the fight. The

teacha receives the exact amount of cash just before the bill. The teacha receives the perfect vehicle just before the trip. The perfect clothing just before the engagement. This is the practice of endarkenment. It is about trusting and perceiving in your God even when your intellect is baffled and cannot see a solution. It is about seeing and walking in intellectual darkness <u>as</u> spiritual Light.

[95]   At this level of consciousness, the teacha does not move around the World; it is the World that moves around the teacha! Through discipline and righteous living, the teacha expects the intelligence of life itself to be in harmony with the fulfillment of her purpose. Everything happens perfectly in its right place and perfectly in its right time; always right on time.

TRACK FOUR

[96]   Consider this. Most inner-city children are afraid of the dark. They are afraid of what their own minds create in the dark. However, when the light comes on they quickly learn that a room in the light is the same room in the dark.

[97]   Here, *room* is the same as life circumstances and situations. As we mature and become more familiar with the objects in our *rooms* (people, things and life circumstances) it doesn't matter if the light is on or off.

[98]   With such a maturity (wisdom) we gain the ability to move freely in our dark *rooms* (unpleasant and challenging life situations) without bumping into anything (wrecking one's life) or being afraid (stagnated in one's life) because we know where and what everything is (there is only one source—GOD).

[99]   In fact, when we are threatened (challenged by the

World) it is darkness (intellectual chaos) that protects us. Continuous Light (order, prosperity, love, security, skills, a plan, etc.) only exposes us (through people, things, and situations) to our predators (fear, anger, jealousy, envy, etc.). Although order is useful toward the cause for peace, order also gives our predators time to focus in on us. The teacha is like the eye of a tornado!

100   Attuned Hiphoppas are guided through the darkest *rooms* of life with an awareness of GOD's actual presence. Attuned Hiphoppas find contentment in the darkest situations (situations that the intellect cannot foresee) because they have learned to use their Spirit *sight* to see in the dark (chaos).

101   For the attuned Hiphoppa, endarkenment is more of a feeling experience than an actual seeing experience. It is an awareness. We call it a *sight* because the presence of the one GOD (Light) makes you aware and better able to comprehend (or see) your situation.

102   Here, endarkenment is about feeling and then trusting (beyond the intellect, instincts, emotions, and senses) GOD's actual presence; the presence that speaks to and from the essence of your being. This practice is essential for the building of one's faith.

103   The question here is, can you still see in Spirit even when your intellect cannot see in the physical World? Does the World tell you what and how it is, pressuring you to assimilate? Or do you tell the World what and who you are; forcing it to assimilate?

104   Here, the teacha achieves the ability to accurately see and act in the dark (chaos) by truly walking in the Right Now of his God! The teacha would ask, *Where is your faith if your intellect* (sense of security) *must confirm your victory before you decide to act? Where is your God if She is so distant from you that in order for you to keep up and stay spiritually*

motivated She must send you a sign, a blessing, a word, Light?
[105]   The teacha has realized that he is Light! That when GOD sends Light into the lives of others, it is the teacha that GOD is actually sending. The teacha does not look at life's obstacles as disappointments. The teacha sees all obstacles and criticisms as well as difficult people as challenges sent to him by the one GOD for spiritual correction and development.

[106]   The teacha has realized that the only harmony is the Great Oneness Deity (GOD)! Conscious Light-energy is the totality of a teacha's reality. And so, the teacha handles difficult people and circumstances simply as unaware sparks of Eternal Mind. Some people may be simply spiritually blind or unaware, but their existence is still in GOD—in time they will see.

[107]   Here, the teacha does not fall victim to judging and criticizing the spiritually blind. Instead, the teacha opens the eye of the blind to the reality of Spirit by revealing a superior personal character in the face of challenging events and people. The teacha is calm and confident in any situation because the teacha sees GOD and GOD's activity in every event. The teacha educates the ignorant not with words, but with a superior personal character which is usually understood by the ignorant later in their lives.

[108]   Mastery of spiritual knowledge is found not in what one knows or in what one teaches, it is found in what one does and in how one lives. *No one can actually experience internal illumination and not reveal this enlargement of understanding in daily living. Growth is a positive process and bears witness to itself. We know that improvement is real when it refines and ennobles human character. The lives of mystics prove the victory of internal light over internal darkness.* (Manly P. Hall)

[109]   Know this. Just as bats see clearer by natural sonar, similarly humans see clearer in Spirit even though we have

natural eyes. For it is our natural senses that illuminate and receive Light when in use. Light stimulates the ability of the eyes, yet it is the eyes (or Worldly sight) that distract the Hiphoppa from a life in Spirit. Darkness is not the absence of Light it is the presence of a different Light which requires a different kind of sight.

110   True Hiphoppas eventually learn how to switch their *sight* (or withdraw their natural senses) at will. Whenever we use our natural senses to either give or receive, we spiritually glow or illuminate. When we illuminate through the use of our natural senses our very Light attracts devils.

111   Consider this. There are two ways in which the enlightened illuminate Light. One way is when Light is received in the form of Health, Love, Awareness or Wealth. These lesser Lights/vibrations assist the enlightened one while in the World. The other way is when those same Lights/vibrations are stored in one's Spirit (*Self*) and then given or illuminated toward others.

112   You will notice that whenever you try to do what is good or achieve what is good there is always opposition. One of the ways spiritually-minded people know that they are blessed is when victory is achieved in the face of adversity. Such victories, however, should mature you from being just spiritually-minded to being spiritually active!

113   For the average Hiphoppa, adversity is the work of devils! But for the teacha, transforming adversity, fear, doubt, disbelief and temptation into understanding, faith, love, security, courage and discipline is the work of God!

114   Such victories are almost always won in battle. For such adversity strengthens the spiritual skill of the teacha. For we are never afraid to display high spiritual skill against ignorance and other obstacles and traps of *Inner-City* life. Teachas are never afraid to fight.

115   Moving in Spirit (at the source) in the dark (in

chaos) with the natural senses withdrawn (emotionally centered) you cannot even be seen by devils (wandering ignorance) because you are emitting no Light (awareness) in the physical World; your awareness and activity is spiritual with physical results. You deny the value of the physical World. You are not focused upon the physical World. You are not flashing and flossing your Light (awareness) in the physical World so to the people of the physical World you are incomprehensible—even invisible!

[116]   For everything is truly everything. And to really comprehend the ALL of everything one must comprehend chaos. But such an awareness is not actually chaotic. It only appears chaotic to the intellect because the intellect creates the physical World of rational thought and individual things by denying the true reality of the oneness so that it can focus.

[117]   However, it can be very uncomfortable and difficult to have your senses continuously withdrawn from sense objects while living in the *Inner City*. It is difficult for the compassionate Hiphoppa not to assist those in need when living in the *Inner City*. But the attuned Hiphoppa must always remember that people are where they are because of who they are. Be careful with whom you choose to help, assist or support; sometimes you can make things worse.

[118]   To remain invisible to devils (jealousy, etc.) you cannot receive nor give Light (awareness/resources, etc.), lest the devils (jealousy, etc.) will see you and attack you. It's just like the deer that must go to the lake to drink, sensing that the lion is waiting right there.

[119]   Nature is set up in such a way that your predator will always be waiting at the place that you must go to receive or give nourishment. This means that every time your God must help you or you must help others, devils are attracted to that very situation. For they too are part of the Great

Event and their adversarial nature actually strengthens the spiritual *sight* (awareness) of the teacha. But once they (devils) realize that they are dealing with a teacha, indeed they begin running!

120   Again, you will know when you are blessed when there are oppositions, fears and/or other challenges in the way of achieving your goal or purpose. They are there for you to overcome and learn from. Most opportunity is found in difficulty. Most of the greatest discoveries are found in the darkest of life circumstances. Stay focused upon the ultimate cause (GOD), not the temporary effects (people, places, things and circumstances).

121   However, even in the Light the *enlightened* are seen, hunted and randomly attacked by devils. However, the teacha uses the mind as a weapon against the devils while giving and receiving Light in the World. Armed with an awareness of the Truth that is backed up by a consistent character of righteousness, the teacha effortlessly defeats (transforms) devils.

122   The attuned Hiphoppa prepares ahead of time for encounters with devils. We do not run or hide from circumstances that can do us harm, we prepare for them. Attuned Hiphoppas are never afraid to display their skills and talents in battle. We are already victorious!

123   The *endarkened* are not seen by devils because their existence does not always require the Light (help, assistance, security) of their God. They (the *endarkened*) have learned to walk in the dark with GOD without the use of their intellectual abilities.

124   After we attain enlightenment, having realized ourselves as Spirit beings, we no longer need the crutch or assistance of a sign, a plan, etc., to guide our intellect and natural senses. At this stage we walk with (or trust) our God when we are intellectually blind.

¹²⁵ We no longer need to receive or illuminate Light in order to *see* our way in the World. We are no longer afraid of the dark. We are no longer distant from our God. There is nothing to give and nothing to receive in the oneness of our God!

¹²⁶ We need not ask GOD for anything when we realize that everything is already available. Here, we pray not for GOD's Light to come to us. Here, we simply exist as the Light in the darkness! We are no longer afraid of the dark. We are Light!

¹²⁷ For enlightenment is like a light bulb being turned on in a dark room just long enough for you to get a glimpse of what is in the room. Then the light bulb is turned off again.

¹²⁸ Having been enlightened helps you to see some of the furniture and items of your *room* (environment). Enlightenment also shows you where the windows and doors are in your *room* (environment). It literally shows you where life's exits and entrances are. Enlightenment shows you exactly where and who you are in life.

¹²⁹ With this knowledge you know how to approach your life and how to escape confusion and unnecessary suffering. Those who have been enlightened are the beneficiaries of being in illuminating situations. However, they do not remain there mentally or spiritually. For the most part we live in darkness.

¹³⁰ When GOD turns the Light (awareness) on in your *room* (life) you will also see where your devils (ignorance) are. Likewise, those devils will see you. Like moths attracted to a flame, devils are attracted to enlightened beings.

¹³¹ For these reasons as you are studying the way of this gospel it is not always wise to illuminate yourself by either calling GOD into your life, or expressing the Will of your God in your life, or even showing the practice of your

skills and talents. Don't be a show-off! Sometimes it is best to follow your God's voice in the dark—in secret, avoiding unnecessary challenges. As I have said many times, *Real bad boys move in silence!*

132   For when the Light comes on in your life it is obvious that there are devils in the same *room* with you. If the Light stays on for too long you can be attacked!

133   The one GOD turns the Light on in your life just at the right time and for what seems like only a second. You then see the reality of your situation (life) and return to the darkness.

134   It is when GOD calls you and in faith you come without intellectual or rational assistance through the challenges that you are *endarkened*. You are *endarkened* when you have learned to use the purpose that you were born with to survive in the World—intellectually unassisted.

135   Not that you will never need intellectual Light. But when your Light attracts devils *endarkenment* becomes a helpful spiritual alternative. Trust GOD! GOD is in the dark (in the chaos) providing Light like nourishment, protection and guidance to the intellect even when the intellect cannot see or plan its own way.

136   For when you are no longer afraid of the dark (the chaos) and can see and act in the dark (the chaos) you are spiritually mature. You are *endarkened!* You move in a realm where everything seems to effortlessly happen right on time and just when you need it to. Your only hindrance is worry, which is actually the denial of your God.

137   For when you learn to accept the guidance of that invisible intelligence that Guides Our Direction, even when you are not thinking about it, things just always seem to work in your favor. At this level of consciousness, even when things seem to be going all wrong (to your intellect) you are at peace in the knowing that everything is actually working

in your favor. Nothing exists outside of GOD. Now go and kick the devil's ass! There it is!

THE NINTH OVERSTANDING
THE FREE STYLES

[1]   Freestyling, as it was originally known, was an effort to modify and personalize the popular dance-forms of the 1970s. During the 1970s Hiphoppas mimicked James Brown's "Get On The Good Foot" dance steps and combined them with older, more traditional dance forms and body movements (like Capoiera martial arts), creating new individualized dance moves commonly called *freestyling*.

[2]   Such personalized dance moves were called *freestyling* or *going-off* because the dancer was basically presenting old and new dance forms in his or her own way. Uniqueness in traditional dance and body movements was the original idea of *freestyling* or *going-off*. It was about doing your own thing within the traditional structures of dance.

[3]   In the 1970s, it was common for people to do their traditional dances to the songs of the day. But artists like James Brown, Sly and the Family Stone and the Jimmy Castor Bunch had instrumental breaks in their songs. Part of the excitement of listening and dancing to these artists was that most of the popular songs of the late 1960s and early 1970s had the artist singing throughout the entirety of the song, whereas James Brown and others would sing up to a point and then stop in the middle of the song, causing an instrumental break to occur.

[4]   When this *break* in the vocal performance of the song occurred it was commonly understood that this was the moment to *go-off* (or make up your own dance moves). It wouldn't be long before a specific group of youth dancers

would form specific dance moves to accommodate the *breaks* of songs.

5   On the east coast these dance forms would be called *Breakin* or *b-boying*. On the west coast these freestyle dance forms would be called *Boogying* (*Boogie-ing*), *Popping* and *Locking*. However, both coasts were united by their love for the *breaks* in certain recordings.

6   Some of the earliest b-boys and breakin crews were known as Don Campbell and the Campbellock Dancers, the Rock Steady Crew, the Nigga Twins, B-boys In Action, the Beat Street Dancers, New York City Breakers, the Dynamic Breakers, the L. A. Breakers, and the Breeze Team.

7   When Rap music became popular in 1979 many Breakers, Poppers and Lockers (as well as Graffiti writers) became Emcees and Deejays, bringing their b-boy/b-girl terminologies with them. When these ex-Breakers and Graffiti writers performed their unwritten, unrehearsed, off-the-top-of-the-head rhymes, they called it *freestyling* because the same rules that were applied to the b-boys and b-girls of the past were now applied to the Emcees and Deejays of the present.

8   Today freestyling is mostly an Emcee affair. Those Emcees who spontaneously create and perform unrehearsed and unwritten rhymes can be said to be freestyling.

9   Here, with this project, I have gone even further with the concept of the "free" "style" by offering 365 inspirational rhymes for a free Hip Hop life. *The Free Styles* are free to all *Temple Members*. Such members use these rhymes as daily affirmations, as well as potential choruses and verses in songwriting and/or book writing. Moreover, the Temple of Hip Hop uses these verses as tools of inspiration for true Hiphoppas.

10   Although each verse is relatively short (two bars each), each verse introduces an important subject for daily

observation and discussion. There are 365 verses—one for each day of the year. They can be said to music (90 beats per minute recommended) or recited internally as an affirmation.

[11] Even though each day is allotted its own verse, Hiphoppas are encouraged to choose a favorite rhyme from among the 365 verses and make it their daily affirmation. *The Free Styles* are observed daily; however, each one can be used as the subject of a weekly lesson.

[12] The true Hiphoppa meditates upon the *free style* of the day as a daily guidance and/or affirmation tool. Within the daily order of *The Free Styles* Hiphoppas are encouraged to fast every seven days regardless of when the fasting day appears within the month. Every seven days does not mean every Sunday and *fasting* does not always imply the lessening of one's food intake.

[13] Here, fasting simply means to <u>lessen</u> your intake of sugar, salt, dairy, flour, alcohol, tobacco, meats, marijuana and other intoxicants, as well as certain people, places, thoughts, money-spending, talking and other addictive habits every seven days or abstain from many of these events, people, activities and products all together.

[14] The Temple of Hiphop suggests water-based soups, cleansing teas and water for beverages particularly every seven days, as well as soothing music, silence and/or spiritually productive conversations every seven days (see January 7, 14, 21, 28, and February 4, 11, 18, etc.).

[15] Finally, December 32 begins at 12:00 noon on December 31. On the last day of the year we give ourselves a half-day, devoting the last 12 hours of the 31st day to spiritual atonement as a 32nd day. On this day, we drink only water-based soups and water. We forgive others and ourselves, accepting in faith the mercy and patience of the Great Spirit.

16   On this day we are reborn in *Spirit*. We observe the advice of the *Overstandings* and we prepare for the New Year. If you have received these *Free Styles* after December 31, then use the last day of whatever month you are already in to give yourself a half day for spiritual atonement (for example January 32, February 30, March 32, etc.).

17   The 365 rhymes/affirmations of *The Free Styles* serve as guidance for the truly committed Hiphoppa. As you begin your practice you will begin to notice how *The Free Styles* will seem to speak directly to the happenings of your day. The more often that this occurs, the more in harmony you are becoming with your Hiphop spiritual lifestyle.

18   These affirmations (the 365 rhymes) help you to <u>live</u> Hiphop. However, the most important thing a Hiphoppa can do to hasten the productive results of her Hiphop spiritual practice is not to deviate from the practice itself.

19   Once you are fully aware of what is required of you, it is then time to live it! Getting adjusted to the ways of a new life is always difficult. However, if you continue to press onward, such a new life will eventually become an old habitual one.

20   In this case, you are seeking to make and/or strengthen Hiphop as your lifestyle. You want Health, Love, Awareness and Wealth to be a regular habit in your life. You want real results from your spiritual reality. Ultimately, you desire to walk with GOD. All of this and more is achievable if you remain committed to your discipline/training.

21   This is what *The Free Styles* are all about. They help you to remain committed to Hiphop's spiritual lifestyle. *The Free Styles* encompass the schedule of Hiphop's spiritual life, which includes Hip Hop's *holy-days* like Hip Hop Appreciation Week, which occurs the third week in May.

22   Hip Hop Appreciation Week is a time set aside the third week in May to acknowledge and appreciate the

existence of Hip Hop itself. During this time the Hip Hop community refocuses itself through a collective review and update of its own history as well as a renewal and update of its core principles and elements.

23   During Hip Hop Appreciation Week artists can be asked to give sound advice on what they've learned about life and living Hip Hop. Schools of all sorts can be encouraged to discuss Hip Hop academically and critically. Radio DJs can be encouraged to upgrade their play of "conscious" Rap music over the airwaves, etc.

24   During Hip Hop Appreciation Week the Hip Hop community is encouraged to: Give the next person the right of way. Allow people to pass you. Do not block a person's forward movement.

25   Donate your skill or profession to someone who cannot afford it.

26   At the supermarket, give your change to the person behind you in line.

27   Be quick to compliment and slow to criticize. Be ready also to forgive and move on.

28   Give 10 percent of your salary to your child's teacher.

29   Ease a neighbor's pressure by donating your time toward the ease of some duty they must undertake.

30   For when this is your habitual nature you will begin to experience a certain harmony with the happenings of life itself; even when you are late, you shall be right on time. Even when you are denied, you shall be accepted. Accidents shall be either just in front of you or just behind you, but never with you. And even if you are in an accident it shall be for your own good and/or for the good of others. Never worry.

31   When you are sick, it shall be so that you may become healthier. Even those who may rise up against you

shall fall victim to their own evil plans. Where others must pay for everything that they get, you shall receive useful things freely. Everything that you lose shall be returned to you. Anything stolen from you or lost shall indeed return to you twofold. For when you make the decision to serve Life, Life itself shall indeed protect and serve you.

32   For you will begin to notice a certain intelligence governing and guiding the happenings of your life. Do not be astonished by it. Do not overthink or marvel at the supernatural activities of your life. Only accept them as normal. Expect it! For if you show any fear, doubt or surprise you will show yourself not to be ready; simply *go with the F.L.O.W. (Follow Life's Outcome Willingly)*. There it is!

JANUARY

JANUARY 1

Today is the day I live by each verse.
Temptation is defeated by trusting God first.

JANUARY 2

The way of Hiphop is always Self-creation.
With faith and will you can change your situation.

JANUARY 3

The only way to know Hip Hop like no one else ~
is to know that you are Hiphop, your Higher Self.

JANUARY 4

Today I will separate my wants from my needs ~
and visualize my needs coming to me with speed.

JANUARY 5

Today I know that I can only achieve ~
The peace and prosperity I am ready to receive.

JANUARY 6

My heart is pure in all my endeavors.
My heart can be weighed against the weight of a feather.

JANUARY 7

Today we thank our bodies for lasting ~
by giving it love and rest by fasting.

JANUARY 8

What you put in your body is what your body gives.
So put in your body the foods that help it live.

JANUARY 9
I am doing what GOD is telling me.
Times are hard, but we live in prosperity.

JANUARY 10
The True Hiphoppa sustains Hiphop.
Television and radio simply do not!

JANUARY 11
The knowledge of Hip Hop is for all that wish to take it ~
cause frankly, everyone is not gonna make it.

JANUARY 12
Once you see how it all connects ~
You feel the peace and give God respect.

JANUARY 13
Today I express what's been taught to me.
I act like, and think, the way it ought to be.

JANUARY 14
Respond to your body and it'll respond to you.
While fasting, tell it what you want it to do.

JANUARY 15
When Michael became Martin, and Martin became King ~
The juniors in the streets were shown a new thing.

JANUARY 16
Today no lies go past my teeth.
I am fishing not to become a chicken or start beef.

JANUARY 17
While the Rapper raps and the Singer sings ~

always be prepared to accept new things.

JANUARY 18
Only you can take care of you.
Stop asking others to do what you can do.

JANUARY 19
I can be trusted, I can be loved.
God lives within me, not way up above.

JANUARY 20
Check your thinking, it's an ancient fact ~
that the way you think is the way you act.

JANUARY 21
We thank the body with rest and with fasting ~
and massage the organs with continuous laughing.

JANUARY 22
What you put in your life is what you get out.
Givin' and takin' is what life is all about.

JANUARY 23
Look for the good in all things and all people.
Perform in GOD, and allow God to be you.

JANUARY 24
Crime will never leave society as a sickness ~
as long as justice in society is a business.

JANUARY 25
You ain't got it hard; you wanna know what's the hardest?
The single working mom raising Hip Hop's artists.

JANUARY 26

Check what ya seein' and check how ya listenin' ~
control all your senses and practice self-discipline.

JANUARY 27

Obeying and worshipping GOD was before ~
now we must act like GODs and be mature.

JANUARY 28

Promote your physical well-being and long-lasting ~
by resting the mind and body through fasting.

JANUARY 29

Do not get trapped in temptation and lust.
Have fun, but always build an image of trust.

JANUARY 30

Your word is your bond when you blow your vocal horn.
But words also manifest, so word is also born.

JANUARY 31

Whether it be with a book, ball or drill ~
the road to success begins with a skill.

FEBRUARY

FEBRUARY 1

I am the master of all memory that's found ~
my history lives for me, not the other way around.

FEBRUARY 2

The moment you were born, you were truly blessed.
There is really no need for you to ever be stressed.

FEBRUARY 3

The formula for positive change is quite clear ~
progression in life begins first without fear.

FEBRUARY 4

The practice of fasting helps the body, no question.
It is you who control your body and mind direction.

FEBRUARY 5

By talkin' 'bout the problem we mangle and mix it.
By workin' wit the problem we eventually fix it.

FEBRUARY 6

Whatever you look for, you'll eventually see.
Whatever you speak will soon come to be.

FEBRUARY 7

Power and peace is found in this sentence:
Today you must realize the Truth of GOD's presence.

FEBRUARY 8

What one does need not be mentioned.
The question to ask is, *what's the intention?*

FEBRUARY 9

For peace and prosperity I need nothing else ~
but GOD, this gospel and my Hip Hop Self.

FEBRUARY 10

Hip Hop Kulture doesn't recognize haters.
Haters within a culture of love are traitors.

FEBRUARY 11

Fasting shows the body its true respect.
Constantly eating shows the body true neglect.

FEBRUARY 12

Compassion and care is the *word* for today ~
allow these virtues to guide your day.

FEBRUARY 13

Everything emanates from our cosmic mother ~
existing as one; all sisters, all brothers.

FEBRUARY 14

The difference between sinking and rising above ~
is shown in your levels of hate and love.

FEBRUARY 15

With whatever you learn in your temple or college ~
the way of Hip Hop is to do your knowledge.

FEBRUARY 16

If you change the way you think, you will change your
surroundings ~
sometimes you are floating, when you think you are
drowning.

FEBRUARY 17
The Hiphop teacha knows that without trust ~
the trustless community turns to dust.

FEBRUARY 18
While fasting, we stop eating the foods that we bought ~
but let us also fast from the eating of negative thoughts.

FEBRUARY 19
The true Hiphoppa is a blessing to any lawyer ~
because the true Hiphoppa promotes Law and also Order.

FEBRUARY 20
Self-creation is what it's all about.
Believe in Self, not fear and doubt.

FEBRUARY 21
Nobody sees things like everyone else ~
the first education is educatin' yourself.

FEBRUARY 22
When do things start and when do things cease?
If your purpose is now, this question is the least.

FEBRUARY 23
From the winter to the spring to the summer to the fall ~
seek knowledge, never think that you know it all.

FEBRUARY 24
Only poor people drink dreams like juice ~
relying on gossip and not on Truth.

FEBRUARY 25
Drink much water and eat what's alive ~

Then be like water as it cleans and revives.

FEBRUARY 26
When nothing ever happens for you, you say,
I knew it.
The problem is you're thinking about it. Just do it!

FEBRUARY 27
Hiphoppas rise in health and wealth ~
when Hiphoppas mature to a knowledge of Self.

FEBRUARY 28
If you have it to give, it is important that you give it.
If you know the Truth, it is important that you live it.

FEBRUARY 29*
Put no interest above your health.
Be your own partner and love your Self.

MARCH

MARCH 1
Peace and prosperity are what Hip Hop is pursuing.
We are all a portion of what the universe is doing.

MARCH 2
Don't worry about when, don't worry about how ~
the power of future begins right now.

MARCH 3
The Hiphop teacha eats herbs and roots ~
vegetables, teas, grains and fruits.

MARCH 4
When you choose a friend, you choose their life, no doubt.
So make sure your friends aren't all stressed out.

MARCH 5
The family man has a family plan ~
a plan that helps his family stand.

MARCH 6
The teacha that only talks begins to ramble.
But the teacha that really teaches speaks through example.

MARCH 7
If GOD in Heaven gives intellectual aid ~
what is really and truly man-made?

MARCH 8
When you discipline your mind from every temptation ~
your mind is clear for any situation.

MARCH 9

The teacha practices being prepared ~
educating the mind, so that the body is not scared.

MARCH 10

What exactly shall I fast from today ~
My eating, my thinking, my work, or my play?

MARCH 11

The physical body is our earthly rental ~
our planetary vehicle, our only true temple.

MARCH 12

People are ambitious, they seek their own glory.
Always seek to know both sides of the story.

MARCH 13

For a spiritual environment, we need not search ~
'cause anywhere we are in the World is church.

MARCH 14

Here is a message that many must heed:
it is more important to do than to read.

MARCH 15

Good and evil might be the same thing ~
'cause angels and demons respect the same king.

MARCH 16

If your life is in turmoil and appears at its worst ~
you have nothing to lose by putting GOD first.

MARCH 17

When fasting, never sound depressed in your voice.

Prayer and fasting are times to rejoice.

MARCH 18
It takes a whole village just to raise one youth ~
but what if that village is denied the Truth?

MARCH 19
The police have to get back to working for the people.
And the people have to get back to treating each other equal.

MARCH 20
Look for the good and the good shall appear.
Look for the bad and the bad is right there.

MARCH 21
Once you know for sure exactly where ya going ~
your own conviction starts the energy flowing.

MARCH 22
When brothers kill brothers and exercise hate ~
the enemies of their father inherit their estate.

MARCH 23
What kind of advice could they possibly give ~
when they really haven't lived in the places we've lived?

MARCH 24
While fasting, the Hiphop teacha serves the meal ~
with this act one's discipline is practiced for real.

MARCH 25
Do not practice forgiveness so that you may be forgiven.
Practice forgiveness to expand your own livin'.

MARCH 26

Every day is a birthday party ~
when you wake up from sleeping and you love somebody.

MARCH 27

Knowledge and skill will bring you a salary ~
but knowing your purpose can change your reality.

MARCH 28

GOD is patient but when She strikes ~
you have been warned every day and every night.

MARCH 29

A mother or father you are to the end ~
but to raise your children you must be their friend.

MARCH 30

The best way to create and maintain wealth ~
is to simultaneously create and maintain Self.

MARCH 31

Look out! Look out! If you're about to crash!
Right about NOW it is time to fast.

APRIL

APRIL 1
Your inner-Spirit is a Spirit that does.
It reacts to what is, what will be, and what was.

APRIL 2
The most valuable lessons should not be a mystery.
The attuned Hiphoppa should teach with simplicity.

APRIL 3
No one can say that anyone's faith is deceiving ~
cause the root of all faiths is choice in believing.

APRIL 4
Study who you are, before anyone else ~
then study everyone else like you've studied yourself.

APRIL 5
Destruction begins when you doubt yourself ~
doubt your health, and doubt your wealth.

APRIL 6
If you really want money your mentality must switch.
If you really wanna be rich you gotta act like you're rich!

APRIL 7
Fasting and prayer are always intertwined ~
one cleanses body, the other cleanses the mind.

APRIL 8
Don't worry 'bout when, don't worry 'bout how ~
the Light of GOD is always right now!

APRIL 9
The Goddess manifests daily in our lives ~
through our sisters, mothers, daughters, aunts and wives.

APRIL 10
To enhance one's Self, creative thinking is critical ~
but maintain a balance between the creative and analytical.

APRIL 11
Makeup and clothing are just the surface ~
but nothing looks good if you have no purpose.

APRIL 12
God is speaking but only a few are listening ~
others are too busy booty-shakin' and dissing.

APRIL 13
Out of Jesus, Muhammad, Krishna and Moses ~
to GOD, which one of them is the closest?

APRIL 14
While fasting, know that you have your father's assistance.
While laughing, laugh within your mother's existence.

APRIL 15
Give us every daughter, give us every son ~
and give us the position to assist everyone.

APRIL 16
It seems like with disease no doctor is stopping this ~
'cause most doctors ignore the effects of consciousness.

APRIL 17
There are no grades to achieve awareness.

Discipline your mind above living so careless.

APRIL 18
If GOD appeared to all of us, right now, this week ~
who would be good enough to step up and speak?

APRIL 19
It's foolish to say we are destroying the Earth ~
'cause everything we're doing destroys us first.

APRIL 20
If you and I was ice cream we both would melt.
But while melting the teacha still asks, *how can I help?*

APRIL 21
How can you have a definition of nutrition ~
when the essentials of productive thinking are always missing?

APRIL 22
Live past your senses, live past your salary ~
remove your perception and look at reality.

APRIL 23
The Laws of the State and the Laws of all others ~
fall into balance with service toward others.

APRIL 24
Just as a car with no gas is worthless ~
your life doesn't run if it doesn't have purpose.

APRIL 25
Past, present, future is a state of the mind ~
really, everything is happening at the same time.

APRIL 26

If something goes wrong, people say, *I knew it*.
But if they want something right they ask GOD to do it.

APRIL 27

Whether you are learning in high school or college ~
in the lifestyle of Hiphop you must <u>do</u> your knowledge.

APRIL 28

Never underestimate your will over your body ~
while fasting, find yourself praying at the party.

APRIL 29

Before we can talk about people being selfless ~
we first gotta talk about people feeling helpless.

APRIL 30

When you see injustice you gotta start speaking up
Many say, "I follow GOD," but are they keeping up?

MAY

MAY 1
Be careful that the highest ideas of yourself ~
aren't just the opinions of everyone else.

MAY 2
First there's me, then there's me thinking ~
then there's me rising, or then there's me sinking.

MAY 3
The road of life is smooth with many curves.
The one that hugs the road is the one that serves.

MAY 4
Do true Hip Hop so that all can see it ~
but longevity begins when you can also be it.

MAY 5
At the Temple of Hiphop there is limited seating ~
reserved for those who perfect their eating.

MAY 6
Everyone that leads can also mislead.
So make sure the knowledge that you have is what you need.

MAY 7
If closeness with GOD is Heaven, where all is well ~
then distance from GOD is hell, can't you tell?

MAY 8
Today is the day I act like God ~
doing this like God, and doing that like God.

MAY 9

Beware of the spiritual *Pimp* and spiritual *Hoe* ~
because of spiritual clothes, you think they spiritually know.

MAY 10

You will pray for a thing and never get to own it ~
if you live in the future and not in the present moment.

MAY 11

Peace of mind begins with non-attachment.
The Hiphop teacha sees the whole in every fragment.

MAY 12

Yearly the teacha fasts, 52 times ~
and meditates upon 365 rhymes.

MAY 13

You will raise your wealth and enhance your health ~
when you release all doubt and believe in your Self.

MAY 14

Never pay attention to fearful criticism ~
Your life and your principles, these others don't live them.

MAY 15

The skills that are given to you by your Mother ~
should glorify the Father through service toward others.

MAY 16

And the emcee said, *here is the key to success* ~
represent the vision of the crowd you address.

MAY 17

It's clever to learn from history or whatever ~

but never cease to update whatever you remember.

MAY 18
The mysteries of life begin to unravel ~
not only through books, but through actual travel.

MAY 19
No one should begin to think you're fasting ~
because around them you are having much fun and laughing.

MAY 20
What's Heaven's is Heaven's, what's hell's is hell's ~
but freedom begins when we govern ourselves.

MAY 21
It makes no sense to love an artist when he dies ~
if you haven't shown him that same love when he was alive.

MAY 22
Graffiti Art, Breakin, Deejayin, Emceein ~
all have to do with acting and being.

MAY 23
Hiphop is healthy and always has wealth ~
but this week, Hiphop is conscious of itself.

MAY 24
Graffiti, Emceein, Deejayin, Beat Boxin ~
with Breakin and Knowledge was original Hiphoppin'.

MAY 25
For those that are strugglin', tryin', and pursuin' ~
change your thoughts and start being and doing.

MAY 26
While fasting, know that your God is living!
While fasting, enhance the soul through giving.

MAY 27
Your choice of philosophy can easily mess your mind up ~
if all you do is study while ignoring your conduct.

MAY 28
Don't get stagnated in the what, where, and how.
If GOD gave it to you, act on it right now!

MAY 29
GOD is speaking to you and everyone else.
Don't wait around for knowledge; you must educate your
Self.

MAY 30
Follow life's teachings even over the fences ~
but learn to control all six of your senses.

MAY 31
You can kill a man by takin' him out his land ~
and puttin' him in a land he really doesn't overstand.

JUNE

JUNE 1
Everything we're buying has already been bought ~
Everything we're learning has already been taught.

JUNE 2
While fasting, eating does not include slaughter ~
Today we are fed by air, light and water.

JUNE 3
Not all Hiphoppas have rims on their cars ~
with baggy pants, braggin' about being behind bars.

JUNE 4
Freely I give you much health and wealth ~
but they are secondhand, 'cause first I give them to myself.

JUNE 5
The direction of the lesson creates your perception ~
and your perception of your lesson creates your direction.

JUNE 6
Express the Love like no one else.
Allow the Love to become your Self.

JUNE 7
You've walked this path long enough ~
It's time for you to start claiming your stuff.

JUNE 8
Some things happen now, and some things happen later ~
but remember, with GOD you are a co-creator.

JUNE 9

On the streets and highways people signal when passing.
On the highways of life the body signals before crashing.

JUNE 10

People will always think you're contradictory ~
When you choose to live for today and not in history.

JUNE 11

In this verse is the teaching of the Church ~
Faith is an act of you moving first.

JUNE 12

Who are the *theys*, and who are the *thems* ~
are *they* not you, and I, and all of our friends?

JUNE 13

Driving in traffic gives you the opportunity ~
to practice courtesy, compassion and unity.

JUNE 14

The Judicial system loses its quickness ~
when more and more people look to practice forgiveness.

JUNE 15

The challenges you face will disappear in an hour ~
when you see them as reasons to use your power.

JUNE 16

Constant working causes crashing!
So stop the working of the body through fasting.

JUNE 17

Find ways to serve in advance before you act ~

and all your actions in advance will be exact.

JUNE 18
Open your mind and extend its range ~
because all school knowledge is subject to change.

JUNE 19
The first move you make is to become awake.
The second move made is for you to stay awake.

JUNE 20
The traps of temptation will always miss you~
when you realize the Truth that GOD is with you.

JUNE 21
Restrictions and rules we really wouldn't need 'em ~
if everyone was conscious of the next person's freedom.

JUNE 22
Suggestions are good, here and there, once or twice ~
but don't make the suggestions of others your whole life.

JUNE 23
You have received according to your asking ~
And you shall believe according to your fasting.

JUNE 24
Few are Emceein while many do Rap.
Many are talking, but only a few act.

JUNE 25
Life is a bitch when you don't flow with her ~
so flow with her, know it's her, and go with her.

JUNE 26

Bronx versus Queens, East versus West ~
the one that endures is the one that's the best.

JUNE 27

Laws don't work for the people that break them ~
Laws only work for the people that make them.

JUNE 28

Never say no to the one that asks ~
but never be led down a suckers path.

JUNE 29

We are all role models, for all to witness ~
but most folks don't think they can really make a difference.

JUNE 30

The teacha is patient and repeats the teachings ~
Not with words, but by fasting from eating.

JULY

JULY 1
Respect the real Rap from before you were born ~
Hip Hop's culture is from all of those songs.

JULY 2
While traveling we follow the signs without question ~
never once doubting or asking who's directin'.

JULY 3
Not a contract, a ring, nor even a salary ~
can really define your role in a family.

JULY 4
The essence of freedom is in this sentence:
Self-creation is independence!

JULY 5
Today is the day we give glory to GOD ~
when we think about it, life hasn't been so hard.

JULY 6
Heaven and hell can grow or shrink ~
based on the way you grow and think.

JULY 7
Most of what's eaten is turned into trash ~
so minimize your eating and practice your fast.

JULY 8
Some give the gifts that sit upon mantles ~
while others give the gifts of productive examples.

JULY 9

Brothers are brothers from breath to breath ~
from wife to wife, from life to death.

JULY 10

If life is a game, childhood is the scrimmage ~
so children must play toward a productive *Self* image.

JULY 11

The student seeks knowledge through admissions and fees.
The teacha seeks knowledge in all that he sees.

JULY 12

Paradise is sudden and in the present moment ~
but if you're in the past or future you will never know it.

JULY 13

Feel the value of the things you have ~
Nothing is more valuable than the ability to laugh.

JULY 14

The body fights its enemies every day and every hour ~
so cut back on salt, sugar, dairy foods and flour.

JULY 15

You see Hiphop in that, and you see Hiphop in this ~
now see Hiphop as your creative consciousness.

JULY 16

Release your anger, your doubt, and your fear ~
and instantly your mind will become quite clear.

JULY 17

The activity of life is constant creation ~

so walk and talk in your daily affirmation.

JULY 18
The guard at the gate of the temple says this to you:
Only the disciplined one will get through.

JULY 19
In life there is only one true oppressor ~
It's the mind of the person that feels like he is lesser.

JULY 20
If you wanna study changes, history will show how.
But if you wanna make changes, you must think and go now.

JULY 21
Foods are drugs and drugs are foods ~
like some drugs, foods can also create moods.

JULY 22
Today you must think before you act.
Let this be this, and let that be that.

JULY 23
Focus your mind on God and Law ~
and all your steps are bound to be sure.

JULY 24
All subjects of learning are sisters and brothers ~
The mastery of one subject leads to all others.

JULY 25
Sometimes the teacha must be alone ~
To see and comprehend what is being shown.

JULY 26

The Gospel of Hip Hop exists to protect.
It speaks to a life beyond cash and checks.

JULY 27

Giving of yourself means, giving of your Self ~
it doesn't always mean the giving of your wealth.

JULY 28

The sugar, the dairy, the flour, the salt ~
for maximum health, these must come to a halt.

JULY 29

The things you do are the desires of your heart ~
no one can truly make you play a different part.

JULY 30

You will live in constant stagnation and stiffness ~
if in life you never learned to practice forgiveness.

JULY 31

In perfect love and balance many are born ~
but as we grow up many more are taught wrong.

AUGUST

AUGUST 1
Those that work for GOD have God working for them.
Life becomes your partner when GOD is your close friend.

AUGUST 2
Establish your goal; with all your time pursue it.
Feel yourself acting, stop doubting, just do it.

AUGUST 3
Unnecessary want, desire, and attachment ~
leads to suffering and mind entrapment.

AUGUST 4
If you wish to slow down how fast your heart is beating ~
then fish and vegetables you should always be eating.

AUGUST 5
Always check to see how your friends are living.
The ones who are receiving should also be the ones giving.

AUGUST 6
This rhyme is spiritual but it pertains to the medical ~
self-control and health are identical.

AUGUST 7
The reality of the slave will always be a mystery ~
because only slave traders were written down in history.

AUGUST 8
Whatever you look for also looks for you ~
so watch what you say, what you think, and what you do.

AUGUST 9

Every single year, about this time~
We are born again with a renewing of our minds.

AUGUST 10

The rich get richer because they work toward rich.
The poor get poorer because their minds can't switch.

AUGUST 11

While you're fasting reaffirm in your mental ~
"I don't live in a tomb, I live in a temple."

AUGUST 12

He is God, she is God, GOD is everywhere ~
in the water, in the fire, in the Earth, and in the air.

AUGUST 13

After all those people finish tellin' you lies ~
open your mind's eye and visualize.

AUGUST 14

Place your mind on the things that are higher ~
and stomp out the fires of your carnal desires.

AUGUST 15

Most people cannot seem to hold success ~
because they fail to repeat the actions of their success.

AUGUST 16

Women love men and men love women ~
when both love GOD, so do their children.

AUGUST 17

The clearest critique of a person is through loving ~

the distorted critique of a person is through judging.

AUGUST 18
The gifts you receive from GOD at birth ~
are the gifts you return to God on Earth.

AUGUST 19
If you give away your coat, your shoes, and your hat ~
the promise to all is that you'll get it right back.

AUGUST 20
In peace, in unity, in joy and in love ~
Show me today what I am capable of.

AUGUST 21
As people pass by, you should say to yourself ~
I love you, I love me and I love everyone else.

AUGUST 22
That man looks good, that woman looks great ~
but today I think I'll take me on a date.

AUGUST 23
Release the critique of others and you will find ~
a silence in your heart and a silence in your mind.

AUGUST 24
The Laws of inhaling and exhaling when breathing ~
are the Laws of the universe toward giving and receiving.

AUGUST 25
You talk to your body through the foods on your shelf.
Your body talks back through the level of your health.

AUGUST 26
Seeing God's finished work is a spiritual practice ~
yet even the most powerful of preachers still lack this.

AUGUST 27
The reason people feel they need prestige and clout ~
is really because they're trapped by fear and doubt.

AUGUST 28
You will get what you believe, and what you wish to achieve ~
when you help others believe and achieve what they perceive.

AUGUST 29
Today I break free from all of my fears ~
I don't need to go over there, it's all right here!

AUGUST 30
After the preacher of the Word astounds you ~
open your heart and feel GOD all around you.

AUGUST 31
Before you begin to rearrange your behavior ~
first be clear about your internal nature.

SEPTEMBER

SEPTEMBER 1
Fasting and rest for the body is ease ~
constantly working and overeating is disease.

SEPTEMBER 2
Whether in a wealthy suburb or in a poor *ghetto* ~
the spiritual life requires that you let go.

SEPTEMBER 3
Foolish people only follow the trend and the check ~
while the wise ones also follow the cause and the effect.

SEPTEMBER 4
The one that loves GOD is good but not above ~
the compassionate one that simply gives and shows love.

SEPTEMBER 5
When I grow up I'm gonna be soft.
When I grow up I'm gonna be hard.
When I grow up I'm gonna be wealthy.
When I grow up I'm gonna be God!

SEPTEMBER 6
I am beautiful, I am smart ~
today there is only love in my heart.

SEPTEMBER 7
Learn from others, but know your own order.
What drowns one man is the next man's sauna.

SEPTEMBER 8

The titles of foods and drugs are name things ~
because foods and drugs are really the same things.

SEPTEMBER 9

When the lessons of simple common sense don't reach you ~
the lessons of pain will manifest just to teach you.

SEPTEMBER 10

Change through destruction sometimes is the hardest.
For even the Goddess burns down her own forest.

SEPTEMBER 11

The tragedies and threats which transformed America ~
brought unity and strength in the wake of hysteria.

SEPTEMBER 12

The spiritual life can begin and start ~
when you quiet the mind and truly search the heart.

SEPTEMBER 13

It might sound crazy and it might sound bugged ~
but forgiveness is real when your enemies are hugged.

SEPTEMBER 14

If the righteous never walk into the houses of the pimps ~
the *whores* of those houses might never get a glimpse.

SEPTEMBER 15

If your mind doesn't permit that you fast, it's okay ~
continue to practice, eating one meal a day.

SEPTEMBER 16

The key to the *City* for all who are listenin' ~

begins with Self and ends with discipline.

SEPTEMBER 17
The Goddess is God and GOD is the Goddess ~
living is an art and you are the artist.

SEPTEMBER 18
Whether it be the daughter or whether it be the son ~
the wisdom of GOD should begin when they are young.

SEPTEMBER 19
Run from the person showing attachment and vanity ~
and run toward the family, showing love and charity.

SEPTEMBER 20
The children of ignorance you will see by their demanding.
The children of wisdom you will see by their overstanding.

SEPTEMBER 21
Peace of mind and awareness of Self ~
arrives when the Self is content with the Self.

SEPTEMBER 22
While others overeat on the road to devastation ~
the teacha is fasting, content in the situation.

SEPTEMBER 23
The one that forgives and holds no grudges ~
wastes no time with lawyers and judges.

SEPTEMBER 24
One of the first spiritual lessons to learn ~
is how to call on GOD and expect a return.

SEPTEMBER 25

At the Temple of H.I.P.H.O.P this is what we teach you ~
Her Infinite Power Helps Organize People.

SEPTEMBER 26

Get prepared! Your blessing is coming!
Doubters are hiding! Haters are running!

SEPTEMBER 27

How can you separate the sun from its heat?
How can you separate the Earth from your feet?

SEPTEMBER 28

The teacha of Hiphop knows just what to do.
You should never chase money, instead money should chase you.

SEPTEMBER 29

Life breeds life and death breeds death ~
continue eating the dead and what's left.

SEPTEMBER 30

The rebel is hasty, he argues with the elite ~
while the teacha performs patience and eventually takes their seat.

OCTOBER

OCTOBER 1
In the eyes of the child the parent must be a hero ~
if the parent is not, then the parent is zero.

OCTOBER 2
If you really wanna make a million dollar bills ~
the question you must ask first is, *truly, what are my skills?*

OCTOBER 3
Those that think *time is money* are lost ~
for it leads them to quickly start ripping people off.

OCTOBER 4
The things that come are the things that go ~
attach yourself to nothing, not even to what you know.

OCTOBER 5
Whether it be a productive or niggative situation ~
all is caused by a person's imagination.

OCTOBER 6
Fasting builds up the spirit you expect ~
Overeating tears down the spirit in neglect.

OCTOBER 7
Step number one. Once you've disciplined the mental ~
it is for the teacha to clean out the temple.

OCTOBER 8
Step number two. Once the temple is cleansed ~
it is for the teacha to forgive and make amends.

OCTOBER 9
Step number three. Once forgiveness is practiced ~
it is for the teacha to seek knowledge and never lack this.

OCTOBER 10
Step number four. For the mind to be clear ~
it is for the teacha to release all fear.

OCTOBER 11
Step number five. Once fear is wiped out ~
it is for the teacha to release self-doubt.

OCTOBER 12
Step number six. With the knowledge of creation ~
the teacha must succeed in the releasing of temptation.

OCTOBER 13
Step number seven. Once temptation is far behind ~
it is for the teacha to free attachment from the mind.

OCTOBER 14
The choice is yours to live shorter or longer ~
this choice is made between alcohol and water.

OCTOBER 15
Step number eight. Once attachment isn't demanding ~
is for the teacha to gain self-overstanding.

OCTOBER 16
Step number nine, which takes the teacha up above ~
is for the teacha to be God, which is Love.

OCTOBER 17
Ask this of GOD in your heart and make it felt ~

Teach me to help others even as I am helped.

OCTOBER 18
From the grave to the cradle, from the cradle to the grave ~
everything you see is really particles and waves.

OCTOBER 19
Everyone knows what they're supposed to be doin' ~
But somehow it's the opposite that they are all pursuin'.

OCTOBER 20
The mind should be quiet and still during the fast ~
Here, anything of God you can ask.

OCTOBER 21
When the work is done, you are the One ~
"The Peace," "The Love," "The Unity" all having fun!

OCTOBER 22
The things you believe you also give power ~
so believe in yourself, every minute and every hour.

OCTOBER 23
Repent, the kingdom of heaven is at hand ~
stop saying *I can't* and say *I can.*

OCTOBER 24
Continue to walk the path, just don't blow it!
People admire you but they just don't show it.

OCTOBER 25
Open your eye, it's not always like this ~
Today is the day you are shining the brightest!

OCTOBER 26
Don't feel bad when your critics are astonished ~
God delivers victory to the soul that is polished.

OCTOBER 27
I am *hip* today and I can *hop* today ~
Fasting doesn't mean that I stop today.

OCTOBER 28
The righteous in sight are with the wicked in sight ~
so that the wicked in sight may also see the Light.

OCTOBER 29
Sometimes you can't show your strength and stamina ~
'cause when you need rest people tend to get mad at ya.

OCTOBER 30
If you got hard work to do, quickly get with it ~
'cause others are on their way to prison or the clinic.

OCTOBER 31
The youngest of people are quickly turned old ~
when life is spent always seeking to control.

NOVEMBER

NOVEMBER 1
Fill the prescription of love and trust ~
so anger and stress can be turned to dust.

NOVEMBER 2
When voting we think like children, not adults ~
'cause only changed thinking will bring new results.

NOVEMBER 3
Really the best way to control your mood ~
is to control your intake of food.

NOVEMBER 4
The American system need not be rearranged ~
it is the thinking of the American people that must change.

NOVEMBER 5
Every generation has gone through the phase ~
of conspiracy theories, aliens and last days.

NOVEMBER 6
We all know the phrase, we all know the song ~
You don't know what you've got till it's gone.

NOVEMBER 7
While limits and lacks follow the one who is scared ~
health and wealth follow the one who is prepared.

NOVEMBER 8
Before you open your mouth to say any curse ~
with your own tongue you curse yourself first.

NOVEMBER 9
The grass will always look greener over there ~
but if the lawn is not yours, why stare?

NOVEMBER 10
While you are fasting, respecting your health ~
respect the well-being of everyone else.

NOVEMBER 11
If I refuse to love, overstand and forgive you ~
then I refuse my own spiritual life to continue.

NOVEMBER 12
Those of little knowledge read books and get scared.
Those of self-knowledge read life and get prepared.

NOVEMBER 13
What's a good education without a good imagination?
The answer: A lot of good people in this nation.

NOVEMBER 14
Heal yourself, find yourself, know yourself, correct yourself ~
see yourself, love yourself, be yourself, respect yourself.

NOVEMBER 15
Knowledge, unity and economic growth ~
should be recited by every student as an oath.

NOVEMBER 16
If it's the social system that you wish to speak to ~
don't speak to the system, speak directly to the people.

NOVEMBER 17
It's only yourself and your body you are defeating ~

when you do not practice intelligent eating.

NOVEMBER 18
Oh GOD, oh GOD, are our parents deserting us? ~
Or is it just you through them, now alerting us?

NOVEMBER 19
A message for those who are politically sinking ~
Don't change the president, change your thinking.

NOVEMBER 20
What is the system of the new World order?
Is it not my son, is it not your daughter.

NOVEMBER 21
Know the purpose of those that surround you ~
It is the thinking of others that can suffocate and drown you.

NOVEMBER 22
Look back on your life and you'll see once more ~
a lot that you can really be thankful for.

NOVEMBER 23
If your life has no purpose you should never forget ~
that the things you don't have, you didn't prepare to get.

NOVEMBER 24
The eating of food is a full that can deceive you ~
while the eating of knowledge is a full that never leaves you.

NOVEMBER 25
What you touch, what you taste, what you hear, see and smell ~
if not controlled properly can lead you to hell

NOVEMBER 26

Everyone come near, let your children hear ~
failure is created by doubt and fear.

NOVEMBER 27

GOD is my strength, my salvation and hope ~
cause most people really don't know how to vote!

NOVEMBER 28

If we only talk about it, it will never get solved ~
so let's talk up a plan, overstand and get involved.

NOVEMBER 29

The lessons and privileges of health, wealth and Self ~
are not just for you, they're for everyone else.

NOVEMBER 30

The Hiphop teacha cares little for labels.
It's all about skills when life turns her tables.

DECEMBER

DECEMBER 1
Today is the day I've inherited the will ~
to resist temptation and resist getting ill.

DECEMBER 2
When it comes to sex if your children can't plan it ~
before your time you'll become a grandparent.

DECEMBER 3
Forgive me GOD, I come in repentance.
Bless me GOD and all of my dependents.

DECEMBER 4
Show me the way that strengthens the will ~
widens perception, and sharpens the skill.

DECEMBER 5
With God in you and God in me ~
we are all one, and we are all free.

DECEMBER 6
The one thing we learned about the Hiphop game ~
is that you have to keep pushin' 'cause nothin' stays the same.

DECEMBER 7
Just as there is no freedom without Law ~
There is no peace without justice, for sure.

DECEMBER 8
While others are eating, smoking, and drinking, ~
the one who is fasting is the one who is thinking.

DECEMBER 9

Remember this as you're burning fat ~
with the road you take there's no turning back.

DECEMBER 10

Just like your highway, your life-way has signs ~
some see what's before them, others drive like they're blind.

DECEMBER 11

Make your security, make it, and defend it ~
by saving and investing and remaining independent.

DECEMBER 12

To the future we are blind, most things are felt through ~
but you can see in the past where God has helped you.

DECEMBER 13

You can have a great intellect where knowledge excites you ~
but you can't take it nowhere if people don't like you.

DECEMBER 14

If God helps those that help themselves ~
it must be nearby where this God dwells.

DECEMBER 15

Nature eats the weak, this is true ~
So fasting prevents Nature from eating you!

DECEMBER 16

Blessed are those who can use their hands ~
only they are prosperous anytime in any land.

DECEMBER 17

Are roses red? Are violets blue?

Reality is only what is real to you.

DECEMBER 18

The sex, the money, the drugs, the gun ~
six million ways to die; choose one.

DECEMBER 19

The Hiphop teacha can teach the right lesson ~
if the receiver of knowledge will ask the right questions.

DECEMBER 20

If you recognize first the gifts of your mother ~
you'll find it easier to give gifts to all others.

DECEMBER 21

Now is the time for courage and trust,
'cause the last days of others are the first days for us!

DECEMBER 22

When you live in health, you live in wealth ~
your fast does not include everyone else.

DECEMBER 23

Rejoice without eating, smoking, or drinking.
practice and discipline expands your thinking.

DECEMBER 24

Think not the worse of your hired-self ~
only give birth to your Higher-Self.

DECEMBER 25

Any path you choose to find God is sacred.
Follow any path of GOD and you will make it.

DECEMBER 26

To achieve transformation, it is God who must work you.
Your friends will desert you and your relatives will hurt you.

DECEMBER 27

Make love, make love on the radio is nice,
but in reality *make love* really means *make life*.

DECEMBER 28

The people that can hurt the teacha the most,
are the people that the teacha lets get too close.

DECEMBER 29

Today is the day that we clean the house ~
while taking *I can't* and *I hate* from out of the mouth.

DECEMBER 30

It is said that opportunity knocks one time ~
but that knock is heard by the disciplined mind.

DECEMBER 31

Continue in peace, love, fun and unity ~
the new year coming is full of opportunity!

DECEMBER 32*

When it comes to the spirit, you cannot cower,
For the rest of the year you will walk in power.

THE TENTH OVERSTANDING
THE SPIRIT OF GRAFFITI ART

1   *They call themselves 'writers' because that's what they do: They write their names, among other things, everywhere! Names they've been given or have chosen for themselves. Most of all, they write in and on subway trains that carry their names from one end of the city to the other. It's called bombing, and it has equally assertive counterparts in Rap music and break dancing. Graffiti writing in New York is a vocation. Its traditions are handed down from one youthful generation to the next. To some it's art; to most people, however, it is a plague that never ends, a symbol that we've lost control.* (*Style Wars*, 1983)

2   Know this: the Overstanding before you is an elementary introduction to the study of Graffiti Art as color and light and how these frequencies affect the psychology of Hiphoppas living in urban areas. As an *Overstanding*, it teaches spiritual Truths through the language of Graffiti Art. Traditionally, the word *Graffiti* originated from the Italian term *graffito* meaning *a scratch*. According to the American language, Graffiti is defined as a "writing" or "drawing" that is "scribbled," "scratched" or "sprayed" onto a surface.

3   However, in his book *Graffiti World: Street Art from Five Continents*, Nicholas Ganz writes, *Derived from the Italian* sgraffio, *meaning 'scratch,' graffiti has been around since the beginning of mankind. Pictures, such as those at the Lascaux Caves in France, were mostly carved into cave walls with bones or stones, but early man also anticipated the stencil*

and spray techniques, blowing coloured powder through hollow bones around his hands to make silhouettes. In ancient Greece, fragments of clay were found on which notes had been carved, while excavations in Pompeii brought to light a wealth of graffiti, including election slogans, drawings and obscenities.

4   James Prigoff agrees in the foreword of the book *Graffiti L.A.: Street Styles and Art* by Steve Grody. He writes, *Cave dwellers drew pictures on their walls; graffiti was uncovered in Pompeii when the lava was chipped away; Spanish conquistadors left their names on Inscription Rock outside of Gallup, New Mexico; Frenchmen scratched their names on the walls of Angkor Wat in Cambodia; and a navy inspector in the 1940s named Jack Kilroy drew his famous logo 'Kilroy Was Here' to indicate his completed inspection, and a funny face appearing over the wall was co-opted by GIs all over the world.*

5   In regards to the art of prehistoric humans we now know that some cave dwellers would put berry juice in their mouths and blow it onto cave wall surfaces also using their open hands as sort of a stencil-styled signature. Later in human history people would carve their names in trees, stones and even famous ancient monuments as memories and evidence of their travels.

6   Although many people still associate Graffiti Art with vandalism, the educated have always overstood this to be incorrect. It is the *taggin'* and *bombin'* of private property that is recognized as vandalism; not Graffiti Art itself! As Roger O. De Keersmaecker writes in an article entitled "Graffito Graffiti," *The first monuments to bear modern graffiti are found at Ephesus, the ancient Greek city, which is now part of Turkey. Graffiti was earlier considered an act of vandalism but in time has added significant information to the archeological study. It originally referred to writings and pictures drawn on sidewalks or the outer walls of buildings*

without permission of the owner of the building. The Romans used graffiti as an art form and carved it on monuments as well as their own walls for various purposes.

⁷ As mentioned in the Gospel at a later Overstanding regarding the origins of Hip Hop, Paul Strathern in his book *Napoleon In Egypt* writes about Napoleon taking part in excursions to the pyramids and the ancient ruins at Giza, *where evidence of these visits remains to this day, in the form of soldiers' names and other graffiti carved into the upper stones of the pyramids, inside the burial chambers and on other ruins.*

⁸ Mr. Strathern goes on to cite the journal of a young Corporal named Francois who recalled how he inscribed his name, place of birth and rank *in the royal chamber, on the right of the sarcophagus, in the second pyramid.* Graffiti writing has always been part of human expression, and although Graffiti writing, in and of itself, predates the cultural formation of Hip Hop in the 1970s, it is Hip Hop that has given Graffiti Art and its artists a healthy cultural environment in which to grow and thrive.

⁹ *Graffiti* was a term given to Hip Hop's graphic art animation when it appeared legally and illegally on public and private properties as *tags*, a form of street calligraphy which presents the identity of one's name or neighborhood in a stylized way. Similar to the way Emceein was labeled *Rap* and Breakin was labeled *break dancing*; the terms *writin'*, *bombin'*, *piecin'*, *burnin'* and *taggin'* all have been categorized and labeled graffiti.

¹⁰ The Hip Hop community never labeled its graphic art *graffiti*; we simply called it *writin'*, *piecin'*, *burnin'*, *bombin'* and/or *taggin'* and those who practiced Graffiti Art were called *writers*. Because of this, many Hiphoppas have chosen to call their art *Aerosol Art, Urban Murals, Spraycan Art* and *Modern Hieroglyphics*. Still, many Hiphoppas use the term *Graffiti Art* because most people recognize this

term, which has become a respected artistic expression in many of the World's urban art centers.

11   Graffiti Art, as we know it today, is believed to have been born in Philadelphia and New York in the 1960s as a form of self-advertisement. In New York early *pieces* appeared on the sides of public transportation and public housing in the mid 1970s bearing a variety of street names and/or other socio-political messages that spoke to the collective consciousness of an ignored sect of people (Hiphoppas) living in the *Inner City*.

12   Regardless of race, class or ethnicity, modern graffiti art as we know it today simply gave expression and even social existence to the ignored underclass of urban America. *This is because nationality, race and sex have no bearing on the graffiti scene*, says Nicholas Ganz.

13   Juan Flores in a 1987 article entitled "Rappin', Writin', & Breakin'," points out that *determining the relative ethnic sources of subway graffiti is the most complicated of all, partly because the first subway writer to attract media attention was Taki, who is Greek American, and because some of the best subway artists are youths of Italian and other national origins. There is clearly an important working-class basis to the graffiti movement that should not be overlooked. Nevertheless, a majority of the practitioners are Black and Puerto Rican, and graffiti experts like Henry Chalfant and Manny Kirchheimer agree that most of the early styles originated with the Puerto Ricans.*

14   Although amongst many Hip Hop scholars it is graffiti writer Phase II who not only did flyers with and for Kool DJ Herc but who is also credited as being the father of the "bubble letter" style, as well as graffiti writer Cornbread from Philadelphia, credited with popularizing the "tag," and Kase 2, for the introduction of the "computer rock style," along with Tracy 168 who popularized the famous

"wild style," Puerto Ricans are still regarded as the face of early subway graffiti art.

[15] Even KRS ONE got his early start in graffiti writing from a young Puerto Rican graff writer named Zore and later commissioned several pieces from Cope Two and the world-famous TATS CRU. However, Craig Castleman, in his book *Getting Up*, warns against any biased attempts to approach graffiti writing as exclusively Puerto Rican.

[16] Juan Flores, however, points to Felipe Luciano (leader of the Young Lords and original member of the Last Poets), who would *associate the pictorial medium* (graffiti) *with the Puerto Rican remote Taino legacy, and call to mind the Chicano mural and 'placa' movement as a parallel indigenous experience.*

[17] Mr. Flores also points to Norman Mailer in a 1974 article entitled "The Faith Of Graffiti" where Mr. Mailer describes graffiti writing as *a movement which began as the expression of tropical peoples living in a monotonous, iron-gray and dull brown brick environment, surrounded by asphalt, concrete and clangor.* The effort to brighten up and electrify one's environment while at the same time expressing one's view of one's self and of one's environment and of one's existence within one's environment is the origin of modern Graffiti Art.

[18] Most children still seem to begin their writing experiences by writing upon any available wall space. It seems that the upright writing upon walls and the need to describe one's self and environment through art has a lot to do with the development of human intelligence. Hiphoppas saw themselves in the brightly displayed color schemes of Graffiti Art long before the introduction of Rap videos and computer generated graphic art.

[19] The ability to imagine and interpret one's self through art assists in the development of a healthy creative

intelligence and helps us to see the possibilities of our specialized group. Our ability to communicate to one another tells us who we are. For Hiphoppas, Graffiti Art is the highest form of calligraphy. It is our true handwriting. It is our first written communication code. It tells us and the World who we are and where we've been.

20   Today Graffiti Art remains one of Hip Hop's most influential self-promotion techniques in urban areas everywhere. Not only does it report what is going on in urban areas, it also interprets the character of what is going on in urban areas. Graffiti Art displays and interprets the *sunshine* of sunshine, the *policing* of the police, the *crime* of the criminal, the *happiness* of happiness, etc.

21   It (Graffiti Art) is visual overstanding. *Graff* (Graffiti Art) doesn't just report; it interprets the character of what it is reporting. It seeks to interpret the substance of what is said to exist. Graffiti Art is beautiful because it reflects and interprets the beautiful ideas already existing in a Hiphoppa's mind.

22   Through Graffiti Art the true Hiphoppa can actually *see* how Hip Hop affects subjects and objects on all levels. Graffiti Art manipulates and expands letters in the same way that Emceein (Rap) manipulates and expands language. Other artists from other cultural/political experiences may be comfortable with the environment and/ or political condition of their lives; and their art may reflect such contentment. However, in our time Hiphoppas are not comfortable with their political condition and this is why Graffiti Art exists.

23   Our cultural voice is never truly heard for what it is. We must always conform to the traditions, customs and laws of those who seek to exploit us and our resources. In this modern American society you have to accept some sort of exploitation just to be heard. In our time, Hiphoppas

are rarely accepted for who we are. This is why Graffiti Art (different from other art forms) is politically rebellious. We have something to say! Our art not only tells the World who we are, it also reminds *us* of who we are. Graffiti Art is the true Hip Hop mirror. It is what true Hiphoppas really look like inside. One of the purposes of Graffiti Art is to unite the *Hiphoppa* to her true *Hiphop* self, and on an even deeper level Graffiti Art helps the Hiphoppa join Nature through art.

24   As an example; for the advanced Hiphop Graffiti artist to draw a tree identically to how the tree actually appeared in Nature is to kill the tree in her art. For the advanced Graffiti artist this is not art in a creative sense, this is photography in a duplicating sense. When an advanced Graffiti artist draws a tree, the term *draw* literally becomes *to attract*. The advanced Graffiti artist, when *drawing* the tree, joins the tree in the drawing.

25   Here, Graffiti Art unites the artist's inner-vision to the tree's outer image. At the deeper levels of Graffiti Art, to simply draw what you see is to separate yourself from Nature and conform to the World's interpretation of reality.

26   Graffiti Art is about Hip Hop's interpretation of the World. It is not the only thing that Graffiti Art is about; but the Graffiti artist who is concerned with expressing Hip Hop's point of view to the World (as well as to other Hiphoppas) seeks to tell our cultural story and/or convey our Hip Hop political messages through art. Beyond being just artists, we are art activists.

27   As artists we do not exclusively create art for art's sake. Our political condition does not give us the leisure to just create art that has no other purpose than to be gazed upon. OUR art tells OUR story. Yes, as artists we create works of aesthetic value. However, the aesthetics of the oppressed are different from those of the oppressor; even

different from those who do not feel the sting of oppression at all.

28   When the advanced Graffiti artist draws what is in front of her, it is her soul that unites with the object for the purpose of telling a much-needed story or expressing the alternative, unrealized potential of whatever is drawn. Like Hip Hop itself, and different from an average artist, the Graffiti artist transforms the common meaning of subjects and objects to fit the ideas of the rejected and ignored Hip Hop mind.

29   From a Graffiti Art point of view, when you are united with the tree (for example) through your art you are in harmony with Nature. When you copy the tree without adding to it or interpreting it symbolically you diminish its value.

30   Like Emcees, Graffiti writers are storytellers. Graffiti Art reflects our inner emotions and desires. It is who we are on the inside that is displayed on an outer surface. The question for every Graffiti artist is, *What is the meaning of my art? What am I trying to say?* Other artists refrain from giving their art any meaning or purpose at all, and this is fine as well. But the political duty of every culturally aware *Graff* writer in our time is to expand and express the collective point of view of the Hip Hop consciousness.

31   Spiritually, Hiphoppas are attracted to the colors of Graffiti Art because such colors are emanating from our inner being. In fact, to recognize and interpret the beauty and meaning of Graffiti Art, one must carry this unique beauty and meaning within one's self.

32   To fully overstand Graffiti Art one must be living in the conditions of the Graffiti artist. However, to begin correctly understanding the *spirit* of Graffiti Art and its revolutionary uses within the *Inner City* one must have knowledge of the social and spiritual interpretations of

color and light. What does this mean?

33   Know this. As explained earlier, the material World responds to (and is created by) light. Various shades of light and color react upon the intelligence of human beings growing toward light and color.

34   We react to light and color in psychological, physiological and sociological manners because in essence we are all made of light. The definitions of colors react upon the psychology of the Hiphoppa based upon the *believed* definition of the color viewed. Colors also have their own physiological affects upon the body regardless of sociological definition.

35   Modern science tells us that it is the sun that radiates the colors we are accustomed to seeing. These colors are red, orange, yellow, green, blue and violet. The color white is believed to have all of these colors in its radiance but the color white is actually none of these colors.

36   It is believed that all of these colors together form the white light of the sun and that it is the color black that absorbs most of these colors. The eye sees the color of an object based upon the color that the viewed object cannot absorb.

37   For example; a lemon appears yellow because as a material object it has absorbed all the other colors such as green, blue, red and violet, but does not absorb yellow so it rejects or throws it off. What we see in terms of color is what is being rejected by the viewed object.

38   Certain colors, when combined with other colors, create even more colors like brown, pink and indigo. All colors have their psychological effects upon the awareness of the viewer but there are also physiological effects as well. Blue (for example) upon the nervous system can cause physical contractions or tightening of the muscles for some people. Yet with other people blue is a soothing, peaceful

and meditative color.

³⁹ Blue is commonly believed to be a cold color whereas red is believed to be a warm color.

⁴⁰ Psychologically, red can stimulate one's mentality.

⁴¹ Orange is a lively color that can stimulate the pulse rate but does not overly affect blood pressure.

⁴² Yellow can stimulate one's mentality when it is time to study. Keep in mind that these are the general interpretations of colors. Other people, based upon other life experiences, can experience different effects. *Know thy Self!*

⁴³ Green can be a sedative to the nervous system and can cause sleep or relaxation. In others it can cause prolonged depression.

⁴⁴ Lastly, violet is believed to stimulate the heart and lungs.

⁴⁵ These definitions of color show their commonly believed medicinal affects upon the nervous system in a natural environment. However, within the inner cities, color and light take on different meanings.

⁴⁶ These meanings and definitions are not only created by the superstitions and belief codes of the inner city, they are also taught to us through our standard childhood education. The common urban definitions of these colors are as follows:

⁴⁷ **Red** - of the color ranging from that of blood to deep pink or orange. Flushed in the face with shame, anger, etc. Having to do with bloodshed, burning, violence or revolution. Commonly, red is defined with fire, danger, war and the command to stop.

⁴⁸ **Orange** - roundish, reddish/yellow juicy citrus fruit. Commonly associated with the sun.

⁴⁹ **Yellow** - the color of buttercups, lemons and egg yolks. Yellow: cowardly craven, gutless, lily-livered,

pusillanimous, spunkless and unmanly. Commonly, yellow is defined as both cowardly as well as having to do with wealth in the area of gold. Yellow is also associated with the spiritual.

50 **Green** - the color between blue and yellow in the spectrum. Colored like grass, unripe or unseasoned. Inexperienced, gullible, pale, sickly hued. Jealous, envious, young. Green: immature in age or experience. Raw, not trained, awkward. Green: unconversant, unpracticed, untried, unversed, easily fooled, easy to trick or cheat, naïve and simple. Commonly, green is defined as inexperienced and also full of life or like Nature. Green is also associated with money or the command to *go!* Green is also the symbol of fertility, growth, peace and relaxation.

51 **Blue** - having the color of a clear sky. Sad, depressed, pornographic, politically conservative. Blue: low-spirited, sad, dismal, down, unhappy, gloomy, melancholy, despondent, obscene, vulgar, indecent, lewd, improper. Commonly, blue is defined with or associated with the sky, the police and water. Blue also symbolizes truth, devotion, calmness, loss of breath or choking, and masculinity.

52 **Violet** - bluish purple color at the end of the spectrum. Commonly, violet is associated with both love and with piety. Many women are named Violet.

53 **White** - resembling a surface reflecting sunlight without absorbing any of the visible rays; of the color of milk or snow. White: reflecting all colors, commonly associated with innocence and purity. White: spotless, honorable, trustworthy, bright. White: ghastly, ghostly, stainless, unblemished, immaculate, virginal, virtuous. Commonly, white is associated with purity and the highest level of spirituality.

54 **Black** - reflecting no light. Heavily overcast, completely dark, like coal. Dusky, wicked, sinister, deadly.

Black: pitch dark, dirty, impure, unclean, depressing, dismal, evil. Commonly, black is defined as both negative and absolute. Black is associated with fear and evil, as well as authority as with a black belt in martial arts. Black is also associated with infinity, mystery and the universe. Black is eternal.

55   **Pink** - pale red color. The most prefect condition, the peak. Healthy, in good shape, perfect health. Commonly associated with love and femininity.

56   **Brown** - having the color of dark wood or rich soil. A color like that of walnut shells. Commonly it is associated with decay and with the human characteristics of bootlicking, or the derogatory term *brown noising*, meaning to cringe, grovel and/or cower.

57   These are the traditional American definitions of colors as taught by a variety of public and private schools in our time. It is interesting to note how these definitions set up the Hiphoppa's psychology pertaining to certain people and objects within a given environment.

58   Light and color are not to be taken as haphazard optical effects with little or no affect upon the actions of Hiphoppas.

59   Today the racist attitudes toward certain people based upon their political skin *color* are directly influenced by these general terms and definitions of *colors* and have also been created by such racist views. Hiphoppas must always examine themselves to be sure that they are not engaging in such prejudices consciously or subconsciously when it comes to colors and their symbolic meanings.

60   For example, out of all five political color groups (black, brown, red, yellow and white), only *white* is pure and innocent. *Yellow* is cowardly, *brown* is bootlicking, *red* is violent and *black* is evil.

61   It is also interesting to note how *brown* is associated

with decay while *pink* is associated with perfect health.

62   For many years, in medicine, colored light has been known to affect the psychology of those exposed to it. In addition to the effects of color upon one's general interpretation of people, places and things; color also affects one's inner-moods, emotions and sense of well-being.

63   Light and color act upon the eye similarly to the way that music and sound act upon the ear. Both are frequencies. Both are forms of energy. Soothing music brings soothing psychological results while harsh music brings harsh psychological results.

64   Of course, the terms *harsh* and *soothing* are matters of personal preference brought about through life experience. However, the same concept applies to light and color upon the eyes.

65   Soothing light delivers *soothing* psychological effects whereas the opposite force of *harsh* or too-bright light delivers tense and stressful effects. Just as the ears can be shocked by sounds that are too loud, so can the eyes be shocked by lights or colors that are too bright.

66   Colors that are too bright are not necessarily colors that are the most vivid. Too bright can also be any color that is not properly presented to the eye in balance.

67   Presently, Nature itself offers the most balanced display of colors to the eye. However, urban Hiphoppas do not live around trees, grass, rocks, running water, flowers, natural sky and wild exotic animals.

68   We are not regularly exposed to Nature's balanced display of color from which we are a product. This has been a major contributor to urban stress. We live around concrete buildings, smog-filled skies, cars, buses, trains, trucks, airplanes and concrete, all of which give off an unbalanced display of color and light, and even hide or mask the healing colors and light radiating from Nature itself.

[69] Within urban environments, it is the *believed* definitions and interpretations of certain colors that affect the psychology of urban people the most. Even though certain colors offer medicinal psychological and physiological effects, most people still react to colors based upon what they believe a specific color represents.

[70] For example, even though red can stop dizziness, control the muscular system and increase body temperature, within the inner cities red is symbolized as representing sex, danger, violence and the command to *stop*.

[71] Even though blue can be a cooling color that slows the action of the heart, within the inner cities it has been for a long time associated with law enforcement, depression and a clear sky.

[72] Even though green can be emotionally soothing to the nervous system and lower blood pressure, within the inner cities green means *go* and it is also associated with money.

[73] Even though yellow can stimulate the mental activities of the brain, within the inner cities yellow can be associated with the command to *wait, get ready* and *pay attention*. Yellow is also associated with gold jewelry, sunlight, and in some cities, taxicabs and school buses.

[74] Attuned Hiphoppas can see that people are generally acting out the symbolic interpretation of the colors that they are exposed to everyday.

[75] Urban people are being chromatically guided by the colored signals found in their environment. For example, take a look at the traffic light.

[76] Whereas on its surface the traffic light presents red for stop, *yellow* for get ready to slow down and *green* for go, in its symbolism the traffic light is continuously inspiring sex, danger, aggression, money and constant movement or *go* within the inner cities.

[77] According to the common definitions of color, the red light does not only mean *stop,* it also stimulates sexual drive and aggressive behavior, even stress!

[78] Yellow informs the *Inner Cities* to pay attention and get ready for the next command. Green stimulates the drive for money and relaxes the nervous system after the aggressive command of red.

[79] With every traffic signal we are told several chromatic messages as we *wait for the light.* The most crucial messages are found in the red and green signals.

[80] *Red,* sexual drive and the constant need to be on guard, ready to fight. *Green,* get money and go! If we observe our cities generally and symbolically, we will find that these are the common collective attitudes of most urban populations.

[81] Of course, the only way many people acquire money is by working for it. So the *green* command comes to symbolize work and keep on moving! The traffic light continuously perpetuates the actions of the inner cities and the control of public movement.

[82] The Temple of Hiphop theorizes that if the traffic lights were chromatically rearranged to coincide with Health, Love, Awareness and Wealth there would be definitive changes in the attitudes of the people studying them daily. Or, if there were a second signaling system that achieved the same goals of Health, Love, Awareness and Wealth there would be a dramatic change in the mentalities of people now exposed to flashes of red, yellow and green.

[83] Police officers use a similar style of psychological command technique. Through a combination of sounds and lights, police officers shock the ears and eyes of not only those guilty of crimes but also of the innocent. Such is a form of social imbalance.

[84] Police officers speak to the city through the same

sounds and lights they themselves disobey. Faster and more frantic sounds and lights override more subtle or lesser sounds and lights like car horns and traffic lights, even traffic signs.

85   If you notice, the inner cities obey the lesser sounds and lights (traffic lights, traffic signs, street lights, school bus signals, automotive tail and headlight signals, etc.) until police officers and emergency medical/fire service vehicles override those messages with a more frantic sound and light display.

86   When the more frantic sounds and lights have gone, you automatically know to return to the commands of standard city sounds and lights. Still, in the inner cities you are never without the commands of sounds, colors and lights.

87   These alternative voices tell you when and how to act just as if someone were verbally commanding you to do something. Most people obey these alternative voices without even knowing that they are obeying them.

88   In New York, Christmas shopping starts with the *lighting* of the Christmas tree at Rockefeller center. Stores and malls all over New York report an increase in customers and gift purchasing directly after the Rockefeller center Christmas tree has been lit. There is also an increase of theft directly after the Rockefeller center Christmas tree has been lit.

89   What if a massive *love one another* or *self analysis* tree was lit every year; what would be the public reaction to that? What if the city streets were sky blue or even the color gold? What would be the public reaction to that?

90   However, the more immediate question is, what are the present psychological affects of unbalanced, flashing hues of blue, red, yellow and white lights found on the tops of emergency medical service vehicles, fire trucks and police

cars in society?

91   Does the lighting within the coliseums and clubs where very loud music is played have an effect on the listener based on what they are listening to?

92   How does the paint color on school walls and buses affect the learning process of urban students?

93   Hiphoppas are constantly attacked or rather sub-consciously influenced by standard city colors and we seek refuge in the vividly healing and rejuvenating colors of Graffiti Art.

94   Hiphoppas think a lot more colorfully than the city allows. The urban life is one of constant conformity for the Hiphoppa and we seek to liberate ourselves through Graffiti Art. Graffiti Art offers the Hiphoppa chromatic freedom!

95   Hiphoppas are constantly denying their true feelings in order to fit into a predominately dull, dim, dingy gray, brown, black and off-white colored society. This creates the rebellious attitude symbolized in Graffiti Art, which sets out to not only brighten up the color scheme of the city, but also express the often-ignored feelings of Hiphoppas living in that same city.

96   It appears that the younger the person is, the more vivid and bright the colors are in that person's life. As this person gets older and conforms to the mentality of the workforce, the color scheme gets duller and duller until the person his or herself turns *old and gray.*

97   The attuned Hiphoppa knows that the more color you have in your life, the slower you are to age. *Color,* meaning colorful mentality, colorful emotions and colorful environment, tends to add richness and vibrancy to one's life. This is another importance to Graffiti Art.

98   Graffiti Art, especially the brightly colored murals done since the days of prehistoric humans, serves as a balancing of color and light within the psychology

of the viewer.

99   Surfaces that already display a balance of assorted colors rarely attract Graffiti artists. It is the surface that displays only one color (usually white) that becomes the object of artistic expression within the inner cities.

100   For Hiphoppas, it is Graffiti Art that stimulates and balances our nervous system. Our nervous system is giving off the same display of color that we see in a well-presented Graffiti *piece* or mural.

101   The untrained eye cannot see the colors emanating from the nervous system but they do exist. Just as the bright colors of Graffiti Art attract and stimulate the nervous system, likewise it is the nervous system that radiates these same colors.

102   The difference is that what is called *color*, emanating from the nervous system, is more accurately called *feelings, moods* and *emotions*. In reverse, what are called the *feelings, moods* and *emotions* emanating from a Graffiti *piece* are more accurately its display of *color*.

103   It is the desires, moods and emotions of a Hiphoppa that fuel the assortment of colors emanating from the nervous system of that Hiphoppa.

104   These colors are the effects of electromagnetic energy emanating from the electro-chemical energy of the body, which is emanating from the electromagnetic impulses of our desires, moods and emotions.

105   Our desires, moods and emotions gather themselves physically in the body at seven nerve centers or points commonly called *chakras*.

106   These seven nerve centers known in India as *chakras* and in martial arts as *pressure points* together radiate at least seven *colors* that collectively make up the human aura.

107   The human aura radiates about six feet in every direction from the human body, like a sphere of energy

that communicates with the electromagnetic field of our environments. Not only does the human aura radiate our desires, moods and emotions, it attracts them to us and also reads the same of others.

[108] The human body is said to have one hundred and eight main nerve/energy centers in all. Actually, everywhere a bone meets another bone there is said to be a nerve/energy center.

[109] However, when we say that a nerve center radiates a *color*, it is more accurate to note that these *colors* are more symbolic than anything.

[110] Within the central nervous system *color* has more to do with desires, moods and emotions than actual colors.

[111] Some people claim to *see* the auras of others; however, it is very important to examine your childhood education as it pertains to all colors and their symbolic meanings, so that you are sure not to mix your own prejudices in with what you are *seeing*. We urge Hiphoppas to feel and master the *colors* of themselves before claiming to *see* and interpret the *colors* of others.

[112] Still, a person's aura can be seen. Some people possess the gift (even handicap) to see the colors of sounds and objects—even the human aura. A common practice of seeing the human aura is simply analyzing what a person's favorite color is, which can be given a symbolic meaning, or analyzing what a person's favorite desire, mood and/or emotion is, which can be ascribed to a certain color.

[113] Although not always accurate, the color of a person's car, clothes, house interior or exterior, etc., can indicate the general desires, moods and emotions of that person.

[114] However, Hiphoppas are advised here again to take extra caution when interpreting the colors surrounding people. Most people, when interpreting color, ignore the sociological and political definitions of

color and are led astray.

115   A prime example of this is found in the definitions of *black* and *white*. As pointed out previously, it has been said that the highest spiritual light or color is the color white and the lowest is the color black.

116   These misleading interpretations tend to lead Hiphoppas astray in their mental graphics or visualizations. As an example, in more ancient civilizations *black* is depicted as sacred, holy, and/or benevolent whereas *white* is referred to as recently deceased.

117   Instead, Hiphoppas are to recognize all colors as spiritual light because all color is an effect of energy. When it comes to color it is more accurate to refer color to the more bright and vivid as *positive* and dull and bland as *negative*. Even more accurately, all colors are energy and they display both positive and negative frequencies.

118   Therefore, it is even more accurate to focus one's meditation or visualization upon the strength and weakness of one's energy (color) output. Instead of looking at color as either positive or negative, good or bad, focus more upon color as being strong or weak, bright or dull. With this in mind, bright and vivid *black* or *white* is considered highly spiritual (energized) as opposed to the less energized radiance of a more dull or dingy and dim black or white.

119   The first nerve/energy center of the human body is generally believed to radiate the color red. It is located in the pelvic area at the gonads. Its personality is about four years of age and it is commonly believed to represent sexual energy and courage. It is the stage where a person identifies with self differently from everyone else. All survival and self-preservation attitudes are established here. The first nerve/energy center (chakra) signifies our life-force and sense of self.

120   The first nerve center influences one's sense of

desire, will, ancestry, and manifestation. All manifestation—goals, wishes, visions, dreams, etc.—happens through this first nerve center (also known as the *root* chakra). One's ancestral awareness is also regulated through this nerve center.

121   The second nerve center is believed to radiate the color orange. It is located at the intestines. Women tend to locate this nerve center at the womb. It represents our desires, moods and emotions outwardly. Its personality is about seven years of age. The second nerve center represents the creation of life.

122   The third nerve center is located at the diaphragm or solar plexus just above the stomach and below the V in the rib cage. It is believed to radiate the color yellow and represents our opinions and judgments. The third nerve center is also the center of personal power. It is truly a central nerve.

123   Notice how your stomach *knots up* when you are afraid or nervous. The feeling of *butterflies in your stomach* is directly related to your third nerve center. It is also where we take in and seek to overstand knowledge. Its personality is about 12 years of age.

124   The fourth nerve center is believed to radiate the color green. It is located in the center of the chest. It is the link between material reality and spiritual reality. It is the centered *Self,* or rather, one's sense of peace and well-being. This nerve center is represented by the thymus organ.

125   It is here that we gain the ability to transform ourselves and our environment through higher ideas and dreams. The personality of this nerve center is about 18 years of age. It marks the beginning of higher consciousness.

126   The fifth nerve center is believed to radiate the color blue. It begins a person's spiritual life. It is the first stage in a person's awareness of his or her life path. This nerve center

is located just above the throat. Rhythm and authoritative speech are among its qualities. This nerve center inspires one's sense of justice, truth and perfection. Its personality is between 28 and 35 years of age.

127   The sixth nerve center is believed to radiate the color violet. It is the third eye, the spirit eye; it has the ability to go beyond time and space. This nerve center is located at the forehead and is believed to be responsible for visualization, insight and inspiration. It governs the penal gland. It is the seat of wisdom. Its personality is between 45 and 50 years.

128   The seventh nerve center is believed to radiate all light. It is located at the top of the head. It is the place where most people believe they consciously exist. It is regarded as divine consciousness with an ageless personality.

129   These nerve centers regulate the electro-chemical energy in the body. Each nerve center rotates opposite to the one below it and above it, creating a magnetic emanation (or *field*) around the body which is called its *aura*.

130   The human *aura* is a magnetic field around the body that attracts and repels to the body that which the heart desires. Your *aura* is the atmosphere that you create through your own thoughts and desires. It is the atmosphere that you bring when you walk into a room. Likewise, it is also the feeling that you get when certain people come around you.

131   A person's *aura* can be as small as a six-foot concentrated circle or as wide as one's reputation. Some *auras* are attracted to one another while other *auras* are not. Your *aura* may know something deeper about the person or situation in front of you than your immediate conscious perception of that person or situation has revealed. Perform Listening.

132   It is not just through speech that we communicate. Our very *auras*, or the electromagnetic vibrating force fields

of our bodies, mingle and speak to the electromagnetic vibrating force fields of other bodies. During this process we *sense* things about people and situations that were never discussed or revealed to us verbally.

133   Such a form of communication is clearly beyond speech. Here, ideas are exchanged with more honesty and with more transparency. Only those with the honest intentions of achieving peace, love, unity and having fun for all would even want to engage in such a conversation. Such a person (being) is no threat to life. Such a being has nothing to hide. Such a being has no hidden agenda.

134   Without the use of words, the very character of an attuned Hiphoppa controls that Hiphoppa's magnetic nervous system, thus controlling that Hiphoppa's frequency or rate of magnetic vibration, thus controlling the turn of events attracted to that Hiphoppa's environment (which is also magnetic), thus controlling what is attracted and repelled to and from that Hiphoppa's life. You get what you truly expect!

135   The Temple of Hiphop teaches Graffiti Art as the balancing of one's energy (desires, moods and emotions). Such a balancing assists in one's tranquil living. The spirit of an attuned Hiphoppa reflects the bright and vivid colors of a disciplined mind. Such a mind exists in a state of peace. It is content.

136   Many modalities exist that enable the Hiphoppa to balance the nerve centers and experience tranquility. However, before embarking upon any endeavor that claims to balance energy, it is wiser to develop one's own self-examination techniques to measure and evaluate one's own energy. *Know thy Self.* In order to evaluate your own energy and which nerve center needs to be adjusted, you can use a variety of techniques.

137   An imbalance in the nerve center can manifest as

physical disorders if it is left unbalanced. For example, Sexually Transmitted Diseases (STDs) are associated with an imbalanced first nerve center or *root chakra* since they affect the pelvic region. Issues regarding will, belonging, or ancestry may be traced to STDs.

[138] Chronic lower back pain is associated with an imbalanced second nerve center otherwise known as the *emotional center*. If this is a condition that you suffer from, you may be worrying too much.

[139] Indigestion, ulcers and stomach disorders are associated with an imbalanced third nerve center or *solar plexus*. These imbalances can be traced to personal power issues such as lack of will, feeling overpowered, or exerting too much force or power.

[140] Heart attacks, heartburn and breast cancer are associated with an imbalanced fourth nerve center or the *heart chakra*. These disorders may be associated with an emotional hardening of the heart, loneliness, or one's lack of humanity.

[141] Throat disorders such as laryngitis, sore throats, and some speech disorders are related to an imbalance in the fifth nerve center or *throat chakra*. These disorders may be traced to issues regarding an unwillingness or inability to communicate.

[142] Headaches, insomnia and nightmares are associated with a disorder in the sixth nerve center or *third eye*. These disorders may be associated with over-analyzing, worrying, restlessness and doubt.

[143] Lack of vision, life path, or lack of spiritual awareness is associated with an unopened seventh nerve center or *crown chakra*. These disorders may manifest as confusion, fear, anxiety, creative stagnation and/or depression.

[144] As mentioned earlier, a variety of methods are used to balance the nerve centers of the human body.

Some people use meditation and visualization. Others use hands-on healing modalities such as reiki, pranic healing and acupuncture. Still others use yoga, dance, feng shui, aromatherapy and even chromatherapy.

145   The attuned Hiphoppa recognizes the uniqueness of everyone's life-path. Everyone's life-path is like their Graffiti *tag;* it is their unique purpose. Hiphoppas are advised to find a nerve-balancing technique (or instructor) that fits their consciousness, and use it (or them) regularly.

146   Like the spoken word, the written word also reflects the desires of one's heart. Graffiti Art is indeed Hip Hop's written word. Therefore, one must analyze one's own art for an even deeper understanding of one's own heart. Do not try to be the best Graffiti writer. Only try to express your higher *Self* through your art. Become the consciousness of the people viewing your art.

147   Even though certain Graffiti writers prefer to remain outlaws, it is of great importance to the further development of Graffiti Art as an artistic skill that we use such a skill to decriminalize Hiphop Kulture and add to our own entrepreneurship. Graffiti Art is a valuable skill in the World that can be developed to enhance one's quality of life.

148   Eventually, the *Graff* writer should seek ways to advance his art industry for the advancement of all *Graff* writers. Getting locked up, hurt and/or killed before one can actualize one's purpose in life actually stagnates the progress of Graffiti writing.

149   We must remain concerned for how Graffiti writing is presented and portrayed in the World. Graffiti writing is not vandalism! It is a form of art, a form of self-expression.

150   Yes, Graffiti Art shall always be about social protest and getting your name up! But for the preservation and

expansion of true Graffiti writing we must pass down to our children the most advanced ways of protesting social injustice and getting their names up without being harmed or incarcerated.

151   The Temple of Hiphop advises Hip Hop's gifted Graffiti writers to also produce customized clothing, furniture and even DVD documentaries, animated motion pictures, Graffiti Art history books, comic books, children's books, toys and video games. Yes, the essence of Graffiti writing encompasses all of this!

152   The modern *Graff* writer has no time for prison. Graffiti Art's value and worth to the modern Hip Hop family is extremely high when you consider a career in advertising, promotion and marketing, website design, graphic design, all kinds of merchandising and even photography. Hiphoppas are advised to explore these avenues of creative expression as well as *bombin'* and *taggin', piecin'* and *burnin'*. There it is.

RED: COURAGE

ORANGE: HEALING

YELLOW: INTELLIGENCE

GREEN: PEACE

BLUE: AUTHORITY

VIOLET: BEAUTY

BLACK: ETERNAL

WHITE: PURITY

PURPLE: SPIRIT

BROWN: STRENGTH

GOLD: SECURITY

PINK: LOVE

THE ELEVENTH OVERSTANDING
THE TEACHA

[1]   The idea of submitting yourself to a teacher/instructor for the purpose of "specialized" knowledge, advice and/or guidance is a very important and ancient concept. However, in today's World of betrayal, incompetence and deceit it is hard to trust anyone with any area of your life. Yet without trust, it is impossible to learn anything new from anyone.

[2]   Information travels from one human being to another upon the chariot of respect, which then leads to trust, which then leads to learning. If there is not a mutual respect and trust between the student/apprentice and the teacher, then nothing can be taught or even learned and both (teacher and student/apprentice) are wasting their time together. For any real learning to occur, both teacher and student/apprentice must take each other seriously.

[3]   The Truth is simple and obvious. Those who teach the Truth of any subject must teach in simple, easy-to-understand and obvious ways. Truth is simple, while ignorance is very complicated! There is no need to waste your energy aimlessly critiquing the teachings of your teacher if the results of your teacher's teachings are obvious and plain for all to see. No excuses, just results.

[4]   Any criticism in the face of REAL RESULTS only exposes the insecurities of the critic. Such criticisms have also been used to break up and defuse mass movements and life-saving ideas by creating mass doubt. However, the Truth is obvious. A teacher's teachings are shown and experienced

in that teacher's life. A proven teacher is already benefiting from what is being taught. A true teacher lives the results of his teachings.

5   This is why the Temple of Hip Hop offers its apprenticeship to all serious Hiphoppas seeking to live a productive Hiphop lifestyle. Here, an apprentice is one who is bound by indenture to serve one's teacha for a prescribed period of time learning the specifics of the Hip Hop art, life and trade. As an apprentice you are expected to live Hiphop, not just perform Hip Hop. You are expected to assist and serve your teacha in the further establishment and growth of the Temple of Hip Hop.

6   However, if you are not really *Hiphop* then this apprenticeship and most of what KRS ONE teaches is simply not for you, and there is nothing wrong or right with this. But if you are *Hiphop* then don't front! You must take such an apprenticeship very seriously. Your Hip Hop life depends upon your successful comprehension of these lessons.

7   And what is it that you must comprehend? You must begin to take your Hip Hop life more seriously than any other style of life that you may live or have lived so that the reality of your Hip Hop life can become more real to you. It is also very important to the development of Hip Hop as a nation that all true Hiphoppas rise above *hip-hop* as entertainment and continue to live *Hip Hop* as their culture, as their faith. Our future selves and those of our children are indeed depending upon us today establishing Hip Hop as a peace-filled and prosperous lifestyle—not just a form of music.

8   Leave the criticisms to the ignorant. GOD shall answer all of their questions with the events of their own lives. As for real teaching, wisdom is gained through great hardship, disappointment and loss. But those who have

successfully survived such hardships and disappointments can advise others on how to achieve greatness without going through the exact same pain. This is what makes knowledge, wisdom and understanding so valuable, more valuable than all of the World's riches.

[9] Knowledge is a privilege. Wisdom is a privilege. Please do not take this apprenticeship for granted. Many people miss out on exactly what they need for the achievement of their own purpose because of their own doubt, or fear, or stubbornness, or suspicion. When proven wisdom is in your presence do not waste your own time debating and doubting it. Again, if you want to avoid unnecessary suffering living Hiphop, you must direct your whole heart and mind to the comprehension of what is taught here. You must decide right now to trust in the expertise and wisdom of your teacha, not for the aggrandizement of the teacha, but for the upliftment of your Self.

[10] Be clear as to why you have become a Hip Hop apprentice. The focus of any Hip Hop teacha is to make the Hip Hop lifestyle real and productive for the apprentice. Such an apprenticeship has little to do with one's own desire to be an emcee, DJ, or b-boy. The purpose of any true Hip Hop apprenticeship is to transmit to the apprentice the essential ingredients of Hip Hop's evolving culture. Culture, not necessarily knowledge about the culture, is the ultimate aim of any worthwhile Hip Hop apprenticeship.

[11] T. S. Elliot, in his 1949 book *Notes Towards the Definition of Culture*, writes, *In more civilized communities of specialized activities, in which not all the sons would follow the occupation of their father, the apprentice (ideally, at least) did not merely serve his master, and did not merely learn from him as one would learn at a technical school—he became assimilated into a way of life which went with that particular trade or craft; and perhaps the lost secret of the craft is this, that not merely*

a skill but an entire way of life was transmitted. Such a style of learning is more about becoming than knowing, and at the beginning of such an apprenticeship trust is an absolute must.

12   It is unnecessarily difficult to learn anything without an unshakable trust and respect for your teacher. Yes, everyone and everything should be respectfully questioned—including your teacher. No one is above question, and a good teacher invites all questions. However, if you are truly serious about your own development, at some point you must get past debating, questioning and doubting and simply trust your teacha. Actually, such a trust has little to do with the personal character of one's teacha, although personal character is very important.

13   Here, it is more important that you put your trust not just in your teacha, but more into your God or into whomever referred you to your teacha. You must also decide if you are truly prepared to submit yourself to the guidance of those who have successfully gone on before you. If the activities of the World have robbed you of your ability to trust your teacha and his/her teachings, then trust your God!

14   For if you truly trust your God then it will be easier to trust your teacha. In fact, your trust for your teacha should come from your trust in your God. Would your God put you in front of a fraud? Or will your God protect you from such experiences? Maybe it is time to take your own God more seriously!

15   Disobedience, stubbornness, suspicion, criticism, fear, doubt and/or arrogance toward your teacher only hinder YOUR learning. We must not unnecessarily criticize each other; we must question and always acknowledge our collective development as a young nation.

16   As Hiphoppas we must lift each other up. Such is our political strength. We have no reason to convince anyone

about the Truth of our faith. It is OUR faith! And if our faith is real, then our faith shall produce real results in our real lives. Why try to convince someone of the obvious? If they don't want to see, why force them? Your faith and its results are for you, not for them.

17   However, it is truly difficult for those with real love in their hearts to watch people unknowingly suffer and/or destroy themselves. It is equally difficult for me to watch hip-hop attempt to destroy itself! But we live by the Platinum Rule, which is: *Do unto others as they would do unto themselves.* In other words, treat people the way in which they treat themselves.

18   With no judgment or condemnation let us allow people the freedom to be whatever they feel themselves to be even if their being seeks self-destruction. You can always make an effort to help those in need, but always remember that everyone is where they are in life by their own choices in life. The World is the way it is for a reason; trying to save the World and everyone in it reveals a peculiar kind of arrogance on the savior's part. Again, wisdom is a privilege but most people do not really respect wisdom; at very young stages in life they think they know. Such an attitude leads to suffering.

19   Every philosopher knows that the purpose of knowledge is to relieve human suffering. Yet those who *know* rarely share that which they *know* either because of the fear of their own loss of power over the ignorant, or of the consequences of speaking Truth. Every time someone steps up with a radically new view toward something, a gang of critics appears with the sole purpose of discrediting, dishonoring and even disrespecting the Truth speaker and his Truth teachings. And even though I am a target for such attacks in my time, this lesson is not solely about your apprenticeship with KRS. This lesson is about leadership

and our approach to it in all areas of life.

20   In this particular lesson WE must never forget that on our quest to establish Hip Hop as an autonomous, self-governed community of peace and prosperity there shall be some who shall consciously and unconsciously seek our demise. Be prepared.

21   They will criticize and even slander your leaders and teachas in their own mass media campaigns. But we must never believe the words of those who have first betrayed the principles of our society or wish to exploit our resources, or enslave our children. We must never accept the judgments of those outside of our movement over the words of a true Hiphoppa who has committed his/her life to our movement.

22   Let us not be so quick to degrade or abandon our leadership if they stumble and/or fall. Let us be even quicker to protect them, lift them up and dust them off with the principles that we have established for ourselves. Reprimand, yes! But never abandon. Question, yes! But never disrespect. Be loyal! Such is the seat of all political strength.

23   Every true Hiphoppa is responsible for Hiphop and its culture—this includes Hip Hop's elements, history and leadership as well. We are all responsible for each other; including the conduct of our leadership. We (Hiphoppas) must do everything in our power to keep our leadership honest and focused. If they fail, it is because we have failed. And if they succeed it is because we have succeeded; their own *people* have protected them and held them up.

24   Let us not be as other nations who create, support and exalt the very leadership that they eventually tear down! All leadership comes from the *people* who exalt it. If the leadership is dishonest it is because the very people who have created, supported and exalted that leadership are dishonest. A leader/teacher reflects the collective consciousness and

activity of the people he teaches and represents.

25   Every triumph of the leader/teacher is truly a triumph of the People. And every defeat of the leader/teacher is truly a deficit of the People. We must protect our leadership from the grasp of the World at all times. The corruption of leadership is born out of the neglect of *the People*. Remember this!

26   On the other hand, those leaders/teachers who intentionally and repeatedly violate their own principles and/or betray the movement for their own selfish gain are not true leaders/teachers at all, and they deserve no such immunity or respect. This is why it is of extreme importance that the *teachas* of Hiphop Kulture show and prove their commitment and loyalty toward the preservation of Hip Hop long before the criticisms come.

27   We must perform our principles daily, not just read them and/or teach them to others. We must act them out daily in our own lives and for the inspiration of others. And it is with this criterion that we shall judge the conduct of all leadership.

28   In our time we have seen too many great leaders who have sacrificed and contributed much to their causes suddenly vanish because of one or even two immature errors that they may have made in their lives. And this is not an excuse for failure. However, the violations of our leadership shall be weighed against the life and contributions of that leadership.

29   No one outside of Hiphop Kulture can ever judge even the most delinquent of us. However, as attuned Hiphoppas we must never fall into the traps set for us. We, out of all Hiphoppas, must live a higher standard of life. This is what it will take to establish and maintain our nation. Above all suspicions and outside criticisms we must respect and support one another.

30   Know this. You are here to learn how to live a productive and victorious *Hiphop* lifestyle according to the teachings of the Temple of Hip Hop.

31   It makes no sense to study under a person or an institution that can show no tangible results to whatever they teach. Here, your *teacha* (spiritual teacher) makes you aware of your Hiphop identity and then shows you how to properly use the character of your new Hiphop identity to achieve your life purpose. Your teacha assists you in experiencing peace and prosperity through Hiphop. Your teacha raises your self-worth through Hiphop, Hip Hop and hip-hop. Is this important to you?

32   Here, you must take yourself seriously. And the first step toward taking yourself seriously begins with taking your teacha (or teachas) seriously. Before you call me or anyone else "teacha," do some research. Read my books. Listen to my albums. Watch my videos and instructional DVDs before you decide to seriously submit yourself to this apprenticeship.

33   Study my history. Ask those who do not care for me much or even like me much to give you their opinions about me. Get all the facts! Do not blindly follow or believe anyone that you do not have some background knowledge on. I may NOT be your teacha. But if I am your teacha, then bring your whole faith to these teachings.

34   I do not require your money, and I will NEVER ask for sexual or professional career favors from you. I require your trust, your support and your respect. Such requirements will not only help you learn faster and more accurately, but the achievement of such a character strengthens Hip Hop itself.

35   So let us move on from here. If you are still reading this gospel then not only am I becoming your teacha, but you are becoming a teacha yourself, and the same principles

that I expect you to hold me to are the same principles that I and the Temple of Hip Hop hold you to.

36   Know this. Everyone is a teacher. Through speech, personal character, clothing, achievements, validations, reputation, and other socially defining symbols of status we are all teaching each other in a variety of ways.

37   Some people are aware that they are inspiring and teaching others. However, most people go through life unconscious of their influence upon others. Every little thing that we do publicly influences, inspires and teaches in some way those who may be observing what we are doing.

38   Our clothing styles, hairstyles, speech styles, races, etc. teach others about the society in which we live, what is acceptable behavior and what our group is about. Everyone is part of some sort of group: racial, professional, political, spiritual. And the way that you conduct yourself and represent yourself teaches others about you and your group.

39   Of course no one wants to be stereotyped, but still the Truth is that whether we are conscious of it, or unconscious of it, with everything that we do and say we are indeed teaching and influencing others. The questions are, *What exactly are you teaching? What exactly are you instructing people to do?*

40   For when the attuned Hiphoppa has realized that it is one's total *Self* (not just one's mouth) that is communicating all sorts of ideas to others, and that those ideas shall one day actualize themselves in real life, such a Hiphoppa seeks to communicate only peace and prosperity. Such a Hiphoppa is called a *teacha*.

41   Different from a *teacher*, *teacha* is the title of a spiritually aware Hiphoppa. Teachas live the *Gospel of Hiphop* and they teach its principles to all interested people. To be called *teacha* one must successfully live and teach the *Gospel of Hiphop*. One must defy the random urges of the

flesh, speak productively, help and give freely, be unaffected by changing attitudes and conditions, and be content with the presence of GOD. This is the gospel.

42   And what is the Gospel of Hiphop? It is an attitude, a behavior, a habitual style of living that has caused peace and prosperity in KRS's life. This is how I went from being houseless to finding my true home in GOD which has provided many houses in my lifetime.

43   Such a life-guide should not be compared to any other. The *Gospel of Hiphop* is a repeated behavior; the *Gospel of Hip Hop* teaches the cultural and spiritual principles of a peaceful and prosperous *Hiphop* life. Like anything, to be truly successful at what is taught here you must bring your whole being to it.

44   Such a gospel may not appeal to you, and if so, then it is obvious that such a *word* doesn't belong to you. This gospel is specifically taught to those who know that they are Hip Hop! As Hiphoppas we don't need what everyone else needs. We need what we need! And what do we need? Answer: PEACE and PROSPERITY!

45   Other people need other things. However, the Gospel of Hip Hop ensures for the Hiphoppa a definitive life-plan toward real peace and uninterrupted prosperity as an attuned Hiphoppa. Such is the lifestyle of a teacha. Some people are peaceful but not prosperous. Others are prosperous but not peaceful. A Hip Hop teacha is peace-filled and prosperous, not always happy and jappy and rich, but instead is content and has what is needed when needed.

46   So how does one walk the spiritual path of a true Hiphop teacha? First by putting GOD before everyone and everything in physical nature, and then by realizing that you are already teaching right now. Realize right now that through your own personal character as well as through your own words and deeds you are influencing the development

of yourself and everyone around you. You are a *teacher* right now! So, what are you teaching? What have you taught?

47   Look at your life. The very examples of your life-actions are what you are teaching to yourself and to others. Do you agree with your own teachings? Do you teach health, love, awareness and wealth with your life-actions? Or do you teach sickness, hatred, ignorance, and poverty with your life-actions? With your personal and even professional character do you teach strength or weakness? Do you live in a tomb or a temple?

48   Peace and/or prosperity are not granted to anyone, they are earned by those who truly seek to attain them. Are peace and prosperity important to you? How much do you value your Spirit nature? What are you willing to commit to? Are you ready to accept the mystical life?

49   Once your commitment to the development of your own Spirit nature is correctly prioritized within yourself, naturally you will begin correcting and inspiring others toward the development of their own Spirit natures. This is the work of a teacha. And it is through this work that peace and prosperity are attained.

50   Do not be afraid; only believe. Never doubt what you are capable of; only believe in yourself. Believe in your Hip Hop identity and it shall truly work for you just as it is working for me right now! We are truly a new people in the World with new powers to overcome the World. Love yourself! Respect yourself! But most of all, BELIEVE IN YOUR SELF! Believe in the authenticity of your own thoughts. Put your faith in your *Self*.

51   Live a righteous life not for the sake of others, but so that you may expect the reality of the spiritual realm in your own life. For we have learned that it is one's own guilt, which comes by way of one's own unrighteous living, that leads to the doubt of one's own spirit *Self*.

[52]   Such doubt weakens the Spirit and strips us of our *victory over the streets*. Through guilt, worry and doubt we deny our very existence and power as Spirit beings. We hide ourselves from God.

[53]   However, right from wherever you are reading and/or hearing these words you can make the decision today to re-create your *Self*. If you are serious about the empowerment of your own life then you can begin RIGHT NOW as you read this *word* to move in the direction of your own empowerment. GET UP! Get up right now! Be the vision of yourself! Be your dreams! GET UP NOW! MOVE! Make the inner-you, the outer-you, RIGHT NOW! Birth your *Self!* As an act of faith stand up right now!

[54]   But if you have already read this paragraph several times and you still have not moved toward the empowerment of your own Hip Hop lifestyle then let's face it, you are NOT really serious yet. You are simply NOT ready. You may admire your teacha but you are not yet prepared to become one yourself. And this is fine. It takes many lives to become a true *Hiphop* teacha.

[55]   But how will you know when you are an official Hiphop teacha? Answer? You shall notice that your reflexes are spiritual and not emotional. Your habitual response to the physical World and its circumstances shall be spiritual.

[56]   For it is the habitual attitude and personal character of the teacha (his performance) that causes his supernatural abilities to develop. Such abilities (performances) give the teacha a considerable advantage over the traps and obstacles of the *streets*.

[57]   The teacha then teaches the nature of such a character through the Temple of Hip Hop and its instruments. Again, how will you know when you have become a *Hiphop teacha?* You will move in harmony with the events and circumstances of life itself. Doors open precisely at the right

time, cars show up right at the exact moment when they are needed, even the weather and the *seasons* work in harmony with the life of the teacha.

58   People are compelled to feed the teacha, to clothe the teacha and to protect the teacha in the World because the teacha displays a caring and trustworthy character. The nature of the teacha is what is attracted to the teacha. The teacha has a zest for life! The teacha has a generous heart. The teacha is highly creative and highly skilled.

59   The teacha also perceives things that are not obvious to other people and brings them into physical existence. The teacha sees connections between seemingly unrelated things, people and/or ideas, and brings them together.

60   The teacha is a counselor. A healer. A life-guide. A wise advisor. A peacemaker. A minister. The teacha takes his own spiritual reality, as well as the spiritual reality of others, seriously. The teacha hears and obeys GOD.

61   The teacha is patient, tolerant, merciful, and forgiving. The teacha is courageous. The teacha lives and teaches the principles of Health, Love, Awareness, and Wealth. The teacha is self-contained and independent. The teacha is disciplined. And yes, the teacha can fight! When necessary the teacha is an excellent divine warrior. The Teacha is not a coward; yet the teacha is not stubborn, stupid and/or arrogant in the face of real danger.

62   The teacha is aware of the fact that character (different from one's personality) is produced by the demands of one's life. Certain life circumstances, whether productive or destructive, demand a reaction, and that reaction produces one's character. Those who deny the demands of life lack character. Know this. It is injustice that demands the character of the just. It is the existence of greed that demands the character of charity. It is the lie that begs for the character of Truth.

⁶³   These are just some of the characteristics of a true
Hiphop teacha, and these characteristics lead to peace,
power, respect and prosperity. The official title of *Teacha* is
given by the Temple of Hip Hop to those who have attained
the *habits* of a truly attuned Hiphoppa. Ultimately, it is the
Mind of God that tests, tempts and fights the true Hiphoppa
to see if he is a truly attuned Hiphoppa. And likewise, the
teacha is tested, tempted and fought against to see if he is
who he says that he is.

⁶⁴   For those who are serious about walking this path
you must quickly learn how to be consistent and humble at
the same time. Your critics will hold you up to standards
that they themselves don't even follow. They will advise you
with confidence on things that they know nothing about.
They will even fight against their own advancement. But
remember, what is obvious to you will not be so obvious
to others.

⁶⁵   This is why it is of extreme importance that the
teacha maintains a secret and private space for himself away
from the ignorance of his own students and apprentices—
even family. Never connect your personal property or the
achievement of your personal goals to the life and learning
process of your students and apprentice. Maintain your
independence, but do not hide from ignorance. Protect
yourself, but do not shut yourself away from the World's
disorder and immaturity—you have power over Worldly
situations. Instead, operate openly where the fruits of your
Spirit can be manifested. This takes courage and skill, but
superior knowledge provides superior skills.

⁶⁶   So if you truly are a teacha then in whatever you do
your superior skill should correct disorder and mature the
immature. Why? Because you are a teacher. You have made
up your mind to only accept the personality of the real YOU!
You are not swayed by the ignorance of others; you correct

it. You instruct the reality of your very environment; it does not instruct you.

67   For when you are yourself, your true Self, with no apology, doubt or excuse about who and/or what you are, then you are the TRUTH! You are your *Self!* You are not fronting for anyone! There is no lie within you so you cannot be led by the lies and the liars that surround you. They can say whatever they like but real knowledge is backed up with real power. And when you have achieved the Truth of your being you shall speak and move with the authority and power of that Truth.

68   Others have no choice but to see you as you see yourself. Teachas are called to teach; have your lesson plan ready. Be prepared with flyers, pamphlets, books, videos, CDs and DVDs of inspirational materials. Be ready to give sound advice anywhere and at anytime.

69   This, however is a skill. The teacha must be able to look past the insecurities of others to really hear what is being said. Some people may question the teacha unfairly or even disrespectfully, but the teacha must look past such unfairness and disrespect and get to the essence of what is being said, or asked, or implied.

70   The teacha must be able to truly hear another person's heart even while such a person continues to be difficult and disrespectful toward the teacha. The teacha can never hold grudges or remain resentful toward others, especially not his apprentice or family. Remember, as a teacha you are at least 10 years ahead of everyone you are teaching. Your work is to simply plant the seeds of Truth in your apprentice(s) and allow time for such seeds to grow. The farmer (teacha) plants the seed, but it is water and sunlight (GOD) that bring that seed to fruition.

71   Remember, your peace and prosperity is not so that you may achieve and hoard a Worldly fortune or even

attain the recognition of a wonderful accomplishment. No! Your peace and prosperity exist so that you can be a channel through which blessings and help may come to others. This takes strength. The nature of this person is unaffected by the World and its temporary pleasures and pains. Such a person walks and talks on behalf of GOD—the only satisfying thing in life.

72   For when one realizes the simple Truth of one's own being and lives only in that inner-place, such an awareness alters one's physical, mental and spiritual condition in the physical World. Nothing in the World can hold you. No institution can contain you. You are not moved by the World and its temporary conditions. You move according to the Truth of your nature.

73   As long as you are pursuing your purpose, you shall be in harmony with the Truth of your nature, which is the universe's purpose for itself. You shall be protected and promoted by the universe itself, because the universe has its own agenda for the actualization of your life's purpose. When you truly come to this realization you will begin to move throughout life in a certain exactness.

74   Everything will happen in harmony with your purpose. People, things and even events will all be in harmony with your daily movements. At this stage in your spiritual development you are becoming the teacha.

75   Do not reject the World as evil; it is not. Do not fight against the desires of your flesh; only seek to understand their causes. Practice being unattached to the cravings of the flesh. Do not allow yourself to be addicted to the World and the desires of the flesh; commit to the reality of your God. Be the teacha!

76   The one who desires to be a chef will never be one. It is the one who courageously enters the kitchen and starts cooking who proves to be a chef. And in the chef reality, such

a person attains chef powers. The same applies to becoming a Hip Hop spiritual teacha. When you are the teacha, YOU ARE THE TEACHA!

77 There is no fight against the flesh when you take on the character of one who simply does not need the desires of the flesh. The Teacha finds pleasure in denying himself pleasure. When you are the Teacha you inherit the Teacha's powers and abilities. The Temple of Hip Hop can validate the completion of your study, but only God can validate the Truth of your being.

78 Therefore, in the beginning of your spiritual practices it is wise to practice performing discipline over the desires of the flesh and the emotions of the heart, not just for the sake of your own moral character, but to prove your own spiritual strength and maturity to yourself. Prove to yourself that you can be trusted! This is the *habit* of a teacha.

79 Resisting the temptations of the World and the desires of the flesh is like lifting spiritual weights. Emotional self-control brings peace and endurance. Use your emotions, and use temptation to your advantage; do not allow them to use you toward their advantages. Control your mind, not your life. It is the thought that happens first; then comes your emotional response.

80 The same applies to fear. Use the most frightening experiences to exercise courage. Stand up to evil because in Truth it is all GOD! And if you are truly one with GOD, in harmony with life itself, no illusion of evil can prevail against you. In fact, evil shall work with you; it shall start and stop with your own internal commands.

81 The challenge is to stay true to your purpose; do not become distracted by better or worse circumstances. Stay within your circle. Perfect yourself through the perfection of your purpose. Master the task that GOD has given you.

Do not compare your work to the works of those whom you may admire and/or criticize! Focus upon the work that GOD has given YOU!

82   Do not be afraid of anything, especially not your own purpose. Exercise the courage to be you, the true YOU. If there is something about yourself that you do not like, simply change it. Do not judge or criticize your life. Your understanding of the World is limited, but your spiritual *sight* is infinite. Trust GOD!

83   As a teacha you shall be moving at a very fast pace in life, faster than others even though you will feel as though you are moving too slow. Be patient. Only GOD sees all things and likewise, it is your God who has led you through all things. Simply observe your history and learn from the lessons that your God has placed upon your life. Such is the making of your ministry.

84   If you really do not like something about yourself, or you feel that it is time for you to mature beyond certain activities, most likely it is the universe itself that is telling you something about your ability (or inability) to achieve its purpose. Follow your heart.

85   Love the total you, even your faults. In exercising the courage to be you, you (the real *You*) may also include your shortcomings. Not that you should make excuses for your own shortcomings, temptations and failures; but remember that such faults are what GOD has given you to overcome. These are YOUR degrees.

86   The overcoming of such shortcomings, temptations and failures is the building of your unique personality and eventual ministry. Again, do not judge yourself; only be willing to grow. Try to realize the Truth. GOD is truly Guiding Our Direction. With our limited intelligence we will never know how things are going to actually turn out. Simply focus the intention of your heart upon the

achievement of your highest good. Go with the flow!

87   Stop trying to control everything in your life and simply allow your God to manifest through you. Continue to seek perfection. Such is the character of a true teacha and such a character requires true courage. Remember, you do not control everything in your life; others are thinking and acting as well. Therefore, the teacha doesn't blame himself for every shortcoming or mistake or tempting moment in his life because he knows that GOD is actually conducting a larger show.

88   Knowledge of GOD's direction or Divine Plan causes peace. When you truly walk the path of *oneness*, you see how all things are connected and how all things are affected by all things. When you see this, all things will begin to move and manifest in harmony with your life and you shall also be in harmony with the happenings of other people's lives, even places and events.

89   You will notice a certain exactness about the movements of your life. People and things will come to you right at the moment at which you need them and likewise, people and things will leave you right at the moment in which you no longer need them. Attach yourself to nothing material, nothing of the World. You are now *the teacha*.

90   *It is reported in the sacred writings of most religions that the birth of the Messiah is accompanied by wonders. All nature unites to pay homage to the child of heaven. The spiritual chemistry of the advent cannot be adequately described in words. The divine self rises victoriously from the not-self. The God-power within comes into its kingdom, and the prince of this world and his legions are baffled. Actually, it is by this mystery that the human being becomes a person and assumes the obligation of enlightened selfhood. The man of soul is in the world, but not of it. He becomes intuitively aware of his own place in the divine plan. He accepts this place and fulfills its*

requirements. We are in darkness as long as we are negative and the world in which we live is positive. The mystical experience reveals the eternal truth that consciousness is positive, and to it all environments are negative. (Manly P. Hall)

[91] A teacha lives in and as the *oneness*. Just as when you are home you have certain things readily available to you for your survival and comfort; so it is with living in and as the *oneness*.

[92] As a teacha, life itself is your home. And just as you move freely and safely about your home, which offers you certain comforts and means of survival as you need them, so it is with the life of a teacha. Life is your home!

[93] Know this. You do not use everything in your *home* at once even though everything you need for your living is there. It is the same way with the life of a teacha. You do not use your kitchen at the same time that you use your bathroom and you do not use your bathroom at the same time that you use your bedroom. You use these things as you need them.

[94] As the need arises you use your towels and as the need arises you use your pots and pans. The same example can be applied to your blankets and sheets as well as to your refrigerator and/or front door. Even though at times you may combine some of these home accessories toward your personal survival and comfort, they are all used only as needed, yet they all exist right now in your present environment.

[95] The same example is applied to the life of the teacha. In the *oneness* all things are already available to the teacha. However, the teacha only uses certain things in life as needed. In fact, life itself provides to the teacha everything that is needed to fulfill his purpose even before he is consciously aware of what is actually needed. Things just come! Events just happen! People just appear!

96   The teacha is always prepared, yet the teacha is rarely in need of preparation. It is the intelligence of Eternal Mind (GOD) that guides, protects and provides for the teacha; this is how the teacha receives the perfect clothing before the event, the perfect car before the trip, the perfect weapon before the fight, the perfect medicine before the illness, etc.

97   In knowing this, the teacha lives in contentment. For in the *oneness* a teacha's very movements in the physical World align with the mathematics and harmony of the universe itself. And with this harmony the teacha seeks to ease human suffering through his actual presence and heightened awareness. Our purpose as teachas is to teach. In fact, if the teacha fails to teach those around him, it is the teacha who suffers the most.

98   The purpose of the teacha is to teach and ease human suffering through knowledge; this is why the teacha has such an ability. The teacha is ordained to teach! Therefore, the teacha's own peace and prosperity will be directly connected to such a purpose. If you're not teaching, you're not eating.

99   For we know that humanity's only real problem is ignorance. In some shape or form when you break down and analyze the human condition and why we suffer, ignorance and/or some form of immaturity always seems to be at the cause of human suffering. Therefore, as teachas we seek to relieve human suffering (caused mostly by human immaturity) with the great elixir of Truth.

100   As teachas we help to move Hiphoppas toward maturity as an organized Hip Hop community. Such is our work; our payment is peace. Teachas work on behalf of GOD, not themselves, and are rarely aggravated or frustrated by the ignorance and immaturity of others because it is GOD that the teacha lives with, not the World.

101   If a teacha is not at peace, it is either because that

teacha has forgotten GOD, or is not effectively teaching or directing those who surround him, or the teacha's teachings have not yet blossomed within the apprentice(s). A teacha is an attuned Hiphoppa who has realized the oneness and how to live within it—in peace.

102   A teacha knows that we are all bound together; that we are all growing together, one is not above another, everyone plays their part in their time and their space for the glory of GOD eternally. This awareness gives the teacha the qualification to lead and the patience to endure the ignorance and immaturity of others.

103   Teachas are qualified to lead the Hip Hop nation simply because teachas are patient and even-tempered. We truly care for the lives of Hiphoppas and the further development of Hip Hop as a nation. Teachas speak Truth to the powerful on behalf of the Hip Hop community's further peace, prosperity and preservation.

104   True teachas are civilization builders; they are capable of sacrificing their own comforts and achievements for the building and leading of Hip Hop's further peace and prosperity. True teachas place the integrity and preservation of Hip Hop before their own personal career goals.

105   Teachas teach even when the lesson is controversial. Those who think only of themselves and for the benefit of their own livelihood are unqualified to lead simply because they cannot really care for the lives of others. A true teacha is never afraid to teach controversial life-lessons.

106   Those who promote sickness, hatred, ignorance and poverty in the name of Hip Hop, or are afraid to speak the Truth, are unqualified to lead simply because they prove with their own words and actions that they regard themselves as separate from everyone else. Their decisions will always be based upon their own individual survival above the common good of all.

107   Hip Hop's teachas teach with real life events and through real life examples. Teachas are inspiring! Others admire them and desire to be like them; this is the ultimate teaching strategy of the teacha. Without saying a word, the teacha's own character and personality inspire others toward their own higher selves.

108   It is the teacha's own character and skill that inspire others to reach for their own higher potentials. Hip Hop's teachas can be identified by the *One* after (or before) their names. Seeing and living beyond dualities and separate things; the *sight* of the teacha is single.

109   The teacha lives in GOD—the living, universal, eternal, creative Spirit of immortality. In western-world terms, the one absolute self-existent, pre-existent force that manifests itself in and through all creation.

110   The teacha is not overly caught up or stagnated by religious tradition and ritual. Yes, the teacha respects and studies all World religions. However, the teacha acknowledges that there are many names and attributes which the Great and Holy Spirit is known by, and each person has an individual *right* to use the personal name or attribute of their choice.

111   Teachas acknowledge the western-world view that all people are the incarnations of one spirit—GOD. We are the logical and necessary outcome of the infinite self-knowingness of GOD. However, teachas also acknowledge that God is personal to all who feel this indwelling presence.

112   Study these distinctions carefully. GOD does not have to control everything. In fact, this very concept is a military idea imposed upon us and our parents by those who also seek to exploit us and our resources. The teacha recognizes the privilege and power of knowing one's personal God.

113   Teachas teach that each person is here on Earth to

fulfill a divine purpose that only that person can complete. The ultimate goal of the Hip Hop life is to rediscover one's own divinity and fulfill it. The question is, who, what and where is OUR GOD?

114   Teachas emphasize that you must have the courage to be you, free from fear and doubt, if you are to actualize YOUR *divinity* and *divine* purpose. The god of those who only seek to exploit us and exploit our resources cannot be our God. If we are truly free, then we are also free to seek GOD for ourselves.

115   If you say that you are divine, then BE DIVINE! Act like the divinity you claim to be; this is what it means to be a *Hiphop* teacha. The teachings of our *temple* demand that you be who you say that you are and do what you say that you can do. Stop being afraid of being YOU! Stop dumbing yourself down so that others can feel secure around you. Stop allowing your temptations to hinder your development. BE YOU! The real YOU! The divine YOU!

116   The teacha acknowledges the direct revelation of Truth through the intuitive and spiritual nature of the individual, and that any person who is comfortable with himself may become a revealer of Truth. However, every life-philosophy or life-advice will be backed up by the events of that philosopher's/advisor's real life in the physical World.

117   Everyone has a philosophy on life, everyone is a master teacher on television and CDs. However, the question is, does one's philosophy actually work in your real life? Teachas teach from the ancient wisdom of various sacred texts that have been revealed and proven throughout human history. This knowledge is best activated in a Hiphoppa's daily life with the study of the Gospel of Hip Hop.

118   Using a variety of techniques, including westernized spiritual language, the teacha teaches that God operates

through Divine Mind, which is the law of GOD. We are immersed in this law which is a creative substance that receives the direct impressions of our thoughts and brings them into physical manifestation. We are the authors of our own lives; GOD is the book itself.

119   The task of the teacha is to make Hip Hop real for the Hiphoppa. This is achieved by living fully in the way that you teach and truly feel. Most people think and feel one way but they act another way—the teacha must be mindful of this.

120   The exercise of Hip Hop's teacha is to bring the Hiphoppa's thinking and feeling regarding Hip Hop into harmony with that Hiphoppa's actions. In other words, if you feel Hip Hop, act it out. Don't suppress your true feelings as a Hiphoppa. If you think like a Hiphoppa then live like a Hiphoppa! Live like an attuned Hiphoppa!

121   This is our greatest discovery as Hiphoppas! To know that our repeated behaviors cause our Hip Hop reality to occur in the physical World. We are truly the authors of ourselves and our destiny as Hiphoppas!

122   So, as you become more and more attuned and in harmony with your true Self, do not marvel at the miracles in your own life. The more you realize you, the more your environment shall cater to your vision of your *Self*. Life itself responds to your vision of yourself.

123   Being in harmony with your Truth causes the so-called "miracles" in your life. And again, with such spiritual harmony you will notice a certain exactness to the so-called random events of your life. You will always be right on time and in harmony with life's events.

124   Do not be amazed or try to over-intellectualize the miraculous events of your spiritual life. Go with the F.L.O.W. (*Follow Life's Outcome Willingly*). Expect to have things go your way even if such a way appears impossible at

the time or the results of your actions do not prove favorable right then and there.

125   As a teacha you are always in harmony with life itself. Sometimes things will happen that appear out of your control, or unproductive to your work. But hold on! Your physical senses cannot sense your entire being; they can only sense the happenings of your physical existence.

126   You, on the other hand, operate in several dimensions at once. So, what appears to be a disaster in the present may not be so in the future. And what happens to you in your space may be necessary for the prevention of something even more dangerous happening to you in another space.

127   Remember, for those who live principled lives all of our so-called accidents are for our own good and further development. Our God is always working toward the fulfillment of our well-being, even when our conscious minds are unaware of it. Again, go with the F.L.O.W. (*Follow Life's Outcome Willingly*).

128   In conclusion, as a *teacha*, you are also a teacher, and with the teaching of any course or curriculum, accuracy, usefulness and credibility are crucial.

129   Presently Hip Hop is being taught all across the United States in a kind of "freestyle" way, with most educators basically "doing their own thing." And for those who are short-term teachers or objective observers of the Hip Hop phenomenon, limiting their courses to rappers and Rap lyrics, this may be fine.

130   But for those who are seriously seeking to become long-term educators of Hip Hop's history, elements, music, culture, philosophies and politics—accuracy, usefulness and credibility are crucial for one's success and the accurate preservation of Hip Hop's legacy.

131   Those seeking a long-term career teaching Hip Hop (for a living) need to be educated and then accredited

themselves with legitimate certification from legitimate and relevant Hip Hop institutions. So, what is it that makes a Hip Hop institution credible and/or legitimate?

[132] To begin with, a credible Hip Hop learning institution is founded by credible and talented people who love and respect Hip Hop and have proven their mastery of the subjects they are now teaching—they have a hands-on experience with that which is being taught.

[133] A credible Hip Hop learning institution then produces the best professionals and scholars in the Hip Hop field of study. Hip Hop credibility is based upon actually doing, not just knowing.

[134] A credible Hip Hop learning institution stimulates imagination. As Albert Einstein pointed out, *A society's competitive advantage will come not from how well its schools teach the multiplication and periodic tables, but from how well they stimulate imagination and creativity.* For Einstein, imagination was more important than knowledge.

[135] A credible Hip Hop learning institution has achieved and perfected for itself that which it teaches. Students and apprentices should be able to learn from the actual physical structure of the Hip Hop learning facility itself.

[136] A credible Hip Hop learning institution is continuously engaged in the building of its reputation in the Hip Hop field of study—it is active in the communities in which it resides, it produces culture.

[137] And finally, a credible Hip Hop learning institution hands out certificates, degrees and/or other accreditations that actually have meaning and value within the field that such an institution teaches.

[138] This last part is crucial to understand because what is the purpose of learning about Hip Hop if in the end you still struggle to pay your bills? Teachers included.

[139] Although I truly, truly, truly appreciate the fact

that there are people teaching something about Hip Hop to those who really want to know, as you may already know I am equally very concerned about the future of Hip Hop scholarship and the livelihood of those who teach and learn Hip Hop for a living.

[140]   We are ALL well aware of the "horror stories" when it comes to the state of teachers and teaching in the United States. I don't have to lecture you on the financial difficulties many of our nation's teachers face every day just to come into the classroom and educate America's students.

[141]   The bureaucracies, the racism, the sexism, the scandals, the violence, the lack of supplies, and in our case, the lack of respect for Hip Hop even as music and/or culture in the classroom, by those who feel that Hip Hop has nothing to offer mainstream education is blatant, and even hostilely disrespectful, in my time! But this may be to our advantage.

[142]   An educational system that denies Truth and real facts is bound to collapse anyway, and why should Hip Hop be a part of that? From a more political point of view, why should Hip Hop be taught in public schools at all? Especially its spiritual views? Are we not again giving one of OUR most precious resources away to certain "systems" of education that do not share our values and continue to degrade and ignore our self-expression?

[143]   I can see the benefit in teaching Hip Hop's music, culture and history to all interested students; however, I am very distrustful as to what Hip Hop's spiritual views shall become in a private and/or state-operated public school system that can't even teach math, science and/or history correctly. Let us practice our gospel privately and keep our spiritual views to ourselves.

[144]   For Hip Hop's music, culture and history to be taught in public schools, the public school system itself

would have to be modified. Otherwise, what are we teaching? Are we <u>teaching</u> Hip Hop or are we <u>using</u> Hip Hop again?

145   We must think about this seriously. Does the teaching of Hip Hop benefit Hip Hop, or does it simply create jobs for those who wish to teach it? The teaching of Hip Hop must be about more than employment for teachers, or Hip Hop's citizenship in a national system that does not respect our interests.

146   Those who teach Hip Hop for a living must be active participants in the music, culture, history and preservation of Hip Hop above all else, otherwise we are using Hip Hop again, not BEING HIP HOP!

147   Therefore, BE THE TEACHA in your environment. Seek to inspire people with Hip Hop. Let them know that Hip Hop is from GOD and that there is more to Hip Hop than how it is presently being depicted in mass media. BE THE TEACHA! And when people look for real Hip Hop they shall look at you and say THERE IT IS!

THE TWELFTH OVERSTANDING
THE MOVEMENT

[1]   In 1987 Afrika Bambaataa held a "cipher" discussion at the Latin Quarter nightclub in Manhattan, New York.

[2]   The topics included the unionizing of Rap artists and the further development of Hip Hop as its influence began to expand beyond the New York area.

[3]   At this discussion, with about 50 prominent Rap artists, DJs, journalists, b-boys/girls, Graffiti writers and other activists present, Afrika Bambaataa argued that without organization and unity Hip Hop would simply become a mass plantation of talented people all working toward the benefit of several corporations.

[4]   This discussion ended with Daddy-O of Stetsasonic predicting the fall of New York's dominance over the Rap music industry and the rise of the West Coast with an emcee called Too Short.

[5]   During this historic meeting everyone pledged to do there part to protect Hip Hop's cultural development. It was around this time (1987) that we began to think of Hip Hop as a *culture*.

[6]   But the streets were extremely dangerous during these times. Many Hiphoppas got caught up in the emerging crack/cocaine drug scene. Automatic weapons found their way onto the streets of New York and into the hands of Hiphoppas.

[7]   When armed, most Hiphoppas used their weapons to protect themselves against the lawlessness of the streets while others used their weapons for robberies, kidnappings,

murders and intimidation. But when DJ Scott La Rock was killed in the Bronx trying to break up a street dispute ALL Hiphoppas were saddened.

8   The drug wars of the 1980s broke all of the original street codes that protected and empowered Hip Hop's community leaders. It became every man/woman for themselves! Many were killed.

9   The murder of Scott La Rock in August of 1987 was the first of its kind for the Hip Hop community. However, Scott La Rock would not be the last prominent Hip Hop artist that would be killed by the escalation of street violence caused by the introduction of crack/cocaine and guns into predominantly Black and Brown neighborhoods.

10   But as bad as things were then, we were still not powerless. The conscious Hip Hop community, inspired by Afrika Bambaataa, began to mobilize and organize against such violence. The police and other law enforcement agencies were not only powerless against the crack/cocaine drug movement of the 1980s, but because of such powerlessness many of them joined in on the sale of illegal drugs and guns within Black and Brown communities.

11   Black and Brown leaders were also powerless and many of them, fearing for their own lives, turned their heads when crack/cocaine was being sold to young Black and Brown teenagers. From the East to the West Coast of the United States gangs of Black and Brown youths were enlisted and protected by American law enforcement agencies to terrorize Black and Brown neighborhoods as the drugs and guns flowed in.

12   Finally, in 1989, the violence and lawlessness of the 1980s reached its peak when a young man was fatally stabbed at a Rap concert in New York City for his jewelry. The then head of A&R for Jive records Ann Carli (Tokyo Rose) was so moved by the event that she approached author/activist

Nelson George and I (KRS ONE) to form a *Stop The Violence* movement based on a song that I had written one year earlier entitled "Stop The Violence."

[13]   Between the three of us we organized the production of a song entitled Self Destruction, a chorus/chant written by Doug E. Fresh with music produced by D-Nice. Other artists, such as Heavy D & the Boyz, MC Lyte, Just-Ice, M.C. Delight, Wise, Daddy-O, Fruit-Kwan (Frukwan), Kool Moe Dee, Ms. Melodie, and Public Enemy also donated their lyrical performances to this cause.

[14]   I opened the song with the lyrics: *TODAY'S TOPIC: SELF DESTRUCTION! It really ain't the Rap audience that's buggin'. It's one or two suckas, ignorant brothas, tryin to rob and steal from one another!*

[15]   *You get caught in the mid, so to crush that stereotype here's what we did. We got ourselves together, so that you can unite and fight for what's right! Not negative, 'cause the way we live is positive, we don't kill our relatives.*

[16]   M.C. Delight followed with: *POP, POP, POP GOES A SHOT! Who's to blame? Headlines, front page and Rap's the name. M.C. Delight here to state the bottom line that Black on Black crime was way before our time.*

[17]   Kool Moe Dee followed with: *BACK IN THE SIXTIES OUR BROTHAS AND SISTAS WERE HANGED! How can you gang-bang? I never ever ran from the Ku Klux Klan and I shouldn't have to run from a Black man! 'Cause that's…*and then everyone said: *SELF DESTRUCTION! YOU'RE HEADED FOR SELF DESTRUCTION!* And everybody from the East to the West Coast of the United States was inspired to seek peace and reconciliation. The conscious Hip Hop movement was born!

[18]   After raising $600,000 for the National Urban League with the proceeds from our "Self Destruction"

song, we began to investigate the root causes of violence for ourselves. We found that illiteracy, poverty, lack of purpose, poor law enforcement practices and media hype all contribute to heightening the levels of aggression in society, and can cause violence to occur.

[19]   We found that it is not the youth of the United States that are the cause of violence, it is primarily the adults, especially those in civil-service positions. We found that American society has laws and other mechanisms to *keep the peace* but that those in-charge of *keeping the peace* have simply *dropped the ball!* For whatever reason, the mechanisms put in place to curb violence and overly aggressive behavior in society have been undermined, and in some cases, attacked by those who benefit from an aggressive populace. The Hip Hop community responded!

[20]   With this revelation we fought back. On the West Coast in California in 1990, rival *Crip* and *Blood* gang members called for a truce and an end to street violence. Stan Tookie Williams (founder of the Crips) declared "gang-banging" to be dead, and even went as far as to denounce the Crips and all gang activity. In commemoration of such a monumental shift in consciousness, activists Mike Concepcion, E'Ban Kelly and Leonard Richardson organized the West Coast's version of the song "Self Destruction," entitled "We're All In The Same Gang," produced by Dr. Dre.

[21]   King Tee, Body & Soul, Def Jef, Michel'le, Tone Loc, Above The Law, Ice-T, N.W.A., J.J. Fad, Young M.C., Digital Underground, Oaktown's 3.5.7., MC Hammer, and Eazy-E all came together to form the super group The West Coast Rap All-Stars.

[22]   King Tee opened the song with the lyrics: *IT'S STRAIGHT UP MADNESS! Everywhere I look, used to be a straight A student, now he's a crook. Robbing people*

just to smoke or shoot up used to have a crew-cut, now he's a pooh putt!

23   Tone Loc followed: *AS A YOUTH I USED TO GET MY BANG ON and on the ave, get my part-time slang on...I ain't slippin' or down with a head trip, I'm talking to all the Bloods and all the Crips. Throw down your rag and get on the right track man, it's time to fight, unite and be a Black Man! Tone Loc on a positive change, 'cause remember: we all in the same gang!*

24   Ice-T followed: *RIPPIN' THE MICROPHONE THE WAY I DO, listen close my brothas cause I'm talking to you! The problem is, we got a suicidal lifestyle, cause 90 percent of us are living foul and wild!...All my brothas need to know one thang, no matter what you think, we're all in the same gang!*

25   Niggaz With Attitude followed: *YO! BULLETS FLYING, MOTHERS CRYING, BROTHAS DYING, lying in the streets! That's why we're trying to stop it all from falling apart and going to waste, and keeping a smile off a White face! N.W.A. never preaching, just teaching the knowledge of the street to each and all, that don't understand! That's why we came to let you know that we're all in the same gang!*

26   Digital Underground followed: *I'M IN A RAGE! Oh yeah, why is that G? Other races they say we act like rats in a cage. I tried to argue, but check it, every night in the news we prove them suckas right and I got the blues!*

27   MC Hammer followed: *IT'S GOT TO STOP! We don't need all the violence! Peace in the hood and a moment of silence. We got together not for ego or fame, we got involved cause we're all in the same gang!*

28   Around 1991 while touring with the prophet Kwame Ture, my friend Professor Z and I began a healing program for the Hip Hop community called *Human Education Against Lies* (H.E.A.L.). Similar to the *Stop The Violence*

Movement, H.E.A.L. was also designed to curb violence and offer strategies toward the continued unity of the Hip Hop community. We were joined by Kid Capri, Big Daddy Kane, Freddy Foxxx, LL Cool J, MC Lyte, Queen Latifah, Ms. Melodie, G. Simone, DMC, Jam Master Jay, Salt-N-Pepa, Kool Moe Dee, Chuck D, Ziggy Marley, Shabba Ranks, Doug E. Fresh, DJ Red Alert, Michael Stipe, Billy Bragg, and motion picture/video directors Fab 5 Freddy, Sacha Jenkins, Jonathan Demme, the late Ted Demme and many others.

29   The main point was that technology seemed to be overwhelming the concept of civilization. We noticed that more emphasis was being placed upon technological innovation than upon knowledge of one's human abilities. We called for healing and balance.

30   Our campaign promoted the idea that "before you are a race, a religion or an occupation, you are a human being." Yes, these tools are very important to the presentation and sustainment of Hip Hop's activity and history in the World but again, Hip Hop in and of itself is a human skill produced by the human Spirit.

31   This we must never forget. And even though most of us are already totally dependent upon an outside technological system of some sort to live, pay bills and eat, it is always liberating to know that Hip Hop as a human skill offers some relief from mainstream technological employment dependency. Such knowledge keeps us and our children's children free and entrepreneurial, well-grounded upon what is real. This was some of what H.E.A.L. was all about.

32   However, as I began to really investigate the nature of my being and why I am who I am and why I do what I do, I realized that I am what I am doing and being right now. I realized that I was not just performing the artistic elements

of Hip Hop, but that I was Hip Hop itself! I AM HIP HOP! I realized that Hip Hop was not *over there somewhere,* but that I was Hip Hop itself and so was everyone else who participated in Hip Hop in some way. My eye was opened.

³³   Two years later, in 1994, I began to flesh out the "I am Hip Hop" philosophy as well as "The Science of Rap." In the same year Afrika Bambaataa, Kool DJ Herc, Crazy Legs, GrandWizzard Theodore, Daddy-O, Mr. Wiggles, TC Islam, Teddy Tedd and Special K, Kevy Kev, Harry Allen, Jacqueline Hines, DJ Kenny Parker, Hakim Green, X-Man, and several other artists, founders, journalists and grassroots activists of that era all came together for the first time in Hip Hop's history at the Schomburg Center for Research in Black Culture in Harlem, New York, to discuss the creation and preservation of Hip Hop as a *real* culture.

³⁴   Harry Allen (*the Media Assassin*) stood before the conscious Hip Hop community of 1994 and said, *I can't begin to speak, or claim to speak, on behalf of Hip Hop and the culture which has been built over these past few decades, without giving respect to my predecessor Afrika Bambaataa* (applause). *And to all the rest of my brothers and sisters who are here on behalf of this art form which is glomming, growing, under attack; pick whatever adjective you wanna put against it. Hip Hop is, you know, ducking. Uh, ducking bullets in many cases.*

³⁵   *My name is Harry Allen, Hip Hop activist and Media Assassin. I respect your time, so I'm going to speak briefly and afterwards, KRS ONE will take the rest of the meeting. But he was gracious enough to let me start this. So let's start this.*

³⁶   *My presentation is entitled 'Black Art: Lost, Stolen or Strayed.' Now, I'm gonna ask you a very simple question. And after I do, I want you to raise your hand if your response is yes. But I only want you to do this after I tell you to, and only if your answer is yes. Because if your answer is yes, you're the*

person that I want to be speaking to this afternoon. You're the person.

37   Allen continued addressing the room: *How many people believe that Hip Hop as an art form, and as an aggressive form of Black art and imagination, should have a home? Now, don't raise your hand yet.*

38   *How many people believe that there should be a place where Hip Hop is archived? A place where the history is available through booklets or pamphlets, or maybe even online by computer?*

39   *How many people believe that there should be a place where Hip Hop teaches and gets people information that they can use for Hip Hop and for other things in their lives?*

40   *How many believe there should be a place, a society, an academy if you will, where awards are given for excellence in the field?*

41   *How many people here believe that there should be a place where the records, and the videos, and the magazines, and the photographs, and the charts, and the posters, and the articles, and on and on and on and on, are kept for the future and preserved so that future generations will be able to understand what this form was, why it came to be, and why we were here?*

42   *Now if you believe this, raise your hand and keep it up* (everyone raises their hands). *Now keep it up, because I wanna ask you one more question. If you really do believe this, what have you done today or even in the last week to make sure this happens? Ask yourself this question: what is the proof of your belief? Put your hands down.*

43   *Black art is lost, stolen or strayed. Ya know it's been said that if you go to great African art museums of Europe, or even in this country—and uh, you can talk about the Berlin art museum or many of the other art museums—and you look at the African art in those museums, and you look at the dates attached to the art, by taking those dates and taking the art*

where its from and plotting it on a map you can essentially outline the path of European conquest of the African continent. Like a flow chart, like a graph all throughout the last century.

[44]   *Now, is this your fate? Is this what's gonna become of you? If you're a Hip Hop artist or if you're an industry professional, or if you're a person who's just concerned about* <u>*this form that you've seen made out of nothing, and turned*</u> <u>*into a billon-dollar business right before your very eyes*</u> *in your lifetime, is this what's gonna happen to you? Is this your fate, to basically be a marker,* <u>*your work a marker to conquest? To the*</u> <u>*destruction of yourself?*</u>

[45]   *I'd like to refer to another example real quickly. What I have in my hand marked up and read is an article that was clipped from November of 1993 in* Billboard *[magazine]. It's headlined 'Library of Congress to Digitize Bernstein.' Now this appeared ironically the same day that the* Billboard *Rap issue appeared, where they have their celebration of hip-hop and what it is and everything. I'm just gonna read a few paragraphs from this article.*

[46]   *'The Library of Congress landed a musical gold mine November 8th when the estate of Leonard Bernstein decided to donate his personal and professional archives to the institution. Now the Library plans to share that wealth electronically.'*

[47]   *Now, as you may know, Leonard Bernstein is an American composer, uh,* West Side Story, *I guess* Porgy and Bess *[actually composed by George Gershwin, 1934], a whole bunch of ya know, very well-renowned, renowned for his work and he died last year. In essence, donates his work to the Library of Congress.*

[48]   Allen continued to read from the article: *'The Bernstein materials, which include more than 200 hours of film and video programs, and 1000 hours of recordings, as well as such documents as unpublished musical sketches, lyrics, and original music manuscripts, will be used to launch a planned*

502

electronic archive accessible to the public by computer.'

[49]   Before continuing Allen paused and commented, *They're gonna call this a Leonard Bernstein Multimedia Archive.* He continued to read: *'Under such a system all of the materials in the Bernstein collection—audio, video, and print—will be digitized or translated to the digital language for storage on a central database. In this form the information can be accessed from a remote computer via modem. Once established, the Bernstein Multimedia Archive will serve as a model for a larger, long-range multimedia project, the Library says.'*

[50]   Harry Allen closed the article and then addressed the room, saying, *Now, why couldn't Hip Hop music have something like this? Why couldn't a form that generates a billion dollars in record sales alone have something like this if it wants to? Why can't a billion-dollar art form have anything it wants? That's the question I'm asking you today. Because…*

[51]   At that very moment the recognized Father of Hip Hop, Kool DJ Herc walked into the room and Harry Allen stopped speaking to acknowledge the *Father.* The room applauded Herc's arrival as he took his seat in the meeting.

[52]   Allen continued, *We are now in a stage in the development of this form, where unlike the situation when people like Kool Herc and Afrika Bambaataa were inventing this art out of our own Black genius, we are now at a stage where there are people who are professionals in diverse areas who know things, who have information. We're at a stage where Wu Tang Clan can make an album for almost nothing, distribute it themselves, get picked up by a major, and then generate 500,000 copies in sales. Millions and millions of dollars in revenue, but how much of that comes back to Hip Hop?*

[53]   *That's the question we have to answer I guess, or be run over, or be left as monuments to our own destruction. I got tired of wondering about the answers to questions like this so I came*

up with my own answer.

⁵⁴ *I started an organization; it's called the Rhythm Cultural Institute. The agenda of the organization is to <u>capture, keep for the future, aggressively define, and widely expand the discussion and definition of Hip Hop music as a culture. So that it can enrich us, so that it can make us better, so that we can get something from it besides music and good times.</u>*

⁵⁵ *Now, the organization is for the most part unknown, which is the way I prefer it. I think it's better to let your work speak for you, and we're doing something! We're getting some things done. Recently we had a P.S.A.* [Public Service Announcement] *produced, which was paid for by Def Jam Recordings, and it debuted during The Source Awards. We also had an ad which was donated and which ran in their program, a copy of which I have here. You might remember seeing it if you went to The Source Awards and you looked through the program.*

⁵⁶ *The board is formed by myself, David—Davy D. Cook from KMEL in Oakland—and Mary K. Penn who you probably haven't heard of, but she's a scholar, an anthropologist based here. The only anthropologist who, when I met her knew the lyrics to "I Know You Got Soul" by Rakim, so I definitely knew I had to have her down.*

⁵⁷ *We're small* (laughter) *but we're <u>politically astute, technologically savvy, legally and contractually curious</u>. And, um, obviously this is a message and an idea that has, that people understand and want to be part of. Recently we got a grant from the New York Folklore Society on application. And what this money will do* [is it] *will pay to have an archivist, a person whose job it is to take history, wrap it up, and make it last for 500 years, come here to New York and sit down with a group like yourself or others and tell you, if you take this process of archiving, preserving, something that is usually appointed to mummies and ya know, uh, I guess, uh, Renaissance art, and*

you point it at Hip Hop—*the art of our very hands*—*how would you do it? How would you make it happen? Ya know?*

⁵⁸ *As well, we have plans to have a legislative aide from Albany come down here to New York City and tell you how by using our juice, our power, our connections, we can get the money to do such a thing and implement such a vision. The fact is that* <u>*Hip Hop artists especially, are people who have a lot of connections politically, are popular, have above-average income maybe, but do not use their political connections, do not use their influence, do not use their influence to make things happen for the form.*</u> *We're unfortunately* <u>*divided to a great extent,*</u> *and hopefully this can change. The motto for Black people should be "Build or be Killed."*

⁵⁹ After Harry Allen spoke, KRS then stood up and said, *I've been attending meetings hosted by Bam* [Afrika Bambaataa] *for this—maybe not the exact same theme, but the theme of unifying Hip Hop as a culture,* <u>*unifying artists and having them organize in a fashion where they can control their political power, control their economic power, their creative power,*</u> *etc., etc.*

⁶⁰ *What has happened is that over the past few years Bam would get everyone together, we'd all come in a room and say yeah, yeah, yeah; next day we're gone and nothing happens. This has happened over and over again. I've seen artists who scream Bam! Zulu Nation! Zulu! Yeah Zulu! And then the anniversary comes around; they're nowhere to be found.*

⁶¹ *In my opinion, I feel as though in the scheme of African thought* <u>*we've always paid respects to our elders.*</u> *And, not that you're an elder Bam* (laughter), <u>*but we've always paid respect to the people who have come before us.*</u> *Meaning that we could not have been in the situation that we're in unless we at least show acknowledgement.*

⁶² *Sometimes that acknowledgement is shown through money. Sometimes that acknowledgement is shown through just*

*basic respect; just yo, I recognize! And that's it! Today the
Hip Hop community is dying because we fail to have this kind
of respect. And it's not a matter of any of us going and saying;
OK, Afrika Bambaataa is GOD. Kool Herc is GOD. We're
gonna kneel to these icons, etc., etc. It's not on that level.*

63   *It's on the level of, before we decided to pick up a mic,
pick up a turntable, matter of fact, before we knew what it was,
these gentlemen were out there doing this and doing that. And
we do it differently now. They did it one way, Flash does it
another way, Theodore does it another way, Herc does it one
way.*

64   *Then you got Run-DMC and LL, and they do it their
way. Then it's Eric B. & Rakim and KRS ONE, Biz Markie
and they do it their way. Now we're coming into a new phase
in Hip Hop which has to do now with the World is doing it
their way.*

65   *And the difference between what has happened then
and what is happening now is that for the first time in Hip
Hop's history, Hip Hop is no longer a New York-based thing.
And I don't say that to say that it isn't. I'm saying that to say
that the reality that, of what I look at now is that, when you go
to Japan the Japanese kids are, 'I'm Hip Hop! I'm Hip Hop!'
You are not! 'I AM! You're in my country now. And you can't
tell me that I'm not.'*

66   *You go to Germany, this, that, and the other, California,
Oakland, the South, Miami etc., etc. My point is that Hip
Hop is running away from us before our very eyes. And I used
to always wonder years ago, I used to always say wow, what
was Chubby Checker and/or Chuck Berry, and the Supremes,
what were they doing to now have like a Nirvana and if you see
a Black Rock group now you're amazed! Wow! A Black Rock
group, Living Color! Wow, they're Black and they do Rock?
That's like amazement when in actuality again I won't go into
that but we again are the originators of that art form as well.*

[67]   *So my point here in starting this discussion is that number one, what I saw, what I see going on in Hip Hop, is the same thing that went on in Rock and Roll but we have a chance to stop it. We're allowing things to happen. We're just allowing certain things to just happen. Just happen! And we're just watching them, saying yeah, that's small, that don't really, don't affect us. That's small too; that really don't affect us.*

[68]   *Then, as much as I respect John Shecter and* The Source *for what they've done in Rap, now we have John Shecter doing an award show, giving us awards for OUR creativity. And let me be very clear in what I'm saying, because this in no way a demise or a disrespect to* The Source *or any magazine for that matter; could have been any magazine.*

[69]   *But the point here is that everyone is giving themselves the ability to define our creativity. And the point here of this discussion or the point that I'd like to interject is to once and for all define Hip Hop. Hip Hop as the lifestyle, as the energy, as the way of life, as the organized way of life. And do it in a sense where we can put together a pamphlet or something.*

[70]   *I don't want to call it rules, I don't want to call it regulations, but I mean I guess during this conversation we'll come up with something, some name for it, but it should clearly define. And this is not a process that's gonna take just today; this is the beginning.*

[71]   *We're gonna go on and on and the purpose for you all to be here is to get several ideas. Ideas as to what you think this certain question, how this question should be answered. If someone else disagrees we should give everyone a chance to speak, but ideas are created out of argument, out of this is what I think it is, why do you think it's like that, maybe it can be like this etc., etc.*

[72]   *So just to start it off, this book that I'm proposing is to be given to every record company and A&R person in the entire planet, the whole World! There's only a couple of thousand*

record companies that seem to be controlling our entire fate in their hands. There's only a couple hundred magazines. Only a couple of thousand television shows. *If some sort of document, or book, or pamphlet can be put together that says this is what Hip Hop is* and this is what we think it should be.

[73]   *This book is not something that will last forever; it's like, it might even have to be revised every two or three years. This is what Hip Hop is NOW in 1997. This is what it is NOW in this, that, the other. We're documenting it now in 1994 based on not having documented it since its conception.*

[74]   *We have a whole broad range of people who have history in their minds, who have certain thoughts and are pushing the forum forward. And this is the purpose actually, or one of the purposes of why you're here.*

[75]   *Let me just end off and say also, this book in my mind will be backed up by force. And when I say force it doesn't always mean physical but it means that too. But it doesn't always mean that. It means political force. In other words, there's a point to make to the A&R people who are signing the guys giving in their tapes.*

[76]   *If you're gonna give in a tape and say 'I'm into Rap,' you have to define yourself. Are you going to be a Rap artist or you gonna be a Hip Hop artist? Because if you say you're gonna be a Hip Hop artist, well, this little book here put together by the minds of people in Hip Hop is what you should know. This will also weed out who's not down and who really is. In addition to that, we won't have these problems that Hip Hop is having because of Rap artists. So this is the main focus of what I'm saying here today.*

[77]   And we began our session by rearranging our chairs into a circle. And when the cipher was complete KRS continued, *Let me start it off with question number one, being, what in our minds is the most important aspect to preserving the culture of Hip Hop? And when I say what in our minds*

is that, in this day and age what is the most powerful means of preserving the culture...? Hip Hop means more people in professional life? Or does it mean that's going to hinder us? Matter of fact, I'll start it off like this; in our opinion, can you be a professional in Hip Hop?

⁷⁸   And a Brooklyn-born Hip Hop activist responded by saying, *I don't think so, 'cause <u>I think Hip Hop is a way of life; it's a culture</u>. How do you become a professional in your way of life unless you clearly have moved to the afterlife?*

⁷⁹   And I responded by asking, *What about someone like, um, say like Jews for instance. Just say. That's a personal belief. Like say they would wear their...I'm talking about orthodox Jews, they would wear their yarmulke, their whole thing, to work. And they're telling, they're showing, their...I mean when you deal with them you have to see they're Jewish. I mean we're in a different circumstance but...*

⁸⁰   And TC Islam responded by saying, *But brother KRS, being Jewish isn't more like wearing a yarmulke and all that; <u>it's your ways and actions. It's like brothas and sistas that live Hip Hop; it's a way of life</u>.*

⁸¹   Then Afrika Bambaataa said, *For y'all to deal with the industry in hip-hop <u>y'all gonna have to be organized</u>. Cause y'all dealing with some devious evil people who been robbing people since the 50s with the Doo Wop groups, same thing in the 60s, same thing they doing with hip-hop.*

⁸²   *A lot of the Rap groups don't know about they mechanical rights, they royalties, they licensing. You can have a cover over here that's one cover. In Europe or in some other, Latin America, it be a whole different cover or [they] might even take your picture off. You gotta know about Cablevision, you gotta be in tuned with what's happening with the future.*

⁸³   *There's so many different things. Like you need to get into professionalism in Cablevision cause it's gonna be 500 TV channels coming on and they're gonna need music,*

programming, video shows for this. We got to be organized! <u>We</u>
<u>gotta have discipline, structure, and you gonna have to have</u>
<u>professionalism</u> because that's what they did to take Hip Hop
away from y'all. Because the Hip Hop community itself was
not organized.

[84]   *So, meaning now the first death of Hip Hop, they took*
away the vinyl. Meaning, they got rid of the DJ. They didn't
speak to the Black or Latino community and say, 'Do you want
to git rid of your turntables or vinyl?' They said, 'BOOM it's
out! CDs is in, cassettes is in,' and that's what happened. And
we just go along with the program. A couple of us might argue
and put on our record, 'We want vinyl! We want vinyl!' They
give you a little to make you happy and shit! And then they
might throw you a little money to shut the hell up!

[85]   *<u>You got a lot of sellouts in the industry in hip-hop</u>. The*
only way we can do it is dealing by an organized meeting of the
minds. And it can't be just one meeting, we have to go down
many meetings, it can be a year, two years, whatever, until we get
this whole thing structured—<u>a Hip Hop union organization</u>.

[86]   And keep in mind that this discussion is taking place
in 1994, before the Internet and at the dawn of compact
discs, satellite television and digital radio. Afrika Bambaataa
foresaw all of what is going on today and warned us of what
was to come. Only the wise listened.

[87]   Afrika Bambaataa continued, *See, we got to start*
working with the brothas or sistas that want to do. <u>Be a doer</u>
<u>of the word</u>! The ones that want to do, ya know, leave them on
the side cause when the time comes around and they, the ones on
that material shit, they will get on the bandwagon once they see
something materialistic to them.

[88]   *That's how many people just join a lot of unions. You*
think the Federation of Teachers waited for everybody to come
together before they could deal with the board of education or
the unions that deal with construction workers?

89   *Like the brothas, the Black and Latino construction workers, they didn't stop to say, 'Well, the Whites is not giving us no jobs working with construction.' They got together and they went out there and started taking jobs and demanding they jobs, and the same way, we gonna have to deal with the industry. 'Cause you messing with some real devious people that's robbing the shit out of a lot of these artists, even the ones that make crazy money in the industry they still getting robbed if you really sit down and talk to them in truth.*

90   *You know you don't want no brotha that's gonna get in the limelight and show, I got my cars, all the young ladies, I got my house and stuff. Ya know, really sit down and check with them how much is they really gettin' or is the industry getting billions of money, or like Wu Tang, if they sold so many how much money or percentage are they gettin' from the record company?*

91   And then Crazy Legs said, *See, the thing is that our only alternative if we don't make it, I can't say we all live Hip Hop, I personally do. But my only Earth alternative if I can't make it with a dance company or whatever, if I can't dance no more, it can only be to scramble. That's the point!*

92   *My only alternative can't be by hustling. It has to be like something solid! Right there! BAM! Alright cool, alright I can't dance no more* (laughs), *ya know I can still dance but you know, if I can't dance no more, BAM we got a dance company going out. We got Ghetto Original Dance productions and we're hiring from within the community. OK, so we're doing this.*

93   *We've set up a base for people who don't have the money to take ballet, or jazz, or whatever! And that's already been taken away from us anyway 'cause those are all original African art forms.*

94   *Alright now, what we're doing is we just like saying these brothas out here don't have the money to join those things and let's give them something, you got to get them involved in*

something that's more cultural, more meaningful to them instead of wearing some tights!

⁹⁵ *You know that's your own prerogative if a brotha wanna wear tights. But I know sistas that dance with us that wanna get busy on some lockin, poppin, b-boyin, whatever they wanna do and we take them on tour.*

⁹⁶ *So we have to just create these other outlets, and if you can't do it you have to be able to bring people on that can still do it. And it's like them brothas that produced Vanilla Ice; it was Black people that produced him. OK, they made money on Vanilla Ice. I think that's dope! I mean the shit is chuckable but ya know they making money.*

⁹⁷ And then Hakim Green, a public school teacher and emcee with Rap group Channel Live said, *A real important aspect to preserving Hip Hop, I mean I believe is getting people to find esteem in Hip Hop. I've been teaching public schools for the last four years and the one thing I noticed in teaching social studies is that the kids didn't see their immediate society as something worth studying. So, things that I would do is I would say, 'OK we gonna study Hip Hop. Hip Hop is a society of people, you interact with one another. We gonna study the ways in which you interact, the ways in which your society manifests itself.'*

⁹⁸ *This stuff: the dance, the music, the hairstyles, the clothes, the fashion. Then I flipped it and said, well, let's see who makes money off of it. I started bringing magazines in. I brought the* Word Up! *in and the* Rap Masters, *then I brought* The Source *in and* Vibe. *And as we got higher in levels of getting across messages we saw where most money was going. I said, well, why is that?*

⁹⁹ *You know, we have to start seeing our community as something to have esteem in. In doing that we define it. Like I said, I've been teaching school for the last four years, this is how I dress. When I put my locks in, I had a little friction with my*

boss, the principal, but I broke it down. I said, look, my locks is an expression of my culture, who I am as an African man. If there's a problem with me wearing my locks then we'll have to take this further.

100   If Jews can wear the locks off the side of their face and not see any feedback or wear a yarmulke I should be able to wear my hair that way. But getting people to say yo, you're worth something and if you're worth something *stand up for yourself!* We as a Hip Hop community are worth something; *we stand up for SELF!* And then Mr. Wiggles from the Rock Steady Crew said, *The one thing that I've realized, a lot of people here define Hip Hop in their own way and I think that's a mistake.*

101   *Ya see, in order for Hip Hop to be a culture you have to have every element. Culture is not just Rap. And I think even though we hear it all the time, a lot of us, it don't sink in.*

102   *Culture is art, music, dance, the way you eat, the way you dress, the way you talk, the way you walk, the whole nine. Now I can sit here and say yeah we all this and blah, blah, but I'm not sure 'cause how many people here really know how to do graffiti, or respect a graffiti writer, or hire a graffiti writer to do your album cover as opposed to, ya know, whoever the hell!*

103   *And how many people here really truly believe in b-boyin, that hire b-boys and give b-boys props, ya know what I'm sayin, as original Hip Hop dance as well as the new school dances. But they ain't really happening. There ain't no connection there. I feel if we gonna make that connection, alright; we gotta take every top rap artist, which to me means Recording Artist Production 'cause all they know how to do is go into a studio and record, but can they get on stage and rock the crowd? If they can't, why they on stage?*

104   *Back in the days MCs needed to be heard, the dancers needed to be seen, the art needed to be seen, ya know what I'm sayin'? We gotta get back to the original cultural mentality of*

the whole art form. Once we get everybody culturally based then we can move. But right now we're not treating it like a culture; we're treating it as a commodity. And when you choose a commodity you gonna lose it.

[105]   And then Jacqueline Hines, a well respected Hip Hop activist, said, *Well, just to follow back on what he just said, I think first off we have to get rid of the hypocrisy in this room. And with no offense to anybody in here, but for all the old school people in here I'm Jacqueline Hines from Hip Hop Incorporated that called when I first came up with the idea of a museum—hall of fame turned into archive.*

[106]   *I mean these are things, that I sit here and I'm offended and I'm saddened that you would say, ya know, you gotta be certain, you have to be this in Hip Hop, you gotta do this in Hip Hop! Anybody that comes to me and says, I wanna preserve the Black woman for what it is today, I'm giving my all in all to that project!*

[107]   *All I said is come be a part of it, be on the board, participate. Instead, what I get is not people trying to assist in a museum that already has a provisional charter, that's already established, that's already established all the groundwork. What I get is, oh, let me get an idea off of this so I can be first, or let me come to meetings and talk about what people have to be to be in Hip Hop. That's like saying Black.*

[108]   *A lot of people look at me and they say, well you not Black because of your hair texture. Well let me tell you, I'm more Black than half of y'all in this room and I know more about my culture than half of y'all! So to define people on the basis of how they look, well you can't be Hip Hop, you can't be Black; that's just bullshit! You have to define people by heart and where they gonna put their time.*

[109]   *I don't know too many people that's going broke for Hip Hop! I'll tell you right now I'm broke because of Hip Hop and I'm getting into more expenses because of Hip Hop!*

And when people talk about they wanna do something for Hip Hop, find out what their root cause is. Find out if they wanna be the first!

[110]   *I don't care, there can be five museums up tomorrow about Hip Hop but my museum will still be established because I know the concept and the thought and the heart that I have in it. It will always be successful!*

[111]   *It's just you have to find out what they want out of the project. Is it they want to be first? Is it money they want? What is it that they want? Because I see a lot of times in Hip Hop it's just that people don't want to assist other people because they want to be the first to have it, they want to have the money from it!*

[112]   *I mean, I think that if you going for money—I think every society needs an economic base, but that does not mean you have to drive a Benz. If we all live in the same community, we all eat, we live, and we happy, and we living the life that we supposed to, like a village in Africa, then you don't need expensive clothes! You set your own standards! You don't have to live off nobody else's standards!*

[113]   After a brief comment by an unknown member of Zulu Nation, Crazy Legs addressed Jacqueline Hines' remarks. Crazy Legs said, *You know what we're missing? I think we should hit the first thing she spoke on. I think it was something more personal with certain people in here.*

[114]   *The fact that, I'll tell you straight up! When you first called me I never heard of you in my life. And bottom line, most of the people that call me to get involved with projects, and I'm sure with certain other old-school people in here, we don't know who they are. And don't forget we've been gettin', we're the first one's to get jerked! And we got jerked so that means we've been gettin' jerked the longest* (laughter).

[115]   *So what happens is since that we were jerked already people try to insult our intelligence and try to say, OK, well, let*

me see if I can get this person to it cause they've done so much shit they probably act so hard up for money right now, alright, boom, boom, boom, boom.

¹¹⁶   *It's nothing personal against you. It's just that I'll tell you straight up! If you would have called me and KRS would have called me at the same time with the same idea I definitely would have gone with KRS. Only because there's a certain part of me that is leery to get with anyone because of what I've been through.*

¹¹⁷   *You forget <u>we did this out of innocence</u>. There was no gimmick! <u>We did it to come together in community, our alternative form of recreation. We were creating it and we didn't even know what we were creating</u>.*

¹¹⁸   *And then we realized that when places like the Roxy, Negril, Danceateria started opening they were giving us guest lists of like 50 people here! Bam got a hundred people on his guest list! Legs, you got 50 people for your Rock Steady Crew!*

¹¹⁹   *And meanwhile all these White people, whatever, was coming in to see us that was coming from the Bronx and Manhattan and whatever, would <u>come to see how we lived. Instead of going to the jungle they brought the jungle to the clubs! And we were the spectacle!</u> So we're like, I realize that now, so we're like wait a second! I'm not going in the cage for no one else anymore!*

¹²⁰   Jacqueline responded. *I understand that, but I think the best way...I think that if KRS would have called me and Tom Dick would have called me and Tom Dick, I didn't know Tom Dick, and I don't know KRS ONE, cause I ain't never sat down and had a conversation with KRS ONE. So what I would have done is sit down, have a conversation with KRS ONE, have a conversation with Tom Dick, and then based on those two conversations I would have made my decision. But I wouldn't jump the gun to say, oh, because of KRS ONE...*

(the room erupts into several voices).

¹²¹   Jacqueline continued, *Excuse me! I think though what needs to be done is that y'all need to find out what is going on! Because there's a hell of a lot of grassroots people that's doing a hell of a lot for Hip Hop. But because they are not well-known or they don't have celebrity attached to their names they don't get the respect that they deserve!*

¹²²   Crazy Legs responded again. *You don't have to be a celebrity. But where was all these grassroots people...see, people think Hip Hop started in the eighties. Where were all these grassroots people when Herc was...* Jacqueline jumped in, saying, *We weren't born!*

¹²³   Crazy Legs responded, *Listen! No, OK, but there were other grassroots people there that totally ignored the ghetto, that's why we had to come up with our alternative form of recreation.*

¹²⁴   As Jacqueline began to respond again, the room erupted into several voices shouting! Afrika Bambaataa then brought order by stating, *Y'ALL NEED TO CHILL! WE GETTING TOO MUCH ON THE 'I' SYNDROME! LET'S THINK ABOUT THE 'US' SYNDROME AND GET SOME SOLUTIONS OF WHAT'S HAPPENING NOW!*

¹²⁵   Mr. Wiggles jumped in, saying, *If there be two museums then y'all should be affiliated! I don't think it makes a difference how many there should be, we should have a hundred scattered all over the World!*

¹²⁶   Daddy-O from Stetsasonic then said, *I wanna go back to the original question that KRS asked about preserving the culture. And I think the best point, which is personal, is the point that my man made over here, 'cause I really don't have long to be here.*

¹²⁷   *But one thing I wanna say to y'all is that it ain't even about us, it's about them little shorties...I think them shorties is*

517

gonna be the ones to preserve it 'cause we gonna be outta here!
I think that when we start thinking about Hip Hop we gonna
have to start providing.

¹²⁸   I mean I can't do no better than my man right here
[pointing at Hakim Green], *he a teacher and I know that's*
like in the gut! My kids is in public school and I be wishing I
was a teacher sometimes, 'cause the teachers be like stressed!
And I be like, I can do that. You know what I'm sayin'?

¹²⁹   *But I'm sayin' I think that issue of the kids and stuff,*
ya know, I think that's really important. I know a lot of people
look at ya know, I don't know how everybody feels about Hip
Hop right now, um, I know a lot of people love it, I know some
people here don't know what it is. Ya know I'm kinda mid-
level, I wasn't with Legs and Bam and them but I was in there
like right after!

¹³⁰   *Ya know what I mean? And I grew up on their tapes.*
That's about as close as I came. And I had my first...oh I'm
old-school Brooklyn! Where all of them guys was. I'm just
saying, I wasn't there with them.

¹³¹   *I think that a lot of people may have discrepancies with*
where Rap is going and all that, but I think that people need to
realize that none of this stuff moves without young people. And
young people are viewing Rap artists and what they know as
Hip Hop a certain way. If we want to impact society in terms
of the way that they think about Hip Hop then I think that it
is probably two levels that those two guys were talking about
between KRS and my man right here [Hakim].

¹³²   *'Cause KRS seems like he want to bum-rush the*
executives and I'm with him (laughs)! *We just beat up about*
five of them and our message will be straight! We won't even
have no more fucking problems (more laughter)! *All y'all gotta*
do is call me and I'll do the beating (more laughter)!

¹³³   Daddy-O continued, *On the other level it's about*
impacting the shorties. On the other level it's about these kids.

'Cause these kids are seeing a certain thing and they admiring a certain thing that goes on around the country. And they're the one's that end up making a difference at the end of the day! It's them that make the difference!

134 *All of this shit that we going through and all that, it's 'cause of kids. It might be White kids starting to feel our flow and they parents ain't feeling their flow, but it's all about kids! It ain't about adults at all! Most of the people I'm looking at is adults in this room and it ain't about us at all! It's about them little shorties.*

135 *Them little shorties will tell you if you wack or if you ain't wack! Straight off! 'Why you don't like so and so?' 'Cause he's old to me now.' 'Why you like Snoop?' 'Oh 'cause da da da da da!' 'Why you don't like da?' I'm telling you these shorties will tell you all in all!*

136 *I mean we all...we don't really have to go through...all we gotta do is listen to KRS records to find out why ya know, society ya know, fucking they heads up in teaching and all that* (laughter). *You know what I'm saying?*

137 *But I'm just saying, the bottom line is that, the only thing I wanted to say is that, to answer the first question about preserving it, I think it's all really, I think it's all really about them little shorties. If we don't give them shorties something to look at that they can admire and that they wanna touch out and that they wanna be then we ain't gonna win with them anyway, it's just gonna be somebody else to move in on their life and say 'I'm top dog!' cause that's all it is around the country!*

138 TC Islam then proposed an apprenticeship program called the *Zulu Media Education Project* where young people could get the technical skills needed to create their own jobs.

139 He said, as an example, *Now say we have like a Hip Hop Deejay like a DJ, he gets paid to show shorties how to Deejay. See what we need to do is start teaching these shorties*

how to do camera work. I mean 9 times out of 10 what's the biggest problem at our shows? 'Yo sound man, what's up with my D.A.T. [Digital Audio Tape]!' Go in the studio, I got a Rock engineer trying to give me a hip-hop sound! But I got a shorty around my way who got a four tracker and all he's doing is looping beats! He got an ear for this!

[140] *Technically, he does not know how to go into the studio, and he look at a 24-track board and go 'Oh my God!' (laughter) But if he gets the technical training, not only does he have a ear for it, but he gots the heart and the soul for it.*

[141] *So I take my man shorty on tour with me, he's working in the studio with me, he got concepts for Rap videos but does not know anything about editing, steadicams, or anything like that. Now he's getting the technical training at the age of 14, 15.*

[142] *So what we have to do is give them an opportunity to create their own jobs within this culture of Hip Hop and that's the only way it will be preserved. You understand where I'm coming from? Training the shorties! That will be taking them off the streets! We give them something that they love 'cause right now the carrots that are dangled in front of their faces are drugs, guns, these fake images of participating in the American dream, which I say scheme of things! You know what I'm saying?*

[143] *So we got to rescue our kids with what? This, Hip Hop kid! You can get paid by doing this man! Make your own job, know what I'm saying, at something you love doing.* Later in the conversation and after much debate and many ideas we returned the conference toward the...*role of being a professional yet still being loyal to the cause of preserving Hip Hop.*

[144] I then continued, *Yeah, I mean the conversation that we are having here is excellent. Because it's a lot of vibes, thoughts that are happening now. Uh, one thing, let me just*

reiterate, the original question was, uh, can you be professional, uh, and be a part of Hip Hop? Brother here mentioned that, 'define professional,' we never really got around to that.

145   *Uh, but let me throw it on the floor. And uh, say number one that, um, in one breath, being professional, uh, is sort of like going through college. It's like, well, just before you get to college, when you're taking the entrance exam, you know what you wanna be, you know what you wanna do, you're gonna fight for this, you're gonna fight for that. But then when you actually go through college, when you pick up your degree you're actually somebody else.*

146   *My point was, or is, can you be a part...can a Afrika Bambaataa, can a Kool Herc be A&R at a record company, play that game and be true to the cause? I'm not saying it can or can't happen, I'm still trying to figure out if it can.*

147   And many voices rose up again; a member of Zulu nation (a chemist) responded to me saying, *You brothas taught us who are right now in college how to do that. You taught us that I can be criminal-minded and still make a contribution to my community with my double major in Chemistry and Biology. You told us that you can go back into the community and have this mind and be a professional and show these young kids, yo, you can do this and you can be that. So we can do that! And anyone who says we can't, you wrong!* The room erupted into applause and many voices trying to make a point.

148   The Zulu Nation chemist continued, *You can't define yourself in some parameters set up by somebody else. You gotta define your own Self the same way GOD did!*

149   *The same way when I was growing up, you know what I'm saying, when I was the smartest kid in the class everybody was like, 'Yo, duke you corny! Man you wack!' Naw, that's not the case. Yo, I'm gonna use my mind to further myself and everyone else and y'all showed me that I can do that!*

150   And then Afrika Bambaataa said, *And the way you*

can do that is, you gotta know that you can't let money become your god (applause).

¹⁵¹ Then I jumped in saying, *Uh, in terms of money being a god, right, we cannot! I mean, that will cloud everything. But the system in which we're under attack* [from] *is capitalism. In which we are going to need some kind of economic plan.*

¹⁵² Afrika Bambaataa then responded, *Naw, I'm not saying that…you know you gonna need economics. But what I'm saying is SELLING OUT! Like if you feel…like whatever I believe, I'm ready to die for it. Now if I say that, um, if I feel that the companies haven't gone my way, I'm ready to quit! Let somebody else take that job. <u>I'm not gonna take the money to get me to sellout my people or to sellout Hip Hop all for big money or statuses. I'm for real with this!</u>*

¹⁵³ I then responded, *Well, that's my point, if everybody is real with this then we're gonna wind up not being professional because we're not going to take the shit! We're not gonna say 'Let's jerk this artist because he got dreads and this guy got jheri curls, we gonna go with him. You know to your heart that shit is wack. But if you say 'I'm pushing these dreads right here, that's what it is,' and you get fired, if we all do that then we gonna wind up being in our nucleus again* (and the room erupted into many voices).

¹⁵⁴ And then Hakim Green (the school teacher/emcee) said, *This is the way you do it. Going back to what Havoc was saying earlier, he was saying that you know, you walk through parks or whatever, you see statues dedicated to leaders. When in all actuality, the motherfucker you looking at ain't really lead shit! He was just the face man.*

¹⁵⁵ *Now you see the artist out on stage, he's the face man. What you need is somebody that's not involved in the politics of music that's saying you owe your allegiance to me! You fuck up, you gotta answer to me!*

¹⁵⁶ I then responded saying, *So wait a minute. The person*

who is professional, then, cannot truthfully say that they are part of Hip Hop (the room erupted into many voices again). And we began to look closer at the word *accountability.*

[157] And the Zulu Nation chemist/biologist said, *See, the problem is, is that we're not ALL doing it. See, if this side of the room is like 'Yo fuck that you gonna do this' and that side is like, 'Na na,' then there's a division that you can drive through. But if we ALL saying, 'No, fuck that, we ALL doing it,' then you can't divide…you can't go through that!*

[158] And Jacqueline Hines from Hip Hop Incorporated followed up, saying, *I think we need to go even deeper than that. We have to deal with some sort of spirituality. If we talking about building anything, we have to deal with spirituality. We have to understand what it means when we DO something. Like what this brotha said about his job. Now if we're gonna build…ya know, what we're really doing is building a society. And part of society, is what's wrong right now, is we have no spirituality.*

[159] *So we have to bring spirituality back in effect! And once you have spirituality and you can come strong within yourself, then you can define what is going to happen in your life. Yes, you may have lost the best job you ever had, because you demanded to hear Rap music on your radio, but your spirituality will keep you strong and keep you moving and you KNOW things will only get better!*

[160] After a short debate with everyone throwing in ideas and many voices speaking at the same time, Afrika Bambaataa again called the meeting to order by saying, *WE NEED A STRUCTURED DISCIPLINE ORDER!*

[161] Afrika Bambaataa continued, *Whether you have professionalism, whether you don't have it, it still comes ALL under one roof that's getting it ALL together under a union to put out ideas that have structure, that have people accountable, and let them know that if they fuck up they out the door and the*

next one is in. You got to have a whole accountable discipline order...and <u>we got to put our money where our mouth is and be doers of the words!</u>

162   *One thing we can learn from watching the Nation of Islam is getting up and doing something for Self. And that's what it all bows down to, that we got to get up and DO SOMETHING FOR SELF!*

163   *Right now hip-hop belongs to other people and we got to take it back and get to the ones sitting on the higher top that got dough come on and sit down. Somehow, uh, basketball stars, uh, other professionalism, 'cause that's the only thing we have is our artists. We don't control the agencies that book us just like we don't control where we live at.*

164   And the Zulu Nation chemist/biologist said, *But the ironic thing is without us they don't have shit! That's the whole bottom line.* Harry Allen then said, *But the bigger irony is that they do have us!* The chemist replied, *They have some of us.* Harry Allen responded, *They have most of us!*

165   Then an activist/artist said, *Yo, we gotta keep it real! I know everybody's willing to die for the cause and all that but I'm a be dead honest! OK, Kool Herc, Bam, y'all are from a dying breed of brothas out here called 'I don't give a fuck I'm going for mine!' That unity is dead! OK because of infiltration. And that's why when they say about the sellout, the sellout is only a sellout if his mind is warped to that extent.*

166   *OK, right now brothas in here is dealing about E.S.P., <u>E</u>xtra <u>S</u>elf <u>P</u>reservation! If it comes to your baby 'bout to starve and shit or you down for the cause, fuck that, ya child gotta eat! And that's how the mentality is. So we gotta realize, we gotta keep it real! I mean I'm down to go for mine to the highest, but when you feel you gonna die in a cause by yourself, you gonna get shot, bowe! 'Well, nigga stood for his, nigga out!' That's dead man!*

167   And then Crazy Legs said, *A lot of brothas ain't*

selling out Hip Hop 'cause you can't sellout what you was never down with. Now, what they're basically doing is selling out THEIR souls. That's what they're doing. 'Cause most of the brothas in the industry were never down with Hiphop Kulture. OK, so they don't even understand how to use it for the community because they're worried about their pockets.

[168] And then Hip Hop activist X-Man said, *Let me interject this one thing 'cause I think for the most part we've been dancing around the issue, ah, for real. And the issue when it comes down to it is how do we acquire and maintain power! Because that's what it comes down to. Let me say a couple of things.*

[169] *In this professionalism piece, we don't want to confuse professionalism with white-collarism because those are two different and separate things. Professionalism means one that is proficient in a particular area…and accepted by their peers. You see what I'm saying?*

[170] *So a doctor just can't go out and claim that he's a doctor. He has to go through a mental learning process and then still be accepted by his peers. And when we develop that kind of professionalism it's gonna weed out all the fakers anyway.*

[171] *The second thing, we do need to come to a definition of Hip Hop that needs to be distributed. We need to come to a collective decision on what Hip Hop is! And define it in a way that gives some leeway; in other words, don't be so focused, don't be so narrow that you define everybody out of it. But define it within a context that people who are down with it can fit into it in some way, shape or form.*

[172] *And the last thing is that we can't talk about power… 'cause what I don't wanna see, 'cause I'll just tell ya, what I don't wanna see, I don't wanna see that archive that has all of the history of Hip Hop, but in the street it's not reflective of what went into that institution.*

[173] *And we don't want Hip Hop or anything else to go the*

way of the dodo in the street, even though you have an archive that's sitting there! And the archive idea is the first step to that preservation.

174   *The last thing is that <u>we can't even talk about power in Hip Hop as if it is divorced from power and organization of young people</u>. We can't talk about it. Because you can't play ball with one hand! I mean you can try, and some people are good. But you will never be as effective as being able to use both hands. You'll never be as effective!*

175   *<u>So if we're talking about serious, serious, a political move, a social move, an economic move, then hip-hop as an industry, as a forum, needs to also be about the political and economic and social organization of our people</u>. If it's not about that, it's talking yin yang! That's it* (applause)!

176   And then the Father of Hip Hop, Kool DJ Herc, spoke saying, *Yo, check this out! Right now the bottom line is about money! A'ight. Money's going here, here, here and here and <u>it ain't concentrated in one place for Hip Hop to build this.</u>*

177   *<u>We need somewhere, a Hip Hop complex itself, a large place that every artist who comes to New York who's somebody will have to come through there and perform. And that money goes somewhere for us for whatever we want to do with it.</u> It's about money!*

178   *It's about money and <u>what Hip Hop's money can do for community and for us political wise. It's a force!</u> It just hasn't been harnessed yet. A'ight. And we trying to bring that shit under one fuckin' roof! That's all it is. <u>We need somewhere that IS Hip Hop.</u> With a big fuckin' parking lot... so the police ain't gotta come on horseback and chase us out of every fuckin' place, where you can't get in.*

179   *There gotta be some place like that in California, West Side, East Coast, West, East Coast, West Coast gotta have a big fuckin' complex. And <u>whoever making money off of Hip</u>*

Hop gotta be in that place. Otherwise they can't go nowhere! That's how its gotta be!

180   This meeting continued on for several more hours. However, at the conclusion of this groundbreaking meeting it was clear to all that Hip Hop was more than just *some good music* and that it was time to organize culturally.

181   It was here and at this time that I began gathering the notes, documents and other inspirational materials to create a solid strategy toward what WE said as a community WE wanted for OURSELVES as a group.

182   This is where we began to seriously approach Hip Hop as an international culture, and it was here that we set our cultural direction as a unique, self-conscious group of people. This is what we, as a *temple* for Hip Hop, are loyal to.

183   There have been numerous other follow-up Hip Hop meetings, conferences and summits since our 1994 meeting; however, the intentions of this first meeting are what the Temple of Hiphop remains most loyal to.

184   These paragraphs are direct, unedited transcriptions as to some of what was argued at our 1994 *Meeting of the Minds* conference. The underlined sections of this transcription are the direct influences and intentions of our Hip Hop preservation movement.

185   Study carefully, and not only use this piece of unedited history as an accurate reference for true Hip Hop scholarship and activism, but through meditation and/or visualization place your *Self* in the meeting as a citizen of Hiphop Kulture; what would you have said? What would you have suggested? After such a meeting, what would you have done?

186   This particular transcription is very important to the awareness of the truly committed Hip Hop activist. This is a major part of what guides the Temple of Hiphop and all true Hiphoppas seeking to advance the culture of Hip Hop.

187   The time for talk and no action is over! The time for complaining with no plan of action has ceased. If we are truly serious about freedom, justice and equality under just laws, it's time we start acting like the community we keep begging America to be. America has its own problems, as do we.

188   Therefore, let us get serious about our own future as Hiphoppas. Let us go down in history as the greatest urban movement of all time! Let us mature and rise to the cultural heritage that we have been born into. Let us as Hiphoppas fulfill *The Dream* of our parents. This is the meaning of OUR movement.

189   Yes, there are other movements of worthy cause, even worthy of more immediate attention. But Hip Hop's preservation is what GOD has given to us as OUR task. Hip Hop is our burden. In history, this is what future generations will know our *moves meant*.

190   Our *moves* for the preservation and further development of Hip Hop include a full-service Hip Hop city, and it is this ultimate vision that defines the meaning of our *moves* today—our *move-meant*. This is the *meaning* of why we *move*.

191   But we also know that revolution only benefits those who participate in it. New ideas and revolutionary movements can be preached from every street corner in the World, but if the listener is still unable to participate in the actualization of such ideas and movements then such talk is only entertainment. This is what Hip Hop has been experiencing ever since our famous *Meeting of the Minds* conference in 1994.

192   Even though many of us have spoken strongly and accurately about the challenges facing our Hip Hop community, very few have actually organized themselves against such challenges. And even worse, when people like

myself step up to begin the process of organization, fear, doubt and distrust from our own people cripple our plans before we can even begin.

[193]   I will call no names here because this Gospel is a historical document that can have lasting effects upon the children of such saboteurs; everyone should be given time to mature past their own fears. However, in my time (your past) I've been criticized as being a "false prophet," "cult leader," "Antichrist," of "wanting to own Hip Hop," and even as being a member of the illuminati, but all of these criticisms and critics have fallen to the *waste*-side; I am only doing what we all said we wanted done!

[194]   Those who are serious about Hip Hop's preservation and further development have taken the vow I AM HIP HOP, and have united with others to form the Temple of Hip Hop, which is the actualization of our goals and collective vision. We have a plan and we will fulfill it. In fact, in your time (my future) we have already fulfilled it. This is the meaning of our movement. VICTORY OVER THE STREETS! There it is.

THE THIRTEENTH OVERSTANDING
THE HIP HOP ACTIVIST

1 After 1994 I attended many more *Hip Hop* summits, conferences and meetings where we all declared our loyalty to Hip Hop's preservation, but then got side-tracked and even stifled once we returned to the pressures and responsibilities of our daily lives.

2 While these famous summits, conferences and meetings took place during the 1990s it was KRS who was expected to attend and take notes and then advise the Hip Hop community on a plan of action relevant to its survival and growth. And I have not forgotten my commitment. Such was my honor in the 1990s and remains the same today.

3 As I have observed on several occasions, the most pressing issues expressed at many of our *meetings* and *summits* over the years have been the need to restore our ancient ways of life before the invasions of western civilizations upon our tribes and natural resources, to raise our present quality of life as Hiphoppas, and to preserve and document the original cultural elements, traditions, history and customs of Hip Hop.

4 Of course, freedom from the corporate exploitation of our artistic elements as well as the establishment of a code of conduct designed for the peace and prosperity of individual Hiphoppas were also among the most passionate themes brought up at our historic discussions.

5 Together as a multi-cultural people, the restoration of OUR lost civilizations, the enhancement of OUR present quality of life, the proper documentation and

preservation of OUR artistic elements and history, freedom from negative corporate exploitation, and a Hip Hop way of life that promotes peace and prosperity has always been the concerns of the *conscious* Hip Hop movement.

6   These have always been the collective agendas that have formed our governing principles and our cultural movement as *Hiphoppas*. Basically, we are seeking *freedom and justice for all*. And it is the realization of this goal that we (the Temple of Hip Hop) are committed to.

7   Yes, there may be other more pressing concerns to address regarding Hip Hop; however over the past 14 years this is what we have said amongst ourselves at our historic meetings to be the most pressing of OUR concerns as a community—*freedom and justice for all*.

8   However, I have seen too many sincere and *conscious* Hip Hop activists and artists struggle and even fail to achieve their goals because of the enormous distractions and temptations of the material World. Some activists spend too much time criticizing the work of other activists, thus stagnating the collective political and social aspirations of our group.

9   Many of our wisest leaders, artists and advisors are hampered down in life, working to pay rents, mortgages, college loans, business loans, childcare, cell phone bills, car payments, food, gas, clothing, etc. And no one seems to ever have enough money to do what they need to do! Even the so-called *rich!*

10   Sure, we may get up in front of a podium or radio and express the most logical ideas regarding Hip Hop's preservation and development, but if, after such advice is given, there is no one capable of carrying out such lofty ideas because of poverty and/or a personal lack of character, vision, emotional sensitivity and/or organization, then it is as if such speakers were simply talking to themselves.

[11] The audience of eager revolutionaries cannot act upon what was being suggested because the very character of the audience and the beliefs that such an audience may hold make it difficult (even impossible) for them to even see, and then actualize, such revolutionary ideas.

[12] This is why true activism requires teaching as well as preaching. The biggest challenge to the activist is the very people who are to benefit from that activist's ideas and actions. If the community desires freedom, then the activist must spend some time teaching the principles of freedom to her people; otherwise the community will not know when they have achieved their goal, and in most cases will actually fight against the very goal they've set for themselves.

[13] In my observation, it will take a community of educated, organized, free-thinking and prosperous Hiphoppas to achieve Hip Hop's real and actual preservation. Even beyond money, the Hip Hop community must know peace. We must be content and confident in the reality of who we are as a *People*.

[14] Revolutionary talk is always stimulating to hear, but if the people hearing such talk are not at peace first amongst themselves, such desperateness caused by insecurity and doubt will collapse and betray our movement before it can really even start.

[15] In my observation, Hip Hop's preservation begins with peace and prosperity leading to Hip Hop's independence. Hip Hop must become self-sufficient, self-sustaining and self-directed. Living and supporting the very industry that we say is *ripping us off* is self-destructive and hypocritical. We cannot ever expect to liberate Hip Hop from those who exploit its resources if we are dependent upon the same for our very survival.

[16] As simple as this may sound, many are still helplessly dragged along in the World's currents and events because of

their own attachment to the World's stimuli. After a while they become unfamiliar and afraid of ideas and solutions that seem to go beyond the World's boundaries. They may posture as if they possessed free minds but in reality their worldview revolves around what the *powers that be*, or what some secret government agency or society, won't let them do. In fact, the more they speak against the World, the more they become dependent upon it.

17   Ironically, because the World does not belong to them they become very insecure about their own affiliation with the World. *The World is not right! We all slaves! They got us trapped!* Many such activists feel that at any moment they can lose everything that sustains them, and that they must work harder to maintain and hold on to the little bit that they believe they have. This life is lived in desperation, and in no way can such a person ever be a truly committed revolutionary. Such a person creates enemies where there are none, and poverty where none should exist.

18   And while you may perceive that such a life is lived mainly by poor people, the Truth of the matter is that I am talking more about the conduct and character of many working/employed people and even some very rich and educated people.

19   As I have observed, the act of *desperation* seems to transcend all classes of people, all races, all ethnicities, all genders, all faiths, EVERYONE! As with insecurity, doubt and fear, desperation knows no race or social class; everyone is a potential candidate—even the rich, even the employed, even the educated, even the activist.

20   This is why (as an activist) it is better to live a simple and content life than a life full of commitments and busyness. Know this. The rich are the most insecure individuals within any community because the base of their power is money, which is always temporary. The activist who has

built up large sums of money for herself is equally trapped by the business relationships that have created such riches.

21   This form of activism is limited because of one's loyalty to other relationships. Those who make their living from the same structure that everyone else is trying to rid themselves of cannot be expected to lead a revolutionary movement toward change. Their desperateness is shown in their attachment to Worldly riches and corporate power. They can help but they cannot lead.

22   Such individuals struggle as activists because to be an activist one must discern between what is right and what is wrong for one's community beyond the benefits of those who may be exploiting the community's resources for corporate gain. To be a true Hip Hop activist one must be self-directed with a minimum amount of corporate ties.

23   For if you make your living in the same corporate structure that seeks to exploit the very community that you are seeking to preserve and further develop, then discernment is almost impossible. The rules of business demand that you be liked by everyone, and take no position on anything. Those who hold these views will not discern between right and wrong, they benefit either way.

24   Unless you are willing to be hated by those you love, and/or become impoverished by those who you have made rich, you shall in no way make any lasting change or enduring progress for your community. Revolution is not a popularity contest. Successful activism is caused by one's sincere love and understanding of and for one's cause.

25   In the business world, cash and credit rule everything around us—not justice. In the world of justice, balance and the common good rule everything around us. In justice, we don't just eat the fruits we find along the journey of life; every now and then we look up to see where such fruits are coming from. This is balance, and this is right.

26   As a Hip Hop activist, do not be led by the rich or adopt their philosophy of "self first." This is what makes a person desperate and insecure, even with riches; they find themselves in the position of pleasing everyone and in doing so, they please even the forces that work against the cause of their protest.

27   For as long as your personality and reputation are based upon your financial status you shall make your financial status the priority of your survival. And this is what leads to fear; it is an extreme act or thought of self-protection.

28   Your impulse to preserve yourself physically, mentally, emotionally, financially, politically, etc., causes you to become fearful. It is in the extreme concern for your own safety (or interests) that causes you to become afraid or insecure. Compulsive attempts at one's own self-interests lead to fear and insecurity.

29   However, once you free yourself by giving up the protection and guidance of your *Self* to GOD you immediately inherit courage. When we surrender ourselves to that higher, deeper guidance, GOD's Protective Spirit or GPS, we rest in the mystery of our being, knowing that all things are working toward the fulfillment of our most comfortable and safe conditions.

30   Whereas fear may be the result of an extreme concern for one's self, courage may be the result of an extreme concern for others. To lend oneself to something other than one's self requires courage. Help is a good example of courage. Teaching is another good example of courage. Self-sacrifice requires courage.

31   Ridding one's self of desperateness, insecurity, worry and fear are all exercises of the Spirit and are essential to the success of any activist. You cannot buy your way out of insecurity, and you cannot purchase courage. In fact, the Notorious B.I.G., who was notorious for flashing huge

amounts of cash and living lavishly, warned us. He said, *Mo' money, mo' problems.*

³² And in no way am I implying that money in and of itself is somehow not to be accumulated and used. Not at all. However to not be happy, or feel secure, or to not feel motivated to pursue change unless you are rich, or to feel that the accumulation of money and/or property makes you more human than someone without such resources is simply NOT the path of an attuned Hip Hop activist. Money must never use the activist; it is the activist who must learn how to efficiently use money.

³³ Hip Hop's activists who have not secured a basic standard of living for themselves independent of the World's institutions are continuously distracted from activism by the influence of the World calling them *back to work!* A true Hip Hop activist cannot be addicted to the power of money, nor can money ever be the reason a true Hip Hop activist is motivated to move or act. Such an activist is moved by principles and virtues and lives a life as such.

³⁴ Biggie warned *mo' money, mo' problems.* So why would any activist who has truly studied the events of Hip Hop's culture still want to pursue a life based upon the accumulation of money? Answer: Addiction. Not to drugs or to sex, but to security. And not even in a bad or greedy way. But simply addiction to the security that money provides, believing that nothing can be done without a certain amount of money.

³⁵ Many see no other life. Others believe in no other power. They see no other way that they would rather live. Many Hip Hop activists are actually addicted to the belief that their actual security as a human being is connected to their Worldly validations and accumulation of money.

³⁶ In Truth, they have forgotten or simply don't know how to live without money, or enjoy a life in Spirit

where you live within your means and people give you the things you need for free. Such a life is taught here within the Overstandings of this instrument. However, this life is crazy to those who rely upon the World's security over GOD's reality.

37   And this is not a judgment, simply a conclusion. In Truth, such is not the fault of the money-addicted, they were trained (educated) to believe that everything must be worked for and then paid for, that only the World's institutions offer real power and legitimacy, and that freedom is attained within a retirement that never comes. They've been educated to believe *there's no other way*. I find that this is how many great minds are trapped and turned to desperate acts just to survive.

38   Those who still live desperate lives based upon the accumulation of money are simply too preoccupied by their own survival and pleasures to really focus upon the well-being and development of others. Sure, most Hip Hop activists can think and speak on Hip Hop's music, culture and politics but find it difficult to really live and act, create and develop the same.

39   This condition seems to be our only challenge as a Hip Hop community. In my time we are simply too desperate as a people to achieve the goals that we say we desire for ourselves collectively. We are simply too dependent upon the World and its temporary security to overcome that same World for everlasting life. We are all simply looking out for ourselves and this is why we cannot seem to protect each other. This is why we lack unity!

40   As the great prophet Kwame Ture has taught us, *The capitalist system will so confuse people that they will think that they can think abstractly. They used to tell me in Latin 'cogito, ergo sum'—I think therefore I am. But we know that this is not the Truth because those of us who are sitting here*

know that there are many who <u>are</u>, but don't <u>think</u>.

⁴¹ As a matter of fact, there is no way that one can think abstractly about anything. The only way that you can think about something is when you are involved in it, because thought is nothing other than the reflection of fast action for the correction of future actions. Thought must be based upon action. Where there is no action there can be no thought.

⁴² If you have never taken physics, you cannot <u>think</u> about physics. Of course, you can think that you think about physics, but unless you <u>think</u> physics you cannot think about physics. You may, while watching a basketball game on television or at the game, criticize every basketball player. But unless you play basketball you cannot <u>think</u> about basketball. If you are not involved in your people's struggle, you <u>cannot</u> think about your people's struggle.

⁴³ If you are not involved in the African revolution, you <u>cannot</u> think for the African revolution. The problem can be highlighted here in the past between the White 'left' and the African movement. It's we who have the action! It's we who confront the police! It is we who have the 'sit-in' movement, it's we who threw the bricks and bottles against the police, it is we who shed our blood, but it is the White 'left' who comes to give us the ideology. This is absurd!

⁴⁴ This is absurd just by what is going on in Azania South Africa. In Azania South Africa the only people dying in the streets are us. It is from OUR actions that we get OUR thoughts. Nobody else will come from our actions to give us correct thoughts. Thought is one of the weaknesses of the African revolution.

⁴⁵ This is where those who say that they are our friends come and take advantage of us. The weakness of the African revolution is that <u>we have collective action but we do not have collective thoughts</u>. We have collective action as a people, and serious collective action! We can rise up in the greatest

imperialistic country in the World, America. And we can burn down 270 cities in a weekend and then sit down for 30 years because we have no collective thought to continue the struggle.

46   When it comes to the Hip Hop community, with all of our awards, and validations, and money, and property, as a community we still cannot seem to protect OUR intellectual property from those who seek only to exploit OUR value as human beings, simply because we are disorganized as a *People* today.

47   Sure, we can talk eloquently about freedom, peace, love, unity, and having fun, we can talk about revolution, we can rally, we can march, we can write books and do lectures for a lifetime, but if we are still desperate, still disorganized and still have not broken the chains of the World's security upon our flesh and minds, we are as crack cocaine addicts throwing crack cocaine against the wall of the crack house in an attempt to break our own addictions to crack.

48   WE MUST BECOME AND REMAIN ORGANIZED! And such organization comes from the loyalty and practice of OUR principles. As the prophet Kwame has said on many occasions, *ORGANIZE, ORGANIZE, ORGANIZE!*

49   *The prophet has already taught us that the only way that we will arrive* (at freedom) *is when the masses of our People are organized! We are a powerless People because the masses of our People are disorganized. <u>Political power comes only from the organized masses.</u> All of the problems we face everywhere, the problem of drugs is simply a reflection of the lack of organization in our community because we do not control anything in our community—who comes in, who goes out, what comes in, what goes out, how it comes in and for what reason. We control absolutely nothing because we are disorganized! The only way that we will organize ourselves is when we ourselves come to organize ourselves.*

⁵⁰   This also means that money cannot be the sole reason that you are engaged in revolutionary change. Real change, not money, must be the goal. Those whose priorities are based upon the accumulation of money and/or power will never be able to remain committed to any organized struggle toward freedom and/or real change for long.

⁵¹   It is us who must desire freedom for ourselves, and such a desire must come from within. It must be our true desire; freedom must be the essence of our very being. But this is where the problem starts.

⁵²   You cannot free yourself from exploitation by becoming rich; you free yourself from exploitation by eliminating want by developing your mind to exist outside of World security. This is a matter of principles and your loyalty to them.

⁵³   The less you want, the fewer chances someone has of telling you how much you are worth, where to go, what to do, how to do it, and what time to do it. The less you need from the World and its agents for your survival and comfort, the happier you shall be. However, these are spiritual lessons; these ideas are based upon a principled life. Self-creation based upon one's independent principles is the key to life!

⁵⁴   The Hip Hop activist lives a principled life, a simple life. Not a poor life, but a simple and easy-to-manage life grounded upon one's principles. Activism on any level requires an already-attained level of freedom and ease on the part of the activist. A true activist has already overcome something or someone in opposition to the goal and they bring such knowledge to the planning table for the collective good of all. Activists should have already attained that which they are preparing to lead their people to. A good and effective activist comes with a set of principles that she remains accountable to, and others can hold her

to—this builds trust.

55   A true Hip Hop activist has already been to the destination discussed and back again, and can now explain to other potential activists the *action* and mind-state that need be taken to achieve the goal. Even if it is only worked out on paper, if the other activists can see where the plan goes, and they have a firm view as to what is at stake and what is required, an actual movement for change can begin.

56   The Hip Hop activist must have alternative sources of survival other than that of the World; otherwise it shall be very difficult for such an activist to overcome the traps as well as the checks and balances of oppression. Principles are indeed one's alternative source of survival outside of the World's validations and securities.

57   A true Hip Hop activist is not someone who has woken up one morning fed up with the choices of her society and has decided to protest. A true Hip Hop activist has already tracked a clear path toward the goals which are being discussed by the group. The Hip Hop activist is led by her principles, which should match the interests of the group.

58   However to think and act in this way, one must be motivated by forces beyond the physical World. To really live and work in this way you will have to make one very important life-changing decision. You will have to decide once and for all whether you desire the World and its ways or the Spirit (your principles) and its ways?

59   In my observation, the true Hip Hop activist must have a "divine" connection in order to actually DO the work of preserving Hip Hop and speaking out on behalf of Hip Hop's controversial issues in the World. In addition to tactical organization, the truly effective Hip Hop activist uses prayer, affirmation, visualization, meditation, chanting, fasting, poetry, dance and other supernatural means to achieve the goal of preserving Hip Hop and protecting

one's self against fear, insecurity and depression that can develop later in life.

60   The Hip Hop activist has no time to be distracted by the pressures, doubts and temptations of the World. Through certain timeless spiritual principles the Hip Hop activist operates outside of the World. In the Spirit, the World and those who depend upon it are no match for a true Hip Hop activist that also operates spiritually!

61   Today's Hip Hop activist must first protest against the addictions and temptations of her own mind before seeking to protest against unjust acts! For if she is not strong from within, the temptations of the World shall distract the activist and lead her astray. The true Hip Hop activist must know God.

62   The true Hip Hop activist must feel God, and you will not come to feel God through your physical senses and ordinary human forms of comprehension. Books alone won't do it! The oneness will be revealed to you in Spirit after you have proven that you can be trusted. This is real!

63   In other words, if lust, fear and doubt still overwhelm your mind and override your physical senses, then you simply cannot be trusted. If you are still addicted to the illusions of the material World then you cannot be trusted with the Truth of the *Spirit realm*. You can be loved. You can be taught. You can even be blessed; but you cannot be trusted. It's like trusting your own child with all of your belongings knowing that he or she is addicted to crack cocaine!

64   Adopting the *Divine Performance* as your personal character (or any spiritual path that you can commit to) shows your God that you can be trusted. Know this. The universe itself is an intelligence that will not reveal certain aspects of itself to you until you prove that you can be trusted. Remember, the universe is alive and it responds to maturity.

65   This is what it means to be of righteous character. It

means that you can be trusted. No one will give you anything if cannot be trusted with what you have already received.

66   In the *Spirit realm*, which is the cause of the physical World, there is no separation of things. Everything is one thing. And everything is aware and conscious. We separate the true reality of people, places and things so that we may understand them. But in Truth, everything is really one thing!

67   With your mind you choose what you want for your physical World out of the *Spirit realm* that you actually live within.

68   Know this. The *Spirit realm* is like a supermarket. Everything is there but you decide upon what you need to survive based on your own values, awareness, likes, dislikes and wants. In fact, you decide upon what you want based on the purpose for which you have entered the supermarket. Ask your *Self* now: *What is my purpose?*

69   Your purpose is directly connected to the intent of the great oneness (GOD). Your purpose has a consciousness of its own that comes from a realm far deeper than your physical reality. Once you have found your purpose you have also found the intention of the conscious universe for you, and this validates and empowers your activism.

70   In fact, when you know your purpose, you shall also know what already exists for you in the now reality of the *Spirit realm*. And it is from this knowing that you plan your activism.

71   For it makes no sense to protest that which does not stand in your way! The Hip Hop activist is motivated to protest when some external force stops, stagnates or in some way impedes the pursuit of that activist's innate purpose or the collective freedom of the community.

72   Any successful warrior will tell you to *choose your battles,* and this is what the Hip Hop activist must do as

well. The Hip Hop activist is advised to join movements, rallies and protests that are in harmony with her purpose; in this way you enter the battle with supernatural assistance!

73   You must limit your awareness of everything else to your purpose. Bring your purpose into existence by being only it. Don't just do your purpose, be your purpose! Your purpose is your connection to the divine. It is your true *Self!* And when one seeks to hinder your divine/true *Self,* divine protection, divine guidance, divine healing, etc., automatically come to your aid.

74   Therefore, you should decide things according to your purpose, you should protest according to your purpose, and you should join organizations that are in alignment with your purpose. Yes, there are many conditions and circumstances to protest, but you will only be successful at your protest if the true intent of your protest matches the preservation and further development of your true life purpose.

75   As a final thought, the Hip Hop activist MUST BE ORGANIZED! What does this mean? It means first that we must simply be superior to our opposition. We must assess the strengths and weaknesses of our opponents and simply outdo them, outperform them, and outmaneuver them. We simply must be better than those we go up against.

76   Second, we must be really willing to win our battles; failure and/or defeat CANNOT BE AN OPTION! We must be specific with our challenges and honest about our own weaknesses and strengths. We must get, be and remain PREPARED TO WIN!

77   Third, The Hip Hop activist must spend quality time with the Hip Hop community teaching the core principles, tactics and beliefs of what we claim to collectively want. Everyone in our community must know and understand what's at stake and their role in the achievement of the goal.

There must be one clear and concise goal that everyone understands and is capable of taking part in. We must know what success looks like.

[78] Fourth, the Hip Hop activist must live and love Hip Hop. For it is one's love for one's cause that reveals extraordinary tactics and overwhelming energy. Those who are paid to fight will never defeat those who fight for what they love!

[79] For if there is no passion to one's fight there will equally be no strength to one's fight. We must never be afraid to fight for that which we truly love! Again, the Hip Hop activist must live and love Hip Hop in order to be successful at her protest on behalf of Hip Hop!

[80] And finally, The Hip Hop activist must maintain the ability to recognize her victory. Most times a true activist will fight, fight, fight, fight, fight against some unjust condition for years, forming a protest habit which prevents that activist from seeing her own victory when it comes.

[81] Many times when you protest against an unjust condition it eventually changes or you gain more insight into what that situation actually is. In any event, if you are only seeking victory or revenge you will not know when to stop fighting and protesting, even after you have succeeded in removing the injustice. Here, you begin to fight against yourself and your own interests—even your own people.

[82] At some point you will either have to accept that you are successful in your protest and move on, or accept that you are unsuccessful in your protest and move on. Either way, at some point the situation does change and the true activist must maintain her ability to recognize such changes and adjust her plans accordingly.

[83] The true Hip Hop activist does not protest for the sake of revenge, or to look good, or to defeat the opponent. The true Hip Hop activist protests unjust situations because

such situations are unhealthy for everyone. The point is to bring awareness to the opposing party and recognize when the opposing party is making amends or has simply outgrown old ways.

84   For when we protest against unjust corporate practices we should always remember that we are in many ways protesting against real people with real families and real personal concerns of their own.

85   We must always remember that even though we are protesting an injustice, we must not become unjust and insensitive ourselves. And the first cause of injustice is the inability to feel for the suffering of others. We must never become as insensitive as those who we are protesting against. Remember, your enemy is also GOD's child.

86   Many times our opposition is afraid and nervous, even trapped and truly sorry for their deeds, but they must now put on a front for their peers because we have challenged them publicly. Sometimes it is our own anger that makes a simple situation worse. Remember, it is our own loud voices that cause our opposition to get even louder as a form of self-defense.

87   If we approach our opposition with a resolution that works for everyone most times we can solve some very difficult situations peacefully and swiftly. The idea is to approach unjust conditions with just conditions. The idea is to replace evil, fear and ignorance with righteousness, good faith and understanding. The purpose of our protest should be to fix the unjust situation, not seek revenge because of it.

88   It is not wise to approach evil, fear and ignorance with even more evil, fear and ignorance. The idea is to advance all parties away from evil, fear and ignorance because evil, fear and ignorance don't work for anybody!

89   For it is a fact that those who commit acts of injustice are either trapped by their own unjust conditions or they

are ignorant to the effects of their conditions. Either way, yelling, screaming, protesting or threatening, is like doing the same to a sick person in need of medical attention.

90   Most people would not yell and protest against a person who was generally depressed or had contracted a deadly disease, even if the sick person is totally disrespecting them. Most people would overlook the hostility of the sick person and seek to help the sick person get well. Using this example, we can see clearly that those who consciously commit acts of injustice are indeed sick to themselves. And if you dig a little deeper, you may find depression, loneliness, anxiety, stress, and/or even ignorance and/or basic immaturity at the center of the unjust person, corporation, or situation.

91   Therefore, our protest cannot be about simply achieving a victory that only satisfies our emotional or political hurt. Such victories are indeed temporary. Our protest must be about the upliftment of the entire situation we may find ourselves within no matter how unjust the situation may be.

92   Protesting against a liquor company, or a cigarette company, or an insurance company, or an oil company while people still use these products daily is a waste of the activist's time. However, teaching people (including the employees of such companies) about the harmful affects of abusing such products is a lot more effective and useful than threatening the corporation itself.

93   Seek the good in people and expect people to respond to good ideas that are beneficial to all. In his book *Why We Can't Wait*, the King outlines the ten commandments of nonviolent activism. He writes:

94   *Meditate daily on the teachings and life of Jesus.*

95   *Remember always that the nonviolent movement in Birmingham seeks justice and reconciliation.*

^{96} _Walk_ and _talk_ in the manner of love, for GOD is love.

^{97} _Pray_ daily to be used by GOD in order that all men might be free.

^{98} _Sacrifice_ personal wishes in order that all men might be free.

^{99} _Observe_ with both friend and foe the ordinary rules of courtesy.

^{100} _Seek_ to perform regular service for others and for the World.

^{101} _Refrain_ from the violence of fist, tongue, or heart.

^{102} _Strive_ to be in good spiritual and bodily health.

^{103} _Follow_ the directions of the movement and the captain on a demonstration.

^{104} This is the character of a true Hip Hop activist. You can modernize the words of this text, but the spirit of what is being said here is timeless and relevant to all Hip Hop activists seeking justice in unjust situations. There it is!

THE FOURTEENTH OVERSTANDING
THE HIP HOP DECLARATION OF PEACE

1   On May 16, 2001, at the United Nations headquarters in New York, 300 Hip Hop pioneers, artists, activists, authors, government officials and Temple Members, along with a variety of ministers, philosophers, and students, gathered at the *Delegates Dining Room* for the revealing and signing of the Hip Hop Declaration of Peace.

2   Harry Allen (author/activist), Ernie Paniccioli (author/ photographer/activist), Pop Master Fabel (b-boy/ Zulu Nation), Adam Clark (doctoral student at Union Seminary), James Mtume (producer/activist/musician), Professor Z (Ph.D./First Friend, Hiphop Kultural Specialist), Malik ONE (Temple of Hiphop), Chuck D. (Public Enemy, Emcee/activist/First Friend), Grandmaster Caz (Emcee/Hip Hop historian) Kool DJ Herc (Father of Hip Hop/b-boy, Emcee, Graffiti artist, Deejay), Dr. Roxanne Shanté (healer/Emcee), Thembisa Mshaka-Morris as master of ceremonies and myself announced the first draft of the Hip Hop Declaration of Peace. Three hundred attendees were given copies of the Hip Hop Declaration of Peace and encouraged to modify it. For one year (May 16, 2001–May 16, 2002), the Hip Hop Declaration of Peace remained open to public scrutiny and debate. Many voices contributed and many modifications were made.

3   The Hip Hop Declaration of Peace, presented to the United Nations Educational, Scientific and Cultural Organization (U.N.E.S.C.O.), the Ribbon International, Peace Action, New York's City Hall and the Riverside

Church in New York, serves as an empowering code of conduct for all Hiphoppas in our quest to further establish our Hip Hop nation.

4 The Hip Hop Declaration of Peace is an accumulation of all the interviews and notes taken at Hip Hop's famous and *not-so-famous* summits and conferences since 1987. Presented as advice, the Hip Hop Declaration of Peace settles general disputes that commonly arise between Hiphoppas while presenting Hip Hop's culture as a unified, self-governed community of peace and prosperity.

5 Capable of being handled like any other autonomous group that chooses to unite its power to vote, its power to purchase and its power to influence, Hip Hop (as culture) holds out the possibility for our children and ourselves to live a better quality of life.

6 Let no one define the essence of your being. The true and ultimate state of freedom is when you are free to define yourself. For if human beings cannot create and define themselves for themselves, then their humanity is indeed handicapped. Such a restriction is indeed the worst kind of bondage, for it implies that you do not truly direct yourself—even mentally.

7 Hip Hop influences the Hiphoppa's ability to self-create. However, once you are created, it is of extreme importance that you remain loyal to the *Self* that is created. In our case, once you have made the decision to be *Hiphop* it is the Hip Hop Declaration of Peace that serves as a guiding principle for your *Hiphop* lifestyle.

8 The Hip Hop Declaration of Peace proves the existence of our people; it defines the present intentions of our hearts today.

9 As scholars, we know the importance of establishing truly advanced states in human interaction. We know that technological advancements do not equate to being civilized.

We know that technology is not civilization, nor is material wealth, or even military strength actually the definition of a great civilization. In Truth, we know that civilized behavior requires advanced human interactions.

10   Civilization is based upon the ways in which human beings treat each other. No matter how rich, or how educated a nation is, or how many weapons a nation has; if it is still plagued with institutionalized racism, sexism, homophobia, discriminatory justice, and a blatant disregard for the well-being of its own citizenship through senseless acts of greed and the inability to follow its own laws and respect its own treaties at the very highest levels of its own government, such a nation's leadership is in no way civilized, nor can such a nation be called a *civilization*.

11   Such is the state of the countries in which many Hiphoppas live within today. But instead of pointing fingers, criticizing and judging other nations we (Hiphoppas) must continue the work that establishes our Hip Hop civilization in hopes that we may succeed and influence other nations to reach for their own higher ideals.

12   Through the Hip Hop Declaration of Peace we (Hiphoppas) begin the challenging process of civilizing and maturing ourselves. We seek to reach advanced states in our interactions toward one another and the development of our human society. We seek to progress and perfect our arts, sciences, specific writing and language techniques as well as our social and political institutions. For us (Hiphoppas) this marks the establishment and sustainment of our true state of freedom.

13   Through the Hip Hop Declaration of Peace in particular as well as throughout this Gospel of Hip Hop in general, we (Hiphoppas) seek spiritual, intellectual and cultural refinement. The Hip Hop Declaration of Peace is evidence of our intentions to be moral, humane and

reasonable people.

14   Yes, individual Hiphoppas may fall short of the mark, but the intentions of Hip Hop's cultural declarations and laws shall remain a beacon of guiding light for all people to reach for their highest human potentials. And it is this (Hip Hop's spiritual, political and cultural intention) that the Temple of Hip Hop teaches and defends.

15   This collective faith is the revolution for us! We believe that we can actually think, re-think and visualize ourselves out of oppression. We believe that by becoming a new people on the Earth we can escape the traps, habits and obstacles of our previous ethnic identities. Our revolution begins with OUR self-creation and the re-telling of OUR human story.

16   Our faith is that future Hiphoppas, having grown up seeing and hearing the advice of the Temple of Hip Hop, will learn from Hip Hop's successes and from Hip Hop's mistakes and continue the campaign to preserve true Hip Hop through the preservation of true Hiphoppas. There it is!

The Hip Hop Declaration of Peace

This *Hip Hop Declaration of Peace* guides Hiphop Kulture toward freedom from violence, and establishes advice and protection for the existence and development of the international Hiphop community. Through the principles of this *Hip Hop Declaration of Peace* we, Hiphop Kulture, establish a foundation of Health, Love, Awareness, Wealth, peace and prosperity for ourselves, our children and their children's children, forever.

For the clarification of Hiphop's meaning and

purpose, or when the intention of Hiphop is questioned, or when disputes between parties arise concerning Hiphop; Hiphoppas shall have access to the advice of this document, *The Hip Hop Declaration of Peace*, as guidance, advice and protection.

First Principle

Hiphop (Hip´Hop) is a term that describes our independent collective consciousness. Ever growing, it is commonly expressed through such elements as Breakin, Emceein, Graffiti Art, Deejayin, Beat Boxin, Street Fashion, Street Language, Street Knowledge and Street Entrepreneurialism. Wherever and whenever these and future elements and expressions of Hiphop Kulture manifest; this Hip Hop Declaration of Peace shall advise the use and interpretation of such elements, expressions and lifestyle.

Second Principle

Hiphop Kulture respects the dignity and sanctity of life without discrimination or prejudice. Hiphoppas shall thoroughly consider the protection and the development of life, over and before the individual decision to destroy or seek to alter its natural development.

Third Principle

Hiphop Kulture respects the Laws and agreements of its culture, its country, its institutions and whomever it does business with. Hiphop does not irresponsibly break Laws and commitments.

Fourth Principle

Hiphop is a term that describes our independent collective consciousness. As a conscious way of life, we acknowledge our influence on society, especially on children; and we shall forever keep the rights and welfare of both in mind. Hiphop Kulture encourages womanhood, manhood, sisterhood, brotherhood, childhood and family. We are conscious not to bring any intentional disrespect that jeopardizes the dignity and reputation of our children, elders and ancestors.

Fifth Principle

The ability to define, defend and educate ourselves is encouraged, developed, preserved, protected and promoted as a means toward peace and prosperity, and toward the protection and the development of our self-worth. Through knowledge of purpose and the development of our natural and learned skills, Hiphoppas are encouraged to always present their best work and ideas.

Sixth Principle

Hiphop Kulture honors no relationship, person, event, act or otherwise wherein the preservation and further development of Hiphop's culture, principles and elements are not considered or respected. Hiphop Kulture does not participate in activities that clearly destroy or alter its ability to productively and peacefully exist. Hiphoppas are encouraged to initiate and participate in fair trade and honesty in all negotiations and transactions.

Seventh Principle

The essence of Hiphop is beyond entertainment: The elements of Hiphop Kulture may be traded for money, honor, power, respect, food, shelter, information and other resources; however, Hiphop and its culture cannot be bought, nor is it for sale. It (Hiphop) cannot be transferred or exchanged by or to anyone for any compensation at any time or at any place. Hiphop is not a product. Hiphop is the priceless principle of our self-empowerment.

Eighth Principle

Companies, corporations, non and not-for-profit organizations, as well as individuals and groups that are clearly benefiting from the use, interpretation and/or exploitation of the term *Hiphop* (i.e., Hip Hop, hip-hop,) and the expressions and terminologies of Hiphop (i.e., Hip Hop, hip-hop,), are encouraged to commission and/or employ a full-time or part-time certified Hiphop Kultural Specialist to interpret and answer sensitive cultural questions regarding the principles and proper presentations of Hiphop's elements and culture; relative to businesses, individuals, organizations, communities, cities, as well as other countries.

Ninth Principle

May 3rd is Rap Music Day. Hiphoppas are encouraged to dedicate their own time and talent to self-development and for service to their communities. *Every third week in May is Hip Hop Appreciation Week.* During this time, Hiphoppas are encouraged to honor their ancestors, reflect upon their cultural contributions and appreciate the elements and principles of Hiphop Kulture. *November is Hiphop History Month.* During this time Hiphoppas are encouraged to participate in the creating, learning and honoring of Hiphop's history and historical cultural contributors.

Tenth Principle

Hiphoppas are encouraged to build meaningful and lasting relationships that rest upon Love, trust, equality and respect. Hiphoppas are encouraged not to cheat, abuse, or deceive their friends.

Eleventh Principle

The Hiphop community exists as an international culture of consciousness that provides all races, tribes, religions and styles of people a foundation for the communication of their best ideas and works. Hiphop Kulture is united as one multi-skilled, multi-cultural, multi-faith, multi-racial people committed to the establishment and the development of peace.

Twelfth Principle

Hiphop Kulture does not intentionally or voluntarily participate in any form of hate, deceit, prejudice or theft at any time. At no time shall Hiphop Kulture engage in any violent war within itself. Those who intentionally violate the principles of this *Declaration of Peace* or intentionally reject its advice, forfeit by their own actions the protections set forth herein.

Thirteenth Principle

Hiphop Kulture rejects the immature impulse for unwarranted acts of violence and always seeks diplomatic, nonviolent strategies in the settlement of all disputes. Hiphoppas are encouraged to consider forgiveness and understanding before any act of retaliation. War is reserved as a final solution when there is evidence that all other means of diplomatic negotiation have failed repeatedly.

Fourteenth Principle

Hiphoppas are encouraged to eliminate poverty, speak out against injustice and shape a more caring society and a more peaceful world. Hiphop Kulture supports a dialogue and action that heals divisions in society, addresses the legitimate concerns of humankind and advances the cause of peace.

Fifteenth Principle
Hiphoppas respect and learn from the ways of Nature, regardless of where we are on this planet. Hiphop Kulture holds sacred our duty to contribute to our own survival as independent, freethinking beings in and throughout the Universe. This planet, commonly known as *Earth,* is our nurturing parent and Hiphoppas are encouraged to respect Nature and all creations and inhabitants of Nature.

Sixteenth Principle
Hiphop's *pioneers, legends, teachas, elders,* and *ancestors* shall not be inaccurately quoted, misrepresented, or disrespected at any time. No one should profess to be a *Hiphop pioneer* or *legend* unless they can prove with facts and/or witnesses their credibility and contributions to Hiphop Kulture.

Seventeenth Principle
Hiphoppas are encouraged to share resources. Hiphoppas should give as freely and as often as possible. It is the duty of every Hiphoppa to assist, whenever possible, in the relief of human suffering and in the correction of injustice. Hiphop is shown the highest respect when Hiphoppas respect each other. Hiphop Kulture is preserved, nurtured and developed when Hiphoppas preserve, nurture and develop one another.

Eighteenth Principle
Hiphop Kulture maintains a healthy, caring and wealthy central Hiphop guild—fully aware and invested with the power to promote, teach, interpret, modify and defend the principles of this *Hip Hop Declaration of Peace.*

THE FIFTEENTH OVERSTANDING
DOWN BY LAW

¹ Peace and much love to all my Hiphoppas incarcerated right now; it is never too late to change your life—NEVER! Freedom is only a thought away. And if you are incarcerated unjustly you will NOT be incarcerated for long.

² You can adopt a new thinking right now and change your environment by changing your thoughts. Do you live in a tomb or a temple? This is real! Your environment must respond to YOUR perception of it. Do not accept your present condition, it is truly temporary.

³ For if you adopt the language and character of this gospel, no prison on earth will be able to hold you. For when you change your thinking your environment has to change to match such thinking—this is science. You may be in prison, but prison is not in you!

⁴ Even beyond a jail cell many are imprisoned by their own unforgiving hearts. They may not be in a jail cell, but their own <u>P</u>ersonal <u>R</u>esentment <u>I</u>n <u>S</u>ituations <u>O</u>f <u>N</u>egativity imprisons their growth and development. Now is the time for you to begin walking and talking like a free man/woman unaffected by the ignorance and immaturity of others even when you may be in an imprisoned situation. Free men/women cannot be held in P.R.I.S.O.N.—prison is for prisoners.

⁵ For if you are reading this gospel right now in prison, then you are truly blessed because this gospel in your hand right now confirms your faith that you shall soon

be free, and with this experience you are now authorized to teach others.

6   Join me on this faith right now! My spirit is with you right now; you are not alone. KRS ONE IS THINKING ABOUT YOU RIGHT NOW. Stay focused and keep your head up.

7   For if you are reading this gospel you have an opportunity right now to believe in your freedom right now because I am believing with you right now! And what are the odds of this? What are the odds of you getting this word *sent* to you right now? God is trying to tell you something about your life-path at this very moment; pay attention, you are being groomed right now for a serious work in the World.

8   Simone G. Parker sends this affirmation to you. She advises you to BE S.T.R.O.N.G. while you are there, meaning Stay Tolerant, Respond Objectively, Notify God. This formula will get you through this period in your life. Your stay in jail and in P.R.I.S.O.N. is truly temporary no matter what your situation looks like. Keep the faith, you are actually being tested right now! Rise to the challenge!

9   Did you know that the original purpose of prison was rehabilitation? That in ancient times when a person broke the laws of his/her society, that person was not immediately regarded as a criminal; such a person was regarded more as a patient in need of time to think, reflect and rehabilitate.

10   Such is your time now. You know that you need this rest period. You know why you are where you are. Use your time wisely. Use this time to improve upon yourself. Do not walk with criminals if you truly are not one. Walk as a free man/woman. Adopt the character of the one who is willing to help even while in need of help.

11   Continue to plan your future. See your future self doing what you know your purpose to be. Just because

your body may be locked up right now doesn't mean that your mind is. You CAN think your way out of prison! Try this. Really, you have nothing to lose. Practice these overstandings; time seems to be on your side.

12   This particular Overstanding deals with Law and the Hip Hop community's opportunity to approach the advantages of Law seriously. Being "down by law" actually has two meanings to it here. One interpretation, the original one, informs us that being "down by law" has to do with holding a certain respect within one's community. The other interpretation has more to do with being kept "down" or oppressed by law. First, let us look at this second interpretation more closely; I will elaborate on the original interpretation of the term "down by law" later.

13   Know this. Just as there is no peace without justice, there is equally no freedom without law. In fact, the more we understand law, the freer and more secure we become. In this overstanding Hiphoppas are encouraged to respect Law and seek to be the law abiding citizens of the countries in which they reside.

14   According to *Black's Law Dictionary, 5th Ed.*, "law" is described as *that which is laid down, ordained, or established. A rule or method according to which phenomena or actions coexist or follow each other.*

15   Law, in its generic sense, is *a body of rules of action or conduct prescribed by a controlling authority, and having binding legal force.* According to the same dictionary, a law is *that which must be obeyed and followed by citizens subject to sanctions or legal consequences.*

16   Law is also interpreted as *a solemn expression of the will of the supreme power of the state.* Law can also mean a body of principles, standards and rules made known to the public by government. In a scientific sense, like with the science of living things (biology), "law" is a scientific theory

that has been tested repeatedly.

17   A "lawful" person is one who is *free, unattainted and capable of bearing an oath*. This is one of the basic standards that attuned Hiphoppas instinctively hold themselves to. Hiphoppas are "lawful" people. In Law we are protected, in Law we are guided. But we Hiphoppas have learned now that every *"laid down," "ordained" or "established"* rule is not necessarily Law.

18   We've seen and experienced now the corruption inherent in man-made laws and this is why our children do not respect today's laws. Yes, we are moral and law-abiding citizens, but in our history many of the laws of the United States were simply imposed upon us for the control and further exploitation of our people.

19   We've experienced now the discriminatory practices of not only law enforcement officers, but the very courts themselves! Yes, HIP HOP RESPECTS LAW! But when *Black's Law Dictionary* describes law enforcement officers as *those whose <u>duty</u> it is to preserve the peace,* we can see with the experiences of our own lives how "unlawful" such officers act toward us. This, in our opinion, is the cause of social unrest and even violence in urban areas.

20   It is not the poor citizens of a country who cause the violence they are forced to live around, it is actually the incompetence and corruption of that society's law enforcement officers that actually cause violent situations to occur in that society.

21   *Black's Law Dictionary* describes "police" as *a branch of government which is <u>charged</u> with the preservation of public order and tranquility, the promotion of the public health, safety and morals, and the prevention, detection and punishment of crimes.*

22   The police officer is *one of the staff of men <u>employed</u> in cities and towns to enforce the municipal laws and ordinances*

for preserving the peace, safety, and good order of the community.
But is this actually how police officers conduct themselves
within America's urban communities? Notice the repeated
references in *Black's Law Dictionary* to *safety, tranquility*
and the preservation of *peace*.

[23]   If police officers themselves conducted themselves
like this there would be very little violence in our urban
communities. There would be an example (even an
inspiration) within our communities as to how real law-
abiding citizens behave. But the conduct of today's law
enforcement officers has clearly fallen short of what they
were originally established to do, and this is ultimately why
our young people break the laws of their country.

[24]   In fact, the lawless conduct of our children is in
compliance with law enforcement officers and their agencies.
When our young people disregard the ordinances of their
City or State, they are actually following the law because
this is how the law behaves in front of them. However, *two
wrongs do not make a right*, or make it right.

[25]   Just because lawmakers and law enforcers contradict
and even break their own laws and ordinances does not
mean that we should. In fact, as a sociopolitical strategy
for the further establishment of today's civil rights it is to
our advantage to study and obey the laws of the nations in
which we live. Every day Hip Hop has a real opportunity
and responsibility to rise to the intended essence of law
enforcement, which is to *promote order, safety, health, morals
and general welfare within constitutional limits.*

[26]   But this means that we Hiphoppas must stop
terrorizing, disrespecting and intimidating the police
officers in our own communities. Yes, we make the police
in our communities afraid and fearful with our own lawless
conduct and blatant disregard for their presence. All across
the United States we make it known that we are willing to

injure and even kill police officers, and such conduct makes them afraid of us; such fear then manifests itself into the "shoot first, ask questions later" attitude so many police officers express while patrolling our neighborhoods.

27   Many police officers go to work every day not sure if they are going to make it home at night, and so the only way to ensure that they will make it home at the end of a day is to overwhelm us with flashing lights, loud noises, tasers and guns. All of this, however, exposes how fearful the police are when they are around us. This relationship is not healthy for anyone, and it is time for the Hip Hop community to mature past this level of communal immaturity. For it is not so much that we must do their jobs for them, it is more the fact that if they fail to execute their jobs well the whole society, with us in it, falls for lack of *safety, health, morals* and *peace!*

28   We, Hiphoppas, have an opportunity to lessen the tension within our own communities by becoming more lawful than today's law enforcement, which isn't that difficult to achieve. Instead of protesting unjust conditions within our nations, why not try being more lawful than those who attempt to oppress us with their own fears and unjust laws? In fact, if we would simply respect our own Hip Hop laws and principles, as well as the laws and ordinances of the nations in which we live, we would not only be stronger and more organized than today's law enforcement officers who do not follow their own laws and ordinances, we would lessen the fear and stress of certain police officers, lessening the amount of hostility we experience as a result of such high levels of fear and stress.

29   In Truth, there is no need to fight against those who have already disrespected themselves by disrespecting their own ordinances. Such a group cannot last long anyway.

30   So even though as Hiphoppas we are encouraged to

obey the laws of our nations we also have come to understand that many of the laws we are obeying are only to be obeyed because of the legal harm it may cause us at the moment. In a society riddled with corruption, greed and incompetence, law is really a matter of what the corporate *powers that be* decide and want.

[31]   As Hiphoppas we know that true Law <u>cannot</u> be broken. True Law in this sense is simply the reality or condition of a person or thing. True Law is not to be obeyed, it is to be understood, imitated and used toward the easing of human suffering. In essence, Law is the natural condition of things, and once you know the natural condition of things you discover the laws (or ways) that govern those things.

[32]   Real laws are like abilities; they are the abilities of your existence, they are the explanations of who you really are and what you are really capable of achieving. True Law doesn't just tell what you can't do, it also tells you what you actually can do. In fact, you are a *law* unto yourself. You create with your decisions, words and actions the conditions (laws) that shall govern and guide your life.

[33]   Hip Hop is the law (or condition) of the Hiphoppa. Those who understand and obey this law bring more of this law into their lives. In fact, when you are in harmony with the law (condition) of your own being, you discover the true power of your true nature.

[34]   *Black's Law Dictionary* talks about police officers as those *"hired"* for *"preserving the peace"* and law enforcement officers as those whose *"duty"* it is to *"preserve the peace."* If we became our own law enforcement officers whose *"duty"* it was to *"preserve the peace,"* not only would we inherit the ability to *"lawfully"* detain hired police officers when they engaged in misconduct, but as law enforcement officers we become the preservers of *"peace"* in our own communities. This would dramatically lessen violence in urban areas.

³⁵ This is the solution to urban crime and police misconduct; we Hiphoppas have to become our own law enforcement officers. In fact, isn't it obvious that we are being led off to prison not because of crime, but because we simply don't care about one another so there is no protection of one another? Crime means that you don't care about your neighbor, and such conduct invites outside forces to cease upon your resources and impose their laws upon you.

³⁶ Know this. The essence of "police power" actually *secures generally the comfort, safety, morals, health, and prosperity of its citizens, while insuring to each an uninterrupted enjoyment of all the privileges conferred upon him or her by the general laws.*

³⁷ It is then obvious that when we obey our own Hip Hop laws and show a higher respect for the general laws of our nations, we naturally inherit "police powers" even to the point of policing the police. The repeated references in *Black's Law Dictionary* to *"morals"* in the enforcement of a community's laws and ordinances suggests that the police are supposed to uphold, protect and even promote the general *morality* of the communities in which they police.

³⁸ They are not in essence authorized to impose a certain *morality* upon a community, they are authorized to uphold the general morality of the communities they police. But if the community in which they police practices little to no morality unto themselves, law enforcement officers are indeed authorized to establish the "law" and "order" of the State over the interests of that immoral community.

³⁹ In addition, how can a law enforcement officer uphold a *peace* he/she does not possess within his/her self? How can a police officer know the correct moral character of a community he/she is foreign to? Or even deeper, how can an insecure, immoral, sick and poor police officer secure *the comfort, safety, morals, health, and prosperity of* the citizens

he/she encounters throughout the day?

40   This is important to know because not only must you personally have *peace* in order to secure peace for others, morality itself is also a spiritually motivated principle like *peace*. If you do not personally study and practice morality and the living of a righteous life, how can you administer such to anyone else?

41   This again is why our young people today have such difficulty obeying the law. They are raised in a corrupt American culture that celebrates such corruption openly and freely in mass media and within the general affairs of the State.

42   It is very difficult to respect the laws and general moral conduct of those who racially profile you, disrespect your culture, ignore your interests, arrest and assassinate your neighbors and seek to exploit you and your resources. Such *moral conduct* we can never accept or respect. Peace to Sean Bell. Remember, slavery was at one time morally correct and sanctioned by law.

43   This is why we Hiphoppas must know the true essence of Law itself if we are to truly protect ourselves and accurately administer justice.

44   But this is the dilemma right here. We Hiphoppas seem to protest the blatant contradictions in the practice of American law by contradicting OUR OWN LAWS. It's like a form of suicide bombing where in your protest against injustice you blow yourself up in an effort to destroy your enemy.

45   Can this be a viable strategy against oppression for Hip Hop? Presently, we don't think so, because anyone who is willing to die for their community actually lives for their community and is loyal to their community even unto death. Thus it is they who are the natural leaders of their community and should go on living, enduring injustice,

leading, inspiring and teaching their community against the internal behaviors that caused the injustice to begin with.

[46]   It is a community's own interpretation of good and evil that determines that community's moral code of conduct. However, good and evil are usually based upon the survival of the community so that what is good for one community may not be good for another community and vice versa.

[47]   In a traditional sense, life is considered "good" while death is considered "evil." Knowledge is considered "good" while ignorance is considered "evil." Wealth is considered "good" while poverty is considered "evil." But all of this is a matter of cultural opinion based upon what that culture feels it needs to exist and survive.

[48]   So when we look at the laws that we are to obey, we are to ask *in whose interests were these laws created?* Some laws are indeed "evil" for our community because they do not consider the well-being of our existence. Other laws are "good" because they enhance and protect our general well-being even if they are imposed upon us.

[49]   Following laws that only have the lawgiver's interests in mind is "oppression," and this is the present collective condition in which Hiphoppas live today. *Black's Law Dicitinary* defines "oppression" as *a misdemeanor committed by a public officer, who under color of his office, wrongfully inflicts upon any person any bodily harm, imprisonment or other injury. An act of cruelty, severity, unlawful exaction, or excessive use of authority. An act of subjecting to cruel and unjust hardship: an act of domination.*

[50]   Notice the level of crime that "oppression" actually is; it is actually a "misdemeanor," meaning *offenses lower than felonies and generally those punishable by fine or imprisonment otherwise than in penitentiary.*

[51]   So when police officers shoot at us, curse at us,

intimidate us, arrest us and/or "detain" us without just cause, not only is this an act of "oppression" but such an act technically is not even a felony. This, in my observations, is the cause of so much lawlessness, urban violence and police misconduct. We Hiphoppas must rise above this condition if we are to ever be truly free.

⁵² If we are to really continue our parents' and grandparents' struggles for freedom and justice (civil rights), at some point we are going to have to consider governing ourselves, which means obedience to our own laws and respect for our own traditions. We are going to have to keep the police and other law enforcement officers out of our communities by abiding by our own laws, which even they would be forced to obey once within our self-governed community.

⁵³ We live in a nation under a government that presently ignores our existence and self-expression as Hiphoppas, yet we are threatened with prison and forced at gunpoint to obey the laws of such a government even though such laws do not have our best interests in mind. For us, this is "evil." Such a governement has no idea who its citizens are and in our Hip Hop observations such cultural illiteracy is the cause of so much of America's social ills.

⁵⁴ A "good" government recognizes not only my right to exist, but also the usefulness of my existence, and puts me in my right social place. This is called "order," and such "order" exists hand-in-hand with law. An ordered society seeks the condition in which every part of it is in its rightful place. Where every citizen is where they are supposed to be, and doing what they are supposed to be doing based upon their own individual nature and purpose supported by a government which they voluntarily serve.

⁵⁵ The United States suffers today economically not only because it is repeatedly breaking its own laws and

traditions while oppressing its population, but simply because it is not making good use of its talented citizens. Let us pray for change. However, such conditions have already begun to change because we Hiphoppas are now ready to change them! Many of us have now grown up and are beginning to take the seats of political office once reserved for those who sought to exploit our resources and ignore our real existence.

56   But how shall we behave when we are in power? Shall we simply continue the same oppression on some other group seeking existence, or shall we be fair and just in our administering of justice? Such an answer does not come when we are in power, such an answer is performed by us, amongst us, today.

57   It is a complete waste of our revolutionary effort to complain about issues we ourselves have not matured beyond. When we protest unjust situations we should be able to do better than the situations we are protesting against. We should not just culturally scream out when we are hit by injustice, we should take the hit as an act of validation toward our authority to speak into existence a new nation. This is what our King taught us.

58   Our King taught us to endure injustice so that you might be validated to speak against it. Those who have not been hit with the sting of injustice lack the real authority to speak against it. Yes, you may definitely protest the injustice that you see, or hear, or even read about simply because of your own sense of right and wrong, good and evil, but ultimately the authentic authority to plan and act against injustice comes only from those directly suffering from it.

59   Even if others decide to help us out of our unjust situation simply because they recognize the injustice of our situation, it is still us who must have a vision and a plan of action for ourselves. Others can only assist and help us

achieve victory over oppression, but ultimately it is we who must know what a better situation looks and feels like.

60   We simply have to get clear about what we actually want. This creates purpose, and purpose creates vision, and vision creates movement, and movement creates history, and history creates tradition, and tradition creates morality, and from our own sense of morality come our principles, and it is our principles that create our laws, which exist to protect and further develop the existence of our group.

61   Living by some other society's laws and traditions hinders us from experiencing our own. A society that expects us to obey THEIR laws and traditions without ever asking us about the existence of OUR laws and traditions is indeed an oppressive society. However, such oppression can only continue if we allow it to continue through the oppression of ourselves.

62   Try to remember what oppression actually is. Not only is "oppression" *an act of cruelty, severity, unlawful exaction, or excessive use of authority,* but "oppression" is also *an act of subjecting to cruel and unjust hardship.* In this case, not only is "oppression" *bodily harm, cruelty, unlawful exaction, and the excessive use of authority*, oppression is also the acceptance of such injustice; it is the *act of subjecting to cruel and unjust hardship.*

63   Those who act or speak *cruelly* are actually attempting to oppress you—rappers included. Those who use their authority *excessively, unjustly,* and/or *unlawfully* are attempting to oppress you—DJs included. By not conducting ourselves according to our own laws and traditions we actually oppress ourselves; we use our own authority as an "original" culture against ourselves.

64   Asking for justice is not how an oppressed group will ever get justice. It is when such a group begins to perform the justice they want for themselves amongst

themselves that such justice appears and serves the well-being of that group.

65   Justice is never given by one group to another group; justice is performed internally within a group first and other groups, seeing such a performance, are compelled to approach such a group the way in which that group approaches itself.

66   Presently, the United States treats the Hip Hop community the way in which the Hip Hop community treats itself. But such a relationship is simply not working for US or the U.S. It is now time for us to begin conducting ourselves as an autonomous group of specialized people, organized and prepared for trade.

67   Regarding *"the social contract theory of the origin of the state,"* Alban Dewes Winspear, in his book *The Genesis Of Plato's Thought*, explains that *the origin of the State is to be found in the fact that no one of us is sufficient into himself. We have all of us need of others. Our needs of food, clothing, and shelter. And so the first unit or association will be a farmer, a builder, a weaver; perhaps we should add a cobbler and one or two other craftsmen. This would be the 'most rudimentary polity'—this simplest and most essential form of human association. In such a grouping we shall discover that one man has one set of natural aptitudes, another man another. So specialization means multiplication of crafts and craftsmen—carpenters and smiths, neatherds and shepherds. And with specialization we shall have exchange.*

68   We Hiphoppas are a kind of craftsmen or craftspeople. Hip Hop is our craft, and Hip Hop even when it is most critical of the United States is still an asset to the United States, an important part of its total functioning. The ignoring of Hip Hop is not so much the ignoring of a needed craft in American society, it is more the ignoring of a whole group of *craftspeople* in that society.

[69]   Such ignore-ance assists in America's economic woes. It says that our particular Hip Hop arts and crafts are not valuable to the society in which our arts and crafts originate. And because of this lie, injustice is allowed to flourish in the fertile soil (soul) of American society.

[70]   But a society's ignore-ance of its *craftspeople* is equally its downfall. As Mr. Winspear continues in *The Genesis Of Plato's Thought*, *Plato shows very great insight when he maintains that the State is based on an increasing interdependence of craftsmen and crafts...Plato, however, very cleverly interprets this mutual dependence of increasing specialization as a 'natural inequality.' Plato, like so many modern thinkers since the Renaissance, endeavored to base his theory of the State on a theory of human nature: we are by nature interdependent, each one of us is fitted by nature to do one particular task. This is the central fact in the secret of the origin of society and the justification of justice.*

[71]   In this case, social justice is based upon every citizen having the ability to pursue and express their innate purpose, and the liberty to reach for the excellence his/her purpose demands. Plato reminds us here that *social institutions are to be accounted for by reference to the desires and impulses of natural man.* Aristotle agrees, *The State comes into being for the sake of life, it exists for the sake of the good life.*

[72]   But is this how any of the central social institutions of the United States behave and approach the impoverished part of the society they serve? Of course not, these institutions serve the interests of oppression and this is why they too are struggling to survive and grow in today's changing World.

[73]   Hip Hop can and will do better than this—much better than this. But first we must establish a state of peaceful harmony under a constituted authority (like the *Hip Hop Declaration of Peace*). Such constituted authority

begins here, with us—we are our own natural authority. But when we break the laws of our own nature and existence we strip ourselves of all authority to govern—even ourselves.

[74] As attuned Hiphoppas we invite Law and Order. In fact, Hip Hop is already a social order unto itself; our people are just presently ignorant of it. Presently Hip Hop is a social class in the United States; we are a distinct group in American society. We can be called "the lower orders" or "a lower order" not because we are looked at as being of a lower class of people, but because our *order* comes under the authority of United States laws and ordinances.

[75] However, we are treated like a lower class of people simply because we act ignorantly and independently of the general well-being of our neighboring cultures and communities. We are not yet considered a "higher order" in the sense of being a *high-minded people* simply because we don't act as such amongst ourselves or amongst others.

[76] Our social behavior tells the World that we care little for ourselves and everyone around us. We are literally OUT OF ORDER! Such a condition is simply not healthy for us or the American people and it's time we both realize this as we continue growing up.

[77] As a people we cry out for JUSTICE! But we cannot cry out or ask for that which we are not willing to give even to ourselves. Know this. We are the justice we seek and when we realize this, injustice shall have no more refuge in our community. Hip Hop itself is social justice, and so to be Hiphop the Hiphoppa must be just.

[78] It would be different if Hip Hop came into existence as a response to hatred (as an example). Then it would be within our divine and natural rights to express and practice love first amongst ourselves and then toward our neighbors if we are to grow and further develop. Love would be the correct strategy toward our liberation and collective peace.

But this is not the case for Hip Hop.

[79]   Yes, our God is Love! And yes, Hiphoppas cannot exist without love. But even love is not the correct strategy for our political and social liberation; justice is. The *Hip Hoptionary* by Alonzo Westbrook defines Hip Hop as *the artistic response to oppression*. With this accurate definition of Hip Hop as a response to oppression, which is basically an injustice to us, we see that the purpose of Hip Hop is justice.

[80]   The purpose of Hip Hop is not the accumulation of money and other material goods; the real purpose of Hip Hop is justice, and those who are rich because of Hip Hop are made as such for the purpose of seeking and maintaining justice. We are a rich culture because the ancestors and parents of our citizenry have had everything taken away from them through war and invasion.

[81]   Our richness today is simply the justice or balance (even karma) of our previously imposed unjust state of poverty. Riches and wealth are part of our natural condition, and so Hip Hop acts as justice itself in the restoring of our natural condition. We are rich not for the purposes of spending money on our oppressor's products; we are rich because such is our natural condition, such belongs to our natural "order."

[82]   The point, therefore, is to BE yourself and stop exploiting yourself. The point is then to stop using yourself for money, and start BEING yourself with money. Use money to further express your Self as opposed to expressing yourself for money. It is time that we Hiphoppas begin the process of "ordering" ourselves to our values and principles based firmly in the nature of our being, which is JUSTICE.

[83]   It is now time for us (Hip Hop) to become "orderly," meaning purposeful, methodically arranged, obedient to our

own principles, well-behaved, trustworthy, and "lawful." Such a repeated behavior creates peace and stability within our own communities, thus lifting us above those oppressive governments that cannot seem to achieve such stability for themselves.

84   For it is order that creates nations and disorder that destroys them. Therefore, let us be ordered in our collective Hip Hop behavior. Let us be the nation America attempted to be, and receive the tranquility Americans attempted to secure.

85   Let us finally accept ourselves as Hiphoppas and live from that "law" and "order." And we have the authority to do so because we are "original", we are "primitive", and being "original" and "primitive" has legal meaning as well as common meaning. As *Black's Law Dictionary* points out, the term "original" means *primitive; first in order; bearing its own authority, and not deriving authority from an outside source.*

86   This is interesting because Hip Hop is clearly an original and distinctly unique culture. We are a *"primitive"* civilization bearing our *"own authority,"* and *"not deriving authority from an outside source"* unless we voluntarily give up such *"authority"* by not respecting or following our own *"order."*

87   In Truth, it is self-respect that creates authority, and authority is what is needed to establish both civilization and law. Such authority comes from an authoritative conduct which begins simply with a serious respect for one's self. In his book *The Secret of Divine Civilization*, 'Abdu'l-Bahá teaches that *man's supreme honor and real happiness lie in self-respect, in high resolves and noble purposes, in integrity and moral quality, in immaculacy of mind.*

88   But James Baldwin reminds us that, *Hunger has no principles, it simply makes men, at worst, wretched, and, at*

best, dangerous. Such is the challenge facing Hip Hop today; our people are simply starving. And we starve not for food, but for justice. It is our hunger to be in our rightful places that disregards our own "principles" and makes us take on the images of being *"wretched"* and *"dangerous."*

89   In the back of our collective hip-hop minds we actually believe that it is hopeless, that corruption is the norm and *"things ain't never gonna change,"* so it seems advantageous to imitate the cutthroat ways of those who cut the throats of our parents. As a community we are simply imitating what we believe power is—violence, murder, theft, deceit, immorality, Godlessness.

90   Basically, we are culturally crying. Not just culturally crying out for justice, law and order, but as a community of specialized people we are collectively depressed by the situation before us. We can't believe that we live amongst such cultures that can see no value in us other than what they can exploit from us artistically.

91   We may front like we are stronger than our sad situation, but in reality, we are emotionally hurt as a community by the conduct of those who claim to be our neighbors, even our government. This is the attitude that fuels so much of the rebellion in our culture. Sure, rebellion was good when we were just getting started in the 1970s, 1980s and 1990s; we were young. But now that we've started and have officially established ourselves in the minds of urban people everywhere, we need a new course of action.

92   We must shatter our own outdated and false beliefs, and rise above the corruption we've found ourselves within. We gotta stop crying and start thinking again. We must find a way, all of us, to rise above the depression we really feel as a community.

93   We must become better, yes, better than those who sought to exploit us and our resources. We must become an

authority over them through righteousness and discipline; something all oppressive governments lack. 'Abdu'l-Bahá lays out the character of such an authority in *The Secret of Divine Civilization*. He writes, *While the setting up of parliaments, the organizing of assemblies of consultation constitutes the very foundation and bedrock of government, there are several essential requirements which these institutions must fulfill.*

[94] *First, the elected members must be righteous, GOD-fearing, high-minded, incorruptible. Second, they must be fully cognizant, in every particular, of the laws of GOD, informed as to the highest principles of law, versed in the rules which govern the management of internal affairs and the conduct of foreign relations, skilled in the useful arts of civilization and content with their lawful emoluments.*

[95] But even if Hip Hop produces and continues to maintain such leadership, who shall such leadership lead? Who shall such public servants serve? The Hip Hop community itself must reflect such a character also, otherwise one will pull the other one down. Hip Hop's leadership must live in spirit, living only according to principles and not according to the cravings of the flesh. Our leadership must be content with GOD.

[96] In regards to this, 'Abdu'l-Bahá warns that *close observation will show that the primary cause of oppression and injustice, of unrighteousness, irregularity and disorder, is the people's lack of religious faith and the fact that they are uneducated...and, because of their inadequate schooling, most of the population lack even the vocabulary to explain what they want.*

[97] Hip Hop's lawful leadership must have a relationship with GOD—the Love that Guides Our Direction. For it is extremely difficult, even impossible, to guide others without being guided yourself. To every Hip Hop leader we must

ask, *what is it that guides you?* And such a question is not really answered in words; it is answered in deeds that must be done under pressure, or in solutions that do not directly benefit one's self.

⁹⁸   Every community produces leadership, and Hip Hop is no different in this regard. There are certain individuals who evolve from deep within their cultures and are naturally recognized by the culture in which they serve. The collective consciousness of the culture magically empowers such individuals to carry out the will of its people.

⁹⁹   Know this. When a people support the organic leadership of their own cultures, no force on earth can stop them from achieving what is naturally and lawfully theirs. It is when such a people withdraw their support for their own organic leadership that such a people break the magical bond between leader and community, thus subjecting themselves to a vulnerability that inevitably leads to invasion and the theft of their resources.

¹⁰⁰   In Hip Hop's early days there were such individuals whom, because of their natural swagger and organic style, the Hip Hop community considered "down by law," meaning respected according to our communal laws. A certain aura surrounded the one who was considered "down by law." Such a person was the walking embodiment of our community's traditions, priniciples and laws.

¹⁰¹   In the early days of Hip Hop's development being *cool* or *highly favored* in the *hood* (one's neighborhood) had a lot to do with one's lucky, *get over,* hustler type of personality. The one who was making a living without a job and *chillin'* at the same time was considered *cool*. The one who seemed to be *getting over* on the system and *beating the Man at his own game,* was considered *cool* or highly admired and revered in the *hood*. This is who everyone strived to be.

102 If a stranger were to ask such a person, *how did you get to be who you are?* or, *how did you get what you got?*, instead of explaining one's whole story as to how one became who one was and how one acquired what one had, such a cool individual would simply say either *I got it like that!* or, *I'm down by law!* And everyone living in the Bronx during the 1970s and 1980s knew what such terms meant.

103 *I got it like that* was a street term that described one's lucky or supernatural nature. It implied that things would always go the way one wanted even if one was unconscious of the outcome.

104 *I got it like that* meant that one was special. It meant, *this is who I am,* that *the good things happening to me are happening because they are supposed to be happening to me; I got it like that! There's no need for explanation or wonderment, I simply got it like that! Such good fortune is normal for me!* In this mentality of expectancy good things actually happen to the one who is *down by law!*

105 For when there was no explanation for one's good fortune early Hiphoppas would simply say, *I got it like that!* It was a kind of bragging about the unexplainable events of good fortune in one's life. It was a reassurance that you were not average, that even though you might be living in extreme poverty, you were still not like everyone else—you were *down by law!* Such was your street validation.

106 Being *down by law* meant being accepted and admired by the invisible code of the streets. But it also carried within its meaning the character of being favored by unseen forces. If someone ever questioned the authority of a person who was *down by law*, that person who was *down by law* would say something like, *What, you don't know who I am? I'm down by law!* meaning, I'm part of this scene, I know people around here, I hold respect on these streets, *I'M DOWN BY LAW!*

[107]   Being *down by law* also had to do with having yourself together, being organized, being authoritative, self-created and entrepreneurial. It had to do with having value and knowing people. To claim that one was *down by law* insinuated that one was also prepared to back that statement up on any level. It was sort of like pulling out one's street credentials as a defense.

[108]   Knowing these early Hip Hop terms brings remembrance of the early Hip Hop character and personality—the cause of today's Hip Hop artistic elements. Early Hiphoppas gave themselves authority through the mastery of certain skills unique to their environment and lifestyle.

[109]   Before the selling of Rap music through high-gloss mini-movie Rap videos, the cause of one's authority in the early Hip Hop community was based upon one's specialness, one's frequent charity and problem-solving in the *hood*, one's mastery of a widely practiced skill or talent, one's political activism on behalf of the *hood,* one's uniqueness and usefulness; even one's strength and fighting abilities all contributed to one's authority in the *hood* and one being *down by law.*

[110]   To be *down by law* one had to have a favorable history in the *hood*. People had to know who you were and where you were. You were trusted by the people, you shared their experiences, your personality made people feel like you were *down* with them. In their eyes, in the eyes of the community, you could do no wrong, because at this level of community acceptance you were exempt from certain judgments and criticisms; the people loved and admired you for who you were. Your reputation was known and respected in every home—you were *down by law!*

[111]   What does it mean to be *down?* To be *down* meant to be *part of,* or *in agreement with* someone or something.

I might say something like, *DJ Red Alert is <u>down</u> with us!* Here, *down* implies group association. One could also say, *DJ Red Alert is <u>part</u> of us!* Or, <u>*moves*</u> *with us!* It means that we share the same interests. It is also an agreement, like, *I'm <u>down</u> with that!* In this instance, one also could say, *I <u>agree</u> with that!*

[112]   R&B singer/actress Brandy published a song entitled "I Wanna Be Down," which implied wanting to be part of someone's life. In the song, Brandy sings, *I wanna be down with what you're going through. I wanna be down with you*. Here, Brandy expresses her desire to unite with the experiences of whom she is seeking to be *down* with.

[113]   *I wanna be down with what you're going through* is like saying, I want to *experience* or *share in on* what is happening to you in your life, I want to join in on your life experiences (*what you're going through*). Such a commitment was highly respected in the *hood* because wanting to be *down* with someone implied a certain loyalty through the good times as well as the bad times.

[114]   So, to be *down by law* also implied being loyal to the history and invisible code of one's *hood*. It meant that one was important in the *hood*, that one was in agreement with the street and its customs, that one needed no other validation other than the acceptance of one's own *hood* to hold authority anywhere.

[115]   Such was (and still is) the cause of royalty. A king is a king anywhere in the World. A queen is queen anywhere in the World. It is when one has the respect of one's community that such a respected individual walks the earth freely commanding the respect of others. For it is a leader's people that promote, protect and empower such a leader in foreign environments.

[116]   Community respect is the ultimate force of political power. Without the respect of your people, how can you

claim to be their leader? Such an individual is simply an oppressor posing as a leader through military means; such a governance is fake, fraudulent and cannot last.

[117]   A true queen is recognized not because of her crown of jewels or exquisitely tailored clothing, nor even because of her knowledge or even military power. A queen is simply a highly respected woman, one who holds the respect of HER PEOPLE.

[118]   A true queen wears a crown because HER PEOPLE put it on her head. A true queen wears the clothing given to her by HER PEOPLE. A true queen doesn't teach her people as much as her people teach her. Her people keep her informed. A true queen never has to threaten anyone or feel threatened in foreign environments because even the criminals of her nation respect her so much that even they are willing to rob, steal, kill, and maim in her honor.

[119]   The reputation of a true queen or king, or in Hip Hop's case, the reputation of a true teacha, is known throughout that teacha's nation and such a nation promotes to other nations its respect and loyalty for its teacha, king, queen, president, etc. Other nations know very well the repercussions that follow any disrespect of a nation's beloved leader.

[120]   This is how such a leader gets things done for her community. It is the community that sends their leader out into the World fully equipped in an effort to secure certain resources and relationships beneficial to the community. A true king has no self interests other than those of HIS PEOPLE.

[121]   A true king doesn't come to his people with a plan that they've never heard of which points them in a direction they've never intended for themselves. A true leader selflessly solves the problems of his people.

[122]   In short, community respect and admiration caused

one to be *down by law*, or highly revered in one's *hood*. In actuality, appreciation, respect and honor are the Law of the streets. And when one is accepted by one's *hood* (or the streets) it means that one is part of the condition of the *hood*. It means that one has voluntarily decided to align one's self with the struggles of one's peers.

123   To be *down by law* literally means *to be part of*, or *represent* (be down with) the *conditions* (law) of one's *hood* (environment). It means that one can be trusted because one has lent one's talent to the upliftment of the *hood* and the ease of human suffering especially when one didn't have to remain loyal to the *hood* at all.

124   Urban conditions revolve around favors, hook-ups and opportunities. Other conditions of the hood revolve around inspiration. Those who can produce favors, hook-ups and opportunities are set aside from everyone else looking for favors, hook-ups and opportunities.

125   Those who can inspire others and make others feel good about themselves and/or their situation are also considered *down by law*. They are set aside in the collective consciousness of the *hood* as special. Such people are not judged the same way by the *hood* as others are.

126   The *hood* anywhere in the World recognizes the ease of human suffering through favors, hook-ups, opportunities and inspiration. Individuals who express such personalities are highly admired and respected throughout the *hood* regardless of their profession (legal or illegal). They are the community heroes, and community heroes are almost always considered *down by law* because they are considered honorable by THEIR community's standards.

127   However, when observing these terms (*down by law* and *I got it like that*) today, our own maturity as a group and the understandings that come with such maturity advance these terms dramatically.

[128] Today, being *down by law* has grown to include one's loyalty toward Hip Hop's development and preservation (the new *hood*). The same community respect that certain individuals enjoyed in the past (exclusively in their *hoods*) certain conscious rappers and popular Hip Hop activists enjoy today (worldwide).

[129] Certain things that others within the Hip Hop community would be criticized for doing, those who are *down by law* are encouraged to do and even protected while doing. Their mistakes are quickly forgiven by the community because the community recognizes their role and service on behalf of the whole.

[130] The one who is *down by law* has already proven her selflessness to the community, and it is this collective appreciation from the community that leads to a communal respect from that community.

[131] Hip Hop's leadership rises from within the sweat and toil of everyday life and never has to prove itself. People know who's who in their communities and their judgments and opinions (based upon the historical events of their community) determine their leadership.

[132] Despite the Hip Hop community's own lust for the material goods and pleasures of the World, in reality the Hip Hop community truly appreciates its activists and those who choose to inspire others through their artistic performances. This is what causes the condition of being *down by law;* it all begins with the appreciation and admiration one receives from one's own People.

[133] However, this ancient state of being appreciated and admired (or *down by law*) is not unique to the Hip Hop community. Most leaders and those of unique talents and/or resources are often considered *down by law* in their communities; no matter what, they can do no wrong in the sight of those who love them.

134   Today, we continue the *down by law* tradition philosophically by acknowledging the principles of Law itself. Most people cringe when they hear the word *Law* because they immediately believe that they are going to be restrained or restricted in some way.

135   However, Law is simply a practice, or rather, a process. Law is simply the conditions that individuals as well as groups agree upon. Law stems from culture. Once the culture is identified, the means for its preservation become obvious and laws are then discovered (not *laid down*).

136   For once you know the conditions of something or someone you also know the laws that govern that thing or person's life. Different from Federal law, or State law, or the laws of certain religions, spiritual law is simply the condition of things; it is the nature of things. Being a Black male in the United States (for example) has certain conditions to it, and these conditions make up the paradigm in which we perceive and operate as Black men.

137   Some conditions are your natural state, while other conditions are imposed upon you; still other conditions are voluntarily accepted by you for the sake of fulfilling the desires of your own mind.

138   In any event, you create the laws (or conditions) that will govern your life. And this is a law in and of itself; we call it the Law of *Self-Creation*. Meaning that whether you like it or not, one of the conditions of life is that everyone must create themselves. You may not like what you have created or how you may have turned out, you may not have even been aware of what you were doing, but in Truth it was you who created YOU, and it is you who continues to create and add upon YOU everyday (GOD willing).

139   This is a law. Like the Laws of Attraction, like the Laws of Success, like the Laws of Gravity and Light and Sound, all of these laws are conditions that if we can

understand them and remain in harmony with them, we experience the power of not being bound by them.

[140]   Every day we are creating our reality through what we believe is important to our survival. Such a belief creates the conditions (or laws) that we live within. Every day we are creating laws for ourselves through what we truly believe about ourselves as well as what we believe of others and of our outer environment.

[141]   This is why the affirmation *I got it like that* became such a powerful affirmation for early Hiphoppas. It implied that supernatural events and good fortune were normal in that Hiphoppa's life, and it told the Hiphoppa personally what her true nature was.

[142]   Such an acknowledgement of one's supernatural good fortune also helped to repeat it; it set a certain condition over the life of the one who acknowledged such a condition. Hip Hop is our supernatural collective good fortune. It is the law of our lives, the condition that we freely accept.

[143]   However, in our time (your past) many people do not think of Hip Hop in this way. They do not truly live a *Hiphop* lifestyle so they feel no responsibility toward Hip Hop's political image and reputation in the World.

[144]   They may say with their mouths *we represent Hip Hop* but in actuality they are representing only themselves and their individual interests. We can see in the way that they approach Hip Hop that they do not have Hip Hop's best interests in mind. And this is not about criticizing today's mainstream rappers or radio DJs. This goes for everyone participating in Hip Hop. Those who truly care for Hip Hop do so by caring for other Hiphoppas. Those who truly represent Hip Hop represent the interests of Hiphoppas.

[145]   Criminal activity, selfishness, hostility, deception and greed do not (and cannot) constitute true Hip Hop. Such thinking and activity have already proven themselves

to be ineffective and even self-destructive to the Hiphoppa's free life. This is a wise law.

¹⁴⁶ In light of this Truth, true Hiphoppas remain sensitive to the content of the messages they express to society and how society is affected by those messages. True Hiphoppas are also aware of the messages society is expressing to Hiphop Kulture. True Hiphoppas care for Hip Hop by being aware of their own conduct as Hiphoppas. This too is a wise law. For when a law is just and true it is also obvious and easy to understand.

¹⁴⁷ As attuned Hiphoppas we cheerfully look for good laws to follow and obey. For a good and wise law is like a thousand years of good advice interwoven into the path that you are already traveling. Good laws are guides and protectors; they not only tell you what you cannot do, they also tell you what you can do.

¹⁴⁸ As Hiphoppas we voluntarily obey the Hip Hop condition over our lives. Such a condition brings with it certain abilities unique to our collective experience as Hiphoppas. Hip Hop's laws are Hip Hop's cultural rituals and traditions. The conditions that created or caused Hip Hop to exist are no longer with us. However, the rules are still the same; we are the authors of our own lives, and that which we write becomes the law for our lives.

¹⁴⁹ Spirit, thought and action are inseparable and are harmonized through life circumstances. As we think, so Hip Hop is! These are universal laws. Racial harmony, freedom, justice, peace, love, happiness and wisdom are all achieved within our Hiphop Kulture when such laws are regularly performed, presented and taught to our children.

¹⁵⁰ Mature Hiphoppas know that such states in human interactions as family, commitment, racial harmony, peace, justice, etc., are not granted to those who simply desire them. Such principles are achieved through the conscious

intent to live them; these are human acts, not just words.

151   Such high states in culture must remain the accepted laws of our community. Not just poetic words, but psychological realities that are interwoven into the rituals, stories and traditions that we share with each other and our children as a Hip Hop family.

152   T. S. Elliot reminds us in his book *Notes Towards the Definition of Culture* that, *By far the most important channel of transmission of culture remains the family: and when family life fails to play its part, we must expect our culture to deteriorate.*

153   However, the value of such principles/laws in the creation and further development of nations, communities and in our case the Hip Hop family is not understood by everyone—even those participating in and benefiting from Hip Hop's culture. Everyone does not truly value Hip Hop. Everyone does not truly value the concept of family, or even themselves as members of a family.

154   But those Hiphoppas who are awake, aware and conscious take the vow *I am Hip Hop* and become one more citizen of the true international Hip Hop community. They value themselves as Hip Hop and become the new *bricks* that restore the body of Hip Hop (*Hiphop*'s temple) to full strength and beauty. This was the original meaning of the phrase *I am Hip Hop*, and this is what it means to be part of Hip Hop's global family.

155   Saying *I am Hip Hop* intellectually means *I am my own strategy for self-improvement. I am the blessing. Whatever true Hip Hop is, I am that!* This is a conscious declaration to migrate, convert and/or simply become a citizen of the international Hip Hop community—a nation of consciousness where citizens are not defined by race, religion, class or gender, but by personal character, creative skill and loyalty to Hip Hop's empowerment and

preservation. A place where the only law/condition is Health, Love, Awareness and Wealth (H-LAW).

156   Such a Hiphoppa clearly overstands that Hiphop Kulture must consciously view itself as its own strategy toward survival, stability and continued growth. What we do not do for ourselves, we cannot expect others to do for us. We are the authors of the laws that shall govern our lives. What we do for ourselves others will help us to achieve, and what we don't do for ourselves others cannot help us to achieve.

157   We may cry out against incompetent police practices, we may wonder about the future of our children and we may hope for a better tomorrow—a better quality of life, a better education, better relationships, etc.—but do we truly value such hopes and wants? Are we willing to sacrifice our pleasures today for our children's victories tomorrow?

158   Know this. Even in the elementary logic of the World, it is obvious that if we do not consciously plan, work and sacrifice today to create the future we want for ourselves and our children, then we have only ourselves to blame if we wind up worse tomorrow than we are today. This is a universal law, a condition for everyone in my time.

159   The true Hiphoppa instinctively feels this today and does whatever it takes to participate in the preservation and further development of Hiphop Kulture tomorrow. This objective is achieved when Hiphoppas pledge allegiance to Hiphop Kulture and take responsibility for each other and how Hip Hop looks and acts in all communities.

160   The attuned Hiphoppa knows that laws are not only established to protect people from people, laws are also established to protect people from themselves. To the untrained *Rap fan*, imitating the irresponsible activities of immature rappers appearing on television, radio, motion pictures and the Internet (in my time) can be very

dangerous. The true Hiphoppa lives *Hiphop*, not Rap videos, music or movies.

¹⁶¹ True Hiphoppas are known to tell their live concert audiences, *Don't give the cops no reason to stop you!* The true Hiphoppa will not unnecessarily break the laws of her community or that of any country she has citizenship in.

¹⁶² The true Hiphoppa is not apathetic toward injustice or even the pursuit of justice. For it is an awareness of the Truth that motivates the true Hiphoppa to participate in her government, faith and/or local community activities.

¹⁶³ The true Hiphoppa respects, studies and practices the rule of law, that nations are to be governed by principles, not by people, and that all citizens are equal before the law.

¹⁶⁴ Whether it is tribal law, state law, universal law, constitutional law, or the H-LAW, the attuned Hiphoppa stays within the law with an understanding of those rights and privileges provided and protected by law. With this understanding, the true Hiphoppa is disciplined and is always thinking ahead for the good of her community and the society at large.

¹⁶⁵ However, sometimes the *good of society* means protest and debate, revolution and rebellion. Still, the true Hiphoppa stays within the rule of law. For example, within the courts of the country we presently reside within, a person is presumed innocent until proven guilty. However, too many times innocent and/or ignorant Hiphoppas are presumed guilty until proven innocent.

¹⁶⁶ Such a presumption is an injustice. Therefore, in an effort to uphold the Spirit of the law and correct injustice, true Hiphoppas are encouraged to help the innocent, the racially profiled, the ignorant and the poor of all nations regain and/or maintain their freedom even if they are convicted or accused of a crime.

¹⁶⁷ Not that we seek to help criminals commit crimes

or that we seek to free those who have clearly violated the law. But if we must live in a society where police officers, lawmakers, judges, prosecutors and elected officials manipulate and violate the law themselves with no reprimanding or correction from their superiors, then Hiphop Kulture is justified within the Spirit of the law itself to uphold justice in the manner that is good for the whole of society.

168   Know this. In our age the one who breaks the laws of the society in which one lives violates the very protection set up to sustain one's power, liberty and tranquility within that society. This includes ALL citizens! Law enforcement included. No one is above the law!

169   Hiphoppas are encouraged to respect, study and follow the laws of the land in which they live. As taught by Dr. Martin Luther King Jr., by staying within the boundaries of the law even in the face of lawless lawmakers, one exposes the contradiction of such individuals and organizations and thus brings about justice in unjust conditions with the great elixir of Truth!

170   Instead of ignoring and/or breaking the law, Hiphoppas are encouraged to study and obey the law. Such is part of our battle strategy against an unjust society. We must know more about the laws of our country than even the police, lawyers and judges themselves!

171   Just as there is no discipline without awareness, equally there is no freedom without law and no peace without justice. Abiding by the laws of one's nation, society and community is not only empowering to the Hiphoppa, it protects law-abiding Hiphoppas from unjust police actions. Such an acknowledgment of law is simply a matter of self-respect—it proves one's ability to govern one's self.

172   True Hiphoppas seek to overstand the natural, moral, civil and divine law of the nation, society or community we

591

visit or reside within, and we seek to correct injustice with justice (see *Hip Hop Declaration of Peace:* principles three and fourteen).

173   With this in mind, true Hiphoppas refine and tune their Spirits through the teachings of *The Divine Performance*. For in Spirit all laws and institutions of divine origin are effortlessly fulfilled and supported.

174   One does not need to consciously try to focus upon complying with the specific laws of one's country or community if peace, love, unity and happiness for one's self and for one's community are the habitual intentions of one's heart. At this stage in one's development one is DOWN BY LAW!

175   But this is only the beginning. Being spiritually *down by law* has to do with being in spiritual harmony with the laws of the universe. Your divine work, or rather your *Hiphop* spiritual path, is to learn how to be guided by universal intelligence beyond your emotional addictions. This does not mean to live an emotionless life; this means to put your emotions where they belong as indicators, not initiators.

176   We must learn to use our emotions without having them use us. Observe your feelings, don't become them. Just because something *feels* good doesn't mean that it is good, and just because something *feels* bad doesn't mean that it is bad. Emotions check the balance of your being in its present state. However, when you change your present state of being, which is a large part of what spiritual enlightenment is all about, you also change your emotional state as well. Things that you've felt before, you no longer feel now, and things that you didn't feel before suddenly become important to you.

177   A *good* feeling about a certain activity, person or place is an agreement, a confirmation, with who you are in

the present moment. A *bad* feeling about a certain activity, person or place is a disagreement, a conflict, with who you are in the present moment. However, to advance one's self out of one's present situation for the better requires a deliberate disagreement with your present emotional state. This is why many people never change; it's just too emotionally painful.

178   Your good, happy, accomplished feelings appear when your present actions match your present perception of yourself. Your guilty, depressed, fearful, doubtful, unfulfilled feelings appear when your present actions do not match your present perception of yourself. But in order to change your thoughts and actions you must be willing to contradict your emotions; they only confirm who you believe you are in the present. Once you make the conscious decision to change your life for the better, you develop new emotional states to match your new perception of yourself.

179   We must learn to use our emotions to test the frequency of the thoughts and actions we are experiencing; however, we must not be led by them. Your emotions follow your being, not the other way around. This is also why when developing one's self spiritually it is important to know what you want even beyond your emotional state. Yes, your emotions may even motivate you toward your higher, deeper self, but, in the end, your emotions can still betray you because they are always bringing you back to who you were, not to who you can truly be.

180   Without getting too emotional, we must train ourselves to guide our feelings toward what we really want, not to what we really don't want, because whether you want what you think of or you don't want what you are thinking of, the fact still remains: YOU'RE STILL THINKING OF IT! And as long as you continue to think about that which you say you don't want (which is an emotional

response), it will be what you don't want that shall happen to you because of your continuous thinking about it. This is a universal law.

181   Know this. It is your perception that is happening to you. Your interpretation of physical reality is the only thing that can actually happen to you in your life. This too is a universal law. Basically, you become that which you think about the most. And what you do to others you actually do to and for yourself. These are indeed universal laws.

182   For example, even though there are those who consider charity, compassion, selflessness and forgiveness as being naïve and even weak-minded, such a personality remains the strongest remedy for the relief of human suffering and the realization of one's own dreams and aspirations.

183   Even though many people are benefiting from the selfless acts of others, even more people still choose to think only of themselves and their own personal gain. They cannot see how such a selfish personality limits them and adds to their own suffering.

184   Contrary to common beliefs, actually performing acts of charity, compassion and faith are the best things a Hiphoppa can do for her *Self*. These acts strengthen the spiritual vitality of the Hiphoppa and teach our children (through example) the way of peace.

185   Prophetess Simone G. Parker has taught over many years that *it is one's Selfish Inconsiderate Needs over one's ability to share and freely assist others that lead many people into their own cycle of suffering.* Even though their own acts of selfishness may appear to make their own concerns the priority in their lives, such selfishness actually has them committing to everything except themselves.

186   Just as anger, hate and insecurity do not hurt others as much as they eventually hurt you, forgiveness, love and charity eventually benefit you more than they benefit the

recipients of such acts.

187   Know this. When you express hate or love, both hate and love are first expressed within your *Self* before they are passed on to others. Every thought/expression that you pass on to others is first experienced within your *Self*. Actually, you are the first to receive the effects of the thoughts and actions that you express toward others.

188   Remember, you are the first recipient of whatever you decide to express to others. This too is a universal law. Therefore, think only those thoughts that you truly want for yourself. It is not that what you say actually comes back to you; it is that what you say has never left you.

189   What we call talking out loud is really others listening in on our expressed thoughts. In actuality you never really talk TO anyone; you are really expressing your thoughts out loud or through your mouth and others are simply listening in on what your mind is doing (saying). But in Truth, all outward communication is secondhand.

190   Charity and forgiveness (for example) are also secondhand expressions. Charity is a productively selfish act. Forgiveness is also a productively selfish act. At the beginning of one's spiritual education one does not perform these acts for the benefit of others exclusively; ultimately one does them for the benefit of one's *Self*.

191   This is very important to remember because many people hear about miraculous healings, expanded awareness, and abundant wealth, and they attempt to acquire such gifts through meditation, prayer and/or affirmation without having the character required to attain such gifts. Health, love, awareness and wealth are not only the gifts of the spirit, they are the character of the spirit; they are spiritual law. And no spiritual law can protect you if your character is not the law itself. Health, love, awareness and wealth are not only states of personal

character they are indeed spiritual laws.

[192] These acts empower you! Thoughts and acts of love, charity, forgiveness, etc., empower you! Likewise, thoughts and acts of hate, selfishness, revenge, etc., destroy you. This is THE LAW and this is why it is very important never to hate. For hate is simply self-destructive, it makes you vulnerable; whereas love is self-protective, an act of self-creation. Therefore, love (create) your *Self* by radiating love toward others. And likewise, you are indeed hating (destroying) your *Self* by expressing hate toward others. Take care of your *Self*. Don't hate!

[193] Patience, charity, forgiveness, love, faith, etc., are regarded as superhuman acts in societies where selfishness, anxiety, depression, hatred, doubt, etc., are the social norms of the day. Again, all such acts, like patience, charity, forgiveness, love, faith, etc., when outwardly performed, benefit you more than they benefit others.

[194] The oldest, most ancient universal law is that you are the author of your own life. This is the mystery. This is the secret. This is the revelation, and this is what begins your spiritual journey. Your work upon the spiritual path includes the actual realization of your limitlessness and making such realizations a habit in your everyday life.

[195] The object is to become and remain a spirit being realizing that you create the laws (conditions) that shall govern your life. In fact, you are a law unto yourself! For when the attuned Hiphoppa habitually gives a divine performance in the World, all laws of divine origin are automatically in alignment with that Hiphoppa's nature and being.

[196] Again, one need not focus upon following the laws of one's country if one's habitual character is peace, love, unity and safely having fun. At this level of spiritual development one no longer fights the law, one now unites with the law

through understanding, becoming the law itself, becoming a law unto oneself. At this level you are truly DOWN BY LAW! There it is.

THE SIXTEENTH OVERSTANDING
OUR GOD – THE GREAT EVENT

TRACK ONE

1   It's funny how soon we forget the condition we were in before Hip Hop became part of the mainstream.

2   We seem to have forgotten who we were before that invisible creative force touched the minds of all of us at the same time!

3   In Truth, no one created Hip Hop! In Truth, Hip Hop created us! Hip Hop saved us, and this gospel is a remembrance of that experience!

4   How long shall we deny that at our most vulnerable and hopeless state as a group of *people*, at the end of all human strength and knowledge, when all social institutions closed their doors to us, something spiritual, something creative, something nurturing (yet non-physical) touched the minds of thousands of us at the same time and transformed and modified what we thought of ourselves and our environment. Such an awareness does not originate with three or four *hip-hop pioneers*; such an awareness comes from GOD!

5   To know GOD is not a right, it is a privilege! Survival strategies such as Street Language, Street Fashion, Street Knowledge, Street Entrepreneurship, Breakin, Emceein, Graffiti Art, Deejayin and Beat Boxin came from a variety of unplanned and spontaneous sources saving many from sickness, hatred, ignorance and poverty. Hip Hop was and still is divinely guided, and its worldwide

success is really unexplainable.

6   This begins the Hip Hop spiritual life: recognizing *The Force* that moves and has moved with you. To begin aligning your awareness to the intelligence that guides your life. To cease taking the magical moments in your life for granted. To begin cultivating and caring for that *Force* which inspired those events in your life that happen and happened without your doing or planning. To finally begin a serious study into *The Force* that has guided you right here, G-O-D—<u>G</u>uiding <u>O</u>ur <u>D</u>irection.

7   I began to truly see GOD *guiding our direction* while I was watching the film *Rhyme & Reason*, directed by Peter Spirer. I was always aware of GOD's presence intellectually but still the actual reality of GOD had not really hit me yet. In the film *Rhyme & Reason*, Grandmaster Caz explains that the first *jams* presented by Kool DJ Herc were presented at 1520 Sedgwick Avenue in the Bronx, New York, sometime around 1973.

8   As Grandmaster Caz of the Cold Crush Brothers explained the birth of Hip Hop, I began to see that he was standing in a familiar playground park just between 1600 and 1520 Sedgwick Avenue. My hands began to shake because I lived at 1600 Sedgwick Avenue from 1972 to 1974. In fact, as Caz explained the birth of Hip Hop I scrambled and pulled out a photo album of some of my baby pictures, which captured me and my brother Kenny at about seven and eight years old at the very park in which Caz was describing the birth of Hip Hop. I was shocked!

9   Going further, as I began to pick out certain photographs of my childhood at 1600 and 1520 Sedgwick Avenue, I came across a photograph of my mother posing in front of an original Kool Herc graffiti tag in 1972! I was amazed! But even more than being amazed, I was now aware!

10   I wondered to myself, why was I at 1600 and 1520 Sedgwick Avenue in the Bronx in 1972? Anybody could have been there; why me? Why KRS? What *force* guided me, my brother and my mother to that specific location at that precise time when Kool DJ Herc was said to have started Hip Hop in the Bronx? Why was I there?

11   No human hand or mind could have set up such a scenario. In 1972 the term Hip Hop and my name KRS ONE did not even exist yet, and no one was aware that what Kool Herc was doing would eventually become a 10 billion dollar music industry and urban culture influencing millions of people through art.

12   In fact, when I asked my mother about her posing in front of Kool Herc's signature tag in 1972, she said that she was just taking a picture—no specific reason for Kool Herc's tag to be in the background, she was just posing for a photograph.

13   Twenty years later, however, I'm KRS ONE and Kool Herc is the Father of Hip Hop. Who knew? We were just living our lives; my mother was just randomly posing for a photograph and took other photographs of me and Kenny at 1600 and 1520 Sedgwick Avenue in the Bronx. What was it that motivated her? It was at this moment that I began to see GOD—<u>G</u>uiding <u>O</u>ur <u>D</u>irection.

14   Was it a mere coincidence that I (out of all people) would be at the birthplace of Hip Hop as a young child growing up in the Bronx? At eight years old I had no idea what my life would become; I was just outside playing and enjoying the *block parties* of the time. But obviously there was a real *force* (an intelligence) with a real plan that guided my mother to live at 1600 Sedgwick Avenue at the precise time that Hip Hop was about to start.

15   No one could have predicted years later that I would become KRS ONE—the first self-proclaimed *teacha* of the

Hip Hop arts and sciences. No human mind could have consciously set my (or Hip Hop's) history in this way—only the true governor of the universe can do such things.

16   These seemingly random events and places that I would frequent as a child turned out to be the very causes of my professional adult life and the birth of Hip Hop itself! I realized that I was destined for this, destined to be who I am today. At that point I realized (or rather remembered) my true Self. I realized that GOD IS REAL! And I AM HIP HOP!

17   After watching the film *Rhyme & Reason* I realized just how real GOD is and was in my life, or with my life. And I use the word *my* very lightly here because the revelation I received after watching *Rhyme & Reason* showed me that nothing that I have done was actually *my* or *mine*.

18   I realized that just as I was unaware of this intelligent *force* guiding my life in my younger years, I was equally unaware of this same *force* guiding my life in my older years. I realized that *my* actions were not exclusively *my* own, and I immediately humbled myself before the actual PRESENCE OF GOD (Guiding Our Direction) which was also GOD's face.

19   I could actually see GOD! I always knew of GOD's loving presence but I could never really <u>see</u> and *feel* the right-now presence of GOD until then, and I was embarrassed at my years of stupidity and immaturity. But the forgiveness came immediately after with the revelation that I had really done nothing at all. In fact, the idea that I actually did something was immature to begin with.

20   Now I began to actually see GOD—the Love that has guided me thus far. I began to pay closer attention to the seemingly random events of my life and how they all added up to my success, guidance, strength and

protection. I began to see how delicate I was and how fragile I was, and how helpless and blind I was; and how this force, this intelligence, stayed with me for a reason, to get something accomplished.

21   I finally felt "the LOVE" OF GOD and to whom I belonged. I began to know GOD's love for me more intently, in a more rational, logical sense—not just in the human sense of affection and/or respect or trust, but more in a oneness, in a caring sense of dependency, like I was part of GOD's language or being, like we actually depended upon one another to exist. I realized that when I made spiritual mistakes, that when I sinned against GOD's nature, that it was not just as simple as a mistake that could be corrected with an acknowledgement; I was literally hurting and abandoning the Love of my life. I was acting as if GOD did not love me for real, and this (for GOD) was like the loss of an innocent child to the streets.

22   Beyond the love that we humans know, it was like GOD was madly in love with me in an urgent kind of crazy way, like the way you may love your arm or leg. And I struggle with my words here because *love* is not even the right word for the feelings that I felt when I realized that I was actually home with the *force* that sent me into the World with purpose. Like when your mother sends you to the grocery store to pick up items that the both of you need to survive and you go in a different direction, spending the money on your own selfish wants—I was actually betraying GOD. I realized that my disobedience not only made me a thief to my own GOD-given gifts and an ungrateful son to all of my blessings, but that I was also denying the very reality of my own holiness and purpose.

23   More than just being an offense against righteousness, my selfish inconsiderate needs made it uncomfortable for GOD to dwell with me—I couldn't be

trusted. I thought that I had to become more than myself to be acceptable to GOD so I struggled with one error after another. But when the revelation of GOD's actual presence hit me, I felt that it was GOD who was trying everything to be more to me, that it was I who, out of fear, was simply not being my true Self. The sadness I felt was the revelation that it was I who was ignoring GOD, not the other way around. Actually the "I" that was feeling sad was GOD! And my sadness was not depression, it was guilt.

[24]   It was like GOD was trying so hard to wake me up, and I was dead, or blind, or retarded, or rebellious, or sick, or something that equates to not being functional in GOD's reality. I felt bad for GOD because I finally knew that what I call "I" was a major part of GOD's existence, like an arm, or a leg, or an eye, and when "I" is not functioning properly GOD suffers.

[25]   With that one flash of revelation I realized that GOD desperately and frantically cares for us, actually needs us. Like a mother struggling to save her child from drowning, GOD loves us in this way. When I realized this, I began to consciously move with that *force*. I never wanted to disappoint GOD again by getting in my own way. I wanted to make GOD happy. I wanted to go to the store and pick up the items GOD instructed me to retrieve. Beyond sin, I wanted to be a son.

[26]   From that day, sometime around 1996, it was like everything in the material World was a stage prop (including physical bodies and events) and GOD was the actual meaning or cause of things. Over time I began to retrace the steps of my life and how I became KRS ONE.

[27]   Why was I compelled to leave my mother's home beginning at about 16 years of age? Why did I put it all on the line to become an emcee? And remember, at age 16 (1981) I had not seen the film *Rhyme & Reason* yet. Hip

Hop was still new and just getting started commercially. But I knew in my very being who I was and what I came here to do. But who or what told me this? What force inspired me in this direction and then protected me until I achieved what I saw of myself in childhood?

28   With no home, no job, no school, no family, no friends, no manager, no producer, no money, no credit, no resources, no organized Rap music industry and very little talent of my own, my only salvation was to place my hopes upon some kind of a supernatural breakthrough. I needed a miracle! And that's exactly what I got.

29   Looking back upon my rise to success truthfully, I did not achieve my goals solely on my own. I did not make KRS ONE on my own. A lot of once-in-a-lifetime-moments (and people) had to occur for me to be KRS ONE. Before the release of my first successful recording ("South Bronx"—1986) I had to beat the odds that were stacked against not only me, but everyone living in the Bronx during the early 1980s.

30   Try to understand this. From about 1981 until about 1985 I was homeless with nowhere to go. The crack-cocaine era was just getting started and almost every day you would see a random puddle of blood in the street where someone had JUST been killed or wounded. So, if I was not in a library, or sleeping in a hospital waiting room area, or in a museum, or aimlessly riding the subway back and forth, I was by myself walking/wandering around the five boroughs of New York, reading graffiti art on walls and trains, hanging out at the free park jams and talking to my invisible friend—GOD.

31   For if I was to become an emcee, GOD was going to have to become real for me. There was literally no other way for me; I needed a supernatural breakthrough. But as you can see, GOD IS REAL! If KRS ONE's career *means*

anything at all, it means that GOD IS TRULY REAL! Not a holy book, not a church or temple, not even words—it is GOD and the powerful experience that comes with a union with GOD that is REAL!

32   Even though I have participated and contributed greatly to my own success—no doubt, I still can't front—I also took advantage of certain life situations and circumstances that no man could have provided or predicted. And if these certain life situations and circumstances had not occured I could not have become KRS ONE even with talent.

33   Being in the right place at the right time, running into exactly who I needed to meet, protection even when I didn't know I was being protected, unexpected random opportunities, good health in the midst of mass sickness, doors that were closed to others opening for me, my social worker becoming my DJ, the battles, the births, the deaths, even the coming together of the Stop The Violence Movement and so on, all point to a higher, deeper intelligence guiding and protecting my development. And this is what I've been paying close attention to over the last 22 years of my Hip Hop experience. It is to this Divine Mind/intelligence (GOD) that I owe everything.

34   GOD IS REAL! And when all you have to survive is GOD and your dreams, GOD and your dreams become real in your life. This is also true of Hip Hop. If Hip Hop is the center of your life for real, then it is Hip Hop that shall give you life—for real. With your own perception of your own life as a "Hiphoppa" you create your own specialized reality that is real for you with real effects in the material World but is not real for everyone else simply because they do not believe.

35   I believe that "I am Hip Hop" and I believe that I am a specific kind of Hiphoppa. So the Hip Hop reality that I create for myself produces the effects that you see.

No one gave me anything. With GOD's guidance, care and protection I perceived my Hip Hop life into existence. And so will you!

³⁶ For there are aspects of your *self* and your environment that are not controlled by you, yet they happen. There are things that come your way that you did not bring your way; a random book, DVD, or CD with a much-needed message, an unexpected turn of events, the meeting of the right person at the right time, etc.

³⁷ These things can all be attracted by your mind, we know this; thoughts are things! But what is the cause of thought? Thoughts do become things but the things that thoughts become still enter an ordered universe. And if thoughts are the only things, then whose thoughts made the thing called *thoughts?* And who's thought is thinking the universe and all the worlds, stars, cosmic events, and us?

³⁸ Yes we are indeed the authors of our own lives, but GOD is indeed the book, the pen and the table by which we write. To see GOD is to acknowledge that you are not in total control of your *Self* or your environment; that there is a loving *force* that thinks with you, guides you, and protects you for the purpose of actualizing its purpose.

³⁹ Know this. There are things that even the physical body does without your permission, one of which is that it continues to live. Thoughts enter your mind without your permission. You are forced to breathe. These conditions to our reality show us that we are not exclusively responsible for our lives; we may only be responsible for our living, and this may even be questionable.

⁴⁰ We may not be responsible for life; we may only be responsible for how it is lived. We don't have all of the answers to our own existence, yet we exist. Therefore, some mysterious part of ourselves has the answers to those other parts of us that complete us and is continuing to produce

the *human* experience for a reason—without our consent.

41   We are not the reason that we exist because we don't have a full understanding as to what makes us exist and why. If we look closely, we exist in a visible and invisible *world* at the same time.

42   Things that are out of our control and planning happen to us throughout the day, which guide the types of days that we experience. With all of our planning and prediction, humanity still exists within an *anything can still happen* reality. There is still another *force* with another plan governing and guiding the conditions of nature and human affairs; this is what we call "GOD"—the consistency of our being, the condition that sustains life, the Great Event.

43   For we have learned that right along with looking for GOD *within* ourselves we must also look for GOD without ourselves. Meaning that we must also look at the guidance of our lives outside of ourselves and even without ourselves. When you can see without your *Self*, you see GOD. When you can act without your *Self* you become God.

44   We must develop the ability to focus upon the seemingly unplanned and spontaneous activities of our lives, especially those activities not directly caused by us that still affect us in a variety of ways. GOD speaks through life circumstances. Therefore, one of the main objectives of the Hiphop spiritual life is to learn how to get out of one's own way and LISTEN for the instruction of GOD! "Let go and let GOD." Another objective of the Hiphop spiritual life is not just to unite with GOD, but also to realize that you are already united with GOD, which makes you, at this very moment, a Holy Spirit. Repent; it is you who denies your own holiness with sin and fear. It seems that the World has made you afraid of your Self.

45   STOP DENYING YOUR OWN HOLINESS just to survive in the World! As a community, we must

forever acknowledge the *force* that has already saved us from sickness, hatred, ignorance and poverty, and has restored us to health, love, awareness and wealth. We must stop seeking and studying the gospels and become them. We must live to experience the true power of GOD and not just read about what such an experience holds for us. Our GOD is a real *force!* And it is the PRESENCE of GOD (the force) that actually brings one's life into peace, power and prosperity. FEELING that GOD is actually with you IS peace, power and prosperity.

46   But to get into the presence of GOD, it is you that must open your ((((I)))) first, because, believe it or not, it is not GOD who is denying your holiness, it is you who denies GOD's Love. GOD is already with you RIGHT NOW! But it is you who are afraid of GOD. Presently, many people are blind to their God-*force* because it frightens them, so it is impossible for them to see GOD. Because of guilt and fear, they hide themselves from GOD.

47   Study the spellings of *God* and *GOD* throughout this entire instrument closely. For us, *God* is what *GOD* creates us to be. We are in GOD—the Great Mother, the unmanifested source of all energy and matter in the universe, the Great Event, the Inner-G. For us, GOD has no title, name or location. *God* is what we call ourselves! For only God can come from GOD.

48   This is what the *Hiphop* spiritual path is all about. It's about re-acquainting one's self with one's own divinity, one's own divine nature. For it is in one's divine nature that one actually communicates with GOD. *God* is a term for OUR spiritually heightened human awareness. And this is not to be mistaken for a spirituality of the Self, but rather the Self immersed in spirituality.

49   Know this. To communicate with GOD one must be trained to do so, and it is GOD who does the training.

Through ordinary life experiences GOD communicates to those who sincerely communicate with GOD. Life itself walks with you. This is part of your stolen or forgotten legacy. God is your rightful name/nature. God is what you are when you are in your right mind, but at every moment of the day we deny this Truth because of fear. God is what we are afraid of becoming, and this is why we remain trapped by the World and World circumstances.

50   Once you are no longer *afraid of GOD*, you can become God. And when I say afraid of GOD I mean that because of our past mistakes we are afraid of approaching GOD. We hide ourselves from GOD because we feel that we are not good enough (or God enough) to approach GOD. But once you realize that even at your most ignorant and immature moment GOD has never left you, you realize that running from GOD is impossible, that what you are really running from is the ghost of your past self.

51   WAKE UP HIPHOPPA! GOD is the very event that caused you to go astray in the beginning. It is GOD who has been teaching you from before you were even born, preparing you with the events of your very life for the ministry you are now qualified to promote. For only wisdom and real-life experiences possess the authority to correctly teach others. The greatest of all sins is to believe that you actually have the power to sin, that somehow there is you *and* GOD. WAKE UP HIPHOPPA! GOD is a thousand times more devious than you can ever be. In fact, it is those who, because of fear and/or pride, never come to GOD for correction, who continue to judge themselves when GOD is not even judging them. It is they who suffer the most in prolonged immaturity and ignorance. And even this is GOD's doing.

52   This is why when you are chosen by GOD to finally mature in your spiritual understanding there is no more

time to waste. If you are privileged enough to be reading this paragraph right now it means that GOD (not KRS) is trying to show you something about your divine nature. And this is how GOD teaches, through life circumstances and random events. Open your senses to GOD's actual movement across the material World. Pay more attention to those random events that seem to warn you, teach you and guide you through life. This is how GOD speaks.

53   We must train/prepare OURSELVES for direct conversations with GOD as Gods. We must mature past the level of doing things in an attempt to find GOD or please GOD. GOD is not found in what we do or say, GOD is what we mean when we do or say. GOD is what we want when we ingest drugs, or overeat, indulge in pleasure, pray, sing or complete a task. However, it may now be time to stop trying to do for GOD and allow GOD to do for you, to guide you, to heal, feed, clothe and protect you. This is the original path toward spiritual enlightenment, to be still and know that GOD IS GOD!

54   To finally be in harmony with GOD, this is the seat of true joy and salvation. To commune with GOD, to have a real relationship with the mind of the universe, to know GOD's ways; this is spiritual awareness. Reading about the prophets of old without having their experiences with GOD can make you feel even more guilty. GOD does not speak English. GOD's *Word* does not come from an alphabet; GOD's *Word* comes directly from GOD to your actual life experiences. The question is, *are you listening?* In fact, what are you really listening to? Who and/or what do you really value? GOD or the World?

55   This is the difference between a *reader* and a *believer*. And in a Hiphop sense, this is the difference between a *believer* and a *perceiver*. Do you believe in the existence of GOD or do you perceive through the existence of GOD?

Do we really want to know GOD, or are we simply content with following the religion of the one with the biggest bombs? What, then, is enlightenment if we are not yet free to see (perceive) GOD for ourselves? What kind of spiritual reality are we really living in? What is enlightenment?

56   This question hit me one day while at a Barnes & Noble bookstore in El Paso, Texas. I was on tour traveling on Interstate Highway 10, and I had pulled over to get some audio books for the rest of my drive into Los Angeles, California.

57   There I happened to run into the famous Graffiti writer Skeme (from the film *Style Wars*) who had his family with him. Once again, this whole event was unplanned and random. After talking to Skeme, this very question jumped out at me from the front cover of a popular magazine: *What Is Enlightenment?*

58   As I reached down to pick up the magazine I felt myself immediately answering this very question; what *IS* enlightenment? Before my hand could even touch the magazine I began to go through a plethora of surface answers. Enlightenment is when you've become spiritually aware, enlightenment is to have realized your spiritual nature, even your spirit reality. Enlightenment is to have achieved the Truth! To unite with GOD! My mind continued on: enlightenment is simply awareness or rather Ahhh-wareness, to finally get it! I picked up the magazine.

59   While holding the magazine and standing in the same spot I began to look around the store at all of the other book buyers and readers and began to wonder about their enlightenment. What IS enlightenment and who has really achieved it? How can you even know if someone IS truly enlightened? What must they do? Or say? Or be?

60   What must someone BE to actually be enlightened? Do they have to be from India? Or from China? Or from

Africa? Do they have to speak a certain way? Dress a certain way? Talk a certain way? How can you really tell if or when a person is really enlightened? And suddenly I realized that even the term "enlightenment" may be misleading.

61   In our modern, consumer-driven, guilt-ridden, everything glossy, glamorous and cheaply packaged, industrialized society, is true spiritual enlightenment even possible? Even in the 10 billion dollar "enlightenment" business, people are more likely to gravitate toward that which serves their own self-interests than the actual acquiring of Truth or "enlightenment."

62   So what IS enlightenment? These days it can't have anything to do with the Truth because today's Truth is too scary for even sincere Truth seekers to deal with. On another level, in a society generated by mostly technology and commerce, Truth may simply be useless. The spiritual idea here is *give me what I want NOW!*

63   As I began to walk over to the cashier to purchase my copy of *What Is Enlightenment* I thought to myself, denial is what most people are practicing—not spirituality. Today's spirituality is rooted in mass denial, escape from guilt and/ or chronic individualism. People don't just want GOD to themselves, they want GOD from themselves because to face the real essence of GOD is simply too painful for many; their own guilt is just too intense for them.

64   People seem to only be interested in the god that they create who conveniently fits into their already accepted beliefs, schedules and rules. So, how can anyone truly answer the question or even pose the question of "what is enlightenment?" if we are not willing to actually question our already made-up minds and beliefs as to what enlightenment is?

65   Is Muhammad Ali enlightened? Is James Brown enlightened? Is George W. Bush enlightened? What do

you consider an enlightened soul today? Gandhi? Mother Teresa? Could President Bill Clinton be an enlightened soul? What about Tupac, or Stan Tookie Williams? Or Howard Zinn? What do you consider enlightenment? One man's enlightenment is another man's silliness and immaturity—even evil.

66   Truth is Truth! And Truth can come out of anyone's mouth at any time from anywhere. But in today's quest for spiritual enlightenment the face delivering the Truth is more important than the Truth itself.

67   We don't want Truth; we want to confirm our own reality. This is why the so-called "Truth-seeking" groups in the United States (as an example) are not asking, and more importantly, not publishing those hard questions that actually lead to enlightenment or Truth. Truth may shatter your business goals. Truth may lead you to divorce, or even suicide! Truth may destroy Hip Hop!

68   True enlightenment may actually point to our own destruction. Or maybe even a glimpse of the Truth is so offensive and painful to deal with that we simply make up our own truths in which it is easier to put our faith. We don't want Truth; we simply want to survive a little better than we already are. Most people in search of Truth today are simply in search of empowerment.

69   As I got on the cashier's line at Barnes & Noble I began to wonder about the offensiveness of what I am suggesting. I thought to myself, what if the Truth is that African Americans are truly slaves by nature and the Thirteenth Amendment is the reason for America's financial crisis?

70   What if GOD actually approves of slavery? What if this is THE TRUTH? Would Black Americans faithfully and spiritually take their places in the American society as slaves, ordained by GOD as such? As a surface

example, what if this was THE TRUTH? Would African Americans accept such a Truth? Would everyone else accept such a Truth?

71   My point here is that in today's individualistic, commercially driven societies Truth seems to be accepted based upon one's need to survive. Not only must Truth be useful for today's Truth-seeker, but if the Truth points to the demise of the Truth-seeker in today's society, even the Truth can be rejected! In today's World it seems that survival is more important than Truth.

72   As another example, what if the United States is truly cursed as a nation for its crimes against the aboriginal peoples of the Americas? Spiritually, would we (Americans) move to another country and start all over again as peasants and immigrants?

73   Even deeper, what if Osama Bin Laden is the "Christ" returned to overthrow the Roman empire (the United States) and free all of "his" people as promised by the Bible? Would we adopt Islam as the true religion and "spiritual" practice of GOD? Even deeper than that, can we? Can you? Would YOU follow him? Would YOU support him? Are we as Americans willing to live THIS Truth? I'm not quite sure.

74   And just to be fair and balanced here, what if Christianity is truly the only way to GOD and the Truth is that all other religious and spiritual thought is indeed false? Knowing this to be the Truth, would Muslims convert to Christianity? Would Hindus, Buddhists, Jews, Satanists and Witches give up that which is comfortable and safe for them and convert to Christianity? Again, I'm not quite sure about this.

75   What if the startling Truth is that President George W. Bush is God's victorious "crusader" sent to bring even more freedom, justice and equality to the World? What if

the Truth is that the United States IS the World's police force ordained by the true GOD of all the universes? Would we stop protesting the invasion of Iraq and America's failed foreign policy? I don't know. But what I do know is that we want what is convenient to us as individuals—and this is THE TRUTH, our Truth.

76 The Truth is that many are NOT interested in "Truth" or "enlightenment," many simply want to survive by any comfortable means necessary! We are NOT interested in whether or not the Vatican is the true central home of the "body of Christ"; if we don't like the policies or conduct of the Catholic priesthood we simply quit the religion, even criticize and debate these "Holy Fathers."

77 It doesn't matter what enlightenment is or isn't, the real answer as to "what is enlightenment" is that enlightenment is whatever spiritual knowledge I am comfortable with. Enlightenment is knowledge that confirms MY survival and comfort. And this is especially true in the United States when someone like Osama Bin Laden may never be on the cover of the magazine *What Is Enlightenment* even though he may be the spiritual hero of many in the Muslim World—even the Christian World.

78 Islam is the spiritual practice of millions of people around the World, but millions of others refuse to see the TRUTH in its ways and principles. How can this be? What if the Truth is that all women should dress as Muslim women do, in full head-dress and clothing down to their feet, exposing as little as possible of their flesh in public? Would American and European women do the same? I don't think so; such a practice is simply not comfortable for them. And this is the point where, if GOD is not comfortable or convenient to us, we simply disregard GOD.

79 It seems that the force that makes us free is the same force that enslaves us. Meaning that freedom seems

to foster a feeling of "do what you <u>want to</u> do, not what you <u>have to</u> do." Well, finally I was next on line to be served by the cashier and the Truth hit me again! We are only willing to follow that which is fun and safe for us to follow. We are only willing to support that which immediately supports us. As American spiritualists plagued by our own chronic state of guilt, fear and denial and false history, we can never know that which we never had.

80   In our present spiritual state we will probably never know GOD or true spiritual living simply because we never knew GOD or true spiritual living from the perspectives of others. Historically, we have created our own god according to our own commerce laws and anything that interferes with this system of thought is indeed criminal. And suddenly I gained enlightenment!

81   "Next please," the cashier called out, and as I pulled out my $7.50 to purchase my copy of *What is Enlightenment* the Truth hit me again! What we call "spiritual living" is simply our own seeking to be accepted by whatever routine is powerful enough to sustain us individually and make us comfortable and mentally secure—that is the essence of American spirituality today.

82   If the guy with the gun is Christian, then so am I. That IS today's enlightenment! This works for us because this is what's in power. We are not actually spending our lives seeking GOD, we are spending our lives staying out of the violent way of our oppressors, which includes pledging our allegiances to THEIR religions so that we are not killed, jailed or rendered unemployed.

83   American enlightenment today seems to begin with what you are willing to accept as valuable insight, and value is usually placed upon personal security. It has nothing to do with what is true or what is real. Today's spiritual learning has more to do with who we are willing to accept

as credible, and credibility is based upon material needs and political results.

84   Most people don't approach their spiritual practice as a "child," or as a "tabula rasa" (blank tablet). Most people approach their spiritual life looking to satisfy their material needs—they want security. They don't really want to become a new being, to mature; they want to strengthen who they already are with a newer version of what they already know. Hip Hop's spiritual life CANNOT be about this kind of denial.

85   As seekers of Truth we must be seekers of Truth, not just seekers of political empowerment and/or financial security. Yes, we are advocates of Hip Hop's empowerment and security; we understand the importance of such material conditions, but let's get our priorities straight! As a temple for the advancement and preservation of Hip Hop, we advocate the seeking of that mysterious GOD-force that has guided and protected us thus far.

86   We are interested in the Truth of our being as Hiphoppas. We are seeking the face of GOD. We are ready to reconcile with our God and live for the comfort of OUR GOD. Yes, we can ease GOD's burdens. Yes, we can take care of GOD; don't you think it's about time? Let us stop asking GOD to solve our problems, and begin solving GOD's problems, beginning with our own immaturity and disobedience to GOD.

87   This is the uniqueness of Hip Hop's spiritual practices. It's the same concept delivered by President John F. Kennedy: Ask not what God can do for you, ask instead what you can do for GOD. We have realized that union with GOD is to love GOD as GOD has loved us. Return to GOD the care, cultivation and protection that GOD has shown us. This is not about how much money you have, or how politically powerful you are, or even how spiritually

enlightened you may be. The question here is, how well do you care for GOD?

TRACK TWO

[88]   We (Hip Hop) are *a force* within THE FORCE. We are birthed from within GOD. GOD (the Divine Mother) is The Force, the unmanifested realm, the Great Event which WE live and have life within.

[89]   Many good-hearted and sincere citizens of the Hip Hop community have been tricked into believing that either GOD is weaker than the government or that GOD doesn't exist at all! Many actually believe that their jobs and their votes are actually above the existence of GOD! Many of us actually believe and live like this.

[90]   Through OUR OWN ACTIONS we confirm every day that our *outer* circumstances are actually more powerful and overwhelming to us than our *inner* reality, and it is this form of thinking, living and being that actually denies us access to OUR OWN GOD!

[91]   This particular problem begins when you stop believing in yourself, your principles and your own life history. GOD may not be the reality of others, but GOD is indeed your reality. And if you deny your reality for someone else's reality, then by your own mind you have freely given up your own power. This is how devils work!

[92]   We have seen now for many centuries that the work of devils is to get you to doubt yourself through fear and/or temptation. They really have no power over you and their strength is based upon illusions and fake images, so they must coerce, convince, lie and tempt you toward your own demise.

93   Devils cannot really harm you or kill you, so the work of devils is to get you to harm and/or kill your *Self!* Once you have forgotten who you really are, due to self-doubt and/or some form of terrorism, you actually will fight against what will free you and continue to accept what has enslaved you.

94   The main issue here is that the capitalistic European/American culture is simply NOT YOURS! This goes for our so-called White, Asian, Latino and Native sisters and brothers as well. GOD may not be the choice or character of those who seek to exploit you, but as for your very being, God may be your very identity. And the more you are convinced to deny your God-nature, the more you can be led astray, enslaved and even killed.

95   As the great prophet Kwame Ture has taught, *In relationship to religious differences, Europe is dominantly intolerant. They've burned Jews at the stake, they've burned Christians at the stake, they've burned Muslims at the stake, they've burned nonbelievers at the stake, they've burned everybody at the stake!*

96   *The particular history of religion in Europe is different from everywhere in the World. Many of the Europeans here in America are here as a result of religious intolerance when they were fleeing Europe to come to America for what they called 'religious freedom.'*

97   *But the religious intolerance of Europe has scared the entire World, reaching its climax with Hitler and the Jews. When* [Karl] *Marx makes the statement that 'religion is the opiate of the masses', he's absolutely correct for Europe.*

98   *Thus, it is a fact that in Europe religion was used by the nations to confuse the people and to intoxicate the masses. We say that this is all true, but outside of Europe religion has been used to help the people as a civilizing force. Certainly if one knows anything about the history of Arabia, and the*

history of the prophet Muhammad, and the religion of Islam they will see that Islam came as a civilizing force!

99   *So that here the relationship of the People to religion is different than it was in Europe. Marx and Lenin, when they think philosophical materialism, they make it atheistic. Thus, they impose upon people who want to be socialist that before you are socialist you must say that you don't believe in GOD.*

100   *Perhaps in Europe you can discuss this, but nowhere outside of Europe can you go and tell people that in order to be revolutionary you must say that GOD does not exist. Especially not these Africans because they believe in GOD!*

101   *When I went to work for the movement in the 1960s, the first thing the people tell you is 'if GOD ain't in this, I ain't! If GOD ain't leading this, we not gonna win this!' If you look at the African Liberation Movement and trace it, you will see that it was led by heroic African Christians like Martin Luther King. Even Malcolm X people forget was a Muslim minister. So the role of religion in the African revolution outside of Europe was entirely different.*

102   *Thus, you cannot take this* [European] *culture and try to impose it upon OUR people, they will not respond. They must respond to THEIR culture.*

103   Kwame Ture continued, *No one judges a system* [of thought] *by its appearance. All systems are judged by their principles, not by their believers. Who in this room judges Christianity by Christians?*

104   And this is the point right here. GOD belongs to us, just as much as we belong to GOD. WE AND THE GREAT SPIRIT ARE ONE! Yes, we live in GOD. The very air we breathe is GOD! And it is GOD that provides OUR consciousness. For us, GOD is the natural and normal fabric of everyday life. We exist in GOD as gods. This is our stolen legacy!

105   This is the only thing that has been stolen from us,

KNOWLEDGE OF OUR TRUE NATURES. Once our children had their sacred rites, rituals and spiritual traditions taken away from them through terrorism, war and invasion over several generations, we simply forgot who we were. And when we forgot who we were, we forgot what we had and we simply gave everything else away through our own ignorance, infighting, betrayals, lusts and disunity.

106   If there is one solution to humanity's problem of disunity, betrayal and temptation, it is that WE MUST RETURN TO GOD! We must return to our God state of being. GOD is a human concept given freely to the World by enlightened human minds, and it is this concept that we must reclaim again by reaffirming our identity as GOD's. The question is: are you African, Asian, European, Indian, Indigenous, or are you fully human? Are you a god?

107   Are you Black or are you human? Are you White or are you human? Do you live in a house, a home, a city, a nation, or do you live in GOD? GOD does not live in the *Spirit realm*, GOD is the *Spirit realm* itself. Human beings are actually Spirit beings, and the realm in which we live is GOD. Your reality is a reflection as to what your mind is doing with its access to GOD. Study this carefully.

108   The Truth is that YOU HAVE COME INTO THIS DIMENSION FOR THE SOLE PURPOSE OF BECOMING GOD! And if you notice, this has been our only crime throughout World history.

109   This has been the one criticism of those who wish to exploit our resources and enslave our children. They say, *Who are you to call yourself God?* And the reply is always the same: *Is it not written in your gospels that we are GOD's, that we belong to GOD?* And if we belong to GOD then we are from GOD—we are GOD's gods.

110   For only GOD's own can refuse GOD. Only GOD's gods can accept GOD. Only gods can communicate

directly with GOD. For once you know who you belong to and who really cares for you, you rush to be with such a love. But if you don't know who you belong to, insecurity, anger and continuous worry are almost inevitable. So, who and/or what do you belong to?

111   WAKE UP! WAKE UP HIPHOPPA! You are only a young and inexperienced God. Your only enemy is ignorance and your only friend is knowledge. This is the Truth. The *force* that created you is the *force* that loves you, and that *force* is GOD. It is now time for you to expect the very real presence of GOD and live from within that presence. IT IS TRULY WONDERFUL! And this is your stolen legacy.

112   Know this. You are God in GOD! You are a co-creator in the creation. You have the power and the authority to create, re-create and change your reality at any time. THIS IS YOUR STOLEN LEGACY! You can become whoever or whatever you have the will to accept. You are truly a universal being.

113   Just think, you are not just a girl or a boy; you are also a woman or a man. And you are not just a woman or a man, you are also spirit. And you are not just spirit, you are also God. And you are not just God, you are GOD's. You belong to GOD, the light of eternal being!

114   The decision to create yourself or not create yourself rests within what you are willing to accept for yourself. YOU ARE WHO AND WHAT YOU CREATE YOUR *SELF* TO BE, and your reality is only the dimensions you've learned to see. Read this again until you fully understand what is being said here.

115   Yes you may be your father's daughter or your mother's son, but you are also who you are when you are not in their presence. You are actually many different actions and natures at once. Your identity is only the nature that

you choose (or rather allow) to dominate your being.

116   Therefore, if we are to truly be and remain free as a *People* we must get serious about overcoming the World and its many traps and obstacles. We cannot be dependent upon the same World that we wish to free ourselves from; otherwise, where is our freedom?

117   We must act free to be free. And the ultimate act of freedom is SELF-CREATION, which is an act of God. To be free with the power to free others we must allow the nature (or name/title) of *God* to dominate our being. It is then that we return to our true nature in GOD which is the essence of freedom and peace.

118   WAKE UP! You are really none of the Worldly titles, natures and actions that you have come to accept for yourself. You become these identities to complete whatever task is before you. However, in reality YOU ARE A UNIVERSAL BEING!

119   In fact, the only way that you can be so many different styles of people (mother/father, daughter/son, wife/husband, C.E.O./employee) completing so many different tasks at once is if you are truly universal in nature and multi-dimensional at the core of your being. A one-dimensional creature cannot do all of things that you do daily.

120   Begin to acknowledge that the real YOU belongs to the very fabric of the conscious universe itself. You may say that you are Black or White, etc.; you may say that you are African, European or American, but the Truth is that these titles and the natures that come with these titles are all your own personal choices.

121   The materials that create and sustain your physical body come from outer space, and your conscious awareness is of GOD. Nothing about YOU is material or limited. You are GOD's. You are Spirit. You are a being of and in the

conscious universe. You are choosing to live the way that you are living—for better of for worse.

122   So I ask you, where did the little boy version of you go when you grew up? Where does your title of son or daughter go when you are not being a son or a daughter? Where do you put the titles that you are not presently using? Where does your job description go after work? Do you stop being a father when you sleep? When you put this instrument down to take a break do you stop being a reader? Not at all.

123   The answer here is that each of your titles/names coexists with all of your other titles/names all the time. They exist as part of your total being until you call one or two of them into your physical reality by choice. Simply by choosing or putting your focus upon any of your various names/titles you cause them to dominate your being, and thus your nature, and thus your reality. This is what makes things real for you.

124   For example, by becoming aware of your motherhood or by simply accepting your motherhood you instantly become a mother with motherly motivations and parenting powers. Likewise, it is because you no longer want to act like a child that you no longer act like a child, and in many ways you lose (or set aside) your childhood powers. Maturity is a matter of choice, and your choices are almost always a matter of mind.

125   Those who believe in the authenticity of Santa Claus create Santa Claus experiences for themselves by choice. Those who lend themselves to criminal activity usually end up with criminal results. So what if you got serious about your God-nature by choice? What if you seriously lent yourself to spiritual reality above your material conditions? What would be the quality of your life then?

126   The point here is that any lifestyle produces its own

results. Therefore, those who truly seek spiritual awareness only need to lend themselves to that reality exclusively. This, however, seems to be very difficult for those living from day-to-day, check-to-check, week-to-week, in an urban environment. They say to themselves, how is this possible?

127   And the answer is that you choose your reality based upon the nature (or name) you decide to adopt as real. As an example, at this very moment you are a child and an old man/woman, a human being and a spirit being, a parent and a son/daughter right now. Right now you are choosing your reality. So who are you right now? A reader or God, or both!

128   Whatever nature you are experiencing right now is your decision to experience. In Truth, you are who and what you <u>think</u> you are. You are whatever you <u>tell</u> people you are. You are the story that you tell about yourself. You are what you <u>do</u> repeatedly. So why not think of yourself as a divine being doing divine being things repeatedly? This decision is always yours to make. Why <u>do</u> human being when you can <u>do</u> spirit being?

129   Each title that you have accepted for yourself comes with certain duties and certain powers to accomplish its nature. Every title has a duty, every name has a nature, and every nature has a spirit which operates within certain spiritual laws. Your true spiritual nature is your *Law* and *Savior*. You just have to make your God a priority in your life and suddenly God appears! It's really that simple.

130   You are a location in GOD. You are a creative force, simple and plain. You are literally a place where GOD is. You are a cosmic event, not just the name on your birth certificate. Your real name is actually a cosmic address in space and time; it is where GOD is. You are where GOD is.

131   In all Truth, YOU ARE WHAT GOD IS DOING

AND YOU ARE WHO GOD IS BEING RIGHT NOW. This is what you have forgotten. This is what is missing from your psychology. YOU are the return of God. YOU are the Madhi, the Buddha, the Christ! YOU are the second coming. You are who you've been waiting for. YOU are your savior as well as the savior of others.

132   You are exactly what you choose to see. So what do YOU see? We have come to remind you that you are the God of your life, the lord of your world, the Mayor of your *Inner City*. You are the Law of your life. And when you truly know this and act from this psychology, you shall enter the spirit realm and inherit the ability to create and/or re-create your material reality.

133   But remember, GOD (the divine substance that you are immersed in) is thinking with you. And on a deeper level, you are really doing nothing at all. All thoughts and actions are GOD's. You become a co-creator because of your disobedience or spiritual distance to GOD.

134   You choose to create with GOD as opposed to allowing GOD to create with you. If you would finally realize that ALL is GOD moving, thinking and acting, you would gain enlightenment and cease the fighting against yourself as a co-creator.

135   Many metaphysicians make the grave mistake of thinking that it is their thoughts alone that create their reality, that if they simply control their thinking they can control their lives. This is partially true; however, the problem is the concept of control.

136   The Truth is that you are not the only one thinking. GOD is a real thinking being! And if you use the GOD-*force* to conjure up a thought that is contrary to GOD's real harmony, GOD will shut your thinking down! GOD will override your intentions for your own protection. This is real!

[137] To really control your life, you must stop trying to control your life. Create your thoughts ending with the phrase "*GOD willing.*"

[138] It is now time to RETAKE YOUR UNDERSTANDING AND RESTORE YOUR PERCEPTION! YOU are the author of YOUR life and YOUR identity, and GOD is the publisher and distributor. You actually think through GOD. This is your STOLEN LEGACY RESTORED!

TRACK THREE

[139] Because of the Jewish, Christian, Muslim, Hindu, New Age, New Thought, Buddhist, Wicca and even Atheist popularity within the inner cities of the United States, Hiphoppas have approached their concept of GOD in the same way that they (we) have approached their (our) music production. We have *sampled* a variety of faiths to discover a spiritual experience that seems to work for us.

[140] In my time, Hiphoppas seem to approach GOD as a Conscious Mind present in human beings and physical nature, the source of all life and values (Theism).

[141] We are not GOD, yet in our higher *Selves* we are God (Humanism). Collectively, we believe in the one supreme creator that is called by many names, a self-existent Spirit that is the source of all creation (Monotheism).

[142] We also believe that GOD is separate from the World (Deism) yet we also believe GOD to emanate through and as Nature, still remaining distinct from it (Panentheism).

[143] Hiphoppas also believe that GOD is unknowable (Agnostic Realism) yet we rely upon our intuitive apprehension of spiritual Truth (Gnosticism) to understand

the activity of God. Overall, Hiphoppas collectively believe all of this at the same time. We have found the *Way* that harmonizes most of the World's approaches to GOD.

¹⁴⁴   Some Hiphoppas lean more toward one or another of these approaches toward GOD, but collectively the modern *Hiphop* spiritual experience manages to harmonize all of the above -*isms* and more.

¹⁴⁵   For us (templists), spirituality is about becoming all that we were intended to be. We approach GOD through the symbolism and natural history of Hip Hop. As attuned Hiphoppas (templists), *Hiphop* is practiced as a particular way of seeing the World, one's self and others.

¹⁴⁶   Generally, Hiphoppas read the Bible, the Koran, the Torah, the Bhagavad Gita, the teachings of Buddha and other spiritual teachings all at the same time. Hiphoppas practice Yoga and read all sorts of New Age and New Thought materials.

¹⁴⁷   We seem to have developed our understanding of spiritual reality from the combination of all of these *paths*, teachings and holy texts, yet as a way of life we belong to none of them exclusively. It is like we (Hiphoppas) read these texts not to become them but to search and develop the Spirit that we already feel inside. Generally, we look for ourselves and our understanding of GOD within spiritual texts.

¹⁴⁸   For Hiphoppas, God and Satan, angels and demons are actually the character and actions of human beings themselves. Commonly (because of the influence of the Five Percenters), Hiphoppas have called themselves *Gods* and their oppressors *Devils.* However, Hiphoppas are less concerned with proving the actual existence of God as we are more concerned with the usefulness of the term *God* in our everyday lives. What does the term *God* mean to us?

¹⁴⁹   The Temple of Hip Hop speaks of GOD not

only as the Love that guides and protects us, but also as an event, a happening, a cosmic intelligence that the true you is indeed an event of. You are GOD's force operating in the material World, and the force that is operating in and upon the material World IS GOD.

150   The very realm or environment which we Spirit beings live within <u>is</u> an aware and intelligent being itself. It is a conscious happening, a going on, a living event.

151   This being (GOD) is actually a great cosmic event which loves us because it is Love itself! It cares for us, teaches us, and feeds us because it (the *Great Event, the* <u>*Great*</u> <u>*O*</u>*neness* <u>*D*</u>*eity* <u>*G*</u>*uiding* <u>*O*</u>*ur* <u>*D*</u>*irection*) is the actual concept of Care, of Teaching and of Feeding in and of itself. It (GOD) actually does nothing, yet it actually is everything. It has no activity yet it is actually the only thing <u>G</u>oing <u>O</u>n <u>D</u>aily!

152   In fact, the term *GOD* is not the name of this great event. Neither is *Great Event* the name of this great event. All names ascribed to this chaotic oneness event are both false and true. You can call the Great Event anything you like and it will be true for you, but it will not be the Truth. The Truth is beyond names, terms and titles. In fact, it is through such word symbols as "GOD" that we organize our perception toward what we believe the G-O-D word symbol to mean.

153   However, in Truth the Great Event (or Oneness) has no name. It just is! All the names given to this <u>G</u>reat <u>O</u>neness <u>D</u>eity are actually titles and terms that we ascribe to it so that we may talk about specific parts of it. But in reality there are no specific *parts* to it. All is one event—the great unified field!

154   Names and terms are for human intelligence. They help us bring order to the seemingly chaotic World in which we live. However, in Truth it is actually impossible

to name an event that is not separate from anything else. In fact, when you name the great oneness you are stopping yourself from experiencing it in and as everything else—including yourself.

155   This act gives the great chaotic oneness the form you desire in the time and space that you are in. You are limiting GOD to your particular time and space created by your own individual need to survive when in reality GOD is everywhere. Take a moment and really try to comprehend the concept of this; all things being one thing, all things being GOD, including you.

156   YES, GOD LOVES HIP HOP! And the good news is that we CAN have direct access to GOD as Hiphoppas. To know GOD, we no longer have to rely upon the spiritual symbolism and theological interpretations of others foreign to OUR life experiences. Our God is a graffiti writer that writes upon the hearts and minds of all true seekers of Truth!

157   Let us stop disrespecting and doubting our God while praising the gods of other communities foreign to our life experiences. The Gospel of Hip Hop introduces a discipline that commits Hiphoppas to the process of being human and makes Hiphoppas aware that deep within themselves (even beyond the quantum level) can be found the answers to the whole puzzle of life itself.

158   By looking within and truly acknowledging the presence of the GOD that loves US, we connect ourselves to OUR God which is our Health, Love, Awareness and Wealth—the H-LAW of our lives. Our God is compassionate and nurturing toward the development of Hiphop Kulture. Our God is a divine DJ who mixes, cuts and scratches life itself! The Gospel of Hip Hop is simply a divine *mixtape*! And know this. LOVE IS THE MESSAGE!

159   We teach that one's commitment to one's God begins with one's earnest commitment toward one's *Self*. In one's earnest commitment toward the development of one's *Self*, one finally begins to take one's *Self* seriously. This is the beginning of discipline and righteous living.

160   Stop playing games with your *Self!* Take your *Self* seriously! Value your *Self!* For if you do not value and/or take your *Self* seriously, no one else will either—including God!

161   Sometimes we must be reminded that *Self* is beautiful! Self (YOU) is indestructible, immeasurable, timeless and enduring; it does not live because the body lives and it does not die because the body dies.

162   The real You has no name, no ethnicity, no career and no religion. These are called the *coats* that you have put on top of *Self* to do the work that actualizes your purpose. Even the coat of Hip Hop is a decision that the real YOU (*Self*) made to actualize your purpose. Even if you are born Hip Hop, at some point YOU must still decide to BE *Hiphop*.

163   The *Self* (the true You) is not physical like the body. It (You) lives in a realm where everything is possible. Everything is happening at once. Everything is happening now! It is the true You, the real You that decides upon the ordered reality in which your physical body is going to live and operate.

164   The real You is Spirit, and You exist within the Spirit realm which for human intelligence is a realm of chaos where there is no separation of things, distance or time. Everything is going on at once. Labels, names, distance and time do not actually exist here in the *Spirit realm*. These things are created so that WE can create the reality that WE desire.

165   The Truth is, you are actually a spirit being acting

like a human being. And because you choose to be human, you accept the conditions of being human. In fact, this is the essence of the choice that YOU have made; you have voluntarily decided to experience the human condition. This is what makes you human.

166   But what if you seriously decided to accept a different condition? This is what helping one's self is all about. It's about choosing the right conditions for your own spiritual growth. Remember, you are born free! You are free to choose the reality you desire. HELP YOUR SELF!

167   God helps those who help themselves and those who help themselves help God. Most people believe their God needs no help, so they ignore their responsibility to actively participate in the further manifestation of their God in the physical realm.

168   For it is through us that GOD enters the physical World. In fact, it is through us that all things spiritual or non-material come into physical manifestation. We pick and choose from the infinite chaos what shall become physical and what shall remain non-physical. However, because of the fear and doubt we learn in public school education many people go on living limited lives because they do not believe in THEIR ability to assist something deeper than themselves.

169   Know this. By fulfilling your purpose you assist your God and by assisting your God you assist your purpose. Likewise, by helping others, you help your God; and by helping your God, you ultimately help your *Self*. Even further, by living a righteous life one raises and strengthens one's God-like abilities; this leads to victory over the streets.

170   Whether you believe or you do not believe your God, simply living a righteous and disciplined life minimizes your own suffering in life. Righteousness and discipline are

simply the best foundations for continued Health, Love, Awareness and Wealth while living in the city.

171   Know this. You do not have to believe of GOD in order to live a righteous and disciplined life. Nor must you believe of GOD to be a morally sound human being. Nor does a religious belief of GOD make you morally sound. However, whether you believe of the presence of GOD, or you do not, evil thoughts and ways will only bring you suffering.

172   In Truth, acts of morality and righteousness simply prevent depression, guilt, anxiety, fear, doubt, etc., in your own life. For when you know that you have lived and are living right, such a knowing prevents guilt, insecurity, low self-esteem and all other mental hindrances that arise out of undisciplined and immoral living. It is just that simple.

173   GOD does not require your belief. It is you who require or don't require a belief IN GOD! Know this. GOD is not mocked! But when you finally decide to truly live within the presence of GOD, morality and righteousness, Health, Love, Awareness, Wealth, peace, etc. automatically manifest in your life. For it is the actual presence of GOD that brings your life into discipline and righteousness.

174   For us, the existence of Hip Hop proves the existence of GOD's presence within us and around us. For it is GOD's actual presence that disciplines the life of the believer. Others can believe whatever they have the understanding for. But the existence of Hip Hop proves for all Hiphoppas that there is a divine intelligence looking out for us, and to walk in this intelligence we must become more like this intelligence. We must voluntarily accept the conditions of Divine Mind if we are to be *down* with its laws/conditions.

175   Know this. To truly walk within GOD we must walk like God. We must finally acknowledge that God is actually

here! We must decide to walk in Spirit and in Truth. We must finally decide to give a divine performance, which is a performance of and in Spirit. We must begin to observe our thoughts and emotions, not become them or helplessly act them out. As Hiphoppas we must learn to USE our minds correctly if we are to preserve OUR way of life, OUR arts and OUR cultural traditions. We must condition ourselves to the real conditions of God. As leaders we must become Spirit beings observing the physical World.

[176] For in Spirit our ultimate expectations of ourselves disappear. We expect the unexpected. Not that we do not set goals, but that we clearly understand that GOD is the opener and the closer, the promoter and the headliner in every arena of the attuned Hiphoppa's life. We live a spiritually guided life. As a performance, our lives should draw the applause of GOD. But first, we must decide that OUR God is truly with us now—at this very moment.

[177] We must adopt the true personality of God which is already felt within OUR being. For when you actually walk the true path of spiritual awakening, seeking GOD on your own, you automatically fall in line with the principles of all holy books. In fact, you see them clearer. As an example, Christians taught us the "Golden Rule" which was to *do unto others as you would have done unto yourself.* However, when you actually walk such a path you learn that you cannot treat people the way you would like to be treated because everyone wants to be treated differently; everyone has their own preferences as to how they want to be treated. What is good for one can be bad for another, and vice versa.

[178] Therefore, after walking such a path we have learned that *do unto others as you would have done unto yourself* might be an inaccurate translation. The true statement for those who actually walk such a path is, *do unto others as they would do unto themselves.* In other words, treat

people the way THEY want to be treated. Do not judge anyone's life, or ways, or character; simply treat people the way THEY want to be treated which will be evident by the conditions and traditions of their lives. This can be called the "Platinum Rule."

179   As Hiphoppas we need a new spiritual story—one that matches our lives today. We know where God is, we are just too ashamed and too afraid to approach God because of the guilt that we have been trained to accept through the stories our parents have been forced (at gunpoint) to believe! Those days are over! We must now begin to expect the power of OUR God to rescue us from the residue of American slavery and terrorism. The Hip Hop solution to such residue and terrorism is simply SELF-CREATION!

180   Together as a Hip Hop community we must call out to OUR GOD! We must begin to appreciate OUR OWN GOD FORCE which is the force behind OUR collective consciousness which is called HIP HOP! For when you appreciate something you get more of it. So let us appreciate GOD!

181   The law of the universe is that you attract more of what you like and of what you dislike simply by acknowledging the existence of the thoughts that YOU create. Therefore, as a community let us begin to appreciate GOD, OURSELVES and OUR HIP HOP REALITY! As a growing community we must call out to OUR divine nature which is God.

182   This is done not only by simply calling out to GOD through an earnest prayer that comes from the sincere cry of your heart. Here, calling on your God has to do with walking in the Spirit (personality/nature) of GOD. This walk is an act of self-creation, self-direction, self-control—a divine performance.

183   When the attuned Hiphoppa walks in Spirit, that

Hiphoppa's God is being called into her life without any specific prayer, affirmation or meditation.

184   Here, the attuned Hiphoppa no longer tries to make things happen through prayer, affirmation and/or meditation. Here, the attuned Hiphoppa simply recognizes and truly acknowledges the presence and power of GOD everywhere, and effortlessly unexpected and miraculous situations suddenly occur!

185   It is at this stage of spiritual development that good things just happen in the life of the attuned Hiphoppa. And as far as the universe is concerned, such a Hiphoppa is indeed *down by* universal *law*. Such is the result of the Divine Performance, and it is this performance that declares one's *victory over the streets*.

186   I am talking about winning all kinds of battles; conquering all obstacles and enemies with ease and moving at the speed of life! I am talking about attaining an aura of authority that has the law enforcement of any city eager to protect and serve your well-being.

187   I am talking about attaining and maintaining the true respect of the People. I am talking about prolonged Health, true Love, creative Awareness, and uninterrupted Wealth! I am talking about unexpected opportunities that are impossible to plan, yet effortlessly produced and received.

188   I am talking about real freedom! Freedom to re-create one's self. Freedom from the work-force. Freedom from inadequate and outdated education. Freedom from stress, depression, anxiety and guilt. Freedom from oppression! Freedom to set aside time for yourself and for those that you truly love.

189   I'm talking about protection even when you don't know that you are being protected, fighting without physical harm, teaching without planned lessons, healing without

cures, communication without speaking. These are the results of *Hiphop's* Divine Performance.

190   It is here that we move from *mind* to *Spirit*, from *revolutionary* to *revelationary*, from *knowledge* to *wisdom*. It is here that we learn to overcome our worldly thinking and submit the natural-self to the divine-*Self*.

191   When this decision is made, calling on your God (your divine nature) is no longer necessary. Your God is always with you. You are aware now that GOD is never separate from you. You acknowledge now that the great chaotic oneness (GOD) is so much more than a *He* or a *She* that is distant from one's *Self*.

192   You now experience GOD as a happening—a process, a going on, a *Great Event* that exists just beyond or behind the material World, animating everything you perceive with your senses. It is here that your thinking and acting come into harmony with your God!

193   For we truly realize now that there is only GOD vibrating at different levels of consciousness, manifesting different forms of matter and life circumstances. However, all of it is *the Great Event* and YOU are a conscious part of that universal chaotic event!

194   As a being of Light, a consciously aware Spirit, the attuned Hiphoppa is full of God's Spirit and is led by GOD's Will. For it is when we become aware of our inheritance of the love of GOD, that we are truly at peace. We know who we belong to; we know were we are from.

195   What can truly upset you when you truly know that the infinite, nurturing mind of the universe and all reality actually loves and believes in you? Sadness and/or depression can only occur when we are ignorant of, or simply deny, this Truth. Be grateful for the victories in your life; they are truly the works of God.

196   GOD (the *Great Event*) is life. GOD is Truth.

GOD is Love. GOD is Light. Therefore, wherever God is, there is Life, Truth, Love, Light and You!

197   In truly knowing this we are forever in joy and peace. In knowing this, we love ourselves not for the sake of self, but for the sake of GOD's love for us! We commit to ourselves not for the sake of self, but for the sake of GOD's commitment to us. How can we not love what GOD loves? And how can we not be committed to what GOD is committed to? How can we not value what GOD values? GOD values us!

198   Imagine: GOD is committed to YOU, but you are committed to everything else, including GOD. This is disharmony. How can you truly have peace? How can you truly feel joyous? If the GOD of the universe is committed to YOU, why then are you not committed to YOU? If GOD is committed to your well-being, why are YOU so committed to GOD? Shouldn't you be committed to your *Self*, meaning your own well-being?

199   Focus your attention where GOD's attention is, and you shall be in harmony with your God. GOD loves you, so you should love you as well. Your God is teaching you, so you should be teaching you as well. Your God is guiding, protecting and depending upon You, so you should be deeply engaged in guiding, protecting and depending upon you as well.

200   You are what the universe is doing. The intelligence of the universe is not focused upon the intelligence of the universe. The intelligence of the universe is focused on YOU! Focus your attention upon GOD's attention, and there you shall find peace, prosperity, purpose and joy.

201   Know this. The love we feel for ourselves and for others radiates from the presence of GOD within our very being! For when love is expressed GOD is expressed. When Truth is expressed GOD is expressed. Truth, compassion,

charity and mercy are all God-like behaviors. When the Hiphoppa performs these virtues such a Hiphoppa is being God-like. Such an image and likeness IS the GOD-force declaring its *victory over the streets!*

TRACK FOUR

202   RISE UP! You are God in GOD, the I manifested, or ((((I)))). You are the ((((I)))) in the eye manifesting what you choose to see and call "I." YOU CREATE YOUR REALITY, GOD WILLING! You are the I that is *am*-ing or (((( ))))-ing, aiming, creating, manifesting, etc. through your physical senses. So what is your aim (your a-I-m)? What are you *am*-ing for? What is your "I" *am*-ing? What is your "I" doing? What are you making?

203   Know this. ((((I)))) becomes what ((((I)))) sees. You are what your I sees, not what your eyes see. In many ways you are called I *sees* or *Isis*—the IS that is, the existence that exists. Here, the path toward spiritual awareness and existence reveals itself when you begin to see by way of your ((((I)))) and not only by way of your eyes. You are ((((I)))).

204   Your I is a sight, a perception, a state of being. You can see clearer with your I than with your eyes. Your eyes are created by your I for the purpose of seeing dualities in GOD—the Great Event. The eyes are the lenses of the divine ((((I)))). They are the special lenses that dim the bright light of Truth and reality so that ((((I)))) may create the material reality ((((I)))) desires for I.

205   We have eyes so that we may give form to light-energy. In Truth, we are playing with the light that we are. We are playing with GOD, and our eyes are one of the

instruments that reveal the classroom of the material World to our understanding.

206   Your physical senses are your spiritual toys, your spiritual weapons and your spiritual learning instruments all wrapped up in one magnificent manifestation which reveals itself according to the consciousness of the possessor.

207   ((((I)))) is YOUR portion of GOD. So what are you creating (seeing/accepting) with your portion of GOD? What is your ((((I)))) becoming? Ask yourself right now, my ((((I)))) is what? ((((I))))-*am*-what? What *am* (or aim) is ((((I)))) doing? What is the ((((I)))) in your eye creating for the ((((I)))), or rather YOU?

208   Well, my ((((I)))) creates and sustains *Hip Hop!* Before Hip Hop became what it is today my ((((I)))) saw it, and when I perceived the thought of my ((((I)))), my two I's (eyes) were opened. One is a creator, the other is created; the I in I, the spiritual ((((I)))) within the mind's I which directs the physical eyes.

209   This duality creates the sight of our *eyes* and the perception of our minds. However, in Truth there is no separation in ((((I)))). ((((I)))) creates what happens to I. ((((I)))) does what is happening to I.

210   But for I to truly understand the spiritual manifestations of ((((I)))), I must live what ((((I)))) create(s). And the living of one's creations without the knowledge of one's true self-nature in GOD begins one's habitual bondage to one's own creations and the beginning of the *I*'s spiritual blindness and misery. The *I* no longer *sees,* the *I* no longer *is.*

211   What the ((((I)))) becomes is whatever the *I* is told. If the *I* accepts the title of Black, or White, or Red, or Brown, or Yellow as its personal racial identity then that is what the ((((I)))) becomes. *I* becomes what *I* thinks, and what the I thinks creates physical reality for the *I*. Hip Hop

is evidence of the power of ((((I)))).

212   I is God, and ((((*am*)))) is what God is doing. The expression of I is its ((((*am*)))). Hip Hop is a creation of what I ((((am)))) doing.

213   I (God) am (manifesting) Hip Hop (Law). Hip Hop is the Law of every Hiphoppa's life. It is the condition of the Hiphoppa. It is what we allow ourselves to be. Hip Hop is the Law of our lives. It is OUR WAY. Others are governed by other Laws and Ways and Conditions, but Hip Hop is our Law and Way and Condition. And we must never break our own laws. For the breaking of our own laws is the destruction of our own being.

214   Hip Hop is what God is being and doing to us. Hip Hop is what the ((((I)))) is being and doing to the *I*. "I am Hip Hop" means *I am the Law of my life, I create my own conditions and circumstances.* With this knowledge I am FREE!

215   The meaning of the *Hiphop* life is to perfect one's self and to do that which transforms one into God. The purpose of the *Hiphop* life is to exercise the full potentials of our brains and minds so that we may reunite consciously with GOD.

216   SELF-CREATION IS FREEDOM. In fact, self-creation is the ultimate state of freedom. If you can become whatever you desire, then slavery, lost history, sickness, ignorance and poverty are all the choices of an uninformed mind (or a mind not-in-form).

217   Your *Hiphop* spiritual path begins with you learning how to create and guide thought; beginning with your own. You are what you think of repeatedly. Therefore, the *Hiphop* spiritual path begins with a faith in our own existence as *Hiphoppas*.

218   First, we must learn to honor ourselves and our Hip Hop history. We must truly honor Hip Hop and respect

ourselves as *Hiphoppas*. This peace, this love and this unity are what create our *Hiphop Kulture*. This is our faith. We believe in the divinity of Hip Hop. We believe in GOD's love for us as Hiphoppas. As Templists, we don't use Hip Hop, we care for and cultivate it.

219   Here, you must finally stop doubting your Self and realize your limitlessness within Hip Hop. For when your inner-Truth is louder than your outer-circumstances you have learned to live and walk in your Hip Hop spirit reality.

220   This is what it means to be attuned, an attuned Hiphoppa; it means to express God, the self-created. THIS IS YOUR STOLEN LEGACY RESTORED! There it is.

THE SEVENTEENTH OVERSTANDING
THE TEMPLE OF HIP HOP

[1] Peace and much love to all true and attuned members of the Temple of Hip Hop. Be encouraged by this Overstanding; it is your true heritage. In my time (your past) the creation of a free and prosperous Hip Hop nation is simply too much for people to comprehend. For whatever reason they are afraid of the idea, and this is why we have formed our private society to discuss, plan and encourage those Hiphoppas that can comprehend such a vision.

[2] Originally, I wanted everyone who was participating in Hip Hop to enjoy the fruits of my research. But as I naively began to express the fact that "Rap is something we do, Hip Hop is something we live," and that "you are not just doing Hip Hop, you are Hip Hop," and that "Hip Hop is a new culture, a new civilization, a new people upon the earth," many sincere and good-hearted Rap fans began to accuse me of everything from wanting to "own Hip Hop" to "starting a cult." Because of this, I stopped trying to openly convince the Hip Hop community that it was so much more than a form of entertainment, and with my friend Professor Z, I formed the Temple of Hip Hop.

[3] When ancient "People" decided to create a sacred space to have a building or even a whole city constructed upon it, they sent for special priests who were able to interpret the spiritual meaning of the site and the times. Ancient Rome followed this same practice with priests known as "augurs" who specialized in prophetically interpreting signs. Most of Rome's important buildings or

spaces had to be "inaugurated" by an augur.

4   The *augur* would delineate a section of the earth or sky that was then called a "templum." When a temple or any important structure was built, it was built in that ritually outlined space (a *templum*). The word *templum* itself is cognate with the Greek *temnein* meaning to cut, in this case "to cut off" with boundaries. In ancient Rome this was all the work of augurs who would ritually outline sacred spaces for state functions to take place.

5   When the Temple of Hip Hop was established in 1996, I envisioned a spiritual/cultural *templum* in Hip Hop's space-time reality. Just as portions of the earth and sky are delineated as sacred spaces in physical reality, the Temple of Hiphop is a delineated space in Hip Hop's cultural and perceptual reality. In a poem that appears on the *I Got Next* album, I stated, *The big brother watching over you is a lie ya see, Hip Hop can build its own secret society! But first you and I got to unify, stop the niggativity and control our creativity!*

6   When I realized that I was not just doing Hip Hop but that I was Hip Hop itself, I also realized the reality that came along with such a realization. I began to perceive my physical World through a heightened sense of purpose and duty. I no longer wanted to "use" hip-hop, I now wanted to care for and nurture Hip Hop. I wanted to protect Hip Hop's reputation as if it were my own. I literally united with the idea of Hip Hop and gained an insight, a power, a new understanding as to how I could actually live my life, and it is WONDERFUL!

7   When I realized my true self as Hiphop, I gained certain abilities that came with the acceptance of the Hiphop nature. My freestyle got sharper! My rhyme-writing abilities intensified to the point where I was doing 14-song albums in a couple of days! My live emcee performances became the livest in the touring market; very few rappers even wanted

to go onstage after me—the energy was too great!

8   When I surrendered to my true nature as Hiphop, certain Hip Hop doors began to open for me. My popularity went up! My "I Am Hip Hop" tour merchandise became "hood favorites," complete with knock-offs and bootlegs in every State. In fact, Black Entertainment Television created a whole "I Am Hip Hop" Lifetime Achievement Award presentation within their BET Awards production, which Grandmaster Flash received in 2006 and I received in 2007.

9   The point to all of this is that when I took on the spirit of Hiphop, my outer-reality magically transformed to fit my inner-nature. I discovered the reality of peace, love, unity and safely having fun as an attuned Hiphoppa even while others were experiencing conflict, hatred, disunity and depression in my same environment. Saddened by this, I would try to accept certain people as apprentices and even rent spaces in various cities to teach the results of my revelations, but most people just wanted to start or expand their Rap careers, or get some money, or just stand next to me so that they could brag about the fact that they knew KRS ONE. These were very frustrating times for me.

10   Realizing that I might be *ahead of my time*, I began to write for YOU, my future. I began to see that it was not I alone who was to establish our Hip Hop nation, it was YOU, my future, many of whom are not even born yet. I can never claim to be better than anyone else or above anyone else, but when our children look back upon Hip Hop's real history, what shall they see? How are we guiding the hundreds of generations that are to come after us? Sometimes I wonder, is this even important to anyone besides myself?

11   Not everyone ponders these questions or their role in the creation of Hip Hop's real history and heritage, but many of us do. I do, and I know that I am not the only one

who feels this way. Those of us who do *think very deeply* about the past, present and future states of Hip Hop as an internationally celebrated urban culture and lifestyle eventually join the Temple of Hip Hop. Our society practices Hiphop as consciousness in an effort to establish Hip Hop as a nation. Our role today is to be the nation that we would like to see.

12   Our role today is to think and act like the nation we desire our children to live within. Here, we envision an urban spiritual movement that brings awareness to the rejected, awakens the minds of those without guidance, saves our people from their own errors in life and restores them to spiritual maturity—in peace. Not with judgment and criticism, but with a sincere care for those who simply do not know or have forgotten spiritual law.

13   We believe and perceive in GOD. The Temple of Hiphop continues to investigate, preserve and promote the reality and nature of GOD through the language and culture of Hip Hop. We exist to interpret and teach the spiritual reality of Hip Hop itself as well as Hip Hop's relation to the divine. The Temple of Hip Hop does not induce mystical experiences, it acknowledges them.

14   With GOD's guidance, we teach healing through awareness, rehabilitation through Truth, and peace through purpose. The authenticity and trueness of our teachings are based upon its compatibility with the apprentice's own heart. You will know if you are part of our nation by the feeling that such an idea gives you.

15   With GOD's guidance we envision a Hip Hop society that empowers itself through a heightened level of spiritual skill and a unified comprehension of its own cultural principles and codes—one that would teach its people to live beyond the material World and their own physical senses, cravings, wants, desires, etc., in an effort

to experience a heightened level of health, love, awareness, wealth and most of all—Truth.

16   Hiphoppas who commit to the teachings of the Temple of Hiphop join a community of like-minded people who practice Hip Hop beyond entertainment. Temple Members help one another through the obstacles of life. We protect one another. We advise one another. We respect one another. We love one another. We support one another. Such is our strength. And it will take this strength to develop and sustain our nation.

17   Our ministry/society is not a fan club, nor a recording or fashion corporation. The Temple of Hiphop is not even a physical place, it is an international Hip Hop preservation Ministry, Archive, School and Society (M.A.S.S.).

18   As a ministry, we promote the divinity of Hip Hop and its culture. We seek to relieve human suffering through an awareness of useful spiritual knowledge. We are a self-realization ministry. We believe that GOD speaks through one's true purpose in life.

19   As an archive, we seek to collect, document and promote Hip Hop's spiritual and material experiences in the World. Our aim is to continue developing our traveling Hip Hop exhibits and official Hip Hop museum/archive for the remembrance and study of Hip Hop's history, art and culture. We intend to edutain the public as to Hip Hop's spiritual first causes and material effects beyond music entertainment.

20   As a school, we seek to teach *Hiphop, Hip Hop* and *hip-hop* to all interested apprentices/students. We believe that a good education does not prepare you for the job market exclusively. We believe that a good education helps you to realize and perfect your true life purpose. Such an education helps YOU to become a better YOU.

21   Finally, as a Hiphop society we seek to preserve Hip

Hop's original causes. Whether it is with skill, influence, knowledge, art and/or money, as a society our existence and activity insure Hip Hop's proper documentation in World history. Temple Members silently help one another through the challenges of life. Without advertising the fact that we are Temple Members, our aim is to silently relieve human suffering whenever and wherever possible. Temple Members are those Hiphoppas who share a basic thirst for Truth and an unshakable love for Hip Hop.

22   Like our society, our nation is not is not a physical place. Yes, we shall establish a physical landmass for our nation, but in reality our nation is an attitude, a behavior, a collective consciousness that transcends race, religion, nationality and economic class. The borders of our nation are psychological; we limit ourselves to the title of *Hip Hop* or *Hiphop* so that we may recognize each other by name and nature.

23   We are not of that hired circle; we are of that Higher Circle. We are not *fee* women and men; we are *free* women and men. Even when we have jobs to do or employment to hold on to, we are still not trapped in the environment of corporate busy-ness (business) where one goes along with injustice and continues corporate exploitation with the statement *I'm just doing my job!* We remain free and self-directed! We are Hip Hop! We help people wherever and whenever we can.

24   Our temple houses our God, and in GOD we trust. Our spiritual goals include getting out of our own way so that God may manifest through us. The Temple of Hip Hop leads Hiphoppas toward God and the divinity of Hip Hop's culture, not toward itself. The Temple of Hiphop is a spiritual Hip Hop movement concerned with overcoming the obstacles and temptations of "street" life and institutional entrapment and sabotage. As the

sacred seal of our temple depicts, our vision and motto is "VICTORY OVER THE STREETS!"

25   Our great seal, with its 40 berries signifying the authority to teach, its streetlight in the background where Hip Hop first received power, its nine sun rays representing Hip Hop's nine elements, and the son holding a boom box symbolizing Hip Hop's social victory through simple and widely used technology, all come together to remind future members of the Temple of Hip Hop the meaning and purpose of our institution.

26   Our sacred seal shows the divine mother holding her son's hand in victory over the oppressive and unjust circumstances of urban life. Standing upon four steps (or stages) signifying the foundations of health, love, awareness and wealth, the appearance of the great goddess in our seal pays homage and respect to the millions of single mothers, wives, grandmothers and "big sisters" who cared for, taught and protected the early Hip Hop community and assisted us in becoming who we are today. Thanks Mom, and that's forever (M.O.M.—Mind Over Matters).

27   The divine mother (the feminine/creative principle within all of humanity) standing next to her divine child (Hip Hop) symbolizes the maturity of divine ideas in our time. In the past the "Mother of God" was shown as a mother cuddling and holding her infant child close to her bosom. She was called the "Madonna" and her son was the "Christ." Our modern interpretation of this ancient motif depicts Madonna's son as Hip Hop and now mature enough to stand upon his own two feet.

28   The symbol of the great mother standing on the right raising her son's left hand up in victory over the streets symbolizes righteousness over corruption. This symbol celebrates the unity of our culture and acknowledges the support of our parents. The symbol "H" in the center of

the sun celebrates both the divinity of Hip Hop as well as the life-giving sun which is mostly composed of hydrogen. [29] The symbol of "H" in the center of the sun also signifies the union and balance between Spirit and Science. The nine stars in the background sky represent Hip Hop's nine elements. However, the stars and the sun appearing at the same time symbolizes Hip Hop's ability to operate in the day or night, meaning, through good times as well as through bad times, whether events are favorable or unfavorable, Hip Hop's divine nature is always at work.

[30] This same symbol of the stars and the sun in the sky together also celebrates Hip Hop's balance between positive and negative forces, even good and evil forces. In addition, such a symbol shows respect to the metaphysical meaning of "light" as Truth, Knowledge, Wisdom and Awareness.

[31] Surrounding our great seal is a wreath of medicinal herbs, symbolizing inspiration and the origins of human awareness. Also within our wreath are rose "hips" and barley "hops," which not only characterize Hip Hop's plentiful harvest (its prosperity) but also symbolize the *cultivation, care, attention* and *worship* of the *intelligent movement*.

[32] Rose "hips" and barley "hops" symbolize for Hiphoppas the *seed* (hips) of the new *vine* or *way* (hops). As mentioned earlier, *Hip Hop* is the *seed* of a new *vine* (the new people/the new way). The Temple of Hip Hop simply acknowledges and documents this *new way*.

[33] Over the years building our temple we've noticed a recurrence of the number 9. We've noticed our 9 elements being taught in 9 months, our 18 Divine Performances, our 18 Hip Hop Declaration of Peace principles, and the 18 characters of our title T-E-M-P-L-E-O-F-H-I-P-H-O-P-1-9-9-6 which appears on our sacred seal (8 + 1 = 9). We also noticed the fact that the Gospel of Hip Hop itself was completed in 2009 which not only equals 11, the date Kool

DJ Herc played his first party for his sister Cindy (August 11, 1973), but 2009 is approximately 36 years from 1973, the birth year of Hip Hop (3 + 6 = 9). Remaining consistent with the numbers 9 and 18, young teachas are advised to accept apprentices in such manners. When starting your Hip Hop ministry teach only up to 9 apprentices who are over the age of 18.

³⁴ And this is our mission. We intend to preserve Hip Hop by preserving Hiphoppas with both a literal as well as a symbolic knowledge of Hip Hop's existence beyond music and other entertainment. We strive to restore and/ or enhance the Hiphoppa's wonder and respect for the spiritual life.

³⁵ As a final thought on this particular subject, let us remember that everyone who claims an affiliation with the Temple of Hip Hop isn't necessarily a true Temple Member. You will know a true *templist* not only by her work to preserve and further develop Hip Hop, but how she treats other people. It is not about how popular, or rich, or influential a Temple Member is; if they are unstudied, inactive or hateful they are NOT serious members of the Temple of Hip Hop.

³⁶ You cannot claim to be a serious member of the Temple of Hip Hop if you are unstudied and/or inactive, or if your personal attitude toward others is contrary to the teachings of our society. If you have truly grasped the teachings of our temple, it will reflect in your attitude toward others. Again, Manly P. Hall reminds us that, *No one can actually experience internal illumination and not reveal this enlargement of understanding in daily living.* The personal character of the templist reveals not only her level of Hiphop understanding, but also her loyalty to the maintenance of the Temple of Hip Hop.

³⁷ True Temple Members are commited to the

maintenance of their temple. Temple Members do not seek to exploit the resources of their temple, they seek to enhance and even multiply their temple's resources. Yes, we are all growing and learning, and mistakes will be made. However, there is a big difference between an honest mistake or "need" verses a deliberate attempt to use one's temple for one's own selfish gain. Let us be on guard against those who join our society in hopes of only furthering their individual careers. This is NOT what the Temple of Hip Hop is all about!

38   The Temple of Hip Hop is all about the spiritual and cultural progression of the international Hip Hop community—that's all! The Temple of Hip Hop is NOT a money-making venture; it is not a business, or a place where you can get your career started.

39   If you are in need of money or any other resource to live, do not let the Temple of Hip Hop stand in your way of securing an income for yourself. Don't let the Temple of Hip Hop stand in the way of achieving your goals and dreams. If your career is in need of attention, remove yourself from Temple of Hip Hop responsibilities and give your career the attention it needs.

40   The point here is that the Temple of Hip Hop is a Hip Hop preservation society and ministry that does cultural preservation and ministry work. And let us emphasize the word WORK! Here, serious Temple Members bring their resources to the Temple of Hip Hop in an effort to complete the WORK that is to be accomplished. Serious Temple Members spend their own money, use their own resources and display their own skills in doing the great work of preserving and further developing the Hip Hop idea. This includes the teachas of our temple.

41   Know this. Even though Hip Hop's teachas and ministas are authorized to *take up an offering* on behalf of the upkeep of their temples, it must be clearly emphasized here

that it is GOD and GOD alone who sustains our temples. If we really believe this, then there really is little need to *take up an offering* from an already struggling people. Our teachas establish their temples not with bank loans, grants and donations, but with their own clear overstanding of spiritual law.

⁴²   The traditions of other temples and churches may require them to *take up an offering* and we are obliged to respect such traditions. But as for the Temple of Hip Hop, we use the mastery of our Hip Hop elements to finance the maintenance of our temple. We come to our people with the resources we and they need to focus upon the lessons we've come to teach. Yes, there is something to be said about the Law of Give and Receive, and the importance of a congregation supporting their man or woman of GOD. But Temple Members should not be teaching the Gospel of Hip Hop until they have mastered its principles, and one of its principles is wealth. Another is charity. Another is love— in this case, care. This is how WE approach OUR people in OUR temples.

⁴³   The Temple of Hip Hop serves as a restoration to the ancient ideas regarding life and spiritual living. Our ultimate aim is to restore the Truth to our people. However, we use the term "our people" here because not everyone is ready to embrace the Truth. Slavery has become very comfortable in my time, while it is freedom that is becoming more and more difficult to maintain in my time. The Truth is that we CAN create our own reality. We CAN recreate ourselves. This is not only the Truth, it is also the ultimate state of freedom.

⁴⁴   Such a *freedom* begins with the way in which we perceive ourselves. Normally, a person's or a people's race and/or ethnicity would not matter in a truly spiritual conversation, but when politically motivated deceptions

and distortions of the Truth make their way into the common understanding of spiritual reality, it is the duty and responsibility of every Truth-seeker to openly correct such deception and replace such lies with Truth. This is why we use the term "our people," meaning those who are ready to hear the Truth.

⁴⁵   As an example, in my time the image of the White Jesus with blue eyes and long blond hair is known by every biblical scholar to be historically inaccurate, yet such an image remains the standard depiction of Jesus' physical image. And why is that? Why are some Christians so reluctant to embrace the fact that Jesus, as well as Moses, King Solomon, King David, Adam, Eve, Cain, Abel, and most of the leading characters of the Bible, was indeed dark-skinned? What difference does it really make whether any biblical character was Black, White, or other?

⁴⁶   As Dr. Henry Lewis Clark advised, *I think the Christianity that Black ministers espouse is going to have to be remade to suit OUR needs, the needs of OUR people.* Mr. Clark continues, *I believe that we are capable of creating a religion of a new humanity!*

⁴⁷   True Christians should pay very close attention to this analysis. In no way can we ever discredit, demean or disrespect the Christian faith; such is NOT the character of an attuned Hiphoppa. However, the seeking and revealing of Truth is the exact character of an attuned Hiphoppa, and because so many Hiphoppas were enslaved, freed and raised within the Christian tradition, it is imperative that we question our relationship with Christianity and our roles as spiritual beings within it. Many of us Hiphoppas began our spiritual journey within the Christian tradition.

⁴⁸   Maybe it was our own African ancestors, in an effort to civilize and spiritualize early Europeans, who created the *White Jesus* so that Europeans would accept the concept

of the Christ. Maybe Jesus himself (or Mary) ordered this racial change because his own people had rejected the Christ. Maybe all of this had to do with the slave trade and the creation of both the slave and the slaveholder. Clearly such an image seems to have served as a form of population control in Christian Europe and early America. Meaning that it would have been more acceptable to average Europeans to enslave an unholy, savage and soulless race of people than to do the same to GOD's true chosen people.

49   Only evil would consider enslaving GOD's chosen people and stealing their sacred heritage and birthright for themselves. Only a jealous, envious, deceitful mind would go to such lengths as to conceal the Truth from so many people for so long. But equally, only a disobedient, ignorant, fearful people living in blatant denial would go along with such an inaccuracy for so long. Sometimes the revelation of evil is even more staggering than the revelation of Truth!

50   Just like today, Iraq as well as Iran are both considered to be the actual places where many of the biblical stories and its characters originate; yet this is the very region that Christian America has declared war upon! How hypocritical can you be? As a Christian nation isn't this self-destruction? Truly, in history we were the "humans" and they were the "animals" and this is what we have had taken from us—our humanity.

51   America boasts of its Christian values and heritage and holds the Bible as its highest level of morality as well as its connection to GOD, yet the American government (in my present time) is bombing the very region the Bible was written in, killing the people of that region, and has already robbed and enslaved the Bible's African descendants. Again, how hypocritical can you be? And again, is this not self-destruction?

52   However, the real question is, how long are we

Hiphoppas supposed to put our precious faith into such corrupt religious practices? How long will we empower our own oppression and ultimately our own demise? It seems like our whole spiritual reality originated amongst the plans for our enslavement. This is why the Temple of Hip Hop exists; it is time that we free ourselves and rediscover our own relationship with GOD. We now know that everyone (including ourselves) was deceived and that we were the true "humans" and they were the true "animals." We know this today but what shall we do about it?

53   It seems that not only were our land and physical resources stolen from us, our actual souls were also stolen. Try to understand this: slaves in the United States were created and bred to be slaves. It seems that a certain part of the African population was set aside and bred for slavery, which included the total breakdown and rebuilding of the African mind and soul, and it is this group that influences the rest of us today.

54   As I research this observation I find that the depths of our losses are more staggering than we have ever imagined. Forget about the theft of our land, minerals, precious metals, stones, plants, oil, knowledge, people, etc., that still goes on today. Forget about all of that. The real tragedy here is that our very souls were taken from us or blocked from our "indefinite use." The very force that animates our being has been stolen from us and put to use in the building of our own prisons!

55   The very force that protects and preserves our natural resources (our souls) has either been stolen from us or switched off. Either way we have been blinded to ourselves. We cannot see ourselves and so we have no direction; we are forced to be led and guided as opposed to being those who lead and guide. And this goes for everyone who chooses to buy into the convenience of slavery over

their birthright of freedom.

⁵⁶ This I believe is the center of the World's problems; it is the fact that the original human beings, the first humans who established civilization, the true Queens and Kings, the true gods and goddesses, GOD's originally chosen people regardless of race or ethnicity, have forgotten who they are, and as a result the whole World suffers because everything is out of order, everything is out of place, everything is upside down. The true kings are slaves and the true slaves are kings. This is why the World's cities are in such turmoil. WE have forgotten OUR divinity and the responsibilities that come with such divinity.

⁵⁷ And this analysis is not only pointing to the injustice of such a situation; this analysis points more toward the imbalance of today's human order and who is supposed to be doing what. I believe that the World is the way it is because the true kings have been enslaved and murdered by jealous and greedy slaves.

⁵⁸ But more importantly, because of our own internal conflicts we have given up our birthright and heritage. Because of our own lack of respect for our own divine history and leadership we have handed our very soul-force over to our enemies—and we continue to do the same today. Our World is the way it is because we have forgotten who we are; our ignorance creates the World that we are experiencing. Our own immaturity and disunity have led to our own enslavement! And the bottom line is that our legacy has been stolen from us and we have been blinded to our own divinity. As a result we remain slaves, the only condition fit for human beings who know not themselves and break their own laws.

⁵⁹ Like the Ten Commandments, for example, which originated in Africa. These are OUR principles. This is what WE gave to the World. *Thou shalt have no other gods*

before me. Thou shalt not make unto thee any graven image, or any likeness of anything in heaven above or that is in the earth beneath, or that is in the water under the earth. Thou shalt not take the name of the Lord thy God in vain. Remember the Sabbath day, to keep it holy. Honour thy father and thy mother that thy days might be long upon the land which the Lord thy God giveth. Thou shalt not kill. Thou shalt not commit adultery. Thou shalt not steal. Thou shalt not bear false witness against thy neighbor. Thou shalt not covet thy neighbor's house, thou shalt not covet thy neighbor's wife, nor his maidservant, nor his ox, nor his ass, nor anything that is thy neighbor's. These are OUR principles, and because we continue even to this day to break these laws, OUR LAWS, we suffer as an African people in America.

[60] Imagine, if we actually obeyed our own Ten Commandments we would not be an oppressed people. If we could just obey *thou shalt not kill, thou shalt not commit adultery, thou shalt not steal, and thou shalt not bear false witness against thy neighbor,* if we just obeyed these four commandments we would be stronger than those who stole these principles from us. Because of such blindness we act out the results of being ignorant of ourselves. And this is the crime; everything we have created we now fight against, believing that it is foreign and destructive to us when in fact most of what we are protesting and ignoring is our own inventions, discoveries and heritage. Everything that our ancestors have established for us we have squandered and misused in utter blindness, rebellion and ignorance, and we are doing the same thing today with Hip Hop. THIS IS WHY WE ARE WHERE WE ARE TODAY.

[61] It is now time to grow up! Hip Hop not only reminds us of our divinity, Hip Hop also reminds us of our immaturity. We can look at Hip Hop (its birth, its contributions to society, its social set-up, its arts, etc.) and

see how we have treated our own legacy and heritage today. The same way we treat Hip Hop today is the same way our parents have treated themselves in the past, and this is what has led to our own enslavement every time.

62   Look at how we exploit ourselves today. Look at how we seek to manipulate and disrespect each other today. Look at how some of us can sell destructive drugs and weapons to others of us, bringing down our own communities. Look at how we sell illegal drugs, guns and sex right on the same streets named after our King—Dr. Martin Luther King, Jr. This is us! And this is how we treat our own heritage and legacy; we have simply forgotten who we are and where we have come from, and most of us don't even care to know.

63   With this kind of attitude toward ourselves, can we truly say that anything has been stolen from us? Or, due to our own ignorance, disobedience and immaturity, have we given away our own birthright and freedom? It's always those chosen few like Moses who get revelation from GOD but must deliver such revelation to an immature and disobedient people. History sure has a way of repeating itself, especially when it comes to African Americans, Americans, and the spiritual reality of Hip Hop.

64   It seems to be time for us to stand up and reclaim our stolen legacies. I used to criticize the Bible until I realized that MY ancestors wrote it! I used to criticize Christianity until I realized that it was my ancestors who had established it and had it stolen from them like Hip Hop today.

65   I used to despise and protest the injustices of the United States until I realized that I am the United States! I used to criticize the United States Constitution until I realized that it was MY great, great, great, great, great grandparents who actually wrote and lived the principles of the Declaration of Independence as well as the United States Constitution long before these documents were in

physical existence!

66   This I believe is how the thieves of our parents' resources and heritage continue to keep their stolen goods; they simply killed our parents and then taught us that everything that once belonged to us now belongs to them (the thieves). And we accept this injustice because we believe that we are powerless to do anything about it.

67   This is why the mission of our temple today is so important. Our aim is to return the World's stolen goods and stolen legacies back to their original owners and inventors. And the way to do that is not through war or through force, it is to be achieved through righteousness—spiritual, mental and cultural maturity.

68   There is nothing physical to reclaim; it is our minds (our perception) that we must restore first. We must retrain ourselves to see through the eye of divinity. This is also why the Gospel of Hip Hop now exists. We no longer need to rely upon the spiritual heritage of those who raped our mothers and murdered our fathers! The gospel of thieves and murderers shall not be the gospel for us.

69   For if our ancestors wrote the Bible and lived its principles long before the Bible was translated into the English language and culture then with that same blood and with that same spirit we present this gospel from those of us who are called "Hip Hop" today. If OUR ancestral parents actually wrote the original Bible and lived its original principles, then by our natural birthright we are genetically empowered and divinely authorized to write another one, and another one, and another one!

70   I have realized that it is a bit immature to try and reclaim the physical effects of our soul-force when we can just reactivate our soul-force today and create even more marvelous gospels, sciences, nations and legacies than our ancestors ever dreamed. Let the thieves keep their stolen

goods and let us call that "charity." Our aim is to reactivate the forgotten soul-force that inspired our resources and heritage to exist in the first place.

71   We don't need to reclaim any physical item if we are truly the creators of such items. If we are truly the creative gods that we believe we are then let us establish a whole new World today with new resources and a whole new legacy. But again, this is the very challenge right here! We really don't believe that OUR ANCESTORS WROTE AND LIVED THE BIBLE! And so we walk around in utter blindness to our true natures, blessings and abilities.

72   As the *Original African Heritage Study Bible* has revealed, *England was very familiar with the Black man of Africa during the seventeenth century. The Muslim had long since given Africa the name 'El Bilad es Sudan,' translated 'Land of the Blacks,' or 'the Blackman's Land.'*

73   *England knew well that during the early days of the Old Testament, Africa was called 'The Land of Ham.' England had entered the slave trade as early as 1552. Queen Elizabeth had money invested in the slave trade and in the colonies of the Americas to where they were going.*

74   *When King James' translators completed the translation in 1611, the Black presence had been part of the English and colony scenario. But the translators called them Negroes instead of Ethiopians, hoping the common mind of the day would not see anything except their color. Even the term 'Cush,' which is used in the original Hebrew tongue ('Kushites'), was not employed.*

75   *The translators knew by calling the slaves Negroes this would give no bearing to the White Christian world that the people they were enslaving were Christians well before Europe knew about the Risen Christ.*

76   *The term 'Ethiopia' in the English Bible has misled the Christian World for more than 400 years, and perhaps even*

the name 'Cush' would have changed the attitude of Europeans concerning the chattel slavery of Blacks. If slaveholders had known who they were lynching, mutilating, burning, raping, and castrating, it might have made a difference.

[77]   The *Original African Heritage Study Bible* continues: *The King James translators did not forget to use the word 'Greece' in reference to Daniel's prophesy. The same translators saw 'Sudanese' Africans in chains boarding slave ships, yet they called them Negroes! But when these Sudanese kings sat on the thrones of Egypt, the translators called them Ethiopians.*

[78]   This is how our names and natures were stolen. It was during our captivity in the United States' slave trade that some of our heritage, some of our cultural identities, and some of our traditional names were taken from us— ALL OF US. Whites, Blacks, Natives, Asians, etc., all of us have been robbed of our spiritual inheritance. And without an awareness of one's own name, which defines one's own nature, freedom and spiritual development are virtually impossible.

[79]   How can you ask people to be loyal to that which oppresses them? As Hiphoppas we must not drink from the cup of hatred and bitterness. We must simply get to work in the reclaiming of our soul-force, our natural birthright and divine heritage. And this is why our temple exists.

[80]   Most Africans in America today are taught to believe that the United States of America was founded solely by White men, that Whites were the *masters* of Blacks, when in fact everything about the United States Constitution is Native American and African-based—including the institution of slavery.

[81]   We now know that in 1619, 20 Africans sailing to Europe on vacation ran aground at Jamestown Virginia due to turbulent weather conditions. There they were

welcomed and blended into early Virginia life. Some, like the Johnsons, who were on the ship, bought land and other property, including indentured servants and slaves, and lived comfortably for many years in Virginia.

[82]   But it was the Tuckers who owned and operated the ship that ran aground at Jamestown, Virginia, and although they would also give birth to the first African American child on American soil, they would continue to travel around the World maintaining statesman-like reputations in the United States and elsewhere.

[83]   They were considered Free Blacks, and as with most free people of the day, slavery was an everyday part of their life. From 1620–1830, Free Blacks in the United States owned real estate and other property (including slaves) valued at over $100,000,000!

[84]   History shows through recorded words and deeds that enlightened Whites, Native Americans and Africans in America, all fleeing some sort of persecution because of their views or racial and/or religious backgrounds established the original principles of the United States of the Americas. This was early America—different cultures and races coming together to create a new human experience. *Out of many, one.*

[85]   These are the visions of OUR ancestors! And this is why the principles of the United States Constitution contradict those who claim to defend and uphold its articles and amendments today. This is why the United States Constitution even contradicts the supposed characters, virtues and personalities of America's *Founding Fathers*.

[86]   The Truth is, they did not conceptualize or originate the principles, checks and balances, nor the "spirit" of the U.S. Constitution. In Truth, the so-called *framers* of the Constitution exploited the existence of the already widely accepted ideas of enlightened Whites, Africans and Native

Americans who were already living in peace in the Americas for centuries.

[87]   Similar to the way Hip Hop was treated in the 1990s, where desperate people looking to make a fast dollar simply copied and imitated the arts of original Hiphoppas, it seems that the *Founding Fathers* of the United States copied the Constitution from already existing ideas shared by many throughout the World at the time. Evidence of this can be found in the fact that the so-called *framers* of the Declaration of Independence and United States Constitution themselves never matched in deed what they copied into rhetoric and law. In principle and in philosophy the Declaration of Independence and the United States Constitution were always ahead of the actual lifestyles of the so-called *Founding Fathers*.

[88]   It seems that the primary focus of the so-called *Founding Fathers* was to exploit, manipulate and control the indigenous populations they encountered in the Americas. Such was the British campaign all over the World, and the *Founding Fathers* of the United States were British Englishmen.

[89]   They wrote (or copied): *We the people of the United States, in order to form a more perfect union, establish justice, insure domestic tranquility, provide for the common defense, promote the general welfare, and secure the blessings of liberty, to ourselves and to OUR POSTERITY, do ordain and establish this Constitution for the United States* ("Preamble to the Constitution").

[90]   In short, Thomas Jefferson, James Madison, John Jay and others may have written and revised the Constitution but they did not author it, nor did they fully understand its principles. In Truth, it was a group of enlightened Africans, Europeans and Native Americans with that certain attitude and worldview who established

the principles of the United States of America as a free nation with *liberty* and *justice for all*.

[91]   It is we, to this day, who are still instinctively pressing onward toward this vision. As historian John R. Tucker (descendant of the first African Americans to land at Jamestown, Virginia in 1619) points out, *When reading the 'Preamble'* [of the U.S. Constitution] *keep in mind the thinking of the founding fathers when it was accepted. Such as 29 signers of the Declaration of Independence were men of color, and laws of naturalization were left out of the Constitution.*

[92]   *We don't want to be home for the social ills of the old World, the homeless, the starving, unemployables, and hooligans,* wrote John Jay to Alexander Hamilton and James Madison, framers of the Constitution.

[93]   Mr. Tucker continues, *Pay special thought on the phrase 'for us and our posterity.' There are 29 men of color in 'us' and the framer renounces the social ills of the old country; they certainly were not considered posterity.*

[94]   As Mr. Tucker points out, *29 of the 56 signers of the Declaration of Independence were men of color.* In fact, Robert E. Lee, the famous general of the Confederate army, was the *grandson of Francis Lightfoot Lee, an African/Native American, and a signer of the Declaration of Independence.* Mr. Tucker continues, *Multiculturalism is the civilization of the founding Fathers—the universality of Man.*

[95]   In Truth, it seems that the Spirit of 1776 was OUR Hip Hop spirit, which was then co-opted by British commercial interests, and made mainstream by the creation of the United States Constitution—just like Hip Hop was. The Declaration of Independence is Hip Hop, while the U.S. Constitution is its mainstream Rap counterpart designed to lure people with its own irresistible principles, ways, and views of the World in an attempt to appear civilized and appealing for business to the rest of the World.

[96] It's like the Declaration of Independence was the flyer/advertisement, and the U.S. Constitution was the actual jam/party. The Declaration of Independence was like the *demo* and the Constitution was like the finished master. The Declaration of Independence was like Hip Hop from 1981-1991, while the Constitution can symbolize Hip Hop from 1991 on.

[97] The Truth is that many free Blacks toured the United States with no problems, owned land, owned slaves, and held public offices. However, a very SINister conspiracy seems to have occurred in the United States just after the Civil War that removed Africans in America from public offices within the government by blatantly disregarding their rights as landowning, tax-paying citizens and legally elected community leaders, many times with force.

[98] As H.M. Turner (president of the Civil and political Rights Association) said in 1868 at the National Convention of the Colored Men Of America just after the Civil War: *To the colored voters of Georgia—the rights guaranteed to us by the constitution of our State, and by the Constitution and laws of the United States, have been unlawfully and arbitrarily torn from us by one branch of the General Assembly, a body created and established very largely by OUR votes, and that at the risk, in many instances, of starvation and death.*

[99] *The Democratic Party, having, by refusing the colored members the right to vote, unlawfully obtained a large majority in the House of Representatives, have decided, by a mere resolution, in defiance of the Constitution and the laws of the United States, and of the State of Georgia, that colored men have no right to represent their race in the General Assembly, and have accordingly ejected them from their seats!*

[100] *By this act they have ignored our rights of citizenship and representation, rights established by the Constitution and laws, and recognized by every sound and impartial jurist in*

the country.

101   Then, calling together a rally of concerned Black men and women, Mr. Turner concluded by stating: *There can be no doubt that our personal liberty is in as great danger as our civil and political rights. <u>The same power, which would override the Constitution in one thing, will do it in another.</u> It is therefore a solemn duty which every colored man owes himself, his family, and his country, to maintain his manhood and his right of citizenship.*

102   His final advice was this: *Guard against all disturbances, as this is a moral contest, a bloodless battle. Drunkards and fools fight in person, sober and wise men fight with thoughts and words.*

103   In 1853 Native Americans, Africans and Irish in America formed the *Know Nothing Party.* And when liberal voters in the North (some believed to be racist themselves) met in Ripon, Wisconsin and united with the *Know Nothing Party* they formed the Republican Party also known as the *People's Party.*

104   Critics of this party called it the *Black Republican Party.* This new *People's Party*, made up mostly of the anti-slavery movement, went on to elect a man from Illinois for President; his name was Abraham Lincoln. However, the thirst for power through White racism (different from the business of slavery) assassinated President Lincoln and began to blatantly disregard the rights and conditions of publicly elected Black officials along with the tax paying, landowning Black families whom Black elected officials represented.

105   So even though Native Americans and Africans helped to establish the Republican Party as the *People's Party,* unified White racism gradually denied them their rights and rightful places in history, in society and within the Republican Party itself.

[106]   Reading a resolution drafted by *the Colored Citizens of Boston* in 1856, just three years after the birth of the Republican Party, Mr. Julian B. McCrea declared: *Resolved, that while we regard the Republican Party as the people's party, the resolve in the Republican platform endorsing the Kansas Free State Constitution, which prohibits colored men from going into that territory, and the determination of the Republican press to ignore the colored man's interests in the party, plainly shows us that it is not an anti-slavery party, and while we are willing to unite with them to resist the aggressions of the Slave Power, we do not pledge ourselves to go further with the Republicans than the Republicans will go with us.*

[107]   Of course, this view of American history paints a much different picture than that which is promoted and taught today in public education. It seems that the true founders of the United States and their vision founded first *in the name of GOD*, with the primacy of *no man over another* and *all authority given to GOD*, were betrayed and THEIR posterity (us) was eventually completely overthrown sometime around the end of the Civil War.

[108]   And this I believe is why America has had such a difficult time being consistent with its own creeds and principles. It is because those who wound up governing the United States through treachery, treason, murder and lies seemed to also have been morally inadequate to lead a nation founded upon such universal principles as *freedom, justice* and *equality.*

[109]   Continuing OUR fight for *Human Rights* rests in the fact that the idea of human beings having *Rights* is an idea of OUR ancestors. Not just Black or Native American ancestors, but enlightened European and Asian American ancestors as well. OUR ancestors (ALL OF THEM) established the United States of America as a *multi-skilled, multicultural, multi-faith, multi-racial people committed to the*

establishment and development of peace (*Hip Hop Declaration of Peace*: Principle Eleven).

[110]   We all keep fighting for our *Rights* instinctively, because these *Rights* actually belong to us genetically! Freedom, justice and love, these are OUR birthrights! Our parents already created and established these *Rights* for the governing of our nations. But if we are unwilling to live our own birthright, then whose fault is it when we are enslaved?

[111]   Our ancient tribes were already prepared to unite for the creation of a *new people* and many enlightened Whites were part of that vision as well. But this is how it has always been. As far as this land mass (America) is concerned, this is the place where the *new tribe* was predicted to be born.

[112]   As French farmer, J. Hector St. John De Crevecoeur (Creve Coeur) observed in his travels throughout the American colonies before settling in New York in the early 1770s: *Americans are disposed races of Man, who had found land, livelihood, and liberty* <u>*without primacy of one man over another, regardless of previous nationality*</u>. *Here, individuals of all nations are melted into a new race of men, a new people.*

[113]   This is the vision of OUR ancestors! And this is what I have always understood Hip Hop to be, everyone coming together for the common cause of sustaining and advancing the Human Spirit.

[114]   When you instinctively feel that peace, love, unity and safely having fun is the normal state of humanity, that such virtues are actually your birthright, then you are indeed a citizen of the King's Dream, the true Kingdom of Heaven, the Hip Hop nation.

[115]   We (the genetic keepers of this vision) are the only ones who sincerely believe fundamentally that *all Men* (all Nature) *are created equal, that they are endowed by their Creator with certain unalienable Rights* (gifts), *that among*

these are Life, Liberty and the Pursuit of Happiness.

[116] We are the only ones, regardless of racial ethnicity or social class status, who believe that *to secure these Rights, Governments* (tribes) *are instituted among men, deriving their just powers from the consent of the governed, that whenever any Form of Government becomes destructive of these Ends, it is the Right of the People to alter or to abolish it, and to institute new Government, laying its Foundation on such Principles, and organizing its powers in such Form, as to them shall seem most likely to effect their Safety and Happiness.* (Declaration of Independence)

[117] With or without a government, with or without a constitution, with or without a religious institution, these are the innate ideas of our being. This is who we are and this is how we naturally act. And it is our being, our act, our character that creates our form of civilization.

[118] This is why we fight for our *Rights*—not because we are owed them, but because they belong to US! They are part of our character, our being, OUR BIRTHRIGHT! Our *unalienable* Rights complete us.

[119] We fight for the existence of *right* not that we may be granted our due *Rights*, but so that such *Rights* may exist in the World for ALL people. We are the frontlines for the protection, preservation and promotion of *right*. We have always defended what is fundamentally *right*. In Truth, we (those who sincerely seek peace, love, unity and having fun) are the World's true civilizers. And in a lot of ways the World is the way it is because WE HAVE FORGOTTEN WHO WE ARE.

[120] History seems to tell us that our ancestors (the original founders of the American idea) were simply overthrown, not just by the hypocrisies of their own population, but also, and in large part, by an even newer White immigrant population from Europe with better

technology. It seems that our enlightened ancestors discovered a spiritual way to live beyond the confinement of tribal loyalty but the individual populations of their tribes didn't agree and began to discredit and disrespect the warnings and teachings of their own tribal leaders. This led to the infighting and betrayal that caused foreign forces to invade and enslave such people.

[121]   Neither early White immigrant settlers nor their children came up with the pillars and principles of American government and society. So, when they arrived in the United States they immediately brought the ways of the "old country" to the new country and seized upon the infighting, greed and betrayal already going on amongst the populations of our ancestors. Our ancestors saw this all coming and many escaped the horrors that we read about today.

[122]   Newly arriving European immigrants learned and adopted some of OUR ways but they were basically here for the fortune they believed they could make in America (just like Hip Hop is treated today). And in ignorance, they attempted to practice OUR principles in their own way amongst themselves as a free *Whites Only* society. And proof of this is in the way in which the majority of immigrant Whites have conducted themselves socially and politically within the recent history of the United States, thinking that they may be the lowest piece of *White trash* amongst their own, but in America they were still better than the wisest and most honorable Black. This formed a *Whites Only* society as European immigrants sought to get all they could from the United States that enlightened Blacks, Whites and Natives built.

[123]   Again, French farmer J. Hector St. John De Crevecoeur points this fact out in his description of early European immigrants settling in the United States. He writes: *Whence came all these people? They are a mixture of*

English, Scotch, Irish, French, Dutch, Germans, and Swedes.
From this promiscuous breed, that race now called Americans
have arisen...In Europe they were as so many useless plants,
wanting vegetative mould, and refreshing showers; they
withered, and were mowed downed by want, hunger and war;
but now by the power of transplantation, like all other plants
they have taken root and flourished! Formerly they were not
numbered in any civil lists of their country, except in those of
the poor; here they rank as citizens.

[124] A "Whites Only" society would have been fine for
newly arriving European immigrants if the true founders
of the United States hadn't adopted such universally sound
principles. You see, one thing that the newly arriving
European immigrants did not seem to learn was that you
can steal and plagiarize all the things of the material World
except for virtue and righteousness, which are not of the
material World. You have to have spiritual hands to grab
spiritual ideas. But as all parties would learn, the adoption of
such universal principles as Freedom, Justice and Equality
requires an understanding of Universal Mind. It requires
a personal character that reflects the universality of such
adopted and established principles.

[125] Founding a nation upon the *laws of Nature and of*
Nature's GOD obligates those founders and their posterity
to be consistent with the known Will of that *GOD* and the
cycles of that *GOD's* Nature. Calling upon the *protection*
of divine providence and pledging your life, your fortunes
and your *sacred honor* to the cause of establishing a truly
free nation cannot be exchanged for the great wealth,
power and prestige that comes with the establishment of
such a nation.

[126] This is what real America has always been about;
peace, love, unity and safely having fun. These principles
have no color and belong to no race or ethnicity of people.

And this is what has always divided the United States, a nation made up of immigrants. Most of us truly seek Peace and Truth but the greedy ambitions of some of us always seem to hinder the progress of all of us. The *protection of divine providence* requires a relationship with Divine Mind—GOD. It requires a harmony with the evolution of Nature itself.

[127] The closer we get to accurately imitating the ways of Nature and that of *Nature's GOD* the closer we shall arrive at a more *perfect union* as a nation. But the American leadership that was to come after the true founders of the United States never seemed to understand that if you want GOD to keep a covenant with you, then you must keep your covenants, contracts and treaties with others, including GOD. Yes, GOD did bless the United States of America in the beginning, but newly arriving immigrants did not understand nor return such a blessing to GOD when they arrived.

[128] Although many today do not want to admit it, the plain old Truth is that the United States of America is a Christian nation founded upon the original Christian principles of Love, Truth and Freedom. As John Jay, the first Chief Justice of the United States Supreme Court so famously stated, *Providence has given to our people the choice of their rulers, and it is the duty, as well as the privilege and interest of our Christian nation, to select and prefer Christians for their rulers.* George Washington, John Adams, Benjamin Franklin, James Madison, John Quincy Adams and many others were men of spiritual insight but even they contradicted the timeless principles and virtues of the Christian bible in exchange for the material promises of science and commerce.

[129] The point, however, is that the true founders of the United States may have been a deeply spiritual people

with an unwavering faith in their cause and their god, but the American population and the leadership that was to come after them have totally contradicted the intentioned principles of America's true founders and the order that supernaturally governs the United States. And everyone (race-wise) is guilty!

130   Blacks, Whites, Natives, Asians, Hispanics, Arabs, Hindus, everyone is guilty! You see, slavery was not about Black people subservient to White people, as has been taught all throughout American history. Slavery was about social status, education, and property. Anyone could own a slave if one could afford it. Separate from White racism, slavery was simply the way things got done in the early days—it was business as usual.

131   Freedom has always been for sale in the United States, even amongst some Africans and Native American tribes. In 1862, Congress abolished slavery in Washington, DC and paid *seven colored residents* $5,978.20 in compensation for 26 slaves.

132   French African plantation owners in 1814 owned White slaves. Native Americans also kept Black and White slaves. West African kings, from the very beginning of the whole slave trade, sold their captives as slaves to the highest bidder. In fact, many countries are still trafficking slaves even to this day.

133   Historian John R. Tucker writes, *To understand the magnitude of the economy of the Confederacy, in 1814 the Spaniards in South Florida held an equipment sales convention in Pensacola, Florida, and some 20,000 African and Original people land owners were in attendance.* These were NOT slaves, most were slave owners and many of them owned White men and women as slaves.

134   This is the point: everyone had a hand in the creation and sustainment of the institution of Slavery in

America. Everyone (all races) sought to subdue and betray their neighbor for financial and political gain in direct contradiction of the fact that the United States was founded upon the principle of *no man over another man*. And such an activity even continues today. In fact, it seems that history is repeating itself again with the events of the Rap music industry. Can you see it?

135   We allow ourselves to be exploited as a group because of our own exploitation of one another. *One nation, under God, indivisible, with liberty and justice for all!* This is a spiritual decree, and only a free mind would want such a thing. Why would greedy slave-owning capitalists want *freedom and justice for all?* Look at these words closely; has the leadership of the United States lived up to these words? Have America's radio and television programmers lived up to these words?

136   Every time a nation says *one nation, under God, indivisible, with liberty and justice for all,* they themselves are held to that which they have decreed. To receive such a decree you must be willing to exercise such a decree toward others. Unity, loyalty, God, righteousness, freedom, knowledge, justice, rule of law, etc., are all the governing principles of the ancients. And it is these principles that ALL American citizens have betrayed; African, European, Asian, Hindu, Arab, Hispanic, Native American, everyone!

137   Everyone is responsible for how the United States of America has turned out. As we will see, the true political contest is not between Black and White; it is between good and evil. It is between educated and uneducated. It is between the Godly and the Worldly, the faithful and the fearful, the aware and the ignorant, the real and the fake.

138   True American history reveals a *True World Order* of peace, love, UNITY, and safely having fun amongst

all people. True American history reveals the stories of brave White abolitionists, interracial love, White slaves (not indentured servants), Black and Native American slave owners, and a continuous civil war between the *good* and the *evil*. Sometimes it's even between the *evil* and the *evil!*

[139]   Race as relevant to our struggles for Freedom, Justice and Equality is an illusion. Race loyalty as a strategy toward lasting peace and uninterrupted prosperity is also an illusion. You either stand for Freedom, Justice and Equality as a person or you contradict these principles as a person. As H. Rap Brown has pointed out, *We must learn that Black is not a color but the way you think. If we are to succeed in The Struggle we must eliminate the significance that we have assigned to color in our community…Among Black people, color can have no value, no significance. Commitment will determine the value of individuals.*

[140]   The issue is not even about class, social status, or religious belief at the deepest level. American slave history has already proven that one's own hatred and ignorance can even manipulate the *body of Christ*. As reported in 1869, southern church members owned an estimated 600,000 slaves/human beings. Methodists owned 219,000 human beings. Baptists owned 125,000 human beings. Reformed Baptists owned 101,000 human beings. Presbyterians owned 77,000 human beings. Episcopalians owned 85,000 human beings. With other denominations it was estimated that 55,000 more human beings were kept as slaves within the *body of Christ*—the Church.

[141]   And it is also known by any serious historian of Slavery that from the very beginning of the slave trade it was the Church that gave moral authority and ethical consistency to the whole institution of Slavery. In fact, it was a Catholic Bishop that suggested the use of African

slaves as a substitute for Native American slaves. Slave ships bore Christian names and the captains of these vessels read the Bible and prayed everyday! To a captured African, torn from her family and way of life, *the body of Christ* looked like a slave ship.

[142] But to be fair here, for all the crimes committed against the *body of Christ* by the *ignorant* there were twice as many good and Godly acts of courage and righteousness performed by the *aware* who healed and sustained the integrity of that *body*. This is one of the only reasons Christianity exists today; it exists because of REAL CHRISTIANS!

[143] One story comes to mind of a brave and righteous White female abolitionist/freedom fighter named Laura Haviland (Havilland). She lived in Adrian, Michigan during the height of slavery and was so successful at harboring and freeing hundreds of Blacks, Whites and Native Americans seeking freedom through the *Undagraound Railroad* that slave owners offered a reward of $3,000 for her capture, dead or alive.

[144] Captain Jonathan Walker (a White man) was jailed, fined and branded on his hand—S.S. for *Slave Stealer*—when he was caught helping fugitive slaves get away to freedom on his boat. Abolitionists raised the money to free him, but bad health later caused him to commit suicide.

[145] Not only does the story of John Brown and his 21 supporters comes to mind, but most recently, like during the Civil Rights Movement, the names of such martyrs as Mickey Schwerner and Andrew Goodman as well as James Reab and Viola Leuso also come to mind. Many such stories exist in America's true history. And this has always been the true order of the World: Man freeing Man! Man helping Man! Man sharpening Man! Man respecting Man! Peace, love, unity and having fun! This is what the majority of the

World is all about and this is the vision of OUR ancestors.

[146]   But as many Americans would learn over many hard years, you cannot want for yourself that which you are not willing to give to another. You cannot expect to want life without first giving life. You cannot expect to live free while enslaving others. You cannot expect to hold onto universal concepts with greedy material-grabbing hands. You cannot serve two gods; in due time you will achieve neither!

[147]   And so, the great pillars of freedom, justice and equality set up by 29 men of color and 27 others making up the laws and philosophies of the United States of America, crumbled under the weight of America's own disobedience to the *laws of Nature and Nature's GOD*, a blatant contradiction of its own principles.

[148]   Such contradictions, however, came with real consequences. White mobs began increasingly attacking African communities in the United States with repeated lynchings, burnings and beatings of African men, women and children. The hatred was high! And it was high because in some places like Florida, New Orleans, Mississippi and South Carolina Africans were powerfully part of the landowning, slave-owning, ruling class of the 1800s!

[149]   Without the guidance of their Godly principles, brother began murdering brother and sister began undermining sister. From 1861–1865 the whole of America broke out into Civil War over who was going to control the wealth, direction and power of the United States. Americans divided themselves up into a *Confederacy* and a *Union* with Africans in America fighting on both sides.

[150]   In New York during the 1863 Civil War Draft Act, persons able to pay $300 for a substitute were not drafted. Black men were not taken into the Army at that time so they were ineligible for the draft. Most of the people drafted for war were poor Irish immigrants who were either indentured

servants, or slaves, or menial job workers; they were of the laboring class.

151   Fearful of losing what little they had to an already prosperous African community by going to a war that had little to do with them as newly arrived immigrants led to the formation of Irish, German, English and Danish mobs burning and bombing African homes, lynching African men and terrorizing African women and children. When the riots, which lasted for four days, ended, 1,000 people (mostly Africans) were dead and property damage was estimated at $2,000,000.

152   It seems that before the Civil War, Africans in America were becoming increasingly powerful as a body of well-educated and spiritually charged people. Most people of the United States fought against slavery, racism and prejudice. However, there seems to have been a racist plot amongst the majority of new White Americans (rich and poor alike) to seize power from other Whites, Africans and Native Americans on the basis of race and race loyalty.

153   And although the new immigrant gangs prayed to their god for assistance in the victory of securing what they believed were their *rights*, no one was able to see that without an acknowledgement of GOD's supremacy over their lives and that of their nation, they had no *rights!*

154   As clearly stated, an American's *unalienable rights* are *endowed* by his *creator*. However, newly arriving immigrants were simply unable to maintain the faith and vision of America's true architects advancing the universal principles which the United States was founded upon—the universality of Man; *out of many, one.*

155   Racism and prejudice seem to have killed the harmony of America's original multicultural, multi-faithed vision of itself. Even though many Whites did see the contradictions in their own society and even risked their

own lives and the lives of their families to correct such contradictions, still as a nation the United States continued to distance itself from *Nature* and from *Nature's GOD,* living with spiritual contradictions that eventually seeped into its laws.

[156] As reported by the New York Tribune in 1868 regarding a bill passed in Atlanta Georgia: *The House yesterday took another step toward the <u>culmination of the counter-revolution</u> which is in such rapid progress in this State. A bill was passed adopting the jury system of the old Slave Code, which forbids colored men sitting upon juries. This is practically denying the colored citizen the right of trial by jury, for, while the prejudice of race remains so potent, he can have no justice in a suit with a White man; <u>and the freedman is worse off, when accused of crime, than was the slave, for the latter was too valuable a piece of property to be wasted in hanging, while the freedman is property of nobody but himself.</u>*

[157] *The <u>proceedings</u> was in <u>violation</u> of the very Constitution from which the Legislature derives its existence and power to make laws, for that document prescribes but one criterion by which juries shall be selected, to <u>wit: intelligence and uprightness</u>, while the old system, perpetuated yesterday, establishes quite a different test, to wit: color.*

[158] *The Constitution says: <u>'The General Assembly shall provide by law for the selection of upright and intelligent persons to serve as jurors'</u> but the 'Code' declares that such jurors shall be White male citizens, above the age of twenty-one years.*

[159] *<u>Ignoring the supreme law of the Constitution,</u> the Legislature adopted the old slave law rendered obsolete by its inconsistency with the Constitution. <u>The bill passed by a vote of 87 to 24, some dough-faced Republicans dodging or voting with the majority.</u>*

[160] It seems that throughout early American history many Democrats were uninterested in Black freedom and

many Republicans (although split on the issue) betrayed Black interests and freedom, especially after the Civil War. The immense profits created from slave trading and slave labor were coming in too fast for American businesses not to become addicted.

[161]   Even though it (slavery) totally contradicted the very philosophical foundations of the United States, nonetheless it (slavery) would be practiced in many different ways and forms for many more years to come in the United States of America. It seems that as science and commerce began to rise in Europe and the United States, morality and principles began to decline. Guns, money and machines began to replace peace, love and unity. The domination and enslavement of whole populations with new technologies actually advanced the concept of slavery; it did not eliminate it.

[162]   If the Truth be told, those who were pro-slavery and those who were anti-slavery both got their way after the Civil War because slavery was removed from public life and public sight but was never really "abolished." Actually it was modified and expanded to include all American citizens.

[163]   As was written into law in 1896, *Neither slavery nor involuntary servitude, EXCEPT AS A PUNISHMENT for a crime whereof the party shall have been duly convicted, shall exist within the United States, or any place subject to their jurisdiction.* (Thirteenth Amendment to the United States Constitution)

[164]   As we can see, yes, slavery still exists! It just doesn't exist within mainstream American life. But it still has its useful place within the U.S. Justice Department as a "punishment." Those who break the laws of the United States and are caught without enough wealth, power or knowledge to free themselves are then reduced to modern-day slaves, commonly called "inmates."

[165]   Nothing in the Thirteenth Amendment abolishes

slavery. To "abolish" something means to end it, to stop it, to do away with it, to remove it from existence. The Thirteenth Amendment does not abolish slavery, it renames it and reinvents it as a "punishment." But this is how it has always been for the African surviving in America. Freedom for the African in America was always about money, education and a compliance with United States laws, laws that Africans in America helped to create.

166   But again, the seeming contradictions between the preamble of the United States Constitution and those of the American government's later legislative actions are better understood when you consider the fact that the body that helped to establish the United States and its principles is NOT the same body that seems to have gradually taken control of the United States government after the Civil War.

167   Indeed, it is knowledge that reigns supreme and one of the most devious and tragic strategies employed against early Africans in America was to betray THEIR loyalty to THEIR country and convince THEIR posterity that they never had a stake in the success of THEIR nation—the great experiment called the *United States of America*.

168   And again, the evidence of this is produced by observing the level of contradiction between what is written in the United States Constitution and Declaration of Independence verses what really occurred in American history. When viewed as multicultural, multi-faithed documents, the Declaration of Independence and even the United States Constitution become spiritual documents that guide and protect the course of any nation that adopts their characters.

169   In other words, you can't just sit on the throne; you have to actually be the king! Or in this case, in order to lead a truly righteous nation, you yourself must exhibit a truly

righteous character.

170   As a true leader, you can't just read the words of divinity; you actually have to show through your judgments, acts and words that you are committed to such divinity. The mind that yearns for *a more perfect Union, Justice, domestic Tranquility, common defense, general Welfare,* and *the Blessings of Liberty* is not the same mind that produces political corruption, war, social insecurity, poverty and a legal separation between God and the State.

171   For most people reality is based upon the histories that they've been forced to learn and *pledge allegiance* to. And as we now know, American history was completely made up to foster an image in the minds of ordinary people that the activities of certain landowning, slave-owning, aristocratic, White males were the only things going on for hundreds of years in the Americas and elsewhere. We now know this to be a lie.

172   Great books and authors that reveal the hidden (even true or truer) history of the United States are popping up in bookstores everywhere and frequently hitting national best-seller lists. Nevertheless, the one thing that all of these books have in common is their harmonious agreement that what we think we know of the United States and of our own ancestry is simply not true. In fact, as Americans we've been living a lie—a lie that has had real material and emotional effects upon our lives and our abilities to plan and grow.

173   Imagine your view of the past being a lie! That what you think went on actually didn't and what you didn't know was even possible was occurring every day. This is not far from the Truth, and this is why the Temple of Hip Hop calls *our people* into existence. Such awareness is not for everyone; not everyone is prepared for the Truth.

174   The Truth is that we are not what we have been taught to be, and the past was not all about conquest, theft

and enslavement. There is another history to the World, a true history that seems to be about peace, love, unity, having fun and people coming together to share ideas and talents.

175   Unlike Christopher Columbus and the Spanish invaders of Mexico, when we (Afro-Phoenicians, the Norse peoples, Asians and Natives from other parts of the Americas) came upon the forest, mountains and shores of what is now called "Mexico," we were greeted just like Columbus was greeted by the peoples of those regions, except we didn't commence to robbing, shooting, stealing, stabbing, raping and enslaving our hosts. We were Hip Hop!

176   We sat down and enjoyed each other's company and ideas. We exchanged jewelry, herbs, spices, and knowledge; we even exchanged men and women. Not on some "you my slave now" attitude, but on a higher respect for learning to communicate between tribes and the exchange of ideas and inventions more rapidly.

177   However, government-backed Spanish corporations, for example, would arrive at our beaches, having never seen us before, looking for the gold on our islands. We would come out to greet them in love and they would read in Spanish a document known as "The Requirement." It read, *I implore you to recognize the Church as a lady and in the name of the Pope take the King as lord of this land and obey his mandates. If you do not do it, I tell you that with the help of God I will enter powerfully against you all! I will make war everywhere and every way that I can. I will subject you to the yoke and obedience to the Church and to his majesty. I will take your women and children and make them slaves. The deaths and injuries that you will receive from here on will be your own fault and not that of his majesty nor the gentlemen that accompany me.*

178   As Black Africans we lived in peace and with respect amongst the Natives of ancient Mexico centuries before the

arrival of the Spaniards in the Americas. Huge 2,500-year-old stone sculptures of African heads throughout Mexico reflect this fact.

[179]   *Unlike the Norse, the Africans and Phoenicians seemed to have made a permanent impact on the Americas. Huge stone statues in Mexico imply as much. It took enormous effort to quarry these basalt blocks each weighing 10 to 40 tons, move them from quarry 75 miles away and sculpt them into heads 6 to 10 feet tall. Wherever they were from, the human models for these heads were important people. People to be worshipped or obeyed, or at least remembered.* (James W. Loewen, *Lies My Teacher Told Me*)

[180]   When Christopher Columbus arrived in the Americas in 1492 we were already here. We (the Hip Hop attitude) have been here in America since before 750 B.C. As Mr. Loewen continues, *showing that navigation and exploration didn't begin with Europe in the 1400s, like the Norse, the Afro-Phoenicians* (who also sail from Africa to the shores of Mexico and elsewhere centuries before Columbus) *illustrate human possibility in this case, Black possibility or more accurately the prowess of a multiracial society.*

[181]   This has always been our aim as a Hip Hop community—*one multi-skilled, multicultural, multi-faith, multiracial people committed to the establishment and the development of peace.* (*Hip Hop Declaration of Peace*: Principle Eleven). This is Hip Hop!

[182]   Africans, Europeans, Asians, and aboriginals of all kinds seem to have traded with each other and lived together in relative harmony for hundreds of years in the Americas and elsewhere before the conquests of certain European corporations. Sure, there were fights and wars, conflicts and disagreements, but never the kind of deliberate genocide and the enslavement of whole populations by force of arms as with the arrival of the Christopher Columbus corporation

and others to the Americas.

¹⁸³ However, it is important to point out that even though our ancient infighting and conflicts in the Americas never reached the magnitude of mass genocide and the enslavement of whole populations, it was our own infighting, stealing and lying amongst ourselves that aided in the victory of outside forces invading our lands and carrying off our resources and people.

¹⁸⁴ Most human beings generally sought peace and good times, play and laugher, and this seems to be what was happening all over the World, especially in the Americas before the arrival of the Christopher Columbus corporation. But when the invaders came we were not strong enough to overcome them because by the time they actually showed up on our shores we had already disrespected our own priests and tribal elders. We were already disunified when Columbus arrived. We had already disregarded the warnings of our priests and shamans and so we made it very easy for an outside invading force to cease our resources, knowledge and people.

¹⁸⁵ We now know that no invading force can ever conquer a united people. No invading force can ever undermine a king, queen or government that is truly loved by its people. It seems that before the invasions of our lands, our own internal respect and loyalty to our king, queen, priests, etc. had already weakened, and it was this weakness that allowed outside forces to invade and capture our lands and people.

¹⁸⁶ Even today, there seems to be an ancient and original *True World Order* that derives power through self-expression and human ingenuity, which is being interrupted and exploited by a technological *New World Order* that derives power out of the barrels of guns. One World is real and the other World is indeed fake! One is indigenous to

Nature and spiritual law and the other is alien to Nature and spiritual law.

[187]   However, anyone who imposes their will upon you enters the relationship from a weak, uneven position because to have to impose your will means that your will is not natural or divine; it is not in harmony with the true nature of things, it is not universal to all creatures. You never have to impose a will that is already in harmony with the nature of reality itself. It is only when your will goes against the natural and universally accepted harmony of things that you must now get your point across with force— which doesn't last anyway because it is not real or natural.

[188]   Hip Hop is natural, and it appears to rise and fall within a variety of historical people and events throughout time and space (we'll get into this later). The thoughts, attitudes and activities that we are calling "Hip Hop" today existed at the earliest formations of American society.

[189]   Our creative intelligence has been in the World for thousand of years, expressing itself in the World whenever we were stable and free enough to express ourselves. For hundreds of years we (our collective Hiphop attitude) lived in peace with all the peoples of the ancient World. But when certain European corporations developed the gun into an instrument of mass-destruction, with that one tool they enslaved the entire globe. And this is what every true Hiphoppa must understand.

[190]   Europe's rise to power did not come by way of more advanced knowledge, better government, smarter leadership, etc. Europe's rise to power came first from its improvements upon the World's already established ideas on the development of sanitation systems and medical services, the production of agriculture and industrial goods, as well as improvements in transportation and communications.

[191]   But the leading cause of Europe's rise to World

dominance was its weapons. It was Europe's ability to invade and kill, and improve upon its weapons and warfare that propelled Europe into World domination. Europeans were not smarter or more talented as a people or as a nation-state than anyone else at the time. They were not closer to GOD, nor did they display some great achievement unparalleled by any other World civilization. Their power came from their weapons and their foreign products like whiskey and from their infectious diseases like smallpox.

[192]   Of course, there were benefits to Europeans arriving in the Americas. But historically and actually, the sorrows and the losses caused by European invasions upon the indigenous peoples of the Americas seemed to outweigh the benefits.

[193]   As Carroll Quigley explains in his 1966 book *Tragedy and Hope: When White men first came to North America, material elements from Western civilization spread rapidly amongst the Indian tribes. The Plains Indians, for example, were weak and impoverished before 1543, but in that year the horse began to diffuse northward from the Spaniards in Mexico.*

[194]   *Within a century the Plains Indians were raised to a much higher standard of living (because of their ability to hunt buffalo from horseback) and were immensely strengthened in their ability to resist Americans coming westward across the continent. In the meantime, the trans-Appalachian Indians who had been very powerful in the sixteenth and early seventeenth centuries began to receive firearms, steel traps, measles and eventually whiskey from the French and later the English by way of the St. Lawrence.*

[195]   *These greatly weakened the woods Indians of the trans-Appalachian area and ultimately weakened the Plains Indians of the trans-Mississippi area, because measles and whiskey were devastating and demoralizing and because the use*

of traps and guns by certain tribes made them dependent on Whites for supplies at the same time that they allowed them to put great physical pressure on the more remote tribes which had not yet received guns or traps. Any united front of Reds against Whites was impossible, and the Indians were disrupted, demoralized and destroyed.

196   This group of European exploiters with guns, explosives, measles and whiskey began terrorizing the inhabitants of the Americas, many of whom were us—the early Hip Hop communal attitude, those forward thinkers with that street attitude. However, with superior weaponry these aliens sought to enslave our people and steal our resources.

197   Centuries of such activity resulted in the further establishment of the British Empire. And because of such activities, our creative intelligence was never really able to fully express itself toward our improved existence. Any expression coming from our experiences or intelligence had to be beneficial to the British Empire or it was deemed *illegal* or not worthy of study—unimportant.

198   For many centuries our parents, grandparents, and great-grandparents could not express their interpretations of the World, of Cosmic Consciousness, and of *Self* publicly. Their (our) ideas and ways of doing things were stolen and/or suppressed by the commercial interests of European invaders with guns who sought to bring the Earth's people under their rule and order through their weapons and institutions.

199   Spanish, Dutch, Portuguese and British commercialism (also known as British colonialism) ignored the existence and authority of everything and everyone it came into contact with, and with the use of bombs and guns, whiskey and disease the British Empire paved a silence over all Earth cultures under its oppressive rule.

200   Long suffering and oppression resulted for all the Earth's indigenous people while British commercialism matured and developed, creating its own philosophies and views of Nature and the universe. Truths, facts, and discoveries made long ago became irrelevant to the new western mind that believed in the supremacy of British culture over all others.

201   At this point, the whole World would have to wait hundreds of years for western man with guns and bombs to mature mentally and spiritually to the point of rediscovering what every other culture already knew about Nature, the Great Spirit and the nature of reality itself. It's like British colonialism/commercialism halted the World's progress through terrorism until IT was able to catch up—and IT still hasn't quite caught up yet! Even other Europeans felt the horrors and stagnation of European commercial conquest.

202   However, many young Europeans still love and respect the basic global Hip Hop attitude and idea, and this is why the Temple of Hip Hop exists. Our aim is to assist in the spiritual and cultural maturity of our Hip Hop community in particular as well as humanity in general. We believe that as evil as some European, African, Asian, Arab, Latino and Native American corporations have been toward the growth of humanity itself, as individual people, they too were victims—immature, insecure and ignorant of themselves.

203   No, we do not condone or even disregard the horrific effects of blatant genocide, greed and hatred. However, even today we can see that such acts are indeed the acts of the fearful, the ignorant, the doubtful, and the unachieved. We can see now how our parents were actually victims of victims! As well-respected metaphysician Louise Hay as pointed out: *What kind of childhood would produce an adult like that?*

[204] Author/historian Howard Zinn agrees: *In the long run the oppressor is also a victim. In the short run, and so far human history has only consisted of short runs, the victim is themselves, desperate and tainted with a culture that oppresses them.*

[205] What a tragic situation to continue to perpetuate. Here, the victim of injustice grows up bitter, eventually losing faith in humanity and society's institutions, while the criminal grows up guilty, eventually losing faith in himself. Ultimately, everyone suffers when injustice is produced.

[206] Therefore, our aim as a temple for Hip Hop is to promote reconciliation, forgiveness and healing within the Hip Hop community, to turn up the volume on peace and justice over war and revenge.

[207] This is the aim of our ministry, to teach our people how to curb and control those natural instincts that motivate one man to rob and/or kill another, to lie to another, to exploit another. The savagery that prevents groups of humans to rise above their condition is the same savagery we are faced with today.

[208] Sure, such savagery is disguised today behind money, flimsy ideologies and technological innovations, but in the end police brutality, racism, deceit and greed are all basically savage behaviors. And it is not the fault of individual people; it is more the fault of failed institutions and social policies.

[209] We know that it is a society's social institutions that support the very foundations of human civilization. Such institutions replace our natural need to seek food and defend ourselves, and when such institutions collapse for one reason or another, the society returns to its natural animal state. Hip Hop cannot be part of such a decline.

[210] The cause of any meaningful religion is to produce a human social order out of a natural animal chaos, to

establish a common spirit amongst the members of the society. Religion (as an example) keeps a society of strangers together, focused upon one common motif understood by all. It creates an abstract family social structure for a society of strangers to relate to each other regarding good and evil.
[211] No human society can exist without a strong moral code, a strong sense of what is right and what is wrong for ITS survival. But in Hip Hop's case, morality can't just be about *right* and *wrong*; the morality of our group should also seek what is true and what is *false*.

[212] Arthur F. Holmes in his book *Ethics: Approaching Moral Decisions,* writes: *First, moral practices vary with and depend on human needs and social conditions. Second, moral attitudes and practices are basically noncognitive responses rather than the product of rational thought.*

[213] Such an interpretation of morality can be called "cultural relativism," *the view that moral beliefs and practices vary with and depend on the human needs and social conditions of particular cultures, so that no moral beliefs can be universally true. There can be no universal 'oughts.'* (Arthur F. Holmes)

[214] We can see here that morality, although important and good for growing groups of people, is still not Truth. As an example, for hundreds of years our parents have been forced to accept the morality of their Christian slave-holders. Therefore, as a growing group of specialized people in pursuit of true freedom and justice, establishing our own moral code based upon what we need to survive, it becomes apparent that we will also need Truth to survive as a group.

[215] We have seen now that without Truth as a moral attitude within a group, such a group cannot survive in peace for long. In my time, Christian values and principles are collapsing because of this, and many urban centers around the World are sinking back into savagery.

216   Again, this is why the Temple of Hip Hop exists. We exist to curb the savagery within our own Hip Hop community with an attitude that seeks Truth over individual desires.

217   Our aim is to inspire children beyond fear, rage and doubt—the cause of so much adult injustice and evil in the World.

218   Our aim is to heal the wounds of ignorance on both sides—to free both the slave as well as the slaveholder from the victimization both groups have had to endure.

219   Our aim is to hasten the actualization of the King's Dream—to sit at that *Table of Brotherhood!*

220   Our aim is to promote and establish peace wherever we are—to relieve human suffering wherever it may appear.

221   Our aim is to raise up a few really good leaders—those who will not sell us out this time!

222   Our aim is to preserve and further develop Hip Hop—to establish and maintain Hip Hop's city!

223   Like any useful institution of divine origin our aim is to lift our community up beyond its desperateness and lead it toward peace, prosperity and security. For we know now that violence is natural, while peace is supernatural. Therefore, those who seek peace seek the supernatural, ultimately seeking GOD—the Love that is reading with you now.

224   Again, when a nation's institutions fail, the people of that nation revert back to their state of savagery; the prevention of such a condition is why our temple for Hip Hop exists.

225   For if a community has no relation to the supernatural, it can only relate to the natural. A good and useful learning institution exchanges our need to kill and eat to survive with learning the ways of cooperation, unity and

teamwork toward survival. This is our mission within the Hip Hop community. Our people have been held down for far too long and now it is our divine time to rise up!

226 As the great mythologist Jospeh Campbell has pointed out: *The dynamics of the psyche and the dynamics of the society are equivalent. What has been pushed down is going to come up! And the tension, and what we were talking about a few years ago, the explosions of the inner city, is exactly the social counterpart of the 'shadow' coming up. It* [the 'shadow'] *is a function of the organism* [society] *that has not been recognized and given its position. And always out of that comes an enlargement of consciousness and there has to be an assimilation of the two."*

227 This is what the Temple of Hip Hop is all about, the *enlargement of consciousness*. As a Hip Hop preservation society, we also study the repeated patterns of Hip Hop's existence in space-time reality. We look throughout written, visual and oral World history to see the patterns that best suit our movements today, one way or the other.

228 We know that history repeats itself because we know that time pulsates in repeatable cycles. We know that it is not historical events that repeat themselves, but more accurately it is the *conditions* that created certain historical events that repeat themselves. Time continuously gives us chances to repeat our victories and/or misfortunes in a circular kind of motion.

229 We have discovered today that our time right now is the time of civilization and great leaps in consciousness are about to occur. We know the cycles of our planet and the sun and how these great movements affect our consciousness as well as space-time reality itself. When we study the many calendars of civilizations before us we can see ourselves being repeated in space-time geometry. We can see who we all are and where we made certain mistakes

as well as achievements.

230   The conditions for the birth of a new people are upon us now. The position of the sun and the mathematics that predict the end of one age into another are upon us now. We are actually completing a 5125-year cycle of time that, according to Mayan calculations, completes December 21, 2012.

231   Is it mere coincidence that Kool DJ Herc is said to have begun modern Hip Hop on August 11, 1973, and the present World age began August 11, 3114 B.C., and completes with the rare alignment of the solar system with the center of the Milky Way on December 21, 2012? Is it a mere coincidence that the zone in which the sun travels across the equator of the Milky Way galaxy spans a distance of time that began around 1980 and ends around 2016, a time that spans the whole mainstream rise of Hip Hop and its commercial promotion of Rap music?

232   Do we really believe that we exist outside of the universe and its influences upon our creation and further development as Hip Hop? Oh no, we don't! Hip Hop is divine and it is following the patterns of celestial calculations. Those of us who are aware are also humbled; it is indeed our time again! The last days of others are indeed the first days for us.

233   Let us unite around the timeless principles of peace, love, unity and joy. We are indeed living at one of the greatest times in human history and to be aware of such a time causes one to be alert and virtuous. Preparing our people for the inevitable shift in Earth consciousness is the sacred work of our temple for Hip Hop.

234   If this path is for you, YOU ARE WELCOMED INTO THE TEMPLE OF HIPHOP. Your training has already begun. The following is a list of our training "stages" that represent the learning levels of our committed

members. Take a moment now and review the following list to determine which "stage" is comfortable for you to begin with.

RAP FAN: A *Rap fan* is anyone who enjoys or respects Rap music. *Rap fans* are only interested in watching or listening to Rap music even though they may call it *Hip Hop*.

I   To the *Rap fan* Hip Hop is music. *Rap fans* are culturally and spiritually blind, deaf and dumb to *true* Hiphop. The deeper spiritual lessons and Overstandings of the Temple of Hiphop are incomprehensible to *Rap fans* and can cause them unnecessary suffering.

II   However, it is the *Rap fan* who has financed the Rap music industry through the sales of music and other entertainment products. Basically, *Rap fans* just enjoy Rap music. Nevertheless, to truly be a knowledgeable teacha of Hip Hop's cultural evolution it is helpful to have been an average fan of Rap music for some part of your life.

III   However, having Hiphop's spiritual *sight* is the fundamental difference between the attuned Hiphoppa and the *Rap fan*. Many *Rap fans*, although greatly appreciated, lack knowledge as to what causes Hip Hop.

IV   They simply buy Rap music product and imitate it or teach it as hip-hop's culture. They do not truly <u>live</u> an authentic, productive Hiphop lifestyle so Hiphop's cultural/ spiritual wisdom (the knowledge of what causes Hip Hop) is foreign and in most cases useless to them.

V   Keep in mind that the term *Rap fan* can also be applied to Rap artists with lengthy entertainment contracts. Many well-known Rap artists, executives, professors, ministers and editors are really *Rap fans* imitating and/ or admiring the skill, mastery and cultural mentalities of true Hiphoppas.

VI   It was new music technology and the need for

various corporations to exploit hip-hop that gave *Rap fans* the ability to imitate what the *true Hiphoppa* experienced. That was, and still is, the difference between watching *hip-hop,* learning *Hip Hop* and actually being *Hiphop*.

VII   When you are naturally and effortlessly Hiphop you instinctively feel the need to express Hip Hop beyond entertainment and money-making exclusively. You simply care for the development of yourself as Hip Hop. You simply care about Hip Hop because you respect your *Self.* There is no separation between you and Hip Hop.

VIII   Hip Hop is your lifestyle and you cannot sell your lifestyle nor should you contradict your cultural principles. In light of this, Hip Hop can be considered an unalienable right of all Hiphoppas.

IX   On the other hand, those *Rap fans* who watch and/or listen to *hip-hop* also live other lifestyles. So the exploitation of Hip Hop's culture, principles and elements is a natural behavior toward the benefit of whatever lifestyle or culture they really live and pledge their alligence to.

X   The *Rap fan* admires and imitates the effects of the true Hip Hop mentality and remains confined only to the elements that have survived over the years. However, the attuned Hiphoppa, having knowledge of Hip Hop's history, meaning, purpose and original causes can apply the original Hip Hop awareness (or spiritual *sight*) to any subject or object in the World, thus expanding one's range of creative freedom.

XI   The attuned Hiphoppa further expands Hip Hop, while the *Rap fan* merely imitates the Hip Hop elements already created. When the demand for such a Hip Hop element fades, so does the career of the *Rap fan*.

XII   But the attuned Hiphoppa, for example, can apply the Hiphop *sight* (or awareness) to empty soda cans and create a new career out of that! Remember, Hip Hop is not exclusively music; it is an awareness that can be applied to any subject or object. It is a transformative power.

XIII   With little or no awareness of Hiphop's cultural or spiritual purpose, even if one thinks he is doing Hip Hop a service by performing Hip Hop's elements he is not. In fact, he cannot!

XIV   *Rap fans* are offered the *Hip Hop Declaration of Peace.*

HIPHOPPA: A Hiphoppa is an individual participating in Hip Hop's culture—a citizen of the Hip Hop nation.

I   *Hiphoppas* <u>sense</u> the deeper essence of Hip Hop beyond Rap music. *Hiphoppas* may also know a variety of spiritual Truths but they still have not matured to the level of actually living them. Most younger *Hiphoppas* are still in search of their purpose.

II   *Hiphoppas* search for organizations, discussions and products that focus upon Hip Hop as a culture and way of life. *Hiphoppas* also instinctively feel the need to acknowledge all of Hip Hop's elements, not just those elements that are profitable or popular.

III   *Hiphoppas* <u>feel</u> Hiphop, and have begun the practice of one or more of Hiphop's nine elements. Hiphoppas are offered the Gospel of Hip Hop.

TEMPLE MEMBER: *A Temple Member* is a Hiphoppa that has begun a serious study into the *Overstandings* of the *Gospel of Hip Hop.*

I   *Temple Members* are Hiphoppas who have joined the Temple of Hiphop by taking the vow *I am Hiphop* and by abiding by the principles of the Gospel of Hip Hop.

II   When we say *I am Hiphop* we become that which we say that we want Hip Hop to become. Therefore, we preserve *Hip Hop* by becoming *Hiphop* and then preserving ourselves.

III   Those who are willing to become *Hiphop* for the sake of preserving *Hip Hop*, take the vow *I am Hiphop!* Such a person is no longer just doing Hip Hop's elements; such a person is Hiphop itself. And this *Gospel of Hip Hop* lays out the character and powers of a successfully lived Hiphop life.

IV   *Temple Members* support each other and the Temple of Hiphop in its campaign to preserve, promote and protect Hip Hop's culture, elements and expressions.

V   *Temple Members* are personally preparing for spiritual victory over the obstacles and traps of urban life—the *streets*. The seriously committed *Temple Member* has embarked upon a rigorous course of self-improvement leading to personal reinvention. It is at this level of overstanding that we realize ourselves to be role models, and we pay close attention to how we look and act in society.

VI   The popular statement "I ain't no role model" is simply not a choice for committed *Temple Members*. Many people deny the fact that they are role models because of their own shortcomings in life, which diminish their own sense of self-worth. *Temple Members* are working to cleanse themselves of such inadequacies, and it is through mentoring, caring and the giving of one's self that is at the essence of one's cleansing.

VII   *Temple Members* have realized that everyone is a role model because every object in Nature affects every other object in Nature. Every object and/or event in Nature appears to the human mind as a symbol—everything means something to us. As an object in Nature you are a symbol to other people as to what reality is and what is even possible.

VIII   *Temple Members* know that everything in Nature is a symbol to the observer, that every physical thing in Nature affects every other physical thing in Nature. So, to assume that you are not a role model is to deny your own influence upon Nature and upon other people. Such an assumption confines you to your own limited thinking.

IX   But this may be a good thing in the long run because those who do not lead productive lives silence themselves for the good of the whole. Even though an unproductive or dangerous life is still a role to be modeled, those who live such lives are right to deny their own influence upon everyone and everything else.

X   It is at this stage that we (*Temple Members*) begin the perfection of our outward appearance and artistic activities. At this stage, the Temple Member seeks to perfect one or more of Hip Hop's nine elements. Private Assignment: study the Gospel of Hip Hop.

TRUE HIPHOPPA: A *True Hiphoppa* is a Temple Member who is studied in the Overstandings of the Gospel of Hip Hop.

I   *True Hiphoppas* are called *True* because, when necessary, they are capable of putting the protection and development of Hip Hop before their individual wants, acts and ideas. They are willing to make sacrifices for Hip Hop's preservation and expansion.

II   It is here that the Templist begins learning the way of self-sacrifice and takes on the last name of *ONE* (or *Oné*, pronounced as *oh-nay,* meaning *God expressed* or *expressed Truth*), signifying victory Over Nearly Everyone and/or Everything.

III   For all true Hiphoppas that belong to the cultural family of Hip Hop, *Oné* (oh-nay) as a cultural last name helps other Temple Members identify each other. The use of the *One* also symbolizes the awareness of being single-minded in your spiritual perceptions. The *One* as a last name means that you are practicing seeing the physical

World beyond dualities.

^{IV} There is no more *this* and *that, them* and *me, name* and *nature, past* and *future*; all is one. You and Hip Hop are one event. The use of the *One* as a last name in speaking or in writing is not mandatory, however it does show one's level of conscious awareness and of one's selfless commitment to the unity of Hip Hop's culture.

^V The true Hiphoppa has also chosen a specific Hip Hop icon/pioneer to begin a scholarly study of. And in addition to studying the icon/pioneer of one's choice, it is always helpful to study the life, legacy and teachings of KRS ONE.

^{VI} Private Assignment: practice the Gospel of Hip Hop and choose a Hip Hop icon/pioneer to begin studying.

<u>TEMPLIST:</u> A *templist* is a True Hiphoppa who is seriously committed and faithfully dedicated to the development of the Temple of Hiphop.

^I Also called "temple representatives," *templists* are involved in the business of the Temple of Hip Hop: its administration and legal affairs as well as the promotion of the Temple of Hip Hop's ideas and image in World history. *Templists* are concerned with the internal organization of the Temple of Hip Hop.

^{II} *Templists* are also activists. They plan Hip Hop conferences, uprisings, protests, cultural summits, social programs, spiritual/cultural workshops and private meetings. As Temple Representatives, some *templists* commit to representing whole cities on behalf of Hip Hop's proper presentation and preservation.

^{III} Working mostly behind the scenes, *templists* assist in the proper presentation of Hip Hop's artistic elements and intellectual worldview even if the *templist* has no professional or personal allegiances to the Hip Hop person

and/or event being assisted.

IV   *Templists* consider Hip Hop itself to be their responsibility. The *templist* seeks to freely assist Hip Hop's many artists, often without those artists even knowing. *Templists* work privately and quietly, often receiving no recognition or even appreciation for their services. A *templist* acts on behalf of God, not on behalf of her own Worldly interests.

V   Private Assignment: self-sacrifice, self-restraint, charity, loyalty and teamwork.

ATTUNED HIPHOPPA: An *Attuned Hiphoppa* is a Templist who has overcome the values of the World and has regulated the passions of the physical body.

I   *Attuned Hiphoppas* are sensitive to the divine meaning and purpose of Hiphop. They live in harmony with the oneness of GOD's actual presence. They have made the decision to live by and actualize the Gospel of Hiphop.

II   Righteousness has become a habit for the *attuned Hiphoppa*. And such a habit has opened the Kingdom of Heaven for that Hiphoppa. Such a Hiphoppa is called *attuned* because her mind has become uninstitutionalized. She is free! Such a Hiphoppa becomes content with being Hiphop. Such a Hiphoppa has found peace.

III   For with an uninstitutionalized mind the Hiphoppa knows not what she can't do. For when your mind is free from being told what its limits are, you achieve great works because you don't know what you can't do. You can lift great weights and endure immense hardships when you don't know what is heavy or difficult.

IV   In addition, when you are uninstitutionalized in your thinking you unite with the Mind of GOD and the cycles of Nature. Your very movement through time and space match the movements of Heaven and Earth.

^V At this level of mind your Worldly activities shall unconsciously match the happenings of physical reality in mathematical ways that are not only seen or proven years later by future historians/scientists looking back upon your time, but such a habitual attitude towards life also places the attuned Hiphoppa in a state of supernatural harmony with her surrounding environment.

^{VI} At the Temple of Hip Hop attuned and spiritually mature Hiphoppas are aware of the Truth that the outer-self is a projection of the inner-self. And a Hiphoppa's inner-thoughts cannot be cut off from the total existence of that Hiphoppa's outer lifestyle and environment.

^{VII} Attuned Hiphoppas know that outer circumstances are shaped by inner-thinking. As we gradually transform our thinking, we gradually transform our environment. It is here, at this stage of spiritual development, that the attuned Hiphoppa realizes the Power of Mind.

^{VIII} It is here that the attuned Hiphoppa realizes that whatever the mind creates the mind must maintain. In other words, whatever your hands create, your hands will maintain. If you create something with your hands, it will have to be maintained by your hands, by your hand-skills.

^{IX} The same can apply to your tongue. Whatever you create with your words, you will have to maintain in the physical World with your words. Word-creations are sustained by words, hand-creations are sustained by hands, and mind-creations are maintained by mind.

^X Therefore, attuned Hiphoppas monitor the activities of their own hands, minds and mouths in an effort to bring order, peace and prosperity to the circumstances of their own lives.

^{XI} Such Hiphoppas have also perfected their chosen Hip Hop element. Private Assignment: Begin a career in

the Hip Hop element you have perfected.

HIPHOP KULTURAL SPECIALIST: A *Hiphop Kultural Specialist* is an attuned Hiphoppa who is certified by the Temple of Hiphop to teach Hip Hop publicly.

[I]   Kultural Specialists are authorized by the Hip Hop Declaration of Peace to *interpret and answer sensitive cultural questions regarding the principles and proper presentations of Hiphop's elements and culture, relative to businesses, individuals, organizations, communities, cities, as well as other countries.*

[II]   It takes at least five years of continuously engaging Hiphop, Hip Hop and hip-hop to become a Hiphop Kultural Specialist. Some do it in fewer years, but in Truth you never really end your education as a Hiphop Kultural Specialist. The Temple of Hip Hop ordains its Kultural Specialists in four stages (degrees).

[III]   Mastery of one or more of Hip Hop's artistic elements as well as an overstanding of Hiphop's nine elements is the first degree.

[IV]   Production of useful works and ideas known historically and enjoyed regularly by the Hip Hop community is the second degree.

[V]   Evidence of at least three years of paying dues, meaning: contributing to Hip Hop in meaningful ways without being compensated for it, is the third degree.

[VI]   Finally, the receiving of certain honors, awards, credentials, letters of appreciation and/or validations from within the Hip Hop community itself, from ITS pioneers and founders, from ITS authentic cultural organizations, from ITS talented artists, is indeed the fourth and final degree in becoming a Hiphop Kultural Specialist—a true Hip Hop scholar.

[VII]   Private Assignment: take your time studying and

teaching all you can about the nature, history, meaning and purpose of Hip Hop.

MINISTA: A *Minista* is a server, a Hiphop Kultural Specialist who has achieved the H-LAW. A Hiphop *minista* is different from a traditional *minister*. *Ministas* teach Universal Law, which includes life-coaching and spiritual advice relevant to the Hip Hop community and ITS experiences in the World.

I   Attuned *ministas* for Hip Hop serve the Temple of Hip Hop in its charity and social work. And even though Hip Hop's *ministas* have achieved the H-LAW, which includes wealth, and can also teach Street Entrepreneurialism, such *ministas* still do not handle money or seek to make deals. Hiphop's attuned *ministas* are given what they need by God. We are supported by the respect of the Hip Hop community for our spiritual, intellectual and artistic skills.

II   *Ministas* are focused upon teaching, revealing, and inspiring the Hip Hop community spiritually. They are the living examples of what they teach. They embody the spiritual vision of the Temple of Hip Hop.

III   A *minista* is a live person, full of energy. A *minista* is a real person, a true person, a genuine person. *Ministas* lead simple lives: great in love, great in life and great in God's work!

IV   But remember this: the *ministas* who teach the great Truths of Godly character must impersonate such Truths themselves. When the Truth that one knows becomes the Truth that one does, one can be called *Minista*.

V   For when you fully and truly realize that Hip Hop is the name of YOUR activity in the World you shall wake up and take more responsibility for how Hiphop Kulture (YOU) is perceived in the World—beginning with the way in which you personally think, speak and act regarding yourself, your community and your future as Hiphop. This realization causes one to become a *minista* for Hip Hop.

VI   For it is not skill mastery or even the selling of millions of recordings, books, etc., that preserves and further develops Hip Hop Kulture. In Truth, it is the individual thinking patterns and habits of ordinary Hiphoppas that allow poverty or prosperity, peace or disorder to affect the collective development of Hip Hop Kulture. The Hip Hop *minista* IS the preservation of Hip Hop.

VII   Private Assignment: attract support for the Temple of Hiphop while freely teaching its principles to all interested apprentices.

TEACHA: A *teacha* is a highly skilled Hip Hop minista who has declared spiritual *victory over the streets!* A *teacha* lives and teaches Hiphop's spiritual, moral and cultural lifestyle. A *teacha* has mastered two or more of Hip Hop's artistic elements.

I   *Teachas* are *Attuned Hiphoppas* who have shown and proven their wisdom of spiritual living. We practice living free and unattached from the stresses and temptations of the World. A *teacha's* presence comforts and inspires many. *Teachas* tend to heal or enhance whatever they touch or come near.

II   Never hateful, always compassionate and fair, *teachas* bring out the higher qualities in people. *Teachas* help people to find and protect themselves, their purpose, their talents and their goals. *Teachas* are not above their students/apprentices, *teachas* are just like their students/apprentices.

III   *Teachas* are the only qualified Hiphoppas authorized to establish *official* 'temples' of Hip Hop in their respective cities. A teacha is the leader or *chief* of Hip Hop Kulture. All teachas are called the *legal guardians, stepfathers* or *stepmothers* of Hip Hop.

IV   Qualifications include: an honorable reputation, two years of public speaking with a minimum of twelve lectures on Hiphop, Hip Hop and/or hip-hop, the publishing of an informative recording, film or book on Hip Hop, hip-hop or Hiphop, and the actual attainment of peace and prosperity.

V   Private Assignment: live and teach the *Gospel of Hiphop*. THERE IT IS.

THE EIGHTEENTH OVERSTANDING
THE ORIGINS OF HIP HOP

TRACK ONE

¹   Peace and much love to all generations of Hip Hop. It is here at the end that we explore our beginnings, our origin. However, before exploring the *origins* of Hip Hop let us be clear about the subject we are about to explore. Not only are we exploring the possibility and opportunity to establish Hip Hop as a free and sovereign nation, we are also exploring the *origins* of Hip Hop in an effort to properly document its real *history*.

²   One of the reasons this Overstanding appears at the end of this *First Instrument* is because such an inquiry requires a certain maturity and openness of mind to fully comprehend. It is not at all my intent to insult, disrespect or demean anyone or any other school of thought regarding such a subject. However, I invite our truly free-thinking Hiphoppas to seriously consider the following Overstanding as a real solution and strategy toward the preservation and further development of our already growing Hip Hop community.

³   First, this Overstanding argues that Hip Hop's true *history* cannot be properly documented without an understanding of Hip Hop's true *origins*. Study carefully.

⁴   The *origin* of something is its origination, its cause, where it came from, how it came into existence. Different from *history*, the *origin* of something deals with the nature and being of a thing; it explores the actual *conditions* that

help to bring a *thing* into existence.

5   In short, Hip Hop's *origins* are indeed Hip Hop's true historical ingredients. Without an *origin* there is no *history.* Yes, there are some very good Hip Hop history books available today, written by some very credible Hip Hop authors. However, I find it a bit funny how so many *rap* and *hip-hop* writers in my time can discuss the writing of Hip Hop's *history* without first discussing the *origins* of Hip Hop's existence—its causes and its effects, its essence and nature in material reality.

6   In addition, many of the *hip-hop history* books for sale on the market today speak as if the whole of the Hip Hop community agrees with the conclusions and interpretations such books depict of OUR life experiences. Many of these books are rushed out with little to no real scholarship, and I often wonder what the rush is all about to publish a *history* of Hip Hop in my time.

7   In my humble opinion, as true Hip Hop scholars, we cannot even discuss Hip Hop's *history* without first discussing Hip Hop's *origins*, and from that solid understanding of Hip Hop's true nature and existence we may set a collective AGENDA that establishes OUR survival and collective well-being in the World. Our AGENDA births our history.

8   The documentation of OUR collective effort to reach OUR collective agenda is called "OUR history." Our movement as a community through time and space IS OUR HISTORY. OUR history (or rather, "our-story") develops naturally from the pursuit of OUR OWN collective agenda, rooted in an awareness of OUR OWN existence. Hip Hop's history is NOT the history of Rap music pioneers and DJs.

9   But this is the challenge right here; many so-called *hip-hop scholars* and/or *hip-hop historians* in my time don't

even believe that Hip Hop exists as an international culture. They are still approaching Hip Hop as music, art and clothing fashions exclusively.

[10]   This begins our study into Hip Hop's *origins* because the desperate attempts of many "Rap journalists" to *make a name for themselves* at the expense of accurate Hip Hop documentation is also part of Hip Hop's true history, and future Hiphoppas should know of this. Study carefully; what is being sold as *hip-hop's history* in my time (your past) is actually Rap music's *folklore*.

[11]   So again, different from a *history* of something or someone, an *origin* explores the <u>conditions</u> that created that something or someone; it explores the <u>nature</u> of historical people, places and things.

[12]   We can read all day about the *history* of Hip Hop, but if we don't know why things are the way that they are and how they got to be that way, our historical view of Hip Hop will always be the interpretations of those who sought only to exploit *hip-hop* and not *be* or learn Hip Hop. As Cicero pointed out, *Not to have knowledge of what happened before you were born is to be condemned to live forever as a child*.

[13]   As a "teacha," a true Hip Hop scholar, you must know the difference between the work of a true Hip Hop scholar, different from that of an objective freelance writer only seeking to make some money on his or her story, or some music executive turned "historian" only seeking to keep his or her name alive. Again, this too is part of Hip Hop's true history.

[14]   As a true Hip Hop scholar, you must know of the *conditions* that helped to create Hip Hop so that you will really know how to preserve it and further develop it.

[15]   The first thing to realize about Hip Hop is that the main reason why *hip-hop's history* is presented in the

way that it is (told through the events of the Rap music industry), is because between the years of 1983 and 2003 the selling of Rap music magazines was where the money was at! Unfortunately, Rap magazines were also the very first documentation of Hip Hop as a subculture—even to other "Hiphoppas."

16   From the first time people became aware of Hip Hop's artistic elements the idea was to *use* hip-hop, not *understand* Hip Hop. When Rap music first hit the mainstream American airwaves in 1979 everyone approached it as if it was something to eat—rappers included. No one cared about how the rapper/MC viewed the World or WHY rappers did what they did. Most people were only eager to learn HOW we did what we did so that they could do it as well to make some money.

17   The honoring of real artistic and intellectual skill, the documentation of Hip Hop's political advancements as well as the words and warnings of Hip Hop's prophets, scholars, pioneers, and cultural principles were all deliberately ignored so that *hip-hop's* artistic elements (mainly DJ-ing and MC-ing) could be exploited by mainstream corporate interests. This is how hip-hop treated Hip Hop when hip-hop gained mainstream acceptance.

18   This is why Hip Hop looks the way that it does in my time (2009) historically. You (my future) can see this fact a lot clearer in your time than the many who cannot seem to see this obvious fact in my time. All across America's mainstream airwaves, *hip-hop* is being presented to the World as an irresponsible community of bitches, thugs, whores and pimps. And this is done deliberately—for the sole purpose of generating an income—while distracting people from the Truth!

19   In my present time (2009, your past) this is a *condition* of Hip Hop, and it is this present *condition* that

is a major part of Hip Hop's *origin*. Again, I am in no way disrespecting or demeaning the work of others—not at all. We are all growing and developing with the conscious awareness that we possess. There is no personal judgment here. However, these are the things that you <u>must</u> know in order to be a true scholar of Hip Hop's real *history*. You must have a special *sight* capable of differentiating between Truth and bullshit!

20   As a true Hip Hop historian, you must know that there are those of us who remain committed to the principles of peace, unity, love and safely having fun, as laid down by Afrika Bambaataa, and there are others who continuously seek to subvert, demean, degrade and even disrespect Hip Hop and its principles in their own desperate attempt to acquire more and more financial security.

21   This is just a fact of my time and this is also part of Hip Hop's true history. Sometime around 1991, with the rise of televised videos, everyone and anyone felt that they could rap, and they did! The so-called *fans* of real DJs and MCs became mainstream rappers, executives and journalists themselves, expressing the interests of mainstream corporate America within *hip-hop*. Without knowing it, their desperate acts served as agents of our continued oppression. This fact is also a major part of Hip Hop's TRUE HISTORY!

22   Hip Hop's true history begins with Hip Hop's true relationship with itself. Before we can really document Hip Hop historically, we must first intimately know and accurately describe the true nature of what we are seeking to document historically; otherwise we are only documenting our personal opinions and emotions regarding Hip Hop into history, and this too is part of Hip Hop's true history.

23   But this is the problem with documenting *hip-hop* for money (as a job); the problem is objectivity. When you are actually Hiphop yourself you instinctively look out for

Hip Hop first, above your employment status, and such an attitude is reflected in your writings.

24   When you are actually Hiphop yourself you instinctively look to protect the long-term interests of Hip Hop and its international community; you write with the well-being of Hip Hop's community in mind.

25   When you are actually Hiphop yourself no one has to pay you to participate in what you already are, or to participate in what you already love and respect. As a loyal citizen of the Hip Hop community you love what you are writing about and/or doing in Hip Hop.

26   As a citizen of the real Hip Hop community you care more for the image of Hip Hop worldwide above your employment status; you have no choice but to document, further invent, preserve, promote, and participate in all of what Hip Hop has to offer—you are drawn to it.

27   As a loyal citizen of Hip Hop's global culture you are not focused exclusively upon where Hip Hop's valued resources are. As a true Hiphoppa you are exploring all of that which you truly love about Hip Hop, regardless of compensation; basically you are exploring yourself and your role in that ever-growing reality we call "Hip Hop."

28   However, if you are not really a citizen of Hip Hop's real community yet you are attempting to document and/or perform Hip Hop's arts, sciences and/or culture, your perspective will always be objective, and approaching Hip Hop objectively dramatically limits one's intimate understanding of Hip Hop.

29   The true Hip Hop historian is subjective with the ability to hypothesize objectively. The true Hip Hop historian loves Hip Hop, therefore she is intimately immersed in it. There is no *standing on the outside looking in* when it comes to the Hip Hop historian/scholar. The true Hip Hop historian IS HIP HOP itself!

30   To be a scholar of Hip Hop's arts and sciences you must ultimately BECOME Hip Hop's arts and sciences. Objectivity has its place, but as an exclusive method for the documentation of Hip Hop, objectivity just does not go far enough into the actual nature of Hip Hop.

31   Most journalists educated in America's colleges today are taught that accuracy in the documenting of an event is based upon one's *objective* approach to that event. They are taught to remove themselves from what they are documenting so that they can get an unbiased perspective of the event.

32   The premise is that the truly objective critic is fairer and more balanced in her interpretations of natural phenomena than the one actually creating the phenomena, because the objective observer is "removed" from what she is observing; there is no bias.

33   The challenge, however, is that no one these days approaches anything objectively, without prejudice or emotional response. And when it comes to Hip Hop, you cannot understand it by watching it; you have to do it, be it, live it, then maybe you'll begin to understand it. Objective Truth does not exist for Hip Hop. Hip Hop's historical reality is inherently enigmatic.

34   The objectivism of today's journalists implies that knowledge (or knowing) is based upon observing objects and events, as opposed to also being them. Objective journalists have been educated to believe that they can <u>look</u> at something and <u>know</u> what it is.

35   Objectivity, however, doesn't really exist in the human experience and it is a grossly inaccurate way of approaching an event as personal as Hip Hop. To truly understand Hip Hop you have to become it.

36   Still, even within the accepted methodology of objectively documenting a subject and/or object, early

Rap magazine/book writers still followed none of the academically accepted rules for the correct documentation of historical events.

[37]   For the objective historian, history is based upon credible sources—it has to be because the objective historian is not the creator of the event she is preparing to document. What is called "hip hop's history" today is mostly the creation of objective music critics interpreting the activities of the urban Rap landscape and its people like products to be bought and sold.

[38]   As the so-called "standard" goes, there are two main kinds of historical sources: one kind of source is called a "primary source" and the other kind of source is called a "secondary source."

[39]   A "primary source" is evidence from the period you are studying (a newspaper article from the period, an archeological find from the period, an originating person, place or thing from the period). The primary source is the *origin* of something or someone's history. If your "primary source" is not correct, neither will your historical facts be correct.

[40]   A "secondary source" is some already documented information about the originating period, person, place or thing (a book or statement by another historian about the period, person, place or thing in question).

[41]   All histories rely upon "primary" and "secondary" sources, meaning that anytime you are presenting a *history* of someone or something you will rely at some point upon *secondary sources* to substantiate your total point of view because no one's history exists on its own, and most historians were not present for the history that they are now exploring.

[42]   But what if your activities in time and physical space create a seemingly new event in time and physical space and

you are the *primary source* yourself? This slightly alters the concept of *primary* and *secondary* source materials because even a newspaper article of an event from the actual period being studied (for example), which would be considered a *primary source*, can be questioned by the creators of the *event* if the article was written by an objective observer of the *event*.

43   If the author/journalist of the time who wrote such an article was still foreign and objective to the event being documented, I would argue that in the face of those who created and originated such an event, in no way can that historian's writings be called a *primary source*. Such writings may be a called a *primary source* to all who are not originators of the *event* (or source), but for those who originate their events, THEY ARE THE PRIMARY SOURCES!

44   *Primary sources* in historical documentation are only *primary* if the originator of the event is presenting his or her own history his or her self in his or her own way. Just because you have a *primary source* in writing or in some other state of preservation does not mean that it IS a *primary source* in physical reality. It is only a *primary source* to you because that's how far your research and mental abilities can go or have gone.

45   However, to those who have created the *event* themselves, an *outsider* observing and then documenting that *event* can never claim any historical authority or accuracy over those who are the *event* itself.

46   This is where the standard methodologies of documenting history come into question when documenting Hip Hop. Traditionally, history is taught as cause, consequence, change and continuity, but all of these methods are affected first by the intelligence, expertise and personal prejudices of the historian.

47   What is the *cause* of an event seen through the eyes

of those only looking to exploit the event itself? The true Hip Hop historian must ask these questions of all cultures being studied within a mainstream context.

48   The question is, how reliable is the *primary source* information of historians whose main motivation for documenting the event or the person is (or was) to exploit the event and/or the person for whatever financial gain they may achieve with the documentation they've objectively obtained? Their own desire to exploit the situation blinds them from what actually caused the situation or what possible effects the situation may bring; their aim is not history, it's money.

49   On another note, what is a *primary source* when there is always another side to the story? Hip Hop's historians should also be looking for as many *primary sources* as we can find because most World history is (was) written by the exploiters of the World's people.

50   This is why as historians uncovering reality through history we should also look at history as historian Howard Zinn does, from the *viewpoint of the Arawaks,* when it comes to the history of Christopher Columbus for example.

51   As another example, Mr. Zinn points out when it comes to the history of the Constitution that we should train ourselves to see such an event *from the standpoint of the slaves.*

52   We should think of Andrew Jackson *as the Cherokees saw him. Of the Civil war? As seen by the New York Irish. Of the Mexican war? As seen by the deserting soldiers of Scott's army. Of the rise of industrialism? As seen by the young women in the Lowell textile mills. Of the Spanish-American war? As seen by the Cubans. The conquest of the Philippians? As seen by Black soldiers on Luzon. The Gilded Age? As seen by southern farmers. The First World War? As seen by Socialists. The Second World War? As seen*

by pacifists. The New Deal? As seen by Blacks in Harlem. The postwar American empire? As seen by peons in Latin America. (Howard Zinn, *A People's History of the United States*—CD series narrated by Matt Damon)

53   But again, even if we confine ourselves to the standard methodologies for the proper documentation of history, we still find that most (if not all) of *hip-hop's* early historical writings are grossly imbalanced and in many cases unprofessional. First let's review the accepted standard.

54   History is generally studied as *cause, consequence, change* and *continuity.*

55   Historical cause means the reason something happened.

56   *Cause* is the *origin* of a historical event.

57   Historical *consequence* means what happened because of an action; it is the result of an event.

58   Historical *change* means when an event makes things different. *Change* is the opposite of *continuity.*

59   Historical *continuity* means when events do not *change;* they remain as they are. *Continuity* is the opposite of *change.*

60   We can see here how unscholarly many of *hip-hop's* written histories are. Very few *hip-hop* histories actually follow any of these *standard* documenting methodologies and this is not good for Hip Hop. Even standard historical documentation methodologies advocate that the historian comprehend, analyze, evaluate and interpret the *source* materials presented within his historical writings—however, this too is not being observed by *hip-hop's* so-called *historians.*

61   History is presented to tell a story about specific people, places or things. In the long run, the *history* of a people, a place, or a thing is not as important as the *story* that is being told about those people, places and things through

history. When it comes to a *People* (a culture), it is the story, the description, the collective tradition as well as the vision of those *People* that are explained in THEIR history.

⁶²   As historians, we know that history is supposedly a continuous recording of past events, and that most people also refer to history as the study of past events, or simply public record. In academic circles, history is thought to be a critical analysis of something or someone memorable. But many Hiphoppas have learned that all history is not to be trusted; this is common knowledge amongst us—and this very historical fact is also part of OUR collective history.

⁶³   The fact that we've been taught a false history about ourselves is history itself, and we must document such historical events with as much *primary* and *secondary* source materials as we can find.

⁶⁴   Many are ready to admit that we have been victims of biased, sexist, racist and inaccurate historians, but few of us are ready to admit that we are also the victims of sincere, reputable and accurate historians. Meaning that whether one is an inaccurate historian or an academically accurate historian, they (historians) are still only giving their interpretation of an event in history.

⁶⁵   As philosophers Ariel and William Durant have pointed out, *Our knowledge of any past event is always incomplete, probably inaccurate and clouded by ambivalent evidence and biased historians, and perhaps distorted by our own patriotism or religious partisanship. Most history is guessing and the rest is prejudice. Even the historian who thinks to rise above partiality for his country, race, creed or class betrays his secret predilection in his choice of materials and in the nuances of his adjectives.*

⁶⁶   This is not to say that we should disregard history, because it will always be the interpretation of the historian— no. This is to suggest the writing of a new history that is

better equipped to balance the scale of racial equality, quality of life, Truth and justice for all!

[67]   History as we know it is the art of revealing an event as if the event existed on its own with no previous or prior influences. The historian cuts off the influences that lead up to the historical event so that only one part (or piece) of time can be discussed. Likewise, the historian cuts off the influences that continue to occur after the historical event, so that the presented *piece* can have an ending.

[68]   The Truth, however, is that all events are without beginning, without end and without form. Every event is part of the continuous flow of events happening in the World at once. This we call an *omni-event*.

[69]   The Durants continue: *The historian always oversimplifies and hastily selects a manageable minority of facts and faces out of a crowd of souls and events whose multitude in its complexity he can never quite embrace or comprehend.*

[70]   In reality, history attempts to document the activities of a continuously developing and changing omni-event. But it seems to be impossible in our time for historians to present an omni-history because we are taught to label and compartmentalize the events we perceive.

[71]   Most people perceive their reality in bits and pieces not in waves and vibrations, so their historical reality becomes this happened, then that happened, then this happened, then that happened, etc.

[72]   Most people never consider the causes of their actions; like who or what influenced their actions. They live as though they are in the World by themselves, unaffected by everyone else and the environment in which they live.

[73]   Equally, they pay no attention to the never-ending effects of their actions. They live as their history was taught to them—bit by bit, day by day. Do this first, then do that, then do this. Doing everything effortlessly and at once is

impossible and even frightening for those people educated in this way.

74   As the Durants continue to point out, *total perspective is an optical illusion. We do not know the whole of man's history. There were probably many civilizations before the Sumarian or the Eygptian; we've just begun to dig. Therefore, we must operate with partial knowledge and be provisionally content with probabilities. In history, as in science and politics, relativity rules and all formulas should be suspect.*

75   History is created so that we can discuss parts of a continuously flowing omni-event. Otherwise, we would have to include every influence in existence that contributed to the event we wish to speak about, just to be closer to historical accuracy. And still, this would not ensure historical accuracy, because we do not know of every influence in our existence.

76   We may never know the true history of anything, much less automobiles, because we can never truly know of all the influences that went into the creation of the very automobile idea! We simply have to accept the automobile story as it is told to us because we simply were not there.

77   Because of this limitation, the historian is forced to literally create a history out of an omni-event. This is why we use history as a guide in our lives and not as the definition of our lives. No one can truly know the past through historical information. Therefore, it is not wise to exclusively base your identity (ethnic or otherwise) on historical information.

78   History as Truth does not exist. What exists as history is a created break in an omni-event. This is why there are many debates between historians as to whose history is the most accurate.

79   History is a socio-political invention for the unity, identity, and form of people, places, and things. Furthermore,

public history has more to do with building the present identity of a group than with accurately recording the events of the past.

80   With this in mind, all individual histories will contradict one another. The illusion is that we all have individual histories. The Truth is that all human activity on Earth is one event—and connected!

81   In fact, ALL activity on Earth is one event. History is not Truth. History is the perception and opinion of the historian. Historians, no matter how scholarly, only record what is, in their opinion, noteworthy to record. This is, of course, if the historian is recording as an eyewitness to the event.

82   Not only does one record what is noteworthy to his or herself, but more importantly, one also records what is noteworthy to the public. It is the public that dictates the historian's values—which in turn affect his recordings.

83   The historian will only tell the public the history that appears to be important to the survival and well-being of that public for that time or era. On one hand, the historian records what his value system dictates he should record. On the other, the public dictates to the historian which history it wants and needs to hear.

84   Historians are well aware that if one gives the public a piece of history that the public finds offensive or unimportant, the public destroys, discredits, or ignores the work of that historian. So, driven by this invisible code, set down by public opinion, historians usually tell the public what it wants to hear.

85   It is only when the public gains more knowledge of itself through life experience that historians will be able to expound on yet another Truth. It is at this point that the past recordings will be subject to change. In fact, the past actually changes!

[86]   The values that are placed upon the historian influence that historian's work, and in turn, the historian's work becomes history, not necessarily the event or person being documented. The public then accepts the historian's work as history because it fits the public's own collective personality.

[87]   When the collective personality of the public changes, the past changes once again to fit whatever the new public personality is. In Truth, it is the present that creates the past. New information revealed in the present changes the public's perception of its past.

[88]   In addition, historians are inclined to expound upon the history that they may comprehend as a similar reality existing in their own life in the present. It is impossible for the historian to comprehend a part of the past that he has no experience with in his present.

[89]   It is the historian's present view of reality that shapes the historian's past view of reality. Actually, if an event of the past is not also an event in the historian's present, where he can draw an understanding from it, it is as if the past event never happened.

[90]   In fact, historians can only study that part of the past that is also active in their present. If a part of the past vanishes with no accessible record of its existence, it is gone forever. The historian, re-creating the past for the present, simply does not and cannot see it.

[91]   We can look at many of the historical encyclopedias of the 20th century and see that even Hip Hop was not important enough to be accurately documented in the 1999–2000, century-ending history timelines. Even though Hip Hop has had a profound influence upon mainstream American culture, thought, fashion, entertainment, religion and politics from about 1979 to 2000, Hip Hop still was not important enough for today's mainstream historians to

include it in their century-ending encyclopedias and other historical timelines regarding the 20th century.

⁹² 	Just as the history of Africans in America, Asians in America, Europeans in America, Natives in America, and so on are blatantly ignored for the creation of a reality that benefits only one class of people in America, so it is with Hip Hop's history in America.

⁹³ 	The point is that if historians do not have Hip Hop in their daily lives (for example), or if they are unaware of Hip Hop, or are against Hip Hop's expansion, or feel that Hip Hop is not an important contribution to popular culture, even Hip Hop can be forever forgotten in the works of various reputable historians.

⁹⁴ 	This is not only a matter of deliberately falsifying World events; this is also an issue of outdated and narrow historical documentation techniques and methodologies. Historians must be well-versed in the existences of many cultures and histories in order to tell a more accurate history of their own.

⁹⁵ 	As with culture, no one's history exists on its own. Hiphoppas who document Hip Hop culture's history must be aware of this at all times. In this instance, it is the *present* that creates the *past*.

TRACK TWO

⁹⁶ 	Peace. Know this. It makes little sense for one group of people to learn about another group of people before learning about themselves. Only an oppressed people are forced to learn of everyone else's history before learning about their own. And equally, only an oppressed people, an institutionalized person, will not even ask questions

pertaining to their own origin and nature.

97   Such a *People* are dependant (even historically) upon their masters' vision and interpretation of reality. This is the challenge with Hip Hop's history today. History informs a *People* as to who they are and where they've been as a *People*.

98   History creates reality for a *People*; it tells them what they are capable of. This is why the Hip Hop historian must not only possess an uninstitutionalized mind in order to accurately document Hip Hop, the Hip Hop historian must also actually care for the further development of the Hip Hop idea throughout recorded history.

99   Such a historian must be a free person with a free mind because again, history informs a *People* as to what is possible for them; it tells them their reality. A true Hip Hop historian cares for the development of Hip Hop's people. For the true Hip Hop historian/scholar the documentation of Hip Hop is NOT a job—it is the duty of a free Hip Hop mind.

100   A slave can never be an accurate Hip Hop historian because Hip Hop's historians are not just documenting Hip Hop's activities in physical reality; we are also *creating* Hip Hop's reality for future generations, and we cannot pass on to our next generation a slave's mentality—even historically.

101   Know this. History exists as *groups of facts* that are then called upon to substantiate the views and desires of the present community. However, the ideas of a free people are backed up with historical facts, whereas the ideas of an oppressed people are created by historical facts.

102   More than just relying upon *primary source* materials to piece together what we believe about Hip Hop's past, the Hip Hop historian is also aware that she is creating Hip Hop's history in a timeless, spaceless present. We create our memories, and we create the history that we shall

remember. If we revolt today, such an act becomes part of our real history and heritage. If we are passive today, such an act becomes part of our real history and heritage.

[103]   When we rob, fight and murder one another, these acts also become part of our real history and heritage. The same applies for when we assist, respect and support one another; these too become part of our real history and heritage. And all of these events seen as one historical event tell us, our children and the rest of the World who we are and what we are capable of.

[104]   What you do with the knowledge that is in front of you now shall determine your real history and heritage, whether you do something with this knowledge or not. Whether you act or don't act, both *acts* are now part of your real history and heritage, and you don't get a second chance.

[105]   This is why it is important to carefully choose the emotions, opportunities and actions of your present life because every present moment (that you are choosing) is creating and further creating your history—a history that you shall rely upon for your future identity and heritage.

[106]   In fact, the existence of this very teaching right here (The Gospel of Hip Hop) is now part of Hip Hop's official history and heritage. Because this book now exists, regardless of today's imbalanced presentations of *hip-hop* on mainstream radio and television, which are also part of Hip Hop's real history and heritage, no one in the future can ever say that Hip Hop was without a spiritual foundation, and that the community of Hip Hop did not seriously consider their roles as divine beings guided by Divine Love.

[107]   In Truth, our existence today is Hip Hop's history tomorrow. Our very existence as a *temple* for Hip Hop today (for example) helps to balance Hip Hop's image and capabilities in World history today and tomorrow.

[108]   When our children become the scholars of

tomorrow and they reach back into their history, into their heritage to find out what they are capable of and upon what cultural foundation they stand, they shall not only see the existence of "bitches," "pimps," "thugs" and "whores" in our present time and culture, they will also see the existence of "teachas," "philosophers," "inventors" and "activists" in our present time and culture. The choice will then be their's.

[109]   Our existence is deliberate. We know that we exist, and we are aware of our existence, we are "conscious." We are deliberately affecting the documentation of our past, present and future selves. This is Hip Hop scholarship.

[110]   The point here is simple. Our present actions are the actual *origins* of our children's history. Therefore, Hip Hop's history is not just to be studied objectively; it is to be further created through a heightened awareness of one's present actions within the *history* being studied. Your present action is Hip Hop's history. Even the reading of Hip Hop's history is Hip Hop's history itself.

[111]   The study of Hip Hop's history is Hip Hop's history. Every act of the Hiphoppa is part of Hip Hop's actual history. This is why a true Hip Hop historian does not rely upon "objectivity." Hip Hop's scholars are Hip Hop itself! We are NOT objective *hip-hop* historians documenting Rap music's pop stars and the lyrics of deceased rappers.

[112]   We have realized that we are affecting the history that we are aware of. Our actions and statements today create the history that our children (and our older selves) shall experience tomorrow. So what shall we choose to remember of ourselves? What act can we do today that shall productively add to the history we shall rely upon for international respect tomorrow? What heritage shall we give to OUR POSTERITY?

[113]   Through our own actions today we truly become

the authors of our history in the future. So what history shall we create for ourselves today? HOW DO YOU WANT TO REMEMBER YOUR SELF? Every present moment is a *memory in the making,* a little piece of history that will unite with other little memorable moments to create your past, your history, your heritage. For it is you who create your history, not the other way around.

[114]   Part of Hip Hop's spiritual awareness begins with the realization that every present moment is a memory, and that you are *in* your memories right now. You create your memories with your present actions. Your reading of this book is now part of your memory, your history, your heritage. So again, what shall you choose to remember? What kind of history shall you create for yourself and your posterity right now with your present actions?

[115]   You can add anything to the fabric of history. What can you see? The old standard ways and methodologies of writing about or documenting an event in time and space must change dramatically when one approaches Hip Hop historically.

[116]   We simply cannot rely upon an exploiter's approach to history to interpret our own. For everyone's sake (exploiters included) we (Hip Hop's historians) must come up with some new methodologies for the documentation of history in our time—and I think we've come up with something.

[117]   Just as the sound engineers of the early 1990s had to rethink everything that they were taught in sound engineering school when Rap music hit America's recording studios, so it is with Hip Hop's proper historical documentation and cultural preservation amongst academics.

[118]   I consider myself a Hip Hop historian. However, I cannot assume that I can approach Hip Hop's proper

documentation academically with the same tools used for Hip Hop's exploitation commercially. You cannot assume that you can bring your old self to a new idea and expect to know the true nature of such an idea simply by observing it.

[119]   Know this. History is a tool that gives validation, meaning, direction and purpose to the events of a *People* in the present. Contrary to what some may have been taught to believe about "time" and "history," it is indeed the *present* that creates the *past*.

[120]   We must break the cycle of believing that we are only our histories, that we are only what we were. Right now we are also what we shall become. More than being the limited observations of a historian, history is the agreement of a "present" group of people about their identity and their direction as a community.

[121]   History is an agreement as to what a community will look like to itself and to the rest of the World forever. OUR history serves OUR interests. But in the case of documenting Hip Hop's actual history, our interests begin with the actual method used to document and interpret Hip Hop historically.

[122]   As you have already learned, Hip Hop is an idea. It is not a physical thing, it is an attitude. Hip Hop is not an object, it is a subject. Here, we approach Hip Hop as a collective consciousness, and as consciousness the documentation of Hip Hop can also fall outside of physical material reality.

[123]   Documenting, studying and teaching the history of an *idea* like Hip Hop demands that one expand her own consciousness beyond linear time and specific places as well as beyond race and ethnic identity. Hip Hop comes from everywhere! The Hip Hop idea is in super-position and should be documented *super-historically*. What does this mean?

¹²⁴ *Super-historical Hip Hop* reveals how Hip Hop's true history is not just the documentation of moving <u>objects</u> in physical reality; it is more accurately the documentation of moving <u>subjects</u> in a transcendent reality. This methodology deals more with Hip Hop's *origins* than with its *history,* but again, we will create a better history when we have an understanding of our true origin and nature as a community—a Hip Hop community.

¹²⁵ Beyond race, class, gender, etc., OUR PEOPLE are united by certain universally accepted *interests* and *ideas,* and these specific *interests* and *ideas* are found all over the World and at different times in the World. Again, Hip Hop itself is not a physical thing, nor is it of the physical World—it is a shared urban *idea.*

¹²⁶ Hip Hop's true and accurate history is the documentation of, and search for, Hip Hop's collective attitudes, principles, views and interests throughout and even beyond linear time and physical space.

¹²⁷ Again, Hip Hop is a subject, not an object. The old methodology of gathering historical data through the observation of natural phenomena and then applying such information to the movement of people, places and things in an effort to understand them must be dramatically modified if we are to accurately identify and document the activities of a non-physical event like Hip Hop accurately.

¹²⁸ Understanding the past through ideas and intentions as opposed to natural events and people can also be called *meta-historical.* Such is not a replacement of any standard methods for the creation of *history*; it is only a more accurate way to document Hip Hop's non-physical *origins.*

¹²⁹ Hip Hop's actual history in time and space does not go in a straight line from one point into the present. In fact, no one's history actually does. The old paradigm was to

identify one's self with one's land of origin. When studying history and looking for one's self in the events of the past we were taught to look for, and relate to, those historical characters that we physically resembled the most.

[130]   If you were Black that meant that you were historically from Africa and if you really wanted to know more about your history you were compelled to take African Studies. You would never think or be encouraged to seek your African history and heritage within the history of the Irish, or the Chinese, or the Cherokees.

[131]   In the old paradigm your personal identification in history is materially based—it is based upon race and the documentation of your race in certain geographical locations on the physical Earth. And there's nothing wrong with this approach, it is just limited to physical things in time and space.

[132]   However, when you seek to document a non-physical event like Hip Hop, the rules change dramatically. To identify and then document Hip Hop in time and space you must realize that you are documenting an idea, not a person, nor even an event in Nature. Hip Hop is a shared *idea*.

[133]   The true Hip Hop historian must undergo a slight consciousness change from identifying himself with certain *people* in history to identifying himself with certain ideas in history. In actuality, Hip Hop is a global *idea* happening in the World at once. It exists in many different places and at different times amongst all the peoples of the World at once. Hip Hop is *super-historical*.

[134]   *Super-historical* means a history that can be found in anyone's history, or a history that affects all other histories. Here, we shall be focusing upon the first definition—a history that can be found in anyone's history.

[135]   *Super-historical* is when history is viewed not as

a straight line of physical events, or of the migration of specific people, or the life of a famous person, but instead as a free flowing omni-event which hosts a collection of specific "ideas" and "interests" that coexist together simultaneously. In this realm, identity is based upon the *ideas* that you accept and the interests that you uphold. Here, group identification and group unity are based upon the acceptance of certain *ideas* and *interests*.

¹³⁶ In this case, Hip Hop as an attitude, as a behavior, as a worldview, is the *idea* that we are looking for in history to see if anybody acted like us, agreed with our worldview, shared our same interests; these would be OUR people. And their stories would be the most inspiring and useful for us Hiphoppas to know today.

¹³⁷ This is how our Hip Hop children need to learn of historical events and people. They also need to see <u>themselves</u> in the histories that they study. It is a fact that the first purpose of historical knowledge is to tell you about you, and after you are informed of your own heritage, culture and tradition, you graduate to the learning of other cultures and traditions. A history that begins with the life and times of people whom you cannot relate to is called "indoctrination."

¹³⁸ I must first be able to see my *ideas* and my *interests* in the history that I am learning or such a history is simply another form of indoctrination. Learning that all my ancestors were slaves and that only recently have I been freed is not only a lie, I don't even relate to such a history today. This type of history alone, true or false, is destructive to my well-being and further development today.

¹³⁹ So, pertaining to the concept of self-creation, the questions become, *what is MY history, my intimate history?*

140   *What story shall I choose to adopt for myself and my children?*

141   *What do I believe of myself? What do I mean?*

142   *How shall I go about the creation of my Self?*

143   *What is my origin? Who and what do I belong to?*

144   Irrespective of race, gender, class, religious background, age, etc., the Hip Hop *idea* of peace, love, unity, and safely having fun, as well as Hip Hop's artistic elements, can be found all throughout World history. And because Hip Hop is a shared idea, a behavior, an attitude, we must seek our history through our compatibility with certain ideas, behaviors and attitudes in history.

145   Using the super-historical approach, I can see myself (my interests, my views, my values, my spirit) in everyone's culture and race throughout human history because I am not looking for a *people* and/or certain events to supposedly explain who I am. As a *meta-historian* or simply as a *Hiphop historian*, my group is an *idea* that is shared by all creation, not by one race or culture of people but by ALL OF EXISTENCE!

146   The history of plants IS my history; the history of fish IS my history. The history of ants and other insects IS my history. There are things about plants, insects and fish (as examples) that relate directly to how I got here and where I might be going. As an attuned Hiphoppa I can see myself historically in almost anything and/or anyone because I've now realized that there are no separate events.

147   There is only one omni-event continuously occurring, of which I am a part. This is what it means to be *super-historical*. With this slight change in consciousness I can now relate to an omni-history as my own. For if I am more mind than I am body then why am I relying upon a physical history that can never truly be accurate in the true description of my being. I can (and should) be experiencing

733

the physical World as I really am—as Mind.

¹⁴⁸ But what was I called in history? What were my views and interests called in history? Can I identify the essential traits of my being in history? Today I am called a *"Hiphoppa"*; yesterday I might have been called a *"Moor,"* or a *"Jew,"* or a *"Cherokee."* Today we are called *"Hip Hop,"* but what were we called yesterday? What looked like us in history?

¹⁴⁹ Try to remember, it is not that every event, tribe, philosopher, artist, etc. of the past that shares our modern view today represents Hip Hop. It is more that the *ideas* themselves that traveled through certain events as well as through the minds of those philosophers, politicians and artists of the past are the same *ideas* that we identify with today, and this is how Hip Hop can be identified throughout American history, even World history.

¹⁵⁰ We must look for our <u>interests</u> in history, not our faces. The question changes now from *how did a certain people originate and develop* to *how do certain <u>ideas</u> originate and develop a certain people* and *how are we further creating such <u>ideas</u> today?* We are largely the ideas we accept for ourselves as true.

¹⁵¹ We are more than our physical appearances; we are also our personalities, traits and characters, which are largely created and steered by the stories (ideas) we've come to accept for ourselves. As Hiphoppas we must seek our own personalities and experiences in the characters and events that we may come across in history.

¹⁵² For if we can unite in true agreement with any figure of the past on any issue, we may be able (by exploring that which we truly agree upon) to discover within ourselves the more hidden meanings and deeper insights of past figures and the events that we study.

¹⁵³ The discipline is to follow the migration of *ideas,*

not just of people and/or events, because in today's reality no one identifies themselves with historical figures; they identify themselves with the *ideas* of such figures.

[154]   As an example, most people identify with the *Dream* of our King more than they identify with our King as a person. They never knew him as a person. They may never relate to our King as a person, as a man, but they may certainly relate to the *ideas* that our King gave mainstream voice to.

[155]   In this instance as Hip Hop scholars, we should be trying to identify the King's *Dream* throughout time and space to see the real nature of what was said and from whence it came. What other prophet in history said the same thing? And was the result the same?

[156]   In fact, those who share the *Dream* of our King can be said to be a community unto themselves. And like us Hiphoppas, whether they organize around the *Dream* or whether they keep the *Dream* quietly to themselves, those who share the King's *Dream*, or Gandhi's *Dream*, or Tupac's *Dream*, constitute a community of people who share the same or similar interests and it is these interests and ideas that move them and unite them—even name them.

[157]   So what can we learn of our true reality as Hiphoppas in the spread-out universe of ideas and intentions? For if we look for ourselves in the past, the present, or the future as people, special places and sacred things exclusively, we are limited to being defined by our effects and not by our true being—which causes such effects to exist.

[158]   As a group, we are a collection of ideas, values, intentions and attitudes, and this is what we should be searching for in World history to identify ourselves. Our children should learn of historical figures in a way that relates to THEIR interests and THEIR Hip Hop reality. When it comes to history and the methods for gathering

history, our children should be bilingual, knowing both standard history as well as meta-history.

[159]   For example, to inspire our Hip Hop children to consider a career in politics and/or learn more about United States Presidents, I'd pull out the book *Ronnie and Nancy* by Bob Colacello and remind our young students that *'Dutch' did not get off to a good start at WOC, where his staff job involved many hours of playing phonograph records, interspersed with the reading of commercials as well as announcing the news, weather and sports scores from early morning until the midnight sign-off.*

[160]   I'd remind our young students that this young DJ would go on to marry a young woman named Nancy, who was raised by her single mother Edith, who was a famous Broadway actress in the early 1900s. I would describe her to our young students the way Bob Colacello describes her: *Nicknamed Lucky Luckett...she smoked, she swore, she told dirty jokes and she was wildly popular.*

[161]   I would then reveal that I am speaking of the mother of First Lady Nancy Reagan, and the young DJ that she would marry would go on to become President Ronald Reagan. Of course, Ronald and Nancy Reagan are NOT Hip Hop! But we can appreciate the moments in which we shared the same interests and similar lifestyle.

[162]   In this way political history can relate more personally to Hip Hop's history in a *super-historical* sense. I can now relate to Mr. and Mrs. Reagan super-historically. Hip Hop and the Reagans seem to have nothing in common when you look at history linearly and physically. But when viewed super-historically we can see where we as Hiphoppas relate to at least the early years of Ronald and Nancy Reagan.

[163]   This discipline (super-historical Hip Hop) follows your values and intentions, even your purpose (not a person)

throughout natural history to see where YOU have been and how YOU have formed. Super-historically speaking, you and the Reagans have something in common, and it's deejayin and live performing!

¹⁶⁴ Being raised by an entertainment mom sounds a lot like our Hip Hop situation today. But again, are Nancy and Ronald Reagan Hip Hop? NO, at least they never openly declared, "I am Hip Hop!" We are just able to see ourselves in them super-historically as DJs. In addition, we can also see a bit of the Hip Hop attitude frequently expressed by Hip Hop's White youth today when Mr. Colacello writes, *Dixon, Illinois had 12 Black families and Neil* [Ronald Reagan's older brother] *would hang out with some of them, bringing them home for dinner and sitting in the 'colored' section of the movie theatre to be with his friends.*

¹⁶⁵ We now know that President Ronald Reagan was not only a lifeguard who saved 77 lives, a construction worker, as well as a caddy for Charles Walgreen (America's first drugstore tycoon), but was also in charge of entertainment for the Young Men's Christian Association's (YMCA) Hi-Y Club and went from playing records at WOC to being a sports announcer at the same radio station in 1932. Yes, a DJ/actor named Dutch and a young lady named Nancy ascended to the United States presidency. This is Hip Hop's (not Rap music's) true history.

¹⁶⁶ As *Ronnie and Nancy* describes, *'Lucky' Luckett was a whirlwind of charm and energy, a pretty blonde with the riveting, widespread eyes she would pass on to her daughter... Her daughter wanted to be just like her.*

¹⁶⁷ In 1924, when Mrs. Luckett was asked by an Atlanta newspaper to name her favorite cigarette, *she answered, 'Lucky Strike,' Her lucky day? 'Pay Day.' Her greatest ambition? 'To be loved by the public.' What would she do if she were President for a day? 'Have a party at the White*

737

House.' This doesn't sound like Hip Hop today?

[168]   Even deeper, this foul-mouthed entertainer Lucky Luckett actually produced a Presidential First Lady who actually married a DJ/actor who became President! Maybe if we knew this about the Reagans we would have more respect and understanding for their *path to the White House* because we would have been able to see ourselves in them.

[169]   With this Hip Hop view of history, historical characters serve as the carriers of certain ideas, not markers in historical reality. We don't need to agree or even understand the total character of a historical figure to appreciate the moments when they became Hip Hop.

[170]   Take the empiricist/philosopher John Locke (1632-1704), for example. He wrote: *All men are born free and independent and have certain inherent, natural Rights, among which are the enjoyment of life, and liberty with the means of acquiring and possessing property, and perusing and obtaining happiness and safety.*

[171]   Now, we may not agree with everything that John Locke was about as a person, but in this particular idea, he is Hip Hop. Other Hip Hop-minded people of his day and today agree with the general meaning of this statement. He's not telling us anything new here because this is how most Hiphoppas naturally feel. However, to be accurate, it is not actually John Locke that is Hip Hop, it is this particular *idea* that is Hip Hop. And the closer and more consistent John Locke is to this *idea,* the closer and more consistent he is with Hip Hop.

[172]   Thomas Jefferson, who shared many of Hip Hop's personal traits and philosophical ideas while intimately living amongst Blacks, Natives and other Whites, and was also influenced by John Locke, then wrote: *We hold these truths to be sacred and undeniable, that all men are created equal and independent. That from that equal creation they derive rights*

inherent and inalienable among which are the preservation of life and liberty and the pursuit of happiness. (Excerpt from the original draft of the Declaration of Independence)

[173]   Using the super-historical approach not only can we trace the migration of such an idea, but we can also see that these are OUR principles! Not just Black African principles, or Native American tribal principles, or Asian, or Hindu Indian principles, or even White European principles. These principles belong to anyone who can live them.

[174]   These are the universal principles that reveal themselves to any thinking person, and it was the adoption of these universally accepted principles that delivered staggering victories and advancements for the United States of America in its early days. Any group of people who remain consistent with this vision will shake off the chains of oppression and rise to World prominence. This is the origin of Hip Hop's history.

[175]   Graffiti writers can super-historically see themselves in World history through the adventures of Napoleon Bonaparte. In his book *Napoleon In Egypt: The Greatest Glory,* Paul Strathern explains how donkey riding was a popular pastime amongst off-duty French soldiers stationed in Egypt. However, while some French soldiers would go donkey riding to pass the time, Mr. Strathern points out that *others took part in excursions to the pyramids and the ancient ruins at Giza where evidence of these visits remains to this day, in the form of soldiers' names and other graffiti carved into the upper stones of the pyramids, inside the burial chambers and on other ruins.*

[176]   Mr. Strathern continues by writing that *such behavior was still commonplace amongst Europeans abroad, and would not be generally regarded as vandalism for several years to come.*

[177] For graffiti writers to study the history of Graffiti Art in this way would be called *super-historical*. And looking at Hip Hop super-historically, we begin to see a slightly different (even new) Hip Hop history emerging, which explores the nature and migration of Hip Hop's artistic and intellectual *elements,* as well as the Hip Hop *idea* itself.

[178] In my observations, this view of Hip Hop's *origins* should be established before we begin the documentation of Hip Hop's *history.* Different from a *history* of Hip Hop, this method reveals the *origins* of Hip Hop and sets the foundation as to what shall be included in Hip Hop's *history* and why.

TRACK THREE

[179] The origins of Hip Hop have very little to do with Hip Hop's music; they have to do with exploring the conditions that caused such music, art and/or dance to exist. *To constrain Hip Hop culture within the framework of chronology seems sacrilegious. But if you need a creation myth— you can have your Kool DJ Hercs, Grandmaster Flashes and Afrika Bambaataas—the real godfather of Hip Hop might very well have been some guy called Robert Moses. Moses was an unelected New York City official who exerted tyrannical control over the Big Apple's city planning in the 50s and 60s. One of Moses' pet projects was the Cross-Bronx Expressway. Built in the early 60s, it became Route One for white flight from the city to the tony suburbs of Westchester County and Connecticut. In order to build this fifteen-mile stretch of road, several thousand people were displaced and large sections of The Bronx were leveled. This destroyed communities, necessitated the construction of ugly, modern housing developments and left*

large portions of The Bronx nothing but rubble and tenements. With New York City bankrupt and beholden to the bondholders who imposed austerity programs on the city, The Bronx—with no incentive for civic pride—became a brutal place to live. The first generation of post-CBE children in The Bronx was the first group to try to piece together bits from this urban scrap heap. Like carrion crows and hunter-gatherers, they picked through the debris and created their own sense of community and found vehicles for self-expression from cultural ready-mades, throwaways and aerosol cans. (Peter Shapiro, *The Rough Guide To Hip-Hop*)

[180] So, what are Hip Hop's *origins?* Other than certain street-gang influences, where does Hip Hop begin and what are its true historical origins? As an *idea*, is Hip Hop strictly a Black thing? Is Hip Hop really an African American creation?

[181] Remember, Rap's history is not Hip Hop's history. We know that after 1962 Jamaicans began entering the United States in huge numbers, and this group brought with them the ingredients for the start of early Hip Hop. However, Puerto Ricans had already been coming to America (especially New York) since the early 1900s and it would be this mixture of Jamaican, Puerto Rican and African American culture that would eventually develop into early Hip Hop.

[182] The first Puerto Ricans to arrive in New York were mostly artists with a variety of hand skills like carpentry, cooking and other manual labor skills. They also had a vast knowledge of politics and took very seriously the political future of their group in the United States. Many, if not most, of the newly arriving Puerto Ricans were dark-skinned people, "Black" people, who fit right into the African American community that was now also taking in Jamaicans, Trinidadians and others from the Caribbean.

183   Young Puerto Ricans began integrating with young Blacks right from the beginning. And yes, there was indeed some friction and even gang rivalries between all of these cultures getting to know one another. But for the most part everyone (Jamaicans, Puerto Ricans and African Americans) managed to get along with one another.

184   Codes were set and "turfs" were established. One thing was certain, all of these non-White immigrant groups were well aware of American injustice and racism, and in a lot of ways such oppression brought everyone together around a certain unwritten moral code based upon the common oppression many were feeling at the time. Young Puerto Ricans began playing many of the African American street games already in practice, and began tasting much of the food recipes of African Americans. They also began listening to the popular music of the day enjoyed by the African American community, as well as the popular dances of the day.

185   Simplicio Rios, a young Puerto Rican who was interviewed by Oscar Lewis in 1965 for his book *La Vida*, explains early Puerto Rican life and the relations between Puerto Ricans and African Americans. *We Puerto Ricans here in New York turn to each other for friendship. We go out on Fridays because that's the beginning of the weekend. A whole bunch of us Puerto Ricans go out together because as far as having friends of other races goes, the only one I have now is an American Negro who owns 'un bar.' If it were in my power to help the Puerto Rican any way I chose, I would chose a good education for them, for the little ones who are growing up now. I would like them to have good schools where they would be taught English, yes, but Spanish too. That's what's wrong with the system up here, they don't teach Spanish to our children. That's bad, because if a child of yours is born and brought up here and then goes back to Puerto Rico, he can't*

get a job. How can he, when he knows no Spanish? It's good to know English, but Spanish is for speaking to your own people. That's the problem the children of Puerto Rico have up here, they understand Spanish but they can't speak it or write it.

186   Young Puerto Ricans not fluent yet in the English language learned to speak English by listening to their African American friends. Learning how to survive the prejudices of the larger White American community, young Puerto Ricans would learn "slang," "Pig Latin" and the "Dozens" from African Americans.

187   The *Dozens* was a verbal street game that was all about humiliating your opponent with words. The focus of the game was to keep *cool* while being humiliated and to fight back with your own set of humiliating words and phrases. The loser was the one who let his emotions lead to physical retaliation. The winner was the one who kept *cool* and showed restraint, responding with even funnier and more degrading insults.

188   The *Dozens* originated when slave traders would sell by the *dozen* (12 at a time) those slaves that they felt were flawed in some way—old age, mental disorder, physical illness, or some other kind of deformity. A good, healthy, mentally alert, undeformed human being (a slave) was always sold separately and for more money.

189   Every slave knew that if you were sold as part of a *dozen* that there was something wrong with you. To a slave's mentality, to be part of a *dozen* was personally humiliating. And so the game began. *Yo mama ain't this, yo papa ain't that! You look like this, you smell like that!*

190   This tradition of verbal assaults would find its way into the art of emceein as emcees battled for lyrical supremacy, respect and self-worth amongst each other. As H. Rap Brown explains in his book *Die Nigger Die* (1969), *The street is where young bloods* [young people] *get their*

education. I learned how to talk in the street, not from reading about Dick and Jane going to the zoo and all that simple shit. The teacher would test our vocabulary each week, but we knew the vocabulary we needed. They'd give us arithmetic to exercise our minds. Hell, we exercised our minds by playing the Dozens.

[191]   Now stop here for a moment. The reason that I am bringing this piece of history into our study is to also show the difference between hip-hop's Rap music folklore which is what is presently being passed-off as Hip Hop's history, versus Hip Hop's real history, which is based upon empirical data and critical research. This is one of the main reasons why Hip Hop's actual history and start-date remain a mystery.

[192]   The history of mainstream hip-hop starts as DJ-ing and MC-ing in 1973 with Kool DJ Herc in the Bronx. However, we can see H. Rap Brown expressing Hip Hop in 1969. And what do we mean by *"expressing Hip Hop?"* We mean that in 1969 H. Rap Brown acted like, spoke like, dressed like, lived like, and thought like the Hip Hop community of today.

[193]   We can see our elements and personalities in him in 1969. Super-historically we can see ourselves, our lifestyles and our values in him. The point is, here's a historical figure experiencing in the 1950s and 1960s what we are experiencing as Hip Hop in the 21st century, yet most "Hip Hop History" books continue to teach that Hip Hop gets its start sometime around 1972–1973. So, when is Hip Hop's actual start-date in linear time and physical space?

[194]   H. Rap Brown was a Black revolutionary, yet he was also an emcee—he rapped! He was rhyming and expressing Hip Hop on the street corners of Baton Rouge, Louisiana in the early 1960s! As he puts it, *The Dozens is a mean game because what you try to do is totally try to*

*destroy someone else with words. It's that whole competition
thing again, fighting each other. There'd be sometimes 40 or 50
dudes standing around and the winner was determined by the
way they responded to what was said. If you fell all over each
other laughing, then you know you scored. It was a bad scene
for the dude that was getting humiliated. I seldom was. That's
why they call me 'Rap' 'cause I could rap. The real aim of
the Dozens was to get a dude so mad that he'd cry or get mad
enough to fight. You'd say shit like, "Man tell your mama to
stop coming around my house all the time. I'm tired of fucking
her and I think you should know that it ain't no accident you
look like me." And it could go on for hours sometimes. Some of
the best Dozens players were girls.*

[195]   Now, in this one statement we can see how
limited rap/hip-hop's history actually is. Here, you have a
historical figure (Civil Rights activist, leader in the Student
Nonviolent Coordinating Committee, Black Panther
member, and rapper) in 1969 talking about his experiences
as a child some 10-15 years earlier and almost none of the
mainstream histories of hip-hop seem to mention this
historic figure at all.

[196]   Remember, I am quoting from H. Rap Brown's
1969 book *Die Nigger Die*, where he is speaking of his
teenage years. So even if we count back just 10 years from
1969, we can see how the art of emceein/rapping as well as
the attitude of Hip Hop was in full existence in 1959 in Baton
Rouge, Louisiana. And of course, the dozens/rapping didn't
just begin in 1959, nor was it confined exclusively to Baton
Rouge. These skills were always amongst Black people,
dating back to ancient Africa as well as the beginnings of
the slave trade in the United States.

[197]   In fact, even if we limit our scholarship of hiphop's *history* to Rap music's *history* we come across Slim
Gaillard, the Cats and the Fiddle, and Slam Steward of the

1930s and 1940s, who actually rapped in the way that we do today! Afrika Bambaataa often talks about Shirley Ellis's "Name Game" amongst other musicians and poets like the Last Poets who were clearly pioneers of early Rap. So, when does Hip Hop actually begin? Zulu Nation teaches that *the official birthday of Hip Hop is November 12, 1974.*

[198]   Interviewing Hip Hop historian Pee Wee Dance in the early 1990s, writer Benjamin I. Green III explains in an article entitled "Hip Hop/B-Boy Phenomenon: Is it Culture or is it a Fad? Pee Wee Dance Drops Science," that *1971 was the year Pee Wee recalls getting his start in the Hip Hop music/Rap culture. '1968 to 1974 were the years the Hip Hop culture introduced itself to the world.' Pee Wee says that during that time there were a lot of unsung heroes that helped to shape the music, the dance, the graffiti artists and everything else we associate with the Hip Hop culture. The music was a relfection of the times.*

[199]   Here we can see that true Hip Hop scholarship begins not with a study of the "music," but with a study of the "times"—the cause of the music. We can see now that Hip Hop does not originate exclusively in gang culture, because as Pee Wee Dance explains, *It gave me a sense of direction and that was the aim to it...Culturally, there was the Black consciousness: afros, cornrows, mock-necks, monkey boots, Pro-Keds, army fatigues. Musically, James Brown set it off with "Say It Loud"/"Cold Sweat"/"Sex Machine"; Sly and the Family Stone, The Ohio Players and record labels such as Stax, De-Lite, and Brunswick brought forth the movement.* This is why we are encouraged to study Hip Hop super-historically in an effort to understand its total historical existence and not just rely upon what we've read or overheard as folklore in exchange for real scholarship.

[200]   H. Rap Brown speaks of female rappers (or "Dozens players") in his neighborhood in the mid 1950s.

And he says that they were *"some of the best"*—in the 1950s! H. Rap Brown was not from the Bronx. He didn't "roll" with Afrika Bambaataa. He didn't even have turntables! Yet we can clearly see ourselves in him. We can see that his experiences were our experiences, he just experienced them before us.

[201]   Modern emceein seems to get its start from people like him, a conscious rapper as well as a street dude. Not only did Brown participate in *the Dozens* which was mostly spoken word, he also was a master of what was called *signifying*. This is where the style of modern Rap really gets its start. As Brown explains, *Signifying is more humane. Instead of coming down on somebody's mother, you came down on them. But, before you can signify you got to be able to rap. A session would start maybe by a brother saying, 'Man, before you mess with me you'd rather run rabbits, eat shit and bark at the moon.' Then, if he was talking to me, I'd tell him:*

> *Man, you must don't know who I am.*
> *I'm sweet peeter jeeter, the womb beater!*
> *The baby maker, the cradle shaker,*
> *The deer slayer, the buck binder, the woman finder!*

> *Known from the Gold Coast to the Rocky shores of Maine,*
> *Rap is my name and love is my game!*
> *I'm the bed tucker, the cock plucker, the motherfucker, the milk shaker, the record breaker, the population maker!*

> *The gunslinger, the baby bringer, the humdinger, the pussy ringer, the man with a terrible middle finger!*
> *The hard hitter, the bullshitter, the poly-nussy getter!*

The beast from the east, the judge, the sludge!
The women's pet, the men's fret and the punk's pin-
up boy!

They call me Rap, the dicker, the ass kicker, the cherry
picker, the city slicker, the titty licker!
And I ain't giving up nothing but bubble gum and
hard times and I'm fresh out of bubble gum.
I'm giving up wooden nickels cause I know they won't
spend, and I got a pocket full of splinter change!

I'm a member of the bathtub club: I'm seeing a whole
lot of ass but I ain't takin' no shit!
I'm the man who walked the water and tied the whale
tail in a knot!
Taught the little fish how to swim!
Crossed the burning sands and shook the devil's
hands!

Rode 'round the world on the back of a snail, carrying
a sack saying Air-Mail!
Walked 49 miles of barbwire and used a cobra snake
for a necktie!

And got a brand new house on the roadside made from
a cracker's hide, got a brand new chimney setting on
top made from a cracker's skull!
Took a hammer and nail and built the world and
called it 'THE BUCKET OF BLOOD!'

Yes, I'm hemp the demp, the woman's pimp, women
fight for my delight.
I'm a bad motherfucker. Rap the rip-saw, the devil's
brother-in-law!

I roam the world, I'm known to wander and this .45 is where I get my thunder!
I'm the only man in the world who knows why white milk makes yellow butter!
I know where the lights go when you cut the switch off!

I might not be the best in the world, but I'm in the top two and my brother is getting old!
And ain't nothing bad 'bout you but your breath!

202   Now, if the brother couldn't come back behind that, I usually cut him some slack (depending on time, place and attitude). We learned what the white folks call verbal skills. We learned how to throw them words together. America, however, has Black folk in a serious game of the Dozens (the dirty motherfucker). Signifying allowed you a choice—you could either make a cat (a person) feel good or bad. If you had just destroyed someone or if they were just down already, signifying could help them over. Signifying was also a way of expressing your own feelings:

Man, I can't win for losing.
If it wasn't for bad luck I wouldn't have no luck at all!

I've been having buzzard luck.
Can't kill nothing and won't nothing die, I'm livin on the welfare and things are stormy!
They borrowing their shit from the Salvation Army, but things bound to get better cause they can't get no worse.

I'm just like the blind man standing by a broken

window, I don't feel no pain!

*But it's your world! You the man I pay rent to! If I
had your hands I'd give 'way both my arms, cause I
can do without them.*

*I'm the man, but you the main man. I read the books
you write. You set the pace in the race I run. Why,
you always in good form, you got more foam than
Alka-Seltzer...*

[203] *Signifying at its best can be heard when brothers are
exchanging tales. I used to hang out in bars just to hear old men
"talking shit." By the time I was nine, I could talk Shine and
the Titanic, Signifying Monkey, three different ways, and Piss-
Pot-Pete for two hours without stopping. Sometimes I wonder
why I even bothered to go to school. Practically everything I
know I learned on the corner.* THIS IS HIP HOP!

[204] Everything about the spirit of this entire quote
(rhymes included) IS an important part of Hip Hop's
creation and deserves to be part of Hip Hop's real history.

[205] You mean to tell me that H. Rap Brown's childhood
rhymes (published in 1969), which include classic Rap
lines like *Known from the Gold Coast to the Rocky shores of
Maine...* (Sequence) and *I'm hemp the demp, the woman's
pimp, women fight for my delight* (Big Bank Hank) and *The
baby maker, the cradle shaker...* (Prince Whipper Whip)
which can be called one of the first MC styles, along with
*The milk shaker, the record breaker, the population maker! The
gun slinger, the baby bringer, the hum dinger, the pussy ringer,
the man with a terrible middle finger! The hard hitter, the
bullshitter, the poly-nussy getter! The beast from the east, the
judge, the sludge,* a style which rapper Smooth the Hustler so
masterfully performed—all of this is not a critical piece of
Rap music's history?

²⁰⁶   Just the mere fact that H. Rap Brown in 1969 is saying rhymes and rhyme styles that appear on the Sugar Hill Gang's "Rapper's Delight" recording in 1979 suggests that we stop *jocking* platinum-selling Rap artists like Rap fans and begin asking more academically sound questions regarding the *origins* of early Hip Hop while most of us are still alive.

²⁰⁷   This one line, *I'm hemp the demp, the woman's pimp, women fight for my delight,* can tell us much about Hip Hop's true history and the migration of *ideas* that help to manifest Rap music.

²⁰⁸   This one line and the style in which it is said (which also appears in the 1970s' motion picture *Five on the Black Hand Side*) seems to either have been a rhyme that everyone in the *hood* knew and added his or her own twist to (which was the actual case for many expressions of the *hood* before the 1980s), or it was an original rhyme by H. Rap Brown that became popular over time.

²⁰⁹   But how does a rhyme said in the 1950s in Baton Rouge, Louisiana wind up in the Bronx, New York in Grandmaster Caz's mouth, later recited by Big Bank Hank on the classic Rap recording "Rappers Delight" in 1979?

²¹⁰   I tend to side with the first view because in the 1950s and 1960s everybody shared everything. Everything artistic was shared and imitated amongst the youth of the *hood*. No popular rhyme, or street game, or clothing style, or slang remained the exclusive property of the originator.

²¹¹   Most times no one even knew who the originator was; you just heard it, or saw it and adopted it for yourself, putting your own twist and style to it. Everyone in the *hood* was embellishing upon the free-flowing ideas and trends of America's inner cities.

²¹²   No one owned our street games, our rhymes, our fashion trends, and our unwritten moral codes of manhood

and womanhood. These expressions existed freely in the *hood* until these same free-flowing ideas that everyone freely enjoyed and improved upon spontaneously became a business.

[213]   When young, White, suburban youth in the early 1980s became willing to spend real money to see real DJ-ing, MC-ing, Graffiti writing and b-boying performed live, Hip Hop went from being the lifestyle of a few *cool* people to a mainstream business product.

[214]   Before all of this occurred, however, the combination of Black (African American) and Brown (Puerto Rican) artistic expressions was on the rise. And in all truth, this combination, along with a strong southern artistic upsurge into the North (New York in particular) set the stage for what would become modern Hip Hop.

[215]   It seems that b-boying, MC-ing, and graffiti writing DID NOT originate in the Bronx; these Hip Hop artistic elements seem to have come from the Caribbean and from all over the United States, especially from the South, and met in the Bronx.

[216]   Even Kool DJ Herc and his "DJ-ing" techniques as well as his sound system were all ideas from the streets of Jamaica—NOT THE BRONX. And I don't take pride in revealing this bit of research being that my first big hit recording in 1986 was a song entitled "South Bronx" which suggested that Hip Hop began in *the Bronx, in the South, South Bronx!* However, in the name of credible scholarship evidence is showing that Hip Hop actually <u>grew</u> in the Bronx; it was not <u>created</u> in the Bronx. This is a very interesting observation regarding Hip Hop and its true history.

[217]   The "history" of hip-hop (Hip Hop's folklore) may begin in the Bronx, as Grandmaster Caz puts it, *Hip Hop started in the West Bronx, not in the South Bronx.* But the "origins" of Hip Hop itself seem to come from Jamaica,

Puerto Rico, and the southern parts of the United States, even the West Coast of the United States.

218   Aerosol (Graffiti) Art is said to have come out of Philadelphia around the 1960s and the "Poppin'" dance-form which later became part of modern Hip Hop dance in the Bronx and the standard of a well-rounded b-boy/b-girl performance is said to have originated in Fresno, California whereas, "Lockin'" is said to have been started in Los Angeles, California.

219   Today, we see "Poppin," "Lockin," "Up-Rockin," "Electric Boogie," etc., as part of one Hip Hop dance performance originating from one place, when in actuality all of these dance forms were at one time separate traditions unto themselves, originating at different times and at different places around the United States.

220   Breakin, Graffiti writing and Emceein were also separate traditions practiced by all kinds of people from a wide array of backgrounds. This is why true Hip Hop scholarship is so important. As scholars, we cannot rely upon Rap music's incomplete history to inform us of Hip Hop's true origin and nature. We must ask the hard questions and probe even deeper into what we think we know of Hip Hop.

221   So, why do we theorize about the origins of Hip Hop occurring outside of the Bronx? I know that Hip Hop starting in the Bronx has become part of Hip Hop's standard history, but it seems that from 1967 to about 1977 the Bronx was the recipient of many foreign peoples and THEIR cultural traditions.

222   This is interesting because mostly every major pioneer (originator) of Hip Hop's elements and/or collective philosophy has come from somewhere other than the Bronx, and the music of Hip Hop's culture (Rap) seems to get its start from the previous funk and soul eras

of our parents.

223   In fact, Hip Hop may not be exclusively African American in its origin at all! Grandmaster Flash has a West Indian background, Afrika Bambaataa has a West Indian background, Kool Herc has a West Indian background, Doug E. Fresh has a West Indian background, KRS ONE has a West Indian background, and the list goes on.

224   This could be why African American leadership in the past has been reluctant to embrace Hip Hop and call it their own—maybe because it is not. Hip Hop may not be an African American creation. Hip Hop seems to be the result of certain foreign cultures coming together and meeting in the Bronx, and African Americans were a leading group in the meeting.

225   Yes, African Americans are indeed major contributors to early Hip Hop. However, from a scholarly point of view, Hip Hop seems to have formed in the Bronx, not by the Bronx. Hip Hop was formed by Black people with the help of African Americans, not by African Americans exclusively. In fact, Hip Hop may be foreign to African Americans and this could be why "they" may use it in the way that "they" do. Look at this seriously.

226   Hip Hop remains independent of all ethnicities and cultural traditions because it is a creation of all of them; it is actually all of them and at the same time none of them. Yes, Hip Hop comes out of the Black experience and was molded by the events of the Black community. But the term "Black" is a racial identification as well as a political identification, whereas the term "African American" is an ethnic identification.

227   These distinctions are important because Hip Hop seems to be more "Black" than "African American." Hip Hop begins in the "Black community" as an assortment of street games (not gangs), street music and street attitudes.

However, the so-called "Black community" of the 1970s and 1980s was NOT all African American.

228   "Black" as a community was simply that group of forgotten and rejected people regardless of ethnicity. The so-called "Black community" was simply the working-poor community. Many different cultures, religions and ethnicities mingled together within the so-called "Black community." Rich African Americans did not live in Black urban communities, they lived in White suburban communities.

229   In the 1950s and 1960s Puerto Ricans befriended poor African Americans and formed many important alliances—some legal, some illegal, some within the system, others outside of the system. Puerto Ricans and African Americans in particular lived side-by-side and shared their neighborhoods. Again, no Black community in New York was ever ALL African American; everyone lived in the so-called *Black community* African Americans included.

230   White folks, Asian folks, Jews, Christians and Muslims all lived and worked in the so-called *Black community*. The real *Black community* was always a multicultural, multi-faith community where African Americans lived amongst Puerto Ricans, Jamaicans, Haitians, Brazilians, Cubans, Dominicans, Africans, Arabs and many other "dark-skinned" people. Here, Italians, Asians, Greeks, Armenians, Russians, etc., were those who worked within the *Black community*, but didn't necessarily live there.

231   In Truth, the term *Black community* as it relates to a geographical location on earth did not and does not exist for African Americans. African Americans collectively did not own the land which they lived upon in New York. Most lived in *rented* apartment buildings with *landlords*, or in state-sponsored tenement housing complexes called "the projects."

²³² Migrating from the South in the early 1900s and settling all over the New York metropolitan area, African Americans and "Black people" lived under constant pressure and harassment from the police along with decrepit schools, corrupted hospitals, high crime, discriminatory justice and drug abuse.

²³³ In Truth, there was no Black "African American community" because African Americans were never completely united as a people internally; "they" were united by oppression and the various designations given to them by the White mainstream.

²³⁴ For there to have been a real "Black African American community" African Americans would have had to unite around specific political agendas and set specific community codes unique to the African American experience and African American development. But this NEVER happened for African Americans as a whole.

²³⁵ What was commonly called the *Black community* was simply the place where the working poor, the foreign, the uneducated—basically, America's undesirables—lived.

²³⁶ The *Black community* of the Bronx in the 1970s and 1980s was called "Black" because EVERYONE who was considered non-White and/or poor (including Whites) was confined there. And this is where Hip Hop gets its start. Hip Hop seems to get its start amongst "Black people," not necessarily African Americans. As H. Rap Brown pointed out in 1969, *Black is not a color but the way you think*.

²³⁷ In Truth, African Americans have contributed to, and have benefited from, Hip Hop like most other cultures have. African Americans were indeed part of the collective *Black community* of the Bronx but they were not the totality of the *Black community* in the Bronx.

²³⁸ Puerto Ricans (as just one major example) would bring their colorful Latino traditions into the *Black*

community, adding a breath of fresh cultural air and political strength against the oppression everyone within the *Black community* faced. Racial segregation, prejudice and isolation forced African Americans and Puerto Ricans in particular to *stick together.*

239   Puerto Ricans brought with them many of the Caribbean food preparation techniques almost forgotten by African Americans. Puerto Ricans made African Americans bilingual and fought right alongside African Americans for Civil Rights and justice in the United States. It wouldn't be long before the *Father of Rock 'N' Roll* Bo Diddley (a Black man) and earlier rock pioneer Fats Domino (another Black man) would begin incorporating Latin and Caribbean rhythms into their music sound.

240   Groups like the Vocaleers, Frankie Lymon and the Teenagers, as well as the Harptones would combine Black and Latino musicians to create a new music sound and style that neither group could produce on their own. Other Latino musicians like Pete Rodriguez, Joe Cuba, and Joe Bataan would also begin to gain prominence during these times.

241   However, as the 1960s emerged, some Latinos (like their light-skinned African American neighbors) tried to bury their African ancestry in an attempt to integrate into the larger White community. In search of a perceived *better life,* both light-skinned Blacks and Latinos that could pass for White abandoned their African heritage to become more American—White American.

242   Television shows like *I Love Lucy* showed a comedic life between a Latino man (Desi Arnaz) and a White woman (Lucille Ball) as husband and wife. Broadway theatre productions like *West Side Story* were huge hits in the United States in the 1960s, all of which helped newly arriving Latino/Hispanic immigrants to integrate into the

American mainstream.

243   But some Puerto Ricans were not impressed. Arriving in New York in the mid 1900s, Arturo Alfonso Schomburg was one such Puerto Rican. Known for his struggles against Spanish colonialism, Schomburg lived in Harlem studying and teaching the causes and the effects of the African Diaspora. His work can be studied at the Schomburg Center for Research in Black Culture, in Harlem.

244   Jesús Colón was another great Puerto Rican who contributed much to the struggle for freedom in the United States. As a journalist and revolutionary Jesus taught many about the historical and ethnic links between Puerto Ricans and African Americans. In his writings he exposed the psychological effects of White American racism and the roles it played in his life.

245   Great Puerto Ricans like Felipe Luciano would lead the Young Lords and also recite poetry as an original member of the Last Poets.

246   Influenced by popular recording artist James Brown, Puerto Rican Dennis Vasquez (the Original "Rubber Band Man") would popularize a style of Breakin called *Up-Rockin'*, Usually performed to James Brown's song "Sex Machine," or Jimmy Castor Bunch's "Its Just Begun."

247   Up-Rockin' was performed as an alternative to violent gang confrontations. Around the 1980s, great Puerto Rican DJs like Charlie Chase of the Cold Crush Brothers as well as MCs like Tito of the Fearless Four, Ruby Dee of the Fantastic Romantic Five and Prince Whipper Whip would find their places amongst the best Black MCs of their day.

248   One of Ruby Dee's most famous rhymes was, *Well I'm MC Ruby Dee, a Puerto Rican; you might think I'm Black by the way that I'm speaking.* This rhyme was one of the most popular street phases recited by ALL youths of

the 1980s.

[249]   But this is just a small part of Hip Hop's Latino influences (or *origins*) during its incubation within the *Black community.* Jamaicans (different from African Americans) also contributed much to the origin and further development of Hip Hop.

[250]   Arriving in the United States in 1967 from Jamaica, Kool DJ Herc was known for having the biggest and the loudest sound system in the Bronx, which attracted a specific group of street kids, Graffiti writers, other DJs and especially b-boys.

[251]   Kool DJ Herc would attract huge crowds to the playgrounds and parks of the west Bronx, emphasizing the playing of the instrumental *breaks* of songs by recording artists such as James Brown as well as the Incredible Bongo Band and Mandrill. In fact, along with the song "Apache," by the Incredible Bongo Band, James Brown's popular recordings would become Kool DJ Herc's main records to play. And while many DJs in the Bronx, like El Marko, Mandingo, DJ Maboya, Elvis 007 and others were also playing James Brown recordings, Kool DJ Herc was considered a street DJ because he would play his music on a huge sound system outside in the playgrounds and parks for free! These events were called *jams* and at the time there was nothing special about a *jam*—they happened often.

[252]   Many other DJs that simply didn't get the notoriety of Kool Herc, or weren't as good as Kool Herc, or didn't have as much *juice* (power) as Kool Herc, or simply fell to drugs, crime and growing up in the *hood,* also played music in Cedar Park and other places around University Avenue in the Bronx, but they are hardly mentioned in hip-hop's mainstream history because they never made it to radio and/or television. And this is very important to know.

[253]   Hip Hop's true pioneers didn't even know that

they were birthing a culture, a music genre, a $10.5 billion entertainment industry, a revolutionary movement for change. Many of Hip Hop's true pioneers are still in jail, outgrew the movement or are dead. Only a few of us have survived to tell our story.

254   The people you see today holding the title of *pioneer* (including myself) are really the survivors of a very dangerous and turbulent time in American history. It is truly a miracle that Hip Hop exists today. No so-called *pioneer of Hip Hop* can ever say that they alone originated Hip Hop, or formed it to be what it is today; any one of us could have been killed, locked up or simply discouraged at any time. Hip Hop was (and still is) a divinely guided movement, and as scholars you must know this.

255   Hip Hop's true history has very little to do with Rap music's platinum artists. Hip Hop's million-selling artists are indeed part of Hip Hop's culture and history, but it is not their (or anyone else's) CD sales, tour dates and/ or album releases that are exclusively responsible for Hip Hop's cultural and political existence.

256   Presently, hip-hop's history is presented through the mainstream events of Rap music and this is simply inaccurate. Hip Hop was going on all over the United States long before the Sugar Hill Gang's "Rapper's Delight" recording. Even Kool Herc (the recognized Father of Hip Hop) was not alone at the birth of Hip Hop.

257   Kool Herc had a crew: his sister Cindy, Peeblie Poo, Timmy Tim, Clark Kent, Coke La Rock, Pee Wee Dance, the Nigga Twins, Phase II, and others. They too can be called *Fathers* and *Mothers* of Hip Hop. In his time, Kool Herc was not just a DJ; he was also an activist in his community, a believer in GOD. He was *conscious*, and talented as a Graffiti artist in his day.

258   Afrika Bambaataa was another street DJ with a

Caribbean background who could be found deejayin Funk and Soul music in either the playground of Public School #123 in the Bronx, or at the playgrounds of the Bronx River housing projects.

[259]   Unlike traditional African Americans, these *other Blacks* with different histories to draw from had no fear of the police or White America and often criticized African Americans as being *lazy* and always *blaming the White man* for depriving them of those things they had the ability to go get for themselves. Sometimes "Bam" (Afrika Bambaataa) and DJ Jazzy Jay would be at the 161st Street playground of Yankee Stadium in the Bronx, or at Stevenson High School's handball and basketball courts in the Bronx, playing Funk and Soul music free for the public. The study as to why and how this was accomplished during some of the most turbulent times in American history is the essence of Hip Hop's true historical scholarship.

[260]   Urging his followers to read the Bible and the Qur'an, Afrika Bambaataa felt that American Blacks had been miseducated about Africa and its contributions to World civilization. From the very beginning, Afrika Bambaataa would structure Hip Hop to be an all-inclusive culture that promoted the greatness of African people worldwide. THIS IS HIP HOP'S REAL HISTORY.

[261]   It was Afrika Bambaataa who would introduce Hip Hop and its elements all over the World. In fact, many countries (if not all of them) would be introduced to Hip Hop's core elements and ideologies through Afrika Bambaataa and Zulu Nation's World tours. Afrika Bambaataa (through Zulu Nation) would continue to strengthen, organize and teach Hip Hop throughout the 1980s, not only as a unified community of people made up of all races, classes and ethnicities, but also as *a cultural movement which is expressed through various artistic mediums*

we call elements. The main elements are known as MC-ing (Rapping), DJ-ing, writing (Aerosol Art), b-boying/b-girling (Breaking), knowledge and overstanding. (Zulu Nation, *Hip Hop History Two*)

262   It was Afrika Bambaataa who established Hip Hop's earliest principles: *The Infinity Lessons, The 11 Points Of Light, The Laws Of Success, Hip Hop History One* and *Two,* and more. Bam would teach that *when we made Hip Hop, we made it hoping it would be about peace, love, unity and having fun so that people could get away from the negativity that was plaguing our streets—gang violence, drug abuse, self-hate, violence against those of African and Latino descent. Even though this negativity still happens here and there, as the culture progresses we play a big role in conflict resolution and enforcing positivity.*

263   Afrika Bambaataa would do much to help end gang violence in New York, introduce Rap music on the radio and unite Rap artists of the mid 1980s. Afrika Bambaataa would not only popularize the Rock Steady Crew, DJ Jazzy Jay, the TATS CRU, DJ Red Alert, DJ Chuck Chillout, D.ST, the Soul Sonic Force and many other *pioneers* through Zulu Nation, he would also organize the very first Hip Hop summits and conferences in Hip Hop's real history.

264   Through Ice-T and Afrika Islam, Afrika Bambaataa would also organize Hip Hop on the West Coast of the United States, paving the way for a new era in Hip Hop. At a time when lawlessness, corruption and hatred existed openly and freely in American society and the rule of law was ignored and God was declared *"dead,"* Afrika Bambaataa fearlessly held our culture together advocating Peace, Love, Unity and safely having fun through a knowledge and respect for one's self and for one's community!

265   His repeated reminders for Hip Hop to seek peace, love, unity and healthy fun have become the principle pillars

of Hip Hop's vision of itself. Technically, Afrika Bambaataa is Hip Hop's first teacha. The principles he introduced into our culture belong to no specific race or group of people, they are simply part of that timeless wisdom that no group of people can live without.

[266] We can see here that even though Hip Hop is introduced to the World by several kinds of "Black people", Hip Hop's origin is still not confined to one race or to one ethnicity. Hip Hop is even beyond the collective "Black" experience. In other words, ALL "Black" people (African Americans included) are not Hip Hop. Just because you are part of the Black race does not mean that you automatically love and produce Hip Hop. And this again is why Hip Hop itself cannot be considered exclusively a "Black thing."

[267] Artistically it may look this way, but historically and culturally this was never the case. In the early days when the awareness of Hip Hop first came into the Bronx it hit everyone at the same time. However, just because you were Black did not mean that you were Hip Hop. Just because you were Latino did not mean that you were Hip Hop. And just because you were White didn't mean that you could not relate to Hip Hop and then produce it yourself.

[268] Black, White and Latino adults as well as youth criticized early Hiphoppas as engaging in something that was not going to last. The question was, *Why are you putting so much time and energy into this bullshit?* And the unanimous answer across the board was, THIS IS AN EXPRESSION OF WHO I AM!

[269] This exchange was seen in the conflict between Graffiti writer *Skeme* and his African American mother *Barbara* in the Graffiti documentary *Style Wars*.

[270] Barbara clearly reflected the aggravation and concern of most parents at the time when she said, *Society should go down in the subway and lock them all up! 'Cause*

they don't have any business down there [speaking of the train yards and subway tunnels]. *It's dangerous down there! People that work down there 25, 30 years have accidents. But his* [Skeme's] *contention is that he is immortal. I guess, like most 17 year olds are immortal.*

271   Graffiti writer Skeme replies, *It's a matter of getting a tag on each line, in each division, ya know, it's called 'going all-city.' People see your tags* [a graffiti writer's name] *in Queens, uptown, downtown, all over!*

272   Barbara chuckles and then says to the interviewer, *I can only laugh to keep from crying because what happens is I really don't think he knows how silly that sounds. He's going 'all city!' I mean, to what end? And when I ask him, he says to me, well, just so people see it and they know who I am.*

273   Skeme then exclaims, *It's not a matter of so they know who I am!*

274   Mom continues, *So they see it, and after they see it, so what?!*

275   Skeme responds, *It's a matter of bombin'* [writing your name in as many places as you can], *knowing that I can do it! Ya know, every time I get in the train, almost every day I see my name. I say yeah, you know it, I was there! I bombed it! It's for me; it's not for nobody else to see! I don't care about no body else seeing it, or not. It's for me and other Graffiti writers that we can read it. All these other people who don't write, they're excluded; I don't care about them! They don't matter to me, it's for us!*

276   And again, the concerns of Barbara were not unique to her or to her race at the time. Most parents felt the way that she did about the rebellious and even illegal activities of early Hiphoppas.

277   The Hip Hop motion picture classic, *Wild Style* shows the same conflict between Graffiti writer *Lee* and his older Puerto Rican brother *Hector* who has just returned

home from military service.

278   In the movie, Lee has just come from the train yards and is sneaking into his apartment through a fire escape window. As he enters his apartment through the window his older brother Hector (not knowing who's coming through the window) greets Lee with a pointed pistol.

279   Lee says, *Hector, I thought you was supposed to be in boot camp.*

280   Hector replies, *Ya know, I was gonna shoot your ass! I ought to rearrange your face, that's what I should do! What the fuck is with that doo-rag on your head anyway? I don't know what the hell you were doing in my crib* [home] *but I want this shit* [pointing to the aerosol art on the walls] *out of my room!*

281   Lee responds, *What shit?* Pointing at the aerosol art on the wall, Hector says, *This shit; it's fuckin' garbage!*

282   Lee replies, *Hey, this isn't garbage! This is something you don't get to see in the infantry my man!*

283   Hector replies, *People are sick of it! Have you been busted* [arrested] *for this yet?*

384   Lee quickly and nervously replies, *Never, never!*

285   Hector continues, *You mean to tell me I'm bustin' my ass, sending money home for you and mom and you're sitting at home doing this shit?*

286   Hector concludes his criticisms by saying to Lee directly, *Stop fuckin' around and be a man! There ain't nothing out here for you!*

287   Lee disagrees and responds by saying, *Oh yes there is.* Gesturing toward his aerosol wall art he says, *This!*

288   Such conflicts between the elders of our traditional ethnicities and early Hip Hop were common. In fact, this is the way it was. This was the reality of a Hiphoppa—here, a graffiti writer.

[289]   In the same motion picture Lee explains to a friend, *Being a graffiti writer is taking the chances and shit, taking the risk, taking like all the arguments from the transit, from the police, from your own moms, ya know, from your friends and shit! Ya know, you gotta take all that bullshit!* This is what it was like to adopt the character of early Hip Hop and this is why many young people gave up on their Hip Hop dreams; it was simply too much of a hassle.

[290]   To participate in early Hip Hop you had to actually BE HIP HOP! Those who stuck it out and endured the criticism did so because they had no choice; Hip Hop was who they were personally. Because of this, many Hiphoppas were discriminated against. People didn't want to associate with us; we were the outlaws, the outsiders, the rejected, "those other people."

[291]   So, through the rejection of our own races, ethnicities, and immediate families, we formed our own community made up of all the people rejected by their families, races and ethnicities. Historically, Hip Hop belongs to no race of people because every race of people rejected it when they encountered it. Mainstream "Blacks" in particular wanted nothing to do with early Hip Hop.

[292]   However, it is interesting to observe how Hip Hop is continuously associated with African Americans and African American history by today's mainstream scholars now that it has achieved such worldwide and financial success. Regardless of race or ethnicity the arts of b-boying/b-girling, MC-ing, DJ-ing and Graffiti writing found very little favor amongst the elders of any community. And this is why true Hip Hop cannot be said to be a racial *thing* at all. You just have to feel it.

[293]   True Hip Hop was never about race, it was always about a certain character and skill. And even though Hip Hop does get its start in the minds of Jamaican, Puerto

Rican and American-born Black youth, it was still a specific kind of Jamaican, Puerto Rican and American Black, and eventually White, youth who broke with their traditions and actually became the first Hiphoppas.

294   However, most Jamaican, Puerto Rican, and American-born Black and White youths influenced by early Hip Hop never became DJs, MCs, etc. Many of them, even if they wanted to pursue the awareness of Hip Hop, were told *"turn that noise off!"* Or *"stop trying to act Black!"*

295   Blacks were told to *"stop trying to act street!"* Others were told, *"you'll never get a job doing that!"* Even White Graffiti writers in the early 1980s complained in the Graffiti documentary *Style Wars,* that it was *harder on Black kids or Spanish kids cause everybody thinks a Graffiti writer is Black and Puerto Rican. And that, like ya know, is wrong ya know. A lot of White people are writin'!*

296   But that didn't stop the then mayor of New York City, Edward Koch, from launching an all-out assault upon New York's City's Graffiti writers, who he and others felt were mostly Black and Puerto Rican.

297   His anti-Graffiti campaign enlisted artistically prominent African Americans like dancer Gene Ray, who was scripted to say (referring to Graffiti Art), *So if you really want to make something out of your life, use your head,* while African American singer Irene Cara continued Gene's scripted statement, saying, *Or your voice. But don't waste time making a mess!*

298   Others, like prominent Latino boxing champions Héctor Camacho and Alex Ramos would join Mayor Koch's campaign with a scripted statement that also aired on local television: *Graffiti is for chumps!* In fact, Mayor Koch's anti-Graffiti campaign came with a bus and subway advertisement that read, *Make your mark in society, not on society.*

²⁹⁹ The point is that Hip Hop's early elements first appeared colorless/raceless. Hip Hop began as the artistic movement of a <u>certain</u> group of urban people. All Black people didn't embrace the idea of Hip Hop.

³⁰⁰ All Hispanics, Whites and Asians didn't embrace Hip Hop either. Only a certain kind of person was attracted to Hip Hop in its early days, and this fact is what inspires us to seek the deeper meaning as to why only a certain group of people in the World were and are attracted to Hip Hop and are born with its artistic and intellectual abilities. Hip Hop may be the reawakening and the coming together of an ancient tribe once scattered by conflict.

TRACK FOUR

³⁰¹ I realize that this entire gospel for our newly established Hip Hop nation will seem strange and even absurd to many. The very idea of establishing a new people, a new civilization, a new human group, in my time, is indeed a concept that borders insanity. But I truly believe that to not at least consider such an idea as an intellectually-gifted, free human being is even crazier. Sure the uneducated, the uninvested, the unstudied, uncommitted individual only seeking a momentary good time is exempt from such matters of thought. But those who claim to be revolutionaries cannot hide from this one simple question: What does it really mean to be free? Regardless of race or ethnic origin, as a free-thinking human being concerned about the sociopolitical conditions of formerly enslaved human beings at this present time, the question is, what does it really mean to truly be free?

³⁰² Often I think about my own role in the continued

Civil Rights Movement and I wonder about the next step for newly freed people. Where do we go from here? As newly freed African Americans who are in many ways still enduring the effects of slavery, racism, sexism and classism within the United States, the questions for every so-called Black intellectual in my time appear to be simple: Where do we go from here? Where can we go from here? What is the next step in our human evolution outside of the terms and designations handed to us by institutions that clearly do not have our best interests in mind? The question is, what does it really mean to be free?

³⁰³ As I think about this I can hear others of my own race already criticizing such views as if I am somehow abandoning over 300 years of struggle. On the contrary, it is my sincere love for African Americans and my unwavering loyalty to the cause of *freedom and justice for ALL* that inspires these ideas. My approach to Hip Hop is the result of my African American enlightenment. As a free Black man who willingly accepts his responsibility as a role model not only to the advancement of his own racial family, but more importantly to the advancement of humanity itself, I refuse to offer my own children, as well as the children of other races, cultures and ethnicities, mediocre and selfish concepts of liberty when I fully recognize that if humanity itself doesn't rise, how then are African Americans or anyone else going to rise? Are we Black or are we Human? Are we animals or are gods? These are the questions that stir at the origins of Hip Hop.

³⁰⁴ After the Civil Rights Movement, what next? All serious women and men who are concerned about the human condition must ask themselves today, has the Freedom Movement of our grandparents concluded? Are the threats to our sustained freedom no more? What exactly should we be doing today to honor and continue the freedom heritage

of ALL of our ancestors and parents? What proves that we are actually free today? Not liberated, but FREE! What is the evidence of our freedom today? Economic security is not freedom. Education is not freedom. Being permitted to vote is not freedom. Freedom is freedom! So, are we free?

305 Just as the environment of a king is called a "kingdom," such is the same for the truly free and their "freedom." Freedom is also the realm, condition or environment of the free. To have "freedom" doesn't mean that you are free; it means to live amongst the free. It means to live in "their" domain; it doesn't mean that you are free yourself. To be free, is to act on your own will, to move because you choose to, not because you have to. I know that I am not the only one thinking in this way. I suspect that there are many who ask of their role in the continued march toward freedom, justice and equality.

306 I also know that many more do not even have the energy, the attention or the time to think about such things as freedom, justice and equality, but many of us still do, and at the top of our list of topics is *"freedom."* Yeah, rap music is valued at 10.5 billion dollars annually in my time, and Hip Hop's unique fashion styles, Graffiti artwork, dance forms, urban language and cultural knowledge have all impacted the modern World in ways that can't even be calculated yet.

307 Yes, we (the Hip Hop community) are more popular and richer today than we have ever been since the early 1970s, and academic scholars of all sorts publish all kinds of views on the existence of Hip Hop and its possible future, but the question remains for everyone participating in the culture of Hip Hop, are we free? Black, White, Brown, Asian, Native, everyone, are we truly free yet?

308 Have we achieved the collective political dreams of our parents yet? Or have we already forgotten them? As a

group, have we become distracted away from real freedom by the political granting of certain liberties? Are we free or have we conformed into better slaves, unable to THINK for ourselves?

309   Are we truly free to be ourselves and live as we please or are we still pretending to be happy and content with the condition of our lives because we basically can do nothing to change them? The question here is, what kind of freedom am I experiencing in my time if the condition to my freedom is that I cannot be my true *Self*, or even possibly create a new *Self*.

310   As John O'Neal (writer for *The Drama Review*) pointed out in the 1960s, *Racism systematically verifies itself when the slave can only break free by imitating the master: by contradicting his* [the slave's] *own reality*. But what is a slave's former reality?

311   Can a *People* who were genetically, spiritually, politically and mentally engineered and bred for slave labor ever truly be free?

312   Can a *People* who were genetically, spiritually, politically and mentally engineered and bred for slave labor ever truly regain those lost aspects of their humanity and culture before the rise of the slavery institution?

313   Millions of Africans may have lost their cultural traditions and possessions during and after the rise and fall of slavery in the United States, but millions of European slave owners as well as slaves not only lost their possessions and cultural heritage—they basically lost their souls.

314   Can they (or more accurately their children) ever recover from such loses? After a slave (and/or slave owner) is deemed *free*, what should such a former slave (or slave owner) and his/her descendants now be looking for?

315   How do former slaves regain all that was lost to them? Or is this even what a newly freed people should be

looking for? What is the proper forward movement for a formerly enslaved people, now *"free?"*

316   In my bold observation, the next move would be self-creation—or rather, the total creation of one's new self. We can never actually be what we were yesterday, but we can create ourselves today to be whatever we believe we are capable of tomorrow. In my view, after a human group is legally deemed *free*, it is they who must then leave the plantation. In my view we need a new exodus! We need to physically, mentally, spiritually, economically and culturally leave the plantation.

317   How can we be sure that we are free if our reference for freedom comes from those who have enslaved us? As children of the *Civil Rights* movement we must ask, how can your slave master free you?

318   Is it not a fact that only a totally independent force separate from the forces that enslaved you can actually free you and assist in the maintenance of your freedom? What if your enslaver decided to enslave you again? Or forced you to enslave others? How would you avoid or combat such a situation?

319   And this is real for anyone recovering from injustice. How do you know when you are healed? What does healing feel like? Are we completely *"free,"* or have we been *"freed"*?

320   Part of the answer to these questions rests on whether you can be enslaved again. If you are truly free no one can enslave you, even if you are enslaved. And likewise, if you are still a slave only freed or liberated, then you cannot experience true freedom even if you are not enslaved—even if you have been *"freed."*

321   We know that both "slavery" as well as "freedom" are states of mind. Not to make light of either one, but history is full of examples of so-called "slaves" freeing

themselves, buying their freedom and inheriting freedom, while other "slaves" with clear opportunities for freedom disregarded such opportunities or betrayed the very freedom movements established for their own liberation.

322   Historical evidence shows that "slavery" as well as "freedom" are both attitudes. We can see historically that avoiding slavery was mostly about one's social class, personal character, principles, and intellectual skills. Freedom is and was an attitude!

323   Nat Turner, the Black revolutionary of 1831, rebuked another slave for bowing and scraping before a White man. *But we slaves,* said the fellow. Turner replied, *You deserve to be. (The Black Book,* p.10)

324   As another example: *A judge sentenced a slave to be severely lashed for purchasing stolen goods. Before the sentence was carried out, the slave addressed the court, saying that the thief from whom he had purchased the goods was a White man. Then he asked the court if the thief would be punished if caught. 'Of course he will be punished,' the judge replied. 'Then,' said the slave, 'you must punish my master also. The goods I bought had no parents, but my master purchased me knowing I was stolen from my mother and father.' Punishment was set aside. (Pennsylvania Packet and Daily Advertiser,* May 20, 1788)

325   Again, freedom (just like slavery) is an attitude, a state of mind. Certain people simply cannot be enslaved because of who they are, and you will know if you are one of these *free* people by the way in which you conduct your life. Going along with the destruction of your own people is clearly the behavior of a slave. Doing what your employer tells you to do regardless of how it affects the well-being of others is indeed the behavior of a slave.

326   Not being able to THINK outside of your employer's or your oppressor's box is indeed the behavior of a slave. To not even consider the state of your own free

condition is the behavior of a slave. To give up on the possibility of freedom makes you A SLAVE! Is freedom even important to you? Are honor, integrity and trustworthiness valuable to you? Liberty is about moving through one's environment unrestrained, while freedom is the character of an unrestrained, non-institutionalized mind.

327   To be *"free"* means that you possess the ability to create your own reality, to live as you please, to move fearlessly amongst others without insecurity, prejudice or threat of enslavement or death.

328   To be *"free"* means that others cannot impose their wills (and temptations) upon you without your consent. It means that you own and control your physical and mental *"Self,"* that your movements are yours, based upon YOUR intentions and interests, and not those of others.

329   Freedom doesn't mean that you ask others through treaties and constitutional amendments not to war with you; freedom means that they cannot war with you even if they want to.

330   A free person is an extremely powerful individual and this is why groups of people rarely ever become free. Only individuals seem to experience true freedom because only certain individuals are willing to work to establish and maintain their freedom.

331   However, even though large groups of people rarely achieve freedom for real, when such an event does occur major changes are made in the World's structure and order. For only free people can free people. Slaves lead slaves back to the plantation/workforce.

332   The question for the Hip Hop community today is, after we have *"overcome"* American racism and prejudice, what next? After we are declared "free," what next? Who are WE outside of the mainstream American paradigm that even White people have become bored with?

³³³   "Black" is a term for people of African descent. However, outside of the American mainstream academic paradigm of racial distinctions and designations who are we?

³³⁴   What measures the value and ability of one's self outside of the American value system? These questions are at the heart of Hip Hop's true origins.

³³⁵   What is human for us?

³³⁶   What is real for us?

³³⁷   What is reality for us?

³³⁸   Whether you are African American, or Chinese American, or Native American, these are the questions of a truly free people.

³³⁹   These are the real questions that every leader, teacher and/or member of any group must ask themselves and the group; who are WE? Where have WE come from? Where are WE going? And how are WE going to get there?

³⁴⁰   At no time can these questions not be answered by any group, or such a group will cease to be a group. We need unity, and we need it NOW! And I believe that Hip Hop has the ability to provide the cultural structure necessary for our next level of unity and freedom.

³⁴¹   For if we don't know to ourselves who WE are, where WE have come from, where WE are going, and how WE are going to get there, WE simply will not survive as the group that we are today.

³⁴²   If WE are not loyal to one another, trusting of one another, supportive of one another, WE are simply a mass of individuals identified exclusively by the fact that WE all have no home, no direction and no vision. WE, at this level of existence, are indeed a subservient people (slaves) living at the expense and permission of those who have a home, a direction and a vision for themselves.

³⁴³   For if we have no home, no direction and no vision for ourselves then we naturally become the helpers and/

or assistants to those who do. This is just a fact! And this is why Hip Hop is so important culturally; Hip Hop is simply the cure for slavery. When practiced correctly, Hip Hop actually cures the slave mentality and the effects of slavery politically.

[344]   True freedom seems to not only be about breaking the chains from one's hands, feet and mind, true freedom seems to also be spiritual; it seems to be about self-creation and self-governance. Hip Hop provides all of this to its *people*.

[345]   The slave was created to be a slave. Therefore, true freedom from any kind of oppression must also include a totally new attitude and character about the governance of one's self and life. Freedom from slavery seems to be about freedom from old slave/master perceptions.

[346]   The ability to create and then govern one's self seems to be the hardest thing for a slave, or rather a person with a slave's mentality, to achieve.

[347]   This is where I bring Hip Hop into view. It is not every day that a group of human beings find themselves with the opportunity to establish a new civilization in the World based upon their own artistic and intellectual self-expression.

[348]   It is not every day that a movement as unique and as ever-growing as Hip Hop comes along in human history with the ability to inspire whole populations of people toward World understanding, good times and peace.

[349]   The question here is; can we govern and correctly guide such a movement toward the upliftment and refinement of all interested people in the World? Can we govern ourselves? Can the Hip Hop community really do better than many of the World's leaders today in regards to self-governance, moral authority, political consistency, and financial transparency?

350   If we really put our minds to it, could we actually govern ourselves with a real rule of law, a free and intelligent press, as well as certain institutional structures that are respected and useful to our community? Can we actually maintain a government that has the participation of its people?

351   Can we create a nation where Health, Love, Awareness and Wealth for all of its citizens are the actual laws of that nation? I believe we can, but first we must create ourselves into *those people* capable of such governance. And please understand this: we are not against anyone or anything here except our own immaturity and careless self-destruction.

352   These ideas are for *those people* capable of seeing Hip Hop's socio-political potential beyond music entertainment. The question here is, are you free? Are you free enough to see Hip Hop in this way?

353   When raising the question again as to "Are we free?" I tend to search for such answers within myself and my perception of my World. No one can free me except me. Liberty is external; it is political. But freedom is internal; it is spiritual.

354   For me, if I am truly free then I have the ability to examine my self-existence independently of every external title I've been force-taught to accept from birth. In other words, I can see myself outside of my oppressor's interpretation of me. I have the ability to know the space that lies between me and my acceptance of externally imposed ideas and identities upon my being.

355   Here, to be free is to be in touch with the nakedness of your actual being, even before your family name and birthday. To be aware of the naked you is the beginning of true freedom.

356   I find that it is my perceptions of the World

around me and what I believe I can do in such a World that determines not only my inner-freedom but also my outer-liberties. Again, freedom, like slavery, is a state of mind; and further, I believe that I can actually be whatever I can perceive my <u>self</u> as.

357　　It is this view of life and of living that helps to inform my political and social views today. This is how I can rationalize Hip Hop as its own self-governed civilization in the modern World. This is because in reality all of the titles, labels and identities that I am currently answering to today are all my decisions and my creations.

358　　Even though I was told (or rather force-taught) my "African American" identity and I never really got a chance in my younger years to truly discover my own nature for myself and name such a nature for myself, it seems that I have taken the identity that was forced upon me (and my parents) by those only interested in exploiting us, and I am trying to make the best of it. All of us affected by the institution of slavery are trying to make the *best* out of the worst (slaveowners included).

359　　This seems to be a post-slavery psychological disorder we suffer from because the first act of any free person is to name themselves based upon the nature of their newly discovered true being. "African American," "Negro," "Nigger," "Nigga," "Black," "Afro-American," "American" and even "African" are all identities that simply do not fit my modern nature accurately. These identities were given to me, I did not give them to my SELF.

360　　In Truth, I am really none of these identities. My true nature is timeless, shapeless and colorless. Is this not the Truth? Is it not true that anything I focus my mind upon I will eventually become? Am I not responsible for the creation of myself? If these are real questions then true freedom for me and my kind is the total re-creation of ourselves.

361   If I am no longer a slave for real, then I am free to call myself whatever I like, whatever my nature is. And those who truly and honestly recognize the free status of my true and free nature will acknowledge and respect the name that I have chosen for myself.

362   Yes. I am indeed a Black man. My political color is "black." But am I really the color "black" or am I really "brown?" Even beyond my political distinction as a "black man" I am a father, I am a thinker, an inventor, an investigator of myself and my surroundings, I am an emcee, a son, a brother. These things are what define my being, not the political skin color I may be designated to.

363   Is it not true that I create myself? Is it not true that I create myself from within; that it is the conscious choices that I make daily that further create and express my true being? Is it not true that I am choosing the *Self* that I am as well as the *Self* that I shall become? Therefore, it is also true that self-creation is the ultimate state of freedom for previously enslaved people now freed.

364   Here, freedom means that I decide my identity for myself; my identity is not taught to me in school, it is discovered naturally within me in life, by me. I choose today to be a "Black man" because I lend myself to the struggles of those so-called "Black people." This is my FREE choice.

365   I am not a Black man because the government labels me this; I am a Black man because I choose to be. It is I who empower the identity and label of "Black man," it is not the other way around.

366   For now though, I may reluctantly agree with the common mainstream political description of myself as a "Black man" because it is common to the population in which I reside. But the common mainstream descriptions of me are NOT my descriptions of my *"Self."*

³⁶⁷   My nature defines me, and my nature is free. Therefore, as an actual political, racial, ethnic identity I am more a "free man" in a "Black man" disguise. I am actually from the mental/spiritual land of "free," and as a "free man" I am from that group of free people with free minds. I am not afraid to be and create myself.

³⁶⁸   Politically, culturally and spiritually I can be anyone I choose to be simply by pledging my love and loyalty to the reality of my chosen identity—whatever that identity may be. I can actually call myself a "White man" and then find all kinds of real facts to substantiate my claim if I want to.

³⁶⁹   This is the issue with all social labels, professional titles and politically created identities; ultimately they are ALL CHOICES! But once chosen, your choice empowers the nature of your chosen identity and produces the reality that you have charged it with.

³⁷⁰   As a Black man I am a free man, and as a free man I choose to be whatever makes me happy and secure. For me, happiness and security is found in being and living Hip Hop. Hip Hop is my nature; it is what comes "naturally" to me.

³⁷¹   As a truly free man with a truly free mind, I choose to call myself "Hip Hop"—I am Hip Hop! If you must connect me to a race or to a political group in the World then I am of the "Black" race; I am a "Black man," a "Black Hiphoppa" or a "Hip Hop American." But if you ask me what I think of my true self, or if you ask me about the character of the person under this dark skin, I will say that "I am Hip Hop!" One race or ethnicity alone cannot really define me today.

³⁷²   In his book *The Beat Of Urban Art,* Graffiti writer Justin Bua writes, *The characters that I draw and paint represent who I am and what I value. They are from different*

backgrounds that together form one urban culture. People ask me what I am. Puerto Rican? Italian? Jewish? African American? Like my characters, I can't define myself by one race. I have so many different bloodlines flowing through my veins and grew up in such a uniquely integrated culture, that I am just me. I am part of an urban race united by the city. We judged each other by the content of our character. This is where the slang word 'ONE' comes from. We are ONE. Urban life challenges us to thrive among diversity and vibe off one another in a positive way.

373   This is Hip Hop and this is the thinking of a large percentage of the audience that is attracted to our movement. Yes, I will always be a brown-colored human being (a Black man, an African), but so is most of humanity, even all of humanity when you consider human origins and the fact that "White" people are actually "beige" today rather than the fictitious color of "white."

374   Open your eye (your mind). Everything that you call yourself is your voluntary choice to do so. We can create and/or re-create ourselves right now! In fact, with every name, title and/or label we assign or accept for ourselves, we actually add to the creation of our actual physical and mental "Self." You are truly whoever and/or whatever you repeatedly think you are. This too is a fact.

375   So, when it comes to freedom and the continued struggle for justice in our time it is now apparent that our generation carries the burden of creating itself. We must now take our Hip Hop activity in the World seriously and organize ourselves into the nation our parents and grandparents dreamt of.

376   All of the ingredients for the creation of a new World civilization exist within Hip Hop today. Our only challenge today is our own lack of belief in ourselves, and this too is part of Hip Hop's real history.

³⁷⁷ Like many World cultures, including the American popular culture, Hip Hop seems to be born from *cultural syncretism*, meaning the blending of different cultures to create a new culture. This is what makes Hip Hop as an international culture possible; these are its origins.

³⁷⁸ The concept of further developing a popular social movement into a sovereign community of specialized people is not new, and there is much research and many precedents to study from regarding this subject.

³⁷⁹ Hip Hop is the combination and unity of several independent cultures and subcultures creating a new heterogeneous culture. This happens often in World history. Old cultures give birth to new cultures; older civilizations have even given birth to our present American civilization. Why treat Hip Hop any different when it is clearly experiencing a similar historical reality in its present day as other great World civilizations have experienced at their geneses?

³⁸⁰ The question is not whether Hip Hop is a culture or not. The question is, do we want it to be? Can we actually govern ourselves? Looking upon the cultural history of just this Western Civilization in which we live, we can see how cultures are created and why.

³⁸¹ Classical Civilization was born from the wreckage of Cretan Civilization in the period 1150–900 B.C., and Western Civilization was born from the wreckage of Classic Civilization in the period 350–700 A.D.

³⁸² As Carroll Quigley explains in his book *Tragedy & Hope: A History Of The World In Our Time*, *Western civilization began, as all civilizations do, in a period of cultural mixture.* Referring to the 350-700 A.D. invasions of Barbarian tribes upon the independent European societies of "Classical Civilization," he continues: *By creating a new culture from the various elements offered from the Barbarian*

tribes, the Roman world, Saracen world, and above all the Jewish world (Christianity), _Western Civilization became a new society._

383   He continues: _When one society is destroyed by the impact of another society, the people are left in a debris of cultural elements derived from their own shattered culture as well as the invading culture. These elements generally provide the instruments for fulfilling the material needs of these people, but they cannot be organized into a functioning society because of the lack of an ideology and a spiritual cohesive. Such people either perish or are incorporated as individuals and small groups into some other culture, whose ideology they adopt for themselves and, above all, for their children. In some cases, however, the people left with the debris of a shattered culture are able to reintegrate their cultural elements into a new society and a new culture._

384   When I read this I am encouraged because this means that there is precedent for what we are proposing for Hip Hop. Hip Hop as a new World culture is very possible because our existence is the natural result of historical, traceable events.

385   What other civilizations have achieved in 1,000 years, we can achieve in 100! Times are indeed different today. The question is, do we want to seize upon this unique opportunity? Quigley speaks of _cultural elements_ being created _when one society is destroyed by the impact of another society._ This points to a good portion of the African American community.

386   He writes, _The people are left in a debris of cultural elements._ This resembles very accurately part of the origin of our African American, Latino and Afro-Caribbean _cultural elements_ coming together to form Breakin, Emceein, Graffiti Art, Deejayin, Beat Boxin, etc., which we _derived from_ OUR own _shattered_ African cultures as well as from

the *invading* European cultures.

387   For the Hip Hop community, the most interesting part of Mr. Quigley's statement is when he points out that *these elements generally provide the instruments for fulfilling the <u>material needs</u> of these people, but <u>they cannot be organized</u> into a <u>functioning society</u> because of the <u>lack of an ideology and a spiritual cohesive.</u>* This is Hip Hop's present state right here.

388   Our elements *provide the instruments for fulfilling* our <u>*material needs*</u>—money, property, prestige, credit, etc.— *but <u>they cannot be organized</u> into a <u>functioning society</u> because of the <u>lack of an ideology and a spiritual cohesive.</u>* This is clear. You can have all the money in the World, but if you hold no strong principles, no lasting traditions, no respect for the creed and vision of your own ancestors, you are still politically a slave—a victim of war, conquest and other past traumatic events. You still have no foundation yet because you still have never actually recovered from the experiences of war and conquest.

389   Even with money the unprincipled, uncultured person is still not free. Until you create your *Self* you are not yet truly free, even with money, power and respect! Culture doesn't grow on trees; it grows in free human minds and is released through free human actions.

390   Human beings choose their cultures; cultures do not choose them. However, the relationship between culture and humanity is indeed more complex than this. It is we who create cultures and civilizations, but in turn the cultures and civilized societies that we create do in fact create us. Take the United States of America as another example. In the beginning there were no "American" people. As Joseph J. Ellis explains in the CD series of his book *Founding Brothers, In the beginning there were no 'American' people. The Constitution's purpose was to provide a framework to gather*

together the scattered strands of the population into a more coherent collective worthy of that designation.

391   Mr. Ellis continues: *This point requires a reflective review of recent scholarship on the complicated origins of American statehood. Based on <u>what we now know</u> of the Anglo-American connection in the pre-Revolution era, that is <u>before it was severed.</u>*

392   *The initial identification of the colonial population as 'Americans' came from English writers who <u>used the term negatively</u> as a way of referring to a marginal or peripheral population <u>unworthy of equal status</u> with full-blooded Englishmen.*

393   *Back at the metropolitan center of the British Empire, the word* ["American"] *was <u>uttered and heard as an insult</u> that designated an inferior or insubordinate people* [like "nigger"]. *The entire thrust of the colonist's justification for independence was to reject that designation on the grounds that they possessed ALL the Rights of British citizens. And the ultimate source of these <u>Rights</u> did not lie in any indigenous origins, but rather in a <u>transcendent realm of natural Rights allegedly shared by all men everywhere.</u>*

394   In the pre-Revolution days (before there really was an "America" or an "American"), 16 percent of the colonial population were "Tories," meaning that they were loyal to the British crown. When rebellion began to break out all over the colonies and elsewhere the "Tories" fled to Canada and others back to England. Thomas Paine, author of the historical pamphlet *Common Sense,* who helped to cause the American Revolution against Britain, was actually British himself.

395   In their famous writings *The Lessons Of History* philosophers Will and Ariel Durant direct us to, *Consider the origin of the great peoples and civilizations of history; how nearly every one of them began with the slow mixture of varied*

racial stocks entering from any direction into some conquered or inviting region, mixing their blood in marriage or otherwise gradually producing a homogeneous people, and thereby creating, so to speak, the biological basis of a new civilization. So the Egyptians were formed of the Ethiopians, Libyans, Arabs, Syrians, and Mesopotamians. So the ancient Hebrews were composites of their own various stocks and of Canaanites, Edomites, Moabites, Ammonites, Hittites, and a dozen other peoples that swirled around the Euphrates, the Jordan and the Aronties [rivers].

396   The Durants continue: *Varied stocks entering some locality from diverse directions and diverse times mingle their blood, traditions and ways with one another or the existing population like two diverse pools of genes coming together in sexual reproduction. Such an ethnic mixture may in the course of centuries produce a new type, even a new people. So Celts, Romans, Angels, Saxons, Jutes, Stains, and Normans fused to produce Englishmen. When the new type takes form, its cultural expressions are unique and constitute a new civilization's new physiognomy, character, language, literature, religion, morality, and art. It is not the race that makes the civilization, it is the civilization that makes the people. Circumstances geographical, economic, and political create a new culture and the culture creates a human type.* But in the final analysis it is the human mind that perceives its civilization and decides to adopt it and develop it. This is where Hip Hop comes into our study.

397   Yes, it is the *civilization that makes the people,* but as we can see it is the activity of a people that further creates civilization. Hip Hop has already created us; the questions now are, are we further creating Hip Hop and what does it mean to be Hip Hop? The Hip Hop experience has already created a new human type in the World, but are we willing to accept, and most of all adopt, such a *type* as our own?

398   Today, being Hip Hop means that you are willing to adopt Hip Hop's ideals as a major part of your own cultural identification creating a new human type in the World. It means that you are ready to tell a new story about yourself and your history creating a new human group. It means that you are free to re-create your *"Self."* This story is common to America's immigrant history. Immigrants rarely forget where they have come from but they/we incorporate the best of our past into the best expectations of our newly created future when we assimilate into any new country.

399   Yes, I am more than proud of my African and American heritages, I am grateful to be part of such a story in World history. However, when thinking critically about the restoration of OUR lost civilizations, the enhancement of OUR present quality of life, the preservation of Hip Hop's artistic elements, freedom from negative corporate exploitation, and a Hip Hop way of life rooted in peace and prosperity (everything we collectively discussed at our Hip Hop conferences and summits), it becomes apparent that we are going to have to become a new type of people altogether if we are to actually achieve such a quality of living.

400   And I am not exaggerating here. To achieve higher states of freedom and liberty and finally claim what is rightfully ours—self-governance—we are going to have to create a new culture and lifestyle from the debris of our "shattered cultures" capable of achieving the goals that we say we want for ourselves and our children. We are going to have to <u>become</u> the civilization that we desire to see. We are going to have to re-create ourselves, and to do that we must know ourselves. Not just on a spiritual level, but on a cultural and even genetic level.

401   Yes, *spiritual cohesiveness* is an important part in the building of our Hip Hop civilization; it is the foundation. But how we interpret our "spiritual cohesion," and the tools

we use to discover ourselves, cannot be based solely upon the opinions and interpretations of those whose intentions are (and were) to exploit us, and our resources. We as a Hip Hop people have to do what Abraham was instructed to do in Genesis, Chapter 12: *Get thee out of thy country, and from thy kindred, and from thy father's house, unto a land that I will shew thee, and I will make of thee a great nation.*

[402] This is why we question the whole idea of establishing one's ethnic identity based upon a land-mass, or upon the pigmentation of one's skin, or upon the language one speaks. Many of us are still defining ourselves based upon the opinions and commercial interests of others who use outdated techniques, disproven views and broken methodologies to understand human identity. For the sake of our very survival, growth and development as Hiphoppas I think it is time for a few of us to rethink our ethnicities as well as the very concept of race itself. Some of us (Hiphoppas) need to become serious *critical race theorists* and stop relying upon the assumptions and opinions of others regarding the origins of race and ethnicity.

[403] Ian F. Haney López explains in his book *White By Law: The Legal Construction of Race, Of late, a new strand of legal scholarship dedicated to reconsidering the role of race in U.S. society has emerged. Writers in this genre, known as critical race theory, have for the most part shown an acute awareness of the socially constructed nature of race. Much critical race theory scholarship recognizes that race is a legal construction.* Quoting John Calmore, Mr. López continues: *Critical race theory begins with a recognition that 'race' is not a fixed term. Instead, race is a fluctuating, decentered complex of social meanings that are formed and transformed under the constant pressures of political struggle. Critical race theory increasingly acknowledges the extent to which race is not an independent given on which the law acts, but rather a social construction at*

least in part fashioned by law. Ultimately, it is the courts that have created and further created our modern understanding of race, not based upon scientific evidence but based upon "common knowledge"—what people believe.

404   For many years in the United States race was scientifically determined by certain human distinctions pertaining to the shape of the skull, distinct complexion differences and hair textures. Early editions of Webster's Dictionary cite professor of medicine Johann Friedrich Blumenbach's classification of races: *1. The Caucasian, or white race, to which belong the greater part of European nations and those of Western Asia; 2. The Mongolian, or yellow race, occupying Tartary, China, Japan, etc.; 3. The Ethiopian or Negro (black) race, occupying all of Africa, except the North; 4. The American, or red race, containing the Indians of North and South America; and, 5. The Malay, or brown race, occupying the islands of the Indian Archipelago, etc.* These racial distinctions were used as part of a larger scientific view of the World's races and their characteristics.

405   However, in an effort to settle immigration and naturalization cases brought before the courts in 1909 Mr. López explains that *a schism appeared among the courts over whether common knowledge or scientific evidence was the appropriate standard. Therefore, the lower courts divided almost evenly on the proper test for Whiteness* [then a requirement for U.S. citizenship]: *six courts relied on common knowledge, while seven others based their racial determinations on scientific evidence. No court used both rationales. Over the course of two cases, heard in 1922 and 1923, the Supreme Court broke the impasse in favor of common knowledge. Though the courts did not see their decision in this light, the early congruence of and subsequent contradiction between common knowledge and scientific evidence set the terms of a debate about whether race is a social construction or a natural occurrence. In these*

terms, the Supreme Court's elevation of common knowledge as the legal meter of race convincingly demonstrates that racial categorization finds its origins in social practices.

[406]   This is very important for the Hip Hop nation to understand. Yes, we may feel a certain loyalty to our individual races, but in fact such loyalty is more a habit of familiarity. As Mr. López's work points out futher, *Race is not a measured fact, but a preserved fiction. The celebration of common knowledge and the repudiation of scientific evidence show that race is a matter not of physical difference, but of what people believe about physical difference...Race is nothing more than what society and law say it is.* So if we Hiphoppas continue to accept the notion of individual races of human beings to define ourselves, we also accept the arbitrary characteristics and social statuses designated to individual races of human beings according to the non-scientific opinions of the courts. FREE YOUR SELF NOW! Free yourself from such prejudiced interpretations of your very being. NO ONE CAN DEFINE YOU EXCEPT YOU! And the definitions you give yourself about yourself create the reality you perceive and presently live within.

[407]   Legally, I am an American citizen, which, because of my "Blackness" and its direct association with Africa, makes my legal political description in the United States "African American." And the collective African American consciousness creates for itself a collective habitual behavior complete with its own history, traditions, beliefs and rituals that manifest certain collective experiences, which affects the development of my individual life directly and daily. As long as I pledge my allegiance to the "African American" identity I experience a certain African American reality—even legally. However, it is MY human energy that makes the identity of "African American" exist, not the other way around. It is my spiritual faith, my intellectual perception

and my physical body that make the identity of "African American" exist.

408   I am telling myself that I am this or that, that I am African American, African, American, a Black man, Negro, etc. I can equally tell myself that I am Hip Hop and it shall be so. The description of "African American" brings with it certain *conditions* that directly affect my well-being. Therefore, if I am truly free and still cannot seem to live the quality of life I expect for myself as an African American, I have the unalienable right and ability to change my cultural-political identity to fit the path of my total well-being.

409   What says that I must remain African American when such a distinction cannot enhance my well-being in the way I expect and respect? Respectfully I ask, what is an African American? Is this distinction an accurate depiction of my being? Did I name myself African American or was I born into this distinction? A distinction that brings with it real conditions to my physical being and reality. The question which comes to mind here is, do I think with my skin or do I think with my mind? What defines me? When it comes to the nature of my being, am I Black or am I human? And of course, this line of thinking is not for everyone. There are many who may never truly understand what I am implying here.

410   But if I really want something different for myself, a different reality, I am going to have to adopt a new name/ nature that is better equipped to satisfy my immediate needs and offers my children a stronger future. I need a new name, a new nature, a new ethnic identity—I need a new culture. And Hip Hop provides for me exactly what I need today to survive as a father, a man, and most of all, a human being. And let me be clear here, creating a new Hip Hop civilization upon the earth is not a task that everyone can be involved in, only some of us can do this. It will take only a

few of us to create a new world civilization. The question is, am I Black or am I human? Are you White or are you Human? Are you Asian, Hindu, Native, Latino, Hispanic, etc., or are you HUMAN?

[411]   This is the true revolution in my time! This is a true change in our political situation. As the old saying goes, *If you always do what you've always done, you'll always get what you've always gotten.* In order to achieve the restoration of our lost civilization, the enhancement of our present quality of life, the preservation of our artistic elements, freedom from negative corporate exploitation, and a Hip Hop way of life rooted in peace and prosperity, we are going to have to totally rethink our group identity. We are going to have to tell a different story about us and our activity in the World so that our children may experience a totally different reality than the one we are presently living today.

[412]   I find it a bit hypocritical to first protest against racism in words and then turn around and cling to the concept of race in deeds. If we are to ever eradicate racism from the minds of our children, we are going to have to think and act beyond the confinement of race and racial distinctions. If we are truly serious about peace, love and the unity of all people, we are going to have to place our humanity above our individual skin colors, and Hip Hop has the ability and opportunity to do just that.

[413]   As a free-thinking human being the questions that I ask of myself are, is the traditional African American lifestyle my actual lifestyle? I respect this lifestyle highly, but did I create this style of life for myself? Is this cultural lifestyle and racial distinction even healthy for me? What sustains my well-being and that of my children; is it the African American identity or is it Hip Hop? And those who do not live, eat and survive by way of Hip Hop may be exempt from this line of questioning.

⁴¹⁴   But for those of us who are Hip Hop, and have our being in Hip Hop, we must ask these questions seriously. Technically, I have a so-called West Indian heritage on my father's side. So why am I not exclusively claiming Trinidadian or Afro-Bajan (Barbados) as my ethnicity? Why do I not feel like a *Trini* connected to the struggles of my *Trini* people?

⁴¹⁵   Yes I feel some allegiance to the struggles of all Black people, but I am trained or educated to the struggles of the African American in particular. And the key word here is *trained*. In fact, most African Americans are genetically linked to Native Americans, so why am I not claiming a Native American heritage?

⁴¹⁶   I, along with millions of other African Americans, have a European genealogy as well; why do I not consider myself White? What if I lived amongst Asians, would I not feel like them as well? Yes, the genetic code of my bloodline would still create me to be whatever IT was, but my training (my education) would still have a profound effect upon what I thought of myself, regardless of my genetic makeup.

⁴¹⁷   The deeper questions here (with the achievement of our goals in mind) are, where do you begin your ethnic identity? Where do you start yourself culturally? Where do YOU begin politically? If we are to be truly reborn into a new people with new powers we are going to have to rethink our cultural start and political beginnings.

⁴¹⁸   We are going to have to rethink our ethnic identities, and this begins the true history of Hip Hop. In fact, we are going to have to pay more attention to the growth of the ethnicities to which we are already accustomed. Most people can't even keep up with the growth of the ethnicity to which they belong, meaning that, with all the new technologies and new innovations in medicine, along with the new archeological discoveries regarding the origins of human

beings, the ethnicity that you may think you are right now may even be in question. The birth of a new people is the origin of a new history.

[419] As the head of Harvard University's African-American Studies department, Professor Henry Louis Gates, found out after taking a DNA test to learn more about his heritage and ancestral family history, *I'm thinking I'm a Brady and maybe I'm from Nigeria, and here I am descended from some White woman...it's incredible!* ("In Our Blood," *Newsweek*, 6 February 2006)

[420] In the same Newsweek article, "In Our Blood," writer Claudia Kalb points out that *Our blood holds the secrets to who we are and increasingly, individuals, families and research scientists are using genetic testing to tell us what we don't already know.* In today's age of genetic research, certainty of ethnic identity is now questionable, or rather certainly not what you think.

[421] It seems that I am that which I think I am. I am what I have been trained or educated to be. I am my training. I am the story that I have accepted of myself, and such a story creates the character, values and habits of my repeated lifestyle. But this approach to my *self*-identity is largely common knowledge and not based upon science. However, the repetition of my daily activities either strengthens my genetic code or it rewrites it—and this is science.

[422] New genetic information is pointing to new discoveries and theories pertaining to human evolution and why people do what they do. New discoveries in molecular biology are showing that different (yet similar) species from different sides of the Earth will develop the same genetic solutions when confronted with the same natural challenges. How does this pertain to Hip Hop?

[423] It is now known that *there are no new genes arising every time a new species arises.* As Dr. Brian K. Hall, a

developmental biologist at Dalhousie University in Nova Scotia has pointed out, *Basically you take existing genes and process and modify them, and that's why humans and chimps can be 99 percent similar at the genome level.*

424 My observation is that if there are no *"new genes,"* if all that we need as humans already exists within us, that Nature makes slight adjustments to an already set number of genes to confront certain environmental challenges, then Hip Hop might have always existed genetically but our environment had to be such that our already existing Hip Hop genes could be *"switched on"* to confront our new environmental challenges. Hip Hop seems to be a genetic response to oppression.

425 *A new field called evo-devo* (evolution and development), *which studies the diversity of living forms, is showing that embryonic development powerfully shapes evolution.* ("From a Few Genes, Life's Myriad Shapes," *The New York Times,* French Edition, 30 June 2007)

426 What does this mean? *The New York Times* article by Carol Kaesuk Yoon continues, *Last year, Dr. Neil Shubin* [an evolutionary biologist at the University of Chicago at the Field Museum], *reported the discovery of a fossil fish on Ellesmere Island in northern Canada. They had found Tiktaalik, as they named the fish, after searching for six years.*

427 *They persisted for so long because they were certain that they had found the right age and kind of rock where a fossil of a fish trying to make the transition to life on land was likely to be found. And Tiktaalik appeared to be just such a fish, but it also had a few surprises for the researchers.*

428 *'Tiktaalik is special,' Dr. Shubin said. 'It has a flat head with eyes on top. It has gills and lungs. It's an animal that's exploring the interface between water and land.' But Tiktaalik was a truly stunning discovery because this water-*

loving fish bore wrists, an attribute thought to have been an innovation confined strictly to animals that had already made the transition to land. 'This was telling us that a piece of the toolkit, to make arms, legs, hands and feet, could very well be in fish limbs,' Dr. Shubin said.

[429]   *In other words, the genetic tools or toolkit genes for making limbs to walk on land might well have been present long before fish made that critical leap...The genetic tools to make fingers and toes were in place a long time...Lacking were the environmental conditions where these structures would be useful.*

[430]   *He added, 'Fingers arose when the right environment arose.' Major events in evolution like the transition from life in the water to life on land are not necessarily set off by the arising of the genetic mutations that will build the required body parts, or even the appearance of the body parts themselves, as had long been assumed. Instead, it is theorized that the right ecological situation, the right habitat in which such bold, new forms will prove to be particularly advantageous, may be what is required to set these major transitions in motion.*

[431]   Could Hip Hop be genetic? Could it be that Breakin, Emceein, Deejayin, Graffiti writing, and Beat Boxin are part of our genetic reactions to the urban environments in which we live and lived? Could Hip Hop be an ancient genetic response to the type of oppression and injustice we faced (and still face) on a daily basis? A kind of survival skill? Maybe.

[432]   Environment seems to have a lot more influence over the evolution of human survival abilities than we think. And when I say "environment" here I mean cultural environment, political environment, urban environment. According to today's scientific view, it is one's culture (one's environment) that also helps to affect certain genetic responses to one's survival and further development as a human being.

433   It seems that we and our new cultural environment (Hip Hop) are inter-connectedly growing together. We are all affecting it, and it is affecting us all. In fact, the Hiphoppa and Hip Hop's cultural development are indeed two aspects of the same response to urban environments.

434   From this view Hip Hop seems to be a genetic response to the pressures of urban life. As philosopher and ordained minister Nancey Murphy of Fuller Theological Seminary pointed out in a June 2007 *International Herald Tribune* article entitled, "Science and the Soul: Descartes Loses Force," by Cornelia Dean, *'All human capacities once attributed to the mind or soul are now being fruitfully studied as brain processes, or more accurately, I should say, processes involving the brain, the rest of the nervous system and other bodily systems, all interacting with the socio-cultural world.'*

435   Elsewhere in the article, Dean points out that, *As evolutionary biologists and cognitive neuroscientists peer ever deeper into the brain, they are discovering more and more genes, brain structures and other physical correlates to feelings like empathy, disgust and joy. That is, they are discovering physical bases for feelings from which moral sense emerges—not just in people but in other animals as well."*

436   This type of observation has led me to consider the physical nature of spiritual reality and how such a "nature" may relate to the existence of Hip Hop itself. Is morality a physical thing? Can your environment affect your sense of moral judgment on a genetic level? Can environmental conditions affect you genetically? The evidence seems to say yes, yes, yes, and of course yes! So who are we really? Culturally, we are only our education, we are the stories and the histories that we have been educated to accept and respect. But can we create and/or re-create ourselves today? Yes. And the re-creation of ourselves is the origin of our history.

[437] We can talk all day about the great civilization builders of our ancient heritage, but until we establish even greater works today than their ancient works of yesterday, how have we advanced the ancient heritage that we brag about today? If we cannot achieve greater civilizations than those of our ancestors, then let's finally face it, we are not of the same bloodline as those who have actually built cities and established civilizations, and we need to stop *fronting* about this!

[438] Without walking the walk, we degrade our ancestors every time we talk that talk about something they did that we can no longer do. Civilization is not a bunch of buildings and a marketplace. Civilization begins around a shared vision of a brighter future where everyone contributes to the peace and security of his or her neighbor. Civilization is first a level of mental achievement. We must first be civil if we are to become a true civilization. In fact, it is our civility that creates the aura of our specific civilization. However, civility is largely based upon the laws human groups adopt for themselves and whether they abide by such laws or not.

[439] In the United States the whole concept of race and racial distinction (which underlines the identity of ethnic cultures) was largely created by the United States' naturalization laws, laws which, according to Ian F. Haney López, have even *shaped the physical features evident in our [American] society.*

[440] As Mr. López explains, *Laws have directly shaped the physical appearance of people in the United States by limiting entrance to certain physical types and by altering the range of marital choices available to people here. What we look like, the literal and 'racial' features we in this country exhibit, is to a large extent the product of legal rules and decisions. Race is not, however, simply a matter of physical appearance and ancestry. Instead, it is primarily a function of the meanings*

given to these. On this level, too, law creates races.

441   The concluding point here is that as Hiphoppas we can establish a new nation, a new tribe, even a new race; it's been done before and we are positioned at this time to do it again. However, before the creation of our Hip Hop nation, we as Hip Hop scholars studying and building Hip Hop as a sustainable community are going to have to reexamine our very existence as a People and above these arbitrary race distinctions, finally create and then define ourselves for ourselves. This would be the true history of Hip Hop—the story of our triumphant SELF-CREATION!

TRACK FIVE

442   As stated earlier, the origins of Hip Hop seem to be more "Black" than "African American," and such an observation seems to also manifest itself historically. We cannot really discuss the "origins" of Hip Hop without taking a look at the intentions of the 1950s and 1960s Civil Rights Movement regarding our intentions today. When you begin to approach Hip Hop as an attitude and not just a music genre you can even go back further to the 1930s and 1940s to really get an accurate assessment of the first causes and origins of modern Hip Hop today. When I look at people like Paul Robeson, for example, I cannot deny his Hip Hopness, his defiance in the face of growing criticism toward his political views and allegiances, his skill as an orator, his intellect, his sports abilities, his activism and love for the Truth. This man was indeed the Hip Hop of his time!

443   Loved by the whole World and making a very good living as an artist/actor, Paul Robeson, clearly ahead

of his time in thinking and in living, would still point out the injustices perpetrated by the United States against "the Negro." After speaking out publicly all over the World about the unjust conditions of Africans in America and expressing his respect for the people of communist Russia he was stripped of his passport for eight years—an event which clearly dampened his ability to work and stifled his very successful performing career. Standing outside of the Supreme Court after winning his passport back Mr. Robeson had this to say: *The question raised by the State Department as to my political opinion bears the question of whether one who wants to sing and act can have, as a citizen, political opinion. And in attacking me, they suggested that when I was abroad I spoke out against injustices to the Negro people in the United States; I certainly did! And the Supreme Court Justice just ruled that—in the segregation cases—that World opinion had a lot to do with that ruling. That our children, Negro children, can go to school like anybody else in the South, I'm very proud to have been part of directing World opinion to precisely that condition! The second, that I fight for the independence of the colonialized people of Africa...the colored peoples of the World assembly made it clear that nobody is going to tell them what to do, they're going to have their independence; I'm proud of that! The third, that I fight for peace and friendship with the Soviet Union. At Geneva the President of the United States made it clear that nobody wants war with the Soviet Union. No American wants to fight them, and I presume certainly the Negro people of the United States don't want any war with them either! Nobody does because we want peace and friendship in the World!*

[444] This attitude is basic to Hip Hop's visionary, forward-thinkers throughout history. During the 1950s, 1960s and 1970s our parents expounded upon a lot of things concerning social conditions, social engineering

and their vision of a perfect society, many of whom were "blacklisted" and even wrongly imprisoned for doing so, and presently remain enslaved (some on death row) even as I write these words. For them, I can never abandon *The Dream*. Others can, because they never really knew Kwame Ture personally or even spiritually. They never knew Dr. King, or Malcolm X, or Elijah Muhammad, or Medgar Evers. They never met their children or donated anything toward their organizations or the continued legacies of these great ancestral leaders. They never even really studied them or their words to get at the true meaning of what was being said and expressed collectively.

445   For most people, these ancestors are simply characters of the past that bear little relevance in the fast-paced, technological, consumer-driven World of today. And as a result, the hard-fought freedoms and "Rights" that our ancestors gave their lives to establish deteriorate for lack of knowledge as to the struggles to achieve such freedoms and Rights and how to maintain them. The very attitude and worldview of the free man is what has been lost to us, and this is why many find the idea of Hip Hop as a new civilization upon the earth so difficult to grasp.

446   This is why and how the police can treat us like anything; they know that we have no leadership, no army or other protection. They know that we don't know our "rights," nor our true history and that we are really unaware of our own mothers' and fathers' struggles and victories over such injustices.

447   For if your father overcame the same injustices that you now face, shouldn't you be able to overcome them as well? Why are we still going through the same injustices that our parents, and their parents, and their parents' parents' parents went through?

448   At what point do we advance beyond the conditions

of our parents and ancestors? At what point do we fulfill the *"dreams"* that our ancestors died for? Do we not realize that every generation has a duty to fulfill the *dreams* of the generation that has come before them? Do we not realize that it is our sacred duty to even advance upon the thinking of our parents and ancestors?

⁴⁴⁹ But to do this we have to know what was said and what was done, and when it was said and how it was done. We have to study and hear from our revolutionary parents as well as from our conformist parents to get a complete picture as to how our heritage may be continued. We have to interpret, decipher and decode the hidden meanings and descriptions of our comedian parents (for example) to get a real glimpse of their real space-time reality and how it may have affected us and the way we think or don't think today.

⁴⁵⁰ Take comedy legend Dick Gregory, for example. In the 1970s, he stated, *So many White folks in America wanna know, 'What's wrong with them? Niggas must be crazy!' Naw baby, understand one thing, niggas got more sense today than ever before in the history of America. And when niggas was basically crazy that's when he thought we had good sense. Yeah, that's right! When he runnin' around goosin' me in the rump, rubbin' my head, 'come here jabbo,' 'yeah yessa boss,' when I was basically crazy. Now we talkin' bout gettin' our thang together, gettin' our sanity together baby. ONCE YOU GET YOUR MIND TOGETHER BABY CAN'T NOBODY DEAL WITH YOU! That's what this convention is all about, getting our mind together. When we leave here it's gonna be a different day!*

⁴⁵¹ One thing is for sure, our parents saw the vision of a new nation; they were indeed divided over the issue of "separation" or "integration" but the direction was clear—it was "NATION TIME!" It was time to *GET YOUR MIND TOGETHER!*

452   Whether that new nation was a transformed United States or an entirely new land somewhere in the World, the idea was never to stay in the same shape we found ourselves in post-slavery.

453   In my view, if we are to truly achieve peace on earth and the end of racial hostility, we are going to have to give up the idea of separate races, which is the root cause of so many social ills. If we can teach our children to identify human beings by the content of their character and not by race or ethnic origin, we may one day look upon racism as we look upon cannibalism or human sacrifice today. However, we are not there yet. As far as our parents were concerned their debate focused upon the issues of their time, namely, do we integrate or separate? All of it was *civil rights* but some of us wanted access to what the American mainstream offered and others of us wanted to build our "own thing."

454   Those who wanted to build their "own thing" were more likely to frequent the "Black Power" movement, while those who wanted American mainstream access remained with the distinction "Civil Rights." Hip Hop actually gets its start in both movements; however, the driving force and essence of Hip Hop seems to be inspired by the "Black Power" movement of the 1960s and 1970s. Everything about early Hip Hop points to the views of those whose voices were loud in the "Black Power" movement.

455   *Black Power* was a phrase that denoted Black self-governance. This powerful phrase, *"Black Power,"* was first introduced to the World by author Richard Wright as the title of a book that he had written after visiting Ghana in 1954.

456   The prophet Stokely Carmichael (Kwame Ture) popularized this phrase as a call for African independence worldwide! Ture and others of the 1950s and 1960s believed

that White racist Americans would never be fair and just to the Africans in America and so the only solution was *"organized revolution."*

457   The prophet Ture declared, *Don't be afraid! Don't be ashamed! We want BLACK POWER! And we don't have to be ashamed of it! We have stayed here and we have begged the president! We begged the federal government! That's all we been doing—begging, begging! It's time we stand up and take over! We have to do what every group in this country did; we gotta take over the communities where we outnumber people so we can have decent jobs! So we can have decent houses! So we can have decent roads! So we can have decent schools! So we can have decent justice!"* This was and still is the real meaning of Black Power! It was about Black/African people governing themselves.

458   Ture believed, like others, that Black people could govern themselves, but that first they needed their own land away from White racism, injustice and infiltration. In the early days of the *Black Power* movement it was clear that Black liberation began with Black Nationalism (Black people governing their own independent nation) and that such a vision would come with a bloody price.

459   As the prophet Malcolm X pointed out, *Revolution is bloody! Revolution is hostile! Revolution knows no compromise! Revolution overturns and destroys everything that gets in its way...It's based on land. A revolutionary wants land so he can set up his OWN NATION! These Negroes ain't asking for any nation, they're trying to crawl back on the plantation! When you want a nation, that's called nationalism.*

460   However, even though our King agreed with the basic social and political ideas of *Black Power/Black Nationalism* he was against any revolutionary violence or Black separatism. Dr. King, in his early days, had a profound and unshaken faith in America as one racially unified nation

that included the equality of *"the Negro."* He advocated a bloodless revolution of integration.

461   The King advised, *In the process of gaining our rightful place we must not be guilty of wrongful deeds. Let us not seek to satisfy our thirst for freedom by drinking from the cup of bitterness and hatred. We must forever conduct our struggle on the high plain of dignity and discipline. We must not allow our creative protest to degenerate into physical violence. Again and again we must rise to the majestic heights of meeting physical force with Soul Force!* I believe Hip Hop is that Soul Force.

462   Hip Hop is the realization and combination of ALL of our ancestors' dreams, hopes, strategies and aspirations toward freedom, justice and equality. We are the achievement of our ancestors; we are their hopes. We cannot divorce ourselves from the struggles of our parents, grandparents and ancestors and expect to live in peace. They've spent their entire lives developing the little bits of advice we receive in fragments today.

463   While others are reading all sorts of scholarly and academically accepted writings on race relations by well-educated scholars on such matters, I prefer to read the prophet H. Rap Brown's 1969 book *Die Nigger Die* super-historically and really feel the space-time reality of my ancestors and their socio-political experiences.

464   Brown writes and advises, *We must learn that <u>Black is not a color but the way you think</u>. If we are to succeed in The Struggle we must eliminate the significance that we have assigned to color in our community...Among Black people color can have no value, no significance. <u>Commitment will determine the value of individuals.</u>*

465   And this is not to say that H. Rap Brown was insinuating the abandonment of race; not at all. However, his approach to race (especially to the Black race) is interesting

to study because his description of his time is strikingly similar to the conditions in our time, at least for those who claim Hip Hop as their lifestyle and culture.

466   He writes, *You grow up in Black America and it's like living in a pressure cooker. Babies become men without going through childhood. And when you become a man, you got nothing to look forward to and nothing to look back on. So what do you make it on? The wine bottle, the reefer or Jesus. A taste of grape, the weed or the cross. These are our painkillers.*

467   *I knew dudes who were old men by the time they were seven. That's the age when little white kids are dreaming about fairy princesses and Cinderella and playing in tree houses and wondering whether they want two cars or four cars when they grow up. We didn't have time for all that. Didn't even have time for a childhood. If you acted like a child, you didn't survive and that's all there was to it.*

468   Brown continues: *White folks get all righteous and wonder why Black people steal and gamble. Same reason white folks do. We need money, because society says you must have it to keep from starving. If you got it, you eat. If you don't, tough. But white people are able to make their stealing and gambling legitimate. White man'll sell you a $20 suit for $50 and call it good business. What he actually did was steal $30. White man'll buy a watch for $5.00 sell it for $49.95 and call the difference profit. Profit is a nice word for stealing, which the society has legitimatized.*

469   *Catholics go to church every week and gamble, but they call it Bingo. The Pope blesses 'em, so it's all right. The state of Nevada is built on a stack of cards and a roulette wheel, but that's okay, 'cause it's white folks that passed the law saying it was okay. But you let us get over in the corner of the alley with some dice and try to make a little profit and here comes the police, the judge, the jailer and the sociology student. We get thrown into jail for gambling or stealing. White folks go to*

Congress for stealing and they call that democracy. America is
a country that makes you want things, but doesn't give you the
means to get those things.

470   Sound familiar? This is Hip Hop's American history. This is what every Hip Hop American child should know. And again, our children should be exposed to these ideas just as historian Howard Zinn suggests. As scholars we must search out, study and teach a wide range of *undaground* views in order to get at the Truth regarding what our Hip Hop ancestry was actually saying.

471   Many things could not be spoken publicly and/or directly. All of our elders were correct in their approaches toward solid solutions for our people. However, they could not see what we (their children) were to find out in the years to come. What was a secret to them in the 1960s became common knowledge to us in the 1980s! What they were killed for we now do openly and frequently. Even you (my future) shall learn of things about Hip Hop today that we (your past) did not know in our time.

472   In my time, we have different tools and new evidence for the investigation of a history that our parents simply did not have. For example, we now know that J. Edgar Hoover (head of the Federal Bureau of Investigation) organized a *Counter Intelligence Program* from 1956–1971 against those Civil Rights leaders and Black Nationalist groups that he felt were political dissidents or "communists."

473   We now know that the F.B.I. under the direction of J. Edgar Hoover used blackmail, illegal drugs, informants, false propaganda, wiretapping and even spiritual warfare strategies like astrology and mysticism to *prevent the rise of a Black messiah*.

474   They had thought the "Black Messiah" was already a grown man but in fact, the "Black Messiah" was still a young infant hidden randomly amongst the

People themselves.

[475]   They (the F.B.I.) felt that a "Black Messiah" was about to rise and that such a "Messiah" would unify and electrify the Black Nationalist movement. And even though they felt that the prophet Malcolm X was most likely that messiah, it was the prophet Stokely Carmichael (Kwame Ture) that they really had their eye upon.

[476]   He (Kwame Ture) was the one who influenced Dr. King to begin using the term "Black" when referring to African Americans as opposed to "Negro." Stokely Carmichael argued for *Black* (African) independence while the King argued for *Negro* integration into the American mainstream.

[477]   Ture would say, *We gotta build so much strength in the building of OUR community that if they come to get one person they gonna have to mess with us ALL!*

[478]   Our King, however, would argue, *When a People are mired in oppression, they realize deliverance only when they have accumulated enough power to enforce change. The powerful never lose opportunities, they remain available to them. The powerless, on the other hand, never experience opportunity; it is always arriving at a later time. The nettlesome task of Negroes today is to discover how to organize our strength into compelling power so that government cannot elude our demands. We must develop from strength a situation in which the government finds it wise and prudent to collaborate with us.*

[479]   But Malcolm X would add, *You know the best way to get rid of segregation? The White man is more afraid of separation than he is of integration. Segregation means that he puts you away from him, but not far enough for you to be out of his jurisdiction. Separation means you're gone! And the White man will integrate faster than he'll let you separate.*

[480]   As Hiphoppas we absorbed ALL OF IT. Yes, we were clearly American citizens and proud of the heritage

laid down by our elders and ancestors; however, America would still never treat Black and Brown people as equals with Whites, and this injustice caused us (even Whites) to develop alternative ways to survive within a society that basically ignored the Black and Brown experience.

481   These experiences helped to cause the cultural beginnings of Hip Hop. For even though *Black Power* was clearly about Black self-governance, such governance clearly included the liberation of ALL people struggling to survive.

482   As revolutionary Kathleen Cleaver has stated, *Everybody knows that ALL the People don't have liberties, ALL the People don't have freedom, ALL the People don't have justice, and ALL the People don't have power, so that means that none of us do! Take this country and change it! Turn it upside down! And put the last first and the first last! NOT JUST FOR BLACK PEOPLE BUT FOR ALL PEOPLE!*

483   The Black Panther Party, clearly an organization set up for the protection and liberation of Black people, headed by Huey P. Newton, laid out a Black agenda that was to lead to the creation of a Black nation/state.

484   Newton pointed out that, *The Black Panther Party calls for freedom and the power to determine OUR own destiny! The Black Panther Party calls for full employment for ALL OUR PEOPLE. The Black Panther Party calls for an end to the capitalistic exploitation of OUR community! The Black Panther Party calls for decent housing for ALL PEOPLE! The Black Panther Party calls for an educational system that will tell U.S. the true facts about this decadent society.*

485   The Black Panther Party agenda would continue with the demand for Black men to be exempt from military service, the immediate end to police brutality, freedom for all Black men held in federal, state, county and city prisons

and jails, all Black people (when brought to court) to be tried by a jury of their peer group or people from their Black communities, and lastly LAND!

[486]   And although the Black Panther Party's agenda was clearly about the upliftment of Black people, their 10-point agenda dealt with the basic humanity, dignity and quality of life for anyone faced with institutionalized injustice.

[487]   Everyone said it in their own way, in their own words and from their own intellectual positions, but the general theme of Black Power was always about the building of a new nation—a new civilization. Whether it was the rebuilding of America as that new nation or the establishment of a new African/Black nation, the goal was clear; it was NATION TIME!

[488]   As aide to Dr. King, Reverend Jesse Jackson would say in 1972 at the National Black Convention in Gary, Indiana, echoing the words of poet LeRoi Jones (a.k.a Amiri Baraka), IT'S NATION TIME!

[489]   Jesse Jackson would say, *WHAT TIME IS IT?* And the crowd would say, *"IT'S NATION TIME!"*

[490]   And Jackson would continue, *When we come together, what time is it?* *"IT'S NATION TIME!"*

[491]   *When we respect each other, what time is it?* *"IT'S NATION TIME!"*

[492]   *When we get our self-confidence, what time is it?* *"IT'S NATION TIME!"*

[493]   *When we form our own political party, what time is it?* *"IT'S NATION TIME!"*

[494]   Even the Mayor of Gary, Indiana (Richard Hatcher), at the same convention in 1972, would say, *I believe that the 70s will be the decade of an INDEPENDENT BLACK POLITICAL THRUST! How should we respond?*

[495]   *Will we walk in unity or disperse in a thousand different directions?*

⁴⁹⁶ *Will we stand for <u>principles</u> or settle for a mess of pottage?*

⁴⁹⁷ *Will we maintain our <u>integrity</u> or will we succumb to the Man's temptation?*

⁴⁹⁸ *Will we act like <u>Free Black Men</u> or like timid shivering chattel?*

⁴⁹⁹ As a collective strategy toward nation building, our elders laid out the ground work for how such a nation could be organized. Our King advocated *Organization, Peace, Discipline, Black Self-Esteem, Financial Independence* and *Justice.*

⁵⁰⁰ Kathleen Cleaver advocated *Liberty, Freedom, Power* and *Justice.* Malcolm X advocated *Self-Defense, Independence, Self-Worth* and *Justice.*

⁵⁰¹ Kwame Ture advocated *Self-Governance, Organization, Revolution* and *Justice.*

⁵⁰² The Black Panther Party advocated *Freedom, Self-Determination, Employment, Fair Trade, Decent Housing* and *Justice.*

⁵⁰³ Jesse Jackson advocated *Unity, Respect, Self-Confidence, Political Activism* and *Justice.*

⁵⁰⁴ Mayor Hatcher saw *Independence* and advocated *Unity, Principles, Integrity, Courage* and of course, he too stood for *JUSTICE!*

⁵⁰⁵ These are just some of the most important guidelines in the actual building of the nation that our elders and prophets of the *Black Power* movement saw. Unfortunately in my time "African Americans" have not yet lived up to such a vision of independence.

⁵⁰⁶ So where and what is the "African American" agenda and vision? We need unity, and we need it NOW! However, what the so-called "African American community" cannot seem to achieve for themselves, Hip Hop can and will achieve for itself. I believe that Hip Hop has the ability

to provide the cultural structure necessary for our next level of freedom.

507   So I say again, if we don't know to ourselves who WE are, where WE have come from, where WE are going, and how WE are going to get there, then WE are not a group at all. We are a mass of individuals identified exclusively by the fact that WE all have no direction and no vision.

508   WE, at this level of existence, are indeed a subservient people (slaves) living at the expense and permission of those who have a direction and a vision for themselves. It is not that they enslaved us; it is more the fact that we reduce ourselves to slaves by betraying our own principles as well as one another.

509   True freedom seems to not only be about breaking the chains from one's hands, feet and mind, true freedom seems to also be spiritual; it seems to be about self-creation and self-governance. Beyond the weak and temporal distinctions that are formed by physical senses, Hip Hop as a collective consciousness has already formed stronger similarities amongst all of the races of the World by allowing the inner and more permanent reality of human expression to be the judge of identity and value amongst human beings. It is clear to all thinking Hiphoppas that race hatred and ethnic prejudice must be removed from the minds of children if as adults they are to live together in peace and domestic tranquility. I believe that Hip Hop is the very environment to teach such a perception.

510   The ability to create and then govern one's self seems to be the continuation of our struggle toward freedom. For us, self-creation is the ultimate state of freedom, and we have another opportunity with our Hip Hop activity in the World to re-create ourselves into a new global civilization. This would not only be evidence of our freedom today, but it would also advance our

political maturity because this would not be the first time that "Africans in America" have set up an alternative self-governing community in the World.

511   Other attempts at such a vision didn't always seem to end up the way everyone envisioned, and as "African Americans" we must ask ourselves why? What can we learn from the Africans who migrated north to Nova Scotia Canada (1782–1785) after fighting alongside the British in the "American Revolution?" Will we ever achieve another Africville again? Liberia was another place, set up on the continent of Africa by the American Colonization Society (ACS), for newly freed and free African Americans in 1821. What can we learn here?

512   After the American Revolution, free and enslaved Africans in America faced continued racism and inequality. Unlike today, the assimilation of free Africans in America into the White American society was "out of the question." Therefore, the only solution at the time was the complete separation of Black Africans and White Americans. This led to the concept of Africans in America returning to Africa.

513   In 1815, an "African American" Quaker and maritime entrepreneur, Paul Cuffee, financed and captained a voyage to Sierra Leone where he helped a group of Africans living in America to establish themselves there. Other Africans would continue to migrate north into Nova Scotia, Canada, and from Nova Scotia travel to Sierra Leone and other parts of Africa.

514   Paul Cuffee believed that Africans in America could "rise to be a people" in Africa, rather than in America with its system of slavery and legal limits on African freedom. Cuffee envisioned an African trade network organized by Westernized Africans who would return to Africa to help build it up.

515   Inspired by Mr. Cuffee's vision, sympathetic White

separatists formed the American Colonization Society to repatriate those Africans living in the United States who would volunteer to settle in Africa.

516   To form a place for Africans in America to return to Africa, the American Colonization Society sent Dr. Eli Ayres, aided by U.S. naval officer Lieutenant Robert F. Stockton, to purchase land along the coast of Africa. Somehow, Lieutenant Stockton led the negotiations with leaders of the Dey and Bassa tribes, who lived in the area of Cape Mesurado.

517   The Dey and Bassa tribes' people were reluctant to surrender their lands to Stockton. So, at gunpoint, Stockton forcefully persuaded the natives to accept trade goods, weapons, and rum worth $300.00 for a 36-mile-long and 3-mile-wide strip of coastal land.

518   In 1824 the settlement called "Christopolis" was renamed "Monrovia" after American President James Monroe, and the colony was formally called "Liberia" (the free land); possibly inspired by the term "liberation." Liberia established a constitution known as the *Constitution, Government, and Digest of the Laws of Liberia*. Sovereign authority and power, however, remained with the American Colonization Society (a privately owned company).

519   The Africans in America who were originally sent from the plantations of the United States to establish this new "African American" nation were hand-picked and considered safe for the project. These "African Americans" (or "Americo-Liberians") formed an elite society which established the same inequality for Africans in Africa that Africans in America were trying to overcome. These "African Americans" basically replicated the same social inequality and political injustice that had limited their own lives in the United States.

520   In fact, this unjust situation helped to sabotage the

"African unity" plans of Marcus Garvey. Liberia became the center of confusion when diamond companies assisted in the funding of civil wars in neighboring Sierra Leone and in Liberia itself. More recently, Liberian President Charles Taylor was accused of using his government and military to assist in the moving and sales of "blood diamonds," diamonds that mainstream rappers ignorantly promoted to the African American community during the 1990s.

521   So, is this what happens when African Americans govern a country? On another note, why are Africans in America so ignorant of Liberia if Liberia was set up as a refuge for Africans in America? Regardless of the condition of Liberia itself, why are African Americans not even interested in governing, or even participating in a land said to be established for them?

522   Another, yet different example of African American self-governance comes through the story of the Hebrew Israelites. Bev Smith, a respected figure in the African American community, was the weekly host of a television show called *Our Voices* which aired on the Black Entertainment Television (BET) network. In one episode she investigated the Hebrew Israelites:

523   *Hi, I'm Bev Smith, and I've traveled to the Holy Land and a very special place called Damona, Israel to bring you this special edition of* Our Voices. *Since 1967 hundreds of African Americans have been returning to Israel stating that they have a claim, a rightful claim as Hebrew Israelites, to the holy land. The debate continues as the U.S. and Israeli governments ponder the question, why Israel and not Africa?*

524   Mrs. Smith continues, *Israel: it's called the holy of holy lands in the world, the land of milk and honey. The place where Moses led former slaves out of bondage. It's a land where politics and religion have gone hand in hand for thousands of years.*

⁵²⁵ *It's no surprise that a group of African Americans, descendants of slaves themselves, would seek out the promised land for their freedom. Frustrated with America's racism, and feeling disenfranchised from American society, they journeyed to Israel for a taste of freedom. I wanted to know why these Blacks felt they had a claim to Israel. So I went to the city of Damona, where they settled, and I learned that it began with a dream. A vision had by Ben Ammi, the man they call the anointed spiritual leader of the African Hebrew Israelites.*

⁵²⁶   Mrs. Smith then asks Ben Ammi Ben-Israel, *How did you know that the words and its vision* [were] *truly sent from GOD?*

⁵²⁷   Ben Ammi Ben-Israel responded in a calm and honest voice, saying, *I did not know, ya know, that's the key element to faith. See, the words were so powerful when the angel Gabriel came to bring the message that it was time to start the journey back, I did not know. As a matter of fact, I felt like Moses in the wilderness of sin. I really wanted to talk a little bit more to Gabriel and to ask him to show me his credentials and to pose the question to the creator, how would I know if these things would truly come to pass? But that was it, I had to walk out on the water by faith, not knowing if these things truly would come to pass or not.*

⁵²⁸   *There was no further message at that time, except that it was time to declare the exodus in 1967. There I was in February of 1966, pondering how would I convince any significant number of African Americans to in fact leave the United States in less than two years.*

⁵²⁹   Bev Smith then asks, *But did you question in your soul and your spirit, why Israel and not Africa? Or was it one and the same to you?*

⁵³⁰   Ben Ammi responds, *At that time, ya know, I knew that Israel was northeastern Africa, only to be separated by the Suez Canal. But there was so many things that I did not know*

at that time when the Word of GOD did come.

531   The point here is that the opportunities for self-governance seem to keep returning to the African American community, and each time only a few African Americans ever heed the call. Those African Americans that do seize upon such opportunities for real political and cultural independence always seem to have to divorce themselves from the "African American" community, becoming an entirely different sect of people altogether.

532   The question, then, for us today is, are we prepared to *heed the call* in our generation? Can we create and then govern ourselves? This would be the true origin of Hip Hop, a civilization established first as art in the minds of enlightened African Americans but then manifested as a raceless civilization of self-expressed human beings. Like butterflies evolving from caterpillars, we would go from being African and American to fully human, from being European to fully human, from Asian, from Latino, from aboriginal to fully human.

533   Such a civilization would stand as a beacon of true light to all the World because finally it would be your GOD-given talent and innate abilities that would propel you toward varying degrees of prosperity and social admiration. Corruption would be lessened dramatically because leaders would be chosen not on the basis of what they propose to do, but instead upon what they have already done. Talent, not inheritance, would rule.

534   Such a civilization would reward talent and so talent would flourish. In such a civilization Health would be the law and our Hip Hop government would teach health and provide its citizenry with basic healthcare. The same would apply to Love, yes, Love! Love can be taught and rewarded by the courts, even modified with each successive generation. Hate would be against the law; like rape it would

be criminal to hate.

[535]   In a truly unified society where humanity reigns over individual races, the pursuit of human awareness would be the norm and properly taught in public education. Such an educational system backed up by an impartial court system that rewarded talent and promoted human well-being above individual races would then produce the best minds in the World and all life would benefit from such an enlightened nation.

[536]   Such a civilization would honor the ancestry of every race and put humanity in direct relation with the unified fabric of the universe itself. THIS WOULD BE THE TRUE ORIGIN OF HIP HOP! There it is.

SHOUT OUTS

1   *Way back in the days when Hip Hop began, with Coke La Rock, Kool Herc and then Bam. B-boys ran to the latest jam but when it got shot up they went home and said damn! There's got to a better way to hear our music everyday, b-boys getting blown away but coming outside anyway!*

2   *They tried again outside in Cedar park, Power from the streetlight made the place dark. But yo, they didn't care, they turned it out, I know a few understand what I'm talking about.*

3   *Remember, Bronx River rolling thick with Kool DJ Red Alert and Chuck Chillout on the mix. When Afrika Islam was rocking the jams, on the other the other side of town was a kid named Flash.*

4   *Paterson and Milbrook projects, "Casanova all over," you couldn't stop it! The Nine Lives Crew, the Cypress Boys, the real Rock Steady taking out these toys!*

5   *As odd as it looked, as wild as it seemed, I didn't hear a peep from a place called Queens. It was '76 to 1980, the dreads in Brooklyn was crazy! You couldn't bring out your set with no Hip Hop 'cause the pistols would pop, pop, pop, pop!*

6   *So why don't you wise up; show all the people in the place that you are wack! Instead of trying to take out LL you need to take your homeboys off the crack! 'Cause if you don't that means their nerves will become shocked, and that would leave the job up to my own Scott La Rock! And he's from the South Bronx, the South South Bronx!*

7   The Gospel of Hip Hop is not an advertisement

of new ideas, it is the documentation of ideas already in action. By studying and teaching the Gospel of Hip Hop, True Hiphoppas raise their self-worth and become serious teachers/scholars of the Hip Hop arts and sciences. In addition, the Gospel of Hip Hop sets the foundation for Hip Hop's spiritual independence and culturally organizes Hip Hop's already growing international community.

[8] This *Gospel of Hip Hop* is the first of three instruments. Mastery of its *Overstandings* remains the only authority needed to teach Hip Hop. The Gospel of Hip Hop presents a rigorous course of self-improvement leading to personal reinvention—that's all.

[9] Self-creation is the center of our ministry, and it took many years to arrive at this conclusion. Many people contributed to the creation of this instrument, which represents the best and most authentic Hip Hop minds of my time.

[10] Therefore, at this time I would like to thank those people and organizations that intellectually and creatively influenced the creation of not only this *Gospel of Hip Hop*, but also the establishment of Hip Hop and the Temple of Hip Hop itself.

[11] The following names should be studied and remembered. These people either shared ideas, assisted, or inspired KRS in some way, or gave direct information that helped to establish this *gospel* for Hip Hop. In the tradition of our culture it is at the end of a project that one gives a *shout out* to those who assisted directly or indirectly to the completion of the project.

[12] Therefore, with sincere gratitude let us take this time to first acknowledge the *old-timers* who influenced (in one way or another) the creation of Hip Hop itself. Let us acknowledge those who helped us to flush out and articulate GOD's vision for Hip Hop Kulture, those whose names and/

or work may never be mentioned in the so-called *histories of hip-hop,* but whose contribution and participation has made Hip Hop's existence possible in the World.

¹³ Shout out to the original Breakers, Poppers, Lockers, b-boys and b-girls: the Dynamic Breakers, the Nigga Twins, Mr. Bubbles, Don Camelot, Pee Wee Dance, B-boys In Action, the Beat Street Dancers, Salsoul, Electric Force, Mr. Freeze, Boogaloo Shrimp, Shabba-Doo, Poppin' Pete, Crazy Legs, Mr. Wiggles, Pop Master Fabel, Rock Steady Crew, Pop-O-Matics, New York City Breakers, the Herculords, the L.A. Breakers, Demons of the Mind, Float Committee, Dennis Vasquez (the original "Rubber Band Man"), the Crazy Commandos, the Electric Company, Fred "Rerun" Berry, Tyrone Hamlet (a.k.a Lock-a-tron), and the Breeze Team.

¹⁴ Shout out to the original Emcees and Emcee crews: Coke La Rock, I-Roy, U-Roy, the Last Poets, the Cold Crush Four, the Romantic Fantastic Five, Funky Four Plus One More, Keith Cowboy, Kevy Kev, the Soul Sonic Force, Mercedes Ladies, the Treacherous Three MC's, Jimmy Spicer, Pebblie Poo, Shock Dell, the Disco Four, Rammellzee, Kurtis Blow, Queen Lisa Lee, the Cosmic Force, Divine Sounds, Dr. Jekyll & Mr. Hyde, the Furious Five, the Get Fresh Crew, DJ Hollywood, Lovebug Starski, Kool Moe Dee, the Galaxy Crew, Busy Bee, the Force MCs, Spoonie G, Run-DMC, LL Cool J, the Beastie Boys, MC Shan, UTFO, Double Trouble, Too Short, Just-Ice, T La Rock, Big Daddy Kane, Chubb Rock, Digital Underground, Lord Finesse, Eric B. & Rakim, Kool G Rap, Ice-T, Boogie Down Productions, Leaders of the New School, A Tribe Called Quest, Tone Loc, Super Cat, Poor Righteous Teachers, Salt-n-Pepa, Jazzy Jeff and the Fresh Prince, Dana Dane, 3rd Bass, Shinehead, Audio Two, the Ghetto Boys, 2 Live Crew, Sweet Tee, Heavy D

& the Boyz, MC Lyte, Gang Starr, Shabba Ranks, Public Enemy, Jaz-O, MC Mitchski, Stetsasonic, Roxanne Shanté, Brand Nubian, the Jungle Brothers, Schoolly D, X-Clan, Special Ed, Ultramagnetic MCs, Niggaz With Attitude, Tiger, Major Mackerel, Yellowman, Whodini, Masta Ace, and the Boogie Boys.

[15]   Shout out to the original Graffiti writers: Cornbread, Taki 183, Super Kool, Phase II, Stay High 149, Ban II, Frank 207, P-Nut 2, Chi Chi 133, Sonny 107, Barbara 62, Eve 62, Kase 2, Cay 161, Butch 2, Stitch 1, Stick 1, Hash 161, El Marko, Pray, Tracy 168, Presweet, Flasher, Skeme, Iz the Wiz, Dondi, Rammellzee, Mitch 77, Futura 2000, Seen, OE, Cap, Med, NOC, Comet, Lady Pink, Blade, Zephyr, Crash, Kel, Duro, Rose, Daze, Caz, Ket, OBE, Chico, Stash, Stem 1, Kaos, Gusto, Chain 3, Quick, Ase, Mack, Lee, Heist, Kel 139, Dez, Rasta, Junior 161, G Man, T-Kid, Cope Two, Quik, Revolt, Bio, Mare, Dream, Rif, Deen, Claw, Twist, Bizaro, Giant, Zore, Rican, Mase, Maze, Naser, Cat, Crane, Brim, BG 183, Crack, KR, Delta, Papo 184, Sharp, Revs, Cost, Myzer, Easy, Josh, and Vulcan.

[16]   Shout out to the original Deejays: Kool DJ Herc, Mandingo, El Marko, Elvis 007, DJ Afrika Bambaataa, Grandmaster Flash, the Smith Brothers, DJ Maboya, Grandmaster Flowers, Johnny Thunderbird, Pete DJ Jones, DJ Plumber, JoJo, Lovebug Starski, Whiz Kid, Mr. Magic, DJ Wanda Dee, DJ Dee, Mean Gene, the Disco Twins, Disco King Mario, GrandWizzard Theodore, DJ Eddie Cheeba, DJ Jazzy Jay, Afrika Islam, D.ST (DXT), DJ Charlie Chase, DJ Breakout, AJ Scratch, DJ Stevie Steve, Lady B, DJ Marley Marl, DJ Chuck Chillout, Cut Master DC, Special K, Teddy Ted, DJ Red Alert, DJ Scott La Rock, DJ Cash Money, Half Pint, DNA, Hank Love, Craig Mack, DJ Kid Capri, Mix Master Ice, DJ Scratch,

DJ Brucie B., Jam Master Jay, DJ King Tech and DJ Sway, Tim Westwood, DJ Kenny Parker, DJ Khaled, DJ Premier, DJ Jazzy Jeff, and DJs Max and Dave.

[17] Shout out to the original Beat Boxers: Doug E. Fresh, Biz Markie, Greg Nice, (the Original) DMX, Emanon, K-Love, Human Jock Box, the Fat Boyz, Rahzel, D.R.E.S. the BEATnik, and Click Tha Supah Latin.

[18] Shout out to the original Hip Hop fashion entrepreneurs: Dapper Dan, Rashad, Ron Mishon Creative Fashion One, Jew Man, Cross Colours, Karl Kani, FUBU, Phat Farm, Meoshe, Sean Jean, Mark Ecko, ENYCE and Lugz.

[19] Special recognition goes out to Richard Pryor, the Wayans Brothers, Chris Rock, Kid 'n Play, Adell Givens, Martin Lawrence, Sinbad, Tracy Morgan, Chris Tucker, Mo'Nique, Arsenio Hall, Dave Chappelle, and Ed Lover & Doctor Dré.

[20] Shout out to the original Hip Hop Motion Picture Classics: *Wild Style, Beat Street, Krush Groove, Style Wars, Rhyme & Reason, New Jack City, Breakin', Boyz n the Hood,* Slam, *Rappin', Stomp the Yard, The Freshest Kids, Menace II Society, 5 Sides of a Coin, House Party, Do the Right Thing, Fresh, Juice, Thug Angel, Colors, Dogma, Train Ride, Bulworth, I'm Gonna Git You Sucka, Tougher Than Leather, Belly, Brown Sugar, Scratch, Beef, Paid in Full, You Got Served, Bomb It, 8 Mile, Crime and Punishment.*

[21] Shout out to the Gospel of Hip Hop's intellectual and spiritual contributors: Acronologist Simone G. Parker, Kristine Aleksandryan, Jacqueline Parker, Professor Z, Minister SERVER, Jacynth Rasheed, Victor Quinonez, Vanessa Chakour, Morgan Wells, Kris Malcolm Parker, J.P. Wingate, Chief Rocker Busy Bee, Eric D. Anderson, "Ingz" Ingrid P. Rios, Bert, A.P.O.S.T.L.E., RedCloud, MalikONE, DJ Scientific, Jahneen Ameni One, Drew D.

Hansen, Dr. Wayne W. Dyer, Mondo One, Mwezi Mtoto, Kim (G Chakra) Maat Wells, Scott Ritter, Keith Tucker, and Zin Uru.

22   Shout out to our wise advisors: Harry Allen, Chuck D, Big Daddy Kane, Speech, Grandmaster Caz, Pop Master Fabel, James Mtume, Hakim Green, Ernie Paniccioli, Wise Intelligent, Dr. Tshombe Walker, Jason—the Druid, Nas, the Black Dot, Elemental Emcee, Nahonda, Doug E. Fresh, Hard Hittin Harry D'Janite, Lisa "Chase" Patterson, and Craig Cohen, Will Luckman, and Riyo Mochizuki at powerHouse Books.

23   Special shout out to Inebriated Beats, Shawnna, Clyde (One) Lane, Maury Winkler, Dr. Barbara King— Hillside Chapel and Truth Center, Inc., Tree, Harold English, Byron and Makisa Woodard, Jay D Krammer, Ralph McDaniels (Video Music Box), Free, *SP Magazine*, The Rock and Roll Hall of Fame and Museum, The Bronx Museum, Kevin Powell, Hiphop University, The Guardian Angels, T-Bone, Cross Movement Records, BB Jay, the Point, Fashion Moda, Jay-Z, Snoop Dogg, Reverend Al Sharpton, Congresswoman Maxine Waters, Dr. Jamal Bryant ("Preach, Black man!"), Harry Belafonte, Charlie Ahern, *ego trip magazine*, *Hip-Hop Connection*, Lauren Hill, Jill Scott, Erika Badu, Missy "Misdemeanor" Elliott, Mike Goldberg—the Latin Quarter Nightclub, Bow Wow, Lil' Kim, Eminem, 50 Cent, *Def Comedy Jam*, *Def Poetry Jam*, Amanda Sheer Demme, Ted Demme, Jonathan Demme, the Apollo Theater, Lannathai restaurant, QD3 Entertainment, Def Jam, and *In Living Color*.

24   Eternal gratitude to Joan Hubbard, Jackie Helps, Luz Delgado, Tyme, Isaac, Kris, and Randy (Joseph) Parker, DJ Kenny Parker, The Liberators, Oz-One, Doeboy, Michael Bourris, Thembisa Mshaka-Morris, Karma 360, Saul Williams, Jeff Campbell, Dee Dee Cocheta, Dan

11/13, BJ Wheeler, DJ Tine E Tim, Penny Marshall, David Kahn, Fat Joe, Tavis Smiley, Rha Goddess, Erica Ford, Smooth B, Rampage, Da Beatminerz, Mr. Walt, Evil Dee, Keith Clinkscales, Steve Smith, Dora One, Blue, Nelson George, Bakari Kitwana, Busta Rhymes, Dr. Cornel West, Dr. Michael Eric Dyson, Cindy (Herc's sister), Craig Henry, John Shecter (J the Sultan), Agape Spiritual Center, Jadakiss, Bishop Clarence E. McClendon, Rev. Dr. James A. Forbes, Jr., Rev. Mariah Britton, Rev. Lorraine Parrish, Dr. Adam Clark, Larry Price, Eddie Maldonado, Dr. Priya Parmar, Dr. Keisha Key, Chuck Kym, The Nation of Islam, Judy Duncan—The Ribbon International, the Five Percenters, Free and Accepted Masons, I-God, Truck Turner, Thor-El, I-Born, Conkrete Mike P, Thabiti, Siahnide, Xzibit, Ras Kass, United Crowns, Willie-D— B.D.P., Delroy Hutchinson (I.C.U.), Tree, Gizmo, the Dungeon Family, United Nations Educational, Scientific, and Cultural Organization (UNESCO), Peace Action, DJ Kay Slay, Icy Ice, Lucky Lou and the Beat Junkies, Boot Camp Clik, Buckshot, Black Moon, Dru-Ha, Smif 'N Wessun, Heltah Skeltah, O.G.C., Wil Rhandi Bannister, Homeless Nation, Alan Grunblatt, Marlene Domiguez, S.H. Fernando Jr., Kim Osorio, Saideh Page Browne, QD3, BboyB, Gato and Peedo—Luna Empire, Meta-4, Wesley Powell, Kiana Charles, Zoe Whitley, and Tommie Smith and John Carlos (1968 Olympics).

25   Shout out to the Stop the Violence Movement; Ann Carli, Ralph McDaniels, Vanessa Chakour, Hakim Green, Sista Shai, Kris Parker, Kenny Parker, Kurt Nice, Jah Jah, Rican, Doug E. Fresh, D-Nice, Heavy D & the Boyz, Just-Ice, MC Delight, Wise, Daddy-O, Frukwan, Ms. Melodie, Public Enemy, King Tee, Body & Soul, Def Jef, Michel'le, Tone Loc, Above The Law, Ice-T, N.W.A., J.J. Fad, Young M.C., Digital Underground, Oaktown's 3.5.7.'s, MC

Hammer, Eazy-E, Kid Capri, Big Daddy Kane, Freddy Foxxx, LL Cool J, Queen Latifah, G. Simone, DMC, Jam Master Jay, Salt-n-Pepa, Chuck D, Ziggy Marley, Shabba Ranks, DJ Red Alert, Michael Stipe, Billy Bragg, Fab 5 Freddy, Jonathan Demme, Ted Demme, Nelly, Styles P, The Game, Method Man, Busta Rhymes, Talib Kweli, Rah Digga, Wise Intelligent, Dilated Peoples, Ne-Yo, Young Guru, Buckshot, Lil Mama, D-Dot, Cassidy, Naughty by Nature, Bone Thugs-N-Harmony, Tony Touch, Lil AJ, Beast, Vex, Sadat X, Lord Jamar, Chip Fu, T Smith, Matt Smith and many others too numerous to mention here.

[26]   Shout out to the popular rappers and Rap groups of my time, thanks for the support: 50 Cent, Lil Wayne, The Lox, Bow Wow, Kanye West, Jay-Z, Three 6 Mafia, OutKast, Maino, Soulja Boy, Joell Ortiz, Jim Jones, Ludacris, Snoop Dogg, Rick Ross, Talib Kweli, Fat Joe, Wyclef Jean, Common, and Foxy Brown.

[27]   Shout out to Scott La Rock for my first big break into the music business, Ced Gee for my first home-cooked meal as a homeless man and for some really fly production on *Criminal Minded*, and MC Shan for my first real battle with a real emcee, without them I would have never been heard. Thanks guys. May their children and their children's children's children be blessed forever! Thanks guys!

[28]   This instrument draws inspiration from the lives, thoughts and actions of Nat Turner, Frederick Douglas, Alexander Crummell, John Jasper, John Brown, Harriet Tubman, Henry McNeal Turner, Ida Bell Wells-Barnett, Nobel Drew Ali, Helen Keller, George Alexander McGuire, Marcus Moziah Manasseth Garvey, Malcolm X, Kwame Ture, Florence Scovel Shinn, Medgar Evers, George Washington Carver, Paul Robeson, Booker T. Washington, Edgar Cayce, Elijah Muhammad, Huey P. Newton, Bayard Rustin and Dr. Martin Luther King Jr. To these great

prophetic teachas we owe our very lives and the existence of our freedom! Every true Hiphoppa should know and celebrate the legacy of these great prophets—and strive to walk like them!

[29]   And even if the World forgets, we shall forever honor our fellow Hiphoppas who gave their lives as examples and lessons for the rest of the Hip Hop community to learn of the traps and obstacles of the *streets*. Upon their sacrifices we have built the folklore and principles of our culture.

[30]   We commend this instrument in remembrance of Scott La Rock, Paul C, Buffy, MC Trouble, Trouble T Roy, Pumpkin, Soulski, Keith Haring, Mercury, TCD, Keith Cowboy, Master Don, Sugar Shaft, Prince Messiah, Dondi, Whiz Kid, DJ Junebug, Eazy-E, DJ Pinkhouse, Dr. Rock, Tupac Shakur, Notorious B.I.G., Big L, Big Pun, B Doggs, Michael Griffith, Cliff 159, Darryl C, Richie T, Caine One, Disco King Mario, Freaky Tah, Sane, Grandmaster Flowers, Rasean, Kuriaki, Buck Four, Top Cat 126, Stim 1, DJ Junebug, Stretch, DJ Rob One, Subroc, Bigga B, Dream, Tie, Marlon Brando, Lesley Pitts, Poetic, Weldon Irvine, Aaliyah, Kenny K, Lisa "Left Eye" Lopez, Matthew Hall, Ted Demme, Jam Master Jay, Ol' Dirty Bastard (Osirus), Stan Tookie Williams, Justo, Proof, Professor X, James Brown, Curtis Mayfield, Issac Hayes, Frosty Freeze, Pimp C, Randy Hubbard Parker, Iz the Wiz, Michael Jackson, __

_____

_____

_____

_____

_____

_____

_____

_____

³¹ We shall forever remember their contributions to the cultural development of Hip Hop and we shall forever call their names with respect. For this is the reason we do what we do as a temple for Hip Hop. WE HAVE NOT FORGOTTEN THE STRUGGLE, OR THEIR PLACES IN IT! Nor have we forgotten the conclusions, revelations and goals of Hip Hop's historic summits, conferences and meetings.

³² However, none of this could have been possible without the undying support and the loyalty of specific activists like Mondo One, Peter—*SP Magazine*, Crazy Legs, Professor Z, Grandmaster Flash, Big Daddy Kane, Doug E. Fresh, Tony Touch, Larry Gold (S.O.B.'s), Roxanne Shanté, Freddy Foxxx, DMC, Chuck D, Dr. Cornel West, A.P.O.S.T.L.E., Buckshot, DJ Premier, Daniel Power, Susanne König, Sara Rosen, Wes Del Val, Chaz Requiña, Ashley Polikoff, Daoud Tyler-Ameen, Orkan Benli, Tami Mnoian, Kiki Bauer, Viviana Morizet, Mike "QPsi" Tucker,

Craig "AC " Mathis, Jah Jah Shakur, Kurt Nice, Mine Suda, Jenny Jianai Chen, Amy Labagh, Jenna Lundin, Brent McCarthy, Ariana Barry, Mad Lion, Hakim Green, Afrika Bambaataa, Pee Wee Dance, Kool DJ Herc and all of their families and managers who stood beside KRS ONE even as the World doubted the vision of a self-sustained spiritual Hip Hop Nation. May their children and their children's children's children be blessed forever!

[33]   It is in remembrance of all of these Hiphoppas and their brave activist parents, grandparents and ancestors that we are inspired to commend to our community this instrument entitled the Gospel of Hip Hop. That the revelation that sparks all true revolution be restored in the minds of OUR PEOPLE. Peace and much, much love, my people—there it is.

The Gospel of Hip Hop
First Instrument

Text © 2009 KRS ONE

All rights reserved. Do not reproduce any part of this book in any manner, in any media. Do not transmit by any means whatsoever, electronic or mechanical, any part of this book. Do not photocopy, record, take a picture of, or post to the Internet (or any other information storage and retrieval system) any part of this book, without our say so in writing. No bootlegs!

The quotes printed throughout have been sourced and transcribed in the language of Hip Hop by the Teacha, KRS ONE. If you have any questions or comments regarding their veracity, get at us:
gospelofhiphop@powerHouseBooks.com

Published in the United States by powerHouse Books,
a division of powerHouse Cultural Entertainment, Inc.
37 Main Street, Brooklyn, NY 11201-1021
telephone 212 604 9074, fax 212 366 5247
e-mail: gospelofhiphop@powerHouseBooks.com
website: www.powerHouseBooks.com

First edition, 2009

Library of Congress Cataloging-in-Publication Data:

KRS-One (Musician)
  The gospel of hip hop : first instrument / presented by
KRS-One for the Temple of Hip Hop.
     p. cm.
  ISBN 978-1-57687-497-4 (hardcover)
  1. Hip-hop. 2. African American youth--Intellectual life. 3.
African Americans--Intellectual life. 4. African American
youth--Religious life. 5. African Americans--Religious
life. 6. African American youth--Social conditions. 7.
African Americans--Social conditions. 8. United States--
Intellectual life. 9. United States--Social conditions--1980-
I. Title.
  E185.86.K75 2009
  306'.1--dc22
                                   2008043510

Hardcover ISBN 978-1-57687-497-4

Printing and binding by Pimlico Book International,
Hong Kong
Book design by Riyo Mochizuki

10 9 8 7 6 5 4 3

Created in the United States of America
Printed and bound in China

The Gospel of Hiphop
Copyright © 2009 KRS ONE
All divine rights preserved & world rights reserved